TRANSPARENCY

Transparency

THE MATERIAL HISTORY OF AN IDEA

Daniel Jütte

Yale

UNIVERSITY PRESS

NEW HAVEN AND LONDON

Published with assistance from the foundation established
in memory of Calvin Chapin of the Class of 1788, Yale College.

Yale University Press books may be purchased in quantity for
educational, business, or promotional use. For information, please e-mail
sales.press@yale.edu (U.S. office) or sales@yaleup.co.uk (U.K. office).

Designed by Sonia Shannon
Set in Fournier type by Motto Publishing Services.
Printed in China.

Library of Congress Control Number: 2022936964
ISBN 978-0-300-23724-5 (hardcover : alk. paper)

Page i: Defaced medieval apostle, Church of St. Mary, Great Massingham,
England. A window at the crossroads: as a result of Protestant iconoclasm,
the face and other significant parts of the originally colorful composition
were replaced with blank, transparent glass (detail; see Fig. 8.4).

Page vi: Fragments of early medieval glass windows found in
the Carolingian monastery of Müstair, Switzerland (probably
dating to the late eighth century) (detail; see Fig. 2.1).

A catalogue record for this book is available from the British Library.

This paper meets the requirements of
ANSI/NISO Z39.48-1992 (Permanence of Paper).

10 9 8 7 6 5 4 3 2 1

Glass is among the materials that rule this world: it divides people into those who live in front of windows and those who live behind them.

—JOSEPH ROTH (1923)

CONTENTS

Transparency

INTRODUCTION

Introduction-opening image: Detail of Fig. I.3

Transparency is a mantra of our day. It is closely tied to the Western understanding of a liberal society, and it informs key areas of our lives: we expect transparency, for instance, from political institutions, corporations, and the media. However, what exactly the term means is not always as transparent as the image of perfect clarity that it invokes. The vision of transparency espoused by politicians and bureaucrats can be quite incongruous with what ordinary citizens associate with the word. Similarly, the policies and products hailed by corporate leaders as "transparent" are often, in reality, rather arcane to investors and consumers.[1] The line between liberal promise and neoliberal reality is, often enough, blurry.

But one thing is clear: despite the difficulties in implementing it, transparency constitutes an ideal in the Western public discourse of our day.[2] After all, who would stand up in public and criticize transparency? Political scientists observe that the term "has attained quasi-religious significance in debate over governance and institutional design."[3] And economists—a tribe that tends to favor facts over feelings—admit that "the general intuition is that transparency is 'good.'"[4] Some activists have gone so far as to argue that we should embrace "global transparency."[5]

This book, of course, is not a manual for transparent governance and management. To the contrary, it is a staunchly historical study. My key interest is to investigate how, historically, people have experienced, conceptualized, and evaluated transparency. Put differently, how did this physical property of certain material objects become a powerful, global metaphor that not only informs our public discourse, but also shapes the way we interact with each other? And why have opacity, ambiguity, and secrecy come to be seen as inferior to transparency?[6]

When I refer to transparency as a "physical property," I mean a material state that is pervious to light and sight, from within and without—in other words, a state that materials-science specialists would characterize as "two-way transparency."[7] One can experience this kind of transparency in a range of different contexts, but we tend to associate it most with one particular material (glass) and one particular medium (architecture). Most people would likely agree with architectural historians that in our age "glass signifies transparency more than any other material."[8]

There are, of course, many other transparent materials, including certain natural minerals and, since the twentieth century, synthetic plastics. Needless to say, transparency can also be experienced in nonarchitectural contexts, as in vessels and eyeglasses. That said, the difference in scale and quality is hard to over-look: as a large-scale and mass experience, transparency first and foremost has been an architectural experience. This experience, in turn, has been inextricably linked to one particular element of architecture: the glass window.

Windows might at first strike us as rather inconspicuous elements of our built environment. They are ubiquitous, and we largely take them for granted. Who, put on the spot, could say precisely how many windows he or she has at home? It is of course even harder to estimate the total number of windows in a particular area or country. For Germany, one recent calculation yielded an estimate of 580 million window units.[9]

The omnipresence of windows in everyday life should not make us under-estimate their practical importance and cultural significance. As the philosopher Gérard Wajcman has argued, the window is "neither a mere 'small object' nor a humble one."[10] He is also right to note that we lack a systematic "fenestrology."[11] There are, to be sure, technical manuals about fenestration, but no single study exists that probes, in a long historical trajectory, how windows have shaped the way we think about domestic and urban space (and the relation between the two). This lacuna is all the more surprising given the crucial role that windows play in the way we experience the spaces in which we live: windows let in the daylight that throws into relief the contours of our rooms; windows provide the air we need to live; and as an aperture in the wall, they provide an important interface between interior and exterior, helping us to locate and contextualize our enclosed domestic spaces in a larger—say, urban—context.[12]

All that said, the window is not an indispensable element of architecture. This distinguishes it from the door, which is absolutely essential for architecture: there can be no house without a door.[13] By contrast, the window—and its de-sign—is a cultural convention that has developed over the course of time. Some societies have dwellings with very small windows or even none at all (fig. I.1).[14] It therefore misses the mark to claim (as some scholars have) that the first appearance of windows must have been comparable in importance and ingenuity to the inven-tion of the wheel and the discovery of fire-making.[15] After all, windowless homes continued to exist for centuries—including in Europe. As late as the first half of the twentieth century, houses without windows could still be found in certain re-mote parts of the British Isles, Scandinavia, and the Balkans.[16] In the Italian pen-

Fig. I.1. House-shaped urn, found in Königsaue (Saxony-Anhalt, Germany), seventh century BCE. Museum für Vor- und Frühgeschichte, Berlin. Several urns of this type have been unearthed in central Germany. They suggest that Iron Age architecture lacked windows, with the door serving as the most important aperture of the house.

insula, windowless *trulli* (stone houses with nothing but a vent in the conical roof) were common sights in the southern region of Puglia. The town of Alberobello, with its particularly large number of well-preserved trulli, is now a UNESCO World Heritage Site (fig. I.2).

Windowless homes might strike us as odd anachronisms from a distant past, worth a touristic visit but unacceptable as a setting for modern life. Such shifting attitudes remind us that the history of the window has never been static, but rather subject to change over time. Le Corbusier, pioneer of modern architecture, was not wrong (albeit typically bold) when he proclaimed that the entire history of architecture could be told as the history of a struggle for windows.[17] He should have added, however, that the desire for ever larger windows, which he considered a driving factor in this history, was a distinctively Western phenomenon—or at least a phenomenon that found its most radical manifestation in Western architec-

Fig. I.2. *Trulli* in Alberobello, a town in southern Italy where a particularly large number of these round, conical-roofed buildings have been preserved. Trulli typically have small vents but no proper windows.

ture: the end point of the "struggle for the window" was the complete dissolution of the window. Indeed, in the twentieth century it became possible to turn entire walls into windows (fig. I.3).

As these introductory remarks indicate, this book is in some ways an attempt to write a broadly conceived "fenestrology." Along these lines, it sets out to cover an ambitious—perhaps overly ambitious—time span: from antiquity to our day. The overarching structure of the book is chronological—but not, I should emphasize, teleological. The "struggle for the window" in Western architecture was a much more convoluted and complex process than one might assume. As I will show, the same holds true for the process by which transparent glass emerged as the standard window sealant in Western architecture.

Scholars of architecture have claimed that "glass is arguably the most remarkable material ever discovered by man."[18] But if one wants to understand why, in modern times, glass has prevailed as the only acceptable kind of window seal-

Fig. I.3. Ludwig Mies van der Rohe, Villa Tugendhat, Brno, Czech Republic, completed 1930. The villa was a pioneering attempt to dissolve exterior walls into fully transparent windows.

ant, any monocausal explanation will inevitably fall flat. In other words, the universal rise of glass cannot be presented as a story of technological or environmental determinism. As we will see, alternatives to glass existed for centuries in Western history. So did alternatives to transparency—to the extent that, for almost a millennium of medieval history, Europeans preferred a particular kind of glass that was not pervious to the gaze: colored glass (Chapters 1–4). The transition from colored to clear glass forms a key theme in this book, for this shift not only had wide-ranging aesthetic repercussions, but also implied a changed attitude toward critical issues such as space, light, vision, and privacy (see Chapters 6, 8–10).

The relativity of architectural glass becomes even clearer if we consider that there were societies in the premodern world—for instance, in East Asia, South America, and parts of the Arab world—where a glass industry existed but where glass was nonetheless rarely used for architectural purposes before industrializa-

Fig. I.4. Window screen (*jali*) carved from stone, Sidi Saiyyed mosque, Ahmedabad, India, 1572–73. The entirely glassless window, which displays intricate vegetal designs, forms part of a series of elaborate jali screens in the Sidi Saiyyed mosque, and is widely considered a masterpiece of Islamic architecture on the Indian subcontinent.

tion (figs. I.4, I.5).[19] Glass manufacturers outside of the Western world tended to focus on portable vessels and other objects of domestic, courtly, imperial, or ritual use, and even in these contexts we notice a taste that was often quite different from that of Europeans: in the High Qing courts of China in the eighteenth century, for example, glass with opaque qualities or a jade-like appearance was considered particularly desirable, as the skill required to make one material mimic another was developed into an imperial aesthetic.[20] As an architectural material, glass played hardly any role in premodern China: the dwellings and cityscapes, as depicted in Chinese paintings from this period, typically featured screens made from a broad array of non-vitreous sealants, ranging from paper to textiles. Of course, this absence of glass in premodern Chinese architecture should not be equated with a lack of comfort; it simply suggests a different lifestyle and architectural tradition.[21]

The global perspective sketched here makes it clear that the rise of glass—and transparent glass, at that—in Western architecture was by no means an inevitable development. It was the result of specific cultural preferences that call for historical study (see especially Chapter 7). In an age of global expansion, Europeans often indulged in the myth that cheap glass beads had helped them to bring entire non-Western societies under their control. In reality, however, the more advanced products of the European glass industry, such as plate glass, did not exert the universal appeal that Europeans assumed. To the contrary, European attempts to introduce or promote architectural glass in other parts of the world often met with considerable resistance.

To return to the case of China: eighteenth-century Europeans were surprised to find that non-vitreous sealants predominated in Chinese domestic architecture. In Western eyes, which increasingly regarded China through the lens of racial and civilizational theories, such sealants were an anachronism thought to "flatter the taste of a vain and puerile people."[22] Driven by the search for tradable goods and a self-proclaimed civilizing mission, Europeans tried hard to sell plate glass in China, but it was considered an "exotic commodity" until the early twentieth century.[23] Where plate glass was installed—for example, in certain Qing-era imperial palaces—this happened as a result of contact with European Jesuits in the sites designated for foreign aesthetics, and sometimes there were explicit specifica-

Fig. I.5. *Shōji* screens in a traditional Japanese house, Meiji-Mura Museum Village, Inuyama, Aichi prefecture, Japan. Spanned with a thin sealant such as rice paper, shōji are translucent. When the sliding screens are opened, the boundary between interior and exterior seems to be canceled.

Fig. I.6. Historical home in north Goa, India. The house features windows that combine local traditions of non-vitreous sealing and European influences. Cut fragments of translucent pearl shell are fitted between the wooden battens, while the central section features a transparent glass pane (see fig. I.7). In Goa, this hybrid type of fenestration may have been introduced by the Portuguese; in other parts of India, windows entirely made of shells existed long before and well after the arrival of European colonists.

tions (as in an imperial edict from the year 1726) that the glass should imitate the wax-like (*shati*) appearance of traditional non-vitreous sealants.[24]

The supposed appeal of glass also fell flat in Mughal India. Visiting northwest India in 1675, an English doctor in the service of the British East India Company found that glass was rare and "scarcely purchaseable (unless by way of Stambole, or Constantinople, from the Venetians)." Instead, local "Windows, except some few of the highest Note, are usually folding Doors, skreened with Cheeks, or Latises, Carved in Wood, or Ising-glass, or more commonly Oister-shells."[25] Elsewhere, too, he noted that buildings featured "Panes of Oister-shells for their Windows (which as they are cut in Squares, and polished, look gracefully enough)."[26] Given the difficulty of obtaining glass windows in India, European merchants and colonists often began to adopt traditional local sealants, realizing that these materials worked just as efficiently as plate glass. Still, the Europeans went to great lengths to approximate the familiar visual effect of glass in their colonial settlements (figs. I.6, I.7). In the Portuguese enclave of Daman in northwest India, a late seventeenth-century Italian visitor observed that "instead of glass [the Portuguese] fit their windows with oyster shells which are finely crafted and transparent [*trasparenti*]."[27]

The situation was similarly complex in Tokugawa Japan, where the Dutch were confined to the island of Dejima (in the bay of Nagasaki) during this period. Their dwellings were constructed by local builders in the traditional Japanese style, which precluded glass. In the late eighteenth century, the Dutch residents obtained permission to install glass in their homes on Dejima.[28] Around that

Fig. I.7. Close-up of a pearl shell window in a historical Goa home (see fig. I.6).

time, the famous Japanese go-between and scholar of the Dutch, Shiba Kōkan, observed this foreign architectural custom with interest, but the fundamental difference between European and Japanese buildings remained firm and unquestioned: the Europeans, Kōkan noted, preferred buildings "all with glass in the windows, just as we use paper."[29] Indeed, in ordinary Japanese residences, window glass was absent until the forced opening of Japan in the second half of the nineteenth century (fig. I.8; see also fig. I.5). By the end of that century, glass windows were still rare and considered a distinctively Western feature of architecture, most likely to be adopted by aristocratic elites.[30]

In Arab countries such as Egypt, Palestine, and Lebanon, we observe a similar reluctance during this period. The reasons were different, but the result was the same: glass remained uncommon in domestic architecture until the late nineteenth century. Here again, westernized elites were the first to embrace it.[31] To this day, one can still find in the Middle East windows sealed with non-vitreous materials, including the *mashrabiya*—the artfully carved wooden latticework characteristic of traditional architecture in parts of the Arab world. The small perforations of the mashrabiya (also found in other kinds of wooden or stone screens, such as the South Asian *jali*) allow air to flow through the window while reducing the exposure to glare and heat.[32]

A close look reveals that concerns about the suitability and supposed superiority of glass also existed in Europe. It is true that, by the nineteenth century, glass had been firmly established as the most common window sealant in European architecture, but preceding centuries had seen criticism and even resistance (see Chapter 11). The opposition to architectural glass forms a subject in European cultural history that has received very little scholarly attention. To probe this resistance, as well as complex traditions of anti-transparency, means not just to provide a fuller historical picture, but also to avoid triumphant teleological narratives about glass and its rise.

Whatever the pitfalls of teleology, one thing cannot be disputed: glass has prevailed in the modern world, in the West and in most non-Western countries alike. In reaching this point, glass superseded a broad array of non-vitreous materials that, for centuries, served as alternatives (see especially Chapter 5). This globalization of architectural glass has not gone without criticism: constructing large glass-faced buildings in, say, hot or tropical non-Western countries might

Fig. I.8. Kitagawa Utamaro, *Shadows on the Shōji*, ca. 1790. The Metropolitan Museum of Art, New York. Due to their characteristic lack of transparency, the *shōji* in the background display the shadow of the young lady.

be a matter of prestige for the commissioning patrons and the Western architects in their service, but it tends to disregard local architectural traditions that were finely attuned to the contingencies of light and climate. It also comes at significant ecological cost, as these glass buildings often require permanent air-conditioning during heat periods and dehumidification in wintertime. Some critics even speak of an "act of (environmental) colonialism."[33] With the acceleration of climate change and global warming, these questions are becoming more pressing, including in places where glass architecture, for much of the past few decades, has been considered a hallmark of modern urban life. In New York, where I am writing these lines, the mayor announced in 2019, "We are going to introduce legislation to ban the glass and steel skyscrapers that have contributed so much to global warming."[34] At this time, in 2022, no such legislation has been put forward.

With all that said, the rise of architectural glass over the past two millennia has in many ways been a fascinating historical process, at least in the West. After all, glass has played a key role in some of the most radical architectural visions and projects in Western history, be it in the soaring cathedrals of the Middle Ages, the vast train stations and "crystal palaces" of the nineteenth century (see Chapter 12), or the glittering high-rises in the megacities of our age (see especially Chapters 13, 15).[35]

It is precisely this potential of glass as a means of architectural innovation that has tended to draw the attention of historians. Focusing on this aspect of glass's history can undoubtedly yield much insight into the architectural ambitions and utopias of different periods of the past. However, such an approach runs the risk of overlooking the more quotidian (if hardly less interesting) history of architectural glass. The "simple" panes of "ordinary" houses can tell us something—actually quite a lot—about social, cultural, and economic realities in a given time. For this reason, this book treats both aspects equally: the use of glass in radically innovative architecture as well as in more conventional, quotidian settings.

The French sociologist Bruno Latour has noted, "We aren't usually very interested in contradictions of mechanisms which we call, quite evasively, 'functional.' We generally prefer discussions about the heart, the soul, or the spirit, which seem to us more dramatic and more aesthetic. This is a pity, because the great moral crises, the great tragedies, the great dramas are occurring today not on movie screens but in machines and appliances."[36] Architectural glass is, I believe, an "appliance" of the kind Latour describes. Put another way, it is a material technology that plays a crucial role in the perpetual dialectic of inside and outside that defines our everyday life and our orientation in space.

Of course, glass is neither a new nor essentially modern material. Western architecture has drawn on it for more than two millennia, and this alone would be a reason to explore how this material has shaped the way we think about the built space that surrounds us. Beatriz Colomina has rightly noted that "any concept of windows implies a notion of the relationships between inside and outside."[37] Glass adds an additional layer of complexity to this issue: unlike translucent sealants, transparent glass enables us to see the outside while we stay comfortably within; in doing so, the transparent window inevitably curates and frames a host of visual impressions. Is it a coincidence that in Western culture, the rectangular frame is a defining feature of both paintings and windows?

At the same time, the transparent window allows people outside to peek in without entering. In other words, transparent windows reveal something about our interiors and private lives, and residents are often acutely aware of this showcasing effect.[38] What people display at or behind their windows can tell us a lot about how they want to be seen. Conversely, a beautiful view from the window is an amenity for which people are sometimes willing to pay an inordinate amount of money—and this, in turn, can reveal a lot about what a society considers desirable to see.

In short, window views and worldviews are more closely entwined than we might assume.[39] There is, more generally, a close link between the technology of the window and the modalities of vision in Western culture. Due to its permanent transparency, the window has become an elaborate apparatus—and metaphor—for vision. As the philosopher Vilém Flusser has noted, the window is the medium par excellence that we associate with seeing the outside: it epitomizes the idea of looking at the world from a protected or otherwise privileged perspective—a seeing that becomes viewing.[40] Indeed, our windows not only frame our image of the outside, but also fuse what the ancient Greeks referred to as "*thea*" (a view) and "*horan*" (to see). The Greek word for this fusion is "*theoria*."[41]

In this sense, my topic is, perhaps, a "theoretical" one. This book is certainly underlain by a methodological ambition that goes beyond the actual theme of transparency. There is a certain tendency among historians to write the history of ideas and then to examine how these ideas influenced the historical reality. My goal is the opposite: a material history of ideas. I would like to explore whether it is possible to trace the material realities without which an idea such as transparency would not have emerged. The question, then, is whether the political and philosophical concept of "transparency" has concrete underpinnings in material culture and, on a more concrete level, in the everyday experience of architecture.[42]

To answer this question one must, I believe, go back far in time. Adrian Forty has argued that "transparent is a wholly modernist term, unknown in architecture before the twentieth century."[43] But this is not correct: the term "transparent" was used in English as early as the fifteenth century.[44] Of course, the term may not have had the exact same meaning it has today; but as we will see, people in the Middle Ages—and, in fact, in antiquity as well—certainly knew what transparency was, and they encountered it in different contexts, even if they used different words to describe this physical property and its experience. What has changed significantly over time is the cultural meaning assigned to transparency and glass.

One final note is due, to prepare (and caution) the reader that in this book I chose a wide rather than a narrow lens. For instance, I will occasionally delve into the question of light—an aspect that seemed too interesting (and too entangled) to separate it pedantically from the history of transparency. There is, of course, an intrinsic link between light and transparency on a physical level: without light there would be no transparency. In other words, whether we perceive a vitreous object as transparent depends on the amount of light on either side of the surface. As a medieval writer put it, "Glass, however clear and transparent it may be, does yet not produce a ray of light of itself."[45] Or in the more technical words of modern materials-science specialists: "If there is more light on the viewer's side than on the reverse side, then it becomes reflective. If, on the other hand, there is more light on the reverse side, then it will be transparent."[46] Beyond the physical nexus between light and transparency, there are also historical reasons why this book explores the perception of, as well as changing attitudes toward, light. After all, the historian must find it curious that narratives of modernity often are based on the claim that we are "enlightened," whereas our premodern ancestors were not.

What does it actually mean that we are (or like to think we are) more "enlightened" than people in the past? To be clear, this book is not a history of the Enlightenment with a capital *E*—a subject on which intellectual historians have written profound (and notoriously long) books. I am more interested in what a morose Hans Sedlmayr called the "enormous thirst for light" that has characterized modernity—not only on an intellectual and metaphorical level, but also on a quotidian level. There were, I believe, links between the intellectual "enlightenment" and the changing experience of light in everyday life. As we will see, in the eighteenth century, it became possible, for the first time in human history, to manufacture windowpanes larger than the human body. Along with other architectural innovations, this made it possible to flood interiors with daylight in a way that was as novel as it was striking. For Sedlmayr, thirst for light constituted a defining feature of modernity, but he also considered it "at heart the compensation for a deep-felt deficiency," and symptomatic of the state of modern man "for whom the light from within as well as from above has died."[47] This verdict might sound harsh, and it is certainly polemical. But it can still serve as a prompt to explore, through the prism of glass, how to link the history of ideas with the history of everyday life, material culture, and architectural change.

But enough about methodology and theoretical considerations. Let us not forget what Latour called the "great tragedies, the great dramas" that arise from quotidian objects and technologies. As far as the window goes, one of these dramas has been the struggle for privacy: after all, ever larger, ever more transparent glass windows have brought us not only pleasure but also considerable anxiety about our privacy. As a result of this dilemma, we spend a fair amount of money on curtains to regain control over our large and often expensive windowpanes. What a paradox—or drama—in the theater that everyday life is! Is it really a coincidence that the stage is another spatial setting in which curtains are common?

There are many other dramas, small and large, in the history of architectural glass. To recall (and vary) Le Corbusier's aperçu, the struggle for the window has also been a struggle *with* windows. Not always did these struggles end with a constructive solution: in some cases, destructive forces prevailed. Indeed, the history of architectural glass is also a history of systematic destructions—whether we consider the iconoclast smashing of church windows during the early modern period or the assaults against the windows of Jewish citizens during Nazi pogroms such as the infamous Kristallnacht (fig. I.9). The intentions behind these violent

Fig. I.9. Smashed windows of a Jewish-owned shop, unknown location, 1938. Across the German Reich, windows of Jewish-owned stores were attacked during the Kristallnacht pogroms of November 9, 1938 (also known as the "Night of Broken Glass").

acts were entirely different, yet such aggressions remind us that glass—a seemingly inconspicuous, "pure" material—has throughout history been endowed in manifold ways with contested political, social, and cultural meaning. Here again, we will see how, across time, the history of vitreous transparency has been inextricably linked to fantasies—and acts—of power, control, and submission (see especially Chapter 14).

How to accommodate this history of power and violence? In a famous passage of his "Theses on the Philosophy of History," Walter Benjamin imagined the "angel of history": "His face is turned toward the past. Where we perceive a chain of events, he sees one single catastrophe which keeps piling wreckage upon wreckage and hurls it in front of his feet. . . . A storm propels him into the future to which his back is turned, while the pile of debris before him grows skyward. This storm is what we call progress."[48]

It is worth keeping this vision of history in mind, even if the topic of this book is infinitely more specialized. For I think that a history of transparency can be written in chronological progression (and with a good conscience) only if we focus not just on progress, but also on backlash and destruction—that is, on the "pile of debris," the glittering pile of shards, that "grows skyward" as we look back to the past.

I

Glass and Architecture
in Ancient Times

Chapter-opening image: Detail of Fig. 1.12

Today, we take architectural glass for granted: when we think of windows, most of us inevitably think of glass. The link between glass and windows is firmly established in modern Western architecture. As we have seen in the introduction, glass has also become the norm in other societies—including non-Western societies where, for centuries, it played little or no role in architecture. Even in Europe, the link between glass and fenestration was by no means as firm in the past as it is today: for millennia, windows were furnished with a variety of different sealants. What is more, glass windows did not come into use until the days of imperial Rome.

Not that glassmaking itself was unknown in antiquity. The first man-made glass dates back to around 2500 BCE and originated in Mesopotamia, more specifically modern-day northern Syria and Iraq. It was produced from the same basic ingredients that, with some modifications, are still used today: a vitrifying agent, typically sand or another source of silica, was the major component; an alkalic fluxing agent such as soda was added to lower the silica's melting temperature in the furnace; and lastly, a source of calcium oxide—for instance, lime—served as a stabilizing agent.

Beads seem to have been the main product of the ancient glass industry, at least initially. Vessels were not produced until a millennium after the beginnings of Middle Eastern glassmaking. This expansion of the product range went hand in hand with the transmission of technological know-how to other parts of the ancient world: from Mesopotamia, glassmaking gradually spread to the Egyptians and later to the Greeks, who further improved it.[1] Yet none of these societies developed glass windows.

Why was glass not used for architectural purposes in pre-Roman antiquity? Technical constraints must have played an important role. Glassblowing, the most efficient method of windowpane production in Roman times, was not yet known. Of course, glassmakers could have relied on other methods to produce panes—for instance, by way of casting. (Ancient Middle Eastern glassmakers were adept at various casting techniques.) However, it seems that the application of these skills to pane production would have been prohibitively expensive.[2] Glass aside, windows in general were an architectural luxury in the ancient Middle East. Because of the limited availability of timber and stone, ancient Mesopotamian and Egyptian houses often were built from bricks made of clay or mud; to ensure structural

Fig. 1.1. Wooden *mashrabiya* screen, Cairo. Such screens were for centuries a common sight in the premodern Islamic world. Nineteenth-century Europeans were both intrigued and perplexed by this alternative to architectural glass. As a result, mashrabiyas became a popular motif for postcards and photographs. The photograph reproduced here was taken in the late nineteenth century by the Bonfils studio.

stability, window openings tended to be relatively small and close to the ceiling.[3] This might explain why the Talmud defines the "Egyptian window" as "any window which is so small that a man's head cannot enter through it."[4]

Climatic factors also influenced fenestration and made glass panes dispensable.[5] In the Middle East, protecting the household from glare and stifling heat was, and still is, a far more pressing issue than shielding the interior from wind and rain. The design of the mashrabiya responds to these concerns (fig. 1.1). The exact historical origins of the mashrabiya are unclear, but the oldest surviving specimens date to the High Medieval period. It is probable that similar kinds of latticework were used in the ancient Mediterranean and Middle East as well.[6] In fact, certain biblical verses suggest that perforated wooden screens may have formed part of the Temple in Jerusalem. We do know of wooden (and metal) grilles in Greek temples.[7]

There are still considerable lacunae in our knowledge of fenestration in the ancient world. This holds true even for Roman times: as Yvon Thébert has noted with regard to Roman provincial architecture, we often "do not know how many windows there were, what size they may have been, or where they were located; in most cases we do not even know how they closed."[8] Indeed, textual sources from antiquity are often terse or ambiguous in their discussion of windows and their sealants. To complicate matters, detailed architectural treatises from this period are scarce. Vitruvius's *De architectura* (On Architecture), written in the first century BCE, is the most comprehensive surviving treatise on Roman architecture. This is precisely why it has been studied extensively since its rediscovery in medieval times—even though Vitruvius was hardly among the most distinguished architects of ancient Rome. In his treatise, Vitruvius discusses windows and their design at various points, but he is silent on the issue of how to seal them.[9] This fits into a general pattern: what we know about Roman houses and their windows often is not derived from textual sources, but rather from archaeological findings.[10]

Taken together, the scattered evidence suggests that it was common among Romans (as it had been among Greeks) to close windows with wooden shutters or, alternatively, to furnish them with iron grilles. Gratings made of timber, terracotta, or carved stone were also in use.[11] This observation, of course, does not justify the sweeping conclusion that "the form of ancient architecture was profoundly affected by the unglazed and stunted window."[12] Nor does it mean that residents had to "shut themselves up in darkness or stay within the brief circles of intense light cast by innumerable oil lamps."[13] Such belittling claims by modern historians tend to ignore the fact that windows were rarely the only sources of daylight in ancient buildings.[14] In early Roman architecture, both public buildings and private homes often received additional light through the open courtyard, the atrium.[15] Well-preserved Roman homes, such as those excavated in Herculaneum and Pompeii, make it clear that even in the absence of outward-facing windows, there was enough light in the interior to enjoy the fashionable—and often elaborate—wall frescoes. The atrium's importance for interior lighting was reinforced by the impluvium in its center: this water basin, often generously sized, served to collect rainwater, but the water surface also reflected the sunlight and thus helped to transmit it into the interior of the building.[16]

Doors, too, played a significant role in interior lighting—and this included the front door as well as those connecting the atrium to the interior rooms. In this respect, early Roman houses stood in the tradition of ancient Greece, where doors often functioned as major sources of light. In ancient Greece, this even left traces in the language: while windows did exist in Greek architecture, there was no special term for them, so the window was referred to either as a mere "opening" (ὀπή) or, tellingly, as a "small door" (θυρίς).[17]

True, there were buildings in Greco-Roman antiquity that featured neither an atrium nor large doors—for example, the multistory apartment buildings that sprouted up in the densely populated neighborhoods of imperial Rome. Under such conditions of urban overcrowding, windows assumed unprecedented importance: every window meant more light. Still, even in these settings, shuttering the windows would not necessarily have implied total darkness. Sophisticated Roman shutters featured intricate latticework that admitted a gentle light even when shut.[18] Simpler versions consisted of two separate, solid leaves. In Ovid's love poetry we read about a room with "one shutter closed tight, the other just ajar," which creates "the light the sort you often see in woods."[19]

Another way of sealing windows without shutting out daylight was to fit them with stretched animal skins or other organic materials, such as thin slices of shell, stretched animal bladders, or occasionally tow or other fibers.[20] A far costlier option was to use panes made from alabaster, selenite, or mica. These minerals often were referred to by the umbrella term "*lapis specularis*," a term literally meaning "mirror stone," but perhaps best rendered as "windowpane stone." Windows sealed with mineral materials accordingly were known as "*specularia*," although this could also denote other kinds of sealants (fig. 1.2).[21]

The use of mineral stones for fenestration may have had precedents in ancient Greece. That much is suggested by documents related to construction work in the sanctuary of Asklepios at Epidaurus in the fourth century BCE. It remains unclear, however, which particular mineral stones were used at the Epidaurus site and whether this was an exceptional choice.[22] We are much better informed about the production and use of mineral windowpanes in Roman times. As Pliny the Elder reports in his *Naturalis historia* (Natural History), lapis specularis was quarried in large blocks, which were then "split into plates as thin as may be wished."[23] This was a relatively easy operation because the blocks—due to their specific crystalline composition—often had a layered internal structure, which lent itself well to the slicing of panes. The final product had advantages over other sealants such as animal membranes: lapis panes admitted more light and provided better insula-

tion while also being more robust and waterproof.[24] Depending on the quality and thinness of the slices, lapis panes could even boast a remarkable degree of transparency (fig. 1.3).[25]

The problem with lapis was its limited availability: the largest natural deposits were located in rather remote areas, and the mining process was challenging. As Pliny detailed, lapis often was "dug at a great depth by means of shafts."[26] For a long time, the main sites of lapis mining were located in the Iberian peninsula. Egypt, too, was known to harbor significant deposits—and indeed, after the Romans conquered the kingdom in the first century BCE, they sentenced criminals to mine lapis there. Smaller centers of lapis mining existed in Italy, Cyprus, and Anatolia.[27]

Due to the high costs of extraction and transport, lapis was an expensive architectural material. To seal one's windows with it was an unmistakable sign of wealth and prestige in Roman society. Indeed, in well-preserved excavation sites such as Pompeii and Herculaneum, archaeologists have found lapis windows (or what remains of them) near houses and villas that belonged to members of the upper class. A particularly important discovery was made in Pompeii's so-called House of C. Cuspius Pansa, where archaeologists unearthed the remnants

Fig. 1.3. A modern attempt to make a window from highly transparent *lapis specularis*. This window was produced with local materials in Brisighella (Emilia-Romagna, Italy) in consultation with historians.

of twenty-five lapis panes. These panes, each sized about six by eight and a half inches, are thought to have been used to seal upper-floor windows.[28] It seems that some Roman lapis panes were as long as thirteen inches (fig. 1.4).[29]

Lapis windows were used not only in domestic but also in horticultural architecture. Growing fruits and vegetables year-round was a hobby of many wealthy Romans (including certain emperors), and the forcing houses in which plants were grown occasionally featured lapis panes.[30] Bathhouses were another common site for specularia.[31] These recreational facilities enjoyed great popularity at the time and were considered "hallmarks of Roman civilization."[32] Their construction was generously funded by political leaders vying for public favor. As a result, Roman bathhouses often displayed the architectural state of the art: they featured sophisticated technology for the circulation of water and steam while also boasting lavish building materials such as marble. It fits into this picture that costly lapis was sometimes used to seal the windows. Of course, this was also a practical choice, as lapis panes helped to preserve the heat and steam crucial for the operation of a bathhouse.[33]

This, in broad strokes, was the state of Roman architecture before the emergence of architectural glass. It is more difficult to date this emergence with precision. The earliest material evidence points to the first half of the first century CE.[34] Experiments with the use of glass in architecture around that time likely were linked to the expansion of the Roman Empire into northern Europe, where the climes were not easily compatible with the Roman lifestyle or balneal culture.[35] Bathhouses always stood to benefit from efficiently sealed windows, but nowhere was this truer than in northern Europe.

The technological foundations for window-glass production, however, were laid in much warmer parts of the Roman Empire: it is thought that Levantine glassmakers pioneered the casting of windowpanes. This is plausible given that the most skilled glassmakers of the ancient world worked in the Levant. The geographical distribution of glassmaking knowledge and skill began to change under Emperor Augustus (r. 27 BCE–14 CE), who created the framework for a flourishing glass industry in the Italian peninsula. Augustus's rise to power had ended a period of political turmoil and inaugurated an era of economic prosperity. Ruling with power unprecedented in Roman history, Augustus promoted the establishment of various crafts in the Italian peninsula. Glassmakers from the Roman provinces of Syria and Iudea were settled in Italy, some of them as slaves.[36] Along with

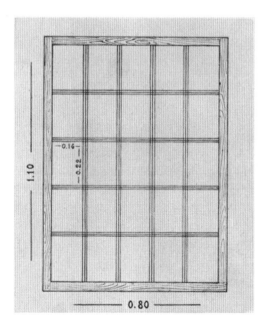

Fig. 1.4. Diagrammatic reconstruction of a large window in the House of C. Cuspius Pansa, Pompeii, first century BCE. The window measured 43 by 31.5 inches. It was sealed with twenty-five rectangular panes of *lapis specularis*, each measuring 6 by 8.5 inches and about 15 millimeters thick. Reconstruction: Vittorio Spinazzola.

their expertise in casting, Levantine glassmakers brought their prized knowledge of glassblowing, a technique that had been discovered in either Lebanon or Israel just a few decades earlier (probably around the mid-first century BCE).[37]

This transfer of technological know-how from the Levant was an enormous boost for the glass industry in Italy. Rome, the Gulf of Naples, and the surrounding regions became important centers of state-of-the-art glassmaking.[38] Within two generations after Augustus, the Roman glass industry turned "from a relatively minor craft to an empire-wide industry."[39] Production sites emerged throughout the Roman Empire, even as far north as England. As a result, glass products, especially vessels, became affordable for most members of Roman society—an unprecedented situation in the ancient world.[40] According to modern estimates, in the second century alone, more than one million glass objects were produced in the Roman Empire. This was a remarkable figure in an empire that counted about fifty million inhabitants.[41]

How did the invention and increasing availability of glass windows change the way people perceived the relation between interior and exterior space? Some scholars have argued that the first view through a glass window must have been a revolutionary moment in the history of mankind.[42] But this is a bold assertion, based on the rather modern idea that windows are by definition transparent. In ancient times, this was not the case: the vast majority of early Roman windowpanes were either semi- or entirely opaque.[43] There is also no reason to assume that the first glass panes were superior to lapis windows, or that they outcompeted them in the market. Quite the contrary: high-quality lapis panes boasted a degree of transparency that even the best first-century glassmakers would have found difficult to achieve in glass panes.[44]

Two factors accounted for the lack of transparency in early Roman window glass. The first was related to the production method—specifically, the fact that the panes were cast. Although no textual description of the casting process has survived, archaeologists conjecture that the molten glass was poured into a solid frame (whether of wood, stone, or metal remains a matter of discussion).[45] A thin layer of sand at the bottom of the mold prevented the glass from adhering. After the molten glass was poured into the form, it was pressed or smoothened out with rollers. Invariably, this meant that the side of the pane facing the sandy surface retained a matte appearance, even after intense grinding and polishing.[46] Casting also made it hard to achieve the degree of thinness that characterized the finest

Fig. 1.5. A Roman windowpane from the mid-first century CE, probably cast. Pieced together from fragments found at Compierre à Champallement, in central France, this pane measures 24 by 17 inches. Due to its bluish-green tint, the window would have provided only a blurred view. Similar glass panes have been discovered at Roman sites across Europe.

mouth-blown glass vessels. At best, cast windowpanes were between two and six millimeters thick; more commonly, they ranged between ten and fifteen millimeters, which was equivalent to the usual thickness of lapis panes (fig. 1.5).[47]

The other obstacle to transparency was that glass panes often displayed natural coloring, most commonly a greenish, yellow, or blue hue. This issue was not specific to panes and was true of the majority of glass products at the time. It resulted from residual iron oxide, which invariably caused discoloration in glass when present, despite typically amounting to less than 1 percent of the ingredients.[48] As early as the sixth century BCE, skilled glassmakers in ancient Greece and Persia had found ways of producing highly transparent glass by adding the right mixture of decolorizing agents.[49] But Roman glassmakers mastered these skills only gradually. Writing in the decades after the first windowpanes appeared, Pliny the Elder observed that "the most highly valued glass is colourless and transparent, as closely as possible resembling rock-crystal."[50] This high degree of transparency, however, remained limited to the most elaborate glass products—an upscale segment of the marketplace to which windowpanes did not belong.[51]

Fig. 1.6. Roman glass jar, ca. 100 CE. The Metropolitan Museum of Art, New York. This 5-inch-high jar was made of decolorized, mouth-blown glass. Vessels with this degree of transparency were mass-produced in the Roman Empire. Blemished by large bubbles, this jar was an object of daily use. Upper-class Romans did not assign much value to imperfect glass vessels of this kind.

Indeed, even with the addition of decolorizers, the panes would have remained at least semi-opaque due to the nature of the casting process. It was far more lucrative for glassmakers to decolorize thin, mouth-blown vessels (fig. 1.6).

Some producers of window glass made a virtue out of a necessity: instead of spending considerable effort on decolorizing cast panes, they embraced the lack of transparency and artificially intensified the coloration. Indeed, inducing or increasing coloration in glass was much easier than eliminating it. For instance, it was well known that adding specific iron oxides during the melting process would induce a range of different colors, such as cobalt blue, amethyst, or the "bloody" red known in Latin as "*hematinum.*"[52] There must have been some demand for colored window glass of this kind, as indicated by fragments found in the ruins of bathhouses and other Roman buildings.[53]

By contrast, lapis panes could not be artificially colored. Nor could they be shaped as easily as molten glass. Glass therefore lent itself better to sealing unconventionally shaped apertures. For example, Roman glassmakers developed convex, mold-cast glass hemispheres (*oculi*), which could reach a diameter of up to twenty inches (figs. 1.7, 1.8).[54] Casting also allowed for the production of large, flat windowpanes, which seem to have enjoyed a certain popularity, especially in bathhouse architecture. They could reach up to twenty-seven and a half by forty inches.[55]

Still, cast panes occupied a relatively small segment in the market for window sealants. Glass gained a greater market share only when mouth-blowing

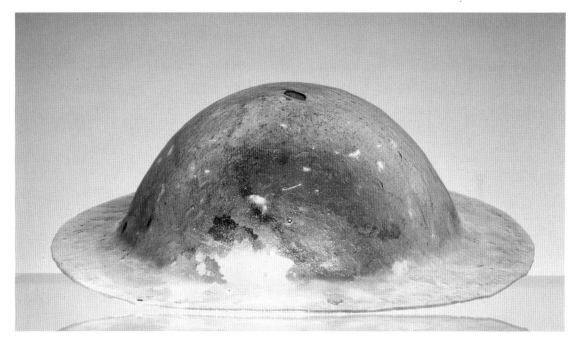

Fig. 1.7. Cast glass hemisphere, early third century CE. Cast glass hemispheres such as this one were used to seal round-shaped windows or roof openings (*oculi*). They have been found in different parts of the Roman Empire. Except for traces of weathering, the one shown here, with a diameter of 20 inches, is exceptionally well preserved. It forms part of a set of eight such hemispheres found by archaeologists in a Roman shipwreck near Embiez (southern France) in 1993.

Fig. 1.8. Round window opening in the women's section of the bathhouse in Herculaneum. These openings may have been sealed with glass hemispheres such as the one shown in fig. 1.7.

techniques were applied to the production of panes, which occurred in the second or third century, thanks to a technological innovation known as the "cylinder method."[56] This method might seem relatively simple in theory, but in practice it required considerable skill: the first step was to blow a cylinder, which was then cut—first on both ends and then longitudinally—so that it could be flattened into a rectangular sheet of glass. This was done while the glass was still hot; in order to obtain panes that were smooth on both sides, it was important to flatten the glass cylinder without making it touch a surface. Not all glassmakers were equally adept (or careful), and as a result some Roman cylinder glass shares a typical feature of cast panes in that one side is smooth while the other is somewhat rough. Also, the edges of the blown panes often display irregularities resulting from pressure applied by the iron tools used during flattening (fig. 1.9).

Gradually, however, the quality of cylinder glass improved, and by the late ancient period, panes produced by this method were the thinnest available in the marketplace, typically ranging from a mere one and a half to three millimeters. Aside from small streaks and bubbles, the resulting panes were highly transparent.[57] In this respect, blown panes were undoubtedly superior to their cast counterparts. They did, however, fall short of the latter in terms of size.[58] The smaller size explains why, in the reality of the marketplace, mouth-blown panes complemented rather than outcompeted cast panes. In other words, cast panes lent themselves to large windows, whereas high-quality lapis panes or mouth-blown glass had the advantage of greater transparency.[59]

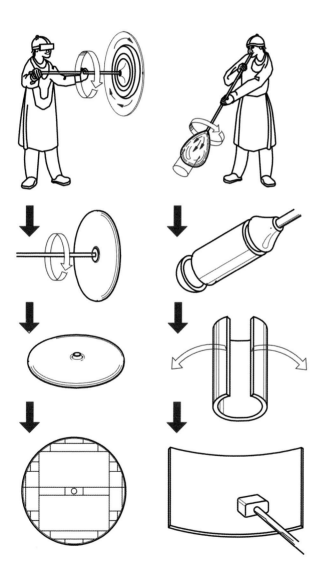

Fig. 1.9. *Left:* Producing a windowpane using the crown method. The glassmaker blows a vitreous sphere and rotates it until it has flattened into a disk. The scar resulting from breaking the disk off the blowpipe is called the bull's-eye. Depending on its size, the disk is then cut into smaller pieces. *Right:* Producing a windowpane using the cylinder method. With a blowpipe, the glassmaker shapes a lump of molten glass into a cylinder. The cylinder is then cut open along its length and flattened. Both methods date back to Roman antiquity, but they remained the most common ways of producing windowpanes well into the nineteenth century. Drawing: Wolfgang Nutsch (partly after Brisac, *Thousand Years of Stained Glass*, 1986).

In late antiquity, a third method of producing glass panes was discovered: the manufacture of so-called crown glass. This innovation completed the basic repertoire of techniques on which European glassmakers would rely for more than a millennium to come (although the term "crown glass" was not coined until the seventeenth century). Glassmakers produced crown windows by blowing a vitreous sphere and spinning it by rapid rotation until it flattened and became a disc. Next, the disk was typically cut into smaller, rectangular panes.[60] Like cylinder glass, crown boasted a high degree of thinness and transparency, depending on the glassmaker's skill. However, the center of the disk was inevitably thicker than the outer parts, and it always featured a lump-like scar (known as the "bull's-eye" or "pontil mark"), which resulted from breaking off the blowpipe (see fig. 1.9).

For a long time, glass scholars believed that the crown method was not invented before the late Middle Ages, and that this happened in northern France. More recent research, however, has made it clear that the first crown windows were produced in Roman times—as early as the fourth century.[61] The diameter of ancient crown disks seems to have varied greatly, reaching up to twenty inches. As in the case of cylinder glass, the windowpanes cut from crown glass were joined with supports made of timber, metal, or plaster.[62]

Was crown easier to manufacture than cylinder glass? Some scholars have argued so, but the archaeological evidence suggests that of all technical options available to Roman glassmakers, crown remained the least common.[63] The discovery of crown glass occurred during a period of a recurrent political and social turmoil, and it is possible that this hampered the transmission of technological knowledge. After the dissolution of the Roman Empire, crown-glass production seems to have fallen into oblivion in western Europe for several centuries.[64] In the medieval eastern Mediterranean, however, crown glass continued to be produced. It became, in fact, a common feature of early Islamic architecture. Through Mediterranean trade channels, Levantine crown panes eventually found their way back to western Europe. In the High Middle Ages, the skills, too, were reimported, perhaps as a result of the Crusades.[65] We will address this revival and its effects in a later chapter (see Chapter 6).

To return to late antiquity: it is safe to conclude that window glass of the highest quality, whether crown or cylinder, boasted a degree of transparency that was not inferior to that of the finest lapis specularis. It is therefore impossible to say with certainty whether the Roman poet Symphosius, active around 400 CE, had glass or lapis in mind when he composed the following short riddle poem about a windowpane (*specular*) distinguished by its transparency:

> I am looked right through and I do not hinder the eye's vision,
> Letting them wander through my body and beyond.
> Although the winter does not pass through me,
> The sun within me nonetheless shines out.[66]

Remarkable as they were, the technical achievements of Roman glassmakers form only one aspect in the multifaceted history of ancient glass. For the cultural historian, it is just as important to probe the cultural effects of glass's increasing availability. Did the greater range and affordability of glass panes lead to changes in architectural taste? Might this in turn explain the greater attention to issues of fenestration that we observe in Roman law from the High Imperial period onward? Indeed, Roman jurists from this period began to clarify in a systematic fashion the enjoyments residents could expect from their windows. Three categories were established: the entitlement to daylight (*lumen*), air (*aër*), and a view (*prospectus*).[67]

Strictly speaking, none of these three enjoyments depended on glass windows. After all, nothing guarantees light, air, and a view better than a completely unsealed window. Glass, of course, had an advantage unmentioned in Roman law: it kept the house "protected against bad weather" (as Pliny the Younger put it in a letter describing the design of his generously fenestrated countryside villa).[68] Or to recall the more poetic words of Symphosius's riddle poem about a windowpane: "Although the winter does not pass through me, / The sun within me nonetheless shines out."

The issue of weatherproofing was closely connected to that of insulation. Minimizing the loss of warmth was particularly important in balneal architecture, especially in the heated areas. Bathhouses featured state-of-the-art insulation, including extra-thick concrete walls.[69] To the same end, windows were sealed with either lapis or glass. They could not be opened, and some even featured double glazing.[70] To ensure sufficient ventilation, bathers operated small windows equipped with movable glass slides (fig. 1.10).[71]

Whether glass windows in bathhouses also provided a view, or prospectus, seems to have depended primarily on the site: archaeological evidence indicates that the issue of prospectus played a greater role in the country than in the city, es-

Fig. 1.10. Diagrammatic reconstruction of the large, arched window in the *sudatorium* (sweating-room) of the baths of Faustina, Miletus (modern Turkey). The sections between the marble bars were glazed. Reconstruction: Dietwulf Baatz.

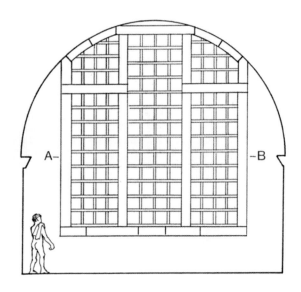

pecially if the location was scenic.[72] It was not, in fact, uncommon to design the baths of private countryside *villae* with specific attention to the view from the windows. This is vividly described in the abovementioned letter by Pliny the Younger, written around the turn of the first century and intended to convey to an urbanite friend the pleasures of Pliny's seaside villa in Laurentum outside of Rome: the villa featured, among other amenities, a "heated swimming-bath which is much admired and from which swimmers can see the sea."[73] As Pliny pointed out, this swimming pool was part of the *caldarium* (a hot, steamy room). This suggests that the windows with a view were both transparent and tightly sealed, which would have required either high-quality glass or lapis.[74] Sealants of this kind likely were used in other parts of Pliny's luxurious villa as well—for instance, in a window alcove (*zotheca*) providing a quasi-panoramic prospect with "the sea at its foot, the neighboring villas behind, and the woods beyond, views which can be seen separately from its many windows or blended into one."[75]

Clearly, not all glass windows in baths and villae were transparent enough to provide a view, but they all admitted generous amounts of light (lumen). It may not be a coincidence that, in addition to the Latin "*fenestra*," the words "*lumina*" and "*luminaria*," plural forms of the term "lumen," became an increasingly common way to refer to windows.[76] The quantity of daylight in baths and villae went well beyond the requirements prescribed in Roman law from the imperial period, where "lumen" is defined simply as the ability to see the sky from one's window.[77] From a practical point of view, solar light also helped to heat interiors. Indeed, it has been argued that the emergence of glass windows in Roman architecture reflected a "special and deliberate attention to sunlight and to climate in general."[78] According to this argument, deforestation had led to soaring prices for firewood, which in turn prompted Romans to make greater use of solar heat. Architectural glass certainly lent itself to this end: shortwave solar radiation easily passes through glass while the reradiated longwave heat is trapped indoors. This effect—known today as the "greenhouse effect"—was ideal for forcing houses and baths.[79] In a poem written around 90 CE, the Roman poet Statius seemed to be referring to this property of glass when he described the baths of a wealthy young contemporary named Claudius Etruscus: "The doorways are not behindhand, the ceilings are effulgent, the topmost parts are alive, shining with figures in vitreous variety. The very fire is amazed at the riches it surrounds and moderates its sway. Daylight everywhere abounds as the unconscionable sun penetrates the roof with all his rays, and is burned by a different heat."[80]

Still, it would be too monocausal an explanation to interpret the rise of architectural glass as a mere function of deforestation and increasing firewood prices. After all, the developing taste for sunlight in Roman society was not just a question of thermal comfort, but also one of prestige and fashion. Indeed, if the desire for more light had been entirely utilitarian, it would hardly have become the subject of criticism. Yet this is precisely what happened. Even Statius's poem, which at first appears to be a panegyric offered to a wealthy contemporary, reveals through tongue-in-cheek hints that it "is in reality an *anti-laudatio*, in which Statius would gently reprove the young man for the misdirected channeling of his admitted ability and wealth."[81] Some Romans raised their concerns in a less subtle fashion than Statius did. Among the harshest critics of abundant light was the first-century philosopher Seneca. In his *Epistulae morales* (Moral Letters), Seneca praised old Roman houses for having "a small bath, buried in darkness according to the old style, for our ancestors did not think that one could have a hot bath except in darkness."[82] In the era before window glass, those who could not afford lapis windows lit their baths primarily with candles and oil lamps. In Pompeii's oldest bathhouse, built in the second century BCE (and renovated around 80 BCE—that is, still in the age before window glass), archaeologists have found more than a thousand lamps, which must have served as the main sources of light.[83] By the time Seneca was writing, tastes had changed, and lighting by means of lamps was considered the "old style." Romans from this period and after sought as much light as possible in baths, a desire Seneca decried as a sign of decadence. Seneca longed for the days of Rome's republican period, when Romans had cultivated a certain disdain of *luxuria*.[84] Contrasting the small, dark baths of the republican past with the new ones from his own, imperial day and age, Seneca asked sarcastically:

> But who in these days could bear to bathe in such a fashion? We think ourselves poor and mean if our walls are not resplendent with large and costly mirrors; if our marbles from Alexandria are not set off by mosaics of Numidian stone, if their borders are not faced over on all sides with difficult patterns, arranged in many colours like paintings; *if our vaulted ceilings are not buried in glass*; if our swimming-pools are not lined with Thasian marble, once a rare and wonderful sight in any temple—pools into which we let down our bodies after they have been drained weak by abundant perspiration; and finally, if the water has not poured from silver spigots.[85]

Seneca's criticism reminds us that Roman balneal architecture underwent a significant transformation in this period—a transformation also reflected in the Latin language: as the traditional word for "bath," "*balneum*," no longer seemed adequate for the ever more lavish bathhouses of the imperial period, it became common to use the Greek-derived term "*thermae*" to refer to these impressive structures.[86] Seneca objected to every aspect of this transformation, including the tendency for larger windows, saying: "Nowadays . . . people regard baths as fit only for moths if they have not been so arranged that they receive the sun all day long through the widest of windows, if men cannot bathe and get a coat of tan at the same time, and if they cannot look out from their bath-tubs over stretches of land and sea."[87]

It is easy to dismiss Seneca's critique—as some historians have done—as the "grumbling" of an "old philosopher" with a nostalgic vision of the past.[88] But Seneca was not alone with his objections. Although the Roman glass industry had achieved an unprecedented level of sophistication, there were contemporaries who harbored reservations about architectural glass. Indeed, window glass at no point became a universal feature of Roman architecture. In the exceptionally well-preserved cities of Pompeii and Herculaneum, for instance, glass was common, but hardly the default in domestic architecture.[89] Excavations have also revealed that, due to security concerns, ground-floor windows tended to be small in the first

instance, often featuring iron bars and grilles instead of glass (fig. 1.11).[90] Pliny noted nostalgically that, in the past, lower-class residents used to grow plants in their windows, but in his time "atrocious burglaries in countless numbers compelled them to bar out all the view" (*praefigi prospectus*), by which he was referring to the installation of shutters and perhaps also iron bars.[91] Glass was more likely to be used in upper-floor windows, but even where that was the case, it did not necessarily apply to all windows.[92] Across the Roman Empire, traditional alternatives to glass—especially wooden shutters and organic sealants, such as skins or other animal membranes—continued to enjoy popularity. Lapis panes likewise remained a widely used option, as we know from both archaeological excavations and textual sources.[93]

Even in the case of bathhouses, the picture that emerges is complex: in Gallia Narbonensis (a Roman province roughly equivalent to the south of modern-day France), archaeologists have found fragments of glass panes in only twelve out of 218 excavated Roman bathhouses—that is, in only about 5 percent of sites. Of course, it is likely that glass shards have not always been correctly identified in these excavations or that they have been overlooked on occasion.[94] But even a generous estimate, taking into account these possibilities, would not justify the conclusion that *all* Roman bathhouses were glazed.

Particularly striking is the fact that religious buildings were rarely glazed. Certain sites of worship did not have windows of any kind: the cult of the (supposedly Persian) god Mithras, which became popular among Romans in the second century, typically convened in subterranean sanctuaries where torches were the main, or even the only, source of light. Such caverns (or *speluncae*, in Latin) epitomized the secretive nature of the cult, which required initiation. But the somber atmosphere also provided a congenial setting for dramatic effects involving artificial light (and sounds). Such carefully engineered effects seem to have played an important role in the worship of Mithras, who was—among other things—a sun deity and thus venerated as the source of true, divine light.[95]

Even the temples that the Romans built above ground—including for their traditional deities, such as the Olympian gods—featured very few windows or none at all. In this respect, the Romans stood in the tradition of the Egyptians and the Greeks, who used windows sparingly in sacred architecture. Typically, where windows appeared in Egyptian and Greek temples, they were located in the upper area of the wall and sealed (if at all) with iron or wooden latticework. Modern reconstructions suggest that the primary purpose of these windows was not lighting, but rather ventilation.[96]

The tall doors of ancient temples often served as the primary source of light. Iron grilles in or above the door panels admitted light even when the doors were shut and locked.[97] In some temples, the interstices between the roof beams were lined with marble sheets that were only a few inches thick and thus pervious to light. This method was employed, for instance, at the Acropolis in Athens.[98] While the marble roofing of the Parthenon does not survive, considerable parts of it were still intact as late as the seventeenth century, as we know from the travelogue of the Ottoman traveler Evliya Çelebi. Describing his visit to the Parthenon, which was used as a mosque at the time, Çelebi expressed his admiration for the ancient Greek architects who were able to build a marble roof that "is finer and shinier than lead, and sparkles in the sun like cut glass."[99]

A small subset of ancient temples received light from unsealed apertures in the roof. According to Vitruvius, temples dedicated to Jupiter Fulgor—that is, Jupiter in his capacity as the god of thunder and heaven—featured a roofless central

room (or *cella*). This allowed worshippers to see the sky and marvel at Jupiter's celestial power.[100] Still, such open-roof designs were rare even in Vitruvius's time. As he noted, "There is no example of this kind in Rome, only the eight-columned temple in Athens, in the Olympian temple."[101] Indeed, it remains unclear what exactly these openings looked like. However, there may have been a link between this type of sanctuary and temples that featured a circular opening, or *opaion*, in the roof. The best-known example of such an opaion survives in a Roman temple built more than a century after Vitruvius: the Pantheon in Rome. While the Pantheon's second level features conventional windows, a closer look reveals that they are bricked up and thus purely decorative; to this day, the only source of light, apart from the main door, is the almost thirty-foot-wide opaion at the apex of the dome (fig. 1.12).[102]

Despite the many continuities between Greek and Roman religion and, by extension, between their sacred architecture, there was one major difference: the Greeks did not produce window glass, whereas the Romans did. Why, then, did this technological advantage leave virtually no imprint on Roman temple architecture? More broadly speaking, why did windows—including glass windows—never become a prominent feature of Roman temples? To tackle these questions, it is important to keep in mind that in Roman times the type of building we now commonly refer to as a "temple" was only one part of a larger sacred precinct. The most important part of this precinct (*templum*) from a liturgical standpoint was the altar (*ara*), which was always located outside of the building and served as the site of regular animal sacrifices. As one scholar of Roman religion has put it, "Today we tend to think of religious services as taking place inside a building, but nearly all Roman religious rituals took place outside."[103] Indeed, the temple building itself—the so-called *aedes*—rarely served the purpose of worship. Its innermost room simply contained the cult statue of a deity or other sacred objects. What is more, Roman religion did not revolve around the recitation of texts, which might be another reason why ample lighting in the interior was not considered a priority.

Even as Rome's political and military rise led to the construction of ever larger temples across the empire, windows remained relatively marginal elements in these architectural designs. Not only was the liturgical need for windows limited, there were also practical concerns that militated against extensive fenestration: after all, the booty amassed by Roman armies often was presented to the gods and thus deposited in temples, which turned many a temple into a vault for precious objects. The Roman state treasury itself was stored in a temple. Unsurprisingly, this concentration of valuables in temples attracted thieves, and it was therefore sensible to limit the number of openings in the (often massive) walls or to insert them far above the ground.[104]

To the extent that Roman temples featured windows, stone *transennae* (latticework) and lapis specularis seem to have been more common than glass panes.[105] Visual depictions of Roman temples with glazed windows are almost nonexistent. On a more general level, representations of architectural glass are rare in Roman art (fig. 1.13). This, to be sure, was not due to artistic limitations on the part of painters: as early as the first century, Roman painters had mastered the art of depicting glass and its transparent effects, as evinced by a number of highly realistic representations of glass vessels.[106]

Why, then, was architectural glass so rarely depicted in Roman art—especially if it was as prestigious as some scholars have claimed it was? And why was glass not universally used in Roman architecture, not even in the houses of the wealthy and certainly not in temples? These questions still beg for an answer, but

Fig. 1.13. Wall painting discovered in a Christian catacomb, Rome, fourth century. The scene shows the biblical hero Samson killing Philistines with an ass's jawbone. The right-hand side depicts a building with glazed windows. Some scholars have identified the building as a pagan temple (more specifically, the one in which Samson died). However, glass windows of this kind were rare in ancient temples, including the Roman temples with which the anonymous artist would have been familiar. It is therefore more likely that the building represents the house of Samson's father-in-law, or (as the drawn curtain might indicate) that it is a symbol of the Promised Land. (Bargebuhr, *Paintings of the "New" Catacomb*, 68–69.)

due to the fragmentary nature of the surviving evidence, we may not find definitive answers.[107] Any explanation, however, will have to take into account that glass held an ambiguous status in the material world of the Romans. In the case of glass vessels, for instance, only the finest mouth-blown products—distinguished as they were by a high degree of transparency and individual finishing—counted as luxury items. Upper-class Romans were unlikely to dine with or drink from glass vessels, unless they were of remarkable artisanal quality.[108] As Stuart Fleming has argued, such exceptional vessels aside, glass "sat low in the hierarchy of Roman material values."[109] It ranked far below noble metals—especially gold and silver—or other precious (and more robust) materials such as marble or alabaster. Emperor Gallienus "always drank out of golden cups, for he scorned glass, declaring that there was nothing more common."[110]

Glass was also considered inferior to rock crystal, which Pliny the Elder praised as "the most costly product . . . of the earth's surface," and which was valued even above gold and silver.[111] There were practical reasons why rock crystal was more valuable than glass: for instance, crystal vessels kept liquids such as wine cool for longer than glass vessels did (by function of their differing thermal conductivities).[112] Such practical aspects aside, the inferior material status of glass also had to do with its ingredients: glass was made of sand, soda, and lime—in other words, materials considered less precious than metals and especially rock crystal (which was believed to be of unmatched purity).[113] According to a widespread ancient view, rock crystal was fossilized water that had frozen shortly after the creation of the world, when the elements had not yet interacted. Indeed, the Greek word "*krystallos*" means "ice." Rock crystal's primeval purity was considered the reason for its remarkable solidity: although ancient people had mastered the skill of melting glass's ingredients, they failed to melt rock crystal. Today, we know that there was a simple chemical reason: rock crystal melts at higher temperatures than ordinary sand—temperatures that ancient furnaces were unable to reach.[114] Lacking this insight, ancient people believed that the difference between crystal and glass was categorical. The venerable prestige of rock crystal extended to lapis specularis: no less an authority than Pliny the Elder declared it "palpably obvious that we have here [in lapis specularis] a liquid which, like rock-crystal, has been frozen and petrified by an exhalation in the earth."[115]

This material hierarchy remained in place even as Roman glassmakers went to great lengths to imitate rock crystal and lapis.[116] In fact, this use of glass to mimic costly materials—including precious stones—may have tarnished glass's reputation among discerning buyers.[117] It certainly did not lead to a decline in prices for real lapis, let alone for crystal products. As Pliny noted, "Glass-ware has now come to resemble rock-crystal in a remarkable manner," but "without diminishing the value of the latter."[118] In the same vein (but with a more pointed pen), the poet Martial captured the predilection for crystal when he portrayed a wealthy Roman who demands "that only large crystal cups be rubbed by my lips."[119] It fits into this picture that the Roman emperors of this period employed a special *praepositus crystallinis*—that is, an official tasked to guard the imperial court's crystalware and keep it in good condition.[120]

In the Roman material world, most glass products seem to have fallen into the same category as pottery. Glass and pottery products also shared a drawback:

they were particularly fragile. In Petronius's *Satyricon*, written in the middle of the first century, the nouveau-riche braggart Trimalchio exclaims that if glass "didn't break, it would be better than gold, but like it is, it's not worth havin'."[121] The historian Strabo related that in Rome some glass vessels could be bought "for a copper."[122] Indeed, the rapid expansion of the glass industry from Augustus's reign onward led to a fall in prices that left traces even on a linguistic level: the word "*vitrum*" (glass) first gained currency in Latin around the time of Augustus, yet a century later it was used in the proverbial phrase "*vitrea fracta*" (broken glass), an expression meaning "trifles."[123] The abundant availability of cheap vitreous tesserae—the small and often brightly colored glass pieces used for mosaics—may have reinforced the impression that glass was a cheap, mass-produced commodity.[124]

We know for a fact that lower-class Romans could afford glass vessels or other small-sized glass products. By the early fourth century, the daily wage of an unskilled laborer would have sufficed to purchase two ordinary glass vessels.[125] Window glass was even cheaper: the so-called Price Edict of Diocletian (issued in 301) indicates that fine "Alexandrian glass cups" cost thirty denarii per pound, whereas "window glass, second quality" fetched a mere fifth of that price (namely, six denarii per pound).[126] For wealthy Romans this was not just cheap—it was probably too cheap.[127] This might also help explain the persistent popularity of windows made of lapis, a material considered purer and more prestigious than glass. The imperial palaces in Rome are a case in point: in a rather unflattering account of an audience with Emperor Caligula, the philosopher Philo of Alexandria described how the erratic emperor "dashed at high speed into the large room of the house, and walked round it and ordered the windows all round to be restored with transparent stones, which in the same way as white glass do not obstruct the light but keep off the wind and the scorching sun."[128] A few years later, Emperor Nero likewise expressed a preference for mineral sealants over glass panes. What is more, he ordered certain windows of his famous Domus Aurea (Golden House) to be sealed with "phengite"—a stone that, according to Pliny, had been discovered only recently in Anatolia and was "as hard as marble, white and, even where deep-yellow vein occurred, translucent."[129]

In sum, the Romans considered window glass neither an indispensable architectural material nor one that necessarily enhanced the building from an aesthetic point of view. Where windows were glazed in the Roman world, this was

Fig. 1.14. Aula Palatina, Trier, Germany, fourth century. Its large windows provided copious daylight for the commercial and legal business transacted in the interior. The windows, now partly reconstructed, were apparently glazed.

done primarily out of practical considerations.[130] Bathhouses were one such setting in which glass was a sensible choice, as it not only provided weatherproofing and protection from heat loss, but also admitted light and solar heat.[131] But even in balneal architecture, glass was never the only option, and it seems to have been used most commonly in those bathhouses that featured oversized windows. The same holds true for basilicas—the public buildings used as market buildings and sometimes also as courthouses and town halls. The commercial and legal transactions taking place in the basilica required good interior lighting, which might be the reason why this building type often featured large windows, as in Trier's Aula Palatina, an audience hall built in the early fourth century and today the largest surviving ancient basilica (fig. 1.14). In these particular architectural contexts, glazing was advantageous and desirable.[132] By contrast, in temples and other sacred buildings, the Romans made only reluctant use of windows and glass. As we have seen, there were practical reasons for this reluctance, but glass's lack of prestige may have played a role as well.

From the perspective of Roman antiquity, nothing indicated that glass would become the most common window sealant in later periods of European history. This remarkable change in the attitude toward glass cannot simply be explained as a result of technological progress. Rather, it resulted from a fundamental reevaluation of glass's aesthetic and material value. It is particularly striking that in the post-Roman world, glass rose to unprecedented prominence in religious buildings—that is, in churches. As the next chapter will show, this architectural and aesthetic paradigm shift was inextricably linked to a transformative historical process: the Christianization of Europe.

2

Dark Ages?

Architectural Glass in Early Medieval Europe

Chapter-opening image: Detail of Fig. 2.2

For a long time, historians believed that the decline of the Roman Empire in the fourth and fifth centuries and the ensuing Migration period resulted in a demise of the glass industry. This assumption has led some scholars to claim that from the fifth century onward, Europe literally entered the "Dark Ages."[1] As recently as 2006, one (otherwise fine) study of the history of windows stated that "the Dark Ages may have been literally dark because there were no glass windows to admit light."[2] Such claims are rather tenuous.[3] And it would be outright wrong to assert, as some scholars have, that the mouth-blowing of window glass was rediscovered in Europe only around the year 1000.[4]

A closer look at the evidence reveals that glassmaking technology was never forgotten in post-Roman Europe. What did change was the geographical distribution of the technological know-how. While crown-glass production continued in the eastern Mediterranean, glassmakers in western Europe specialized in the production of cylinder glass (which, in English, also came to be known as "broad glass" or "muff"). The casting method is thought to have faded into oblivion in the transition to the medieval period, but archaeological findings raise questions about this view: in a number of medieval Viking settlements, such as in Denmark, fragments of cast-glass panes have been unearthed. The panes were probably imported from the Byzantine Empire, which in turn might indicate that cast-glass production was still practiced there at the time, at least on a small scale. By contrast, in western Europe, pane casting was not resumed until the seventeenth century—but when it was, the effect on architecture was dramatic, as a later chapter will show (see Chapter 10).[5]

On the whole, the technological continuities between ancient and medieval glassmaking were considerable. But this is not the only reason why the idea of the Middle Ages as literally being "Dark Ages" is misleading. In fact, the rise of Christianity led to greater demand for window glass than in any historical period before. As we will see, this demand was driven by specific theological ideas, and it is no coincidence that medieval churches became the primary sites for extensive use of architectural glass. This phenomenon is all the more remarkable given that in Roman times, religious edifices were almost never glazed.

The use of glass was not the only difference between Roman sacred architecture and early Christian architecture. The break was also visible on the level of architectural forms. In other words, late ancient and early medieval Christians rejected the Roman temple and instead adopted the basilica—more specifically the market basilica—as the blueprint for the House of God. The basilica, as a building type, had gained currency in the Roman world only from the second century BCE onward. With the rise of Christianity, extant Roman basilicas were frequently re-fashioned and consecrated as churches. In other cases, Roman basilicas served as the model for the construction of new churches.[6] Either way, the tendency was the same: early Christians drew on the tradition of Roman public, rather than religious, architecture—and in doing so, they appropriated a building type that featured more (glazed) windows than the temples had.[7]

Why did the basilica gain such importance in Christian sacred architecture? Some scholars have argued that this building type was particularly suited to meet the needs of the growing Christian communities, as it offered ample space for believers while also allowing for considerable variability and hierarchization in the spatial organization of the interior (for instance, by reserving the choir section and the apse for the clergy).[8] Another explanation stresses that the basilica was a powerful symbol of the imperial judicial system, which Christians invoked to describe God's supreme legal authority.[9] These explanations are plausible and certainly not mutually exclusive. But it is also possible that practical concerns about lighting influenced the Christian preference for the basilica. As we have seen, the interior of Roman temples rarely served as a space for worship, and the most important liturgical rituals were performed outdoors. Christianity, with its focus on communal prayer and text recitation, required a different kind of space. The basilica may have appealed to early Christians because it boasted more windows and, by extension, higher lighting levels than pagan temples did. The typical eastward orientation of Christian basilicas only heightened this effect: the apse—that is, the sanctum featuring the altar—not only was directed toward Jerusalem, but also received the bright light of the rising sun. This tied in with the "sacramental use of dawn and sunset," which characterized Christianity from its earliest days.[10]

It fits into this picture that early Christian churches often emphasized windows even more than traditional Roman basilicas did. For instance, not all Roman basilicas featured windows in the naves, but all major church basilicas from the fifth century onward did.[11] It is also no coincidence that early medieval descriptions of churches—a genre of rather terse and formulaic texts—paid significant attention to matters of fenestration: these texts consistently addressed very few pieces of information, including the building's general measurements, a count of its columns, and the number of windows.[12]

This is not to say that all early Christian churches were glazed or that there were no alternatives to glass. Late ancient Christian authors such as Lactantius and Saint Jerome explicitly distinguished between glass and lapis specularis—an indication that both materials were still known and in use at the time.[13] Early Christian communities also employed other materials from the broad spectrum of sealants that characterized Roman architecture. For instance, there is evidence that well into the early medieval period, church windows were sealed with waxed fabrics, wooden shutters, metal grilles, stone lattices, or lead vents (that is, perforated sheets of lead).[14]

The availability of such alternatives, however, does not contradict the trend of increasing use of glass in Christian churches from the early fifth century onward. Galla Placidia, the daughter of the Roman emperor Theodosius, is said to have financed the insertion of glass into the eastern windows of the church of San Giovanni Evangelista in Ravenna in 426.[15] Slightly more is known about similar measures taken in the church of Saint-Just des Macchabées in Lyon. Like their counterparts in Ravenna, these Lyonnais glass windows have not survived, but we have an account by Bishop Sidonius Apollinaris, who described the church's appearance around the year 469 as follows: "Marble diversified by various shining tints pervades the vaulting, the floor, the windows; forming designs of diverse colour, a verdant grass-green encrustation brings winding lines of sapphire-hued stone over the leek-green glass."[16] From another fifth-century source we know that the papal basilica of San Paolo fuori le Mura in Rome featured glass in various colors. According to the Christian writer and poet Prudentius, these glass windows and their colors reminded churchgoers of flowers in the spring (*sic prata vernis floribus*).[17]

This tendency only increased in the course of the sixth century.[18] We hear of two additional churches in Ravenna (San Vitale and Sant'Apollinare in Classe) furnished with glass in the 540s, and in the case of Sant'Apollinare we know that some of it was uncolored, while the rest was blue, green, brown, or red.[19] A few decades later—but still in the sixth century—the Christian poet Venantius Fortunatus praised the Merovingian king Childebert I for establishing the church of Saint-Vincent in Paris: it was "given eyes by means of glass windows" (*vitreis oc-*

ulata fenestris) and hence the interior (*aula*) was "the first to capture the rays [of the sun]."[20]

As this brief survey reflects, a considerable share of the window glass in early medieval churches seems to have been colored. It is often hard to determine to what extent this was due to the deliberate addition of coloring agents or simply a result of natural chemical residues. In Müstair, Switzerland, excavations in a Carolingian monastery have recently brought to light more than thirteen hundred glass fragments, a large number of which are colored (fig. 2.1).[21] Such findings are all the more significant given that skilled early medieval glassmakers were capable of producing glass that was remarkably colorless. They benefited from the fact that Roman trade networks for Levantine plant ash, a fluxing agent with a decolorizing effect, were still intact.[22] Decolorized glass of this kind, which was also produced in the Byzantine Empire and in the early medieval Islamic world, was no doubt a prized commodity in western Europe. But it served primarily in the production of drinking vessels.[23] Writing around the year 600, Isidore of Seville noted: "The highest esteem is granted to clear glass with its close similarity to crystal."[24] More than two centuries later, Bishop Hrabanus Maurus repeated Isidore's statement almost verbatim—a reminder that crystal-clear vessels remained prestigious objects throughout the Middle Ages.[25]

With respect to architectural glass, however, we observe the opposite tendency: in this segment of the marketplace, colored glass was in growing demand.[26] Was this simply due to economic considerations? True, colorless glass of the highest quality was difficult to produce in large quantities, which made it expensive. But artificially colored glass was hardly cheap either. Certain varieties of colored glass, in fact, were particularly expensive—for instance, red glass, the manufacture of which required great skill. In sum, the relatively rare use of colorless glass in early medieval churches cannot be attributed to economic restraints or technical limitations. Rather, as we will see, the installation of colored glass in a growing number of churches was driven by a specific aesthetic vision.[27]

Church windows often were sealed with numerous small pieces of colored glass embedded in stone tracery or held together by lead lines.[28] Here again, this was not the result of technical limitations, but rather a deliberate choice: early medieval glassmakers certainly had the skills to produce rectangular panes, as the mouth-blowing of such panes was always the first step of the cylinder method. In practice, however, the cooled panes were cut into small, irregularly shaped pieces

Fig. 2.1. Virtually no early medieval glass windows survive in situ. However, fragments such as these, found in the Carolingian monastery of Müstair, Switzerland (probably dating to the late eighth century) give us a sense of the glowing *vitre-mosaïques* (glass mosaics) that adorned windows of churches and monastic chapels in this period.

by means of a hot iron. In the final stage, pieces of different colors were assembled in one window. In other words, the goal was not to produce monochrome, standardized panes (of the type we use today), but rather polychrome, mosaic-like windows. In French, such windows are aptly known as "*vitre-mosaïques*"—that is, "glass mosaics."[29]

From the seventh century onward, glass with a natural tint seems to have lost ground to artificially colored glass (also known as "pot-metal glass," a term reflecting the addition of metallic coloring agents and the subsequent melting in a special clay pot).[30] This is another indication that the polychrome effect of windows was a deliberate aesthetic goal. The glazing of church windows was, in itself, never a solely pragmatic measure. The *Liber pontificalis* (Book of Pontiffs), a medieval chronicle of popes and their deeds, records how around 800 Pope Leo III ordered the insertion of "glass of various colors" into the apsidal windows of St. John Lateran—a commission fulfilling two purposes in that it both "sealed *and* decorated" the windows (*ex vitro diversis coloribus conclusit atque decoravit*).[31]

The decorative aspect of polychrome glass became even more conspicuous when, in the course of the ninth century or perhaps earlier, mosaic-like ornamental designs were complemented by representations of human figures. From a technical point of view, the underlying principle was still the same: glass pieces of different colors were assembled according to a carefully prepared design and usually joined by means of lead lines. New, however, was the way in which the interplay between glass and lead assumed compositional importance: the lead lines helped to accentuate the contours of the human figures, while the colored glass provided volume and contrast.

The first explicit mention of church windows depicting human figures dates to the year 864 and comes from France, a country that had emerged as a center of European glassmaking in this period.[32] The actual windows do not survive; in general, only fragments of figurative windows from this time have come down to us.[33] A century later, Archbishop Adalbero of Reims commissioned for his church "windows depicting various stories" (*fenestris diversas continentibus historias*).[34] The oldest windows of this kind that survive in situ—the so-called Prophet Windows in Augsburg Cathedral—date to a later period, probably around 1100 (fig. 2.2). Still, the Augsburg windows convey a fair impression of what early figurative glass windows must have looked like: the figures—in this case, prophets from the Old Testament—are composed from a multitude of colored glass pieces and are depicted in a static, frontal posture with little interaction with one another. As in all figurative glass of this period, color was not always used in a naturalistic fashion. This, of course, was a concession to technical restraints, as the chromatic spectrum of pot-enamel glass was typically limited to five different colors: blue, red, green, yellow, and purple.[35]

Only in the High Middle Ages did representations of human figures in glass

Fig. 2.2. Detail showing the prophet Hosea from the so-called Prophet Windows of Augsburg Cathedral, Germany, ca. 1060–1135. These dates would make them the oldest figurative stained-glass windows still in situ. The windows, each about 7 feet high, portray five Old Testament figures in a frontal and rather static posture.

windows become more naturalistic and dynamic.[36] The greater ease in depicting narrative scenes owed much to the method of applying dark vitreous paint on glass, as this allowed the artist to devote more attention to pictorial detail and differentiation. These enamel paints consisted of metal oxides (copper or iron oxide), finely ground glass, and a vinegar-based liquid serving as the binding agent. They were applied directly to the glass surface and then fired to ensure permanency.[37] The result is known as "stained glass"—a somewhat misleading, modern term: it would be more accurate to speak of "colored, stained, and painted glass."[38]

The technique itself was not new. Ancient Roman glassmakers had mastered the art of painting on glass, but they seem to have used this skill only for the decoration of vessels.[39] Painting on glass windows was a medieval innovation. It remains difficult, however, to date the emergence of this art with precision. In the 1930s, archaeologists discovered fragments of a painted glass pane showing a blessing Christ in one of Ravenna's oldest churches, and ever since there has been speculation as to whether figurative painting with black enamel paint was practiced as far back as the sixth century.[40] Findings from elsewhere in Europe suggest a later date: the oldest reliably datable fragments of painted glass windows stem from the ninth century, and recent research suggests that the Ravenna pane, too, was produced around that time.[41]

Still, glass painting did not gain currency in Europe before the tenth and eleventh centuries, probably because it required considerable skill to master this technique and apply it on a large scale. Stained-glass artists had to walk a fine line: they were aware of the new possibilities for depicting details such as faces, hands, shadows, or garment folds; at the same time they knew that the dark paint blocked out light—especially when applied in thick layers, as was often the case in early painted glass. Given these challenges, it is not surprising that the art of painting on glass soon became a métier in its own right, separate from glassmaking.[42]

By the High Middle Ages, polychrome glass windows with painted details had become a hallmark of churches, especially large cathedrals, all over Europe. This process went hand in hand with the general proliferation of glass in sacred architecture. According to modern estimates, between the years 1250 and 1500 alone, no less than forty thousand tons of glass were installed in the windows of European churches (fig. 2.3).[43] Unsealed or latticed windows became an increasingly rare sight. True, in rural parish churches they disappeared more slowly than in great cathedrals.[44] And in the southernmost parts of Christian Europe—for in-

Fig. 2.3. Sainte-Chapelle, Paris, 1240s. Commissioned by King Louis IX, this royal chapel in the heart of Paris is one of the most spectacular manifestations of medieval stained glass. More than one thousand separate glass panels (some of which have been restored) depict scenes from the Old and New Testaments; the borders feature vegetal ornament and royal insignia. The effect is stunning: it seems as if the walls have been dissolved into a tapestry of glowing colors.

stance, in Sicily—stone and lead lattices were still common in the twelfth century, primarily for climatic reasons.[45] Such regional traditions, however, do not contradict the broader picture we observe: from around the year 1000 onward, the standard expectation was that church windows were, or should be, glazed. This expectation informed the anonymous chronicler writing around 1060 who, in describing the recently completed abbey church of Saint-Bénigne in Dijon, noted that in the entire church "there is a total of 120 windows, either sealed or *to be sealed* with glass."[46] In older churches where glass had not yet been installed, similar efforts were made. This transition—and the importance assigned to it—is vividly described in a late tenth-century letter written by Gozbert, the abbot of Tegernsee monastery in Bavaria. In this document, Abbot Gozbert profusely thanked a certain Count Arnold of Vogaburg (Vohburg) for financing the glass windows of the church of Tegernsee. Unfortunately, these windows do not survive, as a fire destroyed them just a few decades after their installation.[47] But thanks to Gozbert's letter we get a sense of their visual appearance—as well as of the strong impression they left on contemporaries:

> You have merited that we pray to God for you who has elevated our place with such honorable works which we did not know from the past and did not hope to see ourselves. Up to now the windows of our church were sealed with old pieces of cloth. In your happy days the golden-haired sun has first lightened the floors of our basilica through the colored glass of paintings. The hearts of all those who see it and who express to each other their admiration for the variety of this unfamiliar work are overwhelmed by manifold joy.[48]

As Gozbert's letter makes clear, the transition from non-vitreous sealants to glass was a major caesura in the way the congregation experienced the sacred space. It is indeed no exaggeration to say that the large-scale installation of polychrome, figurative windows in churches was a watershed moment in the history of Western art and architecture. It set into motion what Roland Günter has aptly called the "imagification of windows" (*Verbildlichung des Fensters*)—that is, the process of windows becoming images.[49] This process still resonates in the English word "story," which originates from the Latin term "*historia*" and came to denote the horizontal tiers of a building—a shift in meaning that occurred in the High Middle Ages and is thought to reflect the emergence of narrative stained-glass windows (*historiae*) in these parts of the building.[50]

The increasing demand for polychrome, figurative glass also led to the replacement of church windows made of lapis specularis. Unless the lapis was naturally colored—which was rare—the panes made from it were bound to lack the spectacular visual effect of artificially colored glass. In the ancient world, where polychromy did not yet constitute the aesthetic ideal in window design, lapis's limited color spectrum was not perceived as a shortcoming. Even in the early medieval period, there was still a certain demand for panes made of mineral materials. The *Liber pontificalis* mentions not only the insertion of colored glass into the windows of St. John Lateran in Rome, but also records how Pope Leo III ordered other windows in the same church to be repaired with "metal gypsum" ("*et alias fenestras basilicae ex metallo cyprino reparavit*"). The same pope also commissioned panes of this kind for the windows of San Paolo fuori le Mura.[51] In both cases, the term "metal gypsum" seems to have referred to a certain kind of selenite, which, due to its iridescent qualities, was sometimes compared to metal.[52] Mineral sealants were also employed in some windows of Old St. Peter's in Rome, and the same holds true for prestigious Carolingian churches such as Aachen Cathedral and Corvey Abbey.[53]

With the rise of polychrome—and, subsequently, figurative—glass, mineral sealants fell out of fashion. Even textual sources describing such windows became scarce. In the second half of the eleventh century, we hear about the use of lapis (alongside glass) in the context of reconstruction work at the abbey of Monte Cassino.[54] And in the thirteenth century, an Italian traveler passing through the German lands occasionally spotted old church windows made of selenite.[55] Mineral sealants with colored patterning seem to have survived a little longer, perhaps because they bore greater resemblance to colored glass. In Orvieto's Cathedral—one of the finest examples of Gothic architecture in Italy—some windows in the naves were furnished with panes cut from yellow-veined alabaster as late as the 1320s (fig. 2.4).[56] In the church of St. Vitale and Agricola in Bologna (fig. 2.5), the yellowish alabaster in the windows might date back to the fifth century, but it is more likely that it was installed during later phases of construction (that is, closer to the thirteenth century).

By the end of the Middle Ages, glass—typically, stained glass—had firmly established itself as the standard sealant in church architecture.[57] It was thus a deliberate anachronism when the fifteenth-century Renaissance architect Leon Battista Alberti recommended sealing the windows of churches (or rather "temples," as he called them, in an unmistakably humanist fashion) with "thin slabs of translucent alabaster or a lattice of bronze or marble."[58] Elsewhere in his writings, Alberti was enough of a realist to recommend the glazing of church windows.[59] Indeed, Alberti's musings about lapis windows did not reflect a common architectural practice at the time, but rather his humanist admiration of ancient architecture, which he studied down to the smallest details. Like other humanists, Alberti knew about the importance of lapis specularis in Roman architecture from ancient texts. Similarly, the sixteenth-century artist, architect, and writer Giorgio Vasari was aware of the fact that mineral stones "were used by the ancients for baths and hot-air chambers and for all those places which needed protection against winds."

Fig. 2.4. Orvieto Cathedral, Italy, begun 1290. As late as the 1320s, several windows of side chapels were furnished with yellowish alabaster.

However, even a polymath like Vasari could name only one then-extant building—a church in the Tuscan town of San Miniato—that featured windows of this kind (and these windows were not contemporary, but rather a relict from medieval times).[60] Around the time when Vasari was writing about this subject in Italy, the Englishman William Harrison made similar observations in his *Description of England* (1577): "I find obscure mention of the specular stone also to have been found and applied to this use in England, but in such doubtful sort as I dare not affirm it for certain."[61] A generation later, John Donne invoked that "thing unknown / to our late times, the use of specular stone / through which all things within without were shown.—Of such were temples."[62] Given how rare lapis windows had become in this period, it was no exaggeration when Johann Heinrich

Fig. 2.5. Church of St. Vitale and Agricola, Bologna, Italy, begun fifth century. The dating of the alabaster windows is uncertain, but the thirteenth century seems most likely. As at Orvieto Cathedral (see fig. 2.4), such alabaster windows were a rather anachronistic choice at the time.

Zedler's eighteenth-century *Universal-Lexicon*—perhaps the most comprehensive of all early modern encyclopedias—summarized that the sealing of windows with mineral materials was virtually "unknown."[63]

This does not mean, however, that translucent or transparent stones generally fell out of favor. While they largely disappeared from architecture, they enjoyed great popularity in the field of artistic craftwork, especially in High Medieval reliquaries and other containers for precious objects (fig. 2.6).[64] The demand for solid, transparent containers of this kind was related to a growing visual piety from the twelfth century onward—a piety driven by the Church's intensified promotion of the cult of saints and their relics. In the early Middle Ages, the relics of saints often were preserved in lavishly ornamented metal caskets and shrines.

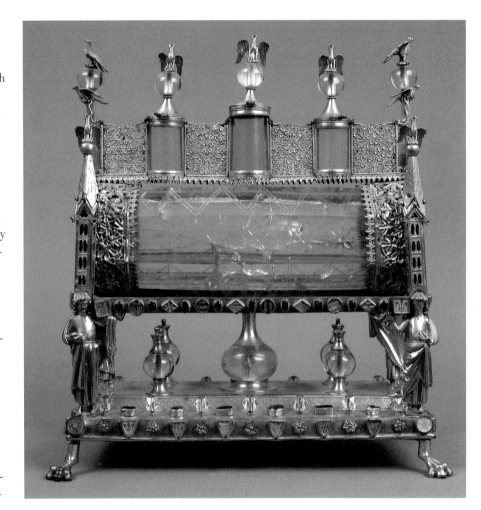

Fig. 2.6. Reliquary, probably produced in France, late twelfth century. The Metropolitan Museum of Art, New York. This reliquary is made of perfectly clear rock crystal. (The gilded copper setting is a nineteenth-century replica.) The crystal capsule held relics of several saints, including Philip the Apostle and Saint Catherine. The use of rock crystal responded to an increasing desire on the part of medieval worshippers to see holy objects such as relics. This visual piety was encouraged by the High Medieval Church and reminds us that, in certain religious contexts, transparency was considered legitimate and, indeed, desirable.

From the twelfth century onward, reliquaries increasingly were designed in a way that allowed worshippers to see the holy objects within. At the same time, these transparent containers reflected increasing restrictions on tactile access to relics, as laid down in the decrees of the Fourth Lateran Council (1215).[65] Reliquaries made of highly transparent rock crystal (so-called ostensories) enjoyed particular popularity.[66] As Michael Camille has put it succinctly, "Gothic reliquaries became like shop-windows."[67] When the term "transparency"—derived from the medieval Latin neologism *"transparentia"*—came into use in late medieval English, it typically referred to such crystal containers rather than to windows.[68]

The demand for crystal-made containers reminds us that there were religious contexts in which medieval people desired material transparency. And in these particular contexts, rock crystal—with its aura of purity and preciousness—was indeed a sensible choice: Christian theologians were aware of the ancient tradition that considered rock crystal nobler and purer than other minerals because it did not require any further improvement by humans.[69] The uniqueness of crystal was, of course, easier to assert in theory than to ascertain in practice—after all, the best medieval glassmakers had mastered the skill of producing glass that closely resembled rock crystal. Tellingly, in thirteenth-century Venice the guild of the *cristellarii* (the workers of rock crystal) complained to the government about local glassmakers who produced glass vessels, beads, and fake gems that could easily be mistaken for rock crystal. Even reliquaries were sometimes made of colorless glass that was almost indistinguishable from crystal.[70]

If such high-quality transparent glass existed, why was it not used for purposes of fenestration? More broadly speaking, why were colorless windows not nearly as popular in medieval times as colored windows were? From a modern perspective, the medieval preference for polychrome window glass might indeed seem puzzling: we appreciate medieval stained-glass windows as historical artifacts, but very few people today would choose polychrome glass for public buildings or homes, as it admits less light than colorless windows do. The modern desire for light is, of course, not an anthropological constant, but rather a historical phenomenon in its own right, as we will see in later chapters (especially Chapter 10). Medieval churchgoers did not seek maximum light, but rather a special kind of light—less bright, but at the same time more variegated than the interior light we are used to today.[71]

It is true that polychrome windows—especially when painted with figurative details—resulted in lower lighting levels than would have been the case had colorless glass been used.[72] Still, this does not mean that church interiors were dark—certainly not by the standards of the time. After all, windows were never the only source of illumination in medieval churches. Myriad candles and lamps contributed to interior lighting, especially during holidays.[73] Even on ordinary days, the effect of dozens or hundreds of candles burning in the interior formed an essential—and intentional—part of the unique sensory, and sometimes mystical, experience associated with church space.[74] This held true not only for major cathedrals, but also for smaller churches such as the Carolingian basilica of Saint-

Denis (now defunct): according to an account from the year 799, the interior of this "early church" (*primitiva ecclesia*) was brightened by no fewer than 1,250 artificial lights (*luminaria*).[75]

Around the same time—the first decade of the ninth century—Charlemagne issued a decree to ensure that sufficient lighting was available in all churches of his empire. Whether he envisioned the light coming from lamps, windows, or both is not specified in the document.[76] We do know, however, that there was a long-standing tradition of using candles to illuminate the shrines and images of saints.[77] In the course of the Middle Ages, new theological ideas and doctrines led to further measures toward enhanced illumination. From the thirteenth century onward, for instance, the Church assigned unprecedented importance to the adoration of the Host during Mass, and this made it necessary to put the Host, as it were, in the limelight. The use of torches was one possible way, and in some dioceses, torch bearers who helped illuminate the Eucharistic liturgy even received an indulgence; in other places, affluent churchgoers left bequests to ensure the ready availability of candles during Mass.[78] This is another reminder that, on a concrete level, the "Dark Ages" were hardly as dark as has been claimed by some modern scholars. Medieval accounts make it clear that contemporaries perceived glazed churches as well-lighted.[79] What is more, Christian churches, seen from the perspective of Greco-Roman antiquity, were, on the whole, much better lit than the sparsely fenestrated pagan temples.[80]

The Christian attention to issues of lighting was not accidental. Nor was the predilection for stained glass and the polychrome light that it engendered. As Michael Camille has put it, "Nothing was more beautiful to the medieval beholder than this colored brightness."[81] This delight in colored glass was not, to be sure, unique to medieval western Europe. We find similar tendencies in Byzantine and Islamic architecture at the time. In Islamic palaces and mosques from the seventh and eight centuries onward (that is, beginning in the Umayyad period), colored crown-glass windows known as "*qamariyya*" were a common feature. As in the Christian tradition, Islamic colored glass evoked notions of divine light while also serving decorative purposes and displaying wealth.[82]

There was one important difference, however, between Islamic and European architectural glass: in medieval Islamic architecture, glass was typically embedded in stucco grilles, whereas in Europe it became common to use lead tracery (fig. 2.7). This difference, which might at first seem a mere technical detail, had

Fig. 2.7. An Islamic *qamariyya* window in the Madrasa of al-Nasir Muhammad, Cairo, late thirteenth century. The stucco surround is original, but the window grille dates to the Ottoman period. The combination of vegetal and geometric forms is characteristic of medieval Islamic window design, making for a striking contrast to the figurative and narrative depictions that became common in European churches of this period.

wide-ranging artistic consequences: the design of Islamic qamariyya windows was determined by the rigid stucco tracery; by contrast, in European windows the malleable lead lines followed the image design. In practice this meant that the qamariyya was well suited to geometrical or patterned designs, while European lead tracery lent itself to the representation of figurative, narrative scenes.[83] Indeed, Christianity deliberately employed figurative images to convey key theological doctrines. The situation was more complicated in Islamic societies, where the visual representation of humans tended to raise concerns about idolatry. It was certainly permissible—and indeed common—in medieval Islamic countries to paint floral or vegetal motifs on glass set in geometric tracery.[84] But it was rare for windows to have a *narrative* function. As Finbarr Barry Flood has shown, medieval Islamic architecture produced glass windows of great beauty and sophistication, but the window in the Islamic tradition did not develop "the complex and canonical symbolic nuances which it had in Byzantium and in the medieval West."[85]

As this observation suggests, any attempt to compare the Islamic and the

Christian tradition must take into account the special case of Byzantium. Located geographically between the Latin West and the Islamic world, Byzantium was not only home to craftsmen and artists of great renown, but also a place where a distinctive tradition of glass art emerged. As in the Islamic tradition, geometrical designs played a prominent role in Byzantine architectural glass, but judging from surviving fragments, representations of humans were not unheard of either. Flexibility also characterized Byzantine technical execution, as glass craftsmen used both stucco and lead tracery. Byzantine stucco windows, with their tendency for geometric patterns, resemble—and, indeed, influenced—their Islamic counterparts; by contrast, the (much rarer) leaded windows of Byzantine churches were more akin to Western stained glass in that they depicted human figures.[86]

Experiments with figurative imagery aside, there were important differences between western European and Byzantine stained glass. Byzantine architecture explored and employed the effects of colored glass, but on the whole "the focus was on interior illumination rather than light from without."[87] Too much bright, colored light from outside threatened to interfere with the visual effect of the elaborate, often gilded mosaics that were essential to the interior decoration of many Byzantine churches. Stained glass could also distract from the glittering and gleaming effect of other precious surface materials—such as gold, silver, and marble—that characterized Byzantine church interiors.[88] These problems were less likely to arise if the windows featured uncolored glass; the same held true for glassless screens or lattice windows, which were also commonly used in Byzantine churches (as was the case in Islamic mosques). Even the Hagia Sophia in Constantinople, for centuries the largest church of Christendom, featured stone transennae that apparently were unglazed.[89] In the transition to the High Medieval period, mystical tendencies gained currency in Byzantium, which led, among other things, to a greater emphasis on nocturnal services. This, in turn, increased the importance of illumination—but the additional light came from the extraordinarily elaborate lamps and candelabra for which Byzantine churches were famed.[90]

Of course, mosaics and other glittering wall surfaces also existed in the West. But as a genre, the mosaic never attained the same importance in western Europe as it held in Byzantine churches. One exception to the rule was Venice, where mosaics featured prominently in many medieval churches. This was a testament to Byzantine artistic influence, but on a more practical level it also reflected the fact that the humidity in the lagoon was not favorable to fresco-style wall painting.[91]

Be that as it may, the prominence of colored mosaics and marble revetments might explain why Venice, despite its highly advanced glass industry, boasted relatively few polychrome church windows.[92]

The Byzantine and Venetian concerns about colored glass and its interfering effect were less pressing elsewhere in Europe: in northern Europe, especially, it was not mosaics, but rather wall paintings, that became the hallmark of church interiors. Murals of this kind lacked the gleam and bright color characteristic of mosaics, such that polychrome light was less likely to distract from the visual effect. Also, the murals often alternated with unpainted wall sections. As art historians have pointed out, in such an architectural setting, conventional daylight would have "highlighted the contours of the church interior in a harsh way."[93] By contrast, a softer, colored light helped to emphasize the contiguous quality of the wall. The windows did not appear as bright, glaring "holes," but rather as harmonically integrated, ornamental elements.[94] Taking this argument a step further, some scholars have argued that medieval stained glass became "just another vehicle for painted decoration, another opportunity for that most important mediaeval aesthetic category, *varietas*, and a further pretext for conspicuous display."[95] This decorative effect, however, was only one of several reasons for the installation of colored glass. The extraordinary prominence of stained glass in medieval churches cannot be fully understood without taking into account the larger theological context of the time—especially the Christian theology of light, which we will turn to in the next chapter.

3

Light from Light

The Theology of Stained Glass

Chapter-opening image: Detail of Fig. 3.2

The rise of stained, figurative glass in the medieval West was an un-precedented—and in many ways unique—phenomenon. So was the prominence that glass, as an architectural material, assumed in churches. Neither in the Byzantine Empire nor in the Otto-man Empire that succeeded it was glass used on the same scale and as conspicuously in sacred architecture as it was in the medieval West. This, of course, was not a matter of technological know-how: throughout the medieval period and beyond, glassmakers in the eastern Mediterranean and the Middle East were just as skilled, and in some respects even more skilled, than their colleagues in the West. Glass's ubiquity in European sacred architecture had reasons well beyond technology.

The sheer amount of architectural glass in European churches, especially from the Gothic period onward, did not fail to draw the attention of foreign observers. As late as 1665, an Ottoman traveler visiting western Europe as a member of a diplomatic delegation recorded the deep impression that the large windows of Christian churches left on him. About St. Stephen's Cathedral in Vienna he wrote: "If man looks at this convent [sic] from a far distance, his eyes will dazzle from the sparkle of the window panes of cut glass and crystal and from the gleam of gold crosses, tall as a man, in 300 places. This great cathedral glitters like the gold mine of Mount Akra in Kurdistan and dazzles the eyes like a mountain of light. It is such a brilliant temple of Messiah-worship."[1]

It would be simplistic to argue that the glazing of churches was merely a pragmatic measure, as it had been in Roman basilicas and bathhouses. True, glazed windows provided the church with protection from inclement weather and heat loss. But from a practical point of view, the glass windows of churches also had drawbacks: most importantly, they often were not openable.[2] This sometimes became a major problem: the generous use of incense for liturgical purposes made the air in churches stuffy or even intolerable, especially when the incense's ingredients were of poor quality (as we know was the case in dioceses and parishes with limited financial means). The problem of poor air quality was particularly likely to arise on important religious occasions that required an elaborate liturgy and attracted large crowds to church—for instance, Mass and church holidays, but also special events such as baptisms, marriages, and funeral services. Even on regular days, the air in churches was hardly clear and fresh, due to the smoke produced by the great number of candles (and sometimes also torches) in the interior. Another problem—especially on an olfactory level—was that poor churchgoers often donated cheap candles made of tallow (as opposed to the higher-quality beeswax candles officially prescribed by the Church).[3]

The glazing of church windows did nothing to remedy the problems of stale air and bad smells. In fact, it only aggravated these issues. Occasionally, large stained-glass lights featured a "vent window"—that is, a small, openable segment.[4] In smaller churches, however, priests sometimes resorted to more drastic measures, such as ordering that unglazed ventilation windows be broken in the walls to ensure a minimum circulation of air. If this was not possible—for either structural or financial reasons—the last resort was to temporarily remove the glass windows on well-attended occasions when ventilation problems threatened to pose a serious obstacle to performing the service. Thus, on the occasion of a large funeral in Norfolk in 1466, a glazier was hired to remove two glass windows "to let out the reek of the torches at the dirge."[5]

Medieval stained-glass windows also fell short of providing a view (or prospectus, in the terminology of Roman law). The multitude of colored glass pieces made it virtually impossible to see anything concrete through these windows.[6] Even when colorless glass formed part of the window, these pieces were often deliberately thick and opaque because glassmakers used them to create the effect of whiteness within the larger, polychrome composition.[7] Writing around 1400, the Italian glass painter Antonio da Pisa argued that one-third of a stained-glass window should consist of uncolored glass, as this would make the composition easier to perceive and more joyous (*allegro*).[8] But even if a window's glass pieces had all been colorless, this would not have resulted in a clear view of the exterior. For one thing, the dense lead tracery inevitably produced a fragmented view. For another, church windows often were placed above eye level, such that churchgoers might see the sky, but usually not the surrounding urban or natural environment.[9]

The tendency to insert windows in the upper wall sections was not dictated by structural exigencies. Here again, it was a deliberate architectural choice. This is particularly apparent in the case of Romanesque single-nave churches, where it would have been structurally possible to extend the windows into the lower parts of the wall, as there was no obstruction from lateral naves and their roofs. Still, fenestration often was reserved for the clerestory (that is, the upper wall sections), with the result that the brightest zone of the church was not where the churchgoer stood, but rather the area to which he or she looked up.[10]

Fig. 3.1. The south rose of Notre-Dame, Paris, 1260s. From the exterior, nothing indicates the spectacular effect that the stained glass creates for those inside the church.

It would have been even more difficult to look through medieval church windows from the outside.[11] This had to do not only with the windows' high position, but also with their coloring: due to the lack of strong backlight from the interior, stained-glass windows appear dark when seen from outside (fig. 3.1). As Johann Wolfgang von Goethe later put it in a poem about painted church windows: "From the market-place there is nothing to see, all is gloomy, vacant of colour."[12] This reminds us that the unique visual effect of medieval stained-glass windows could be experienced only *within* the church (fig. 3.2). Goethe, whose interest in medieval stained glass sprang from his inquiries into the theory of colors, described this visual effect succinctly in the second half of his poem:

> Come but within! Greet, coloured bright,
> The holy chapel in its glory
> Of ornament and sacred story,
> Swift-flashing but untransitory, Significant of nobler light:
> Children of God! Fulfil your mission,
> Thus edify and charm the vision![13]

Goethe's lines capture—albeit from a modern vantage point—the essential purpose of medieval stained glass: its powerful visual effect on those in the interior was meant to inspire a profound religious experience. Indeed, it is only against the backdrop of Christian theology that we can fully understand why stained glass became an increasingly common feature of medieval churches.

The theological reasoning was two-pronged. First, stained-glass windows depicting scenes from the Bible or from the lives of saints were supposed to teach and edify churchgoers. In an age when illiteracy was very common, religious images generally functioned—as Pope Gregory the Great had famously noted—as vehicles for conveying biblical stories and Christian doctrine to ordinary people: "What Scripture is to the educated, images are to the ignorant, who see through them what they must accept; they read in them what they cannot read in books."[14] This didactic quality of visual representations was not, of course, specific to stained glass: paintings or statues could—and did—fulfill just the same function.

Second, what distinguished glass from all other artistic media was its unique relation to light. As Otto von Simson has noted, medieval theology was indebted to Neoplatonic metaphysics in positing that "light is the most noble of natural phenomena, the least material, the closest approximation to pure form. Light moreover is the creative principle in all things."[15] The degree of Neoplatonic influences remains a subject of scholarly debate.[16] One thing, however, is clear: the medieval Church equated light with divine qualities—a belief in line with the New Testament, where Christ famously says: "I am the light of the world" (John 8:12).[17] The Nicene Creed (325) elaborated on this notion when it referred to Christ as the "light from light" (*lumen de lumine*), thereby equating the purest manifestation of light with God the Father.[18]

In the medieval church, light was therefore more than just a practical convenience; it was the vehicle of a theological idea.[19] And stained glass, more than any

Fig. 3.2. The south rose of Notre-Dame seen from within the church. Commissioned by King Louis IX (Saint Louis), this stained-glass rose has a diameter of roughly 40 feet. The visual effect was, and still is, arresting.

other architectural feature, translated this idea of Christ and God the Father as lumen into a concrete physical experience.[20] It reminded churchgoers of the privilege of divine illumination: "Ye were sometimes darkness, but now are ye light in the Lord: walk as children of light."[21] In this vein, the complex light effects were not an accidental quality of stained glass, but rather its raison d'être.[22] Hugh of Saint Victor was merely being rhetorical when he asked in the early twelfth century: "What is more beautiful than light, which, although it does not have color in itself, in some ways gives colors to all the things that it illumines?"[23] The same idea, specifically applied to architecture, informs the anonymous treatise *Speculum virgi-*

num (Mirror of Virgins) from this period: "If it were not for the sun's splendor, colored glass could not display its artful appearance in the dark."[24] This point was well taken and grounded in observation: for whatever the number of candles in the interior, stained glass would not display its visual effect in an environment where the only sources of light were within the building. Only one kind of light, coming from without and associated with divine attributes, enlivened stained glass: sunlight.[25]

The importance assigned to natural light in Christian theology and sacred architecture reflected the Church's attempt to distinguish itself from competing religions and cults. One such competitor was ancient polytheism. From a Christian perspective, it was crucial to ensure that churches received more light than pagan temples typically did. This emphasized Christianity's self-understanding as the true religion and demonstrated its ambition to supersede and, as it were, outshine the deities of pagan antiquity—especially Sol Invictus, the sun god of the late Roman Empire and a target of fierce criticism by Saint Augustine and other early Christian theologians. Indeed, Sol Invictus and the "imperial solar theology" associated with him were supplanted by the idea of a *Christus oriens*—Christ as a rising sun—and, more generally, by an interpretation of light as divine.[26] The sophisticated and generous admission of light that came to characterize church interiors provided a powerful yet sufficiently abstract demonstration of divine enlightenment. The incident light was "immaterial yet at the same time real and visible," thereby evoking a sacred aura without offending the sensibilities of the significant number of early Christians who objected to visual representations of God.[27]

The other rivaling religion from which Christianity sought to distinguish itself was Judaism. In this particular context, the Christian emphasis on light took on an additional dimension: it underscored the Church's claim to be the only true heir of the ancient Jewish Temple—King Solomon's Temple—which, according to medieval theologians, prefigured the Heavenly Jerusalem in that "the glory of God did lighten it" (Rev. 21:23).[28] Based on the Old Testament, the Jewish tradition had long associated light with goodness, wisdom, and divine power.[29] Christianity inherited and incorporated these ideas while at the same time expanding and transforming them. Drawing on the New Testament, the Church construed light as a symbol of Christ's divine nature and his ability to show believers the true way toward salvation.[30] Tellingly, early Christians referred to baptism—the key initiation ritual of the new faith—as "*phōtismos*," a Greek word meaning "enlightenment."[31]

The Christological dimension of light was, of course, absent in Judaism—a difference that also became manifest on an architectural level: while the Talmud requires Jewish synagogues to have windows, there was no reason—and, indeed, no significant desire—for oversized or polychrome windows. Clearly, the close association of such windows with Christian architecture was one factor. But rabbinical warnings against idolatry also played an important role. Although not all Jewish communities abided by the biblical prohibition of images, most did. In the mid-twelfth century, the Jews of Cologne installed in their synagogue stained-glass windows depicting lions and snakes, but this was soon condemned by rabbinical authorities who demanded the removal of what they considered idolatrous decoration.[32] Of course, there were also practical reasons why premodern synagogues did not display the fenestral ambition that characterized medieval churches: synagogues were often remodeled private homes, and as a minority facing both theological and popular hostility, Jews were restrained in their architectural designs by considerable security concerns. Due to fears of stonings and other recurrent (and sometimes officially authorized) forms of vandalism, medieval and early modern synagogues "often only had small windows."[33] Reflecting on the kabbalistic prescription that a synagogue should have twelve windows, the widely traveled seventeenth-century rabbi Joseph Solomon Delmedigo remarked that he had never seen a synagogue with that many windows anywhere in Europe.[34] Delmedigo may have been exaggerating, but the general picture is correct: on the whole, synagogues had far fewer—and far less elaborate—windows than churches did. Needless to say, the small number and size of windows meant relatively low levels of daylight in the interior. Unsurprisingly, in some Jewish communities, members were willing to pay more for seats close to the windows.[35]

To be sure, the Church's fenestral ambition did not constitute an end in itself: the size and design of church windows was never just about the quantity of light, but also about its quality. The medieval Church sought a unique, particularly solemn kind of light that transcended the quotidian experience of light. Stained glass lent itself well to this purpose. While it admitted less light than uncolored windows would, it engendered a polychrome light that was imbued with a sacred aura: after all, the powerful multicolor effect was the result of light passing through vitreous depictions of Christ and the saints.[36] It was, as it were, enhanced light.

Colored glass also allowed churchgoers to notice and admire the changing quality of daylight: red, for instance, has its peak effect in the morning, whereas blue glass reaches its fullest chromatic effect when the sun begins to set.[37] It is no exaggeration to call stained glass "the most ancient and cunning form of kinetic art" or even the "medieval equivalent of the cinema."[38] Indeed, by animating the sacred scenes and figures depicted in the windows, the incident daylight manifested its dynamic, life-giving quality. This powerful experience of light as a supremely active and enlivening force of nature reminded churchgoers that all light ultimately originated in God, who—according to the biblical account—had created it on the first day of the Creation. The powerful effect of light in churches certainly transcended what premodern people were used to from their everyday life.[39] Of course, this special experience was in the Church's interest, as it created an incentive for people to flock to church. As we have seen, stained-glass windows were, and are, entirely unremarkable when seen from without; to experience their full visual effect, the viewer must step inside the church.[40]

The Christian theology of light, sketched in this chapter, provided the general framework for the medieval perception and appreciation of stained glass. But it also served as a starting point for other, more specific interpretations and analogies. Thirteenth-century Bishop Durand de Mende, for instance, noted that the glass windows "are the divine Scriptures that . . . transmit the brightness of the true sun (that is, God) into the church (that is, the hearts of the faithful), they illumine those dwelling there."[41] Writing around the same time in Chartres—a city still famous for its cathedral's resplendent stained glass—the French theologian Pierre de Roissy remarked that "the Church's glass windows, which protect from wind and rain while transmitting the bright light of the sun, signify the Holy Scripture which fends off harmful things and enlightens us."[42] It was also not uncommon to compare church windows to the Doctors of the Church: in this vein, the protection that the windows provided was construed as an analogy to how the venerable exegetes ward off all things evil and heretical. Conversely, just as the light and its warmth will always pass through the glass, so does God's light and grace find its way into the soul of his faithful believers.[43]

Other interpretations fused light symbolism with a Marian understanding of church windows. In his widely read *Etymologiae* (Etymologies), Isidore of Seville characterized glass windows as open to light yet at the same time closed. This definition, in turn, inspired medieval theologians to draw parallels between windowpanes and Mary's virginity: more concretely, the divine sunbeams passing through the window without breaking the glass were seen as an analogy to Mary's virginal motherhood.[44] In the course of the Middle Ages, this Marian interpretation became increasingly popular and was applied not only to church windows, but also to all kinds of glass windows. Consider, for instance, the depiction of a round domestic window in the background of the famous Mérode Altarpiece (ca. 1430; now commonly attributed to the workshop of Robert Campin) (fig. 3.3). At first, the colorless windowpane might appear to be an inconspicuous detail of the Flemish domestic interior that the painter chose as the setting for his depiction of the Annunciation. A closer look, however, reveals a small figure—the prenatal Jesus—carrying a cross and passing, together with the rays of light, through the glass pane without breaking it (fig. 3.4). Contemporary viewers would not have had difficulty reading this pictorial detail as a reference to the virginal conception and linking it to the biblical scene shown in the foreground, where Mary learns of her pregnancy.[45]

The Marian interpretation of glass windows continued to enjoy popularity well into the baroque period, as reflected not only in paintings, but also in iconographic treatises and the rich emblem literature. A seventeenth-century German emblem book, for instance, summarized this symbolic interpretation in straightforward verses geared toward uneducated laymen: "The window with the graceful pane / Signifies Mary the Pure. / For when the sun shines through the glass / There will never be any damage."[46] What is more, in a Marian interpretation, the color of glass had not only a decorative function, but also a profound theological meaning. A passage frequently—if wrongly—attributed to Saint Bernard de Clairvaux explicated: "As a pure ray enters a glass window and emerges unspoiled, but has acquired the color of the glass . . . , the son of God who entered the most chaste womb of the Virgin, emerged pure, but took on the color of the Virgin, that is, the nature of a man and a comeliness of human form."[47]

Church windows were prized beyond their material value precisely because they were endowed with complex religious meaning. True, glass and lead were costly materials, but this alone can hardly explain why stealing or vandalizing a church window was considered a grave crime and, indeed, a sacrilege. Along with altars, relics, chalices, books, and other liturgical objects, the windows formed part of the *ornamenta ecclesiae*, the essential furnishing of a church.[48] Writing in the sixth century, Bishop Gregory of Tours related, as a deterrent, the story of a thief who broke into a church near Poitiers and stole a glass window, which he later sold. God's punishment was not long in coming—and it was harsh: as Gregory noted with approval, the thief "came down with incurable leprosy." But the story did not end there: "For when the first anniversary of his theft was approach-

Fig. 3.3. Workshop of Robert Campin, *The Annunciation* (from the Mérode Altarpiece), ca. 1430. The Metropolitan Museum of Art, New York. The background shows a telling detail: along with rays of light, a small figure—the prenatal Jesus—passes through the glass pane without breaking it.

ing, a tumor grew on his head and his eyes so swelled up that they were thought to have been torn from their sockets. Every year the same thing happened to the man on the day when he performed his theft. The wretch mourned for the glass that he could not recall from the journey on which he had sent it."[49]

The great importance and value assigned to church windows reminds us that architectural glass had turned from the largely secular material that it was in antiquity into one endowed with rich religious meaning. This does not mean that glass was the right material for every ecclesiastical purpose. In some contexts, the ancient hierarchy of privileging "noble metals" over glass lived on. Church councils and papal decrees from the Carolingian period expressly prohibited the use of glass chalices, as these liturgical vessels—which, during Mass, came in contact with the wine transformed into Christ's blood—had to be made of either gold or silver.[50] As for the manufacture of reliquaries, glass was an acceptable material, but as we have seen, the naturally "pure" rock crystal remained a common alternative. Ultimately, then, glass enjoyed unrivaled prominence and prestige only in one particular context: fenestration. This had little to do with glass's intrinsic material value, but much with its complex relationship to light.

The High Gothic period saw the culmination of this process, as stained glass not only became a common feature of European churches, but also reached unprecedented artistic quality.[51] No less remarkable was the growing number and size of church windows during this period. In the preceding Romanesque period, the size of church windows was somewhat limited by the fact that the walls were load-bearing and could not be weakened by fenestration beyond a certain degree.[52] The master builders and stonemasons of the Gothic period addressed this problem with great ingenuity and skill: not only did they find ways to offset the weight of stone vaults onto transverse arches and ribs, but they also added stability to the exterior walls by constructing flying buttresses on the outside (fig. 3.5). These innovations made it possible to build ever-larger cathedrals, with walls that were significantly relieved of the thrust from the ceiling vaults. This also had tangible effects on fenestration: without jeopardizing the structural stability of the

Fig. 3.4. Detail of Workshop of Robert Campin, *The Annunciation* (from the Mérode Altarpiece), ca. 1430 (see fig. 3.3).

Fig. 3.5. Flying buttresses (here at Amiens Cathedral, France, begun ca. 1220) were a Gothic innovation. Thanks to their structural support, it became possible to construct—and glaze—windows of unprecedented size.

church, it became possible to construct windows of unprecedented size and to seal them with the fragile material glass.[53] Improved tracery techniques also contributed to this development, as Gothic church windows featured elaborate stone transoms, mullions, and couronnements, which provided solid structural support for large stained-glass compositions.[54]

A striking example of this fenestral ambition is the thirteenth-century cathedral of Chartres. Its windows were furnished, within three decades, with more than twenty thousand square feet of stained glass. In its heyday, Chartres Cathedral boasted more than 183 stained-glass windows as well as three monumental rose windows (fig. 3.6).[55] That Chartres Cathedral is often considered the pinnacle of High Medieval stained-glass art owes much to the exceptional state of preservation: 152 medieval stained-glass windows have survived the course of time.[56] This makes Chartres one of the finest places to study medieval stained glass in situ. But at the time when the cathedral was built, its artistic decoration was by no means exceptional. Most Gothic cathedrals featured stained glass in spectacular quantities.

The art historian Otto von Simson has argued that the windows of Gothic cathedrals were "structurally and aesthetically not openings in the wall to admit light, but transparent walls."[57] Although this observation captures the increasing size of church windows, the use of the term "transparent" requires qualifications. Stained glass was certainly transparent insofar as it admitted light (a quality perhaps better expressed by the term "translucent"); it did not, however, provide a "clear" view through the window in the way our modern notion of vitreous transparency implies. Quite the contrary, stained-glass windows reinforced, if in a highly artful fashion, the wall's effect as a barrier between interior and exterior.

This barrier to gazing outward aligned with the Church's deep-rooted suspicion of worldly gazes. From a theological perspective, church windows were not supposed to provide, let alone encourage, a view from sacred space onto an outside world tainted by profanity and sin.[58] The glowing polychromism of stained glass helped to achieve this goal. Instead of providing a view, the windows of churches served as colorful, light-emitting walls—an appearance that evoked the walls of the Heavenly Jerusalem, which, according to the New Testament, are "garnished with all manner of precious stones" (Rev. 21:19–20).

Seen from this perspective, the church—the House of God in this world— gave believers a foretaste of the Heavenly City.[59] Inspired by the biblical account, some church windows even featured real (semi-)precious stones—as, for instance, in the sumptuously decorated, fourteenth-century imperial chapel of Karlštejn Castle in Bohemia (fig. 3.7).[60] Karlštejn Chapel was, however, in many ways a rather exceptional case. Situated on a hilltop in the Bohemian countryside, it formed part of a massively fortified castle commissioned by an exceedingly wealthy patron: Holy Roman Emperor Charles IV, who harbored a profound personal interest in the Book of Revelation.[61] In most other settings, the use of precious stones for purposes of fenestration would not have been practicable because of the obvious security concerns; in any event, polychrome glass created a similarly powerful effect.[62] Indeed, regardless of whether stained-glass windows involved geometrical patterns or figurative scenes, they gave the impression that the colorful, radiant imagery was itself the source of the light.[63] Although they were manufactured from cheap materials such as sand and ashes, these windows provided a powerful

Fig. 3.6. Chartres Cathedral, France, begun 1194. Among its more than 180 stained-glass windows, this depiction of the Virgin and Child is probably the most famous. Known and venerated as Notre Dame de la Belle Verrière, this window survived the fire that destroyed the original Romanesque cathedral in 1194. It thus predates the Gothic cathedral built in the immediate aftermath of the fire on the same site. The quantity and quality of the cathedral's medieval stained glass have contributed to its enduring fame.

example of what the thirteenth-century bishop Saint Bonaventure praised as the active quality of luminosity (lumen, as opposed to lux).[64]

These "great tapestries of coloured light" adorning medieval cathedrals were objects of immense fascination for contemporaries.[65] What is more, stained glass came to exert great aesthetic influence on other artistic genres such as wall painting and manuscript illumination. Although the term "illumination" is not an actor's category, it captures medieval miniaturists' goal: to imitate, on parchment, the miraculous effect of color appearing to be the source of light. The use of shining gold and silver in manuscripts (and paintings) was one means to this end.[66]

Ultimately, however, no genre of painting—whether on canvas, walls, or parchment—was able to rival stained glass in luminosity.[67] This observation informed the treatise *De diversis artibus* (On the Various Arts), written by the early twelfth-century German monk Theophilus and now considered one of the most important surviving medieval art treatises. In the first book of this compendium, Theophilus described in great detail different ways of painting on opaque materials such as stone (as in wall frescoes) and parchment (as in manuscripts), but he concluded that "since this kind of painting cannot be translucent, I have, like a diligent seeker, taken particular pains to discover by what ingenious techniques a building may be embellished with a variety of colours, without excluding the light of day and the rays of the sun."[68] Along these lines, Theophilus dedicated several chapters of his treatise to the manufacture of window glass, especially stained glass. As he explained, people entering the church—the House of God—should be impressed not only by paintings on the ceilings and walls, but also by stained-glass windows,

Fig. 3.7. Karlštejn Castle, Czech Republic, 1348–65. The imperial chapel featured walls and windows adorned with (semi-)precious stones, turning the biblical account of the gem-lined Heavenly Jerusalem into a tangible experience. Today, only fragments of the windows survive.

for these offered an even more powerful aesthetic experience to the human eye: "If it [the eye] regards the profusion of light from the window, it marvels at the inestimable beauty of the glass and the infinitely rich and various workmanship."[69]

Around the time Theophilus was writing, Abbot Suger directed the rebuilding of the basilica of Saint-Denis outside of Paris. Suger shared the fascination with stained glass and took great pride in the lavish windows created under his oversight. In his famous account of the construction work, he praised the "very bright variety of the new glass windows." These windows must have been a considerable expense, as they were made by "the distinguished hands of many masters from different countries."[70] Undertaken for the glory of God, such costly efforts were not, of course, lost on the flock. We know that medieval churchgoers looked at stained-glass windows with both thoroughness and awe.[71] The fourteenth-century nun Elisa of Engeltal was "enraptured" by a stained-glass window depicting the Last Judgment. She was particularly struck by the "brilliant radiance" emanating from Christ's face, "as clear as if one thousand suns shone from him, and the heavens stood open above him."[72] The fascination with stained glass is also captured in the travelogue that the fifteenth-century Dominican monk Felix Fabri wrote about his pilgrimage to the Holy Land. Having reached Jerusalem in 1480, Fabri went to see the church of the Holy Sepulchre. During his tour of the interior he paid special attention—in fact, too much attention—to the windows: "I cast my eyes upon the upper windows with curiosity, as ill-bred men stare about in strange places and houses without respect for anyone, and so I stood by myself with wandering eyes." We do not know whether the windows Fabri saw were glass-filled stucco grilles (of the sort common in the surrounding Islamic architecture) or whether they were sealed with European-style stained glass (which the crusaders had produced locally on a limited scale when they had ruled over the Holy Land more than two centuries earlier). Both possibilities are conceivable. In any case, from what we know about the state of the church at the time, the windows must have been relatively small, and they certainly did not rival the splendor of the stained glass adorning the great Gothic cathedrals of western Europe.[73] And still, the windows captured Fabri's attention. In fact, he looked so attentively at them that he accidentally stepped on the stone "whereon Joseph and Nicodemus laid the most precious body of our Lord." When other pilgrims, shocked and "scarce able to speak for weeping," alerted Fabri to this misstep, he was deeply embarrassed and prostrated himself on the floor to kiss the stone upon which he had so carelessly trodden.[74]

Missteps such as Fabri's confirmed the warnings of those who argued that colored glass windows aroused inappropriate "curiosity" (Fabri's term—and one closely associated with sin in medieval theology). In the worst scenario, stained-glass windows could distract worshippers and clergy during services and divert their attention from the liturgy. Some vocal proponents of this critique came from the ranks of the Cistercians, a monastic order that emerged at the end of the eleventh century and promoted a simple and modest monastic life. The Cistercians decried the rise of stained glass as a symptom of a general, objectionable tendency: the construction of ever more lavish churches and monasteries. From the Cistercian point of view, such displays of architectural splendor constituted luxuria—one of the seven deadly sins. In their own building projects, the Cistercians championed architectural and ornamental simplicity. For instance, Cistercian abbeys featured modest ridge turrets instead of soaring church towers.[75] In the same vein, colored windows were frowned upon. As a twelfth-century Cistercian put it, colored glass windows were "not a necessary custom, but rather a result of the lust of the eyes."[76] In line with such criticism, the order's statutes from the 1150s explicitly banned colored as well as figurative windows from Cistercian churches: "The glass windows shall be white and without crosses or images" (*vitreae albae fiant et sine crucibus et picturis*).[77] Only the sparing use of dark enamel paint to add geometric and vegetal ornamentation was tolerated.[78]

In practice, this meant that Cistercian windows had a much "lighter" appearance than their polychrome, heavily ornamented counterparts in the great cathedrals. Still, Cistercian windows were not transparent in the modern sense of the word. In many cases, the glass was not entirely clear to begin with, as natural impurities caused a light hue. Scholars later coined the term "grisaille," a French term denoting the color gray, to refer to such windows, characterized as they are by the interplay between the uncolored glass and the dark-grayish enamel ornamentation (fig. 3.8). Ironically, grisaille panes were sometimes considerably more artistic than the Cistercian statutes originally envisioned. True, unlike polychrome stained-glass windows, Cistercian grisailles did not create the spectacular illusion of gem-like radiance, but nonetheless their ornamental decoration could be impressive in its own—albeit unintended—ways. Tellingly, from the second half of the thirteenth century onward, some non-Cistercian cathedrals adopted grisaille windows—not instead of, but in addition to, their polychrome windows.

The inclusion of grisailles in cathedrals may have been inspired by a desire

Fig. 3.8. Grisaille windows in the choir of the Altenberger Dom, a Cistercian abbey church in central Germany, begun in 1259. The windows date to the period around 1270, when lack of color and figurative representation were the guiding principles for the church's decoration. In later decades, the monks of Altenberg, like many of their fellow Cistercians, began to interpret this principle more liberally, and colored glass made an appearance in various parts of the church.

for greater aesthetic variety. In some cases, budgetary restraints may have played a role as well: even the finest grisaille window usually cost only half the price of a colored stained-glass window.[79] In yet other cases, grisailles were installed to achieve higher lighting levels in the interior than was possible with colored glass: this holds particularly true for churches of the Rayonnant style (ca. 1270–1370), as more light made it easier to appreciate the intricate architectural and sculptural ornamentation characteristic of this particular style of Gothic architecture.[80] Even during the heyday of the Rayonnant, however, the traditional theological hierarchy that considered colored glass superior to noncolored glass remained unquestioned—and indeed, the most prominent windows (such as those in the transept or choir) continued to be reserved for colored glass.[81]

In short, grisaille windows were never the norm in medieval churches.[82] They appeared in certain kinds of non-Cistercian churches more frequently than in others, but usually in some form of interplay with polychrome glass. Whatever specific factors drove their installation, it had little to do with what some historians have called a desire for "transparency."[83] Our modern ideal of transparent window glass is, as we will see, a product of a much later period of history, and it would be misleading to trace its origins back to the Cistercians. It would be equally misleading to argue that the rejection of colored glass formed a nonnegotiable part of the Cistercian "ideology": after all, we do know of Cistercian churches that, in violation of the order's own statutes, featured colored glass.[84] True, in the majority of Cistercian churches the ban on colored glass was enforced, but it is important to remember that the purpose of this ban was to avoid architectural "luxury." Transparency was a side effect and, in any case, depended on the quality of the glass. Typically, the colorless glass installed in Cistercian churches contained too many impurities to qualify as transparent in the modern sense of the word. Even if the glass was clear, damascening or other surface ornamentation often detracted from the transparent effect.[85] Finally, the smoke from candles and torches was bound to blacken the windows over time. This problem resonates in a medieval proverb that holds that "old churches have dark windows" (meaning, on a figurative level, that old religious doctrines can be opaque and difficult to understand).[86]

We will return to the practical challenges of keeping windows clean, and how this made it difficult to achieve transparency of the kind we are used to today. First and foremost, however, we must keep in mind that there were religious and aesthetic reasons why transparency in sacred architecture was neither common nor even desirable: as Francesca Dell'Acqua has noted with respect to medieval churches, "Absolutely transparent windows, which could perform neither as visual nor spiritual filters, would have allowed too much contact with an external and transitory world."[87] While for modern people the experience—and quality—of a window is often tied to its transparency, this was not the expectation during the Middle Ages.[88] As the next chapter will show, color and its interplay with light defined the aesthetics of medieval architectural glass—not just in sacred, but also in domestic spaces.

4

"Closyd well with royall glas"

Medieval Domestic Glass

Chapter-opening image: Detail of Fig. 4.5

Church demand for glass, underpinned by theological motives, was the driving force behind the boom of the medieval glass industry. Glassworks were established in many parts of Europe. By the late Middle Ages, several regions had gained particular distinction for the quality of their glass products, especially Normandy, Lorraine, Venice, and the Low Countries.[1]

Despite this geographical expansion of the industry, prices for glass windows remained relatively high. Even in churches, glazing was often possible only with financial support from affluent donors. (Suffice it to recall the profuse gratitude expressed by the abbot of Tegernsee in his letter to Count Arnold of Vogaburg.) The significant expense associated with glazing was attributable not only to the cost of glass itself, but also to the iron and lead used to assemble the windows.

Theoretically, wood could serve as a support for glass windows, but it was not the most durable material: tellingly, very few wooden transoms from this period have survived the course of time.[2] Stone was a more feasible option. The Romans had demonstrated how to embed window glass in perforated stone screens (transennae) and fix the screens in place with mortar—a method that remained common in the Byzantine Empire and Islamic Middle East throughout the medieval period.[3] Yet neither wood nor stone prevailed in western Europe. Instead, iron emerged as the predominant framing material, and lead as the most common material for joining glass pieces. Like iron, lead was durable and weatherproof.[4] At the same time, lead was more malleable, which facilitated the joining of glass pieces of different, and often irregular, shapes.[5] Here again, however, practical considerations were entangled with an aesthetic vision, for lead also contributed to the window's pictorial composition.[6] To a modern eye, the dense venation of lead lines might seem an anti-naturalistic distraction, but for the medieval glass artist it was a crucial means of achieving the desired pictorial effect. Tellingly, some stained-glass windows even featured dummy lead lines that had no stabilizing function and served a solely decorative or compositional purpose. The downside of lead was its cost: depending on the quantities used, lead could account for almost half of the expense associated with glazing.[7]

Glass, too, remained costly throughout this period, not because of its ingredients (which were relatively common and cheap) but rather because of the significant production costs. Surviving records and bills suggest that medieval glassmakers were significantly better paid than most other craftsmen and artisans (for instance, carpenters or masons).[8] The high wages partly reflected the occupational hazards of this industry. Unfortunately, we have no medieval account of these hazards, but they hardly differed from those described in the eighteenth century by the Italian physician Bernardino Ramazzini, a pioneer in the field of occupational medicine. As Ramazzini knew from firsthand observations, glassmakers were exposed to constant physical challenges: "When they reach the age of forty, just when it is the right time to give up, they say farewell to their craft and spend the rest of their lives enjoying what they have laid by for their leisure and security." The reason for this, Ramazzini explained, was that "no one could endure for long the strain of such work as these men have to do, nor could it be kept up except by robust men in the prime of life."

According to Ramazzini, two aspects of glass production were particularly harmful to human health: "the violent heat of the fire and the addition of certain minerals sometimes used for coloring glass objects." With respect to heat, he said, "The men stand continually half-naked in freezing winter weather near very hot furnaces and keep their eyes fixed on the fire and molten glass; hence they are inevitably attacked by serious disorders." To make things worse, "Because of the heat they are constantly troubled by unquenchable thirst, so that they are obliged to drink too often; they drink an inordinate amount of wine and prefer it to water because they believe that when one is overheated from any cause water is more injurious than wine; they point to the many cases of sudden death from drinking cold water when overheated." The "violent and sudden changes of temperatures" also caused "pleurisy, asthma, and a chronic cough." As if this were not enough, "a far worse fate awaits those who make colored glass." As Ramazzini explained:

> In order to color the crystal they use calcinated borax, antimony, and a certain amount of gold; these they pound together to an impalpable powder and mix it with glass to make the paste needed for this process, and however much they cover and avert their faces while they do this they cannot help breathing in the noxious fumes. Hence it often happens that some of them fall senseless, and sometimes they are suffocated; or in the course of time they suffer from ulcers in the mouth, oesophagus, and trachea. In the end they join the ranks of consumptives, since their lungs become ulcerated, as has been clearly shown by the dissection of their corpses.[9]

Ramazzini's account presents a gloomy picture of the human cost behind the beauty of colored glass. Modern medicine has confirmed that professional glass-

Fig. 4.1. The business of glassmaking, as depicted in an early fifteenth-century illuminated manuscript. British Library, London. The foreground shows the operation of the furnace and the blowing of glass; in the background, the raw materials are assembled and transported to the glassworks. The young boy in the foreground helps to operate the furnace—a reminder that child labor was common in the premodern glass industry. The anguished expression on his face might reflect the physical toll or the painful exposure to heat. Both factors contributed to the below-average life expectancy of premodern glassmakers.

blowing under premodern conditions was bound to lead to health problems, especially as a result of poisonous fumes. As Ramazzini observed, the exposure to average working temperatures of forty to sixty degrees Celsius in itself was problematic: the heat could lead to severe burns, and the glare was responsible for the high frequency of eye complications such as so-called glassblower's cataracts.[10]

Health hazards aside, there were other aspects of the premodern glassmaking industry that we would not tolerate today. In his tenth-century letter, Gozbert mentioned not just the beauty of his church's new stained-glass windows, but also who carried out the wearing, menial tasks in the glassworks: *pueri* (young boys).[11] Of course, child labor was not at all uncommon in the medieval world, and it remained characteristic of the glass industry well into the nineteenth century (fig. 4.1).[12] The typical starting age for boys was ten years, and shifts of twelve hours or more were not rare in premodern glassworks.[13] Here again, we have no medieval account, but the physical toll must have been similar to that among underage laborers in English glassworks in the 1840s (as observed by Friedrich Engels):

> The hard labor, the irregularity of the hours, the frequent night-work, and especially the great heat of the working place (100 to 130 Fahrenheit), engender in children general debility and disease, stunted growth, and especially affections of the eye, bowel complaint, and rheumatic and bronchial affections. Many of the children are pale, have red eyes, often blind for weeks at a time, suffer from violent nausea, vomiting, coughs, colds and rheumatism. When the glass is withdrawn from the fire, the children must often go into such heat that the boards on which they stand catch fire under their feet. The glassblowers usually die young of debility and chest affections.[14]

Criticism of this sort would have been unlikely in the medieval period. Indeed, neither the practice of child labor nor the knowledge about occupational hazards curbed the demand for glass. Colored glass was in particularly high demand in religious as well as private architecture. To the extent that glass windows featured in early medieval secular architecture, they tended to follow the stylistic ideal established by church windows: the more colored glass, the more prestigious. Virtually no secular stained-glass windows from this period survive intact, but excavated fragments provide important insights: for example, in the Paderborn *Kaiserpfalz* (an imperial palace and center of Carolingian power), archaeologists have unearthed fragments of glass windows in bright colors such as emerald green, blue, and red. According to chemical analyses, these fragments date to the earliest phase of construction—that is, between the late eighth and the mid-ninth centuries.[15]

Literary sources from the High Middle Ages underscore how impressed medieval people were by colored glass windows in private—especially palatial—architecture. Windows of this kind seem to have inspired the twelfth-century French trouvère Chrétien de Troyes, who, in his *Le Conte du Graal* (The Story of the Grail), praised a (fictitious) castle in which "the windows were painted in the richest and finest colors that could be created or described."[16] Around the same time, German minnesinger Heinrich von Veldeke, drawing on French literary models, imagined a fantastical funerary monument that featured windows sealed with a variety of precious stones—a vision that invoked biblical descriptions of the Heavenly Jerusalem, but probably also took cues from the experience of stained-glass windows and their gem-like effect.[17] The fourteenth-century English romance *Sir Guy* describes a princess in her chamber adorned with figurative stained glass: "In her oryall there she was, / Closyd well with royall glas, / Fulfyllyd yt was with ymagery, / Every windowe by and by."[18] Also in the fourteenth century, Geoffrey Chaucer, in his *Book of the Duchess*, described a dream in which he found himself in a luxurious chamber adorned with stained glass. Here again, the vivid description is clearly indebted to palatial architecture from this period—a style of architecture with which Chaucer, the widely traveled courtier, was thoroughly familiar.[19] Chaucer praised the windows precisely because they were polychrome and figurative:

> My chambre was
> Ful wel depeynted, and with glas
> Were al the wyndowes wel yglased
> Ful clere, and nat an hoole ycrased,
> That to beholde hyt was gret joye.
> For hoolly al the story of Troye
> Was in the glasynge ywrought thus,
> Of Ector and of kyng Lamedon,
> And eke of Medea and of Jason,
> Of Paris, Eleyne, and of Lavyne.[20]

Monasteries, too, were important sites of early medieval architectural glass. These religious institutions also played a significant role as sites of glass production, not only because they were centers of knowledge and technology, but also because they often owned extensive forests (which supplied the wood needed as fuel for the glass furnaces).[21] In the Frankish Empire, monasteries featuring glass windows are documented as far back as the sixth century.[22] Monastic glazing often was used in chapels, but also in other structures. From as early as the 680s, we have reports about glass windows in the dormitory of the abbey of Jumièges in Normandy. Sources from around the year 900 mention glass panes in the scriptorium of Sankt Gallen as well as in communal spaces in the abbey of Müstair (both in Switzerland). In the central Italian monastery of San Vincenzo al Volturno, the refectory and guest rooms were glazed.[23] The glass windows in monasteries, especially their chapels, were often colored—indeed, this was one of the "luxuries" criticized by the Cistercians. That the Cistercians alone took this view is a testament to the strong theological and aesthetic appreciation for stained glass at the time. Even the Franciscans and Premonstratensians—two orders that shared the vision of a simple, austere monastic life—had no objections to figurative stained glass and employed it prominently in their churches.[24]

Inspired by the beauty of stained glass, the Dominican preacher Giordano da Pisa explained to his flock in Pisa in 1305: "Whoever wants to produce a beautiful glass window, should employ all the colors."[25] This view certainly sat well with medieval glassmakers who focused their ambitions and experiments on perfecting the colors of stained glass. With success: in the early thirteenth century, glassmakers made significant progress in the production of cobalt blue glass; gradually, they also improved the quality of red glass (which, traditionally, was the most difficult-to-produce variety of colored glass).[26]

Costly and time-consuming as they were, these experiments would not have been possible without a strong demand for colored glass—including from secular buyers. For householders who desired (and could afford) glass windows, colored glass held particular prestige—not just because of its price, but also because of the religious aura associated with it. True, some residential buildings featured grisailles or blank panes, but it seems that such choices were often due to financial considerations: uncolored glass—unless of the exceptional quality usually reserved for vessels—was simply cheaper than colored glass. Records concerning the royal apartments at the Tower of London indicate that the blank glass installed in the king's chamber in 1287 cost a third less than the colored glass used in the same room.[27] The account books recording the glazing of St. Stephen's Chapel in Westminster Palace in 1351 suggest an even greater divergence: uncolored (white) glass cost eight pence, whereas red glass was three times more expensive (two shillings, two pence). Blue glass (at three shillings, seven pence) fetched five times the price of uncolored glass.[28] In sum, the Crown spent 145 pounds on the glazing of the chapel—a handsome amount of money, roughly equal to the annual revenue of an affluent knight.[29]

Economic considerations aside, the inclusion of uncolored glass in royal buildings such as the Tower of London and Westminster Palace may also have had practical reasons, such as the desire for higher lighting levels. One thing, however, is clear: most of the time, uncolored glass was not used exclusively, but rather in conjunction with colored glass. A common way of combining these two types of glass was to use stained glass for the window's central segment and relegate uncolored panes to the outer sections. This is another reminder that the inclusion of uncolored glass was often a compromise rather than the ideal. From a practical point of view, of course, it offered all the general conveniences of glass as an architectural sealant. But a closer look revealed imperfections: the lack of color laid bare the streaks and bubbles characteristic of most glass of the period; often there was also the greenish hue resulting from chemical impurities. By contrast, polychrome glass was superior in that it met all the practical expectations associated with glass while at the same time possessing distinct aesthetic qualities and theological connotations.[30]

Very few domestic windows from this period survive, but textual sources confirm how coveted colored glass was among those who could afford to install it at home. For example, in 1324, the Duke of Artois ordered stained glass for his castle in Beuvry, and in 1364 the Duke of Burgundy purchased yellow and red glass—in addition to blank panes—for "the windows of chapels, large rooms, and chambers."[31] The same preferences are attested for the fourteenth-century papal palace in Avignon, where archaeologists have unearthed fragments of window glass in various colors: red accounts for nearly 50 percent, and blue and yellow each for around 12 percent.[32] In the first half of the fifteenth century, Jacques Cœur, the most powerful merchant and financier in the kingdom of France, commissioned lavish stained-glass windows for his stately palais in Bourges. Despite Cœur's later downfall and death in exile, some of the windows survive in situ—including one showing a merchant ship from his fleet (fig. 4.2).[33] Less fortunate was the fate of the glass windows in the Duc de Berry's Château de Bicêtre near Paris: when angry burghers sacked and burned the castle in 1411, they also removed the glass windows—a reminder that the windows had a considerable material value.[34]

Domestic glass windows also imitated their ecclesiastical counterparts in terms of structural design. Held together by lead lines, secular stained glass often was embedded in elaborate stone tracery. While the scale was much smaller than in churches, this tracery derived many forms and patterns from sacred architecture—as evident, for instance, in slender vertical windows crowned by ornamented, pointed arches.[35]

During the thirteenth and fourteenth centuries, Gothic stonemasons significantly expanded and refined the repertoire of tracery techniques. While traditional tracery was carved out of flat stone plates (plate tracery), windows of the new type featured slender stone transoms and mullions (bar tracery) assembled from stone modules that were joined by metal pins (figs. 4.3, 4.4).[36] Bar tracery first appeared in churches but was soon adopted in secular architecture. More efficient and customizable than plate tracery, it expanded not only the range of possible designs, but also the potential size of the window.[37] How to glaze these large apertures was a different question—and, indeed, a challenge. Only wealthy householders could afford the exclusive use of stained glass. A cheaper alternative was to seal the windows with standardized types of panes—bull's-eyes, for instance, or the diamond-shaped panes known as "quarries." Indeed, as the size of

Fig. 4.2. For his lavish mansion in the French city of Bourges, begun 1443, the wealthy merchant Jacques Cœur commissioned secular stained-glass windows such as this one. Depicted here is a merchant ship from his fleet. The window exemplifies the prestige of stained glass, transposed to a domestic setting.

windows increased, such standardized panes gained prominence in medieval domestic architecture. Still, this did not subvert the traditional aesthetic hierarchy: carefully composed stained-glass panels remained the most prestigious way to seal a window. Tellingly, even in a residence featuring generic panes, it was not uncommon to reserve the central section of a window for colored glass (for instance, a representation of the family's coat of arms).[38]

Despite the technical and architectural innovations of the High Middle Ages, the emergence of glass in domestic architecture was, on the whole, a slow and gradual process—and it certainly lagged behind the glazing of churches. In aristocratic residences in the German lands, glass had gained currency by the twelfth century.[39] By contrast, it seems that in the homes of the French nobility this did not happen before the mid-thirteenth century.[40] In England, the lack of a robust local glass industry complicated the situation; high-quality glass had to be imported from the Continent, especially France. Unsurprisingly, then, glass was relatively uncommon in secular architecture in England until the second half of the thirteenth century.[41] As we have seen, even the windows of the king's chamber in the Tower of London were not glazed until the reign of Edward I in the 1280s; and in Winchester (and other royal castles) it was only during the reign of Henry III (1216–72) that the royal apartments received glass windows. In the case of Winchester's royal apartment—adorned as it was by wall paintings—better lighting was cited as a reason for this measure, but the English climate must have played a role as well. Indeed, when glass windows were installed in the wardrobe of Westminster in the 1230s, this was done "so that that chamber may not be so windy [*ventosa*] as it used to be."[42]

In the houses of Europe's nonaristocratic elites—such as the urban upper classes—glass windows rarely appeared before the fourteenth century. Typically, city halls or other municipal buildings set precedents. Consider the case of Nuremberg, one of the largest and most prosperous cities in late medieval Europe: the first recorded evidence of glass windows in the city hall dates to 1388, and in 1433

Fig. 4.3. The thirteenth-century west rose of Chartres Cathedral, France, is an example of plate tracery.

Fig. 4.4. The thirteenth-century rose over the west portal of Reims Cathedral, France, is an example of bar tracery.

the magistrate decided to spend a handsome amount of money on glazing the windows of its library.[43] In the second half of the fifteenth century, glass also gained currency in the private homes of Nuremberg's upper class. The expense was still considerable: according to modern calculations, a Nuremberg mason would have had to spend an entire week's salary to buy ten square feet of window glass.[44]

We find a similar pattern in other major late medieval cities.[45] With respect to the flourishing commercial cities of Flanders, we are particularly well-informed about everyday material culture thanks to the rich visual evidence provided by local paintings from this period. The interior scenes in Flemish paintings illustrate that the emergence of glass in domestic spaces was a piecemeal process: often, the upper segments of a window were the first to be glazed (ideally, with colored glass), while the lower parts continued to be closed by means of wooden shutters or

Fig. 4.5. Detail of Workshop of Robert Campin, Mérode Altarpiece, ca. 1430 (see fig. 3.3). The window features a glazed upper section with heraldic insignia and multi-segment wooden shutters in the lower part. Mixed windows of this kind appear frequently in late medieval paintings. They are reminders that the introduction of glass in domestic architecture was a gradual process.

sealed with textiles or animal membranes (fig. 4.5).[46] As we have seen, such non-vitreous alternatives to glass had been common for centuries, though they have received little attention from historians. From today's perspective, the use of such materials in fenestration might indeed seem rather exotic. This is precisely why we must now take a closer look at these non-vitreous sealants, put them in their historical context, and probe why they enjoyed remarkable popularity.

5

"Glass windows made of fabric"

A Forgotten Tradition

Chapter-opening image: Detail of Fig. 5.6

appiness without glass / How crass!"—these twentieth-century lines in praise of glass (which we will encounter again in Chapter 13) illustrate how difficult it has become to imagine, from a modern perspective, a life without architectural glass. We are bound to find it puzzling that glass was not used universally in medieval architecture. A common way of explaining (away) this historical phenomenon has been to link it to the high cost of glass. But this is too convenient and simplistic an explanation. Economic considerations certainly influenced architectural choices, but we also need to keep in mind that glass was not considered an indispensable feature of architecture. It was one option among others. For theological reasons, glass had emerged as the preferred option for sacred architecture, but in domestic architecture it still competed with a wide range of non-vitreous sealants that, for centuries, had proven practical and effective in their own way.

Ordinary people often relied on wooden shutters. Some also used curtains—or even two sets of curtains—that were hung from a bar above the window lintel.[1] In the historical literature, one often finds the assertion that such glassless windows were associated with the most primitive variety of architecture at the time.[2] In reality, however, the situation was far more complex. Even in aristocratic residences, glazing was done only gradually and sometimes remained unfinished. The twelfth-century French trouvère Chrétien de Troyes described in his *Conte du Graal* a fictitious castle where Sir Gawain encounters both glass windows (painted "in the richest and finest colors") and entirely unsealed windows: "In the palace there were at least four hundred closed windows and a hundred that were open."[3] In the medieval German lands, stately aristocratic buildings such as the imperial palace at Goslar or Wartburg Castle near Eisenach featured a considerable number of unsealed windows.

The fact that some castles had entirely open windows might seem perplexing from a modern point of view. According to one explanation, such windows were limited to assembly rooms—perhaps because, on a symbolic level, unsealed windows invoked older traditions that required that certain legal and political transactions take place publicly.[4] In the residential parts of castles, of course, it would have been less convenient to leave windows unsealed. At the very least there would have been wooden shutters in place. The tenth-century chronicler Thietmar of Merseburg may have had such shuttered windows in mind when he described an episode in which a certain Margrave Ekkehard "broke the windows" (*fractis fenestris*) after being woken by noise from outside a castle in which he was staying.[5]

In urban households, wooden shutters remained common throughout the medieval period, and in rural areas even more so.[6] Consider the small southern French village of Montaillou: thanks to meticulous inquisitorial records that survive, we are well-informed about the local material culture—and thus we know that in the early fourteenth century, even the homes of the most affluent villagers featured only wooden shutters.[7]

Indeed, wooden shutters were considered neither a sign of poverty nor a poor choice. It is important to keep in mind that the windows of medieval homes were, in general, significantly smaller than their modern counterparts, which reduced exposure to environmental impact.[8] In some homes, awnings helped to mitigate the effects of inclement weather (or served as protection from the scorching sun).[9] As for wooden shutters, they came in a range of different qualities and designs. Primitive wooden slabs were no doubt the simplest option available; in a closed position they admitted little or no daylight. But there were also more refined types of shutters that allowed residents to open select segments while keeping others closed. This included louvered shutters, reminiscent of what we today would call roller blinds. Both multi-segment and louvered shutters provided considerable flexibility to control and adjust the admission of light and air.[10]

The flexibility of wooden shutters also proved useful in certain nonresidential contexts, such as artisanal workshops. In France, for instance, craftsmen were required to work "*à fenêtre*"—with open windows—so that their practice and products could be seen and judged by everyone. At the same time, the lowered shutters of artisanal workshops served as sales counters during the day.[11] Tellingly, the blocking up of windows was one way in which guilds punished members who failed to comply with corporation standards.[12]

Early modern sources also mention lattices "made either of wicker or fine rifts of oak in checkerwise."[13] A shutter of this kind is depicted in a painting by the Brunswick Monogrammist (ca. 1540) showing a brothel scene (figs. 5.1, 5.2): the upper parts of the window are glazed, but the lower half is sealed with a finely plaited wicker screen that admits a certain amount of daylight while preventing passersby from looking into the brothel's interior. In a closed state, such wicker screens (or, for that matter, louvered shutters) enabled the person in the interior to peek into the street without being seen. Useful as such screens were in a brothel,

Fig. 5.1. The Brunswick Monogrammist, *A Brothel Scene*, ca. 1540.
Yale University Art Gallery, New
Haven. The windows' upper sections are glazed; the lower parts are
furnished with wicker lattices that
admit light but deny a clear view
in from the outside. The prostitute
standing by the window is taking
advantage of this limited visibility.

Fig. 5.2. Detail of the Brunswick
Monogrammist, *A Brothel Scene*,
ca. 1540 (see fig. 5.1).

they were not unique to this business. Suffice it to recall the meticulously depicted Flemish interior in the Mérode Altarpiece, where the central window displays the state of the art of mixed-technology fenestration: in the upper part, glazed fanlights with polychrome ornamentation; in the lower part, multi-segment wooden shutters and a lattice screen (see fig. 4.5). Other late medieval and early modern paintings—for instance, Carpaccio's *The Dream of St. Ursula*—suggest that wooden screens could be found even in upper-class residential interiors (such as the elegant Venetian bedroom in which Carpaccio depicted the princess Ursula) and that, here again, screens and glass were not considered mutually exclusive.

Wooden shutters and elaborate screens were employed in domestic architecture as early as Roman times, and it is no coincidence that this tradition remained particularly strong in southern Europe throughout the medieval and early modern period. As late as the eighteenth century, the Scottish-Swedish architect William Chambers noted that "in Italy, and some other hot countries, . . . their apartments cannot be made habitable, but by keeping the window shutters almost closed while the sun appears above the horizon."[14] Indeed, many southern Europeans continued to rely on shutters even as window glass became increasingly affordable.[15] The persistence of shutters did not fail to draw the attention of northern European travelers. During his journey through Italy in the 1580s, Michel de Montaigne was surprised to observe that glass windows were, on the whole, much rarer there than in northern Europe. With a certain exaggeration, he noted that Italians have "wooden windows in nearly all the houses" and that even some of the best inns featured "windows large and wide open, except for a big shutter."[16] Montaigne concluded that "their [the Italians'] bedrooms, for lack of glass and proper closing of the windows, are less clean than in France." While Montaigne, a traveler grappling with health issues, found this situation "intolerable," he admitted that the absence of "frequent storms" allowed Italians to hold on to such architectural traditions.[17]

European travelers in the Middle East made similar observations. In this hot, arid part of the world, Europeans encountered a domestic architecture that traditionally favored mashrabiyas and other wooden screens (see fig. 1.1). Writing around 1800, an English visitor to Egypt reported that, with very few exceptions, there were "no panes of glass," and instead almost exclusively "very close wood-work." He added that such wooden latticework "effectually hides the person within" and "makes the rooms very warm, except just at the moment when the sun

Fig. 5.3. This image from Barley Hall, York, shows a rare modern attempt to reconstruct what a medieval horn window would have looked like. In line with the medieval production process, the horn for this window was stripped from the boney horn cores of domestic animals. Windows sealed with animal skins or horn were popular in the premodern period, but virtually none have survived, partly because of weathering and partly because later generations did not consider them worthy of preservation.

happens to shine upon the particular window, then its effects are kept out, and the air admitted."[18] A German contemporary went so far as to claim that "given the heat in Palestine there would be no point of glass windows: they admit solar rays and heat, but at the same time they preclude air drafts, which means that people in the interior would suffocate."[19]

From today's perspective, we might wonder whether shutters implied a heightened security risk for residents. Here again, however, it is important to differentiate. The use of shutters or screens instead of glass did not put residents and their valuables at constant risk. Premodern people were well aware of the need to take precautions, and they did not naively leave the shutters open at all times.[20] In fact, some urban and rural householders also installed iron grilles or stanchions.[21] This is another reminder that there were gradations between "open" and "shut," as well as between the two options of using glass panes or wooden shutters. Indeed, in addition to shutters, medieval and early modern people had a wide range of non-vitreous sealants at their disposal, including stretched canvasses, animal skins and bladders, horn, oiled parchment, and waxed paper (fig. 5.3).[22]

As we have seen, non-vitreous sealants were already known in Roman times, but they also enjoyed popularity outside of Europe. This included mineral materials: in the Middle East—for instance, in Yemen—windows sealed with alabaster, marble, and mica survived well into the twentieth century.[23] In the Philippines, so-called *capiz* windows, made of flattened capiz shells, were common in early modern times.[24] And in a number of other Asian societies, paper- or textile-based sealants (such as the shōji screens characteristic of premodern Japanese architecture) have formed part of domestic architecture for centuries and can still be found in traditional homes (see fig. I.5). In Europe, by contrast, non-vitreous sealants—and their history—have now fallen almost entirely into oblivion. Even historians have rarely addressed this aspect of premodern material culture. This neglect has partly to do with the fact that virtually no examples of such sealants have survived—or rather, that they were not deemed worthy of curatorial preservation.[25] Occasionally, historic window frames survive that display nailing traces, indicating the use of such sealants in the past.[26] But as a general matter, our knowledge about this historical phenomenon stems almost exclusively from textual records (complemented by a small number of visual representations).[27]

The disappearance of non-vitreous sealants from the repertoire of European architecture does not mean that, in the past, they were inherently inferior to glass. And yet, in the limited historical literature discussing such sealants, there is an unfortunate tendency to depict them as anachronistic.[28] Such modern categorizations underscore how powerful the ideal of architectural glass has become in our day, but they do not help us understand the motives of premodern householders who opted for alternatives. For us today, glazing might be a desirable goal—and indeed the norm—in fenestration, but this normativity of architectural glass is in itself the result of a long historical process.

It would, in short, be ahistorical to argue that glass was always a better choice than non-vitreous sealants. The preference for one or the other depended on the geographical location as well as on the architectural and cultural context. In certain respects, non-vitreous sealants had advantages over glass—for instance, in terms of price: glass windows were typically two to four times more expensive than textile sealants.[29] True, non-vitreous sealants lacked perfect transparency (as did the majority of ordinary glass products at the time), but they were always translucent.[30] The translucent effect could be enhanced through varnishing: parchment, for instance, was often coated with linseed oil, and canvas with turpentine or a mix of egg whites and gum water; in the same vein, it was not uncommon to soak paper or parchment in poppy oil or coat it with mutton suet or wax.[31]

Sealants refined by such varnishing were not provisional solutions. Nor were they considered "primitive" at the time—otherwise, it would be hard to explain why they figured prominently in stately residences, such as castles of the Duc de Berry or in the pope's palace in Avignon (to cite just two notable fourteenth-century examples). Upper-class demand for non-vitreous sealants remained strong throughout the fifteenth century: windows with oiled parchment are attested in the palaces of the counts of Savoy as well as in those of Queen Mary of Anjou, and in French royal castles, textile windows coexisted alongside glass windows.[32] Among ordinary Frenchmen, the use of non-vitreous sealants was even more common.[33] The anonymous (and probably bourgeois) author of the mid-fourteenth-century household guidebook *Le ménagier de Paris* (The Good Wife's Guide) explicitly recommended sealing windows "with waxed linen or something like that, or with parchment or other means."[34] And a sixteenth-century English household manual pointed out that parchments windows of the highest quality "keepe the roome verie warm."[35]

A similar picture presents itself in other parts of northern Europe. In prosperous cities such as Bern (1378), Hildesheim (1410), and Wrocław (1471), the windows of municipal buildings were sealed with parchment or cow bladders. In Zurich, the city hall still had canvassed windows in 1504.[36] Around the same time, an anonymous Italian artist active at the court of Urbino painted three famous views of an ideal city, with stately buildings featuring windows sealed with shutters or cloth, not glass (figs. 5.4, 5.5). It is hard to imagine that the artist would have included such sealants in his ambitious architectural vision if they were considered crude or provisional at the time.

Was the persistence of non-vitreous sealants perhaps a sign of "parsimony," as one historian has argued?[37] The use of such materials in aristocratic residences and public buildings seems to undercut this claim. One would do more justice to the historical reality by acknowledging that non-vitreous window sealants offered an acceptable compromise between shutters and glass. Most importantly, they admitted light; but as medieval householder manuals pointed out, waxed paper and oiled canvas also provided efficient protection from mosquitoes and other vermin.[38] Glass windows, of course, offered the same protective effect—but they also had a disadvantage: the larger the window, the more difficult and expensive it was to glaze. As we have seen, glass windows from this period were always composed of smaller segments held together by some kind of tracery.[39] In glazing

Fig. 5.4. Fra Carnevale (attr.), *Architectural Veduta* (View of an Ideal City), ca. 1485. Walters Art Museum, Baltimore.

Fig. 5.5. Textile windows in a Renaissance "Ideal City," detail of Fra Carnevale (attr.), *Architectural Veduta* (View of an Ideal City), ca. 1485 (see fig. 5.4).

windows, moreover, one had to balance a number of different factors, including weight and resistance to wind pressure.[40] By contrast, materials such as canvas or animal membranes, which were typically mounted over simple wooden frames, were far less complicated and time-consuming to apply.[41]

Framing and varnishing certainly required some skill, but the task was hardly beyond an ordinary householder with some experience. The same, of course, could not be said of the production and assembly of glass windows. Tellingly, one *Mayflower* colonist in early seventeenth-century North America advised a friend in England to "bring paper and linseed oil for your windows."[42] Oiled paper was also used in William Penn's Philadelphia.[43] And in some rural areas of the American Midwest, where glass was not easily available, settlers relied on oiled paper well into modern times. This held particularly true for the so-called sod houses, which were usually built in a week and often lasted for decades. As late as the 1970s, residents of sod houses in areas such as Nebraska and western Kansas lived without glass windows—and yet they commended the "environmental comfort of their interiors in all seasons."[44]

In premodern Europe, too, residents sometimes took it in their own hands to install non-vitreous sealants in their windows, but they could also turn to professionals specializing in these tasks. In France, the manufacture and installation of non-vitreous sealants fell in the domain of the "*huchiers*" (sometimes also known as "*châssissiers*"); in the German lands, these craftsmen were known as "*sliemer.*" Interestingly, in some places the sliemer formed part of the local glassmaker guild—a reminder that the line between glass and other sealants was not as categorical and rigid as one might assume from a modern perspective.[45] When necessary, these professionals also carried out maintenance work (such as renewing the varnish or patching holes). Such fixes were inevitable in the long run, but always cheaper and less complicated than repairing broken glass windows.[46]

Windows sealed with lightweight materials such as canvas or parchment were easy to cast open. Of course, whether it was considered desirable to be able to open a given window depended on the broader architectural context. As we have seen, it was a low priority in churches: the theological ideas that underpinned the glazing of churches were not about the flow of air, but rather about the admission of (polychrome) light. Large stained-glass windows were shining manifestations of this theological vision, but their size also meant that it was impossible to open them. In domestic architecture, the priorities were different. Unlike churches, domestic spaces had fireplaces, and they also served as sites of economic activity, which only increased the need for fresh air. Openability was therefore an important concern for householders. This, to be sure, did not preclude the use of glass, as long as the window had hinges and could be cast open. Side-hung windows of this kind were known as "casements"—and the very existence of a special term is a reminder that not all glass windows at the time were openable.[47]

It was much easier to operate non-vitreous windows. Fabric, parchment, and paper all weighed less than glass, and the lighter material also meant lighter window frames. As a result, non-vitreous windows were not only relatively easy to install, but also often openable in a range of different positions. Indeed, they seem to have been the only feasible type of awning window at the time. To this end, the window surface was divided horizontally, so that the lower half could be tilted upward and fastened in this position by means of a cord or metal fixture (figs. 5.6, 5.7).[48] This flexibility must have contributed to the popularity of non-vitreous windows—especially given that standing at open windows was one of the favorite pastimes of premodern people: in an age before telephones, television, and the internet, the window served, for centuries, as the most important interface for communication between house and street, interior and exterior.[49]

There were, of course, situations in which it was wiser to keep the windows shut even if it would have been easy or desirable to open them. The German merchant Hans-Ulrich Krafft experienced this in 1573 when he lived in the city of Tripoli (in modern-day Lebanon), where he worked as the representative of a European trade company. In his autobiography, Krafft recounted that the windows of his apartment were sealed with paper. The lack of transparency does not seem to have bothered him—until the day of a solar eclipse. Krafft was curious to observe this rare natural phenomenon, but he noticed that the event caused great anxiety among the local Muslim population. To avoid provoking suspicion or anger, Krafft decided to observe the eclipse from the privacy of his apartment. Standing at the open window, however, would have drawn too much attention, so Krafft decided "to diligently make a hole in my paper windows so that I would be able to observe the eclipse without being seen by anyone."[50] Krafft's account reminds us that non-vitreous sealants were never fully transparent. But it also suggests that one could afford to damage such windows because, unlike glass windows, they were relatively easy and cheap to repair.

Non-vitreous sealants had another advantage: it was easy to paint them in all

Fig. 5.6. Perugino (workshop), *The Miracles of Saint Bernardino of Siena*, 1473. Galleria Nazionale dell'Umbria, Perugia. The painting shows Saint Bernardino restoring the eyesight of a blind man; the background offers an unusually meticulous depiction of three *impannate* windows in different positions.

Fig. 5.7. Detail of Perugino (workshop), *The Miracles of Saint Bernardino of Siena*, 1473 (see fig. 5.6).

kinds of colors. By contrast, painting on glass posed much greater challenges. Until the emergence of advanced enameling techniques in the fifteenth century, polychrome painting on glass was largely limited to small vessels. This had no effect on architectural glass. As we have seen, stained glass owed its polychrome effect not to the surface application of paint, but rather to the addition of specific chemicals as part of the glassmaking process. In the case of non-vitreous windows, coloring was far less complicated, as the paint was applied directly on the canvas or parchment. Another option was to dye the fabric with one color: a window of this kind admitted a soft, monochrome light, similar to the effect of a monochrome glass window (but much cheaper). In 1416, no less eminent a figure than the queen of France ordered green fabric to seal the windows in one of her châteaux.[51] Other householders sought more variety and commissioned textile windows painted with specific decorative motifs, such as coats of arms or other insignia of power.[52] A Sienese invoice from the year 1555 indicates that a private individual tasked a certain painter, Giovanni Battista di Cristoforo, with "painting three textile windows [*impannate*] with the coat of arms of him and his wife and with a gilded frieze [*fregio d'oro*]."[53] Even complex figurative scenes were possible: to wit, a Florentine inventory from 1417 mentions a window sealed with fabric on which the Annunciation was depicted.[54] A systematic study of inventories along these lines might yield more evidence—including evidence that has previously been misinterpreted. For instance, a Spanish painter's inventory from 1603 mentioning a "primed canvas for a window" (*un lienzo emprimado para una ventana*) might not be a reference to a painting depicting a window (as art historians have assumed), but rather a painting made for a window.[55] And of course there were householders who took the brush in their own hands. In doing so, they could rely on instructions such as those given by Hugh Plat in his 1594 how-to manual, *The Jewell House*: "You may draw anie personage, beast, tree, flower, or coate armour upon the parchment before it bee oyled, and then cutting your Parchment into square panes, and making slight frames for them, they will make a pretty shew in your windowes."[56]

All evidence taken together, it is clear that non-vitreous sealants were considered acceptable alternatives to glass windowpanes.[57] Tellingly, in French, it was not uncommon to refer to non-vitreous windows by the oxymoronic term "*verrières de toiles*" (literally, "glass windows made of fabric")—as, for instance, in the records of the Château d'Hesdin in northern France, where such windows were installed in 1299 in honor of a royal visit.[58] In German how-to manuals, too, instructions for making parchment windows were subsumed under the rubric "glass windows."[59] And in English, the term "pane," now exclusively associated with glass, derives historically from "pan," the Anglo-Norman word for a piece of cloth.[60]

It fits into this general picture that, as late as the sixteenth century, painted paper was sometimes used to replace broken stained-glass windows. True, this was a temporary solution, but it does suggest that non-vitreous sealants—at least those of the highest quality—had the potential to mimic the visual effect of polychrome glass.[61] It was also possible to combine both options—for example, by glazing the upper part of a window and sealing the lower part with fabric.[62] At other times, the two different methods were used in different parts of the same building. The fourteenth-century papal palace in Avignon featured glass windows in some rooms, such as the chapel and reception rooms, while windows in other spaces were sealed with fabric. There is no evidence to indicate that the choice of non-vitreous sealants implied an inferior status of the rooms; indeed, among the fabric-sealed rooms was the Grand Tinel, the vast and stately banquet hall. Similar observations can be made in other Provençal and Iberian palaces from this period, but also in aristocratic residences in the German lands.[63]

Seen from today's vantage point, the use of both glass and non-vitreous sealants in a single building might seem inconsistent. For people at the time, however, it was not: from their perspective, the most prized quality in fenestration was not transparency, but rather the window's appearance as an elaborate polychrome or even figurative image-surface. This visual effect could be achieved by glass, textile, and paper alike.

Colored or not, textile and paper sealants enjoyed great popularity in many parts of Europe, but perhaps nowhere more so than in Italy. To this day, the Italian language has preserved a generic term for this type of window: the "*impannata*" (plural: *impannate*).[64] In premodern times, similar terms also existed in other European languages: speakers of high and late medieval English, for instance, used the word "fenestral."[65] While this English word has long since fallen into oblivion, the term "impannata" is still occasionally remembered in Italian, mostly because such windows have left visible traces in Italy's cultural heritage. For instance, one of Raphael's paintings of the Virgin Mary, dating to the 1510s, is commonly known as the *Madonna dell'Impannata*—a title referencing the large impannata window in the painting's background (fig. 5.8). We cannot tell with certainty which particular kind of sealant Raphael intended, but it appears to be canvas. We also do not know

Fig. 5.8. Raphael, *Madonna dell'Impannata*, ca. 1511–17. Palazzo Pitti, Florence. The painting derives its name from the *impannata* window in the background, which admits a soft, indeterminate light.

whether Raphael had a particular reason to place the impannata window prominently in the painting or whether it served merely as a visual ingredient to make the sacred scene look more commonplace and thus more intimate and authentic. Whatever Raphael's intentions, his is not the only Italian painting from the period featuring a depiction of impannate windows in the context of a realistically rendered urban or domestic scene. Sometimes such paintings even reveal the presence of impannate in prominent locations where we might not expect them. Thus, fifteenth-century views of Florence reveal that several windows of Florence's Palazzo Vecchio were sealed with impannate—an observation confirmed by the palazzo's inventories, which list this type of sealant as late as 1553.[66] Given that virtually no original impannate windows from this period have survived, paintings and other visual depictions are often our only sources of knowledge about the design and appearance of these windows. Unfortunately, however, a systematic survey of this historical phenomenon—and its visual representations—remains a desideratum. Such an overview would no doubt underscore how popular impannate were in the past—but at the same time it would raise a key question to which we must turn next: Why did these non-vitreous sealants ultimately disappear from Western architecture?

6

From the House of God
to the Houses of Burghers

Chapter-opening image: Detail of Fig. 6.6

Given the popularity that non-vitreous window sealants enjoyed for centuries, why did glass ultimately prevail in Western architecture?[1] Monocausal and teleological explanations are bound to remain unsatisfactory. The rise of glass as the standard window sealant in Western architecture was not an inevitable process, as is evident from other premodern societies where glass technology was known but not applied to the production of windows. In Japan, for example, premodern architecture relied exclusively on non-vitreous sealants for centuries, despite intermittent interaction with Westerners. Indeed, shōji screens—translucent, but not transparent—are still a feature of traditional Japanese houses today.[2] The case of Japan makes it clear that, from a long-term perspective, climatic factors alone cannot explain the rise of architectural glass in Europe: even if there were such a thing as a uniformly "European" climate (and a uniformly Japanese climate, for that matter), it would be hard to point to any fundamental differences between the two.[3] In fact, from a climatological perspective, Japan and Europe belong to the same climate zone (that is, one of eight principal zones globally).[4]

Which specific historical factors, then, contributed to the rise of glass in European domestic architecture? Some architectural historians have identified the gradual "brickification" of Europe—that is, the gradual transition from wood-based to stone architecture—as a key factor, arguing that stone walls provided a more stable framework for window openings and the heavy glass windows used to seal them.[5] This is a valid point, but not a complete explanation: after all, the scale and pace of the transition from wood to stone varied greatly across Europe. In addition to architectural change, we must take into account technological improvements in the field of glassmaking.

One such improvement was the rediscovery of crown-glass production (see fig. 1.9). As we have seen, crown glass was pioneered by late ancient glassmakers but fell into oblivion in the following centuries. Only in the medieval Near East did the crown method remain in use, and it is possible that its revival in western Europe, probably in the thirteenth century, was the result of a transfer of technology prompted by crusaders returning from the Levant.[6] What we know for a fact is that Normandy and Venice emerged as centers of crown-glass production in High Medieval Europe.[7] From Normandy, this know-how reached England, the only European country where crown would become the predominant production method and remain so until the nineteenth century.[8] In fact, the English term "crown glass" is thought to have emerged from the small crown embossed on glass products manufactured at one of London's leading seventeenth-century glass factories.[9]

The European rediscovery of the crown-glass method led to an expansion and diversification of the marketplace for window glass. Like cylinder glass, crown was available in a range of different sizes and artificial colors. Early crown-glass disks had a relatively small diameter, but late medieval glassmakers gradually succeeded in producing larger disks with a diameter of up to three feet. These disks were then cut into smaller (and typically rectangular) segments. The segments from the disk's periphery were sometimes as thin as one and a half millimeters, and therefore thinner than most panes produced by means of the cylinder method. Crown glass of the highest quality also surpassed cylinder glass in terms of brilliance, as the hot glass disk was spun without touching a surface.[10]

In other respects, crown proved inferior to cylinder glass: the surface of the disk (and thus the surface of the individual panes) was inevitably slightly curved due to the spinning process. What is more, the disk's center always featured a thick, ungainly segment known as the "bullion" (or "bull's-eye"). Tellingly, in some European languages, this bullion (known as "*boudine*" in French, and as "*Butze*" in German) became the generic term for the round panes cut from the disk's center. Today, bull's-eye windows are often perceived as quintessentially medieval and quaint; in premodern times, however, such roundels were merely the scrap left over after a much larger glass disk had been cut up into rectangular pieces, all of which were thinner than the bullion and fetched higher market prices.[11] In fact, the majority of bullions probably never came on the market, as they were melted down again (fig. 6.1).[12]

This reminds us that there were not only different production methods, but also different qualities of glass. Today, we are used to industrial mass production and fairly firm international standards. In the premodern period, however, the quality of glass was influenced by a variety of different factors, including regional traditions and resources (such as locally available fluxing agents). As far as window glass was concerned, late medieval people considered products from Normandy to be of the highest quality, while German panes were seen as inferior. In the flourishing mercantile city of Antwerp (equidistant from Normandy

Fig. 6.1. Albrecht Dürer House, Nuremberg, Germany, ca. 1420. Although restored in the nineteenth century, the glass windows convey a good sense of what medieval and early modern bull's-eye windows looked like. Nineteenth-century historicism considered bull's-eyes quaint and picturesque (see Chapter 11). In premodern times, however, the round panes, with their characteristic central lump, were usually scrap sold at cheap prices.

and the German Rhineland), guild laws expressly stipulated that only French glass (*franche glas*) was to be used for stained-glass windows, whereas Rhenish glass panes (*Rijns*) were acceptable for bordures or uncolored outer segments of such windows.[13]

In the long term, the diversification of the medieval market for glass certainly had an effect on architecture: sealing windows with glass became more affordable and, by extension, more common. Still, large-scale glazing remained a costly undertaking. In addition to the purchasing costs, one had to factor in the expense of installation and maintenance; the financial investment was significant. This leads to a crucial question: What exactly did householders who made this investment expect from it?

One thing is certain: as in sacred architecture, transparency—that is, a clear view—was not a priority in medieval domestic architecture. Technically, it was possible to produce panes with a remarkably high degree of transparency, but only a small number of people could have afforded them. More importantly, householders of financial means tended to prefer colored glass, which was considered more prestigious.

The low priority of transparency might also reflect legal and urban realities: medieval and early modern building ordinances typically did not entitle residents to a view from the window. This was a departure from Roman law, which, as we have seen, emphasized the right to a view (prospectus) from the window. From a medieval and early modern legal perspective, a resident was entitled to a view only if he or she had expressly secured this right in advance from the owners of neighboring buildings. Securing such an "easement" was a complex legal process, which typically required notarial intermediation.[14] In short, if the purpose of glazing one's windows was to enjoy views of the outside, the legal framework generally provided neither an incentive nor a guarantee.

This does not mean that people were indifferent to the view from their windows. In fact, gazing out and conversing from the window were among the most popular pastimes of premodern people.[15] However, the ability to pursue these pastimes depended not on the transparency of the glass, but rather on the window's openness (fig. 6.2). Consider also the case of a London widow who, in 1341, sued a neighbor for prying into her garden. Tellingly, this visual transgression only became an issue when her neighbor's glass windows were broken.[16] The court ruled in the widow's favor and denied her neighbor the right to this view. Elsewhere in Europe, too, courts and jurists agreed that there was no natural entitlement to a view. Medieval and early modern law did, however, uphold the two other rights enshrined in the ancient Roman Law of Windows (*jus fenestrarum*): the right to air and the right to light. How did these two parameters play into householders' decision to install glass windows?

Let us begin with light. It is no exaggeration to say that natural light was of key importance in an age before electrification. As Daniel Roche has noted, the "ability to control lighting techniques created a greater possibility for organising specialised and separate ways of life."[17] Naturally, there was more daylight available near the windows than anywhere else in the house. The close link between windows and light also left traces on a linguistic level: in French, the word "*jour*"

Fig. 6.2. Interior of the Schlössle in Pfullingen (southern Germany), a timber-framed house with residential and administrative functions, ca. 1450. Despite the generous furnishing with bull's-eyes, one can see outside only when the windows are opened.

(literally meaning "day") was used as a synonym for "fenêtre"—just as, in architectural contexts, the English noun "light" could denote a window.[18] The need for light was particularly pressing in cities: as many cities were walled, urban space was limited and houses often could expand only vertically, with the result that neighborhoods were densely built up. Under these circumstances, windows—and the light they admitted—were crucial for residents' ability to conduct their private and economic life. Unsurprisingly, countless legal quarrels between neighbors revolved around the perceived or real deprivation of daylight.[19]

The invention of printing with movable type in the fifteenth century increased the importance of lighting. In the age of printing, books were more easily and cheaply available than ever before, and literacy rates rose. As a result, reading became a more common activity—but one that was impossible to pursue without sufficient light.[20] There were also many other domestic and economic activities that required good lighting conditions, including, for instance, the day-to-day work of craftsmen and artisans, but also that of physicians who needed daylight to perform certain medical operations, such as uroscopy or dental examination.[21] The growing market for financial services was yet another economic domain where daylight was essential: the anonymous Hebrew *Book of the Rules of the Moneylender and the Borrower*, probably written in the fifteenth century, exhorted pawnbrokers not to appraise pawns and other valuables at moon- or candlelight. According to this manual, only daylight provided adequate lighting levels for an accurate appraisal.[22] In the same spirit, Christian guild regulations often prohibited artisans and craftsmen from working at candlelight.[23]

Customers, too, were advised to transact business only in well-lit spaces: in his famous *Narrenschiff* (Ship of Fools, 1494), the German humanist Sebastian Brant condemned poorly lit premises and stores, as they lent themselves to cheating and manipulation. According to Brant, the lack of proper lighting made it easy for fraudulent storeowners to tamper with scales, clip coins, and pass off merchandise of poor quality as better than it actually was: "The shops are dark, with lights so tiny, / One cannot see the cloth is shiny."[24] Brant was not alone in expressing criticism and suspicion. Martin Luther, the ever-polemical church reformer, accused merchants of using the same fraudulent tricks in selling "woolen goods, silks, fur of marten or sable . . . in dimly-lit vaults or shops, keeping them from the air."[25]

If the manipulation of lighting conditions was malicious, neglect of proper lighting was a sign of outright foolishness. The *Lalebuch* (The Book of Lale), a collection of traditional German lore first published in 1597, included the amusing yet admonitory story of the people of the (fictitious) town of Laleburg who built a city hall but forgot to leave space for windows. When the townspeople inaugurated the building, they were struck by the darkness inside. They decided to remedy the problem by carrying daylight in buckets into the building. When this made no improvement, they untiled the roof to admit light—only to realize that in wintertime they needed to put the tiles back in place. Finally, the townspeople discovered a small crack in the wall through which light entered—and only this made them realize that they had forgotten the windows.[26] Similar farcical stories circulated about other (invented or real) cities and their authorities. Private individuals, too, sometimes became the objects of such mockery. A sixteenth-century German chronicle claims that a certain Count Sigmund von Lupfen built in his territory in Alsace "a stone house without windows and doors."[27] Upon completion, it dawned on him that he would need to break openings into the wall "so that he could see best where the windows were most needed."[28]

The lesson from these tales was clear: a prudent homebuilder avoided embarrassing situations of this sort and gave careful consideration to the issue of lighting. That, of course, is where the real challenge began: finding the right balance in matters of lighting. In his treatise *De re aedificatoria* (On the Art of Building), Leon Battista Alberti, the influential fifteenth-century architectural theorist, tried to steer a middle course. The windows of a home, he argued, "should be appropriate to the requirements of the interior and should take into account the thickness of the wall, so that their frequency and the light they receive are no greater or less than utility demands."[29] To bolster his argument, the humanist Alberti cited the "works of the ancients," who never allowed "openings of any kind to occupy more than a seventh or less than a ninth of a wall's surface."[30]

Alberti's learned arguments notwithstanding, architectural theory and practice often diverged. Consider timber-frame houses, which enjoyed great popularity in northern Europe at the time: these houses often featured a ribbon of windows in the upper stories, as it was structurally possible to exploit the entire space between the timber bars for fenestration. Such designs were evidently not in line with Alberti's vision of architectural proportions, but they reflected residents' attempts to increase the amount of daylight in the interior (figs. 6.3, 6.4).[31]

This brings us back to architectural glass. Clearly, the installation of glass windows—as opposed to, say, wooden shutters—increased the amount of daylight. It has also been argued that by choosing glass, people could "work longer hours and with more precision because they were shielded from the elements."[32] Still, we should not draw the rash conclusion that glass was the most desirable option in each and every setting. Members of certain professional groups continued to prefer paper or textile sealants, as such windows afforded a more even and soft light than glass panes did: this preference was common, for instance, among painters, engravers, and scholars as late as the eighteenth century.[33] In the fifteenth century, Leonardo da Vinci commended the soft light "which passes through translucent matter such as linen, or paper, or similar things." Leonardo distinguished

Fig. 6.3. Maison Kammerzell, Strasbourg, France, fifteenth century. The Kammerzell house is one of the finest surviving timber-framed homes from this period. The almost uninterrupted window ribbons reflect the desire—and, indeed, need—for daylight.

this soft light from the bright, glaring light that passes through "transparent matter, like glass, or crystal, or objects which produce an effect as if nothing were lying between the shadowed body and the light which illuminates it."[34] Indeed, one wonders if Leonardo's preference for this kind of soft light contributed to his mastery of *sfumato* and its blurry visual effects.[35]

In short, the key difference between glass and impannata windows was not so much the quantity of admitted light, but rather its quality. Glass and impannata windows each provided a different kind of light—but either way, the amount of light was considered sufficient for the ordinary needs of domestic life. Here again, it is useful to point to traditional East Asian houses, where non-vitreous sealants were the architectural standard and enjoyed great popularity for centuries. It would be hard to argue that the lack of window glass had negative economic or cultural effects on countries such as China and Japan, which were as technologically and economically advanced as European countries at the time.

To return to the main question: If the view from the window was not a legal entitlement, and the need for daylight could be met with paper or textile windows, then why did glass prevail in premodern European architecture? This question requires us to probe the third item addressed in the Roman Law of Windows: air. As we have seen, medieval and early modern courts considered both the right to air and the right to light nonnegotiable. From an architectural vantage point, builders and theorists such as Alberti concurred, noting that "each individual chamber . . . should have windows, to admit light and to allow a change of air."[36] In practice, however, air turned out to be a much more complicated issue than light, as its circulation was both a necessity and a risk. On the one hand, ventilation was indispensable, especially in an age when domestic activities such as cooking, heat-

Fig. 6.4. Guild houses at the Grote Markt (Great Market), Antwerp, sixteenth and seventeenth centuries. Unlike Strasbourg's Maison Kammerzell (see fig. 6.3), these guild houses were built from stone and used for commercial purposes. Their fenestration, however, displays a similar desire for maximum daylight.

ing, or the use of lamps produced smoke and soot within the house. A medieval proverb captured this in stark terms: *Sunt damna tria domus: imber, mala, fumus* (in an early modern English rendering: "Smoke, rain, and a very curst wife, make a man weary of house and life").[37] On the other hand, the potential influx of "bad air" from the outside was considered a serious danger and linked to a wide range of bodily disorders.[38]

Anxieties about bad air came to the fore during the Black Death in 1348–49 and lingered in its aftermath.[39] In the absence of modern bacteriological knowledge, doctors assumed that epidemics such as the plague spread through so-called miasmata (foul odors). Plague treatises from the fourteenth and fifteenth centuries discussed in great detail how to protect oneself from miasmatic air—and windows played a particularly important role in this context. Protection from foul air was more than just a matter of personal comfort: as the plague could break out at any time, the measures were part of a permanent regimen of medical precaution. One could, in fact, argue that late medieval Europeans understood privacy not so much as the ability to withdraw from other people and their gazes, but rather the ability to seclude oneself from rank air and bad odors.[40] In times of rampant plague, such protection became an issue of vital importance. Physicians advised people in the strongest terms to keep their windows shut to protect the house from miasmatic air, and many city governments made such measures mandatory. Medical personnel and gravediggers, who were in direct contact with infected individuals, were told to stay clear of doors and windows.[41]

During epidemics, nailing one's windows shut was a desperate but common measure. In ordinary times, such extreme steps were not necessary, and instead a tight window sealant promised efficient protection from foul air. Glass was one option, and—according to some contemporaries—the best. The sixteenth-century art theorist Giorgio Vasari, whose writings usually focused on aesthetic issues, emphasized that glass windows (by which he meant stained glass) should not only be pleasing to the eyes, but also supply "a delicate loveliness not less beneficial to health, through securing the rooms from wind and foul airs."[42]

It fits into this picture that, in the decades after the Black Death, the glazing of hospital windows gained traction in Europe. Hospitals at the time served only the indigent who were severely ill or infirm. An outbreak of plague would have had a devastating impact on these particularly vulnerable individuals. As medical historian John Henderson has noted with respect to the Renaissance period, most hospitals came to be "glazed and fixed shut, being designed as a source of light rather than to encourage the circulation of air."[43] It is true that, on an experiential level, doctors knew that fresh air could under certain circumstances prove beneficial to ill people.[44] From this perspective, the emphasis on tightly sealed windows might seem counterintuitive. But at the end of the day, preventive action—that is, protection from miasmata—took precedence over therapeutic experiments. The sealing of hospital windows also responded to deep-rooted anxieties in the population about miasmatic air flowing from hospitals back into public spaces. In fact, any building that was housing an infected person was considered a source of danger. Observing the rampant plague in London in 1666, the diarist Samuel Pepys wrote with great concern in his diary about the rumor that "ill people would breathe in the faces (out of their windows) of well people going by."[45]

Anxieties about foul air flowing through open windows were widespread across Europe well into the modern period. A seventeenth-century physician stationed in Austria observed, "There is a massive fear and loathing of night air as if it were a horrible poison; at all times and without distinction, people go to great pains to cover their windows, doors, and portals."[46] It was not until the late nineteenth century that bacteriological explanations challenged the miasma theory. Some physicians began to fiercely promote the benefits of keeping windows open both day and night. Tellingly, however, such calls for abundant fresh air met with suspicion and even outright rejection—including from other physicians. The doctors at the Hôtel-Dieu in early nineteenth-century Lyon "preserved an invincible prejudice against the free circulation of air."[47] Patients were even harder to convince: in countries as different as nineteenth-century Spain and England, ill people were united in their opposition to open windows.[48] And a Swiss newspaper reported in 1876 that, with respect to the issue of opening windows, "The physician often faces unsurmountable prejudices by both men and women, and by all classes of human society. In popular thinking, the terms 'air draft' and 'night air' are infinite sources of countless diseases, and people are stricken with horror and fear . . . when the doctor orders to open the windows in a patient's room."[49]

These medical discourses and anxieties can help us understand why late medieval hospitals were often among the first secular buildings to receive glass windows. In Florence, this process began in the second half of the fourteenth century—that is, in the aftermath of the devastating plague epidemic of the late 1340s. Before the traumatic experience of the Black Death, the windows of medieval hospitals (as well as leper houses) were often sealed only with stretched animal skins. To be sure, the transition to glass did not happen overnight. In late fourteenth-century Florence, there were still hospitals furnished with impannate—a reminder that what mattered most was that the windows be sealed, not the particular choice of sealant.[50] In the long term, however, it was glass—the most impermeable sealant available at the time—that prevailed in hospital architecture.[51] This pattern can also be observed elsewhere in Europe. As Henderson has noted, "By the later Middle Ages the windows of the larger institutions for the poor sick in both England and France were glazed with clear glass."[52] Once the installation was completed, the commitment to glass was kept up even in times of crisis. When, in 1571, the governors of St. Thomas's Hospital in Southwark grappled with grave financial problems, the only repairs they authorized were those that made the hospital buildings "wind tight and water tight or keep or uphold any house from falling down."[53] Interestingly, the prominence of glass windows in European hospitals did not escape the attention of foreign visitors. Thus, the Ottoman traveler Evliya Çelebi, who visited Christian Europe in the 1660s, observed with great interest that the "hospital of the Stephan Church [in Vienna] . . . was warm and had glass windowpanes."[54]

Of course, the plague was not a problem unique to Europe; it affected societies in different parts of the premodern world. But while the symptoms were the same everywhere, the etiologies differed. As a result, both the preventive and therapeutic responses varied significantly. In Europe, the miasma theory emphasized the need for protection from foul air, encouraging the use of tight sealants such as glass. The cultural relativity of these measures becomes particularly clear if we compare Europe with East Asian societies that developed different responses to the plague or were not affected by the disease in the first place. Consider China: it is not clear whether the plague spread as far east as the Middle Kingdom, but contagious epidemics certainly were not unheard of there. Chinese physicians often attributed such outbreaks to foul air (*qi*) emanating from the soil—an idea not dissimilar to the European miasma theory. However, unlike Western medicine, traditional Chinese medicine recommended mobility instead of isolation in times of epidemics: if the influence of noxious qi could not be dispelled (through geomantic rituals, for instance), then it was better to leave the affected location as quickly as possible.[55] Early modern Japan makes for an even more instructive comparison. There is no evidence of plague outbreaks in Japan before the late nineteenth century.[56] The lack of exposure was probably due to Japan's geographical and economic isolation. As a result, "the Japanese experience with epidemic diseases was different from that of Europe."[57] This also meant that, in premodern Japan, neither the medical reality nor the medical discourse provided an incentive for the use of architectural glass.[58]

By contrast, in Europe, anxieties about miasmata escalated during epidemics. But even during ordinary times the legally guaranteed right to air was a two-sided issue for early modern people. On the one hand, ventilation was a necessity in everyday life; on the other hand, too much air was a source of anxiety and discomfort. Suffice it to recall that Vasari recommended "securing the rooms" not just because of "foul airs," but also because of another—and ultimately more common—issue: the exposure to "wind" and thus to cold. Indeed, the medical literature at the time tended to consider cold more harmful than heat.[59] In a popular health manual composed around the time Vasari was writing, the Italian physician Tommaso Rangone dedicated an entire section to the link between physical well-being and fenestration, admonishing readers to keep windows shut at night and to seal them with "glass, canvas, or paper."[60]

To group all these sealants together, as Rangone did, does not mean that there were no differences between them. But as we have seen, from a medical point of view the main concern was to ensure that windows were sealed, whatever the means. From other (for example, economic) perspectives, the differences between sealants weighed more heavily. Consider the case of bankers and moneylenders. The fifteenth-century *Book of the Rules of the Moneylender and the Borrower* addressed two ways in which a moneylender could achieve good lighting conditions in his premises: either by sealing his windows with oiled paper or by glazing them. According to this manual, both sealants provided sufficient light for conducting business, including for critical tasks such as appraising pawns. Paper had the advantage of being cheap. Glass, however, offered better protection from air drafts—and this, the anonymous author noted, was ultimately more important for a moneylender, as drafts could interfere with the precision of the scales.[61]

In domestic settings, protection from drafts was also a question of thermal comfort. The inconveniences caused by drafts might seem rather abstract to modern Westerners, who are accustomed to weatherproof fenestration and the year-long availability of climate control indoors. By contrast, medieval and early modern householders relied on what today might appear relatively primitive means and strategies for ensuring thermal comfort. The widespread custom of sleeping with a nightcap is evidence of the struggle with drafts and cold. Those who could afford it slept in beds protected by curtains.[62] During the day, people often wore warmer clothes in the interior than we do today. Montaigne noted about his fellow Frenchmen: "We put on our warm furred dressing gowns when we enter the house."[63]

The installation of glass windows was often part of a broader effort to contain the impact of cold weather: remember that the glazing of certain windows at Westminster Palace in the 1230s was ordered "so that the chamber may not be so windy as it used to be."[64] The problem of heat loss, however, persisted. Premodern walls lacked the quality insulation we are used to today. As a result, the advantage of glass windows was relative: they could not remedy heat loss, but compared to other available sealants at the time, they at least offered better—if imperfect—protection from inclement weather.[65]

It was, of course, a humoristic exaggeration when the sixteenth-century Italian writer Pietro Aretino remarked that even the slightest breeze could damage an impannata window.[66] In his 1594 household manual *The Jewell House*, the Englishman Hugh Plat offered a far more nuanced take when he recommended parchment instead of "oyled Paper, because it is more lasting, and will endure the blustring and stormie weather much better then paper."[67] Indeed, in the Château de Joux in the Jura, paper windows had to be replaced in the 1470s after being "torn by violent winds."[68] To prevent such damage, it was not uncommon to install wooden shutters in front of the impannate.[69] Still, glass was the more resilient material. When the French king ordered in 1414 that the oilpaper windows in one of his castles be replaced with glass, the stated goal was "to protect [the windows] from water and the downstream wind against which these windows are [intended]."[70]

Tight-sealing glass windows were particularly useful in rooms that contained a built-in stove or enclosed fireplace. This, to be sure, was not the standard at the time: even in the imposing palace of Urbino—one of the most sophisticated Renaissance palaces—there were far more rooms (two hundred fifty) than fireplaces (forty).[71] In the absence of fireplaces, medieval and early modern people often relied on mobile braziers (that is, metal containers filled with burning charcoals).[72] To install and operate a fixed fireplace or stove was a considerable financial investment, and indeed such expenditures often went hand in hand with increased attention to issues of fenestration. Consider the case of King René of Anjou, the fifteenth-century ruler of Provence. Many of his palaces featured impannate, but in 1478 he ordered the glazing of the windows in his castle at Tarascon after acquiring "a stove in the German style to keep himself warm" (*paesle à la façon d'Allemagne pour se tenir chaudement*).[73] Concerns about the loss of warmth aside, there were also other reasons why glass windows were a sensible option for heated spaces: oiled linen and waxed paper were highly flammable, and having such materials in the vicinity of an open fire posed obvious risks. Tellingly, the high flammability of these materials was occasionally exploited by arsonists or other vandals who set fire to impannate windows from outside.[74]

Today, we think of glass as the only appropriate sealant for windows and assume its universal applicability. But whatever glass's advantages, in the premodern period the demand for it was more local than universal. In other words, glass windows were not considered a sine qua non of architecture, but rather a technology utilized according to regional climate conditions, individual means, and specific domestic needs (for example, sometimes only in one room). Indeed, impannate windows survived much longer in the warmer parts of Europe, such as Mediterranean regions, than they did in the colder, more northerly regions. In the south of France, the glazing of domestic windows did not gain traction until the sixteenth century—and even then, this process advanced only slowly.[75] As the Swiss physician Felix Platter observed in Montpellier in the mid-sixteenth century, the windows in the apartments of university members had "only shutters and the majority of them paper instead of glass." But Platter also noted, "December is less cold than in our town [Basel], there is neither ice nor snow. One warms oneself only by the fire which is at the hearth."[76] As we have seen, the contemporary Montaigne related that wearing warm clothes inside the house was another strategy to cope with the occasional periods of cold.[77]

Even in parts of southern France that were further away from the Mediterranean coast, impannata windows survived well into the eighteenth century: as late as 1717, the episcopal palace in Chambéry—a city in the more mountainous part of southeast France—featured windows sealed with paper.[78] In nearby Lyon, too, paper and canvas were the predominant sealants in domestic architecture through the seventeenth century. Often a building featured both vitreous and non-vitreous windows: in mid-eighteenth-century Lyon, this even held true for the city hall, where paper windows and glass panes sat side by side.[79] It fits into this picture that the guild of châssissiers—craftsmen specializing in the manufacture and repair of non-vitreous windows—still existed in some parts of eighteenth-century France.[80]

But it was in Italy that impannate played a more prominent role than in any other part of early modern Europe. This applied even to sacred architecture: as late as the sixteenth century, "cloth panels" were considered acceptable in Italian churches if there were insufficient funds to purchase glass panes.[81] In general, the window openings of southern European churches tended to be smaller than in northern Europe—perhaps because, as some architectural historians have argued, the warmer climate increased the need for large areas of cooling wall.[82] The most common setting for impannate was, however, domestic architecture, including the residences of the upper classes and the aristocracy. Surviving inventories from the 1430s show that castles of the ducal Este family were equipped with impannate. As we have seen, there is also visual evidence from the same period indicating that some windows of Florence's Palazzo Vecchio (as well as of other palazzi in the city) featured such cloth windows. The use of these sealants in prestigious buildings underscores the fact that impannate were treated as a serious alternative to glass in southern Europe.[83] Northern European visitors did not fail to notice this. Traveling through Italy in 1688, Englishman Sir Robert Worsley noted: "In all ye great towns of Italy except Genoa and in this city [Venice] they have paper in their sashes instead of glass."[84] Goethe, too, encountered windows sealed with oilpaper during his Italian journey in the 1780s.[85]

The persistence of impannate windows reminds us that the history of architectural glass in premodern Europe is, to some extent, the history of a north–south divide. The further south in Europe, the less pressing was the question of domestic glazing. As late as 1727, a French government official visiting the Languedoc region in the country's south reported that glass windows existed "only in the cities, châteaux, and houses of the well-to-do."[86] This observation might have been somewhat exaggerated, but it points to another divide that we need to bear in mind: the divide between country and city. Glass was rarer in rural domestic architecture than it was in the cities. In late seventeenth-century Silesia, the windows of many peasants' homes continued to be sealed with stretched cow bladders, and in the French countryside, paper windows existed well into the nineteenth century.[87] Clearly, this was often due to the cheapness of such sealants. But in contrast to what some historians have assumed, this preference for cheap sealants does not necessarily indicate poverty or destitute living conditions.[88] Travelers such as the English agriculturist Arthur Young, who journeyed through central France on the eve of the French Revolution, considered it "an extraordinary spectacle for English eyes" to see "many houses without glass."[89] At the same time he conceded that these houses were "too good to be cottages."[90] Nor was the rarity of glass in the country necessarily a sign of technological backwardness: nearly everywhere in Europe, the centers of glassmaking were located outside the cities, as the glass industry required a constant supply of fuel in the form of wood. Given the shorter distance from production site to marketplace, glass was often cheaper in the country than in the big cities. If we wish to understand why architectural glass was rarer in the country than in the city, we have to take into account that rural householders had fewer reasons to glaze their homes as the advantages of glazing were fewer than in the city. The problem of miasmata, for instance, was considered less pressing in the country than it was in densely populated cities. Tellingly, during epidemics, the country with its fresh, unpolluted air was the preferred refuge for urbanites who could afford to leave the city.

Precisely because the rise of architectural glass in Europe was not a universal process and involved significant regional differences, it is important to avoid overly generalizing narratives. To say, for instance, that southern Europe "lagged behind" in the use of architectural glass would imply that this was an issue of competence rather than choice. That, however, would be a gross distortion. Italy, in fact, was home to one of the most advanced glass industries at the time. As we have seen, there were secular building types, such as hospitals, where glazing was just as common in southern as it was in northern Europe. By the same token, many Italian doctors of this period agreed that it was advisable to keep windows shut, especially at night, and some architectural theorists, such as Vasari, explicitly recommended the use of glass windows to this end.[91] In everyday life, however, such considerations had to be reconciled with other concerns, such as the need for a breeze and control of heat and glare. Balancing these needs was a considerable challenge for householders in Mediterranean countries such as Italy. Northern Europeans tended to have different priorities. The two key qualities of a window that mattered most to them were succinctly captured in a seventeenth-century Dutch emblem: *Licht en dicht* (Light and closed) (fig. 6.5).[92] Or, as the English schoolmaster William Horman put it in the 1510s: "Glasen wyndowis let in the lyght & kepe out the winde."[93]

Unsurprisingly, southern Europeans occasionally perceived the use of glass in northern European domestic architecture as outlandish and even excessive. Some late medieval and early modern Italians complained sarcastically that one could almost die from the stuffy air in the glazed, stove-heated living rooms of the German lands.[94] The early seventeenth-century Padua-trained physician Hippolytus Guarinonius, who practiced in Tyrol, went so far as to claim that this interior heat "makes healthy people lazy, inert, and sleepy . . . while also contributing to memory loss and dim-wittedness."[95] In the same vein, the sixteenth-century Italian architect Vincenzo Scamozzi argued that this stale air (*aere molto racchiuso*) was responsible for the overly melancholic disposition of northern Europeans.[96] A century earlier, Alberti made similar observations but concluded, on a more diplomatic note, that much in the design of windows depended on the geographical location and climate.[97] This observation remains true to this day—and anthropologists have confirmed it in showing that the notion of comfort varies widely between cultures on a global scale.[98]

Interestingly, even among northern Europeans there was a certain amount of disagreement as to how to strike the right balance between protection from cold air and the need for ventilation. Consider the case of Erasmus of Rotterdam, the sixteenth-century arch-humanist: after several years in Italy, the Dutchman Erasmus moved to Basel, a city in a part of Switzerland known to this day for its mild and sunny climate (by central European standards, at any rate). Occasionally, Erasmus traveled to England, where he found it much more difficult to adjust to the weather. He complained not just about the English climate, but also about what he perceived as an English tendency for excessive glazing: "Their rooms are as a rule so planned as to make a through draught impossible, which Galen especially recommends. Then a great part of the walls consists of translucent glass panes [*vitreis tessellis pellucidam*] which admit light in such a way as to exclude air, and yet admit through chinks what they call filtered air, which is considerably unhealthier and stands there motionless for long periods."[99]

Licht en dicht.

Fig. 6.5. "*Licht en dicht*" (Light and closed): For northern Europeans, these were two key qualities of a window. The widely read emblem book *Sinnepoppen* (1614) by the Dutch author Roemer Visscher likened these qualities to those of an upright Christian who blocks out "the wind of false doctrines and heresies" and instead allows the "light of truth" to enter.

Erasmus's critique is a vivid reminder that attitudes toward fenestration and glazing were often influenced by the observer's geographical and social background. The phenomenon of "too much glass" that Erasmus criticized in England was, of course, limited to the upper-class houses in which the well-connected humanist would have spent most of his time while in England. Such elite homes aside, glass was hardly as ubiquitous in sixteenth-century England as Erasmus polemically suggested. A systematic examination of mid-sixteenth-century Oxfordshire inventories suggests that only 3 percent of poor and average-wealth residents, and only one out of ten affluent householders, had glass windows.[100] The situation was similar in other parts of England—that is, non-vitreous window sealants still predominated, especially in lower- and middle-class homes.[101] Tellingly, even members of the English elite at the time knew very well what such non-vitreous windows looked like. In the words of William Horman, the headmaster of Eton and contemporary of Erasmus: "Paper or lyn clothe straked a crosse with losynges make fenestrals instede of glasen wyndowes."[102] The English Lord Chancellor Thomas More, too, was familiar with such windows. In his *Utopia* (1516), he imagined a society where "glass (of which they have a good supply) is used in windows to keep out the weather; and they also use thin *linen cloth treated with clear oil or gum* so that it has the double advantage of letting in more light and keeping out more wind."[103] More would have had to travel no further than Hampton Court to see horn routinely used to seal the windows of tents and timber houses constructed on the occasion of royal festivities (see fig. 5.3).[104]

By the end of the sixteenth century, however, the situation had changed: the fully glazed window was becoming the standard in the domestic architecture of northern European countries such as England.[105] As John Crowley has noted with respect to England, "During the late sixteenth century glazing underwent the transition from a luxury to a decency as a matter of fashion, not cost."[106] Other historians likewise have observed that by the mid-seventeenth century, glass usage attained "near universality" in England.[107]

Was this process really all about a "fashion"? Or was it, as English social historians have argued, a side effect of the "Great Rebuilding" that occurred under Tudor and Stuart rule?[108] Both aspects certainly played a role. Anxieties about miasmata also mattered. Still, none of these factors provides a complete explanation. Nor was the rise of glass in this period a phenomenon unique to the British Isles.

To the contrary, we observe the same tendency toward extensive domestic glazing in many parts of continental northern Europe.

What, then, was the effect of broader environmental factors? In particular, did the rise of architectural glass correlate with the so-called Little Ice Age? Marked by significantly cooler temperatures and severe winters, the Little Ice Age was felt strongly in northern Europe. Historians (who began to study this climatic phenomenon only a few decades ago) tend to date the gravest phase to the period between 1550 and 1720.[109] It is, of course, impossible to establish with certainty the interrelation between macroclimatic events of the past and changing fashions in domestic architecture, but there is evidence to indicate that changes in "architectural features related to thermal comfort" occurred as a result of the Little Ice Age.[110] New research on early modern English architecture has demonstrated that buildings from this period "reveal subtle accommodations to the climate" and that the greater frequency of glass windows coincided with a growing number of chimneys.[111] Elsewhere in northern Europe, householders began to install double windows and additional wall paneling.[112] Case studies from central and northern Germany suggest that stoves became a common feature in middle-class homes in the period between 1550 and 1620.[113] Concerns about cool air also increased in sixteenth-century medical literature, and entire treatises were dedicated to this subject. This too may have been a reflection of the Little Ice Age.[114]

The prolonged and recurrent periods of cold might explain why, especially in northern Europe, glass windows were no longer seen so much as a matter of personal taste and status, but rather as an indispensable amenity and even a manifestation of civilizing superiority.[115] Samuel Pepys, the mid-seventeenth-century English diarist, noted condescendingly about Portugal that "there is there no glass windows, nor will [they] have any; which makes sport among our merchants there."[116] Writing around the same time, his fellow countryman Edward Chamberlayne proudly observed about England that "the Windowes every where [are] glased, not made of Paper or Wood, as is usual in Italy and Spain."[117] When the English clergyman Gilbert Burnet visited Italy two decades later, he noted with undisguised contempt: "There is one inconvenience in Milan, which throws down all the pleasure that one can find in it; they have no glass windows, so one is either exposed to the Air, or shut up in a Dungeon: and this is so Universal that there is not a House in ten that hath Glass in their Windows: the same defect in Florence, besides all the small towns of Italy, which is an effect of their poverty."[118] A generation later, the philosopher and economic theorist Adam Smith praised glass as "that beautiful and happy invention, without which these northern parts of the world could scarce have afforded a very comfortable habitation."[119] Where non-vitreous sealants survived in seventeenth- and eighteenth-century England, they became the subject of mockery. In contrast to previous periods of history, such sealants were now exclusively associated with low social status and even poverty. In Oxford, unglazed windows still existed in the eighteenth century, but only in the rooms of the so-called servitors, the poorest and least respected members of the student body. Servitors were unable to afford apartments with glass windows and—in the words of a sarcastic poem from 1709—they had no choice but to live in rooms where "their Dormer Windows with Brown-paper / was patch'd to keep out Northern Vapour."[120] This condescending attitude was, to be sure, not unique to England. A growing number of writers from other parts of northern Europe dismissed non-vitreous sealants as inferior and anachronistic.[121] The eighteenth-century German physician and scholar Johann Georg Krünitz wrote, "The paper windows are used so frequently in Italy that one even sees them in ducal palaces, to the discontent of one's eyes. The paper is soaked with oil, both to increase the degree of transparency [sic; *Durchsichtigkeit*] and to prevent the penetration by air from outside, as in many places this air is very unhealthy, especially during nighttime."[122]

The Little Ice Age was not limited to Europe; in fact, its effects must have been felt across the Northern Hemisphere. However, it had different manifestations in different regions: in some parts of Asia, climate change seems to have led to droughts rather than prolonged cold periods.[123] And while the Little Ice Age may have contributed to architectural change in northern Europe, it is not at all clear whether it had a similar effect in, say, China or Japan. In general, the historical impact of climate change on East Asian societies has been studied far less systematically than with respect to Europe.[124] To return to the case of Japan: whatever the effect of the Little Ice Age on early modern Japanese society, it did not prompt the installation of glass windows—partly, perhaps, because the practical advantage of glass was outweighed by cultural resistance to a material that the Japanese elite considered foreign and thus inappropriate.

In the same period, northern Europe saw the opposite development: the glazing of domestic spaces gained unprecedented traction in the sixteenth and sev-

Fig. 6.6. Wollaton Hall, Nottinghamshire, England, 1580s. Built by Robert Smythson, this amply fenestrated "lantern house" is crowned by a "prospect room" providing views in all directions.

enteenth centuries, the heyday of the Little Ice Age. Here again, England is an exemplary case of how glass and class became entangled, for the homes of the English elites made a particularly conspicuous display of architectural glass. This is especially evident in the mansions now known as Elizabethan "lantern houses" or "prodigy houses."[125] One of the earliest examples of this style was Worksop Manor in Nottinghamshire, built around 1589 by the great Elizabethan architect Robert Smythson for the Earl of Shrewsbury. Worksop Manor was destroyed by a fire in 1761, but surviving drawings still convey a sense of the imposing façade with its generously glazed windows.[126] Wollaton Hall near Nottingham, another of Smythson's lantern houses from the 1580s, fared better and has survived to this very day (fig. 6.6).[127] Built for Sir Francis Willoughby, this stately residence features oversized glass windows across the entire upper façade, not only allowing for

Fig. 6.7. Hardwick Hall, Derbyshire, England, 1590s. Arguably the most famous Elizabethan "lantern house," Hardwick Hall was built by Robert Smythson. The spectacular fenestration gave rise to the jingle "Hardwick Hall, more glass than wall."

a splendid view from the inside, but also evoking awe and admiration among visitors approaching from afar.[128]

The best-known surviving example of the conspicuous use of glass in sixteenth-century English architecture, however, is Hardwick Hall, the residence that Smythson built in the 1590s for the wealthy aristocrat Elizabeth Hardwick, Countess of Shrewsbury (fig. 6.7). As architectural historians have noted, Hardwick Hall's façade featured "as much glass as could be provided with structural safety."[129] Inspired by Renaissance ideas about architectural harmony and perfect proportions, Smythson created a façade with strictly symmetrically positioned windows. To this end, he even added false windows to the façade—that is, windows that were glazed but had little or no practical function (for instance, because solid walls or chimneys stood behind them).[130] The total effect of the building was, and still is, impressive. The glazed windows of Hardwick Hall made up such a substantial portion of the façade that they became the subject of an early modern jingle: "Hardwick Hall, more glass than wall."[131]

The generously glazed windows of residences such as Hardwick Hall were undoubtedly a conspicuous status symbol.[132] On special occasions, such as visits by dignitaries, every effort was made to highlight this architectural feature. When, in 1575, Queen Elizabeth visited Kenilworth—another generously glazed English residence, completed just a few years earlier—a contemporary described the brilliant effect of the large, illuminated windows as follows:

> All of the hard quarry-stone: every room so spacious, so well belighted, and so hy roofed within: so seemly too sight by du proportion without: a day tyme, on every syde so torch-light, transparent thro the lyghtsome wyndz, az it wear the Egiptian Pharos relucent untoo all the Alexandrian coast: or else . . . thus radiant az though Phoebus for his eaz woold rest him in the Castl, and not every night so travel dooun unto the Antipodes.[133]

Ostentation, however, was not the only factor driving the spectacular rise of "lantern houses" in England. We also have to take into account the continuing stylistic influence of the Perpendicular Gothic, a late medieval variety of Gothic (church) architecture that emphasized large, vertical windows.[134] Further, the English lantern houses derived prestige from the abundance of the precious resource light. As the account about Kenilworth vividly illustrates, aristocratic residents went to great lengths to impress guests by creating a sophisticated dramaturgy of light. Such carefully staged effects were impossible to achieve for the owners or residents of ordinary houses. Yet even in British rural architecture, historians have observed that the "fashion in the seventeenth century was to place windows on every available wall."[135] The size of these windows was, of course, much smaller than in "prodigy houses," but the sealant used was the same: glass.

This brings us back to the question of climate—a climate that had become noticeably harsher as a result of the Little Ice Age. Admittedly, the link between climate change and glazing might at first seem paradoxical. After all, today we know that "as the number of glazed windows increases, so does the loss of heat through radiation and convection."[136] Applying this observation to the past, however, requires some qualifications (even setting aside the fact that the thermal properties of glass and the laws of convection were not fully understood at the time). True, glass windows could contribute to heat loss—but, as we have seen, the poorly insulated stone walls made heat retention difficult to begin with.[137] We should also keep in mind that our modern concerns about energy efficiency (let alone what we call "green energy") were of no relevance to people at the time. Their main concerns were different—as was vividly captured by Roger North in the 1690s when he remarked about his native England that "wee have generally speaking, too much air, and too little heat."[138] In this struggle with "too much air," glass windows were an imperfect remedy, but the best available. Glass offered the most efficient protection from drafts, and this was particularly crucial in the case of "prodigy houses" such as Hardwick Hall or Wollaton Hall, which were located on hilltops. And with respect to heat retention, glass did as much—or as little—as most other sealants available at the time. At the end of the day, the key factor in ensuring a warm interior was not so much the type of fenestration and sealant used, but rather the availability of in-room fireplaces. As Alberti put it in his widely read *De re aedificatoria*, "If we are to build somewhere very cold, we shall need fires."[139] In other words, all premodern sealants provided imperfect insulation, but this shortcoming could be countered with fireplaces, as long as firewood was easily and cheaply available. At Hardwick Hall, almost every room had its own fireplace. While we today might be concerned about the expense (and the carbon footprint), fireplaces were a natural choice for upper-class residents who had ample financial means and often also owned forests from which they procured their own firewood.

Smythson, the architect of Hardwick Hall and other "prodigy houses," also sought to reduce heat loss by orienting the glass windows in favorable ways: thus, the private apartments of Bess of Hardwick and her family were located in the southern end of the building, where, even on a sunny winter day, the large glass windows had the greatest exposure to solar warmth.[140] Indeed, when a building is optimally sited, glass windows can actually contribute to heating, as vitreous surfaces transmit solar heat without significant loss by absorption or reflection.[141] South-facing windows lent themselves particularly well to this end, as was well known among early modern architects and residents.[142] Windows' contribution to heating depended, of course, on the number of sunshine hours in a given geographical region. With respect to southern England—which enjoys more sunshine hours than other parts of Britain—architectural historians have concluded that oversized windows were not a major source of heat loss "since the gains and losses resulting from the substitution of glass for brickwork were nearly in balance."[143] The only inevitable problem was heat loss during nighttime. This problem, however, could be alleviated by installing curtains—a technology that, as we shall see, began to gain popularity in the early modern period.

In sum, glass windows promised to admit solar heat while shutting out cold air. But to realize this potential, two factors were of crucial importance: proper manufacture and continuous maintenance. True, glass was thicker and more robust than paper or textile sealants, but it was not unbreakable. Vasari noted with regret that window glass "would last in the world an infinite time [if] it were not for the too fragile material."[144] As we have seen, one tried-and-tested way of protecting glass windows was to install wooden shutters in front of them: "I will have a latesse before the glasse for brekyinge," advised the Englishman Horman in 1519.[145] Yet not every homeowner was as precautious. And in the particular case of the English "lantern houses," sufficiently large wooden shutters not only would have presented a technical challenge, but also would have interfered with the façade's grand effect.

The aristocratic owners of residences such as Hardwick Hall were, of course, affluent enough to afford robust glass of fine quality. With glass windows of poorer quality, the risk of breakage was considerably higher. Authorities were aware of this problem and tried to address it by setting quality standards. A decree from mid-sixteenth-century Lorraine ordered glassmakers to ensure that windowpanes "be made stronger so that they break less frequently" (*affin quilz soient plus fortz et moins rompantz*).[146] However, the ingredients used by glassmakers constituted only one of several factors contributing to the window's stability, and even high-quality glass was unlikely to last very long if the lead tracery was poorly fabricated or soldered. Indeed, it was a persistent problem that glaziers used too little lead when leading windowpanes, either out of sloppiness or to save material (as lead was expensive). The result was that such windows sooner or later began to sag and bulge.[147] The seventeenth-century German preacher Abraham a Sancta Clara sarcastically summarized this problem, noting that "not all glaziers are saints, despite their work for holy spaces: they often make the lead lines so thin that they become as transparent [*durchsichtig*] as the glass panes themselves."[148]

Leaky window frames were another source of discomfort for householders. If the window frames were not tight, even the finest glass window would fail to provide efficient protection from the cold. As late as 1705, Madame de Maintenon, the mistress of Louis XIV of France, complained bitterly about the drafts resulting from imperfectly installed glass windows in the royal castle of Marly outside of Paris. Even the king's private chamber was affected: "There is not a door nor window that shuts; one is blown up by a wind that reminds me of American hurricanes."[149] Madame was clearly writing with a pointed pen, but her description contains a kernel of truth: the surviving account books of the French royal court indicate that maintenance work related to glass windows and their frames formed a recurrent and considerable budget item.[150] English monarchs faced the same problem, and during the reign of Elizabeth I, the queen's glazier had his work cut out for him in traveling from one palace to another for the "repairinge and maynteyning of the glasse and glasse-works of the Queenes Majesties mancon howses."[151] German princes, too, had no choice but to foot the bills to preserve their glass windows and the prestige associated with them: the sixteenth-century lords of Rheinfels Castle in Hesse, for instance, paid a glassmaker to visit the castle every few months to clean and "patch" (*flicken*) the windows.[152]

In the long run, the expense of maintaining glass windows and their frames was often as high as the cost of the original installation.[153] Martin Luther, the religious reformer and affluent resident of a large home in Wittenberg, bemoaned toward the end of his life, "I am in constant despair that after my death my [wife] Käthe or my children won't be able to afford [the home], for even during my lifetime I hardly keep up maintaining its roof, glass windows, and ironworks."[154] Repairs were particularly costly when it came to stained-glass windows, as it was a delicate task to replace broken segments with new ones of exactly the same color.[155] Even a dexterous householder would have been overtaxed with the execution of such repairs. Conventional glass windows were easier to repair. Indeed, in his 1698 treatise *On Building*, in a section titled "Requisites about an house," the English writer Roger North recommended that every gentleman's home have storehouses "alltogether in one ordinance of building, and devided so as severall sorts of materialls should be kept by themselves," including "a storehouse for all lead and glass," presumably for window repairs.[156]

The trouble and expense associated with the upkeep of glass windows were all too familiar to Endres Tucher, the chief public building official (*Stadtbaumeister*) of the city of Nuremberg in the second half of the fifteenth century. As part of his job, Tucher was in charge of maintaining all municipal buildings and churches in Nuremberg. In his *Baumeisterbuch* (Master Builder's Book), a handwritten manual containing instructions and advice for his successors, Tucher bemoaned the task of maintaining the windows, which required "much patching, and in all kinds of ways; the building official has to figure out himself how to manage this" (*des flickens vill und an manchen enden, dorein muß sich ein paumeister selber richten*).[157] Speaking from experience, Tucher advised his successors to hire a local glazier as a contractor to deal with these problems.[158]

Ironically, the building requiring the least attention from Tucher was the most prestigious building in Nuremberg: the imperial castle located on a hilltop and visible from every part of the city. The castle traditionally provided accommodation for the Holy Roman Emperor during his visits to the city. But these imperial visits were relatively rare, and often several years passed without one. This in turn served as an excuse for the city authorities to neglect maintenance work in the castle. Broken glass windows were left unrepaired, and Tucher was sent up for repairs only when an imperial visit was imminent. Tucher reports in his *Baumeisterbuch* that he had his hands full on such occasions, for he had to "repair the glass panes in the castle's rooms and chambers as well as clean and replace panes where necessary."[159]

The Holy Roman Emperors, of course, were not the only itinerant rulers at the time. Even among the lesser nobility, it was quite common to govern one's territories and estates by traveling from one castle to another. Maintaining multiple residences, however, was a costly responsibility. Some aristocrats therefore decided to forgo installing permanent glass windows in their residences. In sixteenth-century Alnwick Castle, the glass windows were uninstalled whenever the Duke of Northumberland and his family went elsewhere.[160] Other aristocrats took their windows along when they traveled. In England this was still a common practice in the sixteenth century. In this period, inventories from England (and from other parts of Europe) typically listed glass windows as chattels rather than permanent fixtures of the house.[161]

Putting one's glass windows in storage or traveling with them helped save money on maintenance, but it also protected the windows from vandalism and theft. In the modern world windows rarely get stolen, but in the premodern period this was not at all uncommon. Such thefts reflect the value of glass and lead, two materials that could be melted down and sold.[162] Glass windows, especially of the polychrome variety, were also prized as works of art, which was yet another reason why householders were eager to protect them: in fact, as an artistic creation in its own right, every stained-glass window was unique. The personalized addition of heraldic imagery made such windows even dearer to the owner.

This helps explain why glass windows were considered movables not only for practical purposes, but also from a legal perspective. In England, it was common until the end of the sixteenth century to record glass windows separately (and individually) in the inventories of the deceased.[163] Legal opinion held that if a householder died, his glass windows could be bequeathed separately from the house.[164] This was the case in Doncaster in 1590, when an alderman of the city bequeathed his house to his wife but left the glass windows to his son.[165] We know of similar cases from late medieval Italy and the early modern German lands.[166]

The idea of windows as chattels could become a problem when tenants felt entitled to remove glass windows that technically belonged to their landlord. In Renaissance Venice, religious confraternities operating social housing units had to deal with this problem: the confraternities repeatedly complained about the relatives of deceased residents who carried away not just furniture, but also windows.[167] Such issues were not limited to lower-class tenants. In fifteenth-century France, cathedral chapters found it necessary to remind canons that the glass windows of their residential spaces belonged to the Church and had to remain in place when a canon left the chapter.[168]

Over time, the legal notion of glass windows as movable property gave way to the idea that they formed an integral, permanent part of the house. This new legal understanding ties in with the increasing tendency in northern Europe during the Little Ice Age to perceive a building's lack of window glass as a grave flaw or even as something to "make sport of" (in Pepys's words). Tellingly, perhaps, in England this new legal view emerged around 1600, at the peak of the Little Ice Age: from that time on, English courts considered glass windows an essential part of the house, not to be removed even in the event of a change in ownership. Lord Coke, the most distinguished English legal theorist of this period, summarized this new approach as follows: "Glass annexed to windows by nails, or in any other manner, by the lessor or by the lessee, could not be removed by the lessee, for without glass it is no perfect house."[169]

Precisely because this approach was novel, it was implemented only gradually in places where judicial enforcement of the law was weak (and glass rare). This was the case in Plymouth Colony in North America (now Massachusetts), a settlement that largely adhered to English law but was detached from the changing legal realities in the motherland. According to surviving deeds from Plymouth Colony, as late as the 1640s homebuyers requested written assurances that the windows were included in the transaction and would not be removed by the seller. Thus, in 1645, the seller of a house in the town of Sandwich assured the buyer that the house would come with all "glass, and glass windows, with the wooden shutters to them belonging."[170]

By that time, many European jurisdictions prohibited homeowners who were selling their homes from removing the windows. But while local law in much of Europe came to restrict the *taking* of windows from houses in such circumstances, a cultural practice of *giving* windows as gifts—outside the context of selling one's home—thrived. Indeed, as we will see in the next chapter, one of the most intriguing aspects of the cultural history of premodern architectural glass was the custom of gifting new windows to relatives, friends, and allies. This custom, now almost entirely forgotten, flourished in Europe for centuries. A close examination will help us cast further light not only on the economic costs of glazing, but also on the symbolic meaning and social prestige associated with it.

7

Glass and Class

Personalization and Prestige

Chapter-opening image: Detail of Fig. 7.4

As we have seen, various factors, ranging from technological progress to climate change, led to the increasing use of glass in early modern domestic architecture, especially in northern Europe.[1] Still, glass windows were a costly investment, not least due to the expense associated with maintenance and repairs. Glass and class were entangled, such that glass windows were a marker of prestige.[2] In early modern Spain, a prosperous house was referred to by the proverbial expression "It is glazed."[3] Throughout Europe, glass windows often were installed first in those parts of the building that were particularly visible to visitors and passersby. Façade windows took precedence over lateral or rear windows, which often continued to feature non-vitreous materials.[4]

This approach did not fail to have the desired effect on neighbors, visitors, and passersby. When, in the 1580s, Michel de Montaigne traveled through Alsace, Lorraine, and Switzerland, he was impressed that there was "no village house so small as not to have glass windows; and the good dwellings are greatly ornamented by being well equipped, both inside and out, with these and with panes of glass worked in many fashions."[5] Later in his journey, Montaigne made similar observations in southern Germany and Tyrol.[6] Not that his native France was a backwater in terms of domestic glazing. It is true that in the warmer, southern parts of France non-vitreous sealants were still quite popular. But further north the situation was different: in late sixteenth-century Paris, an Italian visitor was impressed by the profusion of "windows sealed with beautiful glass panes."[7]

The social prestige associated with glass in northern Europe explains why it was common to adorn glass windows with coats of arms, often rendered in color and placed in the central section of the window. Here again, we have a vivid account from Montaigne, ever the thorough observer of local traditions and customs. During his journey through the Holy Roman Empire, he noted that "the Germans are much in love with coats of arms . . . and all their windows are furnished with them."[8] This custom also thrived elsewhere in northern Europe: in England and France, glass windows with heraldic imagery are attested as early as the thirteenth century.[9] Few windows from this period have survived, but documents related to their purchase show how important the heraldic imagery was to buyers. The fifteenth-century dukes of Burgundy, for instance, repeatedly ordered window glass displaying their coat of arms as well as that of the French king (their nominal overlord).[10] The prince-bishop of Basel made a similar request for coats of arms when he ordered a large quantity of windowpanes in 1440.[11]

Coats of arms were objects of great pride and prestige. Families often went to great lengths to display these insignia in a wide range of material contexts, including clothing, bookbinding, and architecture. The house—a term often used interchangeably with the term "family"—was a particularly appropriate and visible place to present one's familial identity to the public.[12] Heraldic windowpanes were one means to this end (fig. 7.1). They enjoyed particular popularity in northern Europe, where architectural glass windows were, in general, more common than in the south. In southern Europe, residents often had their coats of arms painted on impannate windows. It was much easier, of course, to paint on canvas than on glass; unfortunately, the result was also less durable, which is why virtually none of these painted impannate have come down to us.

Southern European buildings that did feature glass windows often also featured heraldic panes. This was true, for instance, of the Palazzo Vecchio in Florence: when Duke Cosimo de' Medici ordered two glass windows for this (otherwise impannate-fitted) building in 1553, he specified that these should display the coat of arms of the Medici as well as that of Charles V, the Holy Roman Emperor (and Cosimo's nominal overlord).[13] Similarly, consider the case of the Mediterranean island of Malta, where canvas had long served as the predominant sealant in domestic architecture. When a French entrepreneur started a glass business on the island in the 1580s, heraldic panes were among his first products. As a contemporary observer reported, "As soon as this happened, the Grand Master [of the island's Knights Hospitaller] ordered beautiful glass windows with his coat of arms . . . to be made at his own expense and to be inserted into the church."[14]

For people at the time—especially in northern Europe—heraldic glass windows combined utility and beauty: the panes protected against cold and drafts while also showcasing the social status and lineage of the owner. Far from being a purely decorative feature, the color formed an essential part of the panes' prestige, as it evoked the venerable tradition of sacred stained glass. Indeed, heraldic windowpanes were indebted to, and inspired by, this religious tradition—first and foremost on a technical level, as heraldic windows were produced in much the same way that church windows were: the image was composed of colored glass pieces and lead lines. Heraldic imagery proved to be an ideal subject for stained glass, as the limited color range of pot-metal glass overlapped with the "tinctures"

Fig. 7.1. Heraldic pane with the arms of the Eberler Family, Switzerland, ca. 1490. J. Paul Getty Museum, Los Angeles. Rendered with great skill and artistic ambition, this pane depicts a courtly woman next to the arms of the Basel-based Eberler family. The family name contains the German word for "boar" (*Eber*)—hence the boar's head in the arms. The pane was likely created in Basel and has been attributed to the circle of Niklaus Manuel Deutsch, a noted Swiss painter of the period.

(colors) traditionally used in the representation of coats of arms: blue (*azure*), red (*gules*), green (*vert/sinople*), and purple (*purpure*). The fifth tincture was black (*sable*), which was rendered on glass by applying dark vitreous paint.[15]

How exactly the limited range of heraldic colors—and the strict rules for combining them—had come into existence is a question still open to scholarly debate.[16] Whatever the origins, medieval and early modern heraldic experts took this color range for granted and did not question it. In fact, they often construed it as a time-honored tradition and associated it with the colors of the gemstones of the Heavenly Jerusalem. This link to the divine city only reinforced the perceived affinity between heraldry and the tradition of sacred stained glass.[17] Heraldic windows also capitalized on the powerful effect of stained glass as a medium: as we have seen, stained glass creates the illusion that the image is not a mere two-dimensional representation, but rather the very source of light.

It is no coincidence that heraldic windows gained popularity in the High Middle Ages—the same period that saw an unprecedented mastery of the art of stained glass. Their popularity only increased during the late medieval period, as technical innovations made it possible to add more pictorial detail to polychrome glass compositions. In early stained glass, the application of black vitreous paint had been the primary means of fleshing out figurative details and creating effects such as shade or volume. In the course of the fourteenth century, glassmakers acquired another technique: the use of yellow stain. This technique originated in the Near East, where Islamic glassmakers had employed it since the early Middle Ages. Through Moorish Spain, this know-how eventually came to Christian Europe. Yellow stain consists of gamboge gum, water, and, most importantly, silver nitrate (which is why it was also known as "silver stain"). Strictly speaking, the application of yellow stain does not constitute painting on glass; rather, yellow stain modifies the color of the glass itself.[18] On firing in the kiln, colorless glass treated with yellow stain typically takes on a golden or yellowish color—a chromatic effect that makes it possible to render details such as blond hair, haloes, or crowns in a naturalistic fashion (fig. 7.2). When applied to certain varieties of pre-colored glass, yellow stain causes a chromatic change in accordance with the laws of complementary colors: for instance, a piece of blue glass treated with yellow stain turns green. This meant it was possible to create different color effects in a single piece of glass—a bi-chromatism that previously could be achieved only by blowing from two varieties of molten glass at the same time or by joining two differently colored

Fig. 7.2. *The Adoration of the Magi*, Cologne, ca. 1510. The Metropolitan Museum of Art, New York. The anonymous artist who created this panel indulged in the effect of yellow stain. Its main chemical agent, silver nitrate, produces a golden or yellow color on clear glass. As this panel demonstrates, yellow stain allowed glass painters to render haloes, hair, and gold vessels with glowing naturalism. Applied to pre-colored glass, yellow stain causes color changes in accordance with the laws of complementary colors. This, in turn, allowed stained-glass artists to work with larger glass pieces and fewer lead cames.

pieces of glass.[19] Yellow stain was the first of several innovations from this period that reduced the need for lead lines, contributing to a gradual shift away from the mosaic-like appearance of windows.

Another major step came around 1400, when European glassmakers became more adept at painting on vitreous surfaces. The method they used was similar to painting on canvas, in that the colors—in this case, enamel colors—were applied directly to the glass surface. The only difference was that these colors were burnt in to ensure permanence. In the words of a seventeenth-century author, the "colors are melted and burned by fire into the glass, in such a permanent fashion that neither weather nor time can erase it."[20]

Painting with enamel colors on glass was, to be sure, not a medieval innovation: Roman glassmakers had mastered this skill as early as the imperial period, and it continued to flourish in the Byzantine and Islamic Near East.[21] In medieval Christian Europe, by contrast, painting with (exceedingly expensive) enamel colors was a rare skill, and one that was typically reserved for the decoration of small, precious ceramic vessels. Only a limited range of enamel colors was available in the first instance, and the technical expertise that burning them into the glass required presented another challenge. In thirteenth- and fourteenth-century Europe, there was only one significant center of enamel-painted glass production: Venice. The Serenissima owed this technological edge to its close relations with the Islamic world.[22]

The breakthrough for enamel painting came in the first half of the fifteenth century, when glass painters in northern Europe caught up with the Venetians. By experimenting with the chemical properties of colors and pigments, northern Europeans not only mastered the art of painting with enamel on glass, but also expanded the range of available colors and developed means of applying them on large surfaces such as windowpanes.[23]

Painting with enamel colors directly on glass panes had practical advantages over the traditional method of assembling windows from small, pre-colored pieces of glass. Most importantly, the need for lead lines was greatly reduced. Some painted panes, in fact, were made from a single piece of glass. But there were other advantages as well. As we have seen, the glass in medieval stained-glass compositions owed its color to metal oxides added during the melting process. The chemical processes that caused coloration during melting were not fully understood, and thus the exact chromatic outcome remained a "hit-or-miss affair."[24] By contrast, enamel painting made it easier to achieve the desired color effect, which in turn allowed for more naturalistic representations.[25] Enamel painting also had advantages over yellow stain: unlike the latter, enamel does not need to permeate the glass and thus is easier to apply. What is more, yellow stain would change the original color of the glass, whereas enamel painting allowed glass painters to apply a wide range of different colors on a single piece of glass (fig. 7.3).[26]

Flemish and French glass painters, who had been at the forefront of the experiments with enamel colors, gained particular distinction across Europe. Their services and skills were sought as far away as Italy—for instance, for prestige projects such as the colored glass windows commissioned for parts of the Vatican under Pope Julius II (r. 1503–13).[27] As Giorgio Vasari noted in the mid-sixteenth century, "Flemings and the French succeeded better than the other nations, seeing that they, with their cunning researches into pigments and the action on them of fire, have managed to burn in the colours that are put on the glass, so that wind,

Fig. 7.3. Window panel, northern Netherlands, 1629. Victoria and Albert Museum, London. This 25-by-25-inch panel is a fine example of enamel painting on glass. The central oval shows Christ as a child with his parents; the bordures are ornamented with festoons of fruit, cupids, and birds (which the anonymous artist copied from contemporary zoological treatises). The figures, animals, and objects are not assembled from small pieces of pre-colored glass, but rather painted with enamel colors directly onto the glass. Accordingly, the lead lines serve solely as mechanical joints and do not form part of the pictorial composition. The aesthetic of medieval stained glass is superseded by an approach indebted to canvas painting.

air, and rain may do them no injury."[28] Enamel painting was a remarkable technical accomplishment, but it also had important aesthetic repercussions. While medieval stained glass was historically linked to the aesthetics of mosaics, the new, enamel-painted windows—in terms of both execution and visual effect—were more akin to painting on two-dimensional media such as canvas or panel.[29] Indeed, enamel painting made it possible to treat a pane of clear glass in much the same way painters treated the surface on their easel. This allowed glass painters to aspire to a degree of realism and detail that could not have been achieved in stained glass.[30] This paradigm shift in the aesthetic of polychrome window glass led Vasari to conclude: "So refined has the skill in this art become, that in our days glass windows are seen as carried to the same perfection that is arrived at in fine pictures upon panel, with all their harmony of colour and finish of execution."[31]

The downside of enamel colors was that they reduced the admission of light. It was therefore expedient to use clear rather than opaque glass as a base. But this should not be taken as an appreciation for transparency as such. In other words, in the case of enamel painting, transparency was not an end in itself, but rather a means toward an end: maximizing the luminous chromatic effect—or, in Vasari's words, "It is better to have the glasses clear in their own substance, rather than obscure, so that when heavily coloured they may not be left too dim."[32]

Enamel-painted panes soon became the most prized products in the marketplace for window glass.[33] High prices reflected the work-intense production process, which required great skill and experience (including a mastery of different painting techniques and the ability to determine the right firing time, which was critical to achieving the desired chromatic effect). As a result, enamel-painted panes were at least twice as expensive as uncolored ones.[34] Still, high prices do not seem to have curbed the demand. Commissions came, for instance, from churches, where colored glass traditionally played an important role. Yet the Church accounted for only a portion of the overall demand. There were practical reasons for this: enamel-painted panes were executed in such a delicate fashion that the full range of pictorial detail could be appreciated only from close-up, which was impractical in most churches. Monumental stained-glass windows of the old style therefore remained a prominent feature in the House of God.[35]

In domestic settings, painted panes could be appreciated from a much closer distance than would have been possible in a church. This helps explain why private demand for painted windowpanes was strong. This holds particularly true for northern Europe, where such panes saw a veritable boom in the fifteenth and sixteenth centuries. Painted domestic windows came in a wide range of different sizes and shapes: a rectangular, painted pane might form part of a *Kabinettscheibe* (cabinet glass), but there were also "roundels" that typically occupied the round, central section of a larger glass window.[36]

Painting with enamel greatly expanded the range of possible motifs and designs. It became common to copy images from other media, such as canvas and engravings, onto glass panes.[37] As in stained glass, religious images—especially biblical scenes or depictions of patron saints—were common. In addition, secular imagery appeared more frequently, including mythological and allegorical scenes, depictions of professions, animal and floral scenes, and illusionist representations of architecture (fig. 7.4; see fig. 7.3).[38] Consider the case of the much-admired Renaissance Belfiore Castle, which belonged to the Este dukes of Ferrara. All windows at Belfiore were glazed (which distinguished the castle from many other Italian aristocratic residences), and in the fifteenth century the windows in one particular room were fitted with painted panes that featured depictions of falconry

Fig. 7.4. Jan Vermeer, *The Glass of Wine*, ca. 1662. Gemäldegalerie, Berlin. A standing man
serves wine to a seated young woman. A closer look reveals that this quotidian Dutch interior scene has a moralistic dimension: the colored glass panel in the window depicts Temper-
antia (Temperance) as a woman holding reins—an admonition that the young woman seems
to disregard. Glass panels with a moralistic meaning enjoyed great popularity in sixteenth-
and seventeenth-century homes, especially in Protestant countries such as the Netherlands.
Enamel painting (as in the glass panel depicted by Vermeer) expanded the possibilities for
such representations.

as well as people chasing herons and quails.[39] A few decades later, on the occasion of an important dynastic marriage in the 1560s, some of the castle's windows were furnished with new painted glass panes; unfortunately we do not know what they depicted, but given the nuptial occasion they likely included heraldic motifs.[40] Heraldic imagery was, in general, exceedingly popular with buyers of painted glass windows. As we have seen, this boom of heraldic glass did not escape the attention of contemporaries such as Montaigne.

The late medieval and early modern demand for heraldic panes—whether painted or made of stained glass—was two-pronged: some people purchased such panes for their own homes, while others presented them as gifts to friends, relatives, or neighbors. Gifts of this kind were particularly common on festive occasions such as weddings or topping-out ceremonies. In the rather scarce historical literature on this subject, the custom of gifting windows is often associated with the southwest of Germany and Switzerland. A closer look, however, reveals that this custom was common across the German lands and other parts of central Europe. As early as the fourteenth century, the presentation of windowpanes is attested in major northern German cities such as Hamburg, Lüneburg, and Braunschweig, and the practice was just as popular in small towns (fig. 7.5).[41]

The historical origins of this custom are difficult to trace, but it likely had roots in the medieval tradition of aristocratic donations of glass windows to churches. Suffice it to recall the story of the tenth-century count Arnold of Vogaburg, whose donation of glass windows to the church of Tegernsee earned him profuse praise from the abbot. Indeed, without financial and material support from affluent individuals, many great medieval churches would not have been glazed (nor constructed in the first place).[42] This holds true not only for continental Europe, but also for the British Isles, as exemplified by Warwick's Beauchamp Chapel, the stained-glass windows of which were financed in the 1440s from the bequest of Richard Beauchamp, the powerful Earl of Warwick. The executors of the will must have had a rather low opinion of English glassmakers, as they explicitly ordered "to glase all the windows in the New Chapell in Warwick with Glasse beyond the Seas, and no Glasse of England." The order also stipulated that the glass should be "of the finest colours of blew, yellow, red, purpure, sanguine, and violet"—a reminder that colored glass was the non plus ultra at the time.[43]

Financial support for glazing became ever more important as the size and

Fig. 7.5. Glass windows from a burgher's house in the northern German town of Alfhausen (Lower Saxony). The windows were purchased and installed with funds raised by neighbors and friends, who recorded their contribution and the year (1766) in the inscriptions. Such window donations were quite common in northern and central Germany, and their completion always coincided with a feast—which is also why such windows were called *"Fensterbierscheiben"* (beer window panes) in German. The execution of these commemorative panes was usually less elaborate than in Switzerland. Indeed, the Alfhausen windows show only one coat of arms, that of the local minister.

number of church windows increased in the course of the Gothic period (fig. 7.6).[44] The Church also began to accept donations from nonaristocratic individuals or entire professional groups (such as guilds). Only in exceptional cases were donors turned away: according to a thirteenth-century source, the bishop of Paris rejected an offer by the city's prostitutes to gift a window to the cathedral.[45] Such delicate offers aside, most donors were respected members of society. Naturally, they expected their generosity to be acknowledged. As in altarpieces and other genres of religious art, a frequent solution was to reserve one section for a depiction of the donor or his coat of arms. Occasionally, the desire for recognition took on excessive forms, as in the case of Henry de Mamesfeld, the fourteenth-century chancellor of Oxford, who donated the stained glass of Merton College Chapel, ensuring that his likeness appeared no fewer than twenty-four times in the win-

Fig. 7.6. Window from Évreux Cathedral, Normandy, France, begun 1220. The donation of glass windows was a mutually beneficial deal: the church received a valuable contribution to the construction work, while the donor gained prestige and, potentially, god's favor. Medieval and early modern donors were eager to see their generosity recorded. The window reproduced here dates to ca. 1325 and shows the contemporary Canon Raoul de Ferrières presenting the window that he donated to the church.

dows.[46] This, however, was the exception rather than the rule. Most depictions of donors and their coats of arms were relatively modest.[47] Still, it was an enormous source of prestige for the benefactor to be acknowledged and memorialized in a church window—after all, the window not only graced, but also protected, the House of God. The central axes of the church were a particularly visible zone of the interior and thus typically reserved for glass donated by aristocrats or other high-ranking donors. As a rule, the higher up the depiction of the donor (or coat of arms), the more elevated his or her social station. This might seem counterintuitive, as increasing height would make it harder for beholders on the ground to appreciate pictorial detail. However, the medieval perception was different: glass windows—including the multi-scene cycles that extended over an entire window wall—were always meant to be "read" from the bottom up. Even illiterate church-goers knew that the higher up the representation of a saint or donor, the closer she or he was to heaven, and thus to God.[48]

The rise of enamel painting expanded the possibilities for depicting donors in a naturalistic and individualized fashion. This provided additional incentives for donors, both among the nobility and among the urban elites of late medieval Europe.[49] The willingness to pay for the glazing of a church window, of course, did not necessarily imply unconditional support for the Church as an institution. In practice, donations were a pragmatic and mutually beneficial deal: donors received the opportunity to display their piety and status in a prestigious location, while the Church secured important financial support for a particularly costly aspect of construction. Only this mutual benefit explains why, in many medieval cities, cathedrals were glazed with the support of local donors at the very same time that bitter conflicts raged between the clergy and the citizens. Chartres Cathedral is a case in point: most of its prized glass windows were donated by burghers and guilds during the 1210s—a period when the city was riven by violent clashes between the cathedral chapter and the city population.[50]

The desire to memorialize one's name and piety in the House of God was a driving factor behind donations—and precisely for this reason, donors were eager to ensure that this material *memoria* would be preserved for future generations. Such concerns prompted some donors to create special endowments for the maintenance of the windows. Maintenance, in this context, meant more than just preservation in the modern sense of the term. It entailed the duty to attend to the memoria as a living and evolving tradition. Thus, if a family's reputation increased—for instance, through a well-arranged marriage or elevation to the nobility—it was only fitting that the descendants hire a glazier to "update" the genealogical and heraldic imagery.[51]

The taste for personalized glass windows also extended to homes. Given the social prestige associated with architectural glass, householders went to great lengths to inscribe their identities in the windows of their domestic spaces. Reserving the central section of a pane for the depiction of an impresa or coat of arms was one way of doing so, but by no means the only one. Some people chose to write their names or mottoes on the panes—a practice John Donne related in his poem "A Valediction of My Name in the Window" (ca. 1600).[52] In Donne's case,

Fig. 7.7. Glass panel from Preston Hall, Suffolk, England, ca. 1600. Victoria and Albert Museum, London. The window shows moralizing texts from the Latin Bible painted onto quarries and roundels; other windows from this stately home are said to have depicted the coat of arms of the Ryece family, the former owners. Glass windows from this period were often inscribed with a wide range of different texts, including expressions of piety and erudition, personal maxims, and poetic creations. Like their heraldic counterparts, such windows displayed the owner's beliefs and status. A physical assault on the windows was a direct assault on the owner's honor.

the window in question was that of his beloved, but one's own windows likewise could serve as the foil for inscriptions (which were created with special writing devices featuring beveled diamonds).[53] Erasmus of Rotterdam explicitly recommended to "write some brief but pithy sayings such as aphorisms, proverbs, and maxims . . . in the glass of a window so that what may aid learning is constantly before the eye" (fig. 7.7).[54]

Irrespective of how a window was personalized, it is hardly surprising that a physical attack against such a window was considered a grave assault on the house and the honor of its owner. That early modern homeowners perceived this kind of violence as a personal affront is vividly captured in Shakespeare's *Richard II*, where Bolingbroke orders the execution of two men who "from my own windows torn my household coat, / Razed out my imprese, leaving me no sign / Save men's opinions and my living blood / To show the world I am a gentleman."[55]

Violence against windows—especially heraldic ones—was a persistent problem in this period. A case study of everyday life in a small northern German town has unearthed numerous court cases revolving around such conflicts while also highlighting the range of possible offenses: smashing was one option, but heraldic windows were also secretly removed, sometimes with the help of a glazier, and then reinserted upside down—a particular humiliation.[56] Whatever the method, such acts offended the honor of the owner, but they also scorned the house as a social institution.[57] It fits into this image that there were jurists who classified the smashing of windows—along with other provocations such as the posting of slanderous images or texts—as a breach of the domestic peace, the *pax domestica*. Assaults on the domestic peace typically called for increased punishment, and in cases where the dishonoring intention of the deed was evident, jurists had even more reason to classify "the smashing or shattering of windows" (*ausschlagung oder auswerffung der Fenster*) as an offense warranting high justice, alongside crimes such as murder, heresy, and treason.[58]

It was not always personal enemies or random vandals who caused damage to windows. Sometimes the troublemakers came from within the family, as was the case for the sixteenth-century Cologne councilman Hermann Weinsberg, whose meticulous diary provides us with rare insight into the complicated entanglement of windows, honor, and family identity. Let us take a closer look at Weinsberg and the world in which he lived.

As was true elsewhere in the German lands, donating glass windows to churches and other public buildings was a widespread custom in early modern Cologne. When Weinsberg decided in the 1570s to make donations of this kind, he chose his parish church of St. James and its school. Weinsberg was an active member of the congregation, and he even held the office of churchwarden (*Kirchmeister*) for some time. His familiarity with the architectural details of this particular church (now defunct) explains why he donated windowpanes that would blend in well with the building's medieval style. More specifically, Weinsberg stipulated that the panes be "old French" (*altfrens*), a term implying some variety of Gothic style. As to the imagery, he requested that a section of one of the windows depict him and his second wife as patrons. A few years later, Weinsberg donated another glass window, this time to commemorate his grandparents and other relatives. In his words, this window was meant to preserve the "memory" (*gedechtnis*) and "honor" (*eren*) of his family.[59]

These donations were in line with Weinsberg's passion for extolling the distinguished origins and achievements of his family—a passion that also led him to compose his massive *Buch Weinsberg* (The Book Weinsberg), a curious mix of diary and family chronicles.[60] Weinsberg's idealized vision of his family's glorious past formed a stark contrast to the family's state in his own time, when the House of Weinsberg was riven by fierce family quarrels. Tellingly, after Hermann's death in 1597, a legal feud about the correct interpretation of his will kept Cologne's courts of justice busy for years. During Hermann's lifetime, the tensions in the Weinsberg family had come to the fore on the occasion of his second donation to the church of St. James. Shortly after the window's installation, Hermann's brother-in-law, Conrad Eck, vented his anger. Conrad had contributed a small amount to defray the expenses for the window, but when he saw the final product, he was unhappy to find himself depicted in the midst of a family with which he did not get along. As Weinsberg recounted in his memoirs:

> Conrad complained vehemently to the pastor, the churchwarden, and the sacristan about the fact that he had been depicted in the image, and next to his wife at that; he could not suffer that he and his coat of arms were depicted. Thus, my sister Sibille had half of the window removed before he would manage to smash it, and we sent the glass painter to him to inquire whether he [Conrad] was serious about it, and with a flurry of useless words he answered in the affirmative; hence, his portrait and coat of arms were removed and only [the portrait and arms of] my sister were reinstalled.

Weinsberg ended his account of this imbroglio with the sarcastic but forgiving conclusion: "Fools are also people."[61]

This frustrating episode did not prevent Hermann from continuing to donate windows, but from that point on these were mostly gifts to private individuals—gifts with which his brother-in-law could not meddle. In 1582, for instance, Hermann presented his brother, who had moved to Worms, with heraldic panes meant to foster "friendship and memory" (*fruntschaft und gedechtnis*). In his capacity as a member of the Cologne city council, Weinsberg must have also been involved in the decision to gift windows with Cologne's coat of arms to Antwerp Cathedral. Cologne's gift fits into a general pattern at the time: it was common for cities to gift heraldic panes, and indeed, Antwerp Cathedral had already received panes from a number of other cities and rulers. For Cologne, it was not only a matter of prestige, but also a politically wise move to join the list of benefactors: the city's leaders hoped that donating a window would ensure "that the city [of Cologne] will be held in honor" in Antwerp, one of the most important commercial centers in early modern Europe.[62]

The phenomenon of political entities—both cities and principalities—presenting each other with heraldic panes was particularly salient in the Holy Roman Empire, with its highly fragmentized political structure. The gradual hollowing out of central imperial power had created a tightly knit web of interdependencies and alliances between the multitude of duchies, counties, cities, and ecclesiastical territories that formed the empire. Even the Emperor himself gifted windows. The majority of such donations, however, were transacted among principalities and cities—typically, with the goal of demonstrating solidarity, power, and wealth.[63] Such donations were particularly common in Switzerland, which was not only a (nominal) part of the Holy Roman Empire until the mid-seventeenth century, but also in itself a complex confederation made up of more than a dozen cantons (*Orte*). In fact, in no other part of Europe was the custom of window donations as popular as it was in late medieval and early modern Switzerland (fig. 7.8). But why was this?

In Switzerland (as elsewhere in Europe), the custom of window gifting seems to have developed from the tradition of donating glass windows to churches.[64] When the domestic demand for glass increased in the late Middle Ages, window donations were adapted to a secular context. Given the considerable cost of glass, donations of this sort offered welcome financial relief for householders. Still, an economic explanation alone cannot explain the boom of heraldic stained-glass windows in late medieval Switzerland. Uniquely Swiss factors came into play, some of which were political. In the second half of the fifteenth century, the Swiss Confederation had emerged victorious from its wars with the Duchy of Burgundy

Fig. 7.8. Glass window emblazoned with the heraldic symbols of Zurich. The magistrate of Zurich gifted this window to the monastery of Muri (Aargau, Switzerland), where it was installed in the cloister. Such window donations were very common in early modern Europe. They enjoyed particular popularity in Switzerland, where the confederate political system encouraged displays of inter-cantonal solidarity as well as strategic diplomatic gifts. Produced in large quantities, the panes typically were individualized with an imprint indicating the year of the donation (in this case, 1557).

(1470s) and from the Swabian War (1499). What is more, Swiss mercenaries—acclaimed for their military abilities—were sought after in Europe and handsomely paid by major political players of the day. Back in Switzerland, this military reputation and strength bolstered a sense of pride and community while also underscoring the confederation's de facto political autonomy. It is no coincidence that the early 1500s saw a brisk domestic output of chronicles and paintings celebrating the Swiss Confederation as well as the bravery of its soldiers. Window glass featuring Helvetic or heraldic imagery fit in this context.

Not all contemporaries approved of this new fashion. The Bern-based chronicler Valerius Anshelm, writing around 1530, bemoaned it as excessive and decadent:

> Not long ago, it was still common in Bern to use thin canvas [*flom*] and cloth, rather than glass. Then came windows with bull's-eyes and panes. . . . Now, however, ill-reputed soldiers have brought foreign arts and luxuries . . . to the Swiss Confederation. Nobody wants to be seen behind small canvas-windows or bull's-eyes anymore. Instead, everyone wants to be seen behind large panes and painted windows, especially in churches, city halls, inns, taverns, baths, and barber shops.[65]

However, critics such as Anshelm were in the minority. Painting on glass windows, and the donation of such windows, flourished in Switzerland—so much so that by the second half of the sixteenth century, the expression "painted windows and glass painters in Switzerland" had become an idiom for abundance.[66] Indeed, leading artists in Switzerland were involved in the design of such panes, including no less than the preeminent, Basel-based Hans Holbein.[67]

Heraldic panes (or *Wappenscheiben*, in German) could be purchased for one's own home, but more commonly one received them as a gift—either from a private individual or from one of the confederation's cantons. Additionally, public or economic institutions such as guilds or marksmen associations sometimes acted as donors. Whoever the donor, such gifts were originally limited to newly built houses. As with church-window donations, this was a mutually beneficial deal: the donee saved money on glazing, while the donor, whose coat of arms figured prominently on the panes, earned prestige by displaying largesse as well as Helvetic solidarity. As historian Valentin Groebner has succinctly noted, heraldic panes served as "political neon signs" in the late medieval and early modern Swiss Confederation.[68]

In practice, a home often received glass windows from several donors, with the result that the cost of glazing was almost completely defrayed. In contrast to the northern parts of the Holy Roman Empire, where window donations were often subject to sumptuary laws and thus capped at a certain level, the Swiss Confederation initially set few limitations on the generosity and taste of private donors.[69] However, stricter rules applied to donations by political bodies, such as city governments or cantons. Magistrates could gift windows either within their own territory or to another city or canton, but—in theory, at least—these gifts were meant to be restricted to public buildings, such as churches, city and guild halls, schools, hospitals, and shooting houses (*Schützenhäuser*); in other words, to buildings that were considered a source of pride and prestige for the entire Swiss Confederation. A new public building of this kind could even receive a set of windows featuring the coats of arms of all cantons—a gift that required approval by the *Tagsatzung*, the Federal Diet of Switzerland.

Taverns and inns, too, were eligible for donations from the Tagsatzung. Even though these establishments were often owned by private individuals, they qualified because they were important sites of public life: taverns and inns served not only as venues for local assemblies, but also as meeting points for town guards during emergencies or other threats. Furthermore, inns were where emissaries and delegates from other cantons stayed on their way to meetings of the Tagsatzung. Given these political functions, it was only natural that the best inn in town would receive a complete set of heraldic panes from the Tagsatzung—a sign of distinction that often evoked the envy of other local inns, and led other inns to vie for similar donations, even if they did not come directly from the Tagsatzung, but rather from individual cantons or private donors. Inns and taverns became, as it were, showcases of Swiss political identity. Sometimes the gifted windows survived in situ well into the eighteenth century—by which time the custom of window donations had long since petered out. As late as 1797, during a journey through Switzerland, Goethe saw "beautiful, painted panes" in a Swiss inn.[70]

By convention, a canton seeking a donation for a new public building had to submit an official application, either by approaching other cantons or by turning to the entire Tagsatzung. Private individuals were not supposed to make similar requests to political bodies. Over time, however, it became increasingly common for ordinary people to take the initiative and approach their cantonal government.

Governments, in turn, realized that such gifts were useful political capital, particularly in cantons (such as Zurich) whose rule extended well beyond the boundaries of the city: by making such donations, the government asserted, in a highly visible fashion, its power over the entire canton, including the rural hinterland. Needless to say, the gift implied the expectation that donees would reciprocate by showing political or military support if needed.

The use of heraldic panes as political capital explains why some cantons kept copious reserves of such panes. Heraldic panes were produced in large quantities and according to specific instructions from the cantonal government. This, of course, was a lucrative business for local glassmakers and glass painters. With the benefit of steady demand, Swiss glass painters developed great skill and enjoyed a distinct reputation far beyond the confederation's borders.[71]

Despite the considerable degree of standardization, the panes required final touches before they could be presented to the donee.[72] At the very least, the year of the donation was added. Only then were the panes sent to the donee, who, in turn, was responsible for hiring a local glazier to install them. Heraldic panes could take a range of different shapes—but whatever their form, the installation was always an expense in its own right. To ensure that the gift would not become a financial burden for the donee, the panes were often accompanied by *Fenstergeld* (window money), a lump sum to be used toward installation. The amount of Fenstergeld was strictly fixed by governments to avoid the impression that some recipients were treated better than others.

There were, of course, affluent householders who could afford window glass and the expense of its installation without having to request government support. The fact that such householders nevertheless applied for donations reflects the honor and prestige associated with this kind of gift. As one supplication to the Zurich government put it, the request was made "for the honor, not out of poverty" (*von Ehren, nicht von Armuth wegen*).[73] Tellingly, suppliants who emphasized the honorific aspect of the gift sometimes chose to forgo the Fenstergeld. In these circles, the donation often resulted in more cost than it defrayed, as the installation typically was followed by an expensive celebration, the so-called *Fensterschmaus* (window feast). The Fensterschmaus served to celebrate the completion of construction and to acknowledge the honor that the donation bestowed upon the house. By convention, all donees, whether poor or rich, held a Fensterschmaus:

the major difference was that this ritual, which started as a small and modest celebration, was gradually turned into a lavish banquet by upper-class donees.

Such extravagant cases aside, most householders did rely on the donation and probably would not have glazed their homes without it. Ordinary homebuilders often solicited gifts from more than a dozen donors, thereby distributing the costs of glazing on many shoulders. Whatever the excesses of the donation system, its architectural effects were hard to overlook: the glazing of domestic buildings was far advanced in early modern Switzerland, including in the homes of ordinary people. This prominence of (painted) glass in Swiss homes, which caught the attention of travelers such as Montaigne, would not have been possible without the complex business of window donations.

As the cantons gave in to more and more requests from private individuals, the number of supplications increased. Eventually, some cantons bemoaned the "begging for windows" (*fensterbetteln*). The Tagsatzung, for its part, passed a resolution in 1517 to reinstate former restrictions on donations, declaring that the "begging for windows shall be terminated once and for all, with the exception of churches, council buildings, and shooting and meeting houses."[74] But implementing these rules proved difficult. The same dilemma can be observed on the level of the individual cantons, which relied on window donations to pursue concrete political goals. Zurich, for instance, prohibited cantonal gifts to private individuals as early as 1487, but—as we have seen—in reality this prohibition was watered down. Similar restrictions were, in theory, in effect in the city-canton of Schaffhausen, but there, too, exceptions were common: in fact, in the period between 1550 and 1630, about 50 percent of all window donations by the Schaffhausen government went to private individuals who were building or renovating their homes. Facing an ever-growing number of solicitations, the government announced in 1593 that henceforth it would approve requests only if a renovation would make a visible contribution to the beautification of the house and if the cost for the renovation would exceed one hundred gulden. This policy clearly reflected budgetary concerns on the part of the government, but it also grew out of the realization that the proliferation of heraldic panes threatened to decrease their honorific value.

The inflation of Wappenscheiben is often considered a key reason for the gradual decline of window donations. Indeed, this decline became apparent in the mid-seventeenth century—yet it cannot be attributed to one factor alone. To understand the erosion of the Swiss donation system, we need to take a holistic perspective and embed the Swiss case into a larger European context—that is, we have to turn our attention to the question of why, across Europe, colored glass in general began to lose its prestige, and why it was increasingly supplanted by blank, transparent glass.

8

From Sacred Material to Secular Commodity

The Reformation of Glass

When did transparency become an aesthetic and architectural ideal in Europe? Some scholars have pointed to the Renaissance, citing, among other things, the mid-fifteenth-century Venetian breakthrough in the production of crystal-clear glass. (We will examine this argument more closely in the next chapter.) Other scholars have traced the origins of transparency as an ideal to an even earlier phase of the Renaissance—namely, the discovery of linear perspective in Western art during the first half of the fifteenth century.[1] But how exactly are perspective and transparency connected?

In the early 1400s, Italian Renaissance artists, spearheaded by Filippo Brunelleschi in Florence, developed a systematic understanding of the laws of linear perspective. In treatises on art theory from this period, the experience of perspective and transparency often seem to be linked. Consider Albrecht Dürer, who was familiar with the Italian literature on linear perspective and offered the following definition: "Perspectiva is a Latin word which means seeing through something" (*Perspectiva ist ein lateinisch Wort, bedeut ein Durchsehung*).[2] This etymologically correct definition harked back to a famous passage in Leon Battista Alberti's treatise *On Painting* (composed in the 1430s and known in Italian as *Della pittura*). There, Alberti likened perspective to a view through a window, writing: "I will say what I myself do when I paint. First I trace as large a quadrangle as I wish, with right angles, on the surface to be painted; in this place, it [the rectangular quadrangle] certainly functions for me as an open window through which the *historia* is observed."[3] There has been a long tradition—among both artists and scholars—of understanding Alberti's definition as if it referred to the view through a real window that is transparent in the modern sense of the word.[4] Most recently, Gérard Wajcman has claimed that Alberti propagated, in a novel way, the view through the window as the foundation of painting, and that this implied nothing less than a "revolution of the gaze" (*révolution du regard*).[5] Wajcman went so far as to argue that there was a "simultaneity between the birth of the modern self" and the "subjectivity of the window onto the street."[6] In a similar fashion, Lutz Koepnick has characterized the Renaissance as a breakthrough moment for transparency, positing, "Post-Renaissance discourse and aesthetic practice championed the window's transparency as a means of offering realist impressions and seemingly detached visions."[7]

But these arguments are hardly tenable if one takes a closer look at the intellectual and material context in which Alberti's and Dürer's discussions of perspective belong. True, in a literal sense the term "perspective" does mean "seeing through," but in the fifteenth and sixteenth centuries the expression "seeing through" was not so much associated with glass windows as it was with Euclidean optics—more specifically, with the idea of a hypothetical plane on which rays emanating from a three-dimensional object cast a two-dimensional image. Indeed, Alberti posited a visual pyramid (with the apex in the eye), and his "window" served as a placeholder for the idea of a cross section through the pyramid.[8]

As we have seen, glass windows—especially transparent ones—were a rare feature of domestic architecture in Renaissance Italy. There is no evidence of a sudden, large-scale introduction of window glass, let alone that any such development informed architects and artists such as Brunelleschi and Alberti in their exploration of perspective. In his influential architectural treatise *On the Art of Building*, Alberti discussed glass windows primarily in the context of church architecture, dedicating little attention to the question of glass in private homes.[9] Indeed, Alberti lived in a part of Europe where the majority of windows featured impannate or other nontransparent sealants. To enjoy the view through such a window, one had to open it. Is this perhaps the reason why Alberti's treatise on perspective explicitly referred to an "open window" (*finestra aperta*)?

It is true that, elsewhere in the same treatise, Alberti likened the painted surface to one made "completely of glass or transparent."[10] But as Joseph Masheck has pointed out, here again Alberti envisioned "a translucent slice through the perspectival pyramid."[11] Indeed, in his practical instructions for using the "open window" method, Alberti did not prescribe the use of glass. Instead, the device he proposed for the study and application of linear perspective was a "veil" (*velum*)—in other words, a device that effectively resembled a thin impannata screen. He wrote: "It is of this kind: a veil woven of very thin threads and loosely intertwined, dyed by any color, subdivided with thicker threads according to parallel partitions, in as many squares as you like, and held stretched by a frame; which [veil] I place, indeed, between the object to be represented and the eye, so that the visual pyramid penetrates through the thinness of the veil."[12] The square grid on the veil enabled the painter to capture a three-dimensional object or scene in line with the rules of perspective.[13] A few decades later, Leonardo da Vinci described a similar device, noting that the fabric could be replaced by glass: "There are some [people] who look at these things produced by nature through sheets of glass."[14] Perhaps the best-known account of how to render three-dimensional objects in

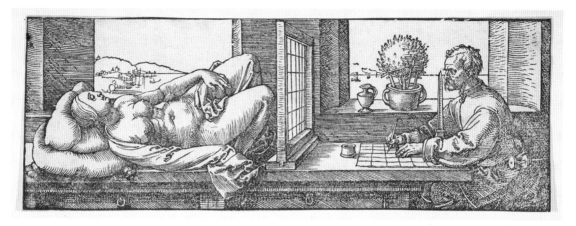

Fig. 8.1. A draftsman making a perspective drawing of a reclining woman in Albrecht Dürer's treatise on perspective, *Underweysung der messung* (Treatise on Measurement, first published 1525). Dürer's contemporary Leonardo da Vinci described how "to look at these things produced by nature through sheets of glass, or other transparent material such as veils." In this image, Dürer provided an illustration of this method. In their day-to-day work, however, accomplished artists such as Dürer and Leonardo scarcely drew on such tools. Dürer, for his part, noted that these devices were "especially for those [painters] who are not sure of themselves."

two-dimensional media can be found in Dürer's treatise on painting and perspective, *Underweysung der messung* (Treatise on Measurement), first published in 1525 (fig. 8.1). Dürer advised aspiring artists to "place a clean flat pane of glass into a quadrangular frame" (*reyn flache glas*) in order to "trace an object."[15] Step by step, the student would then "draw with a brush whatever you wish to paint on the pane of glass."[16] But for Dürer, too, glass was neither indispensable nor even the preferred choice. "There is," he noted, "yet another method of copying an object and of rendering it larger or smaller according to one's wish, and it is more practical than using a glass pane because it is less restricted." This method—reminiscent of Alberti's veil—involved using "a frame with a grid of strong black thread."[17]

It is far from clear how common such auxiliary devices really were, let alone whether they played any significant role in the day-to-day work of professional painters. They are rarely mentioned in sources about the creative process and seem to have been primarily objects of didactic discussion.[18] Dürer noted that his method was suitable "especially for those [painters] who are not sure of themselves."[19] And Leonardo harshly criticized those who used such tools without obtaining a more general understanding of the art of painting, noting, "This invention is to be condemned in those who do not know how to paint without it, nor how to reason about nature with their minds."[20]

What, then, are we to make of the references to windows in the fifteenth- and sixteenth-century discourse about linear perspective? It seems that these references were largely theoretical, and that the window served as a visual and didactic analogy for a rectangular frame, implying "the relation of a fixed viewer to a framed view" according to the rules of single-point perspective.[21] Anne Friedberg has argued that even "Alberti used the window predominantly as a metaphor for the frame."[22] There is no reason to assume that the experience of transparent window glass, rare as it was in Italy at the time, informed Alberti or other Italian theoreticians of perspective. What is more, Alberti employed the view from the window as an analogy, but he did not encourage it in everyday life: for Alberti, looking out of a *real* window—glazed or not—was a social practice acceptable only under certain circumstances. He repeatedly criticized the act of gazing out of windows—especially when it involved women—as a problematic pastime that led to inappropriate contacts across gender and class lines.[23] According to Alberti, open windows in everyday life also encouraged thieves and neighbors to "watch and find out what is being said or done inside," which is why he expressed understanding for the Egyptians, "who built their private houses with no windows looking out."[24] The view through a window onto a bustling, noisy street—the daily reality for most urban residents at the time—was hardly what Alberti envisioned when he used the window as an analogy for a carefully painted, dignified "history" (*historia*).[25]

In short, there is little evidence for a causal relation between the use of glass in domestic architecture and the discovery of linear perspective. True, the skills of glassmakers greatly improved in the course of the fifteenth century—and as we will see in Chapter 9, some glassmakers began to produce transparent glass of unprecedented quality in Alberti's own lifetime.[26] But this kind of crystal-clear glass was typically used to produce vessels rather than panes. Where glass was used in architecture, the traditional aesthetic hierarchy that privileged colored over uncolored glass was still firmly in place in fifteenth-century Europe. For householders who desired vitreous windows, stained glass was the most prestigious option.

The picture that emerges might seem paradoxical: Alberti's notion of the painting as a window became an important trope in art theory, but in architectural practice it was the other way around, as glass windows were, and continued to be, treated as paintings. It was only in the sixteenth century that the popularity of painted glass windows began to wane—a trend that continued in the seventeenth century. Neither technological nor economic factors alone can sufficiently explain this development. Instead, we must take into account fundamental changes on a religious and cultural level.

The Reformation was, without a doubt, a key factor. The rise of Protestantism led to bitter confessional conflicts in sixteenth- and seventeenth-century Europe, affecting almost every aspect of daily life. Here again, the Swiss case provides an instructive example, not only of how Reformation ideas spread, but also of the impact that these ideas had on attitudes toward architecture and fenestration. What was the larger background?

Within a few years of the start of the Reformation in central Germany in 1517, some Swiss cantons became strongholds of Protestantism. The theology they embraced was inspired by, but not identical with, Martin Luther's call for reform. In fact, radical reformers such as Huldrych Zwingli in Zurich and John Calvin in Geneva forged new currents of Protestant theology. By the mid-sixteenth century, the Swiss Confederation was deeply divided in confessional terms: in some cantons, Catholicism held the upper hand; in others, the authorities adopted Protestantism in its Zwinglian or Calvinist variety. This process by which political territories developed different—and rivaling—confessional identities played out across all of northern Europe in the sixteenth century and is now commonly referred to as "confessionalization." In the Swiss case, confessionalization not only transformed a previously uni-confessional confederation into a patchwork of Catholic and Protestant cantons, but also pitted them against each other.

Under these new circumstances, heraldic windowpanes that had been presented by cantons from the opposite confessional camp became contested objects. What is more, they sometimes turned into targets of violence. For the donating canton, the smashing of its heraldic windows constituted a political provocation of the highest order. In 1527, the Protestant magistrate of Zurich bitterly complained about the Catholic cantons and the "infamy and humiliation" that they had "inflicted on the coats of arms and windows given [to them] by [Zurich]," through "smashing and other things."[27] The Catholic cantons, in turn, decried the large-scale smashing of their Wappenscheiben in Protestant Bern.

Both Protestants and Catholics drew the same conclusion from such incidents: they began to consider carefully whether it was opportune to gift heraldic panes to cantons in the opposite confessional camp. In seventeenth-century Zurich, the Small Council, the city's executive body, reviewed requests and had the authority to deny window donations to a Catholic canton. At the same time, cantons expanded donations to their own, confessionally loyal population, and this partly explains why, at least in terms of volume, the heyday of window donations came in the sixteenth century.[28]

In the short term, then, the confessional tensions did not contribute to the decline of glass painting and window donations. In the long run, however, they certainly did—for the Reformation undermined the centuries-old aesthetic hierarchy on which both the artistic genre and the donation system rested: the hierarchy that placed colored glass above blank glass. The traditional superiority of polychrome glass had stemmed from its prominence in sacred space, which endowed it with prestige and aura. It was precisely this traditionally privileged status of polychrome glass that was radically questioned—and ultimately rejected—by radical Protestants across Europe. This holds particularly true for those followers of Calvin and Zwingli who took a literal interpretation of the biblical prohibition on images (Exodus 20:4) and opposed any visual representations associated with the Catholic cult of saints. In practice, this rejection often took violent forms, with Catholic church windows being key targets. The scale of the iconoclast destruction far outweighed the damage done by the occasional smashing of heraldic panes in government or private buildings. In fact, in some parts of Europe, the result was the systematic destruction of religious stained-glass windows in formerly Catholic churches. A vivid (though by no means unique) account of this iconoclasm comes from the southern German city of Biberach, where radical Protestants—with the support of the city magistrate—took action in 1531: "They came with several councilmen and their servants . . . and carried away paintings, large and small relics, vessels, monstrances, altar cloths, and whatever else they found; they smashed the windows that featured painted images of saints."[29] We find the same pattern elsewhere in Europe: along with religious artworks and liturgical objects, thousands of stained-glass windows fell victim to the havoc wreaked by radical Protestant iconoclasts, especially in the confessionally divided German lands and Low Countries.[30] In England under Edward VI (r. 1547–53), Puritan zealots even obtained a royal injunction that authorized them to "destroy all shrines . . . pictures, paintings and all other monuments of feigned miracles . . . so that there remain no memory of the same in walls, glass-windows, or elsewhere within their churches or houses" (fig. 8.2).[31]

Fig. 8.2. Glass and lead cames. Museum of London. This crumpled tangle of glass and lead cames is all that survives of the windows of Merton Priory, London. The priory was vandalized and dismantled in 1538 as part of the Dissolution of the Monasteries ordered by Henry VIII. The fragments shown here were found in a drainage ditch during excavations in the 1980s.

Protestant theologians of a more moderate variety, such as Luther's ally Philipp Melanchthon, criticized these large-scale acts of destruction, reminding iconoclasts that many artworks, including stained-glass windows, had never served as objects of religious veneration.[32] In line with such admonitions, Lutheran Protestants usually abstained from iconoclast actions. This explains why Michel de Montaigne, on his journey through southern Germany in the 1580s, saw figurative stained-glass windows in a number of Lutheran churches, such as in the city of Kempten (Bavaria). Montaigne recalled a conversation with a local Lutheran minister, writing, "Asked why they had Jesus Christ and many images painted on the windows and on the new organ, he replied that they did not prohibit images intended to instruct people, provided people did not worship them" (fig. 8.3).[33]

Radical Protestants, however, paid little heed to such arguments. As the seventeenth-century English Protestant Thomas Fuller put it, stained-glass windows "were in time of Popery the Library of Laymen," and for radical Protestants the continued presence of such "popish" elements in the church was unacceptable.[34] When Jasper Gryffyth—a contemporary and ardent Protestant cleric from

Fig. 8.3. Stained-glass panel depicting the Deposition, 1629. Victoria and Albert Museum, London. The panel was created for Hampton Court Chapel in Herefordshire, England. The German artist Abraham van Linge based the depiction on a painting by Rogier van der Weyden. Both the subject and the medium were a provocation for English Protestants, who considered such depictions "popish." Indeed, in sixteenth-century England, Protestant zealots had destroyed large quantities of ecclesiastical glass. In the first half of the seventeenth century, the Stuart kings promoted a revival of sacred art, including stained glass. To forestall objections from dogmatic Protestants, the panel bears the inscription: "The truth hereof is historicall devine and not superstissious." This line underscored that the image was solely a depiction of a biblical episode and not meant to be venerated. On the Continent, Lutherans would have found such representations acceptable. But English Protestants, especially Puritans, took a more radical position: when they toppled the Stuarts in the 1640s, they also launched a devastating campaign against ecclesiastical glass. It is by sheer chance that this panel survived.

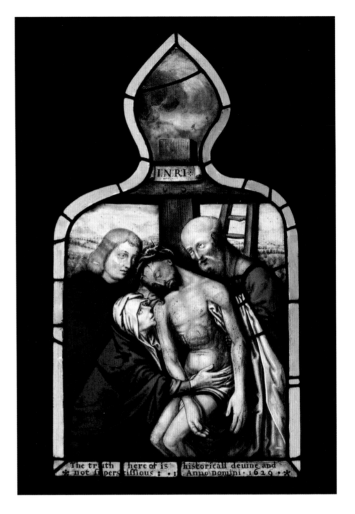

Wales—transcribed medieval poetry that analogized window glass to Mary's virginal conception, he angrily noted in the margins: "The vain opinion of the Papists" and "a fable."[35]

Where radical Protestants refrained from destroying stained-glass windows, this was usually out of practical considerations: many Catholic churches were turned into Protestant houses of worship, and even radical iconoclasts knew that a church with broken windows was exposed to both rain and cold air. After all, replacing stained glass with blank glass required a considerable amount of time and money. For this reason, Protestant iconoclasts sometimes contented themselves with removing only those parts of Catholic stained-glass windows that they found particularly offensive, such as the heads of saints or the Lamb of God (fig. 8.4).[36] With a mixture of frustration and sarcasm, a sixteenth-century English Protestant asked: "Whiche ben the most profytable sayntes in the chyrche?—They that stonde in the glasse windowes, for they kepe out the wynds fro wastynge of the Lyghte."[37]

Still, the devastation was particularly wide-ranging in England, where—according to modern estimates—only 10 percent of medieval stained glass has survived.[38] The extent of this destruction was the result of several waves of iconoclasm, first during the Reformation in the sixteenth century and then, a century later, during the (religiously motivated) civil war of the mid-seventeenth century. Even during the intervening period—that is, during the Stuart reign, with its pro-Catholic leanings—some radical English Protestants did not hide their contempt for stained glass. For example, in 1632, Henry Sherfield, a Puritan politician and government official in Salisbury, considered it his religious duty to smash a parish-church window that showed "little old men in blue and red coats, and naked in hands and feet, for the picture of God the Father," which he deemed blasphemous.[39] Sherfield was fined by the Anglican Church; he did not live to see how his disdain for figural stained glass would become an official government policy just a few years later. Indeed, the Puritan rise to power in the 1640s brought the

Fig. 8.4. Fifteenth-century stained-glass windows depicting four apostles, Church of St. Mary, Great Massingham, Norfolk, England. Sixteenth-century Puritan iconoclasts destroyed the heads and replaced them with blank glass. Pragmatic considerations seem to have prevented further damage.

government-ordered smashing of countless stained-glass windows that had survived the violent excesses of Reformation-era iconoclasts. The Puritan William
Dowsing, who served as the parliamentary commissioner for the destruction of
"monuments of idolatry and superstition," tersely recorded these systematic acts
of destruction in his diary. A typical entry reads: "We brake down 10 mighty great
angels in glass, in all, 80."[40] No less thorough was Richard Culmer, a radical Puritan who oversaw the destruction of stained glass in Canterbury Cathedral. He
took it upon himself to climb up "the top of a citie ladder, near sixty steps high,"
to smash a window depicting the sainted archbishop Thomas Becket. Culmer recorded his delight in "rattling down proud Becket's glassy bones" and considered
it a privilege to destroy these "fruits and occasions of idolatry."[41]

The panes that replaced the smashed stained glass were usually blank, without any ornamental or figural imagery (fig. 8.5). This purist appearance made for
a stark contrast to traditional Catholic sacred space. True, Catholic churches had
seen experiments with blank glass, even before the Reformation. As mentioned
in an earlier chapter, grisaille panes, associated as they were with monastic ideas
about simplicity and modesty, were used in a considerable number of high and
late medieval churches. During the Renaissance, some architects seeking to emulate antiquity experimented with blank glass in churches because they considered
it—unlike stained glass—to be more in line with ancient Roman architecture.[42]
Patrons occasionally encouraged these choices—as did Pope Pius II, a passionate humanist and admirer of ancient architecture. In the 1460s, Pius ordered that
his birthplace, the small town of Corsignano in central Italy, be transformed into
an ideal city inspired by ancient architecture and urban design. The remodeled
town—which the pope self-confidently named "Pienza," after himself—boasted,
among other things, a new cathedral. This sanctuary, a curious blend of Gothic
and Renaissance architecture, featured blank instead of stained glass. In Pius's
own words: "Every chapel has a high and broad window cunningly wrought with
little columns and stone flowers and filled with the glass called crystal. At the ends
of the naves were four similar windows, which when the sun shines admit so much
light that worshippers think they are not in a house of stone but of glass."[43]

Such experiments with the use of blank panes were the exception rather than
the rule in Catholic sacred architecture of this period.[44] And they were certainly
not meant to convey the same theological message that the Protestant removal of
polychrome glass conveyed. The transition from colored glass to blank glass in

Fig. 8.5. Lady Chapel, Ely Cathedral, England, 1321–49. This chapel was the largest attached to any English cathedral. Originally, thanks to its splendid stained-glass windows and polychrome sculptures, the interior of the chapel glowed with color. In the sixteenth and seventeenth centuries, Puritans thoroughly "whitewashed" the chapel and destroyed the stained-glass windows. To the modern visitor, the chapel in its current state may appear solemn; to a late medieval worshipper, it would have looked shockingly bare.

radical Protestant areas was unprecedented in both scale and rigor: never before in the history of Christian Europe were such large quantities of blank glass installed in religious spaces, and never before was the choice between colored and uncolored glass as controversial. For almost one millennium, colored glass had been the norm and ideal in European sacred architecture. In the sixteenth century, this traditional hierarchy was, for the first time, radically questioned—and in the long run, as we will see, this also had massive consequences for domestic architecture.[45]

Aside from fears about image veneration, there were also other, more practical considerations behind the installation of blank glass in Protestant churches. This included the need for more light—a need felt by all Protestant groups, irrespective of their stance on religious imagery. Good interior lighting was critical for Protestant church services, as the liturgy revolved around texts: in line with the idea of *sola scriptura* ("by Scripture alone"), a key idea in Protestant theology, the reading and expounding of the Bible, played a far greater role in Protestant services than it did in Catholic liturgy. Exegesis and sermon formed crucial parts of the minister's duty, but congregants, too, were encouraged to engage in a variety of text-centered activities, such as reading the Bible, praying from a prayer book, or singing psalms or hymns. These reading-based activities required more interior light than Catholic church architecture typically provided. The need for more light was even more pressing because Protestants did away with traditional sources of interior lighting, such as the myriad candles lit in front of Catholic shrines and altarpieces, which Protestants decried as part of the cult of saints and relics. Private chapels—another site of generous candle-lighting in Catholic churches—were likewise drastically reduced.

The copious use of candles and torches during the Eucharist, in particular, was anathema to Protestants, as they rejected this element of Catholic liturgy as a hollow spectacle. Luther approved of candlelight only during the reading of the gospel; during other parts of the service, one or two candles at most were allowed on the altar. Even the Anglican Church under Henry VIII, which retained more Catholic features than any other branch of Protestantism, adopted this stance. Thomas Cromwell—the king's vicar general in charge of establishing the Anglican Church—issued an order to the English populace in the 1530s to ensure that "ye shall . . . suffer from henceforth no candles, tapers, or images of wax to be set afore any image or picture, but only the light that commonly goeth across the Church, by the rood-loft, the light before the Sacrament of the Church, and the light above the Sepulchre."[46]

As the Reformation gave rise to more radical groups, both on the Continent and in England, the opposition to the use of candles in the church grew even stronger. Calvinists and Puritans, in particular, flatly rejected candles as an arch-feature of "Popish" ceremony.[47] The Protestant minister Hugh Latimer, a popular preacher at the court of Edward VI, summarized this tough stance in a 1548 sermon as follows: "Where the devil is resident, there away with books, and up with candles."[48] Latimer's words found sympathetic ears: the pious Edward VI was committed to reforming the Anglican Church in the spirit of "pure" Protestantism, which included not only the destruction of stained glass, but also a total ban on candles. Thus, in 1549, a royal decree prohibited "setting any light upon the Lord's board [the altar] at any time"—and in the same spirit, it was reiterated "that no nave [may] maintain . . . images, relics, lights [or] candles."[49] Admittedly, not every parish implemented these royal orders with the same rigor, and exceptions to the rule continued to exist after Edward's reign.[50] But most churches complied.

From both a theological and practical point of view, the removal of candles from churches marked a major break with the Catholic tradition of interior lighting. As Eamon Duffy has noted, the ban on candles "dramatically changed the appearance of many churches."[51] The absence of candles made it all the more necessary to find other sources of light for the text-oriented Protestant service. This leads us back to the issue of blank glass: while its large-scale use in Protestant churches was initially driven by iconoclast ideas, blank glass proved to have significant practical advantages, as it admitted more light—that is, more unencumbered light—than colored windows did.[52]

True, not all Calvinist and Zwinglian regions in Europe saw acts of iconoclasm; but in all of these regions, churches' demand for polychrome glass declined. Old stained-glass windows may have been left intact in some places, but new windows typically featured blank glass.[53] Where stained- and painted glass windows were still being produced in Protestant areas, they were now predominantly used in domestic architecture.

This decline of religious demand presented a major challenge for manufacturers of stained glass. To adapt to the new situation, they had to gear their production toward the needs and tastes of private, secular clients.[54] Consider the Low Countries, traditionally a center of glass painting: after the sixteenth-century Low Countries broke up into a Catholic southern part and Calvinist northern part, two distinct aesthetics of glass painting emerged. In the south, traditional Catholic motifs—such as depictions of saints or the Virgin—remained frequent and were sought after by both churches and private buyers. By contrast, in the north, demand came almost exclusively from private customers who had no interest in Catholic imagery and instead sought decorative representations of what they considered unproblematic subjects (such as heraldry, moralistic scenes, depictions of professions, floral and animal scenes, or proverbs).[55]

In sum, it is no exaggeration to say that, in Protestant areas, the connotations of window glass were radically redefined. What began as a material endowed with a religious aura became a secular commodity. What is more, blank glass was no longer considered intrinsically inferior to colored glass. For Protestant householders who chose to glaze their windows, the traditional theological hierarchy of colored and blank glass was no longer the yardstick. Blank panes were now a legitimate option in their own right. Whether to install colored or blank glass in one's windows became, first and foremost, a question of aesthetic and pragmatic considerations.

9

The Rise of Cristallo

Chapter-opening image: Detail of Fig. 9.3

I n 2015, the German Protestant Church (EKD) issued an apology for the "destruction of religious images during the Reformation"—including the damage done to stained glass.[1] This, of course, is not how the iconoclasts would have perceived it. They considered their acts constructive, not destructive. Church windows are a case in point: radical Protestants were not against window glass per se; what they opposed was a certain kind of glass. In other words, they destroyed in order to replace. Consequently, blank glass became predominant in Protestant churches, and ultimately also in Protestant homes—a radical paradigm shift, underpinned by theological ideas. But were there also technological factors that contributed to the rise of blank glass in this period?

The age of the Reformation was certainly an age of significant innovation in glassmaking, especially with regard to transparent glass. The Venetians had laid the foundations for this development in the mid-fifteenth century. To be sure, the two manufacturing methods for window glass were still those developed by the ancient Romans: the cylinder method and the crown method. The Venetians' contributions concerned a different aspect: glass's purity. To understand the nature of the Venetian innovations, we must take a closer look at the production process.

Two ingredients are crucial for producing glass: a vitrifying agent and a fluxing agent. Since ancient times, the most common vitrifying agent was siliceous sand. Given Venice's proximity to the coastal shore, sand was easy to obtain for local glassmakers; indeed, sand served for centuries as the basis for glassmaking in Venice, where this craft is documented as early as the ninth century. The fourteenth century, however, saw a major change when Venetian glassmakers began to replace ordinary sand with carefully selected quartz pebbles from the *terraferma* (the mainland). These pebbles consisted of almost pure silica and contained very few impurities. Known as "*cogoli*," they were brought to Venice mainly from the northern Italian rivers Ticino and Adige. To ensure smooth melting in the furnace, the pebbles were roasted, cast into water, ground, and then sieved.[2]

Only after these preparatory steps did the melting process begin—and it had its own challenges. The silicates used for glassmaking have a melting point of around fifteen hundred degrees Celsius, a temperature that premodern furnaces could not reach. Ever since antiquity, glassmakers had been searching for ways to lower the melting point to a workable temperature. The common solution was to add fluxing agents to the glass batch, which helped to reduce the melting point to about eight hundred and fifty degrees Celsius.

Various substances served as fluxing agents. Ancient glassmakers relied primarily on mineral soda, as present in natron (a term derived from Wadi el Natrun in Egypt, an important natural deposit exploited by the Romans). In medieval Europe, Near Eastern natron was much harder to obtain due to the strained relations with the Islamic rulers who had come to control the natural deposits.[3] As a result, many European glassmakers, especially in northern Europe, turned to a different fluxing agent: potash (potassium carbonate), typically made from the ashes of trees, bracken, or underwood.[4] As the sixteenth-century German amateur mineralogist Johannes Mathesius explained, northern European glassmakers produced potash by burning fern "with its roots" or used the "ash of maple, beech, or fir."[5] In *De re metallica* (On the Nature of Metals), a widely read treatise on metallurgy and glassmaking, the humanist and mining expert Georgius Agricola mentioned the same fluxing agents, as well as oak ash (fig. 9.1).[6]

Potash of this kind, which was easy to procure in densely forested northern Europe, was a cheap means to lower glass's melting point. But such fluxing agents also had disadvantages: they contained chemical residues—for instance, iron oxides—that caused unwanted coloration. A greenish hue was the most common characteristic of what came to be known as northern European "forest glass."[7]

In medieval southern Europe, plant ashes were likewise used as fluxing agents. The best glassmakers, however, used only ashes containing a high amount of sodium carbonate (soda ash). Typically, these were ashes of marine plants that grew in waters with a high salt concentration.[8] From the High Middle Ages onward, Venetian glassmakers gained particular expertise in refining and using these ashes, known as "*barilla*," which matched the quality of natron-based soda. Barilla of the highest quality was imported directly from Egypt and especially Syria—regions with which the Venetians maintained privileged trade relations.[9]

As early as the thirteenth century, some Venetian glassmakers enjoyed a reputation for producing glass that resembled rock crystal. Further progress was made in the mid-fifteenth century. In the 1450s, the Murano-based glassmaker Angelo Barovier experimented with different methods of filtering and concentrating barilla, which yielded ash of extremely pure quality. This ash—when combined with decolorizers (such as certain kinds of manganese oxide) and high-quality sources of silica—allowed Barovier and other Muranese glassmakers to achieve what had been out of reach for medieval glassmakers: perfectly decolorized glass that ap-

Fig. 9.1. Illustration showing the operation of a glass furnace and blowing glass from Georgius Agricola's *De re metallica* (On the Nature of Metals, 1621 edition; first published 1556). In his treatise, the German humanist and mining expert Agricola provided one of the most comprehensive introductions to metallurgy and mining. He also devoted a section to glass, including the production of highly transparent Venetian *cristallo*. As his discussion makes clear, the ingredients needed for cristallo were known in northern Europe, but the exact production methods remained the subject of much speculation. Only in the second half of the sixteenth century did the production of transparent glass *à la façon de Venise* gain traction in northern Europe.

peared to be as clear as water—or, in another frequently used analogy, as clear as pure rock crystal. In fact, the latter analogy gave this new kind of glass its name: *cristallo* (crystal glass). Within a few decades, cristallo became the signature product of Venice's glass industry and the foundation of the eminent reputation that Venetian glassmakers enjoyed all over Europe.[10] As the Italian chemical expert

Fig. 9.2. A wineglass made of *cristallo* glass, Murano, sixteenth century. The Metropolitan Museum of Art, New York. Delicate, highly transparent drinking vessels such as this one contributed to the preeminent reputation of Venetian glassmakers.

Vannoccio Biringuccio noted in the sixteenth century, "The best glasswork that is made in our times and that which is of greater beauty, more varied coloring, and more admirable skill than that of any other place is made at Murano."[11]

What did these innovations mean for the production of window glass? In practice, relatively little. Due to the exceedingly high production costs, which stemmed from the use of expensive ingredients, cristallo glass was primarily used for the manufacture of intricate luxury vessels, such as goblets and cups (fig. 9.2). A small number of fifteenth- and sixteenth-century Venetian glassmakers did produce windowpanes made of cristallo—usually by means of the crown method—but this hardly amounted to mass production.[12] When, in the 1560s, the Swiss-German artist Jost Amman created, for an encyclopedia of crafts, a woodcut celebrating the work of early modern glassmakers, he chose to extol the production of Venetian windowpanes as one of the profession's accomplishments. The glassmaker in Amman's woodcut proclaims: "I also [make] Venetian glass panes that are pure / for churches and beautiful halls" (fig. 9.3).

However, contrary to what these verses suggests, there is little evidence to indicate that Venetian cristallo panes were widely used in architecture, let alone that they radically changed the way ordinary people experienced the view through their windows.[13] As we have seen, nontransparent impannate windows predomi-

Fig. 9.3. A glassmaker at work in a woodcut from the so-called *Ständebuch*, an encyclopedia of professions by Hans Sachs and Jost Amman (1568). In the accompanying poem, the glassmaker explains: "I also [make] Venetian glass panes that are pure / for churches and beautiful halls." Venetian glassmakers did indeed produce windowpanes, but rarely from *cristallo*.

nated in Italy throughout the early modern period. The cost of glazing windows with cristallo glass was simply prohibitive for most people. Pope Pius II was all the prouder to note that the newly built cathedral in his model city, Pienza, featured chapel windows "filled with the glass called crystal." And the Ferrarese chronicler quoted earlier (see Chapter 7) found it worthy of special mention that, around 1500, the Este castle of Belfiore boasted "five windows of crystalline glass" (*cinque finestre de cristalino vetro*).[14] A few decades later, the city of Augsburg decided to furnish its new, imposing city hall with Venetian panes that (given their hefty price) were most probably made of cristallo.[15]

High costs, however, were not the only reason why transparency remained a rare architectural feature even after the invention of cristallo. Well into the sixteenth century, colored glass was still the most prestigious variety of window glass. Incidentally, Barovier's reputation rested just as much on his ability to produce fine colored glass as it did on his discovery of cristallo. When the Milanese court architect Filarete, in a treatise from the 1460s, imagined how his "best friend" Barovier could contribute to the planning of an ideal city, he was not thinking of transparent windows, but rather of high-quality colored glass for mosaics, figural glass panels, and glass intarsia imitating precious minerals such as jasper (fig. 9.4).[16]

It was not until the second quarter of the sixteenth century that Protestants in northern Europe began to question the traditional superiority of colored over uncolored window glass. In Catholic regions, by contrast, the close link between polychrome glass and sacred space remained intact and continued to define the aesthetic hierarchy in both religious and domestic architecture. Tellingly, in Catholic places such as Italy, the cristallo panes used in fifteenth- and sixteenth-century private architecture were often chromatically enhanced. In fact, the prized cristallo windowpanes of Belfiore Castle were completely painted.[17]

These observations tie in with a broader trend: painting on crystal-clear glass products—whether panes or vessels—did not decrease their value. Quite the contrary: as Biringuccio noted, Venice's glassmakers owed a good part of their reputation to their ability to produce glass products that were "very clear and transparent like true and natural crystal, and ornament them with paintings and other very fine enamels."[18] In fact, one of the advantages of cristallo panes was that they lent themselves particularly well as surfaces for painting. As Vasari put it, to maximize the polychrome effect of enamel-painted windows, it was best to use "glasses that are clear in themselves."[19]

Fig. 9.4. Wineglass, Murano, ca. 1475–1500. Blue glass, enameled and gilded. The Metropolitan Museum of Art, New York. Made in the same period that saw the rise of transparent *cristallo*, multicolored drinking vessels such as this one were highly prized luxury objects. They are a reminder that cristallo was just one of many varieties of Venetian glass. In terms of production, transparent and colored glass were not mutually exclusive: Angelo Barovier, the fifteenth-century inventor of cristallo, was no less admired for his polychrome creations than he was for his transparent glass.

To paint on fully transparent glass was, of course, a luxury. In other words, "glasses that are clear in themselves" were the optimal surface for enamel painting, but not a sine qua non. As the products of northern European glassmakers demonstrated, fine painting was also possible on panes that were not clear as crystal. This was one reason why the Venetian monopoly on cristallo glass never translated into a dominant position in the market for window glass. It also explains why Venetian glassmakers continued to produce two other kinds of glass that were of lesser quality but significantly cheaper than cristallo. One was known as "*vetro comune*," a lightly tinted "common glass" produced from sand rather than pebbles; the second was referred to as "*vitrum blanchum*," uncolored "white glass" that approximated cristallo in quality, as it was produced from quartz pebbles.[20] Despite the shortcomings vis-à-vis cristallo, both vetro comune and vitrum blanchum were suitable for enamel painting (if so desired). On the whole, such panes, whether painted or not, were used much more frequently for architectural purposes than cristallo was.

Demand for Venetian window glass was traditionally strong in Venice, as the glass industry was a source of pride for the city and its inhabitants. Around 1500, the Venetian chronicler Marino Sanuto described how, along the Canal Grande, "there is an infinite number of houses with . . . all windows of glass. And there are so many of these glass windows that the glaziers are constantly busy taking care of and fitting these panes (which are produced in Murano); there is a glazier's shop in every neighborhood."[21] And a few decades later, the architect Jacopo Sansovino reported that in Venice "all the windows are sealed not with sheets of waxed cloth or paper, but with very blank [*bianchissimi*] and fine glass panes, encased in wooden frames and fixed in place with iron and lead; . . . and all of them are produced by the furnaces of Murano."[22] This common use of window glass in Venetian houses set the city apart from most other early modern Italian cities.

While Venetians generally were committed to purchasing window glass from local manufacturers, buyers elsewhere in Europe chose between several different options. Indeed, in the market for ordinary glass, Venetian glassmakers faced stiff competition from their northern European counterparts. Glassmakers north of the Alps not only produced panes of a quality similar to that of Venetian "common glass," but also had the advantage of operating closer to the main areas of demand in Europe.[23] For these logistical reasons alone, northern European glassmakers maintained an edge in the market for ordinary glass. Vasari—who, as a Tuscan, cultivated a bias against the Venetians—went so far as to claim that for ordinary enamel-painted windowpanes, "French, Flemish, and English glasses are better than the Venetian, because the Flemish are very clear and the Venetian much charged with colour."[24] Vasari's English contemporary William Harrison was less judgmental, but he, too, discussed a broad range of available options: in his observations on window glass in English architecture, he noted that "we have diverse sorts, some brought out of Burgundy, some out of Normandy, much out of Flanders, beside that which is made in England."[25] Venetian glass is noticeably absent from Harrison's list. Whatever the reasons for this omission, Harrison's and Vasari's accounts both make clear that, from a pan-European vantage point, Venetian panes did not play a major role in the market for architectural glass. What is more, the Venetian invention of the luxury product cristallo did not disrupt the business of northern European window-glass manufacturers; it certainly did not affect the way most people experienced architectural glass in everyday life.

Cristallo's impact on architecture was indirect, and it manifested itself only in the long run: the Venetian discovery of this crystal-clear glass sparked an unprecedented competition for innovation in the European glass industry, which—as we shall see—ultimately also affected architecture. Initially, however, this competition revolved entirely around the production of small vessels. Venetian cristallo cups and goblets were widely admired for their elegant design and fetched stupendous prices among affluent buyers across Europe.[26] In this segment of the market, the Venetian monopoly on cristallo was undoubtedly an asset, not least because the republic's glassmakers were long able to keep the production methods secret. This secrecy owed much to the traditional location of the Venetian glass industry on the hard-to-access island of Murano. In the thirteenth century, Venetian authorities had ordered glassmakers to move from Venice to Murano—initially not so much to guard craft secrets, but rather to protect densely settled Venice from fires caused by the operation of furnaces. After the discovery of cristallo in the mid-fifteenth century, Murano's isolated location in the lagoon proved highly effective for preventing industrial espionage. There were also other deterrents: Murano's glassmakers faced grave punishment—including the risk of assassination—if they tried to leave the republic and settle abroad.[27]

As a result of this secrecy, the exact method of producing cristallo remained unknown outside of Venice, even though northern Europeans understood that certain plant ashes played a key role. Writing in mid-sixteenth century Bohemia, Johannes Mathesius related that the Venetians "produce their refined ash from various saline herbs, and this makes the glass clearer and purer."[28] Still, theoretical knowledge about the ash's composition was of little use without the practical know-how necessary to master the multi-staged process of producing cristallo. The Venetian monopoly on cristallo began to erode only in the late sixteenth century, when northern European rulers and governments succeeded in poaching glassmakers from Murano. Once these Muranese glassmakers had set up the necessary technical framework abroad, they began to produce cristallo glass of a quality hard to distinguish from the Venetian original. This northern European cristallo glass came to be known as glass "*à la façon de Venise*" (in a Venetian fashion), a designation still used in modern scholarship (fig. 9.5).[29]

The first successful attempts to produce cristallo glass outside of Venice were made in the sixteenth-century Spanish Netherlands—more specifically in Antwerp, a leading commercial city of northern Europe at the time. Antwerp was, among other things, a hub for the trade in Spanish plant ashes, some of which approximated the quality of the Levantine ashes used by the Venetians.[30] When Antwerp's commercial fortune declined in the seventeenth century, France took the lead—not only with regard to the production of cristallo glass à la façon de Venise, but also in another field in which the Venetians had previously been unrivaled: the production of glass mirrors.[31] In the 1660s, Jean-Baptiste Colbert, the powerful and ambitious minister of finances under Louis XIV, founded the Manufacture Royale de Glaces à Miroirs (Royal Mirror-Glass Company) where formerly Muranese glassmakers helped to produce glass mirrors that surpassed the quality of those made in Venice. As we will see in the next chapter, these skills would also lead to major improvements in the production of window glass.

In the last quarter of the seventeenth century, additional competitors emerged and gained a share in the lucrative market for highly transparent glass vessels: England and Bohemia. The rise of the English glassmaking industry resulted from a homemade crisis earlier in the century: in order to procure wood for firing the furnaces, entire forests had been cut down. As deforestation began to affect ever-larger areas of England, the English navy feared that a shortage of wood would jeopardize the ability to maintain the fleet and build new ships. As a result, a royal proclamation in 1615 prohibited the use of wood as an industrial fuel. Glassmak-

Fig. 9.5. Unknown maker, possibly from the Höchstetter studio in Hall, Austria, Goblet, ca. 1550–60. J. Paul Getty Museum, Los Angeles. This goblet attests to northern European glassmakers' ambition to imitate Venetian *cristallo* glass. The finest vessels of this sort achieved this goal and were known as glass *à la façon de Venise*. These vessels often mimicked Venetian designs, which makes it difficult to distinguish them from original Venetian products. But sometimes the northern products adapted traditional local designs, as in the case of this goblet, which displays certain features (such as the trailed glass bands) that suggest its origins in German lands.

ers (as well as iron founders) were ordered to use coal instead. Initially, the forced transition from wood to coal posed many technical challenges for glassmakers, not least because the smoke and other gases resulting from the burning of coal caused a range of quality issues, including unwanted coloration.[32] Gradually, however, English glassmakers found ways to resolve these problems. What is more, it turned out that the transition from wood to coal offered many advantages—not just in terms of forestation, but also from an economic perspective. For one thing, coal tended to be cheaper than wood (which was needed for many other purposes);

for another, coal—when burnt in special, conical furnaces—allowed glassmakers to attain higher temperatures in the furnace, which in turn decreased the dependence on fluxing agents.[33] In the 1670s, experiments with the addition of lead oxide paved the way for George Ravenscroft's invention of so-called flint glass, which matched the quality of Venetian cristallo.[34] It is perhaps no coincidence that around this time "transparency" became a common word in the English lexicon.[35]

Glassmakers in late seventeenth-century Bohemia took another path: drawing on the Venetian process of ash refinement, they successfully managed to purify ordinary potash by means of lixiviation (that is, by dissolving potash in a solvent and extracting the purified solute). Through further improvements, such as the addition of lime, Bohemian glassmakers soon produced glass that was just as clear as—but much less expensive than—Venetian cristallo.[36] Ironically, by the early eighteenth century, Venetians were importing Bohemian glass in large quantities.[37]

To sum up: in the early modern period, the interplay of two distinct factors laid the foundation for the emergence of transparency as an aesthetic and architectural ideal. The first factor was the Venetian invention of cristallo glass. This invention had neither an immediate nor a direct impact on architecture, but it did set in motion a chain reaction of innovation in the major centers of European glassmaking. Initially, the main goal of Venice's competitors was to produce cristallo for luxury vessels. In the long run, however, the technological knowledge gained along the way made it possible to produce larger and cheaper transparent glass windows (as we will see in the next chapter).

The second key factor was the declining demand for colored glass in many Protestant regions. There was little desire for new stained or painted glass in churches. What is more, surviving medieval glass windows were systematically destroyed in some places (such as the Netherlands and England). The new windowpanes that replaced medieval stained glass were deliberately blank—a material quality that conveyed a clear theological message while providing, on a practical level, more light for the text-centered Protestant service.

As a result of these factors, the centuries-old superiority of colored window glass began to erode. Against this backdrop, the rise of enamel painting turned out to be an innovation with mixed results: while enamel painting greatly expanded the possibilities for detailed, naturalistic depictions on glass, it also implied an emancipation of the color from the glass. In other words, it was no longer necessary to pre-color the window glass, as it was now possible to apply paint in all colors directly on a pane. This was a fundamental change compared to the past: glass was no longer the medium, but rather the vehicle for color.[38] When color fell out of fashion, what remained as the glass industry's default product was the blank pane.

IO

More Light

From the Baroque to the Enlightenment

More light!
— GOETHE'S
(reputed) last words

Chapter-opening image: Detail of Fig. 10.5

The Age of Enlightenment played a key role in the history of transparency, redefining how transparency was experienced and conceptualized. But important foundations were laid well before the Enlightenment. The fifteenth and sixteenth centuries, in particular, saw two transformative processes play out: first, on a technological level, a string of innovations sparked by the Venetian discovery of cristallo; and second, on an aesthetic level, a reevaluation of glass's theological connotations. One feature of windowpanes, however, remained the same: their size. This began to change only in the late seventeenth century—and, as we shall see, it accelerated the decline of colored glass.

For centuries, most panes did not exceed the size of an octavo page.[1] Together, several panes formed one window. But while the panes were much smaller than modern ones, they came in a great variety of shapes. Rectangular panes, diamond-shaped quarries, and roundels were common. And of course there were traditional stained-glass windows, composed of a multitude of small, irregularly shaped pieces of glass.[2] This composite character meant that the window—unlike its modern counterpart—did not form a uniform, continuous surface. This, of course, was not a shortcoming for as long as colored glass was prized. Small panes aligned with the fashion of coloring some sections of a window (especially the central ones) and leaving others (such as the bordures) blank. In the special case of stained glass, the mosaic-like assembly of small pieces was also essential for the pictorial effect. As glass historians Raymond McGrath and Albert Frost have noted, medieval makers of stained glass were "not handicapped by the limited sizes of glass but indebted to them for one of the subtlest and most important effects."[3]

As long as the paradigm of colored glass (and, by extension, the idea of the composite window) dominated, the production of larger panes was not a priority for glassmakers.[4] Windowpanes began to increase in size only when the perceived superiority of colored glass started to erode. This development owed much to technical lessons learned in a different field: mirror production.

Glassmaking and mirror production had not always been closely interrelated. In the ancient and medieval period, most mirrors were made of polished metal or silver sheets, not glass.[5] Metallic materials had disadvantages: such mirrors were often blurry (due to insufficient polishing) or spotty (from rust). A person looking into a cheap ancient mirror was likely to have an experience similar to that described in the First Epistle to the Corinthians, where St. Paul states metaphorically that "for now we see in a mirror dimly" (a verse that older translations of the New Testament famously but inaccurately rendered as "through a glass, darkly").[6]

By contrast, glass had the advantage of being rust-resistant. This was certainly known in ancient and medieval times, and indeed experiments were made with glass as a material for mirrors. Still, the link between mirrors and glass grew closer only in the first half of the sixteenth century, when Venetian glassmakers perfected a method—probably first invented in Flanders—to manufacture mirrors from clear glass plates that were coated with a mixture of mercury and tin on the rear side.[7] The complicated silvering process and the use of cristallo glass made high-quality glass mirrors—or "looking glasses," as they were also called—an exceedingly expensive and prestigious luxury item. Tellingly, glass mirrors were often fitted in gold or silver frames; sometimes they were also enhanced with intricate engravings or covered with protective curtains.[8] In the words of mirror scholar Herbert Grabes, these looking glasses were "a technological marvel of the age."[9]

Glass plates for mirrors were typically produced in the same way as cylinder-blown windowpanes, which means that the size was inevitably limited by human lung capacity. In practice, most Venetian mirror plates did not exceed eight by ten inches.[10] True, the mirrors that were most common in premodern Europe—little handheld mirrors—were even smaller. But the problem for the user was the same: looking into the mirror, one could see only part of one's body. A life-size image required joining several mirror plates, which was very expensive. What is more, the plates' borders formed a grid that spoiled the illusionistic effect of the mirror.

Mirrors served various other practical functions—and in these contexts, too, size played a role. For instance, mirrors amplified interior lighting by reflecting candlelight.[11] As Roger North noted in his 1698 treatise *Of Building*, even a sparingly fenestrated house could be well illuminated if residents installed mirrors in the right places. North went so far as to argue that "no furniture contributes more to the life and spirit of an apartment, than good and well plac'd glasses."[12]

For all these reasons, larger, continuous mirrors were widely desired in premodern Europe, which drove glassmakers to produce larger plates of glass.[13] Indeed, it was not architectural glass, but rather glass mirrors, that Jean-Baptiste Colbert had in mind when he founded the Manufacture Royale de Glaces à Miroirs (1665), which became, within a century, one of the largest manufacturing enterprises in France.[14] The company succeeded in attracting Venetian glassmakers to

France by offering them protection and lucrative salaries. Drawing on Venetian expertise (and on funding by the French Crown), the company soon mastered the manufacture of Venetian-style mirrors made of silvered glass plates. Here again, however, the glass plates did not reach full human size, as they were still produced by the cylinder method.[15]

The company's success was an earthquake for the mirror industry in Murano. Tellingly, the Venetian authorities tried more than once to sabotage the French enterprise. They even set out to assassinate Muranese glassmakers who had settled in France—and they apparently had some success.[16] But in the long run, even sabotage could not turn back the clock, and to the great dismay of the Venetians, the Manufacture Royale and its products became a source of great prestige for the French Crown. The company also paved the way for the creation of the much-admired Galerie des Glaces (Hall of Mirrors, 1678–83) in the royal palace at Versailles (fig. 10.1). The hall boasted no fewer than 357 mirrors, which were installed on the interior wall facing the generously glazed garden front. This spatial arrangement meant that people in the hall saw Versailles's lavish gardens twice: once through the windows, and again in the mirrors. It was as if the boundary between nature and palace was canceled—a marvelous effect that only added to the fame and prestige of Louis XIV, the château's omnipotent master (fig. 10.2).[17] After sunset, the hall was lit by as many as seven thousand wax candles.[18]

Inspired by the celebrated example of Versailles, mirrored halls became a prominent feature of late baroque architecture, especially in the palaces of the aristocracy. A contemporary French chronicler sarcastically related the case of the Countess de Fiesque who, despite her financial troubles, furnished her residence with a large mirror. Asked how she could afford this, she replied that she had sold a piece of farmland, and asked back with surprise, "Have I not done wonderfully? A beautiful mirror instead of wheat!"[19]

The splendor of the royal Hall of Mirrors remained, of course, unsurpassed. Yet even on a smaller scale than at Versailles, mirror-lined halls implied a new relation between interior and exterior space. As Georg Kohlmaier and Barna von Sartory have argued, "With the introduction of the mirror in the baroque period, the continuity of the walls was broken to form an illusion, and a direct connection with the outside world resulted. The cultivated landscape in front of the house became the symbol of control over nature."[20] At Versailles there were also additional layers of meaning: the generous admission of sunlight through the hall's windows

Fig. 10.1. The Galerie des Glaces (Hall of Mirrors), Palace of Versailles, begun 1670s. The hall was the royal palace's prestigious centerpiece; its name comes from the 357 mirrors that line the walls and reflect the views from the lavishly fenestrated garden side. The effect of the mirrors and windows is interlinked and mutually reinforcing.

Fig. 10.2. Hall of Mirrors, Palace of Versailles. The reflection of the windows in the mirrors helps to flood the hall with light while also creating the illusion that the boundary between interior and exterior has been canceled.

and its bright reflection in the mirrors were entirely in line with Louis XIV's monarchical self-fashioning as the Sun King.[21] Indeed, Versailles was designed as an apotheosis of sun and light, and the amplification of sunlight through mirrors was only one of many architectural details conveying this message. Other contrivances included the brightly shining parquet floors; the lavish, scintillating glass chandeliers; and the light-reflecting waterworks and fountains in the gardens. There even were plans to erect a monumental Temple of the Sun in the gardens, with a main hall completely furnished with mirrors.[22]

The dazzling visual effect of mirrors was, of course, best realized in light-flooded rooms.[23] It is no coincidence that the baroque fascination with mirrors went hand in hand with a taste for expansive transparent windows. For both purposes, the production of larger glass plates was key. Indeed, the French Crown promised considerable rewards to glassmakers for finding ways to enlarge the size of glass plates without compromising on quality. In the past, quality issues had been a crucial factor limiting size: the largest mouth-blown panes often suffered from unevenness or featured sections so thin that grinding was difficult, if not impossible.[24] Overcoming these obstacles was not only a matter of technological ambition, but also of political prestige for the French Crown. The prospect of lucrative remuneration attracted some of the finest Italian glassmakers to France, among them Bernard Perrot (originally Perrotto), a native of northern Italy who settled in Orléans. In 1687, Perrot made an innovation that held great promise for the manufacture of both mirrors and windowpanes: a method for producing large glass plates by casting (or "coulage," as it was called in French).[25]

Perrot was not the first person in history to master the casting of windowpanes. As we have seen, ancient Roman glassmakers commanded this skill, and it is possible that pane-casting was still practiced in some parts of early medieval Europe. In the course of the medieval period, however, casting was supplanted by the crown and cylinder method, perhaps because certain features of cast glass came to be seen as undesirable: the panes were relatively thick and heavy, and they invariably had a matte underside. Perrot was aware of these shortcomings and sought to remedy them. His solution—which some historians of technology consider the most important innovation in glassmaking since Roman antiquity—was to pour the molten glass onto a smooth, preheated metal surface (the "casting table"), where it was spread with a heavy iron roller (fig. 10.3).[26] The resulting glass plates were about one centimeter thick. They still required extensive grinding and

Fig. 10.3. Engraving showing casting glass plates according to the *coulage* method invented by Bernard Perrot, in the *Encyclopédie* by Denis Diderot and Jean le Rond d'Alembert, 1762. Arguably the most important innovation in glassmaking since Roman times, the coulage method made it possible to produce mirrors and glass plates of unprecedented size.

polishing, but this menial work was relatively cheap at the time: even before the invention of coulage, the French Crown had no scruples about assigning tasks such as glass-grinding to the crippled veterans living in the Hôpital des Invalides.[27]

As the coulage method was improved, the cast panes became thinner and evener, eventually surpassing the quality of their Roman prototypes. Most importantly, the panes exceeded the typical size of blown window glass. When decolorizers were added to the molten glass and the final product was ground thoroughly, the panes were not only of unprecedented size, but also remarkably transparent.[28] In spring 1687, Perrot first presented his invention to the Académie Royale des Sciences in Paris; a year later he received a royal privilege to produce large glass panes "by means of the invented machines."[29] Soon enough, however, it became clear that the Crown's goal was to exploit this innovation rather than protect the inventor's intellectual property. In 1695, the Crown ordered the seizure of Perrot's equipment, awarding him an annual pension for the rest of his life but prohibiting him from pursuing the production of cast glass. Instead, the king established a new company—the Manufacture Royale des Glaces de France (Royal Plate Glass Company)—which had a virtual monopoly on glass casting.[30] (The company continued to operate under this name until the nineteenth century.)

Large, cast windowpanes necessitated new methods of installation and structural support. Concerns about weight were a major argument against lead or iron frames of the sort that had been used for structural support in the past. A lighter material was far better suited to joining and framing large glass panes: timber. In France, wooden muntins had started gaining popularity in the early seventeenth century, at a time when panes (the so-called *petits carreaux*) were still mouth-blown. The emergence of cast *grands carreaux* further reinforced this fashion.[31]

The size of the first cast plates from the late 1680s hovered around fifty by eighty inches. In the mid-eighteenth century, the typical size increased to sixty by one hundred inches; and another century later (in the 1850s), the largest glass plates reached sizes of 140 by 180 inches.[32] For the first time in history, it became possible to produce continuous glass surfaces (including mirrors) larger than the human body.[33] In practice, plates of this size were often cut into smaller panes. But even these smaller segments tended to exceed the average size of mouth-blown panes of the past (fig. 10.4).

Gradually, cast glass spread beyond France to the rest of Europe. Courtly and public buildings were much more likely than ordinary homes to feature large panes. This, of course, was primarily due to the cost of such panes, which reflected the expensive manufacturing process: after all, the coulage method required specially designed melting furnaces as well as large casting tables made of metal. In the main factory in Paris, for instance, each casting table consisted of almost three tons of copper. The initial investment, before the first pane could even be cast, was substantial.[34]

Mouth-blowing remained a considerably cheaper alternative: the furnaces necessary for producing crown or cylinder glass were much smaller, and the work tools were simple and inexpensive.[35] In practice, then, casting did not immediately supersede blowing and had to compete with it. The cylinder method in particular continued to be practiced in France and elsewhere in Europe. What is more, in England and Spain the authorities took measures to protect local glassmakers and their traditional methods—for instance, by establishing high tariffs on cast panes from France.[36] In England, where crown-glass production traditionally predominated, there was an additional levy: the "glass excise." To illustrate the effect of

Fig. 10.4. Frame for a mirror with two parcloses, France, 1751–53. Oak, carved, gilded, and painted; modern mirror glass. J. Paul Getty Museum, Los Angeles. Measuring 129 by 77 inches, this frame was fitted with two large glass plates, which created the effect of an (almost) seamless reflective surface. Before the late seventeenth century, mirrors of this size would have required assembly from several small glass plates. A label on the back indicates that this mirror was on sale in the shop of François-Charles Darnault, a supplier of luxury goods and furniture to the French royal family.

these levies: in England in the 1750s, an imported cast plate measuring sixty by forty-two inches cost as much as eighty-one pounds, of which the excise duty accounted for the handsome amount of thirty-seven pounds. And in 1794, a polished plate sized one hundred seventeen by seventy-six inches sold for a staggering 404 pounds.[37] (For context, the average London laborer in the 1790s earned thirty pounds per year.)[38] In theory, the glass excise applied to all varieties of glass panes. In practice, however, it privileged blown glass, as the levy was calculated based on weight—and with crown glass being the thinnest variety of glass available on the market, it was also the least affected by the excise.[39] In addition to the tax burden, the high production costs discouraged English entrepreneurs from investing in the manufacture of cast glass. The few attempts to set up cast-glass production in eighteenth-century England all failed.[40]

Even in France, the center of coulage, cast panes remained luxury objects that only the nobility and upper classes could afford. The most important buyer of the Manufacture Royale des Glaces de France's products was, in fact, the king himself. Louis XIV explicitly stated in the original letters patent that the company's main purpose was to supply the royal buildings as well as the "principal houses of our subjects"—with an understanding that the king would be entitled to buy the panes at a significantly discounted rate.[41] The owners of "principal houses," for their part, had to buy at the regular price. Understandably, they were all the more eager to display their acquisitions prominently: large cast panes were installed not only in buildings, but also in the windows of carriages (another status symbol among the elites). It also became common to display large paintings, engravings, or prints under glass—not only to protect the artwork from dust, but here again in a gesture of conspicuous consumption.[42]

The taste for oversized windows with large panes was a testament to the stylistic influence of Versailles, which had defined a new ideal of palatial architecture and fenestration.[43] The downside of this vogue was that the demand for colored and stained glass further declined in the eighteenth century. In the past, upper-class commissions had formed a major and reliable source of income for glass painters. As demand declined, so did this artistic practice.[44] In 1760, Charles-Nicolas Cochin, the French king's "administrator of the arts," justified the court's lack of interest in colored glass as follows: "To be honest, no one has use [for glass-painting] anymore because neither in apartments nor even churches do people want anything that potentially diminishes the light."[45] When, in 1764, the Strasbourg-based artist Jean-Adolphe Dannegger approached the king with a proposal to revive the production of stained glass in Alsace and to supply samples to the court, Cochin flatly rejected the offer. The reply to Dannegger made it clear that the centuries-old hierarchy of colored and uncolored glass had been subverted: "If it were proven that [the art of stained glass] had been lost and is now rediscovered, no one would know what to do with it."[46]

This, of course, is not to say that only panes of the new, larger type were installed in seventeenth- and eighteenth-century royal residences. Versailles boasted hundreds of windows, and most of them were—and remained—furnished with petits carreaux (that is, rectangular panes produced in Normandy by way of the traditional cylinder method). What these smaller panes had in common with the grands carreaux was a high degree of transparency, and they were often assembled in a way that mimicked the effect of an oversized window—for instance, with twenty-four petits carreaux installed in a single window.[47]

The demand for oversized windows also contributed to the development of the "French window," a human-size window with a transom above head level so that the two lower, hinged leaves could be pushed open like a door (fig. 10.5).[48] Large, door-like windows of this type allowed for ingress and egress, but also helped to flood interiors—especially ceremonial rooms—with sunlight. Here again, this vision of abundant light was perfected at Versailles. Louis XIV was virtuosic in using windows for his self-fashioning as the Sun King. Not by chance, his bedroom at Versailles featured large windows oriented to the east, toward the rising sun. These windows enabled the king to enjoy an imperious view down the straight avenue leading to his capital, Paris, but they also flooded the bedroom with light every morning during the famous levée ceremony, so that both king and sun rose in a spectacular (and concerted) way.[49]

Louis XIV closely followed the development of the French glass industry. In 1666, one year after the establishment of the royal glassworks, he personally inspected the production sites and, in a symbolic gesture, helped to blow a glass pane.[50] The Sun King also paid great attention to architectural details and had a particularly sharp eye for issues of fenestration. The Duc de Saint-Simon—the ever-critical chronicler of court life at Versailles—related a telling episode: during a visit to the construction site of the Trianon palace at Versailles, Louis XIV noticed that one window was slightly smaller than the others. The Marquis de Louvois, Louis's minister of war and official overseer of the construction project, was present during the tour and dared to question the accuracy of the royal observation. At the king's order the window was measured, which confirmed that it was too small. According to Saint-Simon, the deeply embarrassed Louvois worried so much about his standing at court that, in order to deflect attention from the issue, he incited the king to enter a military adventure that became the Nine Years' War.[51]

Louis XIV was not, to be sure, the only French king of this period with a keen interest in fenestration and its spectacular visual effects. Under his successor,

Louis XV, the French court spent no less than thirty-six thousand livres per year on the glazing of windows and their maintenance. (For context, a typical manual worker in eighteenth-century Paris earned about three hundred livres per year.) French kings in the Age of Absolutism had no scruples about implementing their grand ideas for lavishly fenestrated castles: apart from enjoying discounted rates for cast panes from the Manufacture Royale des Glaces de France, the kings also required the glassmakers of Normandy to provide a certain amount of ordinary glass panes each year without charge, for use in royal and public construction projects. When the Norman glassmakers failed to comply in 1724 and 1738, Louis XV sent royal agents to Normandy to seize all the glass in their factories.[52]

One can, of course, find aristocratic residences from earlier periods that evince a similar desire to maximize window size and the admission of light. (Suffice it to recall the English "prodigy houses" of the sixteenth century.) However, as architectural historian Hentie Louw has noted, the baroque dramaturgy of light

Fig. 10.5. "French windows" on the garden façade of the Palace of Versailles. Highly fashionable in palatial architecture of this period, this type of door-high window admitted copious light while also reinforcing the perception of a seamless transition between interior and exterior.

marked a new quality, as it drew on the "ability to produce progressively larger sheets of flat clear glass" while benefitting from the "large scale switch from metal to wood as the constructional material in windows."[53] These technical innovations made it easier to construct ever more—and ever larger—windows in aristocratic residences, in the spirit of Versailles.[54] In 1680s England, the poet Charles Cotton sang the praises of Chatsworth, the residence of the Third Earl of Devonshire, where "all these Glories glitter to the sight / By the advantage of a clearer Light / . . . / The Windows now look like so many Suns, / Illustrating the noble Room at once."[55] And when, in the 1690s, Christopher Wren designed new apartments for the royal family at Hampton Court, he spent the extraordinary sum of 4,600 pounds on eighty-four windows with large cast panes. (Another 250 windows were glazed with crown glass, which cost "only" six hundred pounds.)[56]

The taste for glass was similarly conspicuous in the Holy Roman Empire. The Habsburg emperors generously glazed some of their palaces even before their archenemy, the French Crown, began construction of Versailles. The rationale, of course, was the same: to gain prestige. Indeed, when the Turkish traveler and diplomat Evliya Çelebi visited Vienna in 1665 and was admitted to the Habsburg imperial palace, he reported with admiration how "the entire palace is illuminated by thousands of artfully designed windows with exceedingly beautiful small panes which shine brightly."[57] The "small panes" that Çelebi admired were probably ordinary petits carreaux. Had he returned a century later, he would have also found oversized panes: by then, the emperor's main study in Vienna's Hofburg featured a window made of two panes, each as large as a man. Predictably, the effect did not fail to impress visitors and ordinary subjects alike. Even four decades after the empire's collapse, a nineteenth-century Austrian guidebook reminisced: "Rarely did a Viennese walk through the square without looking up to see whether father Francis [Emperor Francis II] was standing behind the windowpane; the well-being of thirty-three million people was encased in this study in which the Emperor worked."[58]

The Hofburg in Vienna was formally the heart of the Holy Roman Empire, but in reality, most of the political power in the empire lay in the hands of its territorial princes. These rulers went to great lengths to assert and display their power by building their own lavish palaces—which, needless to say, often boasted large glass windows.[59] Here again, the effect drew the attention of contemporaries, especially travelers and foreign observers. It is perhaps no coincidence that English

Fig. 10.6. Haus Monheim, Aachen, Germany, begun 1662. The ground floor of this building originally accommodated a pharmacy and drug store; the storeowner and his family lived on the upper floors. The stately façade symbolized the social status and prosperity of the upper-class family. Further windows were added during an upgrade in the 1780s. The ostentatious fenestration imitated aristocratic architecture and went to the limits of what was structurally possible. This might explain why four of the lateral windows are blind windows painted onto the façade.

writers from this period translated, in jest, the German aristocratic salutation *"Ihre Durchlaucht"*—an originally medieval form of address meaning "Your Enlightened Highness"—as "Your Transparency."[60] Of course, this was a pun on overly literal translations, but it might also reflect an awareness of the aristocratic competition for more windows and interior light.

In German cities, affluent burghers certainly tried to emulate this aristocratic fashion (fig. 10.6). Consider the jurist and imperial officer Johann Caspar Goethe, the father of Germany's most famous poet. In the 1750s, the windows of the Goethe family residence in Frankfurt am Main were completely overhauled. More specifically, the father ordered that the old bull's-eye windows be replaced with new, large panes of glass. As his son would later recall, "The large panes of plate-glass contributed towards a perfect lightness, which had been wanting in the old house for many causes, but chiefly on account of the panes which were for the most part round."[61] The upgrade of the windows in the Goethe family residence was in line with the advice given by architectural treatises at the time. In his popular *Anfangs-Gründe der Bau-Kunst* (Introduction to Architecture)—available in the seventh edition when Goethe grew up—the German polymath Christian Wolff stated: "Glass windows have to be made either from large and clear panes, or—even better—from glass plates, for the generous use of lead [lines] deprives the room of light."[62]

Did the baroque infatuation with large, transparent glass windows inaugurate a new chapter in the cultural history of light? There is much evidence to believe so, at least with respect to the aristocracy and upper classes. Daylight was, of course, an indispensable resource throughout premodern times, and some professions and industries could not have operated without it. Traditionally, however, the premodern need for light was pragmatic: in other words, most people needed daylight for specific tasks. As Alberti put it in the fifteenth century, windows "should be appropriate to the requirements of the interior . . . so that their frequency and the light they receive are no greater or less than utility demands."[63] For precisely this reason, practitioners of certain métiers preferred the attenuated light of windows sealed with paper or fabric. The idea of flooding an interior space with daylight may have intrigued baroque aristocrats, but it was not always a priority—and perhaps not even a desire—among ordinary people.

But what about medieval cathedrals? Did their glass walls not anticipate (or even surpass) the baroque dramaturgy of light? From an experiential perspective this objection is legitimate, but it ignores the different conceptual and aesthetic framework. As Hans Blumenberg has pointed out, the light falling into late ancient and medieval churches was meant to edify churchgoers in a quasi-mystical fashion. Man was the passive recipient of light, which seemed to emanate from the colored glass but ultimately originated from God. According to Blumenberg, the baroque period marked a departure from the medieval attitude: from the seventeenth century onward, light was no longer perceived as something "given" by God, but rather as an "available" resource. By extension, the concept of passive receipt of "light" (*Licht*) gave way to active acts of "lighting" (*Beleuchtung*). In Blumenberg's pointed words, "Things no longer stand in the light; they are lit from a certain angle."[64] This "dramaturgy of light" (*Lichtregie*), skillfully operated by humans, manifested itself not only in architecture, but also in the visual arts—for instance, in the works of seventeenth-century painters such as Caravaggio and Rembrandt.[65] (And one could easily add the names of Bernini, Vermeer, Poussin, and Lorrain.) Incidentally, the seventeenth century saw a growing scientific interest in optical phenomena, which in turn laid the foundation for a systematic inquiry into light's physical properties.[66]

The enthusiasm for making light abundantly "available" culminated in the eighteenth century—and it not only affected architecture and the visual arts, but also left an imprint on the term by which the historical period came to be known: the "Enlightenment" ("*Siècle des Lumières*" in French; "*Illuminismo*" and "*Ilustración*" in Italian and Spanish, respectively). The thought and rhetoric of the Enlightenment equated darkness with repression and reaction. Consequently, darkness was to be dispelled by more light, the symbol of Enlightenment values such as progress, liberty, and skepticism. As Michel Foucault has noted, "A fear haunted the latter half of the eighteenth century: the fear of darkened spaces, of the pall of gloom which prevents the full visibility of things, men and truths."[67] Or in Blumenberg's words: "The Enlightenment shifted 'light' into the domain of that which has to be achieved; truth lost the natural *facilitas* with which it used to prevail."[68]

This idealization of light—and the concomitant aversion to darkness—informed learned philosophical discourses, but it also had repercussions in everyday life. The Age of Enlightenment saw concrete attempts by both enlightened reformers and government authorities to subject darkness—especially its prime manifestation, the night—to human control. As we shall see, this project was riddled with contradictions and inconsistencies, not least because different standards were often applied to public and domestic spaces. As far as public space was concerned, the enthusiasm for lighting was almost infinite. Daniel Roche has shown that leading eighteenth-century French enlighteners and government officials were engaged in fierce "battles between light and darkness."[69] One of the front lines was the project to improve and expand street lighting. In France, there were even fantastical plans, inspired by the ancient Pharos of Alexandria, to erect "light-houses" in the principal squares of cities for the purpose of flooding the urban space with light and eliminating darkness.[70]

The idea of turning night into day fascinated eighteenth- and nineteenth-century Europeans.[71] In earlier times, urban space at night was, at best, lit by the fickle flames of torches and portable lanterns. This changed dramatically starting in the eighteenth century, as oil lanterns, permanently installed and unaffected by weather conditions, sprouted up in many European cities. Often funded by monarchs or other aristocratic rulers, street lighting was a prestigious policy project. For centuries, citywide nocturnal illumination had been a spectacle reserved for special ceremonial occasions. Turning such spectacles into a permanent feature cast a positive light, as it were, on the ruler. In Paris, where large-scale street lighting began in the 1660s under Louis XIV, a medallion released on that occasion bore an image of the king on one side and a Latin inscription on the other: *Urbis securitas et nitor* (The City's Security and Beauty). Indeed, beautification of the city was not the only driving factor: well-lit streets were simply safer than dark ones. The desire for safe streets explains why even European cities that did not enjoy royal patronage went to great expense to install street lights.[72] With the beginning of the Industrial Revolution, street lighting also became an issue of increasing economic relevance. Thanks to the permanent availability of artificial light, nightfall did not impede industrial mass production: with illuminated factories and streets, production and transportation were possible around the clock.[73]

The Enlightenment enthusiasm for light went hand in hand with the rise of transparency as a politico-philosophical concept. Of course, transparency as a material experience was not new. Transparent or nearly transparent glass had been produced for centuries; but, as we have seen, it was used primarily for the manufacture of small vessels, and the symbolic connotations were, up to the eighteenth century, largely religious. In medieval and early modern art, transparent goblets and cups were often associated with spiritual purity and thus considered symbols of the Virgin Mary. They could also denote the fragility and transience of worldly things, as attested by the frequent appearance of delicate transparent vessels in *vanitas* still lifes.[74]

In the Age of Enlightenment, transparency took on a broader and certainly more secular meaning. Architectural change—especially the taste for oversized windows and large, clear panes—played a key role in this process. In an unprecedented way, this new type of window allowed residents to experience (the illusion of) seamless continuity between interior and exterior space. This experience was a source of delight for many late seventeenth- and eighteenth-century people, especially when it involved garden views. Leading garden designers such as the seventeenth-century Englishman John Worlidge praised the idea of having a garden with a "small Edifice, usually term'd a Pleasure-house," with its windows and doors "glazed with the best and most transparent Glass, to represent every Object through it the more splendid."[75] As Richard Sennett has summarized, what eighteenth-century upper classes liked to see from their windows was "an exemplary scene" in which "the viewer had aided the landscape to be more of itself."[76]

The idea of maximum visual permeability between home and nature also intrigued Jean-Jacques Rousseau, the champion of the credo later proverbialized (and trivialized) as "back to nature." As Rousseau scholarship has demonstrated, the desire "to preserve or restore a compromised state of transparency" forms a common thread in his philosophical and literary œuvre.[77] For Rousseau, transparency was an intrinsically good quality; like glass, he claimed, his heart was "incapable of ever being able to hide anything that was going on in it."[78] Elsewhere in his *Confessions*, Rousseau declared, "In the whole course of my life one has seen that my heart, transparent as crystal, has never been able to hide for an entire minute a slightly lively feeling that has taken refuge in it."[79]

These invocations of transparency were not mere rhetorical tropes. Quite the contrary, Rousseau had a profound understanding of transparency's material manifestations. Indeed, his reference to "crystal" implies not only transparent minerals, but also man-made crystal glass, a prized commodity at the time. Rousseau scholars have paid little attention to the fact that the philosopher was well informed about the glass industry and its operations: in his *Institutions chimiques* (Chemical Institutions)—a didactical treatise written in the 1740s, but unpublished during his lifetime—Rousseau discussed glassmaking in great detail and included an entire chapter titled "*De la vitrification*" (that is, "On Glassmaking").[80] In this context, he elaborated on the subject of "crystal glass" (*cristal*), highlighting its advantages over "common glass" (*verre commun*).[81] Rousseau concluded that transparency was a key criterion for the quality of glass: "In general, almost all use of glass in practical chemistry, in society and in the arts, is based on transparency."[82]

For Rousseau, then, transparency was more than just a material or aesthetic quality. It served as a model for how to conceptualize interpersonal relations in society. This social transparency, Rousseau hoped, would find expression in an architecture that emphasized visual permeability between interior and exterior. In his popular novel *Julie, ou la nouvelle Héloïse* (Julie, or the New Heloise, 1761), Rousseau declared programmatically: "The first step toward vice is to go about innocent actions in a mysterious manner, and whoever likes secrecy sooner or later has reason to be secretive. A single precept of morality can do for all the others, it is this: Never do or say anything that thou dost not wish everyone to see and hear; and for my part, I have always regarded as the worthiest of men that Roman who wanted his house to be built in such a way that whatever occurred within could be seen."[83] Rousseau's vision of a society in which transparency constituted a key "precept of morality" aligned well with the Enlightenment belief in openness and publicity as social virtues. Immanuel Kant—a close reader of Rousseau—provided the classic formula in his famous essay "What Is Enlightenment?" (1784), calling on each individual to "make public use of his reason in all matters."[84] True, Kant did not explicitly speak of "transparency" in this context, but the term he used—"publicity" (*Publizität*)—was closely linked to contemporary discourses about transparency.[85]

In his 1795 essay "Perpetual Peace," Kant provided a concrete example of what institutional transparency should entail: the inadmissibility of secret treaties.[86] For some Enlightenment sympathizers, however, this was not enough. They interpreted Rousseau's vision of a transparent society as a call for radical political action. This holds particularly true for leading protagonists of the French Revolution who—as Lynn Hunt has observed—propagated "the revolutionary belief in the possibility and desirability of 'transparency' between citizen and citizen, between the citizens and their government, between the individual and the general will."[87] Tellingly, Rousseau's remarks about transparency as a virtue were invoked in May 1789, on the eve of the French Revolution: in the meeting of the French Estates General, the philosopher's vision was explicitly cited as a model for a future national assembly that would ban all secret deliberation and commit to a maximum of openness and transparency (including in terms of architecture).[88] However, as the revolution took a radical turn in the 1790s, the call for institutional and social transparency revealed its dark side: a regime of surveillance and mistrust. Citizens who were thought to be insufficiently transparent or who were suspected of harboring anti-revolutionary ideas had to endure house searches euphemistically known as "domiciliary visits."[89] Forced entry of this kind was the most blatant—and most brutal—way to "open up" private homes to public oversight and to achieve, in a perverted application of Rousseau's words, a state where "whatever occurred within could be seen."

Despite the revolutionary excesses, the enlightened taste for transparency remained strong, on both a metaphorical and architectural level. Daring visions of lavishly glazed, light-flooded buildings continued to intrigue enlighteners. This fascination with transparency even extended to sepulchral designs. Around 1800, Pierre Giraud, a French prison architect and supporter of the revolution, proposed a cemetery design in which the remains of the virtuous dead would be displayed in imperishable urns made of transparent glass. Drawing on alchemical theory, Giraud even sought ways to transmute human remains into transparent glass (an idea that had intrigued Rousseau as well). In Giraud's words, "the mere view" of these dead worthies—that is, of their vitrified remains enshrined in glass—would impress visitors with awe and keep them away from the "route of crime and even of dissipation."[90] Alternatively, the vitreous urns could be claimed by the families and displayed at home to inspire future generations.[91] By contrast, "degenerate beings" faced a miserable afterlife in Giraud's ambitious project: they were doomed to have the "honors of vitrification denied."[92] Instead, their remains would be incinerated in a large cauldron and then buried in a mass grave.[93]

Today, we are likely to find Giraud's vision rather unsettling—not least because the twentieth century has demonstrated that mass burials of the dead are often preceded by inhumane conduct toward the living. In general, the Enlightenment belief in the morally elevating effects of transparency might seem rather naïve or even disturbing to us. True, there may have been noble intentions behind the idealization of transparency. But the practical application of this ideal often revealed an uncanny dimension: the invocation of transparency as a model for social relations and institutional design could easily slip into fantasies about power, control, and surveillance.

Architecture was one area where this ambiguity of transparency became particularly manifest. Of course, fantasies about completely glazed spaces and unlimited visibility existed in earlier periods of history. But given technical constraints, such visions were merely utopian before the dawn of the modern era. In the premodern world, a totally transparent space was conceivable in only one realm—the celestial realm of God.[94] Jewish tradition, for instance, held that the walls of Paradise were made entirely of glass or other crystalline matter.[95] Similar ideas were popular in medieval Islamic theology and literature. The tenth-century Islamic scholar Abu Mansur related that King Solomon, with the help of *jinn*, built a "city or palace of crystal a hundred thousand fathoms in extent and a thousand storeys high, of solid foundations but with a dome airy and lighter than water; the whole to be transparent so that the light of the sun and the moon may penetrate its walls."[96] According to the fourteenth-century historian Al-Nuwayrī, King Solomon also built a palace of justice made entirely of crystal (again, aided by jinn).[97]

In Christian Europe, leading theologians such as Saint Augustine argued that heaven and earth were separated by a stratum of perfectly clear rock crystal.[98] This idea originated in ancient Greek cosmology, but Christian theologians preferred to bolster it with references from the Bible. The Book of Job, for example, relates that the sky is "as a molten looking glass" (37:18). Vitreous imagery of this kind also informs the Book of Revelation (4:6), where the heavenly throne is described as follows: "And before the throne there was a sea of glass like unto crystal: and in the midst of the throne, and round about the throne, were four beasts full of eyes before and behind."[99] Such accounts of a crystalline celestial sphere left an imprint on both the popular imagination and literary visions of heaven. As Milton put it in *Paradise Lost*: "And God made / the firmament, expanse of liquid, pure, transparent, elemental air."[100]

God's omnispective rule—that is, his ability to see everything through the celestial "sea of glass"—made heaven, as it were, a panopticon. In other words, panopticism was imagined as a divine privilege. Only in the eighteenth century did the idea arise of building real structures based on the same principle. Tellingly, the very word "panopticism" did not come into use before this time.[101] No one did more to popularize the term than the English philosopher and social reformer Jeremy Bentham, who used it in the title of a famous treatise first published in 1791. Indebted to Enlightenment rhetoric and driven by unbridled belief in progress, Bentham argued that most moral and economic problems of his time could be remedied "by a simple idea in Architecture": the eponymous Panopticon (fig. 10.7). Bentham illustrated this in the context of penitentiary architecture, describing the Panopticon as a circular building in which the "apartments of the inmates occupy the circumference."[102] The inmates, kept in cells with iron gratings, would be in full view of a guard stationed in a central "inspector's lodge." The Panopticon depended on a maximum of architectural transparency to achieve permanent surveillance: glass windows, iron gratings, and the arrangement of the cells and the inspector's lodge ensured complete visibility—and, by extension, a "new mode of obtaining power of mind over mind," in Bentham's chilling words.[103]

In Bentham's original plan, the windows of the central lodge were supposed to be fully glazed and covered by blinds, to provide the inspector with "the unbounded faculty of seeing without being seen."[104] As Foucault has noted in his seminal study of the "birth of the prison," the "panoptic mechanism arranges spatial unities that make it possible to see constantly and to recognize immediately."[105] In the Panopticon, "visibility is a trap": the inspector takes full advantage of the glass windows' transparency, but the blinds conceal him from the eyes of the inmates.[106] Bentham envisioned this one-way transparency as the key mechanism

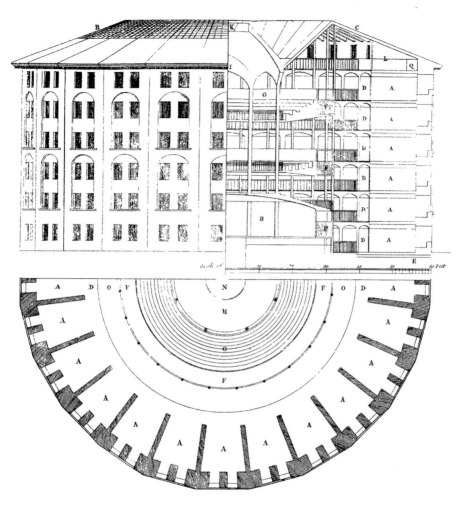

Fig. 10.7. Ground plan and elevation of Jeremy Bentham's Panopticon, 1791. Bentham strongly believed that a wide range of public institutions—from prisons and hospitals to schools—would benefit from this "simple idea in Architecture." The copious use of glass played a key role in Bentham's design and in his chilling project of "obtaining power of mind over mind." The central inspector's lodge was supposed to be "almost all window." This was in line with Bentham's general vision: "Give me as much window as possible."

behind the operation of the Panopticon. He emphasized that the inspector's lodge should be "almost all window." He even contemplated covering the observation platform with a glass "sky-light," as this "might add to the convenience of the lodge."[107]

Bentham was, in general, deeply fascinated by the possibilities that glass offered for surveillance and social engineering. "Give me as much window as possible," he demanded in a postscript to the Panopticon treatise.[108] Indeed, he suggested that "the walls of the building, exterior as well as interior, [be] made as transparent (with windows) as possible," because "the more perfect the application made of the characteristic principle, the less the quantity of strength that will be necessary (both of eyes and hands) in the lodge."[109] As these remarks underscore, transparency was not merely a technical feature of the Panopticon—it was the "characteristic principle" of the whole plan. Bentham summarized, "My prison is transparent: my management no less so."[110] For precisely this reason, the Panopticon was meant to be open and, in more than one sense, fully transparent to visitors. Bentham believed that only such public accountability would ensure the orderly operation of the institution. The incentive for the visitors lay in the voyeuristic opportunity to watch the prisoners through the glass panes of the lodge. The Panopticon would serve as "a spectacle, such as all persons of all classes would, in the way of amusement, be curious to partake of . . . providing thereby a system of inspection, universal, free, and gratuitous, the most effectual and permanent of all securities against abuse."[111]

Such architectural schemes were, of course, easier to draft than to put into practice, as Bentham himself learned the hard way. Despite parliamentary support and Bentham's own fierce advocacy, the Panopticon was not realized in England in his lifetime. Only in the nineteenth century did authorities around the globe—including in the United States—begin to build penitentiaries based on ideas taken from Bentham's treatise. Some prison reformers praised panoptic designs as key to reforming the penitentiary system. In a treatise published in 1840, the French prison architect Nicolas-Philippe Harou-Romain proposed to "place the prisoners in rooms that are *transparent* [*logements transparents*] and that are entirely open onto the galleries; this is to ensure that none of their actions will escape surveillance."[112] This scheme was unmistakably indebted to Bentham, but it also came full circle to Rousseau: Harou-Romain cited the same Plutarch account of a glass house (*la maison de verre du philosophe grec*) that had served as the starting point for Rousseau's praise of architectural transparency. While Rousseau argued that a glass house was the ideal domestic setting for a righteous man, Harou-Romain recommended it as a means of enforcing morality among people who had strayed from the right path: "The sage desired it [the glass house] because none of his actions necessitated the veil of walls: the prisoner, by contrast, lives in it because we do not want him to get used to doing bad things behind the walls; instead, he should get used to doing nothing that could make him fear the view from the outside."[113]

The call for architectural transparency also informed plans for other regimented institutions such as hospitals, workhouses, and schools.[114] Identifying "panopticism" as a major force behind the birth of a "disciplinary society," Foucault noted that "the old simple schema of confinement and enclosure—thick walls, a heavy gate that prevents entering or leaving—began to be replaced by the calculation of openings, of filled and empty spaces, passages and transparencies."[115] Bentham would not have disagreed: he firmly believed in the soundness of his design and enthusiastically recommended the "inspection principle" as a model for other building types, including factories and government buildings.[116] He also acknowledged his sources of inspiration, including the French École Militaire, built in Paris in the mid-eighteenth century.[117] The école systematically employed architectural transparency to enforce discipline—for instance, by ensuring that all corridors and cells lay open to the gaze of school officials. As one of the école's planners put it, the design entailed that "a window be placed on the corridor wall of each room from chest-level to within one or two feet of the ceiling. Not only is it pleasant to have such windows, but one would venture to say that it is useful, in several respects, not to mention the disciplinary reasons that may determine this arrangement."[118]

Bentham considered schools and other educational institutions to be good candidates for panoptical designs. But he was scrupulous (or realistic) enough to concede that "gratings, bars, and bolts, and every circumstance from which an inspection-house can derive a terrific character, have nothing to do here [in institutions of learning]."[119] Such qualifications aside, Bentham insisted that transparency was key to the proper operation of almost every kind of public institution. He was particularly eager to establish transparency as the guiding design principle in government architecture. Bentham felt that the spaces of political decision-making, such as the offices of government ministers, should be fitted with extra-large windows to achieve utmost architectural—and, by extension, institutional—transparency. In his view, architectural transparency and good governance were inextricably linked (a belief that has continued to be remarkably resilient, despite all criticism).[120] Maximal architectural transparency corresponded to the oath that Bentham wanted all legislators to take: "My endeavours shall be constantly directed to the giving to them the greatest degree of *transparency*, and thence of simplicity, possible."[121]

The enthusiasm that Bentham and other enlightened reformers had for architectural glass was tied to the idea that transparency would usher in an age of social, political, and philosophical reform. As Henri Lefebvre has noted, "This illusion of transparency goes hand in hand with a view of space as innocent, as free of traps or secret places. Anything hidden or dissimulated—and hence dangerous—is antagonistic to transparency, under whose reign everything can be taken in by a single glance from that mental eye which illuminates whatever it contemplates."[122] For Lefebvre, the driving force behind this attitude was "philosophical idealism."[123] But it would be more precise to identify the enthusiasm for transparency as a distinctive Enlightenment phenomenon—one that was entirely in line with the enlighteners' goal of fighting obscurantism and bringing light to the (supposedly) dark areas of society.[124]

Indeed, the Age of Enlightenment profoundly affected the way in which darkness was conceived. In previous periods of history, darkness was first and foremost a practical problem—an obstacle to the conduct of certain domestic and professional activities. The night was also bound up with natural and supernatural danger, as reflected by a host of apotropaic beliefs. These traditions were still alive in the eighteenth century, but more than ever, darkness was then associated with cultural backwardness and social inferiority. Indeed, darkness came to be seen as a wholly undesirable and morally problematic state. In an age in which abundant light signified political power (as it did in Versailles) as well as progress and morality (as it did for the enlighteners), it is not surprising that elites mocked villagers because "their houses are dark, more suitable as dungeons for criminals than as homes for free men."[125] These were the words of a Frenchman, but the same discourse existed elsewhere in Enlightenment Europe. Thus, a Dutch writer declared: "Formerly, painted glass was used stupidly and unnecessarily, and most glass windows of churches and houses were so stained that one couldn't see daylight. . . . Our estimation which loves light will never desire to live in the dark, or on a clear day by candlelight, as one must do in many houses."[126] Capturing the same sentiment of superiority, a Swiss savant who had moved to England wrote around 1700:

> When I compare the Modern English Way of Building with the old Way, I cannot but wonder at the Genius of old Times. . . . Of old, they used to dwell in Houses, most of them with a blind Stair-case, low Cielings [sic], and dark Windows; the Rooms built at random, often with Steps from one another. So that one would think the Men of former Ages were afraid of Light and good Air; or loved to play at Hide and Seek. Whereas the Genius of our time is altogether for lightsom Stair-Cases, fine Sash-Windows, and lofty Ceilings.[127]

Glassmakers, of course, had a vested economic interest in supporting the "battle" against darkness. As Roger North noted sarcastically in the late 1690s, "One might know by the visage of the citty houses in the chief streets, of what calling the chief contriver was," as a building "full of windoe, with much glass in compass" indicated that a glassmaker had been overly involved in the design.[128] Some glassmakers went so far as to praise their products as an indispensable, civilizing amenity. In 1744, the glassmakers of Franche-Comté boldly declared, "Without glass, one would still be required to use paper for windows and to live like in prison, without the light of our homes."[129] Of course, self-congratulatory rhetoric of this kind ignored the fact that not all contemporaries actually wanted to live in light-flooded domestic spaces (as we shall see in the next chapter).

In public space, the ideal of transparency and light prevailed. Naturally, this also had consequences for the architecture of power. Medieval and early modern government chambers and courtrooms often featured stained glass, but this tradition of secular polychrome glass declined in the seventeenth and eighteenth centuries, giving way to the idea that good political and legal decision-making required more light—that is, more neutral light or, as some contemporaries called it, "absolute light."[130] Consider the solemn words with which Samuel Sewall, the chief justice of the Massachusetts Bay Colony, described the installation of large glass windows in Boston's new courthouse (now known as the Old State House) in 1713: "May the Judges always discern the Right, and dispense Justice with a most stable, permanent Impartiality; Let this large, transparent, costly Glass serve to oblige the Attorneys alway [sic] to set Things in a True light."[131] Sewall, of course, was a deeply religious Puritan whose praise of untainted light was suffused with Protestant rhetoric. Enlighted thinkers in Europe may not have shared these religious sentiments, but they championed a very similar idiom of pure light. For instance, this desire for unencumbered light underlay the grand projects of Étienne-Louis Boullée, perhaps the most daring of all eighteenth-century French architects. Boullée is best known for his *architecture parlante*, a monumental style that skillfully employed the kinetic and symbolic qualities of natural light. In Boullée's design for a palace of justice—unrealized, as was true of most of his projects—the vast courtrooms were supposed to be lit dramatically from above, and were to be placed, in a triumphant gesture, above the dark world of a "half-buried podium containing the prisons." The envisioned building would be an "august palace raised on the shadowy lair of crime."[132]

But nowhere did the eighteenth-century campaign against darkness manifest itself more forcefully than in sacred architecture, especially in Catholic churches. The "brightening up" of churches in this period often brought about more change than the havoc wreaked by Protestant iconoclasts in preceding centuries. The intentions, too, differed. As we have seen, the installation of blank glass in sixteenth-century Protestant churches was not driven by the desire for more light (though this was a welcome side effect), but rather by theological opposition to images smacking of "popery" and idolatry. Also, Protestant iconoclasm was a regional rather than pan-European phenomenon. In the Catholic Church, stained glass continued to form an integral part of sacred architecture throughout the sixteenth and seventeenth centuries, and Lutherans, for their part, usually tolerated the presence of stained glass in churches that had come under their control. By the eighteenth century, however, the situation had changed: across the entire confessional spectrum (and across Europe), it became fashionable to "brighten up" church interiors by replacing colored with blank glass.[133] This new attitude is palpable in Johann Georg Krünitz's critique of stained glass: "In former times one used to paint the church windows all over with the result that not enough light entered the church. If the painting of windows had not become so rampant and instead had been used sparingly—for instance, by adding a fine, painted bordure in the window's margins—one could put up with it and leave it as it stands."[134] But since this was not the case, Krünitz and many other contemporaries—especially fellow enlighteners—saw fit to remove stained glass that they considered an obstacle to light and a symbol of an outdated, "obscurantist" religious tradition. The desire for brighter church spaces accompanied the pursuit of a more "rational religion—a religion that would find its ideal architectural idiom in the strict symmetry and "purity" of ancient sacred architecture. Forms and elements derived from the Greek and Roman tradition became common features of eighteenth-century church architecture, striking a deliberate contrast to the medieval ("Gothic") style criticized as anachronistic, cluttered, and somber.[135] The new classicist style was, of course, in many ways an "invented tradition" that adopted only those elements from antiquity that appealed to eighteenth-century taste. Ironically, a faithful imitation of ancient sacred architecture would have run counter to the desire for more light, as the interiors of most Greek and Roman temples were darker than many Gothic churches ever were.

Around 1800, churches across the entire confessional spectrum came to stand "in the service of transparency."[136] To illustrate this aesthetic sea change and its effects, let us take a closer look at the case of France, a country that played a key role in defining architectural fashion at the time. In France, most stained glass survived the Reformation. True, even this predominantly Catholic country saw acts of Protestant iconoclasm and window-smashing in the sixteenth century (for instance, in cities with sizable Huguenot communities such as Amiens, Lyon, and Soissons).[137] But on the whole, the scale of Protestant destruction was far more limited than in other places riven by confessional conflict, such as England or the German lands.

From the late seventeenth century onward, however, attitudes toward stained glass shifted dramatically in France—to the negative. The French author and educator Germain Brice, for instance, in his *Description de Paris* (first published in 1684), described the interior of the medieval church of Saint-Gervais as "dark and very filthy," which he attributed mainly to "the windows painted with ornament and the dirty walls."[138] The art critic Henri Souval, writing in the 1720s, polemicized against medieval stained glass in churches more broadly: "Regarding the windows, they were poorly constructed and fitted with quite thick glass; in addition, they were obscured by badly executed and boldly colored figures, so that one barely saw anything."[139] Critics of stained glass were particularly averse to what they perceived as a lack of light in church interiors. But they also showed little or no appreciation for the aesthetic qualities of this particular genre of medieval art, dismissing figural scenes as clumsy and primitive. In the words of the eighteenth-century savant Jean-Aimar Piganiol de La Force: "The most ancient glass windows . . . are nothing but barbaric with respect to the depictions."[140]

Catholic clergymen did little to preserve the centuries-old stained-glass windows entrusted to them. In fact, a considerable number of clergymen agreed with, or even actively supported, the polemics against stained glass—another indicator of the aesthetic paradigm shift that was underway. Admittedly, there were precedents for this elsewhere in Europe. In late sixteenth-century Lombardy, Carlo Borromeo, the archbishop of Milan, pursued a vision of Counter-Reformation Catholicism that rejected unnecessary or distracting ornamentation. The *Instructiones fabricae et supellectilis ecclesiasticae* (Instructions on Ecclesiastical Building) issued under Borromeo's aegis recommended "transparent glass, not painted in any part or at the most with the image of the saint to whom the church or chapel is dedicated, so that more light can be admitted."[141] Borromeo's prescriptions influenced the design of new churches in his diocese, and with his ecclesiastical visitations, he sought to ensure that older churches, too, complied with the new rules. Thus, the wardens of a late-ancient church in the urban periphery of Milan were told "to install a lantern or four windows in the building to illuminate the church which is very dark."[142] On the whole, however, Lombardy under Borromeo was an exception rather than the rule. Borromeo's vision did not find much support among popes of this period, who considered lavishly decorated church buildings—replete with stained glass—an effective way of fighting Protestantism. Tellingly, it was only in the nineteenth century that Borromeo's prescriptions were incorporated into papal doctrine.[143]

The late papal endorsement of Borromeo's *Instructiones* fits into the general trend we observe: from the eighteenth century onward, stained glass became increasingly unfashionable, even in the Catholic Church. Instead, colorless glass and unencumbered daylight emerged as the new ideal. But the desire for brighter church interiors was not the only reason why the clergy showed little interest in preserving stained glass. There were also pecuniary concerns. For one thing, there was the recurring expense of cleaning: all glass needed to be cleaned periodically, but in the case of stained glass it was particularly important given that polychrome windows admitted less light to begin with. Even eighteenth-century defenders of stained glass conceded that irregular cleaning and insufficient upkeep had made some colored glass "so opaque that it resembles slates or roof tiles more than glass."[144] The other maintenance-related problem was that church windows, without the protection of shutters, regularly suffered damage. Inclement weather and material disintegration were two frequent causes. Other common scenarios that led to breakages included collateral damage from construction work (indeed, many churches, especially cathedrals, were sites of permanent construction or maintenance); drunkards hurling stones or other objects; and children shooting at birds with slingshots or playing ball.[145] Accidents of the latter kind were frequent enough to earn mention in early modern city ordinances, such as those of the English town of Kendal, where, in 1641, the magistrate admonished the burghers that "whosoever do play at the football in the street and break any windows shall forfeit . . . the sum of 12*d* for every time every party, and 3*s* 4*d* for every window by the same broken."[146]

Of course, all of these problems existed long before the eighteenth century. But in earlier times it was easier to repair damaged church windows, as there were enough glaziers and glass painters who had experience with stained glass. The

Church traditionally relied on these skilled craftsmen. Suger—the twelfth-century abbot who oversaw the famous remodeling of the basilica of Saint-Denis—reported how he made prospective arrangements to protect the church's prized windows: "Because the windows are precious—due to the marvelous craftsmanship and the considerable cost of the painted glass and the sapphires—we have appointed a master [glazier] to take care of their protection and repairs."[147] Indeed, in most major churches a specially appointed local glazier was in charge of patching damaged sections; he also cleaned the windows at least once a year.[148]

In the eighteenth century, it became increasingly difficult to ensure regular maintenance: the number of glaziers adept at dealing with stained glass had sharply decreased as a result of dwindling demand. In many places, the production of colored glass—whether pot-metal or enamel-painted glass—had devolved into a niche occupation. As early as 1659, a German writer observed that the once-flourishing métier of glass-painting was in decline: "In this craft there used to be distinguished masters in the German lands, especially in Switzerland. But in our time it has slumped because such paintings take away light from the halls and chambers, thereby causing darkness."[149] The same trend was underway in France, where there were fewer and fewer royal and aristocratic commissions, and where the king and his economic advisors showed little interest in granting or renewing royal privileges for the manufacture of colored window glass. In 1731, when two glassmakers from the Franche-Comté applied for a special concession to produce colored glass, the royal council of trade rejected the request because "colored glass is not used very much today, not even in churches."[150] Less than half a century later, in 1768, there was only one practicing glass painter left in the entire metropolitan area of Paris, and he still had trouble making a living.[151]

Medieval stained-glass windows, assembled from a multitude of pre-colored glass pieces, were considered particularly primitive and archaic. Tellingly, they were also the first to fall victim to the changed aesthetic taste (as early as 1650, in some parts of Europe).[152] Enamel-painted windows survived longer: they were generally considered more acceptable, as their greater degree of naturalism made them resemble other, more familiar genres of two-dimensional painting (such as oil-on-canvas painting). Unlike pot-metal glass production, enamel painting continued to be practiced into the eighteenth century, but with notable concessions to the changed taste: instead of painting entire panes or even just the central sections, it was more common for painters to limit their ornamentations to the margins (for instance, by painting colored bordures). During the first half of the eighteenth century, even this restricted use of color petered out. By the end of the century, many early modern enamel-painted windows met the same fate as medieval stained glass and were removed.[153]

While the eighteenth-century removal of colored glass was driven by motives entirely different from those of sixteenth-century Protestant iconoclasts, the result was largely the same: even in an overwhelmingly Catholic country such as France, church interiors came to resemble those of Protestant churches that had seen the destruction of colored glass during the Reformation era. In France, this eighteenth-century removal of colored glass came to be known by a euphemism: "*mise en blanc*" (whitening).[154]

The challenge and expense of maintenance served as a justification for the mise en blanc, but usually this was just a convenient excuse. Consider the church of Saint-Merri in Paris, where the "whitening" began in 1751 (fig. 10.8). The church officials repeatedly complained about the hassle of cleaning and repairing the medieval stained-glass windows, but instead of addressing these particular problems, they chose a much more radical solution: "The interior of the church was so dirty and dark that it was necessary to scrub and whiten it; it was so dark even during noon time that we were forced to remove the majority of the old glass windows and replace them with new ones."[155] In Saint-Gervais, another venerable Parisian church, the same decision was made in 1772. In this case, storm damage served as a welcome justification.[156]

It is difficult for us to imagine how fundamentally such measures changed the traditional appearance of church interiors. Twentieth-century art historians were able to study this dramatic effect in churches where medieval stained glass was briefly removed for preservation (for example, during World War II) or for restoration purposes. One observer noted: "One was forced to experience how the bright daylight admitted by the glassless openings was so glaring that it was at first impossible to visually grasp the dark church interior."[157] Aside from the effects on the spatial experience, the eighteenth-century removal of colored glass also had dramatic consequences for the perception of artwork in the church. Paintings, frescoes, sculptures—all appeared, as it were, in a new light. For more than a millennium, Christian sacred art had been created for spaces characterized by an artful interplay of shadow and attenuated, colored light. Medieval sacred art was not meant to be exposed to bright, unfiltered daylight—in fact, this often negatively

Fig. 10.8. Church of Saint-Merri, Paris, first half of sixteenth century. This parish church originally featured stained glass. Like many other French churches, it underwent the process of *mise en blanc* ("whitening") in the eighteenth century. In 1751, most of Saint-Merri's stained glass was replaced with blank panes. The picture shows the rather bland result. Church officials justified the replacement by citing the cost of maintaining stained glass, but in reality the measure was part of a paradigm shift in sacred architecture: a greater desire for light and transparency.

affects its visual effect.[158] Problems caused by overly bright lighting haunt the presentation of medieval art in many modern museums.

Of course, many medieval paintings and sculptures would not have survived without the protection offered by museums and private collections, many of which were established in the eighteenth and nineteenth centuries. However, these early efforts at preserving medieval art rarely extended to glass windows. Few private collectors were interested in medieval stained glass. Some church officials took to disassembling the removed windows and selling individual pieces of colored glass to smaller churches that had not yet implemented the mise en blanc, for use in occasional repairs.[159] Eventually, "recycling" gave way to outright disposal. This happened not just in France, but also elsewhere in Europe. The case of Salisbury Cathedral is paradigmatic. When the great English architect Christopher Wren toured the cathedral in 1669, he criticized its stained glass and expressed his conviction that "nothing could add Beauty to Light." He did, however, commend the cathedral's windows for being not as badly "obstructed with many mullions and transoms of Tracery-Work" as was common in the "ill-fashion" of the Middle Ages.[160] A century later, in the 1780s, the stained-glass windows of the cathedral were removed and dumped in the town ditch—with the explicit approval of church officials.[161] A similar indifference to the preservation of stained glass prevailed in the German lands. In the second half of the eighteenth century, a visitor to Freiburg's Minster noted with striking nonchalance that "the colored windows are gradually being removed and replaced with blank panes because they are very somber and heavy and because they make the interior dull."[162] Indeed, there was hardly any opposition to these measures in Germany, as one antiquarian with a rare passion for medieval art bemoaned while on a journey in the 1810s:

> The most splendid glass painting is not any more valuable to the people than a white window; in fact, many actually prefer the latter over the former. Whenever a stained-glass panel (or only parts of it) was damaged by the wind, the entire window was removed; the most magnificent heads and [other] representations did not find mercy; children played with them, they were left in shambles or smashed. This way, one stained-glass panel after the other, one window after the other, was lost.[163]

In France, the destruction of colored glass reached a sad climax during the French Revolution. As we have seen, the revolution went hand in hand with a celebration of transparency as a virtue. But it also unleashed a wave of anti-religious violence, culminating in the replacement of Christianity with the secular "Cult of the Supreme Being." Radical revolutionaries wreaked havoc on medieval stained glass in churches that had survived earlier efforts of mise en blanc. Paris was a special case—but not in any positive way: in the French capital there was not much left for radical revolutionaries to destroy, as the mise en blanc of Parisian churches was far advanced even before the revolution began. Indeed, many Parisian churches today display either no medieval stained glass or only mutilated fragments. There were exceptions to the rule, such as the rose windows of Notre-Dame or some of the famous windows of the Sainte-Chapelle. Their survival owes much to their extraordinary aesthetic quality: even at the height of the French Revolution, such magnificent samples of medieval stained-glass art were considered *mirabilia* worthy of preservation.[164] Most stained-glass windows, however, did not fall into this category, and where they did survive, this was often by sheer chance. Thus, the High Medieval windows of Chartres Cathedral—today widely admired as masterpieces of medieval stained glass—remained intact only because the radical phase of the French Revolution ended abruptly, preventing the revolutionaries from achieving all of their destructive goals. Incidentally, these goals included razing Chartres Cathedral to the ground and building in its stead a neoclassical Temple of Wisdom.[165]

On the whole, such fortuitous cases of preservation cannot distract from the fact that more than two-thirds of the surviving polychrome windows in French churches date to the sixteenth century or later. Considered less "archaic" and "primitive" than their medieval counterparts, these windows were more likely to escape the eighteenth-century mise en blanc.[166] The case of France is not unique. Art historians estimate that in all European countries taken together, only 5 percent of medieval stained glass has survived in situ.[167]

Often enough, modern visitors and worshippers do not notice the scale of the past destruction. Indeed, it is easy to be misled: after all, from the nineteenth century onward, stained glass gradually reappeared in some churches as a result of the so-called Gothic Revival. The origins of the Gothic Revival lie in mid-eighteenth-century England, and for the first few decades it remained a rather small and local movement. Only in the nineteenth century, an age of burgeoning nationalism, did the Gothic Revival gain traction—especially in northern Europe, where medieval architecture was now reclaimed (and misconstrued) as an expression of "original" northern art. This contributed to the rise of neo-Gothic architecture as well as to a new taste for medieval-style stained glass. Some of these nineteenth-century windows were executed with great commitment to historical accuracy, so that most church visitors—then as much as today—would find it difficult to tell apart nineteenth-century creations from medieval originals. This commitment to accuracy, however, does not change the fact that the vast majority of medieval glass was already irrecoverably lost at the time. The sad truth is that the nostalgia for medieval stained glass emerged only after most of it had been destroyed.[168]

II

Too Much Glass

The Genealogy of a

Nineteenth-Century Concern

Chapter-opening image: Detail of Fig. 11.5

The eventual success of glass over other window sealants is often cited as a great achievement of Western culture. In the words of one historian: "It must be reckoned the biggest single improvement in the standard of living that has ever taken place."[1] Elsewhere one can read that "without glass we would have spent much of this millennium living in dimly-lit enclosures."[2] And yet another scholar has argued that "the glass pane brought the definitive and complete solution to a fundamental problem of all architecture, namely, the communication between limited and unlimited space."[3]

These celebratory statements hold up the modern windowpane as the telos of architectural glass. In the same vein, one often sees modern glass equated with transparency. Sometimes the teleology is implicit, as is the case in a recent art-historical study stating that "blank glass *triumphed* over colored glass."[4] Elsewhere in the literature the point is made explicitly: for instance, the noted French historian Robert Mandrou has argued that the shift toward "clear-glass panes" and "rooms with better lighting," together with the invention of the telescope and the refinement of optical lenses, marked a crucial step toward the "promotion of sight, which was obviously closely dependent on the rise of modern science."[5] Citing modernity's taste for light, the American historian Warren Scoville deemed it "only natural that the colored-glass industry declined in importance."[6]

It is true that from the eighteenth century onward, transparent window glass was the norm in European architecture. Some historians even speak of an "age of windows."[7] Larger and cheaper glass windows encouraged ever more ambitious architectural designs. At the same time, a closer look shows that the rise of transparent glass was by no means universally greeted at the time. The enthusiasm for more transparency and light was greatest among social reformers and members of the elite, especially those who promoted enlightened or utilitarian ideas.[8] But there were also those who expressed skepticism. In the second half of the nineteenth century, this skepticism grew into a significant stream of opposition.

One controversy revolved around sacred architecture—and this brings us back to the contemporaries who criticized the large-scale removal of stained glass from churches. Admittedly, these critics remained a small minority in the eighteenth century, unable to prevent the havoc wreaked on medieval glass. Still, their arguments deserve attention, as they foreshadowed a critique of transparent glass that would gain traction in the nineteenth century.

The earliest critics of the destruction of stained glass came from conservative clerical circles and from among the small group of glassmakers still committed to the production of colored glass.[9] Foremost among the latter was Pierre Le Vieil, a descendant of an old glass-painter dynasty from Rouen. His treatise *L'art de la peinture sur verre et de la vitrerie* (The Art of Glass-Painting and Glassmaking, 1774) formed part of the multivolume, encyclopedic *Descriptions des arts et métiers* (Descriptions of the Arts and Trades) commissioned by the Académie Royale des Sciences.[10] Le Vieil seized the opportunity to make a vocal plea for the preservation and study of medieval stained glass, writing: "One says that [stained glass] is an entombed art which is no longer of any interest. . . . But wait! . . . In writing about this art, from whose womb I have been born, my goal is to ensure that posterity will not regret the loss of the knowledge that is still extant."[11] Le Vieil saw the mise en blanc as a crusade against a long religious and artistic tradition. The proponents of the mise en blanc, he noted, sought "a more cheerful light, even in holy buildings in which a somber light used to edify their ancestors and inspire their desire for prayer—a desire which their descendants have now so carelessly traded for a desire to see or to be seen."[12] Le Vieil called for the preservation of historical church windows, but he, too, had priorities: for instance, he paid far less attention to medieval stained glass than to sixteenth-century painted glass windows, which, in his view, represented the "heyday" (*meilleur temps*) of polychrome glass.[13]

Glass-painters and conservative clergymen were not the only opponents of the mise en blanc. One ally was the popular writer and playwright Louis-Sébastien Mercier. Mercier criticized the mise en blanc as a rash process, implemented without consultation with the flock and without respect for what he praised as a longstanding French reverence for stained glass. Tellingly, Mercier believed foreigners—especially Italians—were the masterminds behind the mise en blanc. Their goal, he charged, was to impose a foreign aesthetic on French churches:

> Italians have come and whitened our churches. Why whitening, why substitute the white of plaster for the tint of centuries, that venerable tint which announced and indicated that our ancestors prayed where we are praying now? . . . A tiring illumination [*enluminure*] has destroyed the somber and imposing character of these dark and holy spaces. One is no longer in a temple where mysterious shades inspire the soul to lift itself onto the wings of meditation; instead one finds oneself in an almost profane space where everything is illuminated. . . . No, one will never pray in a new temple with as much fervor as one did in an old one.[14]

Mercier's critique addressed the specific situation in France, but similar concerns about "tiring illumination" were raised elsewhere in Europe. The 1788 treatise *Untersuchungen über den Charakter der Gebäude* (On the Character of Buildings)— published anonymously, but probably authored by a Prussian government official—pointed out that "there are cases where low lighting can create very pleasant, sometimes even great expectations from a building; and certain characters [of buildings] can only be evoked by means of low lighting."[15] Conversely, the author decried the "miserable effect" of a building with too many windows, or windows that were too large: "In such a case, we immediately see the size and number of rooms, and the building itself is almost transparent [*durchsichtig*]. Yet even a fairy-tale castle built of rock crystal would hardly intrigue us for too long."[16] The author concluded that "if one wants to give a building a great and noble appearance, there is nothing worse one can do but to construct many large windows; for this reason alone, one should never take the amount of available light as the only yardstick."[17]

Writing around the same time in England, Edmund Burke concurred that too much light spoiled the dignified character of a great building. Burke, a political conservative and professed critic of the Enlightenment, maintained that "all edifices calculated to produce an idea of the sublime, ought to be rather dark and gloomy."[18] But Burke drew a fine line between "sublime" and "terrible" darkness.[19] As he explained, "To make any thing very terrible, obscurity seems in general to be necessary"—an inclination he attributed to "uncivilized" societies: "Those despotic governments, which are founded on the passions of men, and principally upon the passion of fear, keep their chief as much as may be from the public eye. The policy has been the same in many cases of religion. Almost all the heathen temples were dark. Even in the barbarous temples of the Americans at this day, they keep their idol in a dark part of the hut, which is consecrated to his worship."[20] Burke concluded that European architects should choose the middle ground and pursue "well managed darkness."[21] How exactly Burke envisioned this "management of light," and whether his vision involved stained glass, remains unclear.[22]

Leaving such philosophical concerns aside, there was also a pragmatic critique of excessive fenestration. For instance, some contemporaries argued that oversized windows violated canonical rules of architectural symmetry and proportion. As we have seen, Renaissance architectural theory held that windows should not exceed a certain amount of wall space. Structural considerations played a role here, but the building's visual appearance was an even greater concern. After all, the *façade*—a term originating in Renaissance architectural theory—was often explicitly likened to the human *face*. This analogy was more than a mere play on two etymologically related words. It also had prescriptive force: if beauty was the goal, the individual elements of a façade, like those of the face, had to follow certain rules of harmony and symmetry.[23]

Oversized windows were in conflict with this tradition. Writing in the 1690s, the Englishman Roger North sided with tradition in insisting that "aperture is onely [*sic*] for use, and if there be more than the nature of the building declares needful, it is a foolish superfetation."[24] In line with Renaissance architectural theory, North emphasized that the human body provided the yardstick for the right proportions: "Some things will hold proportion with the bodys of men, and not the grandure of a fabrick, and of that sort is lights. For howsoever great an house is, the windoes must not exceed 4½ or 5 foot wide. Else it is a breach and not a windoe." Only for public buildings did North make an exception to this rule: "In publik building, where the windoes are to light the space, and not to be accessible, as in churches, windows hold proportion with the fabrick."[25] But even so, North felt it was better to err on the side of moderation. Thus, he criticized the "extream in our plaister churches in London, where the white walls and much windoe, makes it a pain to sit in them." In his opinion, medieval stained glass "made the light moderate and solemne; but our churches are for light like amphitheaters built abroad."[26] The taste for large windows in domestic architecture was an even greater concern. North reserved his harshest criticism for residences that were "like a bird cage, all windoe."[27]

The financial cost of glazing was another source of concern. The great English philosopher and politician Francis Bacon, a contemporary of Elizabethan "prodigy houses" such as Hardwick Hall, had his share of personal experience with the difficulty and cost of maintaining buildings with too many windows. In Thornage Hall, a stately Norfolk residence that Bacon inherited from his father, the rooms intended for general use were all furnished with blank glass. However, an inventory from Bacon's lifetime indicates that thirty panes in the hall were completely damaged, and the windows in the long gallery were "much broken." In other rooms, the windows were "much decayed." Only the chapel's windows were still intact.[28] The hassle of keeping up a generously fenestrated residence seems to resonate in the sarcastic lines of Bacon's essay "Of Building": "You shall have sometimes fair houses so full of glass, that one cannot tell where to become to be out of the sun or cold." In the same vein, he cautioned his readers to limit the number of windows: "Let them be but few, four in the court, on the sides only."[29]

Bacon's contemporary, the diplomat and politician Henry Wotton, struck a similar note in his *Elements of Architecture*, noting, "There is no part of Structure either more expencefull, then windowes; or more ruinous; not only for that vulgar reason, as being exposed to all violence of weather; but because consisting of so different and unsociable pieces, as Wood, Iron, Leade, and Glasse, and those small and weake, they are heavily shaken."[30] In early modern England, the cost of windows was high—and the deforestation crisis in Bacon and Wotton's time aggravated this problem. Indeed, the shortage of wood drove up not only the market price, but also the ecological cost of glass.[31] A royal proclamation of 1615 decried how "the wast [*sic*] of Wood and Timber hath been exceeding great and intollerable by the Glasse-houses and Glass-workes." It mandated the use of coal as fuel, stating in no uncertain terms that "it were the lesse evill to reduce the times unto the ancient manner of drinking in Stone, and of Latice-windowes, then to suffer the losse of such a treasure [that is, the forests]."[32]

In the seventeenth century, windows became even more expensive: in 1696, the English government introduced the "window tax." Except for the cottages of the very poorest, every dwelling with fewer than ten windows was billed two shillings per year; those with ten to twenty windows were charged six shillings; and those with more than twenty windows owed ten shillings.[33] Later, there came the "glass excise," a sales tax introduced in 1746. The excise was tied to weight, which meant that the tax burden was higher on architectural glass than on glass vessels and other small or hollow glass products.[34]

To be sure, neither the window tax nor the glass excise was intended to enforce the architectural moderation recommended by Bacon, Wotton, and other critics of excessive fenestration. More than anything else, these taxes reflected the constant fiscal crisis of the state. It is no fluke that the glass excise increased sevenfold between 1776 and 1808—a time when public debt soared as a result of Britain's involvement in the American War of Independence and the Napoleonic Wars.[35]

The problem of depleted state budgets was not unique to Britain, of course. Early modern governments constantly sought to tap new sources of revenue—and indeed, glass excises were also levied in other European countries. Yet the window tax was unique to Britain for much of the early modern period.[36] When introduced in 1696, it replaced another highly unpopular tax: the "hearth-money." The levy on hearths had long been a thorn in the side for English householders, not least because the tax assessor needed to enter the house to count the number of taxable fireplaces. In theory, the window tax promised to remedy this situation, for it allowed the tax assessor to inspect the house from outside.

In practice, however, the window tax quickly gained a reputation as the epitome of unfair and even pernicious taxation. True, for the upper classes the financial burden was manageable, and indeed the window tax did not end ostentatious fenestration in the homes of the well-off. But among the lower classes the tax burden was acutely felt, and it prompted a number of householders to brick up windows. "It is a dreadful thing to pay as we do," exclaims a landlady in Henry Fielding's novel *Tom Jones*. "Why now, there is above forty shillings for window-lights, and yet we have stopped up all we could; we have almost blinded the house, I am sure."[37] The bricking up of windows reduced tax liability, but it also decreased quality of life.[38] Some critics charged that the window tax was to blame for light-deficiency diseases among the lower classes. Indeed, rickets was sometimes referred to as the "*mal anglais*" (the English disease).[39]

Of course, neither Bacon nor Wotton knew about the window tax or the glass excise, as both levies came into effect only after their time. What united both men was a more traditional concern—that glass windows, where used excessively, were not only aesthetically extravagant, but also morally questionable. Not that Bacon and Wotton were proponents of austerity in architecture: Wotton, for one, acknowledged that "a Franke Light, can misbecome noe Aedifice whatsoever." Still, he exhorted his readers to "take heede to make a House (though but for civill use) all Eyes, like Argus; which in Northern Climes would be too cold, [i]n Southern, too hot."[40] Bacon for his part emphasized that a gentlemanly residence should display magnificence—but he dismissed oversized windows as vain ostentation.[41]

This moral critique of glass had roots in medieval times. Precisely because glass was a fragile, precious material, it often served as a foil for moralistic reflections about the vanity of worldly goods. Consider the popular moralistic treatise *Ars moriendi* (The Art of Dying), published in several editions and languages in the late fifteenth century. In one episode describing "The Temptation to Avarice," devilish creatures try to distract Moriens (the Dying Man) by making him worry about his worldly goods. Tellingly, his handsome house features glass windows. This detail underscores his wealth, but it also reinforces a general message: a good

Fig. 11.1. Detail of Matthias Grünewald, Isenheim Altarpiece, 1512–16. Musée Unterlinden, Colmar, France.

Christian should not concern himself with worldly and transient possessions, but rather with salvation.[42] Indeed, for all their material value and beauty, glass windows give only an illusion of protection.

A similar spirit pervades Matthias Grünewald's famous Isenheim Altarpiece (1512–16), where the devil effortlessly breaks the glass window of Saint Anthony's study, ready to tempt and torment the saint (fig. 11.1). An ink drawing by the late sixteenth-century Swiss artist Daniel Lindtmayer makes it even clearer that glass windows provide only relative protection: in this scene, Death has climbed through the glass window of a workshop and is about to take the life of a glazier engrossed in the production of his worldly products (fig. 11.2).

Fig. 11.2. Daniel Lindtmayer, *Death and the Glazier*, 1592. Pen and ink on paper. Niedersächsische Staats- und Universitätsbibliothek Göttingen. This preparatory drawing for an (unexecuted) glass roundel forms part of a Dance of Death cycle. The moralistic message is clear and in line with a long tradition: neither the glassmaker nor his worldly products will survive the course of time. The somber scene foreshadowed, as it were, the artist's own fate: the Swiss artist Lindtmayer came from an old glassmaking family but died impoverished and was soon forgotten.

Moralistic warnings about the fragility of glass were not limited to theological discourses. For instance, the sixteenth-century Italian metallurgist and glass connoisseur Vannoccio Biringuccio noted, "Considering its brief and short life, owing to its brittleness, [glass] cannot and must not be given too much love, and it must be used and kept in mind as an example of the life of man and of the things of the world which, though beautiful, are transitory and frail."[43] In even starker terms, the seventeenth-century German poet Andreas Gryphius reminded his readers that human life is just as fragile as glass, and that death is inevitable:

"Strength does not help here—you are glass."[44] Similar admonitions recurred in emblem books, a popular genre of moralistic literature. Consider the *Thesaurus philopoliticus*, a seventeenth-century emblem book that combined moral maxims with (more or less unrelated) views of major European cities. In one example— the view of Erfurt in Germany—we see a house in the foreground with glass panes damaged by a tempest, and the accompanying "inscription" (as the caption was called at the time) reads: *Vitrea Fortuna est, cum splendet frangitur illa* (Luck is like glass—just when it glitters, it is smashed) (fig. 11.3). This point was clearly impor- tant to the book's author, for a slightly rephrased version of this line, adopted from

Fig. 11.3. View of Erfurt from the *Thesaurus philopoliticus* (first published 1623). The fore- ground shows a hailstorm shattering glass windows—an allegorical illustration of the mor- alizing inscription: *Vitrea Fortuna est, cum splendet frangitur illa* (Luck is like glass—just when it glitters, it is smashed). Such warnings about the fragility of glass were common throughout the early modern period and contributed to the critical discourse about ostenta- tious fenestration.

the ancient Roman writer Publilius Syrus, also accompanied the view of the German town of Berncastel.[45]

The moralistic discourse about the vanity of glass lost its force in the eighteenth and nineteenth centuries. To some extent, this may have been due to the emergence of glass insurance. Thanks to this new type of insurance, the installation of large glass windows became a less risky investment. It is certainly no coincidence that glass insurance began to appear precisely when the demand for architectural glass soared: the first glass insurance came on the market in France in 1828, and by the mid-nineteenth century such insurance was available in most European countries.[46]

More than anything else, however, the notion of glass as a luxury waned as a result of the declining cost of glass. Technical progress and increasingly industrialized production methods made window glass ever cheaper, turning it from a costly good into a mass commodity. The rise of glass-casting played an important role in this context: once perfected, the method of casting panes effectively halved production time, compared to glass-blowing, and, unlike glass-blowing, casting could be performed by relatively unskilled workers.[47]

Finally, the improvement of public infrastructure contributed to cheaper prices for glass. The advent of the railway and the ambitious infrastructure projects of nineteenth-century nation-states provided easier and safer means of transporting goods. These improvements were particularly beneficial for the glass industry, as its products were highly fragile. Before the nineteenth century, glass producers had to "price in" the considerable risk of transport-related breakage. The farther away panes were shipped, the higher the risk and, by extension, the higher the price. Tellingly, panes from Normandy cost twice as much in the southern regions of Languedoc and Guyenne as they did in nearby Paris. But even in Paris, transportation-related breakage was a common problem: as late as the eighteenth century, one in four Norman glass panes arrived in the capital broken. This figure rose in the winter and springtime, when roads were particularly rough due to the changing weather conditions. In general, glass manufacturers and merchants preferred to ship their fragile goods over water. That said, roads could not be completely bypassed: after all, many glassworks were not located near rivers, but rather in forested areas, where wood for the furnaces was easy to obtain.

Even manufacturers located close to urban markets were not altogether protected from damage caused by shipping. Take the Manufacture Royale des Glaces de France in Saint-Gobain, a town in the hinterland of Paris. In theory, the company's products had to travel only eighty or so miles to Paris, but in practice, even this relatively short distance was sufficient to cause significant damage to the company's large (and thus particularly fragile) panes. In some years, only twelve out of seventy-two glass plates arrived in Paris intact. The improvement of roads, along with the possibility of railway transportation, greatly reduced such risks—and lower risk, in turn, resulted in lower prices.[48]

Yet falling prices were sometimes canceled out by taxation. This was the case in Britain, where the glass excise kept the cost of window glass artificially high for much of the eighteenth and nineteenth centuries. When the excise was finally repealed in 1845, prices sharply declined and the demand for glass soared.[49] A mere decade later, the *Cyclopaedia of Useful Arts* (1854) observed, "The use of glass in our windows, instead of the louvre-boards of our ancestors, has introduced comfort into the meanest dwelling which previously did not belong to the richest palace."[50] What is more, England now boasted "private houses . . . with single sheets of glass upwards of 20 feet in height and 10 inches width."[51] The 1851 abolition of the window tax (which was replaced by a general house tax) only increased the taste for large windows (fig. 11.4). Writing in 1858, the English architect George Gilbert Scott praised large glass surfaces "as undivided as possible" as "one of the most useful and beautiful inventions of our day."[52]

Soon enough, however, this enthusiasm for generously glazed windows ebbed away in England, and critical attitudes toward excessive fenestration resurfaced. As architectural historian Hentie Louw has noted, from the 1860s onward "a revival of interest occurred in the picturesque effects of the leaded lights and small-paned sashes of the local vernacular styles."[53] A popular English interior decoration guide, published in 1878, remarked that "large sheets of plate-glass have, doubtless, won favor, as affording little or no obstacle to the view," but "they can have no other virtue, for no one could possibly detect properties of beauty in a large sheet of glass."[54] The specter was an "unbroken flood" of light spilling into domestic space. If light was "to be beneficial in our living rooms," it had to be "educated to accord with indoor life."[55] Oscar Wilde struck a similar note in his 1882 lecture "The House Beautiful": "Most modern windows are much too large and glaring, and are made as if you only wanted them to look out of; they annihilate light and let in glare that is destructive to all sense of repose, and by which one cannot write or work or enjoy any comfort. . . . The small, old windows just

A VISION OF THE REPEAL OF THE WINDOW-TAX.

"HOLLO! OLD FELLOW; WE'RE GLAD TO SEE YOU HERE."

let in light enough. If you have big windows in your house, let a portion of them be filled with stained glass."[56] This growing concern about too many—and overly transparent—windows in domestic architecture was not particular to Britain. In continental European homes, too, the wall space occupied by windows declined in the second half of the nineteenth century.[57] As a German treatise on interior decoration from the 1880s noted, "People increasingly felt that all that daylight in the house creates aesthetic problems and that too much brightness can easily turn into banality."[58]

At the same time, the generous use of glass in public buildings continued to enjoy broad support. State officials, planners, and other reformers championed the "enlightenment" rhetoric inherited from the eighteenth century. Large glass surfaces were also considered in tune with the emerging genre of industrial architecture: more light was supposed to create better working conditions and thus increase economic productivity. Tellingly, industrial and commercial spaces were exempt from the window tax not only in Britain, but also in France, which was the only other major European country to adopt the British practice of taxing windows (from 1798 onward).[59]

The result was an increasing divergence between public and private architecture—or, put another way, an architectural dialectic of the Enlightenment: light was idealized as a symbol of progress, particularly in public contexts, but there were concerns, and sometimes even outright anxieties, about overexposure to light in private settings. Even among prominent enlighteners, attitudes toward light at home diverged. The neoclassicist architect William Chambers, an exponent of the "Scottish Enlightenment," noted that in "regions where gloom and clouds prevail eight months of the year, it will always be right to admit a sufficiency of light for these melancholy seasons." But he also cautioned readers to "have recourse to blinds, or shutters, whenever the appearance of the sun renders it too abundant."[60] The anonymous, Enlightenment-minded Prussian who authored the treatise *Untersuchungen über den Charakter der Gebäude* (On the Character of Buildings) likewise considered dim light "very pleasant" in private architecture, and complained about the "miserable effect" of overly large or numerous windows.[61] Yet with respect to monumental architecture, he argued that "a resplendent building [*Prachtgebäude*] needs to be very brightly lit. Therefore you shall give it many and large windows."[62] A similar tension is evident in the writing of his contemporary, the German doctor and polyhistor Johann Georg Krünitz, who argued, "It is an unpleasant thing when a room is like a lantern and open to light from all sides. . . . An outer wall without any or with very few windows is, despite the lack of variety, entirely acceptable, but the abundance of windows . . . is disgusting [*ekelhaft*]."[63]

Concerns about light only grew in the following decades. As the architectural historian Stefan Muthesius has noted, "one of the most astonishing developments" in the second half of the nineteenth century was a "completely new preference for relative darkness" in domestic spaces.[64] But was this preference really "completely new"? There was certainly precedent when it came to health-related anxieties about overexposure to light. Roger North had warned as early as the 1690s that the "mistake of over lighting an house" was "bad for the eyes."[65] A century later, the author of the entry "*Fenêtre*" in the French *Encyclopédie* noted that too much light in one's rooms could severely harm eyesight. Scholars, in particular, were at risk: "They must never work facing the window," he wrote. "Instead they must ensure, first, that the light falls indirectly on their book; and, second, that there is only as much light as is necessary for reading. In this way, they can work as long as they want without harming their health."[66] As a cautionary example, the author mentioned the Chinese, attributing their "half-closed" eye shape to their preference for "large windows" (a reference to the wall-size sliding screens common in traditional Chinese architecture).[67]

Immanuel Kant, for his part, insisted on strict darkness in his bedroom. The eminent German enlightener believed that only complete darkness could provide a healthy sleep environment and prevent the spread of vermin.[68] These and other anxieties about health hazards carried over to the nineteenth century. In the 1880s, a popular guide on interior decoration noted that "some [residents] attenuate the light because they cannot bear it for physical or psychological reasons."[69] Some even worried that the very sight of oversized windows could cause health problems. *Harper's Weekly* reported in the 1860s about a certain Mr. Rogers who fell sick after dining by a large window. The window was glazed, but "such was the force of imagination, that he actually caught a cold."[70] Other writers lamented the fact that "with window glass man leaves his outdoor or semi-outdoor activity and becomes a modern industrial worker or office server." This tendency toward interiority would eventually lead to "muscular degeneration," which "will make its permanent change in the race of to-morrow" and alter "the man of the future . . . just as surely . . . as is the parasite altered by the environment in which it lives."[71] Finally, some critics pointed out that façades with too much glass also had a negative effect on service animals: for instance, the glaring reflection of glass windows startled carriage horses in the street and made them balk.[72]

These concerns were by no means idiosyncratic. In fact, certain professional groups shared the skepticism about too much light. As late as the eighteenth century, some painters and engravers shunned transparent windowpanes in favor of textile and paper sealants, which admitted softer light.[73] Noted architects and architectural writers sympathized. In the 1860s, Richard Lucae, the respected director of the Berlin Bauakademie (Academy of Architecture), decried the effect of having too many front-facing windows in a home, declaring: "Light fills the entire room and illuminates the objects in an almost obtrusive fashion. It does not tolerate a deep shade, and by destroying this contrast, it deprives itself of any poetic effect. Such rooms always have the same conventional smile and therefore lend themselves well to entertaining and showing off, but there is nothing comfortable [*Gemüthliches*] about them."[74] Lateral windows only worsened this effect, in Lucae's view: "In such a room," he argued, "we entirely lose the sense [*Emp-*

findung] that is of utmost importance in a domestic space: the sense of seclusion from the exterior world; indeed, in common parlance such a room is succinctly called a lantern."[75] Around the same time, the widely read architectural writer Jacob von Falke declared: "In our day, thanks to technical perfection, the window has become a hole which lacks any artistic quality whatsoever. . . . It has become one single, large, and sharply delineated mass of light [*Lichtmasse*]—a technical triumph. Still, we are entitled to aesthetic needs and can choose to forgo the celebrated progress. The bright mass of light hurts our eyes; . . . by contrast, what we seek is an attenuated kind of brightness."[76]

In fin-de-siècle England, the architect Baillie Scott offered a similar critique. A proponent of Tudor-style architecture as well as of the Arts and Crafts movement, Scott castigated the type of "modern villa" in which "the windows are almost invariably too large," warning: "Already from the outside we have been made aware of these gashes in the structure which reveal the window arranged, like a shop is, for outside effect. There is the table, with its vase, the lace curtains, and the rest. Inside we are met by a glaring and pitiless light which destroys all sense of repose and shelter. The rain beats in torrents against the glass, and the sun blazes unchecked into the room."[77] Late nineteenth-century critics such as Lucae, Falke, and Scott may not have been aware of it, but their arguments display a remarkable continuity with older discourses about too much light and excessive fenestration. Recall, for instance, Francis Bacon's criticism that in buildings with too many windows one "cannot tell where to become to be out of the sun or cold." And the nineteenth-century dismissal of such buildings as "lanterns" had verbatim precedent in the works of early modern authors.

But there were also new facets to the nineteenth-century critique of excessive fenestration. One such concern was visual privacy. This is not to say that premodern people lacked a sense of privacy. Intrusive views into domestic spaces were no doubt considered a nuisance.[78] The difference was that in premodern times, glass windows did not necessarily expose residents to unwanted gazes. As we have seen, most medieval and early modern glass windows either were colored or lacked the degree of transparency that would have been necessary to see through clearly. As windows became increasingly transparent in the eighteenth and nineteenth centuries, the issue of visual privacy came to the fore.

For aristocrats, the problem was less pressing: their generously glazed palaces were typically surrounded by large gardens inaccessible to the general public.

What is more, a proper aristocratic mansion featured private rooms with limited visual exposure. This, of course, was a luxury that ordinary householders could rarely afford. In the densely built-up cities, it was hard to achieve the spaciousness and compartmentalization that was characteristic of aristocratic residences. Under these circumstances, transparent glass opened up the home to the outside world in unprecedented ways.

Nineteenth-century residents had to learn how to adjust—or resist. As one architectural critic from the 1880s put it, "The more that windows have increased in size, the more transparent the glass and the larger the panes have become, the more necessary it is now to find means to fight against the advantages of this progress [*die errungenen Vortheile zu bekämpfen*]."[79] The most radical option in this struggle was to shun technical progress altogether and to revert to non-transparent window glass. This attitude partly accounts for the revival of opaque panes in late nineteenth-century architecture. In the words of Scott, the vocal proponent of Tudor-inspired architecture: "The beauty of glass depends entirely on its use in small pieces, in a setting which, allowing a slight variation in their planes, will make them sparkle and twinkle. The large sheet, with its blank and vacant stare, should never be used unless under stress of circumstances."[80] In a similar vein, Lucy Orrinsmith, the author of a popular interior decoration manual (1878), recommended glass that was "shaded in green or yellow, and forms a pleasing variation of colour."[81]

It fits into this picture that glass-painting and stained glass became fashionable again in domestic architecture—and not just in Britain, but across the Continent.[82] The Gothic Revival alone does not sufficiently explain this phenomenon. In his *Kunst im Hause* (Art in the House, 1871), Falke pointed out that only colored glass "closes the glaring, gaping hole in the wall; . . . it adds poetry to the room and imbues it with solemnity, thereby removing sobriety and banality."[83] The subsequent editions of Falke's book indicate that the new taste for the old was spreading fast. In the preface to the fifth edition (1883), Falke was pleased to note: "When *Kunst im Hause* first appeared, it would have been futile to say much about glass paintings in our houses. The taste was not yet mature enough to accept such a recommendation. Today things have changed, and this is a sure sign of progress. Especially the most modern, most delicately decorated rooms today demand glass painting, and decorators are pleased and willing to meet this demand."[84]

Even bull's-eye windows became fashionable again. The cheapest product in the medieval market for window glass, bull's-eyes reappeared in nineteenth-century homes—not only out of historical nostalgia, but also because they were thick enough to prevent intrusive gazes.[85] Contemporary observers did not fail to notice this link between the revival of bull's-eyes and heightened concerns about visual privacy.[86]

Residents also experimented with other methods of containing the effects of transparency. One option was to install shutters. However, in an age of transparent glass, the shuttering of windows was a potentially self-defeating measure, as it might only increase curiosity or even arouse suspicions. In his witty novel *Dr. Katzenbergers Badereise* (Dr. Katzenberger's Journey to the Baths, 1809), Jean Paul described the eponymous Doctor Katzenberger as an avid "eavesdropper and peeper" who "declared that the window shutters of ground floors are by far the best opera glasses and hearing devices he knows; and he said, such shutters might fend off thieves, but not the heart. . . . He had never left such window shutters without benefit."[87] Charles Baudelaire, often deemed the quintessential nineteenth-century flâneur, felt similarly drawn to shuttered windows, noting, "Looking from outside into an open window one never sees as much as when one looks through a closed window."[88]

Roller shutters—an innovation based on thin wooden slats held together by cords or chains—were another option for residents. They offered more flexibility than hinged shutters did because the degree of closure could be calibrated.[89] Still, there were downsides: in the words of a nineteenth-century design manual, shutters of this kind had "a stiff, harsh look," while their interior counterparts—known in English as "Venetian blinds"—were "heavy and ugly, and continually out of order."[90]

The easiest solution, then, was to rely on textile curtains, especially those made of gauzy fabric. Indeed, curtains came to enjoy unprecedented popularity in nineteenth-century homes. Here again, the technology was not new: like shutters, curtains had been known for centuries. As we have seen, in the medieval period, it was not uncommon to install heavy curtains *instead* of glass, given that they offered a certain degree of protection from inclement weather and heat loss. The installation of curtains in addition to glass windows was rather uncommon before the fourteenth and fifteenth centuries. Curtains for glass windows—made of fine fabrics and sometimes ornamented with embroidery—were prestige objects afford-able only for members of the upper classes, such as Bess of Hardwick, the aristo-cratic owner of Hardwick Hall, who ordered movable coverlets and "counterpoynt of tapestry" a few years after the completion of her lavishly fenestrated residence.[91]

In southern Europe, even thinner fabrics could be used, given that heat loss was a less pressing concern.[92] In Italy, for instance, curtains served primarily as status symbols, especially if made of delicate materials such as silk. For this rea-son, fine curtains were frequently prohibited under Italian sumptuary laws from this period, which regulated the display of wealth and luxury. In mid-sixteenth-century Venice, the authorities went so far as to ban all types of silk curtains (*panni di seda d'alcuna sorte*), declaring them unnecessary and ostentatious.[93]

In the eighteenth century, the situation began to change. Thermal control and ostentation were no longer the main reasons for the installation of curtains. Instead, curtains increasingly served to regulate lighting levels and ensure visual privacy (fig. 11.5).[94] By the mid-eighteenth century, 81 percent of London homes featured at least one layer of curtains.[95] In Germany, an interior decoration guide from the 1880s noted that "it is the epitome of poverty for a German house if it lacks curtains."[96]

From a practical standpoint, curtains came to function as what modern ar-chitects and interior designers call a "one-way vision screen," enabling residents to see through their windows yet restricting visibility from the outside.[97] As Lucy Orrinsmith noted in her 1878 manual, curtains made of "delicate, soft material, such as white muslin, Tussore silk, or Madras muslin" gave windows a "pleas-ant semi-transparent background."[98] Thanks to mechanical weaving, such fab-rics were cheaper than ever.[99] Still, many nineteenth-century residents went fur-ther and furnished their windows with two (or even more) layers of curtains: one was typically made of a gauzy material, and the other of a heavier fabric. By clos-ing the heavy curtains, residents could achieve total seclusion from daylight and outside gazes.[100]

The nineteenth century, then, was marked by a paradoxical situation: trans-parent glass was cheaper and more common than ever before, but at the same time there was a growing taste for furnishings, such as curtains, that thwarted the effect of vitreous transparency. This paradox was not lost on attentive contemporaries such as the art historian Cornelius Gurlitt, who observed: "The great advantage

Fig. 11.5. The Salon of Baron Jean-Baptiste-Louis Gros. Daguerreotype, ca. 1855. The Metropolitan Museum of Art, New York. A pioneer of photography, Baron Gros's daguerreotype provides a carefully choreographed glimpse into his salon: a nineteenth-century interior of great refinement, yet typical in its heavy reliance on curtains.

provided by large, polished windowpanes is simply eliminated. One can no longer see through them without hindrance, neither from without nor from within. . . . But why, then, does one spend a handsome amount of money on large, crystal-clear glass panes if, at the same time, their effect is cancelled out by the tulle's close meshing and ornamentation?"[101]

Was this observation too sweeping? After all, one could argue that there were exceptions to the rule—and the Netherlands might be the first to come to mind. According to a popular view, Dutch homes have glass windows, but rarely any curtains.[102] Taking cues from Max Weber's influential theory about the links between a specifically Protestant ethic and the "spirit of capitalism," the argument typically goes as follows: in the proto-capitalist, Calvinist Netherlands, people rejected curtains, as they considered a prosperous household to be a sign of divine election and thus worthy of display to neighbors and passersby. In other words, Protestant theology encouraged residents to showcase their homes. This interpretation, however, is both exaggerated and historically inaccurate. While it is true that curtains were relatively rare in twentieth-century Dutch homes, there is no strong evidence to indicate that Dutch people before this period followed the same convention. In fact, in the nineteenth century, curtains seem to have been more common in Protestant areas in the Netherlands than they were in neighboring, predominantly Catholic Belgium. Why and when curtains fell out of favor in Dutch homes is a question still open to further research. In any case, recent studies have shown that "the motivations depicted as Calvinist seem to be a secondary, retrospective explanation for this particular cultural phenomenon."[103]

The Dutch case, then, fits into the general picture. On the one hand, "the idiom of glass had taken over" in nineteenth-century Europe.[104] On the other hand, many people had qualms about or outright trouble adjusting to this new idiom. The ubiquity of curtains in nineteenth-century interiors was symptomatic of these difficulties. Dolf Sternberger has succinctly described the resulting dissonance: "The paradox of the window, the modern, fully transparent window, which both opens up to, and admits, and yet then again locks off the outside, was a constant source of anxiety."[105] According to Sternberger, the history of nineteenth-century domestic architecture is also the history of "troublesome windows."[106]

These concerns hardly disappeared in the twentieth century. Quite the contrary: although the twentieth century saw significant architectural and material innovations in window design, the question of how to manage transparency and ensure visual privacy remained a constant and pressing issue. In a German survey from the 1980s, 70 percent of participants counted curtains among the objects "most important for feeling at home," trailing only indoor plants, and well ahead of TVs—a vivid reminder that curtains have become an almost indispensable feature of the modern home in the "age of windows."[107]

12

Palaces of Glass

Vitreous Visions in an Age of Public Glass

Chapter-opening image: Detail of Fig. 12.5

Attitudes toward architectural glass in the home remained ambivalent throughout the nineteenth century. By contrast, public buildings saw unprecedented architectural experiments with glass. As Isobel Armstrong has noted, "The nineteenth century was the era of public glass," giving rise to public buildings that provided "an environment of mass transparency, never before experienced."[1]

These projects were impressive displays of technical and architectural skills. But they also demonstrated mastery and power in other respects. In the case of Bentham's Panopticon project, the generous use of transparent glass implied total control and power over the inmates. In other architectural contexts, glass demonstrated power over the natural environment. Indeed, some of the earliest glass houses served precisely this purpose: to enshrine nature and allow for enjoyment of it at one's leisure, unencumbered by external factors such as the weather. Glazed greenhouses and winter gardens are a case in point. Any survey of the "era of public glass" must begin with these pioneering building types.

The very term "winter garden" reflects the somewhat paradoxical endeavor to create a natural environment unaffected by the change of seasons.[2] Horticultural glass architecture also engendered other fantasies of power—for instance, the hubristic idea that these encased islands of nature, available year-round, could compensate for the accelerating environmental destruction caused by industrialization and urban growth. Finally, the display of exotic plants demonstrated the colonial power that Europeans wielded across the globe. Greenhouses and winter gardens of this period were "like a museum in which the masterpieces of nature were gathered together, listed in a catalog, and preserved for the future."[3]

The use of glass for horticultural purposes in itself was not new. Two millennia earlier, Romans had constructed small, movable containers to grow cold-sensitive plants. The Roman agricultural writer Columella, active in the middle of the first century, described containers equipped with wheels and "covered with panes of glass [*specularibus*], so that even in cold weather, when the days are clear, they may safely be brought out into the sun." According to Columella, "By this method Tiberius Caesar was supplied with cucumbers during almost the whole year."[4] Even more ambitiously, some Romans built forcing houses that allowed for the year-round cultivation of various fruits and vegetables. The poet Martial, writing in the late first century, complained about having to stay in a cold room at a friend's lavish villa while, in an adjacent part of the building, panes (*specularia*) ensured that the exotic plants housed there did not "lose color in dread of winter," and that "a brisker air [not] bite the tender grove."[5] (Whether these panes were made of glass or lapis remains unclear.) Elsewhere in his *Epigrams*, Martial described the home of an upper-class Roman who had forced "the country inside [his] city mansion," where "the vintage lives enclosed by clear panes."[6]

Roman forcing houses pioneered the principle underlying all subsequent experiments with this building type: the windows—at least the south-facing ones— were sealed with translucent panes that kept out the cold while admitting "clear suns [*sic*] and unadulterated daylight" (Martial's words).[7] Interior temperatures were boosted by burning wood or dried manure in stoves. Of course, this required both staff and a generous budget for constant fuel supply.[8] Some Romans considered such expenses decadent. Seneca, the vocal critic of excessive fenestration, raised the question: "Do not men live contrary to Nature who crave roses in winter, or seek to raise a spring flower like the lily by means of hot-water heaters and artificial changes of temperature?"[9]

Seneca's call for moderation hardly dissuaded upper-class Romans. The eventual decline of Roman horticultural architecture came only with the general demise of Roman civilization in later centuries. In the medieval period that followed, there is no mention of glazed greenhouses. In the early modern period, however, this type of building reemerged. It is no coincidence that this period saw Europe's ascent as a global power: from the fifteenth century onward, the European voyages of discovery and the establishment of colonial trade networks brought a constant stream of new, exotic plants and fruits to Europe. The first greenhouses in post-Roman Europe were closely linked to the process of colonial expansion, as their purpose was to "domesticate" exotic plants such as orange and palm trees.

The desire to cultivate these exotic plants in Europe gave rise to two distinct types of glazed greenhouses: the "orangerie" and the "palm house." Only aristocrats and other exceedingly wealthy individuals could afford to construct and maintain such structures. Indeed, sixteenth- and seventeenth-century greenhouses were typically attached to, and funded by, courts of nobility. Aristocratic patronage also enabled the construction of greenhouses in the botanical gardens at universities such as Pisa (1590), Leiden (1599), Heidelberg (1620), and Altdorf (1635).[10]

The first greenhouses from this period were not completely glazed. Only the side with the greatest sun exposure featured a large glass surface, sometimes

Fig. 12.1. The Orangery, Belton House, Lincolnshire, England, 1820. Designed by Jeffry Wyatville, this orangery exemplifies the new type of glass house that emerged in this period: freestanding, glazed on all sides, and topped with a glass roof. The cutting-edge design relied on cast-iron supports. Unlike later horticultural architects, however, Wyatville went to great lengths to conceal these supports by cladding them with stone.

supplemented by skylights. The other walls were made of either brick or timber.[11] This helped save money on glazing while also limiting the loss of stove-generated heat. In addition, frames with oiled paper were often installed behind the glass to approximate the effect of double-glazing. The concerns about heat retention lost their urgency only in the course of the eighteenth century, as better heating methods and more robust glass plates became affordable.[12]

The more glass they featured, the more popular greenhouses became—not only for horticultural purposes, but also for year-round sociability. Graced with grottoes, fountains, and statues, "greenhouses" became veritable "winter gardens."[13] Horticultural architects enjoyed considerable creative freedom, as their buildings fell outside the traditional architectural canon. Apart from a handful of vague literary mentions of Roman forcing houses, there were no concrete ancient templates on which to draw.[14]

The early nineteenth century also saw the introduction of new, more efficient methods of heating, by means of hot water and steam. This, in turn, made it possible to construct freestanding greenhouses glazed on all sides (fig. 12.1).[15] Yet as the buildings grew in terms of both size and ambition, the question of structural support became more pressing. Traditionally, wooden frames and bars had provided the structural support for skylights and other glazed areas. Timber was cheap, but also prone to deterioration when exposed to high temperatures and humidity.[16] An alternative material, iron, proved far more suitable. It was to revolutionize glass architecture.

The foundations for this revolution were laid in the 1820s, when new casting and rolling methods made the mass production of prefabricated iron supports both easier and cheaper.[17] By the mid-nineteenth century, cast iron had become the most common structural support in glass architecture.[18] The transition to iron—and later steel—opened entirely new architectural possibilities, such as the construction of large-span or even curvilinear glass roofs.[19]

The Jardin d'Hiver in Paris, completed in 1848 and located near the Champs-Élysées, was a pioneering building of this kind. Open to the general public, the garden boasted a length of three hundred feet, but it was even more admired for its almost 130-foot-wide arched glass roof, which relied on cast-iron supports. The Jardin d'Hiver offered much more than its name suggested: far from being a mere "winter garden" with exotic plants, it featured fountains and menageries, as well as cafés, stores, and reading rooms. On special occasions, the garden became a space for concerts or balls, accommodating up to eight thousand people.[20] An article titled "Architecture of the Future," which was published in the leading French architectural journal shortly after the garden's completion, declared: "Glass is destined to play an important role in metal-architecture. In place of thick walls whose solidity and resistance is diminished by a large number of apertures, our houses will be so filled with openings that they will appear diaphanous."[21]

The Jardin d'Hiver drew attention and admiration well beyond France. It inspired, for one, the English gardener and horticultural architect Joseph Paxton, who went on to design the most famous of all nineteenth-century glass houses: the Crystal Palace in London (fig. 12.2).[22] Paxton had made his name as the architect of the Great Conservatory at Chatsworth (1836–40).[23] But the fully glazed Crystal Palace, erected for the 1851 Great Exhibition in London's Hyde Park, was a building of unprecedented ambition. What is more, it was built with an efficiency that is still astonishing.[24] Between July 1850 and February 1851, almost three hundred thousand glass panes were produced for Paxton's project, forming a glazed surface of nine hundred thousand square feet. Thousands of iron joints, with a total weight

Fig. 12.2. John J. E. Mayall, Interior of the Crystal Palace at Hyde Park, London. Daguerreotype, 1851. J. Paul Getty Museum, Los Angeles. As one contemporary visitor noted, the building provided "transparency in all directions."

of 4,500 tons, provided structural stability. With a total length of 1,848 feet and a maximum height of 108 feet, the Crystal Palace dwarfed everything achieved before in the field of glass architecture.[25] As one visitor from the Continent noted, the building provided an experience of "transparency in all directions."[26]

Even contemporaries who were unable to visit the palace were in awe. Reminiscing about his childhood, the nineteenth-century German art historian Julius Lessing recalled the impression that the Crystal Palace made on him: "Such sentiments were registered throughout the world. I myself recall, from my childhood, how the news of the Crystal Palace reached us in Germany, and how pictures of it were hung in the middle-class parlors of distant provincial towns. It seemed then that the world we knew from old fairy tales—of the princess in the glass coffin, of queens and elves dwelling in crystal houses—had come to life."[27] The Crystal Palace was a product of meticulous planning, but it also owed much to felicitous circumstances: the Great Exhibition provided the occasion, and the Crown—especially Prince Consort Albert—was strongly committed to Paxton's daring project. The timing was also favorable in other respects: just a few years earlier, in 1845, the glass excise had been abolished in Britain, clearing the way for projects that otherwise would have been prohibitively costly. Paxton admitted that the repeal of the glass excise "gave an impetus to horticulture which only a short time ago no efforts could have called into action."[28]

Often hailed as a revolutionary building, the Crystal Palace was in many ways indebted to the tradition of horticultural architecture. The palace was, after all, "a direct descendant of the botanical greenhouse."[29] Indeed, Paxton made a number of rather traditional decisions with respect to the technical execution. For instance, he chose to glaze the palace with blown glass plates, which were cheaper and smaller than their cast counterparts—the largest being only four feet long.[30] (For comparison, the exhibition inside the palace boasted an enormous nineteen-by-ten-foot cast plate.)[31] And while iron ensured the building's structural stability, the ridge-and-furrow roof designed by Paxton consisted entirely of timber.[32] Contrary to popular belief, the Crystal Palace was not all iron and glass.

The attention to easy assembly, by contrast, was certainly innovative. When the Great Exhibition ended, the Crystal Palace was dismantled, only to be erected anew (and enlarged) in Sydenham, a suburb of London (fig. 12.3). Paxton's sense of efficiency also showed in the palace's interior design, which maximized floor space.[33] Filled with trees and plants, the Crystal Palace resembled a gigantic win-

Fig. 12.3. Reconstruction (in progress) of the Crystal Palace at Sydenham, London. Silver print, 1854. The Metropolitan Museum of Art, New York. In its reassembled and enlarged version, the Crystal Palace stood on the Sydenham site until it was destroyed by fire in 1936.

ter garden. In its day-to-day operation, both before and after the reconstruction, the palace also served many other ends—for instance, as a concert hall and convention space. In this respect, Paxton's palace epitomized a nineteenth-century tendency: glass houses were no longer merely horticultural structures, but rather became multifunctional spaces. Vast vitreous buildings such as Paris's Jardin d'Hiver and London's Crystal Palace sought to attract large numbers of paying visitors in search of entertainment.[34]

The celebrated contemporary architect Gottfried Semper did not exaggerate when he observed, with respect to the Crystal Palace: "This building is the embodiment of the general direction in which our era is going to move for the time being."[35] Indeed, glass construction emerged as a preferred architectural idiom for new nineteenth-century building types, such as international fair and exhibition spaces, but also train stations.[36] This boom of public glass architecture is amply documented in literary sources and historical photographs. Unfortunately, the buildings themselves have not always survived. Some were destroyed by natural disasters or wars, while others shut down and were dismantled when their continued operation was no longer lucrative. As for Paxton's Crystal Palace, it perished in a fire in 1936. Similar was the fate of the Galerie des Machines, an immense, all-glazed exhibition space erected in Paris for the 1889 Exposition Universelle. Boasting a main span of 370 feet and a length of more than 1,300 feet, the gallery was torn down in 1910 to make space for the redesign of the Champs de Mars.[37]

Certain other glass architecture projects were never realized, but at least they survive in drafts and models. Admirers of Paxton, for instance, sought to erect a one-thousand-foot-high "Prospect Tower," which they envisioned as "an enormous tower of the materials of the glass palace," in the heart of London.[38] Other English cities, such as Manchester, Bath, and Plymouth, contemplated building local versions of Paxton's palace. Some contemporaries even called for a reconstruction of the Crystal Palace over Shakespeare's birthplace in Stratford-upon-Avon.[39]

The nineteenth century also saw grand proposals to cover entire streets and neighborhoods with glass. Hailed as clean and pure, glass seemed an architectural antidote to environmental pollution as well as an aesthetic enhancement of urban space. In 1845, the English entrepreneur Frederick Gye proposed to construct a "glass street" in central London, with a seventy-foot-high roof. This glass-covered promenade would have featured reading rooms, public meeting spaces, concert venues, cafés, shops, and a flower market.[40] The idea was picked up and expanded by Paxton a decade later. In 1855, he proposed the construction of an enormous glass-roofed boulevard in London with stores and an elevated railway. The envisioned length of this "Great Victorian Way" was no less than eleven and a half miles, including three bridges over the Thames. As the *Times* reported, the vitreous loop "would be ventilated and made as perfect, as far as the atmosphere was concerned, as the country itself."[41] A parliamentary committee initially approved the plan, but it was later abandoned when the projected cost soared to thirty-four million pounds.

It proved far easier to realize such ideas on a smaller scale. The arcades— the generously glazed (and often skylighted) shopping passages that sprouted up in many nineteenth-century European cities—are a case in point. The Galerie d'Orléans in Paris, built in 1829 (and destroyed in 1935 as part of urban remodeling), was the first arcade with a completely glazed roof. No less impressive was the Galeries Royales Saint-Hubert (1847), which still stands in the heart of Brussels, featuring three stories under a sixty-foot-high glass roof (fig. 12.4). In Victorian England, too, large cities such as Birmingham, Manchester, and Newcastle built glass arcades. However, the most iconic arcade from this period is the Galleria Vitto-

rio Emanuele II in Milan, which was begun in the 1860s, inspired by the Galerie d'Orléans. Two glass-vaulted streets—approximately six hundred and 350 feet long, respectively—form the core of the galleria, and at their intersection, an imposing glass cupola rises to a height of almost 160 feet (fig. 12.5).

In the late 1880s, in an attempt to outdo Milan, Naples began to construct an even grander arcade: the Galleria Umberto I, crowned by a cupola that is a symbolic ten feet higher than its Milanese counterpart. Around the same time in Paris, the architect Louis-Charles Boileau and the engineer Gustave Eiffel (now primarily remembered for the famous iron tower named after him) joined forces to build the Bon Marché department store, a building featuring extra-large glass panes in unbroken series as well as glass skylights spanning the store's courtyards. By the end of the century, the taste for glass arcades had spread as far as Moscow, where the glass-roofed "Trading Rows"—known today by the Soviet acronym "GUM"—were opened in the 1890s.[42]

Fig. 12.4. Galeries Royales Saint-Hubert, Brussels, opened 1847. The glass-roofed Galeries Royales are among the earliest commercial arcades in Europe.

Fig. 12.5. Galleria Vittorio Emanuele II, Milan, 1865–77. The glass-roofed building is perhaps the most iconic nineteenth-century arcade.

The arcades of this period reflected—and indeed epitomized—a tendency with roots in the eighteenth century: the increasing use of glass in commercial settings. This included the emergence of glazed shop windows. Of course, the custom of displaying merchandise in windows was not new. But before the eighteenth century, shop windows typically featured wooden shutters or iron grilles, which were opened only during business hours. In other words, premodern shop windows were unglazed.[43] In the German lands, this tradition even left traces in the language: the German word for a store is *"Laden,"* a term that originally referred to the wooden shutters (*Fensterladen*) that protected the display window after business hours.[44]

These long-standing architectural conventions began to change in the second half of the eighteenth century. As Wolfgang Schivelbusch has noted, commercial display windows "became a glassed-in stage on which an advertising show was presented."[45] London, one of the foremost commercial cities at the time, is a case in point. In a letter from 1775, the German scientist and enlightener Georg Christoph Lichtenberg described London streets that featured "on both sides high houses with windows made of mirror-quality glass [*Spiegel Glass*]. The lower floors consist of boutiques and seem to be entirely made of glass."[46] Lichtenberg was not alone in these observations. Daniel Defoe had already described this phenomenon a generation earlier—and with a hint of criticism, noting: "That a fine shew of shelves and glass windows should bring customers, that was never made rule in trade till now."[47] The German novelist Sophie von La Roche, too, expressed ambivalent feelings about glazed shop windows, which she first encountered during a visit to London in the 1780s, reporting: "Everything, absolutely everything is on display behind the large plate-glass windows, in such a nice, shiny way, and in such quantities, that one must crave it."[48]

Early glazed shop windows consisted of several medium-sized panes, held together by wooden muntins. By the 1850s, large, cast plates prevailed. As an English observer noted in 1851, stores began to display "an uninterrupted mass of glass from the ceiling to the ground."[49] The same tendency was manifest elsewhere in Europe. In 1850s Paris, the poet Charles Baudelaire, with a mixture of fascination and perplexity, invoked the new "curtains of crystal."[50] In Vienna in the 1860s, a resident who witnessed the construction of the Ringstraße (the famous circular boulevard) recorded the appearance of "display windows made of *one single plate of glass*." He was particularly amazed by the new stores along the Ringstraße: their "shop displays are fairylike, the shop windows are one *Klafter* [ten feet] high and long and *of one single* glass plate. And behind them is an elaborate system of sensory stimuli—. . . there is no alternative, one has to enter."[51]

As such remarks indicate, the response to glazed shop windows oscillated between fascination and skepticism. Some contemporaries flatly opposed what they viewed as the excessive use of glass in commercial settings. For instance, the architectural critic Hans Schliepmann noted in 1901 that the quality of a store was unrelated to its "glass luxury."[52] The term "luxury" was not necessarily exaggerated: after all, some late nineteenth-century department stores featured no fewer than forty large display windows.[53] What is more, shrewd store managers employed professional "window-gawkers"—that is, men and women who were paid to look into the display windows so as to draw the attention of passersby.[54]

Such measures helped to increase sales, yet they also reinforced the impression that shop windows were manipulative and that their sole purpose was to make one "crave" the goods on display (as La Roche had put it). An anonymous newspaper article from 1840s Britain noted, "The beggar in his rags, the street-sweeper bespattered with the mire of the crossings . . . may look, it is true, at the wealth displayed in the windows . . . but they may not enter; they may admire, but they may not touch; and this admiration not infrequently leads to envy and jealousy, and sometimes to a still fiercer feeling."[55] Indeed, retailers had to walk a fine line to entice customers without alienating them. One compromise was to embed the new oversized shop windows in a traditional architectural idiom. Thus, the popular Berlin department store Tietz (1899–1900) featured sixteen extra-large glass windows sized fifty-eight by eighty-six feet, but these windows were reined in by an opulent neo-baroque façade (fig. 12.6).[56]

Stylistic dissonances of this sort were characteristic of nineteenth-century commercial architecture, including in the arcades, which often featured ambitious glass roofs and novel window designs framed by historicist architecture. This dissonance would later become a key subject in Walter Benjamin's *Passagen-Werk* (Arcades Project)—a famous, if unfinished, attempt to take the arcades as a starting point for a cultural history of the nineteenth century. Benjamin was intrigued by the arcades as a cultural phenomenon, but he also sharply criticized what he considered their inherent contradictions, declaring: "Glass before its time, premature iron. In the arcades, both the most brittle and the strongest materials suffered breakage; in a certain sense, they were deflowered. Around the middle of the past century, it was not yet known how to build with glass and iron."[57]

Such criticism aside, nineteenth-century arcades and department stores played an important role for experiments with glass as a construction material. Looking back from the perspective of the mid-twentieth century, the Swiss architectural critic and historian Sigfried Giedion noted: "It was from these store windows that we first learned how to use large glass areas in dwelling houses."[58] What Giedion left unmentioned is that this process was by no means linear. When it came to domestic architecture, advocates of glass faced considerable reluctance and even outright resistance. Writing in 1928, the celebrated American architect Frank Lloyd Wright expressed satisfaction that "crystal plates have generally taken the place of fundamental wall and piers in almost all commercial building." But at the same time Wright admitted that "it is surprising how little this material [glass] has yet modified our sense of architecture beyond the show-windows the shop keeper demands and gets."[59]

Fig. 12.6. Warenhaus Tietz (Tietz department store) at Leipziger Straße, Berlin. Colored postcard, 1900. The Tietz department store, inaugurated 1900, featured extra-large glass windows embedded in a neo-baroque façade. The tension between historicist ornament and the bold use of large glass surfaces is typical of arcades and department stores from this period. Walter Benjamin, who grew up in fin-de-siècle Berlin, argued that at the time, "It was not yet known how to build with glass and iron."

Why these reservations about glass in domestic architecture? As we have seen, nineteenth-century concerns about light, health, and privacy proved hard to dispel. It also did not help that large windows were associated with the architecture of commerce and consumerism.[60] In Germany, the moral unease about commercial glass architecture even left an imprint on the law: window displays had to be covered on Sundays due to religious sensitivities. When the government lifted this blue law shortly before World War I, popular protests ensued.[61]

The critique of commercial glass architecture often drew on the nostalgic notion of a pre-capitalist economy characterized by interpersonal relations (not anonymous displays of goods). In his widely read book *Der Städtebau nach seinen künstlerischen Grundsätzen* (City Building According to Its Artistic Fundamentals, 1889), the Austrian urban theorist Camillo Sitte noted with regret that "the lively activity of merchants and traders has been moved into iron cages and glass market places."[62] For critics of this development, even architectural feats such as Paxton's Crystal Palace were troubling manifestations of a new spirit. Indeed, some dismissed the palace as an enormous waste of money and resources. Others went a step further, casting the building as a dangerous celebration of consumerism and global industrial manufacturing at the expense of local products and workers. Ironically, radical critics from both the left and the right coalesced on this issue. Karl Marx and Friedrich Engels, who lived in England at the time, criticized the Crystal Palace as a modern "pantheon in which the bourgeoisie displays, with proud complacency, the gods that it has made for itself."[63] On the conservative end of the political spectrum, the Tory MP Charles Sibthorpe railed against the Crystal Palace as "that fraud upon the public called a 'Glass House' . . . that accursed building, erected to encourage the foreigner at the expense of the already grievously-distressed English artisan. Would to God—I have often wished it—that a heavy hailstorm or visitation of lightning would put a stop to the further progress of that work."[64] The angry MP and his conservative followers did not change their minds even after the palace proved a great popular success. Quite the contrary, Sibthorpe began to decry the building in an even shriller tone as a place where the poor taste of the masses triumphed. He openly threatened the palace's commissioners:

That miserable Crystal Palace, that wretched place where every species of fraud and immorality will be practised. Let them [the commissioners] beware of man-traps and spring guns. They will have their food robbed—they will have a pie-bald generation, half black and half white; but I can assure them that my arm will be raised to prevent such a violation. They might look for assassinations, for being stabbed in the dark; but careless of that, I am determined to pursue an even, straightforward course, and I would say that my dearest wish is that that confounded building called the Crystal Palace might be dashed to pieces.[65]

Admittedly, few critics were as agitated as Sibthorpe. Semper struck a more moderate tone, paying respect to Paxton's skill as an engineer and architect, while at the same time bemoaning the conceptual hollowness of the "glass covered vacuum."[66] John Ruskin, an admirer of medieval architecture and critic of modern mass culture, voiced similar concerns:

> The quantity of bodily energy which that Crystal Palace expresses is very great. The quantity of thought it expresses is, I suppose, a single and very admirable idea of Mr. Paxton's, probably not brighter than thousands of thoughts which pass through his active and intelligent brain every hour—that it might be possible to build a greenhouse larger than ever a greenhouse was built before. This thought, and some very ordinary algebra, are as much as all that glass can represent of human intellect.[67]

Such criticism may have hurt Paxton, but he did agree with critics that glass should be used sparingly in domestic architecture. Indeed, the residential homes and villas designed by Paxton and other leading glass architects at the time tended to be rather traditional, featuring stone façades and conventional windows.[68] In the same vein, admirers of Paxton's Crystal Palace drew a clear line between public and private architecture, insisting on moderate fenestration in domestic architecture. Richard Lucae, director of Berlin's Bauakademie, praised Paxton's opus magnum as a space where "like in a crystal . . . there is no real inside and outside," and where visitors "are enchanted by its magic, as one would expect in a fairy tale."[69] At the same time, Lucae had no tolerance for residential buildings with oversized windows—a building type which, as we have seen, he mocked as a "lantern." Like most contemporaries, Lucae expected domestic spaces to convey a feeling of "seclusion from the exterior world."[70] Only in the early twentieth century did a new generation of architects begin to challenge this proposition. For this new generation, abundant glass was not a problem; it was the solution.

13

Modernity and the Struggle
for Glass Architecture

What is to come, will be marked by transparency.

—WALTER BENJAMIN,
"The Return of the Flâneur" (1929)

Their outlines softened by distance, the
sky-scrapers raise immense geometrical
façades all of glass, and in them is reflected
the blue glory of the sky. An overwhelming
sensation. Immense but radiant prisms.

—LE CORBUSIER,
The City of To-morrow and Its Planning (1929)

Chapter-opening image: Detail of Fig. 13.3

B enjamin and Le Corbusier's vitreous visions seemed plausible in 1929—at least from a technological and economic perspective.[1] In their own lifetimes, window glass had become more available and more affordable than ever before. As we have seen, a late fifteenth-century German mason would have had to spend a week's salary to buy twenty square feet of window glass, but by the 1930s, a mason's weekly salary could buy two hundred square feet.[2] This unprecedented affordability of window glass owed much to rapid technological progress, especially to automatized methods of mass production.

A particularly important innovation was the Fourcault process, patented in 1904. This method made it possible to "draw" a continuous band of glass by pressing the molten glass vertically through a formed fireclay slot (the so-called debiteuse) and then flattening it with asbestos-covered rollers.[3] The Libbey-Owens process, patented in 1905, was based on a similar principle, but involved horizontal drawing. The resulting glass sheets boasted a width of up to ninety inches and an almost wrinkleless surface. This, in turn, reduced the amount of time needed for grinding and polishing—tasks that, by the 1920s, were also mechanized.[4]

Despite the rise of glass-drawing techniques, casting continued to be practiced. Here, too, there were advances. The traditional seventeenth-century method (of rolling the molten glass into a sheet on a table) was superseded by the Bicheroux process, a method introduced in the early 1920s, which involved flattening the molten glass between two mechanical rollers. The resulting glass plates were smoother and required significantly less post-production grinding.[5]

Unsurprisingly, mechanization and industrial mass production presented a massive challenge for glassblowers (who relied on techniques that went back to Roman times). Indeed, crown-glass production rapidly declined in the twentieth century, as it was no longer efficient or competitive.[6] Cylinder glass—the other traditional type of mouth-blown glass—fared slightly better and survived the advent of the industrial age, but only after significant adjustments: instead of the human lung, it was now a machine—a large, automated air pump—that did the blowing. Consequently, the cylinder's size was no longer restricted by the glassmaker's lung capacity. These machines could blow cylinders with a length of up to fifty feet and a diameter of up to thirty inches; they also handled the subsequent steps, especially the cutting and flattening of the cylinders. Still, mechanically produced cylinder glass failed to be competitive. By the 1930s, casting and drawing had prevailed as the predominant industrial production methods.[7]

The early twentieth century was not just a period of rapid technological innovation. It also saw a widening gulf in the perception of glass architecture. On the one hand, progressive architects hailed the mass production of transparent glass as a breakthrough. Frank Lloyd Wright, for instance, noted enthusiastically in 1928 that "the machine has given to architects, in glass, a new material with which to work."[8] Wright praised glass as a material that was "strictly modern."[9] Similarly, the German modernist architect Arthur Korn proclaimed in 1929, "A new glass age has begun, which is equal in beauty to the old one of Gothic windows."[10] Reinforced-concrete skeletons, in use since the late nineteenth century, encouraged architectural experiments with large glass surfaces and made previously utopian projects feasible.[11] As the Russian avant-garde artist El Lissitzky put it in the 1920s, this was an "age that thirsts after glass, steel, and concrete."[12]

But this enthusiasm was only one side of the story. While glass featured prominently in public architecture, the concerns about its use in private architecture persisted and in some respects increased.[13] Architectural historian John Hix has noted that the "utilitarian and rational use of iron, wood and glass was reserved for industry, transportation and exhibition buildings."[14] Domestic architecture remained largely unaffected by the new possibilities. Most architects accepted this gulf between public and private architecture; some even argued that this categorical difference required clear expression—not least in the design of the windows. Baillie Scott, a champion of the Arts and Crafts movement, declared that "one of the most essential reforms in the modern house is the reduction of its windows to a reasonable size."[15] This call for moderately sized windows aligned with the personal taste of many residents. As Walter Benjamin argued sarcastically, bourgeois homes and apartments of this period were "plush dungeons."[16] These interiors, filled as they were with tapestries and massive, dark furniture, "caught every beam of the light that threatened to sneak into an empty corner."[17] Heavy curtains contributed to a sense of seclusion, as did the bull's-eye windows and neo-medieval stained glass that saw a revival.[18] At the same time, the increasing availability of electricity made residents less dependent on daylight. With electric light just a switch away, windows lost their importance as sources of light.

Around the turn of the century, it was hard to overlook the discrepancy between technological progress and the widespread concerns about too much glass.

The ambition to resolve this tension drove a new generation of early twentieth-century architects and architectural theorists. By propagating more (rather than less) glass as the solution, they sought to reconcile public and private architecture. Indeed, they envisioned not just a new attitude toward glass, but a new kind of architecture.

Among the most vocal proponents of these ideas was Walter Gropius, director of the Bauhaus, the reform-oriented school of arts and design founded in Weimar in 1919 (and reestablished in Dessau in 1925). Driven by a holistic approach to design, art, and architecture, the Bauhaus championed efficient, universally applicable forms and materials. This new aesthetic, it was hoped, would foster positive human interactions and thus help create a better society.[19]

Gropius's first experiments with glass architecture preceded his time at the Bauhaus. They pertained to a building type that was unlikely to become an object of controversy: the industrial factory. In these early projects, Gropius took cues from his mentor, Peter Behrens, whose AEG Turbinenhalle (Turbine Hall) in Berlin (1908–9) had combined three very different construction materials—iron, concrete, and glass—on a monumental scale (fig. 13.1). Its technical sophistication aside, the AEG Turbinenhalle was a curious blend of tradition and innovation. Indeed, in Gropius's circle, the building was admired for its daring use of "modern" construction materials, but at the same time criticized for its display of "classicistic influences" and a "theatrical hint."[20] Behrens's use of glass exemplified this tension: the effect of the large glass front is eclipsed by the monumental cornerstones that emphasize the building's massiveness.

Gropius chose a different path: his goal was to embed glass in a functionalist, "honest" architecture that rejected traditional evocations of gravitas. Identifying light as a key need in industrial architecture, Gropius sought maximum openness in his design. He first realized this approach in the Fagus-Werk, a shoe-last factory near Hanover, which he designed in 1911 together with his partner, Adolf Meyer (fig. 13.2). The slender supporting piers put the glass façade center stage—an effect reinforced by the seamless glazing of the corners. A radical break with traditional aesthetics, the Fagus factory anticipated what came to be known as "curtain-walling" (the construction of façades dominated by large glass surfaces, with the supporting elements receding to the background).[21] In line with Gropius's vision of architectural openness, even the building's interior featured glass walls.[22] With this generous and elegant use of architectural glass, the Fagus factory foreshadowed two later buildings that would bolster Gropius's reputation as a pioneer of curtain-walling: the so-called Fabrik—a model factory designed for an exhibition in Cologne in 1914 (again in cooperation with Meyer)—and the iconic Bauhaus building in Dessau completed in 1926 (fig. 13.3).[23]

To be sure, not all proponents of glass construction were architects. In fact, one of the staunchest advocates was the German fin-de-siècle author Paul Scheerbart. Loosely associated with the expressionist movement, Scheerbart was best known for his fantasy novels and proto-Dadaist poems. His enthusiasm for glass was, to say the least, idiosyncratic. On the surface, it had little in common with the functionalist rhetoric of clear forms and minimal ornament.[24] Quite the contrary, Scheerbart promoted a mystical-utopian cult of glass that sprung directly from his personal *weltanschauung* (or "cosmotheism," as he called it). According to Scheerbart, the cosmos was the future of mankind, and glass architecture could give a

Fig. 13.1. Peter Behrens, AEG Turbinenhalle (Turbine Hall), Berlin, 1908–9. A hybrid between monumental classicism and modern functionalism, the Turbinenhalle demonstrated the potential of glass in industrial architecture. Although critical of the stylistic tension, up-and-coming architects such as Walter Gropius, Le Corbusier, and Mies van der Rohe took inspiration from the Turbinenhalle. All three worked in Behrens's studio around this time.

Fig. 13.2. Walter Gropius and Adolf Meyer, Fagus-Werk, Alfeld, Germany, 1911. An elegant and early demonstration of "curtain walling," the Fagus factory established Gropius's reputation as a pioneer of avant-garde glass architecture. The factory is now a UNESCO World Heritage Site.

foretaste of the cosmic experiences that awaited future generations. True to this multisensory vision, Scheerbart was particularly intrigued by colored glass and its rich visual effects.

Scheerbart's crusade began in the 1890s, with short articles praising glass architecture as the architecture of the future. His enthusiasm found its most systematic expression two decades later, in his manifesto, *Glasarchitektur* (Glass Architecture, 1914), in which he stated:

> If we want our culture to rise to a higher level, we are obliged, for better or for worse, to change our architecture. And this only becomes possible if we take away the closed character from the rooms in which we live. We can only do that by introducing glass architecture, which lets in the light of the sun, the moon, and the stars, not merely through a few windows, but through every possible

Fig. 13.3. Walter Gropius, Bauhaus Dessau, Germany, 1925–26. View from the interior onto the glass façade of the entrance wing. In a charter penned in 1919, Gropius envisioned the Bauhaus bringing about a new kind of architecture and "ris[ing] toward heaven from the hands of a million workers like the crystal symbol of a new faith."

wall, which will be made entirely of glass—of colored glass. This new environment, which we thus create, must bring us a new culture.[25]

And further:

The face of the earth would be much altered if brick architecture were ousted everywhere by glass architecture. It would be as if the earth were adorned with sparkling jewels and enamels. Such glory is unimaginable. All over the world it would be as splendid as in the gardens of the Arabian Nights. We should then have a paradise on earth, and no need to watch in longing expectation for the paradise in heaven.[26]

The most succinct expression of Scheerbart's utopian vision is a poem from 1914 in which he rapturously praised the architectural use of glass, especially colored glass. Take the opening verse: "Happiness without glass / How crass!" (*Glück ohne Glas—wie dumm ist das!*).[27] This may have been an inversion of an older proverb, "Happiness and glass / both break so easily" (*Glück und Glas / wie leicht bricht das*). Originating from Roman antiquity, this proverb was popular throughout medieval and early modern times when the fragility of glass was often invoked as a metaphor for the transience of life.[28] Scheerbart turned the moralistic message upside down, assigning glass a new, quasi-religious function: "Without a glass palace / Life becomes a burden." Tellingly, Scheerbart's poem ends with a passionate call to action: "Glass makes everything light / So use it on site / Glass opens up a new age / Brick building only does harm."[29]

Whatever their literary quality, Scheerbart's fanciful ideas found supporters. Among them was the German architect Bruno Taut (pen name: Glas), the dedicatee of Scheerbart's book *Glasarchitektur*. Taut's vision of glass architecture drew on an eclectic array of sources (in addition to Scheerbart's utopian ideas): his influences included the tradition of Gothic cathedrals, the legacy of nineteenth-century horticultural architecture, and expressionist aesthetics.[30] For Taut, glass architecture promised a much-needed spatial experience—the experience of man and nature coexisting in a setting as barrierless as possible. Nature served as a source of inspiration for Taut's designs, as is particularly evident in his drafts for monumental glass buildings in the shape of alpine crystals. From a practical perspective, most of these projects were entirely unfeasible. On a smaller scale, however, Taut was able to realize the Glashaus, a pavilion for the 1914 Cologne exhibition of the Werkbund (a German association dedicated to reforming the arts and crafts). Taut's Glashaus was a highly original structure, perhaps best described as a fourteen-sided rotunda crowned by a vitreous dome (fig. 13.4). Taut used the project to explore the architectural potential of glass, experimenting, for instance, with double glazing and its positive insulating effect.[31] That said, the technical experiments were subordinated to a daring aesthetic vision: for Taut, glass architecture was not merely about efficiency and practicality, but about achieving an architectural *Gesamtkunstwerk*, a total work of art. To this end, the pavilion combined different varieties of glass, transparent and colored. Gentle background music, polychrome light effects, and water fountains with chains of glass pearls contrib-

Fig. 13.4. Bruno Taut, Glashaus, Cologne, Germany, 1914. One of the most imaginative buildings of this period, the "glass house" epitomized Taut's enthusiasm for vitreous architecture, displaying the entire spectrum of forms and products available to glass architects at the time. The Glashaus was also a testament to Taut's friendship with the like-minded poet Paul Scheerbart: the frieze of the polygonal building displayed verses that Scheerbart had composed in praise of glass.

uted to the multisensory experience. Taut referred to the pavilion as a "garment of the soul," and it fits into this image that the walls—construed as the garments of the structure—were richly decorated. It is also no coincidence that the façade featured four lines from Scheerbart's above-mentioned paean: "Coloured glass destroys hatred"; "Without a glass palace life becomes a burden"; "Brick building only does harm"; "Glass opens up a new age."[32]

Having fulfilled its purpose as a showpiece, the Glashaus was dismantled when the 1914 exhibition concluded. Taut, for his part, remained committed to the belief in the panacean potential of architectural glass. In 1919, he founded Die gläserne Kette (The Glass Chain), a group of twelve architects that included both utopians (such as Taut) and proponents of functionalism (such as Gropius). The Glass Chain's activities revolved around the internal circulation of drafts and eventually petered out about a year after the group was formed.[33] Despite its short existence, the Glass Chain is a reminder that the two major strands underlying the glass-architecture movement—namely, utopian expressionism and functionalist *Sachlichkeit* (objectivity)—were entwined in complex ways. Consider the case of the supposedly strict functionalist Gropius, who not only read Scheerbart and joined the Glass Chain, but indeed took unmistakable cues from the utopian language of Scheerbart and Taut in the Bauhaus charter that he penned in 1919, writing: "Together let us desire, conceive, and create the new structure of the future, which will embrace architecture and sculpture and painting in one unity and which will one day rise toward heaven from the hands of a million workers like the crystal symbol of a new faith."[34]

Admittedly, this grand rhetoric does not explain why the 1920s saw increased experimentation with glass in domestic architecture. The reason was simple: the large-scale destruction caused by World War I. Looking back in 1929, a German architectural writer noted that the magnitude of the war damage required new solutions for how "to build in a more cost-efficient and streamlined way"—which included the use of "artificial materials" such as glass.[35] This, of course, was welcome news for glass manufacturers. Even before the war, they had generously supported experimental projects such as Taut's pavilion.[36] In the face of unprecedented war damage, glass manufacturers emerged as significant supporters of modernist architecture. In Germany, the Verein Deutscher Spiegelglas-Fabriken (Association of German Plate Glass Factories) sponsored events promoting glass architecture while also publishing advertisements that praised glass as a cost-efficient, useful, und modern building material.[37] In fact, the glass walling of Gropius's Bauhaus building in Dessau was made possible through the support of the German glass industry, which donated the bulk of the glass plates.[38]

The 1920s ushered in a new era for glass architecture. Across Europe, avant-garde architects experimented with glass to create a novel, distinctively modern kind of domestic architecture—or, in their own words, a *sachlich* and "honest" style of building, overcoming the world of the nineteenth century, which had irrevocably collapsed as a result of World War I. To be sure, this new architecture came in more national varieties than the commonly used label "International Style" suggests. That said, there were common denominators: the commitment to clear forms, a minimization of ornament, a preponderance of the "clean" color white—and the call for larger windows.

In France, the modernist movement was spearheaded by architect-designers such as Pierre Chareau and Le Corbusier (who was originally Swiss). In different ways, both men experimented with new approaches to fenestration. Chareau's most noted architectural project was the Parisian Maison de Verre (Glass House, 1928–32), built in collaboration with the Dutch architect Bernard Bijvoet as a home for the Dalsace family (fig. 13.5). As its name implies, the façade of the Maison de Verre consisted almost entirely of glass. One contemporary observer remarked that it was "one large window."[39] Yet this façade was not transparent: the so-called Nevada glass blocks admitted light but were too thick to be pervious to gazes. By means of these glass blocks—a brand-new product at the time—Chareau accomplished a balancing act: residents enjoyed both copious light and privacy, and indeed the Maison de Verre offered, despite its name, just as much privacy as a conventional home.[40]

Le Corbusier was similarly eager to adopt the latest technological innovations. Maintaining good working relations with his German colleague Gropius, he closely followed the experiments at the Bauhaus.[41] Indeed, Le Corbusier and Gropius had shared aspirations, but Le Corbusier's rhetoric tended to be more polemical. For instance, he decried the traditional design of "windows of our houses which pierce the wall and create patches of shadow on either side."[42] Never short of grand statements, Le Corbusier considered the entire history of architecture a struggle for larger windows—and he drew a straightforward conclusion: "Teach your children that a house is habitable only when there's abundant light, only when the floors and walls are clean."[43]

Such apodictic rhetoric aside, theory and practice did not always correspond in Le Corbusier's architecture. His window designs from the early 1920s were less radical than those of other contemporary avant-garde architects. Only gradually did large windows become a feature of Le Corbusier's buildings. In the case of his iconic villas La Roche and Jeanneret outside of Paris (1923–25), he decided at a rather late stage to enlarge the windows.[44] If Le Corbusier became a key figure in the interwar controversies about fenestration, this was due less to the size of his windows than to their design.

Le Corbusier was the most fervent advocate of the *fenêtre en longueur*, the horizontal "window ribbon" connecting several rooms. The fenêtre en longueur

Fig. 13.5. Pierre Chareau (with Bernard Bijvoet), Maison de Verre (Glass House), Paris, 1928–32. The "glass house" accommodated both Dr. Dalsace's home and his medical practice. The translucent glass blocks provide ample light to both parts of the building without compromising visual privacy.

had precedents in North American architecture, where it was known as a "strip window."[45] The first American experiments with strip windows dated to the late nineteenth century, when large warehouses and office buildings were shooting up across the United States. The design of these American buildings was pragmatic: instead of featuring a light court, which was considered a waste of space, they were often outfitted with large windows—some with wide bays—to admit light deep into the interior.[46] Particularly common in the Midwest, this fenestration design was, with some modifications, a hallmark of the so-called Chicago School. Chicago became a hotbed of architectural experimentation after a devastating fire ravaged much of the booming city's downtown in 1871. Faced with the challenge of rebuilding the city center from scratch (while also accommodating the needs of a modern metropolis), Chicago-based architects developed a distinctive style—the Commercial style—that redefined the city's appearance. The Commercial style went hand in hand with vertical expansion: thanks to a systematic adoption of steel- and iron-framed construction, Chicago became the birthplace of the modern high-rise. Many of these high-rises featured horizontally elongated, tripartite windows—an innovation known as the "Chicago window" (fig. 13.6). In some buildings, almost 80 percent of the façade was covered by glass.[47]

The Chicago School profoundly influenced the work of early twentieth-century American architects. Chief among them was the Chicago-trained Frank Lloyd Wright, who incorporated the horizontal window in his distinctive Prairie style.[48] By contrast, European architects of this generation were less familiar with the innovations of the Chicago School. According to Sigfried Giedion, a friend and ally to Le Corbusier and Gropius, "Chicago windows and the Chicago skyscraper were unknown" in Europe well into the 1920s.[49] This was a somewhat exaggerated claim, and one that helped Le Corbusier fashion himself as a pioneer in his self-proclaimed struggle for larger windows.[50] Le Corbusier certainly knew how to showcase his architectural ideas. The Villa Le Lac (also known as La petite maison, 1923–24) in Corseaux was an early experiment with horizontal fenestration: this "small house" boasts a window ribbon more than thirty feet long, providing the residents with a splendid view of Lake Geneva.[51] Equally spectacular are the views of the Neckar valley through the horizontal windows of Le Corbusier's model house in Stuttgart's Weißenhofsiedlung (Weissenhof Settlement) (fig. 13.7). The length of these strip windows—made possible thanks to the use of reinforced concrete—determined the experience of the surroundings in a fundamental way: instead of compressing a segment of landscape into a traditional vertical window, the fenêtre en longueur enabled residents to view the landscape in unbroken horizontal continuity.[52] Indeed, Le Corbusier declared the strip window to be "the sole actor of the façade."[53]

In traditional circles, the fenêtre en longueur met with fierce criticism. The French architect Auguste Perret, a proponent of blending nineteenth-century "rationalism" with the neoclassical tradition, argued that his former employee Le Corbusier had sacrificed the venerable tradition of the vertical window (porte-fenêtre)—a tradition that, in Perret's anthropocentric view, expressed the idea that

Fig. 13.6. Holabird and Roche, Chicago Savings Bank Building, Chicago, 1904–5. The building is a fine example of the Chicago School and its innovative use of the elongated and tripartite "Chicago window."

Fig. 13.7. Le Corbusier, two-family house for the Weißenhofsiedlung (Weissenhof Settlement), Stuttgart, Germany, 1927. The horizontal ribbon window provides a panoramic view over Stuttgart. It also evokes the windows of a railway train—a source of inspiration that Le Corbusier, an admirer of modern technology, explicitly acknowledged. The Weißenhofsiedlung house is one of many Le Corbusier buildings from this period that feature horizontal window bands. It served as a demonstration of Le Corbusier's *5 Points d'une architecture nouvelle* (Five Points of a New Architecture, first published 1926): one of these five points was the commitment to the horizontal window.

"a window is a man, it stands upright."[54] For Perret, the horizontal window condemned the residents to a "perpetual panorama."[55] In England around the same time, the Arts and Crafts architect Charles Voysey was more open to experiments with large glass surfaces, but he too preferred windows that were vertical, corresponding to the form of the upright human body. Voysey sarcastically dismissed the modernist penchant for windows that were "lying down on their sides."[56] In the same vein, Paul Schultze-Naumburg, a flagbearer of architectural conservatism in Germany, claimed that Le Corbusier's horizontal windows gave domestic spaces the appearance of "factories behind whose windows there are engine lathes or cutting tables."[57]

Such criticism hardly impressed the self-confident Le Corbusier. In fact, he argued that "the 'glass wall' is the conquest of the Modern Age" and that, consequently, at least one wall of a home should be "entirely glazed."[58] His Immeuble Clarté, a multistory "apartment building of clarity" constructed in Geneva in the early 1930s, exemplified this approach, featuring forty-five apartments in which "the window is the wall, and compromise is eliminated" (as an admiring colleague put it).[59] In an essay titled "Glass, the Fundamental Material of Modern Architecture" (1935), Le Corbusier declared triumphantly: "Modern technology has provided the building with an exceptionally beautiful product that is, it may even be said, miraculously beautiful because it is theoretically perfect: this is plate glass."[60]

Le Corbusier was not the only architect at the time who experimented with floor-to-ceiling transparency. Another who explored that possibility was Mies van der Rohe, in Germany, who knew Le Corbusier from the days both men were apprentices in Behrens's firm. Yet there were differences: while Le Corbusier, in his Immeuble Clarté, pursued architectural transparency by stacking up a series of window ribbons, Mies experimented with uninterrupted glass walls. More specifically, Mies's reputation went back to two projects drafted in 1921/22, but which were impossible to realize at the time. Both projects envisioned an all-glazed skyscraper: one for central Berlin, the other for an unknown location. Published in Taut's journal *Frühlicht* (Dawn's Light), the drafts were met with both fascination and incredulity.[61] Countering critical responses, Mies's admirer Korn praised the design for keeping "the load-bearing elements . . . within the core of the building, leaving the outside wall free to be nothing but a wrapping to enclose and to allow light to penetrate."[62]

Several years passed without an opportunity for Mies to realize his bold ideas about comprehensive glazing—until he received the prestigious commission from the German government to build the country's pavilion for the 1929 International Exposition in Barcelona. Mies seized the opportunity. Although much smaller in scale than the skyscrapers he designed in the early 1920s, the Barcelona Pavilion remains Mies's most iconic building (fig. 13.8). In line with its open floor plan, the pavilion had few interior walls. Reinforcing the impression of openness and permeability, there were also no exterior walls in the traditional sense. Instead, the pavilion was dominated by floor-to-ceiling glass plates (some transparent, others tinted).

The Barcelona Pavilion was a powerful demonstration of Mies's theoretical

Fig. 13.8. Mies van der Rohe, Barcelona Pavilion, Barcelona, 1929 (reconstructed 1986). The instruction that Mies received from the German government was clear: "We need a pavilion. Design it, and not too much glass." Mies ignored the instruction and created one of the most iconic examples of modern glass architecture.

ideas, but it defied the instructions he had received from the German government. As Mies recalled in an interview three decades later: "One day I received a call from the German government. . . . I was told: 'We need a pavilion. Design it, and not too much glass.'"[63] Mies got away with the copious use of glass thanks to the extreme time pressure under which the pavilion was built: his withdrawal would have jeopardized the project and embarrassed the German government. Most importantly, Mies's creation convinced through sweeping elegance. The oversized glass plates not only created a striking sense of lightness, but also cast reflections of the expensive stone surfaces in the pavilion's interior, such as onyx, marble, and travertine. At the official opening ceremony in May 1929, Georg von Schnitzler, the representative of the German government, commended the building as the embodiment of a new, modern Germany, declaring: "We wished here to show what we can do, what we are, how we feel today and see. We do not want anything but clarity, simplicity, honesty."[64] The pavilion was a showpiece. In the course of its short existence, it served no other purpose. The question of temperature control and overheating remained unaddressed; nor was visual privacy a concern, as the building fulfilled no residential function. Freed from any mundane constraints, the Barcelona Pavilion offered a masterful meditation on the art of architecture, but hardly a template for conventional homes.

The practical challenges were far greater in the other major project that Mies tackled at the time: the Villa Tugendhat in Brno (1929–30). Commissioned by an affluent industrialist couple, the villa sits on the top of a slope with magnificent views of the Czech city. Working with an extraordinarily generous budget (and exceptionally open-minded patrons), Mies used the Tugendhat project to demonstrate how he envisioned the dissolution of walls into windows in a domestic setting. Like the interior of the Barcelona Pavilion, the villa's main living area was based on an open floor plan. Rooms in a traditional sense did not exist; curtains created a sense of compartmentalization. The most stunning feature of the villa, however, was its rear, which provided sweeping views through floor-to-ceiling glass: the western glass wall measured fifty-five feet in length, while its southern counterpart extended over eighty feet (fig. 13.9). The bronze-framed glass plates, each fifteen feet wide, were the largest produced in Europe at the time. What is more, two plates could be retracted mechanically into the basement, thereby maximizing the sense of permeability between interior and exterior.[65]

The Villa Tugendhat and other avant-garde glass buildings of the interwar period proclaimed a new ideal: the emancipation of the window from the wall.[66] As the German architect Arthur Korn put it in 1929, it was "now possible to have an independent wall of glass, a skin of glass around a building; no longer a solid wall with windows."[67] Raymond McGrath and Albert Frost, two leading proponents of glass architecture in interwar England, even declared that "the wars of liberation of the window are now virtually over" (fig. 13.10).[68]

Writing around the same time, Walter Benjamin noted approvingly that "the societal prerequisites for the widened applications [of glass] as [a] building mate-

Fig. 13.9. Mies van der Rohe, Villa Tugendhat, Brno, Czech Republic, 1929–30. Reputedly the most expensive private villa built at the time, the Villa Tugendhat featured, among other things, a garden-facing glass front more than 80 feet long. The picture shows how the two movable windowpanes are mechanically lowered into the basement.

rial" had finally been achieved.[69] Benjamin praised avant-garde architects, such as Le Corbusier, as pioneers who had taken up Scheerbart's call for glass architecture while stripping it of its mythical utopianism.[70] In a similar vein, Ludwig Hilberseimer—professor of architecture at the Bauhaus and collaborator of Mies—declared in 1929 that the sachlich style of the interwar period had prevailed over the "glass architecture romanticism" of Scheerbart, for whom "glass was more a decorative than a structural device." Maliciously, Hilberseimer added that the "only good thing" about Scheerbart's vision was that "unlike other kinds of architectural romanticism it was not realized."[71] Indeed, for the supporters of a functional, "objective" architecture, the generous use of glass was not a merely aesthetic choice. Quite the contrary, architectural transparency was meant to signal a radical break with traditional notions of domesticity.

In his 1933 essay "Experience and Poverty," Benjamin spelled out this position, arguing that glass is a "hard, smooth material to which nothing can be fixed," and that "objects made of glass have no 'aura.'"[72] By extension, "glass is, in gencral, the enemy of secrets. It is also the enemy of possession."[73] In Benjamin's opinion, it was precisely these austere, anti-bourgeois qualities that made glass the most suitable building material for his own time: glass architecture promised to do away with the nineteenth-century "plush dungeons" that had signaled to the outsider, "You have no business in this room."[74] In the new age of transparency, seclusion would no longer be an option, consigning the nineteenth-century taste for interiority—with all its inherent contradictions—to the past. Glass would give rise to a new kind of domestic architecture and, by extension, to a new type of resident—men and women who, deprived of nineteenth-century dreams and delusions, would "long for a world in which they can make such pure and decided use of their poverty—their outer poverty, and ultimately also their inner poverty—that it will lead to something respectable."[75] In this process, glass itself would finally be redeemed from an architectural tradition that did not know how to use it properly.[76]

These expectations projected onto architectural glass were no doubt bold—

Fig. 13.10. "Modernization: The house-owner Gieselmann before and after the renovation of his façade." Cartoon from the *Berliner Illustrirte Zeitung*, 1929. As part of the renovation, the building's overloaded historicism is superseded by a sober *sachlich* style. As a result, the windows gain unprecedented prominence and become, despite their uniformity, the only distinct feature of the façade. Writing around the same time, Walter Benjamin hoped that the embrace of glass architecture would bring about a new, more sincere type of resident. The anonymous cartoonist, however, suggests that this transformation will merely lead to a more streamlined and technocratic kind of personality.

too bold to be realistic. Before World War I, Scheerbart had famously erred when he proclaimed: "When glass architecture comes in, there will not be much more talk of windows . . . ; the word 'window' will disappear from the dictionaries."[77] That, of course, did not happen. Similarly, some of the high-flying hopes from the interwar period were dashed. While the proponents of glass architecture were driven by a strong belief in technological and social progress, the public response to their ideas was far more reluctant, and at times outright critical. Gropius, for his part, had confidently forecast that glass's "application will be unlimited and will not remain confined to windows, for it wins the love of creative architects due to its noble properties, its transparent clarity, as well as its light-weight, wafting, and unsubstantial material quality."[78] But to win the "love of creative architects" was of little use without also winning support from homeowners and residents willing to live in glass buildings. Ironically, this reluctance even extended to some of Gropius's colleagues at the Bauhaus. Gropius's Meisterhäuser (Masters' Houses) in Dessau—generously fenestrated, modernist homes built for senior Bauhaus faculty—were not beloved by all occupants. One of them, the painter Lyonel Feininger, complained to his wife: "What is going on here is beyond belief and almost beyond endurance. Crowds of idlers slowly assemble along Burgkühn-auallee, from morning to night, goggling at our houses, not to speak of trespassing in our gardens to stare in the windows." His next-door neighbor, the painter Wassily Kandinsky, was similarly annoyed by the effect of the large windows, and he took it in his own hands to remedy the situation (fig. 13.11). His wife, Nona, recalled: "Gropius had . . . made one large wall of the entrance hall of transparent glass so that anyone could look into the house from the street. That bothered Kandinsky. . . . Right away he painted the glass wall white on the inside."[79]

In short, the nineteenth-century concern about "troublesome windows" remained powerful and could not easily be dispelled. Mies van der Rohe, too, had to learn this lesson. Like other leading modern architects, Mies pinned great hopes on glass as a material that would bring about a "New Dwelling." In a contribution to a prospectus published by the German plate glass industry in 1933, he stated, in his characteristically terse style: "Only a glass skin and glass walls can reveal the simple structural form of the skeletal frame and ensure its architectonic possibilities. And this is true not only of large utilitarian buildings. To be sure, it was with them that a line of development based on function and necessity began that needs no further justifications; it will not end there, however, but will find its fulfillment

Fig. 13.11. Walter Gropius, Meisterhaus (Master's House) Kandinsky, Dessau, Germany, 1926. In his capacity as Bauhaus director, Gropius designed a series of spacious residences for the school's senior faculty, including the Russian painter Wassily Kandinsky. The houses all featured large glass surfaces—a feature that greatly troubled Kandinsky, who decided to paint over one of the "glass walls."

in the realm of residential building."[80] But in practice, Mies faced the same problem as other glass architects: most private clients were skeptical about these new "architectonic possibilities" and preferred traditional designs. Patrons such as the Tugendhats, who gave carte blanche to Mies, were rare. In the villas he designed for the Esters and Lange families in Krefeld around that time (1928–30), Mies was forced to install conventional, albeit large, windows, as the clients rejected his original vision of floor-to-ceiling glass. He later recalled: "I wanted to make [these houses with] more glass, but the client[s] did not like that. I had great trouble."[81]

Given this reluctance among homeowners, public and industrial architecture remained the most important areas for experiments with extensive glazing.[82]

Gropius was known to be "happiest when he [was] planning on a large scale," focusing on "buildings for whole social groups," such as factories and schools.[83] Other members of the Glass Chain found department stores to be a congenial testing ground for glass architecture.[84] In addition, the early twentieth century saw the emergence of an entirely new building type that was predicated on large-scale glazing: movie studios. Consider Berlin, at the time the center of movie production in Europe: on the eve of World War I, the German capital boasted no fewer than six *Glashäuser* (glass houses) built by the movie industry. These factory-size vitreous structures made it possible to shoot films under a range of different light conditions, including the maximum lighting levels that were needed most of the time (figs. 13.12, 13.13). The new, glittering structures even became the subject of a novel, Edmund Edel's *Das Glashaus* (The Glass House, 1917).[85]

In general, commissions by the movie industry provided significant opportunities for avant-garde architects. In his 1918 manifesto "A Program for Architecture," Taut, the founder of the Glass Chain, praised the film industry for encouraging architects to "erect large-scale models of their ideas." On a "well-situated experimental site . . . architectural effects (e.g., glass as building material) shall be tried out, perfected, and exhibited to the masses in full-scale temporary constructions or individual parts of buildings."[86]

The cinematic glass houses were among these "experimental sites," but they were short-lived. They quickly lost their raison d'être when better cameras and improved artificial lighting techniques reduced the dependence on daylight on the set. In addition, the rise of sound film in the late 1920s called for ateliers with maximum soundproofing. Falling short of these requirements, the movie industry's glass houses were either demolished or transformed into massive brick compounds.[87]

Even in their heyday, cinematic glass houses met with mixed reactions. Writing in 1916, the German journalist and stage director Hans Brennert offered a rather negative assessment:

> In a colossal, awkward, and fanciful way, these glass palaces stand in the midst of a bright landscape. The lower part of the building is a mighty, even, and high red-brick structure, and on top there is a second colossal house. The latter is entirely made of glass. It has been wholly constructed from thousands of extra-large glass plates: like a gigantic hothouse, but surrounded by a small gallery with numerous studio doors. The reason for this is that in the summer the heat

is often unbearable, and every now and then the movie people go up to the gallery to get fresh air. On hot days, cold water is sprinkled against the glass walls so that one can bear staying inside.[88]

A few years later, the acclaimed movie director Sergei Eisenstein dismissively noted that "glass belongs to the primitive age and if it continues to be part of the framework of primitivism . . . it can only serve as a primitive material."[89]

On the whole, skeptical attitudes toward glass architecture persisted in Ger-

Fig. 13.12. The glass house of the Union-Film studios, Berlin-Tempelhof, 1918. The ground floor contained storage and office spaces; above it rose the entirely glazed hall, approximately 65 by 130 feet wide and 40 feet high. Glass houses such as this one provided maximum daylight, which was indispensable for movie production at the time. Artificial light could not have met these needs, because it was generated by alternating current electricity, which, apart from being expensive, created a flickering effect on the movie screen. Despite chronic problems with overheating, glass houses remained the preferred venue for movie productions well into the 1920s.

Fig. 13.13. Film shoot in the UFA glass house (built 1912), Babelsberg (near Berlin).

many throughout the time of the Weimar Republic (1918–33), even though modern architecture enjoyed greater political support than before the war. This support was pragmatic: politicians on both the state and local level were in search of efficient and affordable remedies for the postwar *Wohnungsnot* (housing shortage). Taut, who was well connected in progressive political circles, estimated that Germany needed three million new apartments within a decade—and, according to Taut, only modern architecture, with its efficient use of space and materials, could meet this demand.[90] In some cities, these ideas fell on fertile ground and attracted public funding for modernist architecture and urban planning. Model neighborhoods were supposed to showcase affordable housing solutions for the masses.[91]

One of the most ambitious projects of this kind was the Weißenhofsiedlung in Stuttgart. In 1926, the southern German city invited leading European avant-garde architects, among them Gropius and Le Corbusier, to present their vision of a new domestic architecture.[92] Mies was responsible for the master plan. The common denominator of the thirty-three buildings, completed in 1927, was a commitment to a sachlich style and to flat roofs (a signature element of the modern movement). Many houses also displayed innovative approaches to fenestration, including horizontal windows and a generous use of glass (fig. 13.14; see also fig. 13.7).[93] A separate exhibition in downtown Stuttgart gave Mies and his collaborator, Lilly Reich, an opportunity to present their "Glass Room." This project, realized with support of the German plate glass industry, consisted of three sparsely furnished rooms with walls made of oversized glass plates (some perfectly clear, others tinted in light color tones). The "Glass Room" offered a prototype of an interior space defined by glass instead of brick; in fact, some architectural historians consider this experiment with "different degrees of transparency" a milestone toward the Barcelona Pavilion, which Mies began to tackle a year later.[94]

Still, neither the high quality of the Weißenhof buildings nor the concurrent design exhibition impressed critics. Conservative circles decried the settlement as a flat-roofed "Arab village" (*Araberdorf*).[95] The windows in particular were a point

Fig. 13.14. Mies van der Rohe, apartment building for the Weißenhofsiedlung, Stuttgart, Germany, 1927. In addition to creating the master plan for Stuttgart's new, modern neighborhood, Mies also designed this multifamily apartment building. The elongated windows contribute to the elegant appearance of the façade. However, the first residents had to request the installation of curtains, as "tropical temperatures can easily arise behind the ample glass surfaces."

of contention. Before the first house was even built, the city's municipal building department tried, unsuccessfully, to impose smaller windows on Mies's master plan.[96] After the Weißenhof's public opening, the windows remained a target of criticism. A local newspaper noted in an (otherwise balanced) article about the new neighborhood:

> The many high and broad windows, so much feared and criticized, do a very good job fending off rain and wind, but they admit a flood of sun and light. I have been told that the cleaning of the large windows is very easy, but in the case of the large double-windows it is quite laborious. . . . With respect to the approaching summer, several [residents] have called the lack of blinds a great deficit. The inhabitants of the block built by Mies have therefore requested [blinds] from the city, as tropical temperatures can easily arise behind the large glass surfaces.[97]

The controversy about the Weißenhof windows was not limited to Stuttgart. As far away as Breslau (Wrocław, now in Poland), the local branch of the Hausfrauenbund (Association of Housewives) published a pamphlet criticizing the windows and their size, "which makes the maintenance and cleaning significantly more difficult and expensive while affording too little thermal insulation."[98] The Hausfrauenbund generally supported modern architecture, hoping that functional designs would facilitate women's domestic chores. Oversized windows, however, increased rather than reduced the domestic workload of housewives.

The cost of the windows was another target of criticism. There was a certain irony in this, given that early proponents of architectural glass had championed it as an affordable material. To be sure, window glass was cheaper than ever before, thanks to mass production. But in the 1930s, glass was still almost three times more expensive than brick. The advocates of architectural glass maintained that the advantages outweighed the cost.[99] Yet from a strictly economic perspective, it was difficult to justify the generous use of glass as a choice rooted in pragmatism and efficiency.

Indeed, in practice, glass architecture often owed more to aesthetic than to functionalist considerations. For instance, Gropius's iconic glass façade for the Dessau Bauhaus was "unfunctional, despite its considerable appeal."[100] The same is true of his Fagus factory, where corrosion of the steel framework caused the glass panes to break.[101] What is more, some showpieces of interwar glass architecture blatantly contradicted the promise of an affordable architecture. The generous use of glass often coincided with architects' ambition to build unique works of art. Le Corbusier's Villa Savoye cost a fortune by the standards of the time, and these costs were exceeded tenfold by Mies's Villa Tugendhat, the most expensive private residence built in those years. Even supporters of the modernist movement criticized buildings such as the Villa Tugendhat as "the peak of modern snobbism."[102]

Technical issues and excessive costs are a reminder that glass architecture presented more practical challenges than its pioneers had anticipated. In other words, glass architecture often fell short of its own idealistic goals and aspirations. What is more, in the 1930s another problem came to the fore: glass architecture was increasingly co-opted for radical political agendas. As we shall see in the next chapter, this politicization massively tainted the noble (if sometimes naïve) idealism that had characterized the early glass architecture movement.

14

Transparency between Totalitarianism and Democracy

Twentieth-century glass architecture began with a promise: to overcome the contradictions of nineteenth-century domesticity and create a genuinely modern style. As the artist and Bauhaus professor László Moholy-Nagy proclaimed in 1928, transparency was the "path for future architecture," through which "the inside and the outside, the upper and lower, fuse into unity."[1] Transparency, of course, meant glass—that "completely new, pure material in which matter is melted down and recast" (as Adolf Behne, a member of the Glass Chain, put it).[2] This idealistic discourse was not limited to architectural circles: public intellectuals such as Paul Scheerbart and Walter Benjamin praised glass architecture for its purity and the new spatial and social experience it provided. "Virtuous vitreousness" was supposed to level class differences and create a better society.[3]

There was only one problem: glass architecture was met with reluctance. As we have seen, the taste for glass was quite limited in domestic architecture. Practical concerns, such as the cost of installation and cleaning, fed this sentiment. But people also worried that generously glazed spaces would upset traditional notions of domesticity. Architectural transparency could be oppressive through its very openness—a realization that caused considerable unease among people who were used to nineteenth-century interiority.[4]

This unease affected people both inside and out. For people on the streets, especially in dense urban areas, the growing multitude of windows evoked a feeling of permanent surveillance. The German author Edmund Edel captured this feeling in his 1908 urban novel *Neu-Berlin*, where he described Berlin's "colossal houses . . . whose innumerable windows stare at passersby in a hypnotic fashion."[5] Around the same time, Franz Kafka gave a similar description of New York in his unfinished novel *America*. Kafka had never been to the United States, but he drew on accounts by emigrant relatives, imagining New York as a city that gaped at its inhabitants "with the hundred thousand windows of its skyscrapers."[6]

People inside had other concerns. For one thing, more windows meant more glare and heat. In early modern buildings such as the "lantern houses" of sixteenth-century England, solar heat had made a welcome contribution to thermal comfort. But with the rise of electric heating in the early twentieth century, abundant sunlight often meant overheating and discomfort. Windows played a crucial role in this context: the more glass, the more likely the building was to suffer from the "greenhouse effect," especially as air-conditioning was not yet available.

Glass architecture was also associated with visual exposure and a lack of privacy. During a visit in 1906, Maxim Gorky described New York as a city of "transparent prisons of glass."[7] Two decades later, Russian film director Sergei Eisenstein, whose critical attitude toward glass has already been mentioned, even planned a film—half satirical, half tragic—about the feeling of isolation and surveillance in an entirely glass-faced skyscraper. Conceived in 1926, the movie remained unrealized, but Eisenstein's drafts and notes have survived. One of these preparatory sketches defines the movie's subject as follows: "The loneliness related to the permanent display of oneself to others as well as to visibility from all sides. The coldness of objects. The coldness of glass par excellence."[8] Although the film did not materialize, Eisenstein maintained a keen interest in the subject and continued to make notes. As late as 1947, he revisited the project. This time, he envisioned the suicide of a resident of the skyscraper—the desperate gesture of a lonely individual, observed through the windows by neighbors who are just as lonely, yet trapped in their transparent cages.[9]

Concerns about privacy were heightened by the polemical rhetoric that some proponents of transparency employed. In the nineteenth century, the problem of "troublesome windows" was covered up, as it were, with curtains. Twentieth-century advocates of glass architecture rejected such compromises. Walter Benjamin celebrated glass as the "enemy of secrets." His contemporary Adolf Behne did not mince words either, proclaiming, "The European is correct when he fears that glass architecture might become uncomfortable. Certainly, it will be so. And that is not its least advantage. For first the European must be wrenched out of his coziness [Gemütlichkeit]. Not without good reason the adjective 'gemütlich' intensified becomes 'saugemütlich' [swinishly comfortable]. Away with comfort! Only where comfort ends, does humanity begin."[10] The Italian futurist poet Aldo Palazzeschi went even further. Enamored, like most futurists, with the idea of technological progress and radical modernity, Palazzeschi declared in his 1913 poem "La casina di cristallo" (A Little Crystal House): "I dream of a little crystal house . . . A house every common mortal / could possess, / which would have nothing in particular, / but which would be all transparent, / made of crystal. / . . . You would see me eating, you would see me / when I sleep, / uncover my dreams; / you would see me defecating, you would see me changing my shirt."[11]

Compared with these radical visions, even Le Corbusier's rhetoric seemed relatively moderate. That said, Le Corbusier left little doubt that he, too, wanted to supplant traditional notions of privacy and domesticity. In his view, glass architecture was a major step toward implementing the "three eights" system—eight hours of work, eight hours of recreation, and eight hours of sleep each day—which offered only a limited degree of privacy.[12] Large glass windows played an essential role in this system: they would not just provide a pleasant view, but also level the barrier between domestic and professional life. As Georg Kohlmaier and Barna von Sartory have noted, "The window extending along the whole length of the dwelling would remind [the resident] of work and make the outside world permanently present."[13] Some architectural historians have gone further, arguing that Le Corbusier and like-minded contemporaries envisioned an architecture in which the private would become even more public than the public, in a sense.[14] It is certainly true that Le Corbusier considered transparency imperative in the modern home. "Till now," he wrote, "the function of the windows was to provide light and air and to be looked through. Of these classified functions I should retain one only, that of being looked through."[15]

It was precisely this vision of maximum transparency—and, by extension, of privacy undone—that made glass architecture appealing for collectivist ideologies. In other words, the "struggle for windows" attracted allies who harbored distinctively antidemocratic ideas and who co-opted glass architecture for their own political ends. Of course, the glass architecture movement had never been unpolitical: social utopianism and reformist ideas were driving forces since its inception. The hope that more light and transparency would translate into well-organized, accountable institutions harked back to Bentham and other eighteenth-century thinkers. Technological progress in the early twentieth century only fueled the idealism among those who considered architecture a vehicle for political change. A case in point is the 1927 model for the Palace of the League of Nations, submitted by two Bauhaus architects, Hannes Meyer and Hans Wittwer. The unrealized design featured comprehensive glazing, which, in Meyer's words, would ensure that "there won't be any space for the backroom politics of diplomats, but rather open glass rooms for public conversations among open people [*offener Menschen*]."[16]

With regard to domestic architecture, advocates of transparency also cited benefits to public health: homes with larger windows were said to increase quality of life by improving hygienic conditions and admitting more healthy sunlight.[17] Scheerbart even expected that glass architecture would have a civilizing effect and lead to the moral betterment of mankind, declaring: "Our hope is that glass architecture will also improve mankind in ethical respects. . . . The man who sees the splendours of glass every day cannot have ignoble hands."[18]

Scheerbart did not live to see his prediction turned upside down in the 1930s, when glass architecture was not only championed by "ignoble hands," but indeed co-opted for political purposes that did not "improve mankind in ethical respects." Consider the case of fascist Italy, where dictator Benito Mussolini supported the generous use of glass in architecture. In this context of fascist architecture, Benjamin's characterization of glass as "the enemy of secrets" took on a dark, unintended dimension. Transparency came to symbolize the conflation of public and private, of individual life and collectivist mass culture. By Mussolini's own definition, fascism was a "glass house into which everyone can gaze freely."[19] At the same time, glass architecture served as a source of nationalistic pride. In Italy, the Federazione Nazionale Fascista degli Industriali del Vetro (National Fascist Association of Glass Manufacturers) praised window glass as a distinctively Italian contribution to civilization: after all, the ancient Romans, the celebrated models of Mussolini's Italo-fascism, had first used glass in architecture.[20]

Leading Italian avant-garde architects accepted these ideological premises. Some, in fact, helped to shape Mussolini's vision of a distinctively fascist architecture. Among them was Giuseppe Terragni, a longtime champion of glass architecture. In 1932, Terragni received the regime's commission to build Como's Casa del Fascio, a building that would serve both as the headquarters for the local fascist party and as a community center (fig. 14.1).[21] Completed in 1936, the building emphasizes transparency and openness: more than 50 percent of the exterior is glazed, and the interior, too, features glass walls and floors.[22] Terragni hoped that a generously glazed building such as the Casa del Fascio would allow for "instinctive verification" in the relation between the fascist state and its citizens.[23] Citing Il Duce, Terragni declared about the Casa: "Here is an embodiment of Mussolini's idea that fascism is a glass house in which everyone can peek."[24] For Terragni, a "house of glass" ensured that there would be "no encumbrance, no barrier, no obstacle between the political hierarchies and the people."[25]

In fascist Germany, too, issues of fenestration and architectural glass received considerable attention. In the public architecture of the Third Reich, oversized windows underscored the regime's will to architectural monumentality. As in Italy, such windows also served as sites for the theatrical staging of power.[26] Hitler himself was well aware of windows' potential for political self-fashioning.

Fig. 14.1. Giuseppe Terragni, Casa del Fascio, Como, Italy, 1932–36. An admirer of Il Duce, Terragni declared about the Casa del Fascio: "Here is an embodiment of Mussolini's idea that fascism is a glass house into which everyone can peek."

Not by chance did he choose a window—that of his office in the Berlin chancellery—for his first public appearance as German chancellor on January 30, 1933. This wing of the chancellery was a functionalist annex built during the Weimar Republic, and its windows were quite large—but not large enough for Hitler, who dismissed the whole building as a "warehouse or municipal fire station."[27] Later, recalling this first public appearance as chancellor, Hitler remarked to Albert Speer, his master architect: "The window was really too inconvenient. I could not be seen from all sides. After all, I could not very well lean out."[28] This was an unacceptable situation for the führer—especially as his admirers routinely gathered beneath his office to cheer him. But a solution was hard to come by. A larger window would have conflicted with the façade's uniform fenestration. The compromise reached in 1935 was to build a balcony in front of the window.[29] The dictator received an extended stage—but to his great displeasure, the effect was not always as rousing as he anticipated. When, on the eve of the German invasion of Czechoslovakia in 1938, Hitler ordered a military parade through the center of Berlin, a British diplomat heard from German liaisons that "Hitler, who was watching from the window, was disgusted with the crowd for their apathy."[30]

In other settings, Hitler, the artist turned politician, did not have to make compromises and was free to act out his architectural ambition without constraints. An exemplary case is the Berghof, the führer's lavish residence on the Obersalzberg mountain in the Bavarian Alps. Originally a modest Bavarian chalet known as Haus Wachenfeld, the building was massively expanded at Hitler's orders in 1935–36. The new residence assumed the name Berghof (Mountain Court). Hitler had an unflinchingly high opinion of his own architectural skills, and he personally drafted the plans for the alpine retreat. As Despina Stratigakos has shown, Hitler used the idyllic setting and vernacular style of the Berghof to present himself to political guests and the press as a trustworthy, grounded statesman. Indeed, in the 1930s, the Berghof became the subject of countless photo-stories in the national and international press, such that "for a time, Hitler's mountain retreat was arguably the most famous house in the world."[31]

The Berghof's central space was the Great Hall, a space of three thousand square feet, intended for meetings, receptions, and entertainment. The vast hall was furnished with heavy furniture and precious tapestries, but its most spectacular feature was an oversized panoramic window measuring twenty-eight by twelve feet (fig. 14.2).[32] Hitler was intimately involved in the minutiae of the window's design, ignoring the advice of skeptical confidants such as Gerdy Troost, his long-standing interior decorator, and Speer, his master architect. Speer recounted after the war:

> A huge picture window in the living room, famous for its size and the fact that it could be lowered, was Hitler's pride. It offered a view of the Untersberg, Berchtesgarden, and Salzburg. However, Hitler had been inspired to situate his garage underneath this window; when the wind was unfavorable, a strong smell of gasoline penetrated into the living room. All in all, this was a ground plan that would have been graded D by any professor at an institute of technology.[33]

The gasoline smell does not seem to have bothered Hitler, perhaps because it did not interfere with the primary purpose of the window: to afford a grand view and a sense of omnipotence (fig. 14.3). Unlike the office window in the Berlin chancellery, the Berghof window did not serve Hitler's self-presentation to the masses. (The thousands of Germans who made a pilgrimage to Obersalzberg were kept at a distance from Hitler's home, which was heavily guarded by SS men.) However, Hitler much enjoyed showing off the window to acolytes and visitors. In a letter from 1938, Unity Mitford—a British admirer of Hitler and ardent promoter of fascism—recalled her visit to the Berghof, singling out the vast window as the architectural highlight: "The effect is simply extraordinary. The window—the largest piece of

Fig. 14.2. The panorama window of the Great Hall of Hitler's Berghof residence, Obersalzberg, Germany. Postcard, 1930s. Bavarian State Library, Munich. Hitler was closely involved in the design of this large 28-by-12-foot window, which could be mechanically lowered into the basement. Hitler liked to show off the window—one of the most photographed motifs of his alpine retreat—to acolytes and state guests. After the war, the heavily bombed Berghof was razed to the ground; nothing survives of the building and its famous window.

glass ever made—can be wound down like a motor window, as it was yesterday, leaving it quite open. Through it one just sees this huge chain of mountains, and it looks more like an enormous cinema screen than like reality. Needless to say the génial idea was the Führer's own, & he said Frau Troost wanted to insist on having *three* windows."[34] Two years earlier, the panorama window had left a similarly strong impression on David Lloyd George, the former British prime minister, as well as his delegation, during a semiofficial visit to the Berghof. One member of the delegation reported, "What fascinated us all was the vast window at the north end, or rather the absence of it, for it had been wound up or let down out of sight into a groove and there was nothing between us and the open air and sky and mountains and a view of Salzburg in the distance."[35] Lloyd George was so impressed that he ordered a similar picture window for his country house in England.

As Anglo-German relations soured in the course of the 1930s, British visitors grew weary of Hitler's showing off at the Berghof. When a high-ranking British government delegation, alarmed by Hitler's warmongering, met with the dictator at the Berghof in fall 1937, Hitler sought to impress his guests by drawing attention to the window. One member of the delegation later recalled that Hitler "insisted on demonstrating" the window's cutting-edge features; instantly, "a couple of stalwart S.S. men doubled into the room, fixed things like motor-car starting-handles into the sockets and wound violently. The whole structure sank noiselessly into the floor, giving the room the appearance of a covered terrace."[36] However, this demonstration only reinforced the guests' impression that Hitler was behaving "like a spoilt, sulky child."[37]

Hitler's infatuation with oversized windows and their theatrical effect became an object of ridicule in Charlie Chaplin's famous satirical film *The Great Dictator* (1940). One of the movie's central scenes shows the dictator Adenoid Hynkel hosting his fellow fascist leader, Benzino Napaloni, during a state visit. While the two dictators are waiting together for a shave, the following dialogue unfolds in the barber's room:

> HYNKEL: It was the emperor's library.
> NAPALONI: Makes a good a-barbershop.
> HYNKEL: Too old-fashioned, I want something modern.
> NAPALONI: Is that so?
> HYNKEL: You see, when I get shaved, I'm very nervous. I like something to look at. So I'm putting in glass walls in the ceiling. So then when my head is turned this way, I shall have a view of the mountains.

Later, the conversation returns to this subject:

> HYNKEL: And then in my summer palace I have a barbershop.
> NAPALONI: Is that so?
> HYNKEL: Mmh. Yes, that also has glass walls.
> NAPALONI: You don't tell me.
> HYNKEL: Oh yes, with goldfish swimming inside.

Fig. 14.3. Hitler looking out of the picture window at the Berghof. Undated picture from the private photo album of his mistress, Eva Braun. National Archives, Washington, D.C.

NAPALONI: Goldfish swimming inside-a the walls? Mmh. How do you feed 'em?

HYNKEL: You can't. They're all dead. That's why I'm building a new barbershop.[38]

Chaplin brilliantly ridiculed Hitler's penchant for large windows and exposed it as showmanship. But like many contemporaries, Chaplin may have underestimated the political dimension of Hitler's architectural fancies. Far from being a mere extravagance, the Berghof window embodied Hitler's fantasies of unfettered power—including power over nature and, by extension, over the *Lebensraum* that nature provided.[39] Indeed, Nazi propaganda went so far as to proclaim the führer as the "master of the forces of nature" (*Herr der Naturgewalten*).[40] Tellingly, the Berghof window did not remain a unicum. Aware of Hitler's taste for sweeping views, the Nazi Party gave him, on his fiftieth birthday, a mountaintop pavilion on the nearby Kehlstein summit—and here again, the building featured large picture windows that could be lowered mechanically.[41] As Stratigakos has noted, the Nazis "did not tremble before nature, but rather treated it as one more thing to be brought under their dominion."[42] Hitler's panorama windows embodied this will to absolute power.

Traditional alpine architecture, characterized as it was by pragmatic designs, offered no precedent for Hitler's lavish mountain residences, let alone for his fenestral ambitions. The führer's penchant for large windows was far more in line with what might, at first, seem an unlikely context: interwar modernist architecture. The picture window at the Berghof, for instance, bears close resemblance to the famous retractable windows of the Villa Tugendhat—a villa commissioned by a Jewish family and built by the Bauhaus director Mies van der Rohe.[43] And hadn't Le Corbusier gushed about panorama windows conveying "the feeling of lookouts dominating a world in order"?[44]

It might seem counterintuitive that the Nazis adopted rhetorical tropes and stylistic elements of modernist architecture. After all, the official party line denounced this architecture as an aberration. Particularly fierce was the invective against the Bauhaus—both the institution (denounced as a "cathedral of Marxism") and the building named after it. As early as 1932, the Dessau branch of the Nazi Party mocked Gropius's glass-faced Bauhaus building as a "sober glass palace of Oriental taste" and called for its demolition.[45] When the Nazis came to power in

1933, the Bauhaus, as an institution, was shut down within months. However, the flagship building of the Dessau campus survived: instead of demolishing Gropius's "glass palace," the Nazis added a pitched roof (which they considered quintessentially German), and then turned the building into a training center for party leaders. The preservation of the iconic Bauhaus building was symptomatic of the ambivalent and sometimes quite flexible Nazi approach to modernist architecture.[46]

Hitler himself displayed flexibility in this respect. In a cultural policy speech delivered in 1933, the führer castigated interwar art but at the same time declared "crystal-clear functionalism" a yardstick for "the most sublime beauty."[47] Hitler rejected a "purported Sachlichkeit," yet he remained open to certain elements of architectural modernism.[48] After all, he felt, the aesthetics of "function and material" stood alone in having brought about "creations that are modern and at the same time aesthetically satisfying." In a rather convoluted conclusion, Hitler noted, "From new building materials such as steel, iron, glass, concrete, and so on, a development begins which will inevitably lead to an approach suited to the purposes of construction as well as to [the properties of] these materials."[49]

There were further intersections between the fascist vision of architecture and the idiom of interwar modernism. The mantra of rationalization, the use of uniform materials, the lack of ornament, and the idea of functional design—all of these key modernist principles proved compatible with Nazi architecture, if stripped of their original democratic impetus and put in the service of a collectivist ideology.[50] As architectural historian Petra Eisele has observed, in the Third Reich "the agenda of the Bauhaus was rejected in terms of its philosophy, but continued on a formal level."[51] Leading Nazi politicians, such as Propaganda Minister Joseph Goebbels, explicitly defended interwar modernist architecture, commending its emphasis on clear forms and endorsing it as a legitimate source of inspiration for a new fascist architecture. Baldur von Schirach, the leader of the Hitler Youth, commissioned overtly sachlich architecture for his organization. In his opinion, a "youthful" German architecture was to avoid monumentalism and historicism, and instead draw on quintessentially modern materials such as glass, steel, and concrete.[52]

But it would be too simplistic to argue that fascism appropriated interwar modernism in a unilateral fashion. The process was bidirectional. Noted avant-garde architects and architectural theorists flirted with, or even endorsed, the vision of a new, "national" architecture. Le Corbusier, for instance, accepted invitations from Mussolini and tried to interest the Italian dictator in daring projects; and after the Nazi conquest of France, the architect also reached out to the fascist Vichy regime and served for a time as a government adviser.[53] In Germany, too, architects who had supported the liberal democracy of the interwar period sounded out the opportunities in the new political reality. After 1933, both Gropius and Mies—the two most prominent Bauhaus directors of the Weimar period—agreed to participate in exhibitions and competitions sponsored by the Nazi Party. Pandering to the regime, Gropius added swastikas to his designs. Mies likewise adjusted projects to cater to the regime, and the Nazi press in turn commended him as a "representative of Fascism in art."[54] When Gropius and Mies left Germany for good—in 1934 and 1938, respectively—their exits were driven not by categorical opposition to the regime, but rather by financial considerations and the prospect of better opportunities abroad.[55]

Among the modernist architects who stayed in Germany were the brothers Hans and Wassili Luckhardt, former members of the Glass Chain, who had joined the Nazi Party as early as 1933. In the 1934 competition for the National Socialist Haus der Arbeit (House of Labor), the two brothers submitted a design that combined the formally required Thingplatz—a site of assembly meant to invoke medieval Germanic culture—with a secular temple-cum-convention hall in the form of an oversized, vitreous crystal.[56] The project remained unrealized, and the two brothers later fell afoul of the regime. Still, their vitreous design for the Haus der Arbeit indicates that the legacy of Scheerbart, Taut, and others did not end abruptly in 1933.

The case of Otto Völckers has received less attention, but it illustrates particularly well how modernism, and especially glass architecture, could be brought in line with the new political circumstances. During the years of the Weimar Republic, the architect Völckers had made a name for himself in modernist circles and become known as a champion of architectural glass. After the Nazi rise to power, Völckers aligned his lobbying for glass architecture with the regime's architectural vision. The most comprehensive result was his 1939 book *Glas und Fenster* (Glass and Window). Arguably the most detailed account of glass architecture under fascism, this volume deserves closer examination.

Völckers's call for more glass—a sealant that he celebrated as quintessentially German—was published a few months after Nazi officials and sympathizers had smashed the windows of hundreds of Jewish stores, homes, and synagogues during the pogroms euphemistically known as Kristallnacht. The timing was a co-incidence, but not a contradiction. The fenestral violence was the flipside of the vision of a German architecture characterized by glass and light. Precisely because this vitreous architecture was deemed intrinsically German, Nazi ideology would not extend it to Jews and their buildings.

Not only were Jews deprived of their window glass; their contribution to glass architecture was also systematically purged from the historical narrative. In Völckers's generously illustrated volume, buildings designed by Jewish architects are conspicuously missing. This is all the more salient given that Völckers's historical survey provides one of the fullest accounts of the development of window glass from antiquity up to his own time. Also disconcerting are the ideological conclusions that Völckers drew from the millennia-old history of window glass. In his view, "The window is the soul of all northern European architecture, and glass is the soul of the window."[57] Essentialist as they are, such claims reveal the contradictions inherent in fascist narratives about links between glass and "national spirit": after all, in propagating architectural glass, both Italian and German fascists produced conflicting myths of origins. Mussolini's followers took credit for window glass as a Roman contribution to civilization, whereas, in Nazi Germany, authors such as Völckers argued that northern Europeans had displayed a "naturally conditioned predilection for extensive fenestration" from time immemorial.[58]

In Völckers's view, this German predilection for windows had found its greatest manifestation in the country's medieval cathedrals, which epitomized the "Nordic light-loving spirit of the Gothic period" (*nordisch-lichtfrohen Geist der Gotik*).[59] According to Völckers, this intrinsically northern European inclination was gradually suppressed by a very different, southern European taste:

> Mediterranean art originally did not know at all the window as an element of architecture; it was only the Italian Renaissance that turned it into one. The Nordic Gothic, by contrast, founded its architecture on vaults and windows; half-timber construction—based on a similar guiding principle—followed this model. Both approaches, the southern and the northern European, diverge in their principles; and the more we become aware of our own creative potential, the more our architecture distinguishes itself from the architecture that has come to us from the Mediterranean. The South always approached the façade as having a sculptural quality; we in the North see the façade as having a planar quality, and this perception aligns beautifully with the shining evenness of glass. For us, the window is not a necessary evil, not a hole that needs to be framed with ornamental embel-

lishment—quite the contrary, the window is in itself an embellishment. When the building's purpose requires (or does not preclude) it, we even surrender the entire wall to the window, ultimately allowing the window to transform the entire house into a transparent body.[60]

While Völckers credited the Italian Renaissance with treating windows as distinctive architectural elements, this hardly changed his overall negative attitude toward "southern" architecture. In his view, the rise of Palladianism from the late sixteenth century onward had foreshadowed flaws that became fully manifest in Italian baroque architecture—that highly formalized architecture in which "the exterior is everything, and the convenience and quality of life in the interior mean very little." For Völckers, seventeenth- and eighteenth-century Italian architecture saw the "badgering [*Bedrängung*] of the windows by the exterior architectural design."[61]

Völckers concluded that northern Europeans should emancipate themselves from southern European architectural traditions. Citing Goethe, he urged his fellow Germans to "avow themselves to the tribe that seeks the light" (*zu dem Geschlecht bekennen, das ins Helle strebt*).[62] As it happens, this quote was a misattribution: the line—which was also cited by other nationalist authors such as Houston Stewart Chamberlain—was a rather distorted version of a remark that Goethe had made in a completely unrelated context.[63] But Völckers's argument sat well with the Nazis—not only because of its nationalist impetus, but also because the call for more light tied in well with the regime's goal of improving the "health of the people" (*Volksgesundheit*). As we have seen, arguments about public health had long informed the discourse about glass architecture. Advocates of glass routinely claimed that large windows had a beneficial effect on hygiene, creating a framework for healthy working and living conditions.[64] Yet only under fascism did these issues become a distinctively *national* question.

The regime's rationale was simple: more windows meant more light and more air, which were considered crucial for the systematic battle against "diseases that corrupt the people's health" (*volksverderbende Krankheiten*)—that is, the *German people's* health.[65] The main enemy in this battle was rickets, a disease also known at the time as "light deficiency disease" (*Lichtmangelkrankheit*). As Völckers stressed, rickets was "directly correlated to cold, sunless, and damp apartments."[66] The disease could lead to bone softening, which threatened to impair fertility—a specter for a regime that promoted, for ideological reasons, more births and stronger offspring. Tuberculosis and rheumatism were no less dreaded. Here, too, glass architecture was said to have beneficial effects. Striking a rather martial tone, Völckers argued: "We have to welcome even the smallest contribution to our weapons arsenal against diseases that corrupt the people's health, and even if copious light and thorough sunshine exposure can only partly qualify as weapons, we must still use these weapons—by enlarging the windows of our apartments and work spaces and by making them face the sun."[67] Völckers considered light, air, and sun the three "noblest and absolutely irreplaceable life resources," which "must be allocated to every German as much as possible in order to guarantee the flourishing of our people."[68] This radical change should begin with domestic architecture, as people statistically spent most of their time at home. He concluded that, "from a medical perspective, the largest possible window opening—that is, the complete dissolution of the exterior wall into glass—would be an advantage."[69]

Medical doctors at the time were less sure about the validity of such claims, and some pointed out that ordinary window glass transmitted little or none of the ultraviolet rays needed to prevent rickets.[70] Such objections do not seem to have bothered Völckers, whose position was in line with the view of the Nazi Reichsheimstättenamt (Reich Homestead Office), the agency responsible for public housing and planning. In 1940, for instance, the agency declared: "A new approach to residential architecture derived from the principles of National Socialism demands a clear and bright residential space."[71]

Industrial architecture was likewise supposed to benefit from generous use of glass. Speer recalled that Hitler "could become enthusiastic over an industrial building in glass and steel."[72] Völckers's slogan, "Good light—good work" (*Gutes Licht—gute Arbeit*), fully aligned with the mission of the Nazi Reichsamt Schönheit der Arbeit (Office for the Beauty of Labor).[73] The office's name was, of course, a euphemism: the goal of Nazi economic policies was not to achieve "beautiful" working conditions, but rather to prepare Germany for war. In an effort to improve the conditions of industrial production, the office published brochures and pamphlets that encouraged companies to install large windows (figs. 14.4, 14.5). What is more, one of the most iconic industrial glass buildings associated with modernism—Gropius's Fagus factory—was officially declared an "exemplary national-socialist workplace."[74] Indeed, the continuities between interwar modernism and Nazi industrial architecture are hard to overlook.[75] As Speer admitted after the war, the office went so far as to plagiarize Bauhaus ideas and designs.[76]

104 Lichtverteilung in einem einseitig befensterten Fabrikraum. Werbebild des Reichsamtes „Schönheit der Arbeit"

Völckers, the avant-garde architect turned National Socialist, was not directly implicated in the Nazi war machine. Like millions of other Germans, he was a *Mitläufer* (follower), willing to put his ideas and skills into the service of the regime. But support and collaboration were not the only options available. First of all, there were noted non-Jewish artists, architects, and intellectuals who could have stayed in Germany but instead chose to emigrate, as Gropius and Mies eventually did. Another famous emigrant was the novelist and Nobel laureate Thomas Mann, who settled in the United States, from where his fiercely anti-Nazi radio speeches were broadcast to Germany. It is perhaps no coincidence that Mann, repelled by the führer's grandstanding and Nazi monumentalism, referred to these radio speeches as an effort to "tirelessly throw stones into Hitler's windows."[77]

Even artists and intellectuals who decided to stay in Nazi Germany found ways to express opposition to the regime. In this context, windows were used not only as a metaphor (as with Mann), but also as a concrete locus of resistance. A fascinating but almost forgotten example is a church window created by the German artist JoKarl Huber. Huber was a declared opponent of the Nazi regime, as was his wife, the artist Hildegard Huber-Sasse. At their wedding in Munich in 1938, they received the obligatory copy of Hitler's *Mein Kampf*—but they threw it away under the registrar's gaze. Huber's opposition to Nazi ideology was known to the authorities: three years earlier, in 1935, the artist had been branded a "cultural bolshevist" and, as a repressive measure, was prohibited from painting on canvas.[78] Consequently, he resorted to other materials, such as glass. In 1938, through an acquaintance who was a priest, Huber received the commission to create a new

Vorbildliche Montagehalle

Fig. 14.5. "Exemplary assembly hall." Image from the *Taschenbuch Schönheit der Arbeit* (Pocketbook Beauty of Labor), published by the Nazi Office for the Beauty of Labor in 1938. The office used images such as this one to advocate for large windows and ample daylight—features that were considered essential for "the National-Socialist redefinition of the work environment" (as Albert Speer put it in his preface to the pocketbook). As early as October 1933, the office had published the brochure *Gute Beleuchtung am Arbeitsplatz* (Good Lighting at the Workplace); a sequel, titled *Gutes Licht* (Good Light), followed in 1936.

church window for the Catholic church of St. Peter and Paul in the small southern German town of Weil der Stadt. The Nazis did not consider "construction-related art" (*Kunst am Bau*) to be art in the full sense of the word (*freie Kunst*), which allowed the ostracized Huber to accept the commission.[79] Over the next two years, he created a window that recounted the story of Christ, consisting of nine separate stained-glass panels. Of particular interest is the panel with the Temptation of Christ—for it depicts a Satan whose face unmistakably resembles that of Hitler (fig. 14.6). This resemblance did not go unnoticed among locals after the window was unveiled in 1940, and it was clear to everyone that the artist had risked his life. Huber's saving grace was the support of the parish priest, who downplayed the issue. It also turned out be a blessing in disguise that the artist was conscripted a year later and deployed to the front: as a Wehrmacht soldier, he could be tried only in military court, which protected him from the clutches of the Gestapo, the much-feared secret police, which had begun to investigate the case.[80]

To this day, the most striking aspect of Huber's church window cycle is no doubt the daring depiction of the devil as Hitler (an analogy reinforced by the figure's brownish garments and swastika-like bodily contortion). But perhaps there was also a message in the medium? Huber created the window using medieval stained-glass techniques, and the deliberately "archaic," polychrome effect contrasted sharply with the fascist taste for large, transparent glass surfaces and boundless light. Huber's highly colored church window does not maximize the admission of light, but rather harks back to the idea of a solemn, "Christian" light. Interestingly, this vision also reverberates in the work of Huber-Sasse, the artist's wife. She, too, was involved in the artistic remodeling of the church of St. Peter and Paul, frescoing a side chapel dedicated to the Virgin Mary. The frescoes depict female figures as guardians of light, which here serves as a symbol of life. The female figures hold their guarding hands before the flickering light that is threatened by a hostile environment—a subtle reference to what it meant to live a (Christian) life under a dark and hostile regime.[81]

The year 1945 was not "zero hour." True, the Third Reich had collapsed, as had innumerable buildings across Germany. But the two Germanies that emerged from the ruins saw continuities on various levels—including in the field of architecture. In the West, Mitläufer such as Völckers found new opportunities in the newly founded Federal Republic. In fact, Völckers continued his architectural practice and was involved in the reconstruction of Munich. His vision for the new

Fig. 14.6. Detail from JoKarl Huber, *Temptation of Christ by the Devil*, part of a stained-glass cycle depicting scenes from Christ's life, church of St. Peter and Paul, Weil der Stadt, Germany, installed 1940. The panel is traditional in its artistic execution, but extremely daring in content: the resemblance between the devil and Hitler is hard to overlook and could have cost Huber his life. The medium itself—stained glass—runs counter to the fascist taste for monumental, clear glass surfaces.

city center entailed large housing compounds with glass-roofed common spaces for shopping and socializing. When this plan did not materialize, Völckers found an ideal platform for his ideas in the architectural magazine *Glasforum* (Glass Forum), which he edited from 1950 until his death in 1957.[82]

A less tainted proponent of glass architecture was Hans Schwippert. Before the rise of the Nazis, Schwippert had belonged to the avant-garde circle of Bruno Taut and Mies van der Rohe. Unlike Taut and Mies, Schwippert stayed in Germany throughout the Nazi years, adjusting to the new regime without becoming a vocal supporter.[83] After the fall of the Third Reich, Schwippert launched a remarkable career in the Federal Republic, where he played a key role in creating a new architecture for the nascent democratic state. Schwippert considered glass a material particularly well suited to embody West Germany's commitment to democracy. Once again, vitreous transparency was invoked to convey a political message—but this time a message diametrically opposed to that of fascist architecture.

Schwippert's architecture met the expectations of the postwar political establishment. Adolf Arndt, an influential social democratic member of parliament, declared in a 1960 lecture titled "Demokratie als Bauherr" (Democracy as Architect) that political architecture in a democratic state was duty-bound to render the invisible visible. Criticizing traditional façades and their "political purpose to conceal," Arndt demanded a "link between the principle of a democratic public on the one hand, and the exterior and interior transparency [*Durchsichtigkeit*] and accessibility of a democracy's public buildings on the other hand."[84] Arndt articulated a majority view: under new symbolic and political auspices, postwar Germans espoused the architectural mantra that "transparency equals democracy."[85] The architectural historian Deborah Ascher Barnstone has gone so far as to argue that political architecture in West Germany displayed an "obsession with transparency."[86]

Some of the most prominent public buildings in Bonn, the West German capital, featured extensive glass surfaces—including the Bundestag, the federal parliament. The first Bundestag (1949), fitted by Schwippert into a preexisting compound, received an all-glass façade that allowed the public to observe the proceedings in the assembly (fig. 14.7). The second Bundestag, constructed by Günter Behnisch in 1992 as a more spacious successor to Schwippert's parliament building, evoked the same architectural idiom of transparency. So did the courthouse of the Bundesverfassungsgericht (Federal Constitutional Court) in Karlsruhe, built by Paul Baumgarten between 1965 and 1969. Baumgarten's courthouse is still in use, and the architectural design continues to inform the institution's self-understanding. The high court's website explains: "By [the building's] open structure, [Baumgarten] intended to express democratic transparency and to distinguish the building from the 19th-century-style palaces of justice."[87]

This commitment to glass architecture remained strong after the 1989 German reunification—even through the government's relocation from Bonn to Berlin over the next decade. As Lutz Koepnick has observed, glass "emerged as one of the Berlin Republic's most privileged construction materials."[88] Probably the best-known example is the Reichstag, the current seat of the German parliament.

Fig. 14.7. View of the assembly hall of the German Bundestag, Bonn. Postcard, 1950s. Completed by Hans Schwippert in 1949, the assembly hall was the heart of the first postwar West German parliament building. Schwippert faced a difficult task: the hall, along with administrative offices, had to be integrated into a preexisting building complex from the 1930s. At the same time, he added a floor-to-ceiling glass façade through which citizens could watch the parliamentary proceedings.

After the 1990 decision to make Berlin the capital of reunited Germany, a competition was held to solicit proposals for a radical overhaul of the nineteenth-century Reichstag building. British architect Norman Foster won the competition with his proposal to cap the Reichstag's central assembly hall with a glass cupola that would be accessible to visitors and allow them to observe the parliamentary sessions from above (figs. 14.8, 14.9). As Foster noted, the idea of a glass cupola catered to the expectations of both the political establishment and the public: "For security reasons, not every part of the Reichstag can be open to the public, but we have ensured that where possible it is transparent and its activities are on view. It is a building without secrets."[89]

Foster's Reichstag has become one of the most iconic symbols of the "Berlin Republic." It epitomizes postwar Germany's commitment to vitreous transparency as the privileged idiom of the architecture of power. Indeed, Berlin—like Bonn in the past—is home to many other political buildings characterized by expansive glass façades. As the American architectural critic Jane Kramer has noted about the mentality of post-reunification Germans: "They live in a capital from which the worst of Germany's history was decreed, and now that the government

Fig. 14.8. Reichstag, Berlin, renovated by Norman Foster, 1995–99. After the reunification of Germany in 1990, the Reichstag became the seat of the German Bundestag. The late nineteenth-century building received a comprehensive overhaul by British architect Norman Foster. The new Reichstag emphasizes continuity with postwar German architecture by privileging transparent glass over other architectural materials. Indeed, in planning the building, Foster "ensured that where possible it is transparent." This approach finds expression in the amply glazed entrance area and the internal glass partitions, but especially the iconic large glass cupola.

is moving back to that capital they have convinced themselves that the right buildings will somehow produce the right attitudes in the people inside them. They like the transparency of the Reichstag's dome—it's the most visited place in the city now—because they think it will somehow guarantee that openness and democracy thrive in the Reichstag."[90] But is there really a guarantee that architectural transparency will bring about institutional transparency? Are democratic values innate to large glass surfaces? A closer look at German history reminds us that there is little evidence to justify such sweeping assumptions. For one thing, we have seen how the Nazis co-opted glass architecture for a deeply antidemocratic political agenda. For another, the history of postwar Germany cannot be reduced to the history of the Federal Republic. For four decades, there existed another German state, the German Democratic Republic (GDR), where glass architecture also served a political function—but under the auspices of communism.

The communist government of the GDR had its own reasons for encouraging the use of glass, at least in certain genres of architecture. Invoking an argument familiar from early twentieth-century modernist discourses, the party line deemed glass and transparency beneficial to public health. In this vein, the GDR-published booklet *Die Funktion des Fensters von der Romantik bis zur Gegenwart* (The Function of the Window from the Romantic Period to the Present, 1970) ended with the emphatic claim that "socialist public housing" had leveled the differences between ostentatious bourgeois architecture and the poorly lit lower-class dwellings of the past: "Both in generic and experimental buildings, all apartments receive sufficient light through large windows. And those sites of production, where work under bad light conditions was the rule in the past, are now almost forgotten thanks to the use of the newest building techniques."[91]

Creating better living and labor conditions for the working class was not the only objective, of course. As in the Federal Republic, glass carried symbolic meaning in the GDR—especially in Berlin, a city in which the Cold War played out also on an architectural level. Any major building project in the divided city was considered a political statement, even if the building did not have a political purpose. A case in point is the Europa-Center, a large shopping center and office building erected in the 1960s on Kurfürstendamm, West Berlin's central boulevard. The glass-faced complex was perceived as a temple of consumerism, and it embodied "West Berlin's effort to adopt American modernism and lifestyles."[92] In the eastern part of the city, communist leaders sought to counter such architectural symbolism. It is no coincidence that glass figured prominently in the political

Fig. 14.9.
Cupola of the
Reichstag, Berlin
(see fig. 14.8).

Fig. 14.10. The Palast der Republik (Palace of the Republic), East Berlin, 1973–76. Postcard, 1970s. Housing the East German parliament along with cultural spaces and restaurants, the building was meant to embody the spirit of "democratic socialism." The façade, with its iridescent, bronze-colored windows, suggested openness and accountability; in reality, however, it was the visitors who were closely monitored and surveilled.

architecture of the GDR—a communist state that routinely fashioned itself as the "showcase of socialism" (*Schaufenster des Sozialismus*).

As in the West, but with a different ideological impetus, the GDR's conspicuous use of glass in certain political buildings was meant to signal political transparency.[93] Consider the Staatsratgebäude (1960–64), the seat of the state council, built by an architectural collective under the leadership of Roland Korn and Hans Erich Bogatzky. Located in the heart of East Berlin, the building featured a generously glazed main façade, while the central staircase boasted a monumental cycle of colored windows depicting the historical development of German communism. With similar intentions, the façade of the nearby Palast der Republik (Palace of the Republic, 1973–76), built by an architectural collective under the direction of Heinz Graffunder, was lined with iridescent, bronze-colored windows, which, at least from a close distance, provided views into the interior (fig. 14.10). The Palast der Republik served as the official seat of the GDR parliament, and its glass façade suggested that the inner workings of the (rather powerless) legislature were visible to everyone.[94] In line with this appearance of openness, the palace also housed publicly accessible concert halls, theaters, and cafés. The impression of abundant light in the interior was augmented by hundreds of ceiling lamps, which led citizens to quip about the palace as "Erich's lamp shop" (*Erichs Lampenladen*, referencing Erich Honecker, the GDR's leader at the time).

The Palast der Republik—like other amply glazed public buildings in the GDR—was supposed to give an appearance of democratic accountability and good governance. In practice, however, transparency only existed in a very different sense. As we now know in disturbing detail, the interior of the palace was under permanent surveillance by the Stasi, the GDR's feared state security service. In fact, the well-lit interior provided optimal conditions for the Stasi's omnipresent surveillance cameras and informers.[95] It was not the inner life of the GDR's political institutions that was transparent, but rather the private life of the citizenry, which in this setting, and indeed in many others, lay exposed to the eyes of thousands of spies and informants.

Mass surveillance was a tactic that the Stasi had learned from its big brother, the Soviet secret service. It is no coincidence that the Stasi subscribed to the Soviet cult of Felix Dzerzhinsky, the founder and first director of the Cheka, the secret police that ultimately became the KGB.[96] Interestingly, the invocation of vitreous imagery played an important role in this cult. For Dzerzhinsky, being true to the party line meant living a transparent life as a model Soviet citizen, without hiding any secrets from the state. Dzerzhinsky, for his part, was praised by the Soviet propaganda as a "crystally pure person." This notion of crystal-clear commitment to the communist cause was not mere rhetoric. It had tangible effects in the Soviet Union: a crystal-glass factory was named after Dzerzhinsky, and a town specializing in industrial glass production bore his name.[97] Needless to say, none of this vitreous rhetoric translated into institutional transparency in the political system. The Soviet regime remained notoriously secretive. There was no connection—neither historically nor etymologically—between glass and *glasnost*.

15

Postwar Enthusiasm, Postmodernist Rejection— and the Present

Chapter-opening image: Detail of Fig. 15.7

Postwar architecture would be hard to imagine without glass. Few other architectural materials have risen to similar prominence since 1945. As we saw in the preceding chapter, the case of Germany vividly illustrates how glass—that quintessentially "clean" and modern material—assumed a key role in the rebuilding of a world in ruins. Large glass surfaces became a characteristic and highly symbolic feature of postwar German political architecture. In domestic architecture, too, the technical sophistication of German windows has fostered a sense of national pride. When, a few years ago, Angela Merkel was asked in a newspaper interview which qualities she associates with Germany, her answer was as terse as it was telling: "I think of tight windows! No other country is able to design windows as tight and beautiful."[1]

Merkel's answer is, of course, somewhat exaggerated. Innovation in the mid- and late twentieth-century glass industry was hardly limited to Germany. Firms in the United States, the United Kingdom, and France made similarly important contributions. It was precisely this concert of technological innovation that revolutionized glass production from the 1950s onward and paved the way for the ubiquity of glass in postwar architecture. Perhaps the most important of these innovations was the perfection of industrial high-quality production. Ever since the renaissance of glass-casting in the seventeenth century, one technical issue had remained unsolved: how to mass-produce large sheets that are completely even and do not require any finishing. In the search for a solution, the British firm Pilkington Brothers took the lead. In the early 1950s, engineer Alastair Pilkington (no relation to the owners) began to experiment with means of floating molten glass on a bed of liquid tin. Due to the high temperature of the molten glass (around 1,100 degrees Celsius), the tin (with its low melting point of 232 degrees Celsius) would remain liquid and form a perfectly flat surface.[2] The glass film could then be drawn through metal rollers, yielding a thin, clear, and continuous band of glass.[3] As the company explained, "Because the surface of the metal is dead flat, the glass is dead flat too. Natural forces of weight and surface tension bring it to an absolutely uniform thickness."[4]

By the late 1950s, this method, the "float system," was ready for serial production, and Pilkington Brothers began to mass-produce glass plates with a smooth surface and a width of more than eight feet. With minor modifications, the float system soon became the standard method for producing large glass panes— and it remains so still today. Despite the enormous initial investment—the cost of setting up a factory can run into the nine figures—float glass has effectively super-seded centuries-old methods such as blowing and coulage.[5]

There were also, of course, cultural and political factors that contributed to the rise of glass architecture. The case of postwar Germany illustrates some of the political hopes bound up with the use of architectural glass—but here again, the German case is hardly unique. The postwar boom of architectural transparency manifested itself in many other parts of the world, including in the United States.[6] This development was closely related to the rise of "openness" as a shibboleth of postwar political discourse. As Michael Schudson has shown with respect to the United States, the mantra of openness became a "key element in the transformation of politics, society, and culture from the late 1950s through the 1970s."[7] This rhetoric laid the foundation for what Schudson has identified as the "transparency imperative" in modern American politics.[8] Whether this call for institutional transparency has achieved its goals on a practical level is debatable. But it has certainly left its mark on a symbolic level. As this chapter will show, the evocation of institutional transparency through the large-scale use of glass is one of the most common tropes in the postwar architecture of power—both political and corporate power. At the same time, modern glass architecture has come with a range of practical problems that reveal the cracks, as it were, in an architectural aesthetic in which glass must bear not just structural weight, but often also an overload of symbolic meaning.

As in Europe, the postwar "transparency imperative" had precedents in the United States. Terms such as "light" and "publicity" had long carried positive associations in the American political discourse. As early as 1891, Louis Brandeis, the American lawyer (and later Supreme Court justice), argued, "If the broad light of day could be let in upon men's actions, it would purify them as the sun disinfects."[9] In 1913, Brandeis famously synthesized this belief when he said that "sunlight is said to be the best of disinfectants; electric light the most efficient policeman."[10] Brandeis was not alone in this positive view of publicity and openness. For instance, his contemporary, President Woodrow Wilson, repeatedly emphasized the importance of shedding "light" on the government's conduct.[11] Of course, this was metaphorical language. But it is noteworthy that this rhetoric of virtuous openness coincided with the period that also saw the first notable and systematic experiments with open façades and large glass surfaces in American architecture—experiments that were often tied to a vision of bettering individual lives as well as society at large.[12]

Among the earliest and most vocal proponents of glass architecture in the United States was Frank Lloyd Wright. At the beginning of his career, Wright experimented primarily with colored glass, but he soon emerged as a champion of glass architecture in general, extolling it not just for its aesthetic qualities, but also as a remedy for the social and urban problems of his time.[13] Like his German contemporaries Paul Scheerbart and Bruno Taut, Wright was fascinated with the idea of designing entire cities from scratch, with "buildings—shimmering fabrics—woven of rich glass." In Wright's exalted description, "Such a city would clean itself in the rain, would know no fire alarms—nor any glooms."[14] Although this vision remained unrealized, Wright remained convinced of the panacean qualities of glass, reiterating in later years that glass was a "super-material" and that the way "we now use it is a miracle."[15]

This commitment to architectural glass and large windows even provided common ground between Wright and Le Corbusier—a somewhat remarkable fact given that the two men disagreed on a range of other issues and were not on amicable terms. Some of Wright's slogans—for instance, "Fewer doors, fewer window holes, though much greater window areas"—could just as well have been aperçus by Le Corbusier.[16] Both men certainly shared a penchant for polemic. In that vein, Wright argued that only large glass windows would allow modern man to "escape from the prettified cavern of our present domestic life as also from the cave of our past."[17] For Wright, a well-designed home entailed ample access to natural light as well as generous views of the surrounding landscape. To accomplish this goal, he argued, the architect had to eliminate conventional windows and instead replace these "holes in walls"—or even the entire wall—with large glass surfaces.[18]

Wright's experiments with architectural glass remained largely confined to domestic architecture. When, on the eve of the Great Depression, he formulated his vision of an American urban landscape "woven of rich glass," the circumstances were hardly conducive to such bold experiments. It was left to other architects to realize that vision. And in time, the economic recovery and technological progress of the postwar years proved far more favorable to the realization of ambitious projects.

The Equitable Savings and Loan Building in Portland, Oregon (Pietro Belluschi, 1948) stands out as a pioneering attempt to construct a fully glazed office tower. New York and Chicago soon followed suit.[19] The first glass-faced skyscrapers in Manhattan were the Lever House (Gordon Bunshaft and Natalie de Blois,

Fig. 15.1. Wallace Harrison, after designs by Le Corbusier and Oscar Niemeyer, United Nations Secretariat Building, New York, 1948–52. Clad in greenish glass, the tower soars 500 feet high. It is the most prominent building of New York's United Nations campus, which, at the time of its inauguration, appeared to contemporaries as a "city of glass."

1952) and the United Nations Secretariat Building (Wallace Harrison, after designs by Le Corbusier and Oscar Niemeyer, 1952). The latter was described in the press as a veritable "city of glass" and "the most radical building design ever attempted on a huge scale" (fig. 15.1).[20]

In Chicago, glass high-rises began to appear around the same time—and here, too, European architects contributed their expertise. It was thanks to Mies van der Rohe that the United States' "Second City" held its ground as a premier site of architectural innovation. Mies had left Nazi Germany in 1938 and settled in Chicago, where he found ample opportunity to revisit his vitreous skyscraper projects from the 1920s. As Richard Sennett has noted, "Mies van der Rohe was the architect who did more than anyone else to make plate glass the physical stuff through which our century sees."[21] Indeed, Mies's glass-faced American high-rises have become part of the canon of twentieth-century architecture. This holds especially true for the Lake Shore Drive apartment towers in Chicago (1949–51), nicknamed the "Glass Houses," as well as the Seagram Building in New York (1955–57)—both admired for the elegant combination of steel skeleton and glass façade (figs. 15.2, 15.3).[22]

As architectural historian William Curtis has noted, glass façades attained "the status of a leitmotif in the United States in the first decade after the war."[23] The new taste for vitreous façades also aligned well with the needs of corporate architecture: glass-faced high-rises with open floor plans let daylight penetrate deep into the building's core, allowing for a higher density of workers in the interior. For employers, this translated into better "space efficiency; for developers, into higher rents."[24]

The boom of glass architecture in the postwar United States was not limited to corporate buildings, nor was it solely a phenomenon of city centers. The 1950s also saw a large-scale campaign to make oversized windows an essential feature of the suburban home. Both the construction industry and glass manufacturers

Fig. 15.2. Mies van der Rohe, 860–880 Lake Shore Drive, Chicago, 1949–51. The residential complex consists of two glass-faced high-rises. A sales brochure from the 1950s praised the building as "a historic 'first' [that] is further dramatized by its unique lakeside setting." However, the glass windows also produced other, less welcome kinds of drama, including overheating in the summer and water damage during rainstorms. The latter problem forced residents to form a "bucket brigade." Mies dropped his plan to move into the building.

Fig. 15.3. Mies van der Rohe (with the assistance of Philip Johnson), Seagram Building, New York, 1955–57. The Seagram Building is often considered Mies's finest realization of a glass-faced tower—an idea that he had pursued since the 1920s.

promoted the "picture window" as a must-have status object in the rapidly growing suburban communities (figs. 15.4, 15.5).[25] In prewar American homes, large windows were not unheard of, but they were typically made up of several smaller panes held together by wooden muntins. Only in the postwar years did oversized glass plates begin to appear in American homes.[26]

In 1949, a leading manufacturer of such picture windows boasted that three thousand war veterans "stood in line" to buy homes with the "floor-to-ceiling

Frame a pretty picture for the living room — your garden! Now you can use the beauty of the outdoors to charm and cheer your indoor living all year-round. For Twindow—the window with built-in insulation—cuts down heating costs, minimizes downdrafts, virtually eliminates window "steaming."

ARCHITECT:
HENRY W. JOHANSON
ROSLYN, N.Y.

Fig. 15.4. "In every home there is a place for Glass." Thus opens the 1950 sales brochure *How to Give Your Home Glamour with Glass*, published by the Pittsburgh Plate Glass Company, one of the world's largest glass manufacturers at the time. The numerous color images, such as this one, showcase the company's broad range of glass products, including the wall-sized picture windows that are presented as the ultimate status symbol of postwar domesticity.

You'll enjoy living in a "glass house" —with one wall of your living room made completely of Twindow — as shown here. And don't worry about chilling downdrafts, because Twindow has built-in insulation.

ARCHITECTS: FUBNO AND HARRISON, NEW YORK

Fig. 15.5. "You'll enjoy living in a 'glass house'" assures the caption—a promise that began to lose its appeal as residents grew disenchanted with larger-than-life glass windows. Image from the 1950 sales brochure *How to Give Your Home Glamour with Glass* (see fig. 15.4).

5

Thermopane window wall in the living room, a window 8 feet high, 16 feet long."[27] And that same year, the magazine *Architectural Forum* proclaimed that "outdoor space, with a large glass area overlooking it, [should] be considered a minimum standard for modern homes."[28] The *Journal of the American Institute of Architects* went so far as to praise picture windows and the sweeping views they provided as a fulfilment of the deep-rooted American dream that "we are still children of the Great Without." With boundless enthusiasm, the author asked, "How did we exist before the creation of the all-seeing picture window?"[29] As such remarks show, the picture window functioned not just as an economic status symbol, but also as a symbol of American lifestyle and freedom. As the Cold War reached new heights, the question of fenestral design became even more politicized: governmental housing agencies joined the construction industry in arguing that picture windows embodied the "American style." Opting for such windows in a sense meant taking sides in the struggle between freedom and totalitarianism.[30]

Yet the most daring glass architecture from this period was realized neither in the cities nor in suburbs: it was rural America that saw unprecedented experiments with total transparency in domestic architecture. Here again, Mies van der Rohe played a pioneering role—most notably, with his Farnsworth House in a secluded, wooded area in Plano, Illinois. Designed in 1945 but completed only in 1951, the Farnsworth House has been called Mies's "most radical domestic design" (fig. 15.6).[31] By designing a roof that rests on eight steel stanchions, Mies was free to envelop the rest of the house with floor-to-ceiling glass walls. Apart from a central service core (lined with wooden panels to conceal two bathrooms), the Farnsworth House is completely transparent on all sides, offering its residents full, unmediated exposure to the theater of light and nature unfolding outdoors.[32] For Mies, this ever-changing interplay between interior and exterior was a source of inspiration. He declared: "We should attempt to bring nature, houses and human beings together in a higher unity. If you view nature through the glass walls of the Farnsworth House, it gains a more profound significance than if viewed from outside . . . it becomes part of a larger whole."[33]

A seemingly simple design, the Farnsworth House was, in practice, far too costly and radical for serial production. But it did not remain a unicum. While the Farnsworth House was still in the making, Philip Johnson, one of Mies's staunchest American supporters, designed his own version: the Glass House in New Canaan, Connecticut (1948–49) (fig. 15.7). Like its Miesian model, Johnson's Glass

Fig. 15.6. Mies van der Rohe, Farnsworth House, Plano, Illinois, 1950–51. Considered Mies's "most radical domestic design," this glass pavilion in rural Illinois certainly proved too radical for its owner, Edith Farnsworth. She complained about countless small dysfunctions while also noting more generally, "There is a certain brutality about having the outside inside."

House is completely transparent on all four sides. But while the Farnsworth House hovers on a platform five feet aboveground, the Glass House is built on ground level, which reinforces the sense of fluidity between interior and exterior.

From weekend homes in the country to corporate high-rises in the city, glass-faced buildings from this period were bold architectural projects that drew on state-of-the-art construction techniques. Still, the ambition to build with glass often exceeded the technical ability to resolve the practical challenges that arose after completion. However noble (or naïve) its aspirations, glass architecture came with its own set of issues. Particularly pressing was the issue of overheating on warm days.[34] Le Corbusier's buildings are a case in point: as his projects increased in size

Fig. 15.7. Philip Johnson, Glass House, New Canaan, Connecticut, 1948–49. Unmistakably inspired by Mies's Farnsworth House, Johnson's fully transparent Glass House likewise elicited strong responses. Frank Lloyd Wright, a pioneer of glass architecture in the United States, asked his host, Johnson: "Do I take my hat off, or leave it on? I can't tell whether I am indoors or out."

and ambition from the late 1920s onward, so did the problems of overheating. Le Corbusier's Cité de Refuge (Salvation Army Hostel), built in Paris in 1930, was a particularly extreme case: the large glass windows, essential to Le Corbusier's vision of the building as a modern "architectural symphony," could not be opened by the occupants.[35] Cotton curtains and a mechanical ventilation system were supposed to ensure agreeable temperatures in the interior throughout the year. But the ventilation system was flawed. During the summer months, a shutdown of the fans caused unbearable, stifling conditions. Alarmed doctors noted that the temperature in the hostel's crèche rose to thirty-three degrees Celsius. Le Corbusier refused to make changes to the building, let alone sacrifice the ambitious window design. Instead, he argued that faster ventilating fans would solve the problem. In 1935, the municipal authorities finally stepped in and ordered—against the architect's will—the installation of forty sliding windows in the glass façade.[36]

Similar problems arose in Mies's Farnsworth House. Even architectural scholars partial to the elegant design have noted that the house "rewards aesthetic contemplation ahead of domesticity."[37] This, of course, puts it mildly. A blunter characterization is that the "Farnsworth House suffers from serious and elementary design faults."[38] In the absence of air-conditioning (which was still too expensive in the 1940s), and as a result of poor cross-ventilation, "it was perfectly predictable that a badly-ventilated glass box, without sun-shading except for some nearby trees, would become oven-like in the hot Illinois summers."[39] Mies, at least, took the concerns about overheating more seriously than Le Corbusier did. For the Seagram Building in New York, he chose tinted glass, which offered a higher degree of sun and heat protection.[40] Indeed, glass manufacturers at the time increased their efforts to develop heat-absorbing and glare-reducing panes. Tinting was considered particularly effective: thanks to the addition of iron oxide, tinted glass reduced the admission of short-wave infrared, thereby decreasing solar heat.[41]

More than anything else, however, the rise of air-conditioning proved crucial for glass architecture. The first experiments with building-wide electric air-conditioning dated back to the early twentieth century, but the technology only reached maturity after World War II. In the 1950s, air-conditioning became the second-fastest-growing industry in the United States (led only by television manufacturing).[42] Thanks to building-wide air-conditioning, people living or working in glass buildings regained the ability to control and adjust the temperature in the interior.[43] Yet the convenience also had (and has) a downside: a massive energy bill and, by extension, a large carbon footprint. In 1955, the Eisenhower administration strongly encouraged the installation of air-conditioning in government buildings. Two decades later, the government was forced to acknowledge the attendant problems: in 1979, President Jimmy Carter, in the midst of an energy emergency, decreed that thermostats in public and commercial buildings not be set below seventy-eight degrees Fahrenheit.[44]

Heat regulation was not the only challenge in glass-faced buildings. Large-scale transparency also raised the question of how to handle too much daylight—a problem for buildings such as libraries and museums in particular. This problem haunts Mies van der Rohe's last major project, the Neue Nationalgalerie in Berlin (1968). Enclosed by transparent glass, the Nationalgalerie, with its twenty-seven thousand square feet of exhibition space, serves as a museum for Berlin's modern art collections. Eight massive steel columns hold the flat roof and provide the structural support for the unpartitioned interior with its oversized floor-to-ceiling glass walls. The spatial experience is powerful, to be sure—but the building is dysfunctional as a museum space. Mies foresaw this problem but chose to ignore it: "It is such a large hall that of course it means great difficulties for the exhibiting of art. I am fully aware of that. But it has such potential that I simply cannot take those difficulties into account."[45] Curators, of course, cannot afford to be so nonchalant about what Mies dismissed as trite "difficulties": artwork exhibited in the Nationalgalerie is overexposed to light, which not only affects the aesthetic experience but also presents conservational issues. As one Mies biographer has put it, paintings run the risk of being "drowned in the ocean of surrounding space" there.[46] Ironically, "the New National Gallery pavilion is at its best when left entirely empty, or used as a display space for large-scale, free-standing sculpture."[47] To this day, most exhibits in the Nationalgalerie are presented in the lower level, which has relatively few windows.

In domestic architecture, the issue of excessive light was aggravated by concerns about privacy. A 1948 cartoon from the *New Yorker* captured how large picture windows upset traditional notions of privacy: the lady of the house is disturbed in her privacy by a confused brush salesman standing outside the window, who mistook it for the front door.[48] Visual privacy was particularly difficult to achieve in those suburban communities where homes with large picture windows were built back-to-back. In this setting, residents could often look right into their neighbors' living rooms—a problem that came to be known as the "goldfish bowl effect."[49] One critic observed that "the picture window seldom affords a view of anything more picturesque than the picture window of one's neighbor."[50] The construction industry countered this by claiming that large picture windows helped overcome "the former stuffy top-secret idea of boudoir."[51] Homeowners, however, grew increasingly weary of such claims. As we shall see, by the 1960s, a significant disenchantment with picture windows was underway.

The issue of privacy was even more salient in radical architectural designs such as Mies's Farnsworth House. Edith Farnsworth, who commissioned the glass pavilion named after her, soon began to complain that "there is a certain brutality about having the outside inside."[52] With frustration she noted, "Mies talks about his 'free space,' but the space is very fixed. I can't even put a clothes hanger in my house without considering how it affects everything from the outside."[53] Farnsworth eventually decided to install roller blinds instead of the off-white curtains provided by Mies.[54] Still, she remained unhappy with the house and went so far as to sue Mies for what she considered flawed architecture. Today, the Farnsworth House is an uninhabited museum space—both admired and criticized. In the trenchant words of Richard Sennett, the glass pavilion is "a space in which we experience the terror of nature sharpened by a building offering no promise of refuge."[55]

Privacy concerns have also haunted Mies's two glass-faced residential towers on Chicago's Lake Shore Drive. Even before moving in, prospective residents raised questions about visual privacy, and these concerns only grew when, in the course of construction, the translucent glass depicted in the sales brochure was replaced with fully transparent glass.[56] Soon enough, it became clear that the pricey apartments also suffered from overheating during the summer and from water damage during rainstorms, to such an extent that residents were forced to form a "bucket brigade."[57] Some apartment owners sought damages in court for the persistent problems with the glass façade. Mies, for his part, dropped his plan to move into the "Glass Houses" himself. Years later, one of his closest associates admitted that the numerous leaks in the vitreous façade were the result of an "infantile stage of curtain wall design."[58] The leaks were eventually remedied by installing windows with tighter seals (but with the consequence that residents could no longer open them). And the installation of air-conditioning helped offer relief from oven-like temperatures during the summer. Both measures were urgently needed to make the "Glass Houses" livable, but from a purist perspective, they spoiled Mies's original design.[59]

As to privacy concerns, tinted glass could have provided a solution. However, Mies only began using tinted glass in later high-rise projects.[60] Other architects took privacy concerns more seriously and experimented with "mirror glass," which, thanks to a thin metallic layer, can provide one-way transparency—impervious from the outside, but allowing a clear view outward from the interior—as long as the interior is darker than the exterior. When light conditions are reversed—at night, for instance—a curtainless interior will be exposed to views from outside.[61]

But what if privacy was just a petty bourgeois anachronism? Some flagbearers of modernism certainly thought so, hoping that radical glass construction held the promise of obliterating once and for all the old-fashioned distinction between interior and exterior. Glass architecture, in this view, was an "X-ray architecture" that could turn the inside out. Indeed, X-ray technology and avant-garde glass architecture both emerged in the early twentieth century; both innovations relied on the application of vitreous plates; and both were celebrated by proponents as evidence for progress through technology. Tellingly, in the 1930s, an American film promoting the benefits of radiology proclaimed that, for the X-ray patient, "henceforth a glass house should hold no terrors."[62] As Beatriz Colomina has shown, the radical vision of "X-ray architecture"—couched in the language of clean, medical precision—formed an important current in the discourse of modernist architecture.[63] It clearly informed the design of the Farnsworth House, whose resident incidentally complained about a house that "is transparent, like an X-ray."[64] The radical exposure of privacy is also intrinsic to Johnson's Glass House in New Canaan: the ground-level Glass House may in fact be the fullest realization of Jean-Jacques Rousseau's call for a "house to be built in such a way that whatever occurred within could be seen." The radicalism of the Glass House perplexed even that early champion of glass architecture in the United States, Frank Lloyd Wright, Johnson's colleague. On a visit to the house, Wright is said to have remarked, "Do I take my hat off, or leave it on? I can't tell whether I am indoors or out."[65]

As this episode indicates, Johnson enjoyed entertaining guests and visitors in the Glass House. In daily life, however, he was well aware of the challenges that came with living in a fully transparent home. Just steps away from the Glass House, Johnson built the so-called Brick House, which features no windows except for two roundels in the rear. Initially designed as a guest house, the Brick House became the place where Johnson lived and slept while in New Canaan. In Johnson's lifetime, the Glass House was solely a pavilion for sociability.[66] Instead of a unified vision of the avant-garde home, Johnson's New Canaan estate offers two sharply contrasting versions: a brick house for comfort and privacy, and a glass house for maximal experience of the scenic surroundings. For Johnson, this was no contradiction. He envisioned the two buildings as complementing each other, explicitly referring to the Brick House as "an anchor for the Glass House."[67]

This, of course, was a rather eccentric vision of home, neither viable nor affordable for anyone but an independently wealthy bohemian such as Johnson. It was precisely this kind of dogmatic aestheticism, coupled with a neglect of practical concerns, that made Wright increasingly critical about postwar glass architecture.[68] Wright was not alone in his skepticism. As early as 1955, the architectural critic Bernard Rudofsky published a book titled *Behind the Picture Window*, a sharp critique of postwar American architecture, arguing that "glass walls have taken out of life at home its last secret wrinkles and make it as transparent as life in a fish bowl."[69] Six years later, Lewis Mumford expanded on this point in his bestselling work *The City in History* and tied it to a wholesale critique of the modernist movement, asserting: "This movement has perhaps now reached the natural terminus of every such arbitrary interpretation of human needs. In opening our buildings to the untempered glare of daylight and the outdoors, we have forgotten, at our peril and to our loss, the coordinate need for contrast, for quiet, for darkness, for privacy, for an inner retreat."[70] Journalists joined the chorus, sometimes in a shrill pitch: in 1967, the *New York Times* reported that residents of glass-walled buildings were likely to "develop dizziness" as well as "a fear of being watched," and a psychiatrist interviewed for the piece went so far as to say that, after initial excitement, the residents of glass buildings found themselves "depressed all over again."[71]

There were still, to be sure, ardent defenders of the vitreous visions of High Modernism. Britain in the 1950s, for instance, saw the rise of "Anti-Ugly Action," a movement made up of young architecture students and practitioners who condemned any recourse to traditional ("ugly") architecture as a betrayal of modernism and its noble goals. Citing prominent avant-garde architects such as Mies and Le Corbusier as models, the anti-ugly activists considered window size a key indicator of an architect's commitment to modernism. In 1959, anti-ugly activists assembled in Cambridge to protest the new Second Hall at Emmanuel College, which, in their opinion, was a "ghastly new building." Several hundred activists marched through the streets, shouting, "Burn it, burn it!" and carrying banners with slogans such as "Small Windows. Small Minds."[72]

In the United States during those years, a group of young architects and architectural theorists developed a different approach, expressing unease with the mantra of transparency inherited from their teachers. In the late 1950s, two up-and-coming young architectural theorists, Colin Rowe and Robert Slutzky, penned a polemical critique of the phenomenon that they called "literal transparency."[73] For Rowe and Slutzky, transparency was "literal" where large, uniform glass surfaces served primarily to reveal the interior of a building. A case in point was curtain-walling, a technique pioneered by Gropius, Mies, and others. Rowe and Slutzky couched their argument in highly theoretical language, but the thrust was unmistakably critical: "literal transparency" was naïve and anachronistic; in Rowe's words, it was the "holy cow" of the fathers of modernism, but not the answer to the challenges that lay ahead.[74]

As a counter-model to "literal transparency," Rowe and Slutzky promoted "phenomenal transparency"—a notion they borrowed from the wartime writings of the Hungarian designer and art theorist György Kepes. An admirer of cubist deconstruction, Kepes had argued that transparency, in its most complex expression, "means a simultaneous perception of different spatial locations."[75] Inspired by Kepes's notion of transparency, Rowe and Slutzky called for an architecture that "created by implied layers of planes an illusion of spatial depth that was at variance with the spatial reality of the buildings."[76] This kind of transparency would not necessarily require glass, but could be achieved with a range of different architectural materials. As a model of well-done "phenomenal transparency," Rowe and Slutzky cited Le Corbusier's Villa Stein at Garches (1926)—a building that is indeed characterized not so much by large windows, but rather by a sophisticated combination of interlocking planes and viewpoints.

Rowe and Slutzky's "dangerous and explosive little essay" (in Rowe's words) was initially unpublished, and later appeared in installments from the 1960s onward.[77] Gradually, however, the manifesto became a canonical text that influenced an entire generation of young, "postmodern" architects who were disillusioned with the promises and contradictions of "literal transparency."[78] The American architect Victor Hornbein stated in 1975 that the "glass box" was "good in some of the prototypes," but had failed as a building type for "dormitories, office buildings, classrooms, hotels, apartment houses, factories, powerhouses, [and] dwellings." What is more, large-scale, epigonic projects had turned glass façades into "unintentional symbols of the faceless, undifferentiated society that produced them."[79] Around the same time, German architect Gerhard Auer argued, "Today architectural transparency no longer seeks to gratify the searching gaze, no longer turns the inner into the outer, no longer informs us about structural orders." Instead, the time had come for a "more ambitious, more subtle, more relaxed" kind of architectural transparency.[80] The many practical problems that had haunted large-scale glass façades contributed to this critique of "literal transparency"—as did the energy crises of the 1970s, which heightened concerns about thermal efficiency.[81] By the 1980s, it seemed as if "transparency was dead."[82]

Glass-faced buildings from this period often deliberately defied expectations. For instance, instead of transparent glass, they featured dark, reflective panes. Such reflective glass façades suggest transparency while at the same time denying it—precisely the contradictory effect that "postmodern" architects sought. To be sure, this kind of subversion was not what Rowe and Slutzky had envisioned as "phenomenal transparency." Indeed, some critics argued that postmodern façade

Fig. 15.8. John Portman, Westin Bonaventure Hotel, Los Angeles, 1974–76. One of the most controversial glass-faced buildings of the postwar period, the Westin Bonaventure represents a turn away from "literal transparency." The glass façade is not transparent, but rather reflective, and therefore impervious to outside gazes. Architects associated with postmodernism often used reflective surfaces as an ironic gesture to defy conventional expectations. Critics of postmodernism argued that this type of glass skin merely serves to "repel the city outside."

design only made things worse. Take John Portman's Westin Bonaventure Hotel in Los Angeles (1974–76), which became a target of trenchant polemic by the influential cultural critic Fredric Jameson (fig. 15.8). For Jameson, "the way in which the glass skin repels the city outside" was not only aesthetically troubling, but also created "a peculiar and placeless dissociation of the Bonaventure from its neighborhood." He lamented that it was "not even an exterior, inasmuch as when you seek to look at the hotel's outer walls you cannot see the hotel itself but only the distorted images of everything that surrounds it."[83]

As postmodernism's momentum faded, the pendulum swung back: from the late 1980s onward, a re-appreciation of "literal transparency" was underway. Some architectural historians have even spoken of a "purging of postmodernism" that led to "a return of glass skins of unprecedented expanse."[84] Anthony Vidler, who has closely studied postwar discourses on glass architecture, has noted that since that time "we have been once again presented with a revived call for transparency, this time on behalf of the apparently 'good modernism.'"[85] His case in point is France, where the government promoted a "new" glass architecture that found its most iconic expression in I. M. Pei's vitreous pyramid at the Louvre (1989). No expense was spared to realize Pei's daring design. St. Gobain Vitrage SA—the company descending from the glass manufacture established by Louis XIV—was commissioned to produce glass panes with the highest possible degree of transparency. To that end, extremely pure white sand was melted in special furnaces, and the final panes were polished by specialist subcontractors.[86] No less ambitious were the greenhouse buildings known as "Les Serres" (Adrien Fainsilber/RFR, 1986), forming part of the Parisian Cité des Sciences et de l'Industrie and featuring, for the first time ever, a frameless glass façade whose structural support relied solely on cable trusses. Even larger in scale was Dominique Perrault's design for the new Bibliothèque Nationale in Paris (1995), which features four tall glass towers.

In these *grands projets*, the vitreous transparency served to express modern republican values such as openness and accountability. Ironically, however, these projects were commissioned and executed through a rather undemocratic and opaque process. All major decisions were made by François Mitterrand, the French president at the time, often without consultation. Mitterrand was so committed to these projects, which were nicknamed "*la transparence*," that he ignored critics—including those who rightly warned of the damaging effect of storing the Bibliothèque Nationale's light-sensitive book collections in gigantic glass towers.[87] While the architect claimed that the vitreous towers would "show off the 'book' to advantage," librarians predicted inevitable damage to the collections. In the end, wooden shutters were installed in the glass towers. Kept permanently closed, the shutters effectively undo the vitreous transparency that was meant to become the library's hallmark.[88]

To be sure, the French infatuation with glass architecture on a monumental scale was hardly limited to the public grand projets. Privately commissioned buildings from this period display the same tendency. A particularly striking example is the Fondation Cartier in Paris, built in 1994 by Jean Nouvel. The building is a bold experiment with horizontal and vertical transparency—to the extent that female workers wearing skirts have expressed concerns about feeling exposed. What is more, rumor has it that office decoration is subject to strict rules, so as to ensure the uniform appearance of the offices, which are completely visible from the street.[89]

The case of 1980s and 1990s France is in many ways reminiscent of postunification Germany, where projects such as the new Reichstag cupola were driven by similar motivations rooted in political symbolism (and suffer from similar practical problems—rain buckets are a familiar sight in some of the glass-roofed administrative buildings that form part of the Reichstag).[90] Yet the renaissance of large-scale transparency is by no means limited to Europe. Glass architecture has become a *global* phenomenon in the past two decades.[91] There are even calls from some quarters to retrofit this vitreous aesthetic onto buildings of other styles— particularly "brutalist" buildings of the 1950s and 1960s. Whatever one may think about the aesthetics of brutalism (and this is not the place to delve into this controversial subject), it represents an alternative approach to the problem of public and especially political architecture. As a built legacy of the past, it is as worthy of preservation as any other kind of historical architecture. Nevertheless, those who live near these buildings often have strong feelings. For example, Boston City Hall (1968), a building that locals have "long loved to hate," has faced a call for an ostensibly preservationist-friendly "makeover" involving sheathing the building with a glass curtain wall. The proponent—posing the question, "Could City Hall be literally transparent?"—has suggested that this vitreous makeover would make the building "appear luminous and crystalline, transparent, welcoming, sheltering, inclusive—all better metaphors for city government."[92]

But nowhere is the contemporary enthusiasm for glass architecture more evident than in the field of international corporate architecture. Perhaps the most prominent examples of this tendency are Apple's flagship stores, situated in premium, highly visible downtown locations around the world, with their hallmark abundance of glass both inside and out (fig. 15.9). For a global company such as Apple, whose reputation rests on an absolute commitment to clear and efficient design, glass has become a signature material that is supposed to reflect the values and strengths of the company.

The culmination of this corporate mantra is on display at Apple's new headquarters in Cupertino, California—yet again a lavishly glazed building, but this time on an unprecedented scale. Apple Park (or Apple Campus 2), designed by

Fig. 15.9. Bohlin Cywinski Jackson, Apple flagship store at 59th Street and Fifth Avenue, New York, 2006. The iconic glass cube officially received patent protection in 2016.

Fig. 15.10. Foster and Partners, Apple Park, Cupertino, California, 2014–17. The gigantic circular building is the apotheosis of the kind of architectural transparency that Apple has successfully turned into a corporate trademark. In practice, however, access to the completely transparent building is strictly limited, and the company is known for a highly secretive corporate culture.

Norman Foster, is a gigantic glass ring with a circumference of one mile (fig. 15.10). Arranged in unbroken series, the almost nine hundred oversized glass panes (made by a specialized manufacturer in Germany) would span six miles if set in a straight line. Envisioned by Apple's founder, Steve Jobs, as "the best office building in the world," Apple Park offers workspace for more than thirteen thousand employees.[93] In commissioning this entirely transparent environment, Jobs did not just aim for a spectacular aesthetic effect. From the outset, architectural transparency was also meant to signal institutional transparency—or in the words of a top Apple executive, "It will become a very unique working environment and our innovation center, a highly transparent and highly collaborative workspace."[94] This is a rather remarkable understanding of transparency; after all, the completed building is fenced off and inaccessible to the public. What is more, Apple has a reputation as a notoriously secretive company in which even employees are not necessarily allowed to speak with one another about their work. Does the fact that "everyone in the ring will get the same view" really translate into corporate "democracy"?[95]

A similar dynamic is on display in the design of Facebook's sprawling campus in nearby Menlo Park. Consider the most recently completed flagship building, MPK 21, designed by star architect Frank Gehry. According to Facebook, the building boasts "an open workspace designed to foster collaboration between teams," and its "bird-friendly glazing allows for clear views," thereby helping to bring "the outdoors into the office space."[96] Indeed, the building, boasting a total space of more than half a million square feet, is entirely "transparent—one can see through it from one end to the other."[97] Founder and chief executive Mark Zuckerberg presides at its center, in an office entirely encased in bulletproof glass. Like Apple Park, Facebook's MPK 21 apotheosizes the idea of corporate openness, but in practice this openness is strictly limited and guarded. Interested outsiders cannot set foot in the building that strives to "be a good neighbor."[98] They must rely on polished, officially approved images. The building's openness remains a fiction and, for practical purposes, can be experienced only as an online simulation.[99]

Both buildings, then, raise larger questions that lie at the heart of modern glass architecture and its history. What exactly does architectural transparency achieve? And for whom? Most importantly perhaps, is there really a link between architectural and institutional transparency—or is this claim merely a façade?

EPILOGUE

History, the long term, is transparency; it is the absence of secrets." Or so claimed an op-ed in the *New York Times* not long ago.[1] This is a remarkably confident statement, underpinned by the belief that the historian can know the dead "with an intimacy impossible in their day." Personally, I don't share this confidence. Perhaps future historians will be in the lucky position to study a past that is completely transparent to them. For now, I suggest that we start elsewhere—namely, by acknowledging that transparency has a history.

This history of transparency is the history of both an idea and a material experience. And both histories, I have argued, converge in one medium: architectural glass. As we have seen, architectural glass is by no means an indispensable feature of the built environment. Rather, it is a cultural convention that became common under particular historical circumstances.

It was the Romans who first used glass to seal windows. Yet glass remained an ambiguous material in Roman culture. In architectural contexts, it competed with a number of other sealants, some of which were deemed considerably more prestigious. The use of glass also remained limited to particular types of buildings, such as bathhouses and countryside villas. In Roman sacred architecture, glass played virtually no role.

Christianity adopted many elements of Roman architecture, but it chose a different approach with respect to fenestration. In striking contrast to pagan temples, Christian churches featured ever-larger glass windows. This phenomenon reached its apex in the great Gothic cathedrals in which stone walls seem to dissolve into tapestries of polychrome glass. To fully understand this development, one must recognize the complex links between light and color in Christian theology. After all, the function of medieval church windows was not to provide a view, but rather to glorify divine light in all its facets and colors. In other words, unlike modern windows, the church window did not frame the outdoors as an image. It was in itself an image.

Throughout the Middle Ages, this conception of the window remained the aesthetic optimum. It also influenced secular architecture, where polychrome fenestration carried the greatest prestige—a trend that was not limited to glazed windows. Indeed, windows furnished with non-vitreous sealants such as fabrics and parchments were widespread throughout the period, not least because they lent themselves well to colorful and ornamental designs.

The ideal of the window as a polychrome image came under heavy assault during the Reformation. Radical Protestants rejected all visual representations associated with the cult of saints. In some places, church windows, along with other "icons," were systematically destroyed. Although these acts of iconoclasm were limited to certain parts of Europe, the Reformation marked a watershed moment in the history of architectural glass: the aesthetic hegemony of polychrome glass, uncontested for more than a millennium, was literally shattered. The blank, transparent pane emerged as the preferred alternative.

During the same period, glass windows became, as a general matter, more common in European architecture. As we have seen, the reasons were manifold. The recurrent plague outbreaks made well-sealed windows a desirable protection against miasmatic air. The invention of printing with movable type led to the wide circulation of books and, by extension, to a desire for better indoor lighting. Most importantly, the climatic effects of the Little Ice Age spurred the demand for efficient thermal barriers.

Yet none of these factors alone can explain why the early modern period saw an unprecedented—and often ostentatious—use of glass in public architecture. To understand this phenomenon, we must take into account cultural change on two levels. First, on the level of political culture, we observe what Ernst Kantorowicz identified as a distinctively absolutist "heliolatry."[2] The most iconic example is Versailles, the lavishly fenestrated palace of a monarch who employed the maximization and manipulation of light for his elaborate self-fashioning as supreme Sun King. Second, on the level of intellectual culture, we see Enlightenment culture equating visibility with virtue, endowing transparency with moral and political qualities in unprecedented ways. Thinkers such as Jean-Jacques Rousseau and Jeremy Bentham espoused what Michel Foucault would later call "the dream of a transparent society, visible and legible in each of its parts, the dream of there no longer existing any zones of darkness."[3]

Technological progress contributed to the emergence of extensively glazed buildings. In the late seventeenth century, the rediscovery of glass casting made it possible to produce ever-larger panes. In the early nineteenth century, the rise of iron construction enabled architects and engineers to erect colossal glass palaces. Reformers and architects embraced these possibilities, and the nineteenth century became a veritable age of public glass.

By contrast, many homeowners and tenants had qualms about larger windows and more glass, whether because of aesthetic unease, medical anxieties, or concerns about visual privacy. Around 1900, the resulting divergence between public and private architecture was hard to overlook. Bridging this divide was a key goal of a new generation of architects. However, the pioneers of modernism were by no means neutral. They rejected—often in polemical fashion—nineteenth-century interiority as a symptom of a bourgeois world that had outlived itself. Embracing a rhetoric of "openness," the advocates of modernism pinned their hopes on glass as a "simple" and "pure" material, as the "enemy of secrets" (in Walter Benjamin's words).

Whatever the merits of this vision, Benjamin's prediction proved correct: more than any preceding period of history, the twentieth century became the age of vitreous transparency. It is difficult to imagine modern and contemporary architecture without expansive glass façades. In fact, "Transparency has expanded . . . to almost every architectural type imaginable, from office blocks to parliaments, from single-family homes to media centers."[4] What is more, glass architecture has become a global phenomenon.

From a purely technical perspective, then, one might speak of an "ever-upward curve which describes the development of the window."[5] After all, the twentieth century brought about groundbreaking technological innovations that made it possible to realize some of the most daring architectural visions. As the Italian architect Giuseppe Terragni put it in the 1930s, "In a prodigious effort, the glass industry has solved in just a few years problems that for millennia were felt to be inherent to the very nature of the material."[6] Glass panes have become far larger than the humans who look through them. And breakability is no longer a pressing problem: two thousand years after the Roman poet Petronius wrote that if glass "didn't break, it would be better than gold," glass manufacturers have mastered the skill of producing toughened glass that is almost shatterproof.[7] Moreover, glass is no longer necessarily a "thermally inefficient material."[8] New "super windows" double as electric heating systems.[9] Manufacturers have even started to produce "smart windows" that can change their degree of transparency through electrochemical reactions between two thin panes.[10] And self-cleaning glass surfaces are no longer a utopian idea.[11]

With all that said, the future holds unprecedented challenges: climate change is accelerating, and the discussion about the ecological cost of glass-faced buildings will not end anytime soon. Recent studies have shown that in cities such as

New York, "70 percent of the city's greenhouse gas emissions [come] from buildings, and those with glass exteriors [are] among the worst offenders."[12] At the end of the day, as critics put it, "all glass buildings perform against themselves."[13]

And from a historical and cultural perspective, too, the history of glass in modern times, despite all technological innovation, is not a story of linear progress. Modern glass architecture has been called a quintessentially "rational architecture."[14] But there remains a dissonance between what we expect from glass and what it can do. No amount of architectural glass will guarantee a transparent social or institutional culture, and any belief to the contrary has more to do with supernatural thinking than with a realistic assessment of what architecture can accomplish. Where transparency is desired as a communal or institutional reality, it needs to be encouraged and enacted on a social basis. Everything else is mere architectural symbolism—and the benefits of such symbolism are not at all clear. Does it really lead to greater accountability if one can see parliamentary or corporate board meetings but not hear what is said?[15] Often enough, for those outside, "transparency only reveals everything in which you cannot partake."[16] By contrast, for those inside, transparency might not foster an atmosphere of openness, but rather a feeling of relentless exposure. Recent studies in legal sociology have shown that the extensive use of glass in courthouses, far from spurring greater public interest or scrutiny, has created spatial settings in which defendants and spectators "are treated like a contained object on display."[17]

Transparency, then, is not per se a positive or progressive condition. In fact, what Foucault identified as the enlightened "dream of a transparent society" has revealed, at times, in the course of modernity, a nightmarish side. The institutions of surveillance and confinement that Foucault studied are but one aspect of this problem. As we have seen, glass architecture was also co-opted by authoritarian regimes in the twentieth century: in both fascist and communist architecture, large, transparent glass surfaces served political agendas that were deeply undemocratic. Glass architecture, I argue, is at its core an architecture of power. Inherent to it are fantasies of total visibility: fantasies of an interior completely revealed, but also of imperious views of the outside world. In both an architectural and figurative sense, the desire for transparency is bound up with the "feeling that seeing something may lead to control over it."[18]

Far from being a "neutral" interface, the transparent window gives us the impression (or illusion) of such visual control, serving as a neatly framed and tightly sealed barrier between inside and outside. In other words, although glass is a material that pretends to be invisible, the transparent window is a technology of spatial demarcation that helps us to impose a "clear" sense of order on the world that surrounds us. In this sense, the glass window—convenient though it may be—reinforces the antagonistic relation between interior and exterior that runs deep in Western culture.

In certain architectural settings, this categorical distinction between inside and outside is of such fundamental importance that even the presence of windows would threaten to destabilize it. For instance, industrial factories and large office buildings sometimes forgo windows, as these would interfere with the illusion of a permanent, artificially lit day in the interior—and thus interfere with a regimen of shiftwork around the clock.

The situation is similar in department stores, shopping malls, cinemas, and casinos. These building types all form part of an "architecture of introversion."[19] Here again, windows are often omitted because they would distract us from the glittering, artificial interior spaces that are designed to focus our attention on consumption. Like the arcades of the nineteenth century, modern shopping malls and department stores feature only one kind of window: the display window.[20] In the laconic words of a manual for retail-store design: "Enclosed mall stores often have no windows at all. Here, retail establishments open onto a controlled environment."[21] In the end, then, these spaces of consumption and entertainment all follow one rule: the fewer distractions from the outside, the easier to keep people inside.[22] As early as 1938, an article in the industry periodical *Department Store Economist* recognized, "In many ways the elimination of windows adds to the beauty and to the selling efficiency of the store."[23]

One could, of course, argue that not all windowless buildings operate under the manipulative logic of capitalist consumerism. Many spaces associated with "high culture" likewise omit windows to ensure a distraction-free aesthetic experience. Theaters and opera houses, for instance, are spaces in which we sit in total darkness, completely isolated from what is happening outdoors. This, however, is not a timeless observation. For the greater part of Western history, art forms such as theater were associated with outdoor performance, whether in Sophocles's Athens or in Shakespeare's London.

In other words, it was the transition to modernity that brought an extensive drive toward the interior. As one consequence, the categories of interior and exterior became more firmly entrenched—a process that affected spaces of aesthetic experience just as much as spaces of consumption. In the artistic realm, performances moved to indoor spaces, and artworks such as statues, once designed predominantly for outside display, were confined to museums. In the sphere of consumption, sites of commercial exchange moved from the outdoor marketplaces to the largely windowless stores of our day.

And what about domestic architecture? Most nineteenth-century homes reflected the "architecture of introversion," with small windows and heavy curtains attesting to considerable anxiety about exposure to the outside. By contrast, twentieth-century domestic architecture saw more emphasis on openness, pretending to break down the traditional inside–outside antagonism. High-end real estate, for instance, often features ostentatiously oversized glass windows. Yet paradoxically, the larger the windows have become, the less time we spend looking out of them. According to sociological surveys, looking out of windows and watching street life was still one of the favorite pastimes of Europeans around the middle of the twentieth century. In the decades that followed, this pastime completely disappeared from the surveys. It is not farfetched to link this decline of window gazing to the rise of other sources of entertainment and information, such as television, radio, and—most recently—social media.[24] In fact, in the past two decades, the "windows" of our digital screens have become our primary source for what is going on outside of our homes.[25]

In a not-so-distant future, the digital screens might converge with our traditional windows. The director of the German-based Institute for Window Technology envisions domestic life in the year 2030 as follows: "When we come home, the electronic 'butler' will ask us which motif the media wall should display today. We choose the theme 'Mediterranean.' In our living room, the panorama window displays our favorite scene with a blue sea and small dream cove, accentuated by a soft breeze that invites sailing."[26]

Against the backdrop of this prediction, the decline of traditional window-gazing might seem a mere nostalgic concern. Yet the loss of such cultural practices can have significant ramifications. As Jane Jacobs pointed out in her classic *The Death and Life of Great American Cities* (1961), neighbors who look out of their windows and have "eyes on the streets" are a benefit to communities, helping to prevent crime and fostering a sense of mutual support.[27] Will this still be the case if "eyes on the screens" becomes the new norm? Even as it stands, many "conventional" windows—let alone large picture windows—cannot be opened at all, which makes it difficult to engage with life on the street. (This, of course, is by design: busy and noisy street scenes are hardly a selling point, but sweeping and detached views are.)

What makes a view spectacular is different in the city than it is in the country, to be sure. In the country, the window aspires to frame nature in a picturesque way: the more "scenic," the more prestigious and expensive the view. The cult of the scenic view is vividly on display in Philip Johnson's New Canaan Glass House, which, in his own words, "turns the landscape into a kind of wallpaper—expensive wallpaper to be sure—but wallpaper, where the sun and the moon and the stars make different patterns."[28]

In the city, vertical height is an important factor and reinforces the feeling of visual control. Michel de Certeau has described high-rise windows as objects that give us the impression of being "a solar Eye, looking down like god." According to de Certeau, this "scopic drive" fosters the fiction that we can make "the complexity of the city readable," and "immobilizes its opaque mobility in a transparent text."[29] In a similar vein, Richard Sennett has argued that the modern "divide between the inside and the outside" is furthered by the "protected openness" that comes with glass.[30] As Sennett has noted, the "physical sensation aroused by plate [glass] is complete vision without exposure to other senses."[31]

The desire to minimize exposure to the city's complex sensory environment is closely related to the history of glass architecture. Tightly sealed windows keep the city's smells at bay, and the development of soundproof glass has turned windows into highly effective barriers against the exterior soundscape.[32]

As a result, the role of the window has all too often been reduced to that of a visual frame. Among other things, this has led to a significant uniformity of window forms. The construction industry caters to this demand for uniformity. For the Spanish architect Santiago Calatrava, this is a key reason why "we actually have the same windows everywhere."[33] Indeed, the vast majority of windows in our time are conceived not as individual façade elements attuned to their particular surroundings, but rather as geometrical cutouts in the wall or simply as the space between two steel beams.[34] Perhaps the fiercest critique of this uniformity can be found in Friedensreich Hundertwasser's manifesto "Window Dictatorship and Window Rights" (1990). In this programmatic call to action, the Austrian artist-architect argued that residents should have the right to alter the appearance of their windows according to their individual needs and wants.[35] The apartments in Hundertwasser's colorful buildings come with a contractual provision that allows the residents to ornament their windows and the surrounding exterior wall space within an arm's reach. This notion of "window rights" offers an unusual—and certainly imaginative—attempt to think more flexibly about the inside–outside divide. In practice, however, this approach has resulted more in an aestheticization of the problem than in a fundamental reconceptualization of the modern window.

This is precisely why a historical perspective can broaden our conceptual horizon, inviting us to reflect on what we expect from that complex interface that is the window. As we have seen, exploring the history of architectural glass and transparency means, inevitably, confronting the powerful antagonism that has come to characterize the relation between interior and exterior in Western culture. A historical view beyond Europe, though only partly sketched out in this book, makes it even clearer that some architectural traditions were (and are) defined by a more osmotic and multisensory experience of space.[36]

Traditional Japanese architecture is a case in point—and it is no coincidence that it has long intrigued Western architects in search of a counter-model.[37] Traditional Japanese houses do not feature glass windows, but rather shōji—screens made of light-colored paper and reinforced with wooden latticework.[38] Shōji are translucent, not transparent—but this was by no means considered a deficiency in premodern Japan. It is a Western myth that the adoption of glass windows made the Japanese more sensitive to grime and, by extension, more hygiene-conscious. To the contrary, historical sources show that premodern Japanese took great care to keep their houses clean.[39]

In fact, the lack of transparency had a number of advantages. First, the shōji screens are more lightweight than glass windows and easier to install. This proved particularly useful during fire disasters, which broke out with notorious frequency in the densely settled cities of premodern Japan: the screens were easy to dismantle and carry away.[40] During ordinary times, too, shōji offered considerable flexibility: pushed to the side, they even gave the impression that the border between interior and exterior had been canceled. Indeed, traditional Japanese architecture has construed interior and exterior not so much as antagonistic categories, but rather as an organic unity. The introduction of Western glass windows into Japan—a result of the colonial "opening" of Japan—changed this relation to the natural environment. As Timon Screech has shown, "Glass windows promoted a new kind of seeing, removing the spectator from the field of action and turning him into an observer."[41]

The osmotic quality of traditional Japanese homes did not mean a lack of privacy. In domestic architecture, high fences or hedges ensured "relative privacy for the occupants despite the open structure of the house itself."[42] Nor were screen-faced homes more vulnerable than their European counterparts: at nighttime or during severe weather, the screens could be covered with protective panels (*amado*).[43]

The real difference between Japanese and European architecture may be found in the attitude toward light and vision. Unlike the transparent windows that became the norm in European architecture, the traditional, translucent Japanese window provides a soft, diffused light without glare.[44] Often refined by patterned transom and fretwork designs, the shōji screens enable an artful interplay between light and shadow, visibility and concealment.[45] Jun'ichirō Tanizaki, one of the fathers of modern Japanese literature, has powerfully evoked this "beauty in shadows" and the delights of opacity.[46] So has Tadao Ando, perhaps the most renowned Japanese architect of the twentieth century, in his reflections on the "subtle spatial resonance of light and darkness." In this understanding of architectural space, darkness is not a mere lack of light, but rather "imparts on light its character and enhances its brilliance." However, in an age that favors transparency, architecture has become "far too obsessed with homogeneous light."[47]

Under the dogma of transparency, this obsession with unencumbered light converges with the desire for maximal vision—a convergence that can be observed both in architectural reality and in figurative speech. It is no coincidence that advocates of a fully "transparent society" refer to those who have not joined it as "cave dwellers" in need of transforming themselves into "smart, honest, and truly independent creatures of light."[48] Glass-faced buildings of our time are, often enough, the architectural expression of this wishful thinking.

Gaston Bachelard has suggested that one can take "the house as a tool for analysis of the human soul."[49] We might extend this observation to the individual elements of architecture—the window included. Future historians will be in a better position to analyze what the oversized glass windows of our time reveal about our mentality. They will certainly notice the sense of assurance and empowerment that we derive from the ability to maximize lighting levels and oversee our environment. Tellingly, perhaps, we say: to *command* a view. Maybe it is the old Platonic anxiety that still haunts us—the anxiety that we might live in a world where all we see are the shadows of reality, and that only "the light of truth" will reveal how things really are.[50] The Christian tradition, too, has struggled with the idea that "for now we see through a glass darkly" (an image so powerful that it has prevailed over other, more accurate translations of this famous biblical verse). Indeed, Christianity's promise of salvation has, from the earliest days, entailed the vision of a life in which light, clarity, and truth coincide.

Whatever the origins of the Western will to see and to see *through*, it is bound up with deep-seated anxieties about darkness, opacity, and ambiguity. But is not ambiguity often an ingredient that intrigues? Does darkness not sometimes sharpen our sensation? Don't we sometimes see more when we view less? "Limits of the diaphane . . . ," writes Joyce in *Ulysses*. "Shut your eyes and see."[51]

NOTES

INTRODUCTION

1. Christensen and Cornelissen, "Organizational Transparency"; Fenster, "Transparency in Search of a Theory"; Alloa, "Architectures of Transparency," 329–30; Forssbæck and Oxelheim, "Multifaceted Concept of Transparency," esp. 3. The latter also make the useful distinction between transparency as the "mere disclosure of information" (as decision-makers often see it) and transparency as a more demand-based "right to know" (25). For an overview of different approaches to transparency in the business world, see the contributions to their volume: Forssbæck and Oxelheim, *Oxford Handbook*; as well as to the collection by Hood and Heald, *Transparency*. Defining and implementing transparency in institutional contexts is the mission of NGOs such as the Berlin-based organization Transparency International (TI). Founded in 1993, TI's self-declared goal is "to stop corruption and promote transparency, accountability and integrity at all levels and across all sectors of society." See Transparency International, "Mission, Vision, Values," https://www.transparency.org/en/the-organisation/mission-vision-values (accessed March 19, 2022). For an impassionate manifesto along these lines, see Brin, *Transparent Society*.

2. Barnstone calls transparency a "catchword" of our times ("Transparency," 3); Stehr and Wallner speak of it as a "key term of our day" ("Transparenz," 9). See also the other contributions to Jansen, Schröter, and Stehr, *Transparenz*; as well as Schudson, *Rise of the Right to Know*, esp. 4; Barnstone, *Transparent State*, esp. xi; Rzepka, *Die Ordnung der Transparenz*, esp. 7; Han, *Transparenzgesellschaft*. Fukuyama states succinctly: "It is hard to think of a political good that is more universally praised than government transparency" ("Why Transparency Can Be a Dirty Word," *Financial Times*, International Edition, August 9, 2015). A take on the same issues, but with qualifications, is Vattimo, *Transparent Society*.

3. Hood, "Transparency," 3.

4. Forssbæck and Oxelheim, "Multifaceted Concept of Transparency," esp. 5.

5. Brin, *Transparent Society*, esp. 309.

6. Indeed, there were periods in the past in which good knowledge was often equated with secret knowledge: Jütte, *Age of Secrecy*.

7. Rice and Dutton, *Structural Glass*, 10. The opposite would be "one-way transparency"—for example, architectural glass that allows "daylight to penetrate to the interior of buildings" but beyond that "serves as nothing more than a means of preventing the rain from getting in and the heat getting out." By contrast, two-way transparency appears "as soon as

the view to the outside acquires an importance" (10). In most contexts, I will refer to "one-way transparency" as "translucency."

8. Gino, "Changing Rooms," 32. See also Barnstone, "Transparency," 3; Alloa, "Architectures of Transparency."

9. Frank Zimmermann, "Was man nicht sieht," *Frankfurter Allgemeine Zeitung*, March 20, 2012 (suppl. "Faszination Fenster"), 87.

10. Wajcman, *Fenêtre*, 22.

11. Wajcman, *Fenêtre*, 22. See also Wigginton, *Glass in Architecture*, 8: "The story of the window in architecture . . . deserves a book of its own." To the best of my knowledge, such a history has not yet been written. The volume that comes perhaps closest to this goal (but with a focus on modern times) is Lampugnani, *Architecture of the Window*. See also Friedberg, *Virtual Window*; Selbmann, *Kulturgeschichte des Fensters*; Uhlig, Kohler, and Schneider, *Fenster*. There is, however, a fair amount of scholarship on the motif of the window in the visual arts: see especially Gottlieb, *Window in Art*; Schmoll gen. Eisenwerth, "Fensterbilder."

12. Herbig, *Fenster in der Architektur*, 6–7.

13. Jütte, *Strait Gate*, esp. 19.

14. Oliver, *Dwellings*, 78 (discussing the *enkang* houses of the Maasai).

15. Badstübner, *Die Funktion des Fensters*, xv.

16. Völckers, *Glas und Fenster*, 10.

17. Le Corbusier, *Oeuvre complète*, 1:77; Le Corbusier, *Precisions*, 51–52.

18. Wigginton, *Glass in Architecture*, 6. For more assertions along these lines, see the references in Chapter 11.

19. Oliver, *Dwellings*, esp. 138; Macfarlane and Martin, *Glass*, 66, 76, 183. On the potential of non-vitreous sealants for contemporary architecture, see Abdel Gelil, "New Mashrabiyya."

20. Curtis, *Glass Exchange*, esp. 4–5 and chap. 4; Whitehouse, *Short History*, 61–62. My warm thanks to Winnie Wong for invaluable help on the Chinese contexts, here and elsewhere.

21. Knapp, "In Search," 68–69. See also Oliver, *Dwellings*, 130, for a discussion of how the notion of comfort is shaped by cultural and societal parameters.

22. Malte-Brun, *Précis de la géographie universelle*, 5:183.

23. Curtis, *Glass Exchange*, chap. 4; Bao, *Fiery Cinema*, 214 (quote). On Western promotional efforts, see also Liu "Vitreous Views," esp. 23. On the rise of architectural glass in twentieth-century China, see Knapp, "China's Houses," 7. This is all the more remarkable given that in the port of Canton, to which Europeans were confined for trade, painted glass and painted mirrors became new local products, accepted by the Qing court as "local" tribute offerings for officials stationed in this province of the empire.

24. Curtis, *Glass Exchange*, 44. On the interest of Qing elite in Western glass, see also Liu, "Vitreous Views."

25. Fryer, *New Account of East India*, 92.

26. Fryer, *New Account of East India*, 66. See also Dikshit, *History of Indian Glass*, 124, where these observations are confirmed by other European travelers. On European contempt for Philippine windows made of *capiz* shells, see Yamaguchi, "Architecture of the Spanish Philippines," 134.

27. Careri, *Giro del mondo*, 10.

28. Meid, "Einfluß westlicher Architektur," 60–61.

29. Quoted in Screech, "Glass," 29.

30. To be sure, a glass industry existed in Japan: Yamasaki, "Brief History." On the rarity of architectural glass in Japan before the twentieth century, see Sand, *House and Home*, 249; Screech, "Glass"; Meid, "Einfluß westlicher Architektur," 60–61; Enders, "Zur historischen Bauweise," 38–39.

31. Thürlemann, *Das Haremsfenster*, 130; Fuchs and Meyer-Brodnitz, "Emergence," 411.

32. Kenzari and Elsheshtawy, "Ambiguous Veil"; Depaule, *A travers le mur*; Oliver, *Dwellings*, 137–41; especially on *jalis*, see Ruggles, "Making Vision Manifest."

33. Ng, "Cultural Ecology," 497, 521 (quote). On the ecological cost, see also Adrian Lobe, "Architektur: Der falsche Glanz der Transparenz," *Neue Zürcher Zeitung*, February 9, 2017.

34. Mayor Bill de Blasio quoted in Mays, "De Blasio's 'Ban' on Glass."

35. Gannon, "Introduction," 18.

36. Latour, "Moral Dilemmas," 3.

37. Colomina, *Privacy and Publicity*, 134.

38. Erffa, "Die Verwendung des Glasfensters," 2.

39. Jütte, "Window Gazes and World Views." See also Wajcman, *Fenêtre*, 22, which speaks of the window as a *"machine à penser le monde."*

40. Flusser, "Häuser bauen."

41. Flusser, "Häuser bauen," 284; Sennett, *Conscience of the Eye*, 8.

42. To the best of my knowledge, this question has not yet been asked: there are studies on transparency as a notion, but none that probes the complex material genealogy of this idea in Western culture. Most histories of architectural glass, in turn, focus on the technological dimension. A comprehensive, but slightly dated survey is McGrath and Frost, *Glass in Architecture and Decoration*; equally detailed (but more current) is Wigginton, *Glass in Architecture*. See also Hix, *Glasshouse*. On the general history of glass from a global perspective, see Macfarlane and Martin, *Glass*; Whitehouse, *Glass*; Klein and Lloyd, *History of Glass*. There have, however, been recent, stimulating attempts to use other architectural materials as a starting point for a cultural history of the built environment: Campbell, *Brick*; Forty, *Concrete*.

43. Forty, *Word and Buildings*, 286.

44. *Oxford English Dictionary*, s.v. "transparent."

45. Wenzel, ed., *Fasciculus morum*, 39.

46. Rice and Dutton, *Structural Glass*, 15.

47. Sedlmayr, *Das Licht in seinen künstlerischen Manifestationen*, 43. While Vidler operates within a very different theoretical framework, he too has demonstrated that the history of transparency and light (and, by extension, darkness) are entwined in complex ways: Vidler, *Architectural Uncanny*, esp. 168–69, 172.

48. Benjamin, "Theses," 249.

I

GLASS AND ARCHITECTURE IN ANCIENT TIMES

1. Whitehouse, *Short History*, 10, 17; Henderson, *Ancient Glass*, 8; Nightingale, "Glass and the Mycenaean Palaces."

2. On the considerable cost of glass in these periods, see Henderson, *Ancient Glass*, 156.

3. Demangel, "Fenestrarum Imagines," 122–24; Herbig, "Fenster an Tempeln," 239, 252–55; Lim et al., *Environmental Factors*, 2–3; Brödner, *Wohnen in der Antike*, 278–80.

4. Tractate *Baba Batra*, 58b. (English translation from the Schottenstein Edition of the Babylonian Talmud.)

5. Wigginton, *Glass in Architecture*, 12.

6. Kenzari and Elsheshtawy, "Ambiguous Veil," 18, 20; Lim et al., *Environmental Factors*, 8; Mohamed, "Traditional Arts and Crafts," 8; Abdel Gelil, "New Mashrabiyya." Architectural glass was known in the medieval Islamic world, but mostly used in mosques and palaces: Flood, "Palaces of Crystal," passim (and on pierced grilles in Egypt, esp. 42–43). See also Henderson, *Ancient Glass*, esp. 291, 303, 370; Whitehouse, "Window Glass," 38. Occasionally, the upper sections of a mashrabia window are sealed with glass: Danby, "Privacy," 140.

7. Ezekiel's reference to such windows in his vision of the new Temple (Ezek. 13) is vague. St. Jerome, writing around 400, interpreted it as a reference to a wooden screen. The relevant passage from Jerome's commentary on Ezekiel is provided in Dell'Acqua, *"Illuminando colorat,"* 103. For Greek architecture, see Demangel, "Fenestrarum Imagines," 134, 152; Herbig, *Das Fenster in der Architektur*, 27.

8. Thébert, "Private Life," 331. In the same vein, see Vipard, "L'usage du verre"; Beretta, "Between Nature and Technology," 5: "There is no comprehensive study of the diffusion of window glass in the ancient world and particularly in Rome."

9. Vitruvius, *De architectura*, esp. 278.

10. Thébert, "Private Life," 331, Fontaine and Foy, "La modernité," 17; Dell'Acqua, *"Illuminando colorat,"* 16.

11. Veyne, "Roman Home," 315; Fleming, *Roman Glass*, 15; Dell'Acqua, "Finestre invetriate," 113; Löhr, "Griechische Häuser," 12. For security purposes, iron grilles were also used, especially in ground-floor windows: Baatz, "Fensterglastypen," 10–11; Ratzka, "Atrium und Licht," 99; Herbig, "Fensterstudien," 289. For Greek precedents, see Demangel, "Fenestrarum Imagines," 124; Herbig, *Das Fenster in der Architektur*, 27.

12. McGrath and Frost, *Glass in Architecture*, 20.

13. Veyne, "Roman Home," 315. See also Fleming, *Roman Glass*, 15.

14. Ratzka, "Atrium und Licht," 96.

15. Ratzka, "Atrium und Licht"; McGrath, 98, *Glass in Architecture*; Baatz, "Fensterglastypen," 12.

16. Ratzka, "Atrium und Licht," 96–97; Adam, *Roman Building*, 304; Aldrete, *Daily Life*, 75, 228.

17. Löhr, "Griechische Häuser," 11; Skrabei, "Fenster," 35; Herbig, *Das Fenster in der Architektur*, 6. On the importance of doors for lighting in the Greek and early Roman world, see also Steppuhn, "Der (un-)getrübte Blick," 371; Günter, *Wand, Fenster und Licht*, 21; Röver, "Einleitung," xi.

18. Aldrete, *Daily Life*, 227. See also Wimmel, "Luna moraturis," 72.

19. Ovid, *Amores*, I, 6, 3–4: "Pars adaperta fuit, pars altera clausa fenestrae, / Quale fere silvae lumen habere solent."

20. Vipard, "L'usage du verre," 3; Löhr, "Griechische Häuser," 12; Rykwert, "Windows and Architects," 21. Such sealants could be installed in addition to, or in lieu of, wooden shutters.

21. The most comprehensive survey of this phenomenon is Guarnieri, *Il vetro di pietra*. See also McGrath and Frost, *Glass in Architecture*, 29; Whitehouse, "Window Glass," 31; Stern, "Ancient Glass," 344–46.

22. Strobl, *Glastechnik*, 22; Löhr, "Griechische Häuser," 12; Sperl, "Glas und Licht," 64.

23. Pliny, *Natural History*, 36:45.

24. Stern, "Ancient Glass," 344–45 (peeling into sheets); Whitehouse, "Window Glass," 35; Fontaine and Foy, "De pierre et de lumière," 159.

25. Pliny, *Natural History*, 36:45, where this is implied in his statement about lapis from Cappadocia which "produces the largest pieces, but they lack transparency" (*amplissimos magnitudine, sed obscuros*). See also Foy and Fontaine, "Diversité et évolution," 444–49.

26. Pliny, *Natural History*, 36:45.

27. Pliny, *Natural History*, 36:45. On lapis mining in the Roman Empire, see especially the contributions in Guarnieri, *Il vetro di pietra*. See also Kreusch, "Beobachtungen zu Gipsfenstern," 47; Fontaine and Foy, "De pierre et de lumière," 159.

28. Ingravallo and Pisapia, "Trasparenze antiche," 164; Strobl, *Glastechnik*, 22.

29. Guarnieri, "Il lapis specularis," 234.

30. Martial, *Epigrams*, 8.14, 8.68; Strobl, *Glastechnik*, 22; Fontaine and Foy, "Modernité," 19; Sperl, "Glas und Licht," 69. See also below, Chapter 12.

31. Whitehouse, "Window Glass," 31.

32. Aldrete, *Daily Life*, 108–11 (quote at 108); Stambaugh, *Ancient Roman City*, 201–6; Jordan and Perlin, "Solar Energy Use," 588.

33. Baatz, "Fensterglastypen," 6; Fontaine and Foy, "La modernité," 17.

34. Whitehouse, "Window Glass," 31; Fontaine and Foy, "La modernité," 15.

35. Erffa, "Verwendung des Glasfensters," 4; Aldrete, *Daily Life*, 108; Rykwert, "Windows and Architects," 21.

36. Fleming, Roman Glass, 3; Grose, "Early Imperial Roman Cast Glass," 1; Henderson, *Ancient Glass*, 204, 227; Honroth, *Vom Luxusobjekt*, 35; Stern, "I vetrai," 38.

37. Whitehouse, *Short History*, 31. A more detailed account is Stern, "Roman Glassblowing."

38. Honroth, *Luxusobjekt*, 35; Stern, "I vetrai," 38.

39. Grose, "Early Imperial Roman Cast Glass," 1.

40. Henderson, *Ancient Glass*, 204; Whitehouse, *Short History*, 31.

41. Beretta and Di Pasquale, "Introduzione," 24.

42. Selle, *Die eigenen vier Wände*, 47.

43. Schnapp, "Fragments," 176; Grose, "Early Imperial Roman Cast Glass," 14–15; Lagabrielle, "Avant-propos," v.

44. Guarnieri, "Il lapis specularis," 236; Kreusch, "Beobachtungen zu Gipsfenstern," 40; Schwarzenberg, "Cristallo," 64; Whitehouse, "Window Glass," 35; Dell'Acqua, "Finestre invetriate," 111.

45. We have, in general, very little contemporary textual evidence about glassmaking: Fleming, *Roman Glass*, 10. My discussion of the "casting theory" is based on Steppuhn, "Der (un-)getrübte Blick," 372; Gerner and Gärtner, *Historische Fenster*, 10; Whitehouse, "Window Glass," 33; Strobl, *Glastechnik*, 22–26; Fontaine and Foy, "La modernité," 19–20; Dell'Acqua, "Finestre invetriate," 111. Some scholars have disputed this theory, arguing that all Roman window glass was blown. See Harden, "Domestic Window Glass," esp. 44.

46. Friedberg, *Virtual Window*, 107; Gerner and Gärtner, *Historische Fenster*, 10, 56; Adam-Veleni and Ignatiadou, *Glass Cosmos*, 53; Meyer, "Crown Window Panes," 214.

47. Naumann-Steckner, "Depictions of Glass," 86–87; Dell'Acqua, "Finestre invetriate," 111; Baatz, "Fensterglastypen," 7; Strobl, *Glastechnik*, 22.

48. Schnapp, "Fragments," 176; Fleming, *Roman Glass*, 10.

49. Stern, "Ancient Glass," esp. 364.

50. Pliny, *Natural History*, 36:198.

51. Whitehouse, *Short History*, 24, 27 (with ills.); Henderson, *Ancient Glass*, 76; Strobl, *Glastechnik*, 28; Adam-Veleni and Ignatiadou, *Glass Cosmos*, 123; Stern, "I vetri," 47.

52. Vipard, "L'usage du verre," 8; Dell'Acqua, "Nature and Artifice," 99; Steppuhn, "Der (un-)getrübte Blick," 375.

53. Dell'Acqua, "Finestre invetriate," 112; Baatz, "Fensterglastypen," 9, 11.

54. Fontaine and Foy, "Des fermetures de verre."

55. Foy and Fontaine, "Diversité et évolution"; Fontaine and Foy, "La modernité," 22; Strobl, *Glastechnik*, 28; Vipard, "L'usage du verre," 8; Baatz, "Fensterglastypen," 7; Rykwert, "Windows and Architects," 21.

56. Strobl, *Glastechnik*, 28; Meyer, "Crown Window Panes," 214. For a later dating of the discovery, see Foy and Fontaine, "Diversité et évolution," esp. 410.

57. Dell'Acqua, "Nature and Artifice," 97; Dell'Acqua, "Finestre invetriate," 111; Baatz, "Fensterglastypen," 8.

58. Strobl, *Glastechnik*, 106.

59. Strobl, *Glastechnik*, 28; Adam-Veleni and Ignatiadou, *Glass Cosmos*, 53.

60. Adam-Veleni and Ignatiadou, *Glass Cosmos*, 53; Chambon, "Evolution," esp. 165. But see also Whitehouse, who argues that this was relatively rare in Roman times: Whitehouse, "Window Glass," 34, 39.

61. They were probably first produced by glassmakers in the eastern part of the Roman Empire, more specifically in the Levant. Engle, "Light, Lamps and Windows," 80–81; Dell'Acqua, "Finestre invetriate," 111. According to Meyer, crown glass did not emerge before the sixth century: Meyer, "Crown Window Panes."

62. Stern, "Roman Glassblowing," 465; Dell'Acqua, "Finestre invetriate," 115; Meyer, "Crown Window Panes."

63. Whitehouse, "Window Glass," 34. But see also Meyer, "Crown Window Panes," 214, 219.

64. Fontaine and Foy, "La modernité," 19–20; Caviness, *Stained Glass Windows*, 49.

65. Dell'Acqua, "Finestre invetriate," 111; Loibl, "Zur Terminologie," 104; Steppuhn, "Der (un-)getrübte Blick," 374.

66. Symphosius, *Aenigmata*, no. 68: "Perspicior penitus nec luminis arceo visus, / transmittens oculos ultra mea membra meantes; nec me transit hiems, sed sol tamen emicat in me" (*Aenigmata*, Latin, 48; English, 184). That the phrase "perspicior penitus" implies transparency is accepted in modern scholarship: see the editor's commentary (185–86). Translation quoted with permission: © T. J. Leary, trans., 2014, *The Aenigmata*, Bloomsbury Academic, an imprint of Bloomsbury Publishing Plc.

67. Jütte, *Window Gazes* (with further literature).

68. Pliny the Younger, *Letters*, II.17.4 (133). Translation slightly modified. It is not en-

tirely clear whether Pliny is referring here to glass, but the qualities of the sealant he describes certainly apply to glass. See also Baddeley, "Window Glass."

69. Broise, "Vitrages et volets." See also Fontaine and Foy, "La modernité," 17; Vipard, "L'usage du verre," 6, 8; Sperl, "Glas und Licht," 66.

70. Baatz, "Fensterglastypen," 10; Broise, "Vitrages et volets," 62; Dell'Acqua, "Finestre invetriate," 115; Höcker, *Metzler Lexikon*, s.v. "Thermen," 252.

71. Broise, "Vitrages et volets," 62; Baatz, "Fensterglastypen," 10.

72. Broise, "Vitrages et volets," 61. On the Roman enjoyment of framed views of the landscape, see also Pavlovskis, *Man in an Artificial Landscape*, esp. 5–7.

73. Pliny the Younger, *Letters*, II.17.11: "*Calida piscina mirifica, ex qua natantes mare adspiciunt.*"

74. Baatz, "Fensterglastypen," 5; Herbig, *Das Fenster in der Architektur*, 10.

75. Pliny the Younger, *Letters*, II.17.21. See also Baatz, "Fensterglastypen," 5; Pavlovskis, *Man in an Artificial Landscape*, 26–30.

76. *Thesaurus linguae Latinae* (Berlin: De Gruyter, 1900–), s.v. "lumen." See also Vipard, "L'usage du verre," 8; Schwarzenberg, "Cristallo," 68; Wimmel, "Luna mortaturis," 71.

77. Hermansen, *Ostia*, 91–95; Drerup, "Bildraum und Realraum"; Horn, "Respiciens per fenestras." esp. 35–40.

78. Jordan and Perlin, "Solar Energy Use," 588.

79. Jordan and Perlin, "Solar Energy Use," esp. 588–90. On the greenhouse effect from a technical perspective, see Achilles and Navratil, *Glass Construction*, 24.

80. Statius, *Silvae*, I.15 (87).

81. Holtsmark, "Bath," 220.

82. Seneca, *Epistles*, 2:313 (no. 86)

83. Sperl, "Glas und Licht," 65; Adam, *Roman Building*, 274; Herbig, *Das Fenster in der Architektur*, 10.

84. Grose, "Origins," 23.

85. Seneca, *Epistles*, 2:313–15 (no. 86) (emphasis mine).

86. Stambaugh, *Ancient Roman City*, 203; Höcker, *Metzler Lexikon*, s.v. "Thermen," 251–52.

87. Seneca, *Epistles*, 2:315 (no. 86).

88. Völckers, *Glas und Fenster*, 90.

89. Beretta and Di Pasquale, "Introduzione," 25–26; Guarnieri, "Il lapis specularis," 236.

90. Mutz, "Römische Fenstergitter"; Pöhlmann, *Übervölkerung*, 53. Such grilles already existed in Greek architecture: Herbig, Das *Fenster in der Architektur*, 27.

91. Pliny, *Natural History*, 19:59.

92. Adam, *Roman Building*, 304–5.

93. Dell'Acqua, "*Illuminando colorat*," 101–3; Foy and Fontaine, "Diversité et évolution," 449. See also the contributions in Guarnieri, *Il vetro di pietra*.

94. Vipard, "L'usage du verre," 8. For a higher estimate, see Fontaine and Foy, "La modernité," 17. On the lack of attention by archaeologists, see Whitehouse, "Window Glass," 33.

95. Dell'Acqua, "Nature and Artifice," 99; Sedlmayr, *Das Licht*, 13; Aldrete, *Daily Life*, 162; Herbig, "Fenster an Tempeln," 255; Kantorowicz, "Oriens Augusti," 159; Onasch, *Lichthöhle und Sternenhaus*, 39.

96. Herbig, "Fenster an Tempeln," esp. 224, 228; Skrabei, "Fenster in griechischen Tempeln," 40–41; Höcker, *Metzler Lexikon*, s.v. "Fenster," 85; Riegl, *Spätrömische Kunstindustrie*, 38–39, 49; Rykwert, "Windows and Architects," 21 (with a discussion of the exceptional "window of appearances" that formed part of certain Egyptian temples).

97. Beyer, "Die Orientierung," 1; Skrabei, "Fenster in griechischen Tempeln," 39; Demangel, "Fenestrarum Imagines," 149.

98. Heile, "Licht und Dach," 28. For further evidence, see also Schuller, "5000 Jahre," esp. 27.

99. Çelebi, *Ottoman Traveller*, 284. See also Heile, "Licht und Dach," 28. On thinly sliced stone sheets in Roman architecture, see Adam, *Roman Building*, 214–15. Ceilings covered with thin alabaster slabs have also been recovered archaeologically from Yemeni palaces, some of which date back to the pre-Islamic period. Finbarr Barry Flood, personal communication, July 11, 2017.

100. Vitruvius, *De architectura*, I.2.5 (38).

101. Vitruvius, *De architectura*, III.2.8 (144).

102. Lim et al., *Environmental Factors*, 4–5; Günter, *Wand, Fenster und Licht*, 21; Heilmeyer, "Über das Licht," esp. 109. For Greek precedents, see Demangel, "Fenestrarum Imagines," 150.

103. Aldrete, *Daily Life*, 150.

104. Aldrete, *Daily Life*, 150–51.

105. Pliny, *Natural History*, 36:46.

106. A particularly fine example is a wall painting that depicts a glass bowl containing fruit, discovered in the so-called Villa Poppeae at Oplontis. See also Vipard, "L'usage du verre," 7, 10; Beretta and Di Pasquale, "Introduzione," 25.

107. Vipard, "L'usage du verre," 10.

108. Henderson, *Ancient Glass*, 234.

109. Fleming, *Roman Glass*, 12. See also Vickers, "Antiquity and Utopia," esp. 18–19.

110. *Scriptores historiae augustae*, 3:53.

111. Pliny, *Natural History*, 37:204. Stern ("Glass and Rock Crystal") suggests that this hierarchy did not exist in Greek and Hellenistic culture, emerging only in Roman times. Elsewhere she notes that, ironically, today "rock crystal has so little economic value, that it is no longer mined commercially" (Stern, "Ancient Glass," 369).

112. Pliny, *Natural History*, 37:9. On rock crystal in antiquity, see also Schwarzenberg, "Cristallo," 61; Crowley, "Crystalline Aesthetics."

113. Vickers, "Antiquity and Utopia," 19.

114. Schwarzenberg, "Color," 28.

115. Pliny, *Natural History*, 36:45.

116. Schwarzenberg, "Cristallo," 61.

117. Fleming, *Roman Glass*, 12; Schwarzenberg, "Cristallo," 64. On the long tradition of glass imitating precious materials, see Henderson, *Ancient Glass*, 20, 368.

118. Pliny, *Natural History*, 37:29. Translation slightly modified.

119. "Nec labris nisi magna meis crystalla terantur." Martial, *Epigrams*, 9.22.

120. Schwarzenberg, "Cristallo," 61.

121. Petronius, *Satyricon*, 37.

122. Quoted in Stern, "Roman Glassblowing," 478; Adam-Veleni and Ignatiadou, *Glass Cosmos*, 61.

123. Fleming, *Roman Glass*, 12.

124. Grose, "Origins," 26. For a more skeptical take on the "cheapness hypothesis," see Stern, "Roman Glassblowing," esp. 478–79; Stern, "Ancient Glass."

125. Stern, "Ancient Glass," 384.

126. For a discussion of the prices in the Price Edict and their historical context, see the summary in Stern, "Ancient Glass," section 8 (quotes at 385).

127. McGrath and Frost, *Glass in Architecture*, 98.

128. Philo, *Embassy to Gaius*, 45:364 (quote at 181–83).

129. Pliny, *Natural History*, 36:46. This was probably a variety of mica or onyx marble.

130. Stern, "Ancient Glass," 386; Frodl-Kraft, *Glasmalerei*, 6.

131. Herbig, *Das Fenster in der Architektur*, 12; Rykwert, "Windows and Architects," 21.

132. Günter, *Wand, Fenster und Licht*, esp. 8; Adam-Veleni and Ignatiadou, *Glass Cosmos*, 113; Köhler, "Basilika und Thermenfenster," 125; Eder, "Licht und Raumform," 131; Rykwert, "Windows and Architects," 21. On the origins and functions of the basilica in the Roman world, see, for example, Fuchs, "Die Funktion."

2
DARK AGES?

1. See, for instance, Wallace-Dunlop, *Glass*, 55, 90; Völckers, *Glas und Fenster*, 18–20; Schwarz, *Sachgüter*, 76.

2. Friedberg, *Virtual Window*, 107; similarly Kluge-Pinsker, "Wohnen," 214.

3. On the myth of the early Middle Ages as glassless and dark, see Foy, "La suprématie," 59, 64; Macfarlane and Martin, *Glass*, 18. On the continuity of glassmaking, see also Whitehouse, *Short History*, 45; Liefkes, *Glass*, 36.

4. Kohlmaier and Sartory, *Houses of Glass*, 45; Le Dantec, "La transparence," 94. See also Schiaperelli, *Casa fiorentina*, 124.

5. Whitehouse, *Short History*, 45. Steppuhn, "Der (un-)getrübte Blick," 372; Loibl, "Zur Terminologie," 107. Recent findings of Carolingian glass might shed new light on the question of continuity; see Kessler, Wolf, and Trümpler, "Leuchtende Fenster," 226. On the survival of casting techniques in the Islamic world, see Flood, "Stucco and Glass Window-Grills," 7; Franz, "Neue Funde," 308. A fine account of window glass production in the transition from late antiquity to the Middle Ages is Dell'Acqua, *"Illuminando colorat."* On medieval glass from a general perspective, see the contributions in Baumgartner and Krueger, *Phönix aus der Asche*; Lagabrielle, *Le verre*.

6. Neuheuser, "Mundum consecrare," 268; Theis, "Architektur," 19; Höcker, *Metzler Lexikon*, s.v. "Basilika," 33.

7. This was observed by Alberti as early as the mid-fifteenth century: Alberti, *Art of Building*, 230; see also Dell'Acqua, *"Illuminando colorat,"* 14; Herbig, "Fenster an Tempeln," 262; Grodecki, *Romanische Glasmalerei*, 38; Riegl, *Spätrömische Kunstindustrie*, 54; Rykwert, "Windows and Architects," 21. See also Meyer's observation that "architects for the many

new churches founded in the sixth century were quick to adopt the use of a great deal of glass" (Meyer, "Crown Window Panes," 219).

8. Deichmann, "Entstehung," esp. 40–42; Höcker, *Metzler Lexikon*, s.v. "Basilika," 33.

9. Onians, "Sign and Symbol," 513.

10. Dell'Acqua, "Glass and Natural Light," 300 (quote); Wallraff, *Christus verus sol*, 77; Flood, "Palaces of Crystal," 288. Kitschelt argued that, in addition to the eastward orientation to the real Jerusalem, there was a tendency to construe the basilica itself as a representation of the Heavenly Jerusalem: Kitschelt, *Die frühchristliche Basilika*. On the origins of the basilica as a building type, see Fuchs, "Funktion."

11. Günter, *Wand, Fenster und Licht*, 41–42, 61–63. On the prominence of windows in basilicas, see also Dell'Acqua, "Glass and Natural Light," 301.

12. Arnulf, *Architektur- und Kunstbeschreibungen*, 90, 131, 233.

13. In both cases, the context is metaphorical. Dell'Acqua, "*Illuminando colorat*," 101–3. See also Guarnieri, "Il lapis specularis," 237.

14. Schöne, *Über das Licht*, 46; Barnwell, "Low Side Windows," 64, 67; Turner, *Some Account*, xxx; Flood, "Palaces of Crystal," 29; Franz, "Transennae," 67.

15. Strobl, *Glastechnik*, 31; Dell'Acqua, "*Illuminando colorat*," 21, 102–3.

16. Sidonius, *Poems and Letters*, 1:465–67 (letter to Hesperius). The original, which is not easy to interpret, reads: "*Distinctum vario nitore marmor percurrit cameram solum fenestras, ac sub versicoloribus figuris vernans herbida crusta sapphiratos flectit per prasinum vitrum lapillos.*" See also Strobl, *Glastechnik*, 31–32; Dell'Acqua, "*Illuminando colorat*," 103–4.

17. Quoted in Dell'Acqua, "*Illuminando colorat*," 102.

18. The relevant source excerpts are gathered in Dell'Acqua, "*Illuminando colorat*," 93–94, See also *Grove Encyclopedia of Medieval Art and Architecture*, s.v. "stained glass"; Meyer, "Crown Window Panes," 219.

19. Dell'Acqua, "*Illuminando colorat*," 26–28; Meyer, "Crown Window Panes," 217.

20. Quoted in Dell'Acqua, "*Illuminando colorat*," 108–9; see also Barrelet, *La verrerie*, 21.

21. Kessler, Wolf, and Trümpler, "Leuchtende Fenster," 224–25; Hodges, "Fetishism," 77.

22. Ashtor and Cevidalli, "Levantine Alkali Ashes," 483; Foy, "La suprématie," 60; Dell'Acqua, "*Illuminando colorat*," 8; Erffa, "Verwendung des Glasfensters," 37. Early medieval Islamic glassmakers too were capable of producing transparent vessels: Barovier Mentasti, "Enameled Glass," 253.

23. On the production of colorless glass in the eastern Mediterranean, see Flood, "Palaces of Crystal," esp. 36. This production also left traces in late ancient Persian and Jewish literature; see Kiel, "Gazing."

24. Isidore, *Etymologies*, 328.

25. Hrabanus Maurus, *De universo*, quoted in Dell'Acqua, "*Illuminando colorat*," 153.

26. The most comprehensive study is still Erffa, "Verwendung des Glasfensters." See also Harden, "Medieval Glass in the West," 98.

27. Dell'Acqua, "Nature and Artifice," 98; Dell'Acqua, "*Illuminando colorat*," 14.

28. Rauch, "Anmerkungen," 105; Franz, "Neue Funde," 30; Cramp, "Window Glass," 79.

29. Foy, "La suprématie," 60–62; Caviness, *Stained Glass Windows*, 39–41; Kessler,

Wolf, and Trümpler, "Leuchtende Fenster," 227; Langlois and Le Maho, "Les origines du vitrail," 32.

30. *Grove Encyclopedia of Medieval Art and Architecture*, s.v. "stained glass," 647.

31. Quoted in Dell'Acqua, *"Illuminando colorat,"* 121 (emphasis mine). See also Whitehouse, "Window Glass," 36; Frodl-Kraft, *Glasmalerei*, 23.

32. Barrelet, *La verrerie*, 21–22; Dell'Acqua, "Nature and Artifice," 94; Dell'Acqua, *"Illuminando colorat,"* 147; Frodl-Kraft, *Glasmalerei*, 23.

33. *Grove Encyclopedia of Medieval Art and Architecture*, s.v. "stained glass," 650; Binding, *Bedeutung von Licht und Farbe*, 139–40.

34. Richer of Saint-Rémy, *Histories*, 2:30–31.

35. Schwarz, *Sachgüter*, 76; Caviness, *Stained Glass Windows*, 40–41; Frodl-Kraft, *Glasmalerei*, 24.

36. Dell'Acqua, "Nature and Artifice," 102.

37. Brisac, *Thousand Years*, 182.

38. *Grove Encyclopedia of Medieval Art and Architecture*, s.v. "stained glass," 646; see also Kurmann-Schwarz, "'Fenestre vitree,'" 61.

39. Dell'Acqua, *"Illuminando colorat,"* 147.

40. Brisac, *Thousand Years*, 7; Dell'Acqua, *"Illuminando colorat,"* 27–28.

41. Brisac, *Thousand Years*, 7; Dell'Acqua, "Enhancing Luxury," 205–7; Frodl-Kraft, *Glasmalerei*, 27.

42. McGrath and Frost, *Glass in Architecture*, 99–101; Becksmann and Waetzold, *Vitrea dedicata*, 23; Caviness, *Stained Glass Windows*, 38–40, 52.

43. Whitehouse, "Glass in Medieval Europe," 69.

44. Barnwell, "Low Side Windows," 67.

45. Franz, "Transennae," 77.

46. *"Fenestrae clausae vel claudendae vitro centum viginti."* Quoted in Arnulf, *Architektur- und Kunstbeschreibungen*, 234 (emphasis mine).

47. Völckers, *Glas und Fenster*, 19.

48. *Codex epistolarum Tegernseensium*, 25.

49. Günter, *Wand, Fenster und Licht*, 83.

50. *Oxford English Dictionary*, s.v. "storey/story"; Crowley, *Invention of Comfort*, 42.

51. Cited in Dell'Acqua, *"Illuminando colorat,"* 120–21 (quote at 121).

52. Dell'Acqua, *"Illuminando colorat,"* 121.

53. Kreusch, "Beobachtungen," 39–40; Steppuhn, "Der (un-)getrübte Blick," 371.

54. Strobl, *Glastechnik*, 35.

55. Steppuhn, "Der (un-)getrübte Blick," 371 (the German term is *"Marienglas"*).

56. Taylor, "Iconography," 17; Torriti, *Cathedral of Orvieto*, 20.

57. Erffa, "Verwendung des Glasfensters," 36, who dates the beginning of glass's dominance in sacred architecture to the twelfth century.

58. Alberti, *Art of Building*, 228; see also 230, 237–38.

59. Alberti, *Art of Building*, 146.

60. Vasari, *Technique*, 43; see also 264.

61. Harrison, *Description of England*, 198.

62. Donne, *Major Works*, 195 ("To the Countess of Bedford").

63. Zedler, *Grosses vollständiges Universal-Lexicon*, s.v. "Fenster," 538. A rare eighteenth-

century inquiry into this subject is Nixon, "Dissertation." One might object to my argument by pointing to the famous round window above the Cathedra Petri in St. Peter's, created under Bernini's supervision in the 1660s and commonly thought to be made of alabaster. Extant account books, however, do not seem to support the alabaster theory, as the window is referred to as an "Invetriata Grande" the execution of which was carried out by "vetrari" (glaziers). See Battaglia, *La Cattedra Berniniana*, 51–52, 179–80.

64. Gerevini, "Christus crystallus"; Dell'Acqua, "Nature and Artifice," 98.

65. Gerevini, "Sicut crystallus," 256–57.

66. Biernoff, *Sight and Embodiment*, 143; Legner, "Wände aus Edelstein," esp. 182; Westermann-Angerhausen and Täube, *Mittelalter*, 111.

67. Camille, *Gothic Art*, 38.

68. *Oxford English Dictionary*, s.v. "transparency"; "transparent."

69. Schwarzenberg, "Color," 29 (with references to Pseudo-Dionysius the Areopagite and Michael Psellos); Gerevini, "Christus crystallus."

70. McCray, *Glassmaking*, 51.

71. Sedlmayr, *Das Licht*, 12; Erffa, "Die Verwendung des Glasfensters," 39.

72. Schöne, *Über das Licht*, 31–32; Simson, *Gothic Cathedral*, 3.

73. Schwarz, *Sachgüter*, 86; Milner, *Senses*, 103–4.

74. Fichtenau, *Living in the Tenth Century*, 74; Roche, *History*, 117.

75. Speer, "Lux mirabilis," 93.

76. The document is reproduced in Dell'Acqua, *"Illuminando colorat,"* 118.

77. Dendy, *Use of Lights*, 15, and esp. chap. 7.

78. Barnwell, "Low Side Windows," 63.

79. Erffa, "Verwendung des Glasfenster," 10.

80. Dell'Acqua, "Nature and Artifice," 99; Fichtenau, *Living in the Tenth Century*, 74.

81. Camille, *Gothic Art*, 42; Lee, Seddon, and Stephens, *Stained Glass*, esp. 72. See also Binding, *Bedeutung von Licht und Farbe*, esp. 135–36.

82. Flood, "Palaces of Crystal," esp. 28.

83. Flood, "Palaces of Crystal," esp. 1, 33, 56, 188, 297. On the importance of this difference, see also Whitehouse, "Window Glass," 38.

84. Flood, "Palaces of Crystal," 309.

85. Flood, "Palaces of Crystal," 330. See also Franz, "Transennae," 81; Franz, "Neue Funde," 312.

86. Harden, "Medieval Glass in the West," 99; Dell'Acqua, "Plaster Transennae," 345 (who points out that only two significant Byzantine figurative stained-glass windows are known: from Istanbul's Pantocrator and the Chora church, respectively; they probably date to the twelfth century, and only fragments have survived).

87. Flood, "Palaces of Crystal," 41.

88. Dell'Acqua, "Glass and Natural Light," 316; Dell'Acqua, "Plaster Transennae," 345; McGrath and Frost, *Glass in Architecture*, 300; Onasch, *Lichthöhle*, 141–42. See also Rykwert, "Windows and Architects," 22.

89. Franz, "Transennae," esp. 68, 74, 81 (Islam).

90. Theis, "Lampen," esp. 57, 62.

91. Lane, *Venice*, chap. 15, esp. 212.

92. Marinelli, "Trasparenze"; Hills, *Venetian Colour*, 14–16; 109–11; 4; Luchs, "Stained Glass," 222.

93. Erffa, "Verwendung des Glasfensters," 39.

94. Erffa, "Verwendung des Glasfensters," 39. See also Helten, *Mittelalterliches Maß-werk*, 144. On the medieval taste for colored wall paintings, see also Binding, *Bedeutung von Licht und Farbe*, 158–60; Dell'Acqua, "Glass and Natural Light," 316.

95. Gage, "Gothic Glass," 43.

3
LIGHT FROM LIGHT

1. Çelebi, *Ottoman Traveller*, 235. Çelebi erred, however, when he claimed that the church windows were sealed with crystal glass from Murano. (They are Gothic.) This exaggeration probably served the purpose of underscoring the splendor and luxury of the building. See Köhbach, "Beschreibung," 221.

2. Klinkott, "Fenstergeschichte," 39; Rykwert, "Windows and Architects," 23.

3. Barnwell, "Low Side Windows," 63–64. Writing in 1610s Tyrol, the physician Guarinonius complained about (Catholic) churches "where large numbers of people gather . . . , for the breath and transpiration of so many people makes the air half rotten and harmful, especially where music is performed with trumpets and trombones" (*Grewel der Verwüstung*, 492).

4. Wolf et al., "Protective Glazing," 102.

5. Quoted in Barnwell, "Low Side Windows," 64.

6. Kemp, *Sermo Corporeus*, 19; Rykwert, "Windows and Architects," 23.

7. Frodl-Kraft, *Glasmalerei*, 34.

8. Gage, "Gothic Glass," 37.

9. Wigginton, *Glass in Architecture*, 14.

10. Badstübner, *Funktion des Fensters*, viii.

11. This was clearly spelled out during the Counter-Reformation: Mayer-Himmelheber, *Bischöfliche Kunstpolitik*, 105.

12. Goethe, *Poems*, 206.

13. Goethe, *Poems*, 207. On Goethe's collection of stained glass, see Caviness, *Stained Glass Windows*, 65.

14. Letter from Pope Gregory the Great to Bishop Serenus of Marseille, ca. 600, quoted in Caviness, "Biblical Stories in Windows," 105. On the narrative function of church windows, see also Caviness, *Stained Glass Windows*, 58; Dell'Acqua, "Nature and Artifice," 100; and esp. Kemp, *Sermo Corporeus*.

15. Simson, *Gothic Cathedral*, 51–52.

16. For a summary of this discussion, see Helten, *Mittelalterliches Maßwerk*, chap. 7.

17. See also Camille, *Gothic Art*, 54; and Dell'Acqua, "Christ from San Vincenzo," 15, which argues that "glazed windows were essentially christological." On medieval light symbolism, see also Schöne, *Über das Licht*; and Feuerstein, *Open Space*, 22–31.

18. On the Christian theology of light, see esp. Wallraff, *Christus verus sol*; also Sedlmayr, *Das Licht*; Binding, *Bedeutung von Licht und Farbe*.

19. Wolff, "Die Kathedrale," 21; Barry, "House of the Rising Sun," esp. 89–92.

20. Erffa, "Verwendung des Glasfensters," 40.

21. Eph. 5:8.

22. Sedlmayr, *Das Licht*, 12. See also Grodecki, *Romanische Glasmalerei*, 15.

23. Hugh of Saint Victor, "On the Three Days," in Coolman and Coulter, *Trinity and Creation*, 72.

24. "*Nisi enim solis splendor adesset, color vitreus, quod in arte acceperat, in tenebris non monstraret.*" Quoted in Büchsel, "Licht und Metaphysik," 33.

25. Wochnik, "Zur Wechselwirkung," 283.

26. Kantorowicz, "Oriens Augusti," esp. 131; Wallraff, *Christus verus sol*, esp. 48–49. See also Norberg-Schulz, *Meaning in Western Architecture*, 137; Dell'Acqua, "Glass and Natural Light," 303; Onasch, *Lichthöhle*, esp. 36, 39.

27. Dell'Acqua, "Glass and Natural Light," 302.

28. Büchsel, "Eccleasiae symbolorum," 80; Rykwert, "Windows and Architects," 22.

29. Lacerenza, "Simboli del mistero," esp. 185–86; *Grove Encyclopedia of Medieval Art and Architecture*, s.v. "stained glass," 649.

30. *Grove Encyclopedia of Medieval Art and Architecture*, s.v. "stained glass," 649.

31. Dell'Acqua, "Glass and Natural Light," 300; Onasch, *Lichthöhle*, 12.

32. Schmandt, *Judei*, 13.

33. Krinsky, *Synagogues of Europe*, 26.

34. Delmedigo, *Sepher maẓref la-chochma*, 99.

35. For instance, in Haller, ed., *Protokollbuch*, 93–94. See also Jütte, "'They shall not keep.'"

36. Wolff, "Die Kathedrale," 21; Frodl-Kraft, *Glasmalerei*, 6.

37. Wochnik, "Zur Wechselwirkung," 283.

38. Lee, Seddon, and Stephens, *Stained Glass*, 6–7.

39. Camille, *Gothic Art*, 29, 54; Wochnik, "Zur Wechselwirkung," 283; Wolff, "Die Kathedrale," 21.

40. Wochnik, "Zur Wechselwirkung," 312; Kurmann-Schwarz, "'Fenestre vitree,'" 61.

41. Durand de Mende, *Rationale Divinorum*, I.24 (18).

42. Deschamps and Mortet, *Recueil de textes*, 2:185.

43. Sauer, *Symbolik*, 120–21; Dell'Acqua, "Nature and Artifice," 101; Büchsel, "Ecclesiae symbolorum," 80.

44. Isidore, *Etymologies*, XVI.15. This visual analogy was apparently first introduced by Athanasius of Alexandria in the fourth century: Dell'Acqua, "Nature and Artifice," 101. The best survey of the motif is Breeze, "Blessed Virgin." See also Gottlieb, *Window in Art*, 67–68; Camille, *Gothic Art*, 42; McCray, *Glassmaking*, 6; Caviness, *Stained Glass Windows*, 58.

45. For a slightly different interpretation, see also Gottlieb, *Window in Art*, 119.

46. Quoted in Schöne and Henkel, *Emblemata*, 30.

47. Quoted in Luchs, "Stained Glass," 221.

48. Binding, *Bedeutung von Licht und Farbe*, 137. In the late medieval period, some windows even carried an indulgence (that is, remission of temporal punishment). A rare surviving window of this kind can be seen in All Saints' Church, North Street, York.

49. Gregory of Tours, *Glory of the Martyrs*, 83.

50. Wallace-Dunlop, *Glass*, 135; Vose, "Dark Ages," 45.

51. Erffa, "Verwendung des Glasfensters," 13.

52. Lee, Seddon, and Stephens, *Stained Glass*, 64.

53. Lim et al., *Environmental Factors*, 7; McGrath and Frost, *Glass in Architecture*, 104; Helten, *Mittelalterliches Maßwerk*, 158; Rykwert, "Windows and Architects," 23.

54. Lee, Seddon, and Stephens, *Stained Glass*, esp. 20–21; Kurmann-Schwarz, "'Fenestre vitree,'" 26; Kurmann, "Architektur," 35; Lagabrielle, "La timide introduction," 130; Campbell, *Transoms*, 6, 37, who shows that thirteenth- and early fourteenth-century transoms had structural purposes, whereas "after the middle of the fourteenth century, most transoms were built for decorative reasons" (6).

55. Kemp, *Sermo Corporeus*, 13; Barrelet, *La verrerie*, 40; Brisac, *Thousand Years*, 33.

56. Kemp, *Sermo Corporeus*, 13.

57. Simson, *Gothic Cathedral*, 4.

58. Jütte, "Window Gazes."

59. Büchsel, "Eccleasiae symbolorum," 84; Dell'Acqua, "Glass and Natural Light," 304; Kessler, "'They preach not,'" 59–60. On the great importance of the Heavenly Jerusalem as a trope in medieval architectural discourse, see also Lichtenberg, *Architekturdarstellungen*. Of course, this is not to say that all Gothic cathedrals aspired to this ideal or that they all form part of one unified style (as older scholarship sometimes suggested). As Michael Viktor Schwarz has rightly noted, if there had been a blueprint for designing cathedrals as the Heavenly Jerusalem, the extant medieval cathedrals would display "evident disagreement about its appearance" (Schwarz, "Kathedralen verstehen," 49). See also Schlink, "Gothic Cathedral."

60. Möseneder, "Lapides vivi," 43. Fajt, Royt, and Gottfried, *Sacred Halls*, 23.

61. Legner, "Karolinische Edelsteinwände," 359.

62. Westermann-Angerhausen, "Glasmalerei," 99, 102; Camille, *Gothic Art*, 42; Erffa, "Verwendung des Glasfensters," 40. On gems and their sacred aura in the High Middle Ages, see also Legner, "Wände aus Edelstein"; on the medieval fascination with the idea of gem-made windows, both in sacred and secular architecture, see Lichtenberg, *Architekturdarstellungen*, 40–41, 50–51, 98–99.

63. Hutter, *Glasmalerei*, 7; Schnapp, "Fragments," 176; Caviness, *Stained Glass Windows*, 41; Schöne, *Über das Licht*, 38. Light-emitting qualities were also ascribed to gems, which is a reminder of the perceived analogy between gems and stained glass: Lichtenberg, *Architekturdarstellungen*, 12.

64. Gilson, *La philosophie*, esp. 272–74; Simson, *Gothic Cathedral*, 51–52.

65. *Grove Encyclopedia of Medieval Art and Architecture*, s.v. "stained glass," 649; Lichtenberg, *Architekturdarstellungen*.

66. Schöne, *Über das Licht*, 37; Caviness, *Stained Glass Windows*, 43; Brisac, *Thousand Years*, 34.

67. Butts and Hendrix, "Drawn on Paper," 5.

68. Theophilus, *Various Arts*, 37.

69. Theophilus, *Various Arts*, 63.

70. Suger, *Ausgewählte Schriften*, 358.

71. I disagree here with Brisac, who has argued that glass windows rarely fulfilled their function as "catechism of the poor" because they were installed too high up. Brisac, *Thousand Years*, 41.

72. Quoted in Lewis, *By Women*, 92.

73. The church of the Holy Sepulchre's glass windows from this period have not survived. The crusader-period windows may have suffered damage as early as the Muslim reconquest of Jerusalem in the late twelfth century: Schmaltz, *Mater Ecclesiarum*, 163. On the production of stained glass in the Holy Land under the crusaders, see Dell'Acqua, "Enhancing Luxury," 208. On Crusader buildings featuring glass windows from local Islamic production, see Flood, "Ottoman Windows," 432.

74. Fabri, *Wanderings*, 1:342–43.

75. Erffa, "Verwendung des Glasfensters," 11; Schmidt and Dirlmeier, "Geschichte des Wohnens," 268–69.

76. "*Haec omnia non necessarius usus, sed oculorum concupiscentia requirit.*" *Dialogus inter Cluniacensem monachum*, 1584. The term "lust of the eyes" harks back to 1 John 2:16. See also Erffa, "Verwendung des Glasfensters," 11.

77. Thus the order's statutes of 1152, quoted in Scholz, "Ornamentverglasungen," 51. The prohibition goes back to the 1130s.

78. Erffa, "Verwendung des Glasfensters," 11; Hutter, *Glasmalerei*, note to table 11.

79. Brisac, *Thousand Years*, 44–45; Scholz, "Ornamentverglasungen," 51; Erffa, "Verwendung des Glasfensters," 37.

80. Kurmann, "Architektur," 36; Scholz, "Ornamentverglasungen," 53; Gage, "Gothic Glass," esp. 37. That grisailles were not a symptom of "poverty" is stressed by Helten, *Mittelalterliches Maßwerk*, 160.

81. Scholz, "Ornamentverglasungen," 53.

82. Erffa, "Verwendung des Glasfensters," 37.

83. Schöne, *Über das Licht*, 41; Lagabrielle, "La timide introduction," 134. For a nuanced discussion of the main factors driving the installation of grisaille, see Lee, Seddon, and Stephens, *Stained Glass*, 72.

84. For ideology, see Kurmann, "Architektur," 36. See also Brisac, *Thousand Years*, 44–45; Scholz, "Ornamentverglasungen," 51. Frodl-Kraft, *Glasmalerei*, 40, discusses a particularly striking exception to the rule: the polychrome and figurative "Habakuk Window" (ca. 1295) in the Cistercian church of Heiligenkreuz, today in Austria (see Frodl-Kraft, *Glasmalerei*, table 7).

85. Erffa, "Verwendung des Glasfensters," 37.

86. *Thesaurus proverbiorum*, 7:49–52. On the blackening effect of soot in domestic spaces, see also Alberti, *Art of Building*, 147. On the problems this causes from the point of view of modern restoration, see, for example, Lee, Seddon, and Stephens, *Stained Glass*, 190.

87. Dell'Acqua, "Nature and Artifice," 100. See also Helten, *Mittelalterliches Maßwerk*, 124.

88. Crowley, *Invention of Comfort*, 63; Wigginton, *Glass in Architecture*, 14.

4
"CLOSYD WELL WITH ROYALL GLAS"

1. Steppuhn, "Der (un-)getrübte Blick," 375.

2. The downsides of timber are vividly described in a letter by a sixteenth-century nun who commissioned a stained-glass window but ruled out timber, as it would "rot at the places where rain and snow would hit." By contrast, iron frames "also would look more ap-

propriate and craftsmanlike" (quoted in Schleif and Schier, *Katerina's Windows*, 277–78). See also Steppuhn, "Der (un-)getrübte Blick," 375; Brisac, *Thousand Years*, 16; Erffa, "Verwendung des Glasfensters," 33; Vose, "Dark Ages," 45.

3. Flood, "Palaces of Crystal," esp. 56, 188, 293; Dell'Aqcua, "Finestre invetriate," 115; Baatz, "Fensterglastypen," 11.

4. *Grove Encyclopedia of Medieval Art and Architecture*, s.v. "stained glass," 648.

5. Erffa, "Verwendung des Glasfensters," 33.

6. Frodl-Kraft, *Glasmalerei*, esp. 24.

7. See, for instance, the early fifteenth-century expense records of the Austrian monastery Rein, published in Jaritz, "Reiner Rechnungsbücher," 248. See also Kleinmanns, "Fensterglas," 167. On the aesthetic function of lead lines, see McGrath and Frost, *Glass in Architecture*, 105.

8. Scoville, *Capitalism*, 74; Godfrey, *Development*, 4, 186.

9. Ramazzini, *Diseases of Workers*, 62–63, 66.

10. Stern, "Roman Glassblowing," 456; Henke-Bockschatz, *Glashüttenarbeiter*, esp. 104–5.

11. On the hierarchies in the glass industry, see also Strobl, *Glastechnik*, 35; Rauch, "Anmerkungen," 106.

12. Henke-Bockschatz, *Glashüttenarbeiter*, 92–93, 100.

13. Henke-Bockschatz, *Glashüttenarbeiter*, 117, 149.

14. Engels, *Condition of the Working Class*, 499.

15. Gai, "Vitres," 84–85.

16. Chrétien de Troyes, *Complete Romances*, 432.

17. Arnulf, *Architektur- und Kunstbeschreibungen*, 483; Lichtenberg, *Architekturdarstellungen*, 59.

18. Quoted in Warton, *History of English Poetry*, 1:176.

19. Crowley, *Invention of Comfort*, 42.

20. Chaucer, *The Book of the Duchess* (vv. 321–31), in *Riverside Chaucer*, 334.

21. Erffa, "Verwendung des Glasfensters," 30.

22. Barrelet, *La verrerie*, 22. Monasteries also played a pioneering role in the British Isles: Cramp, "Window Glass." On the general importance of monasteries for medieval glazing as well as glass production, see also Crowley, *Invention of Comfort*, 39–40.

23. Erffa, "Verwendung des Glasfensters," 6, 13; Hodges, "Fetishism," 77; McCray, *Glassmaking*, 42–43; Kessler, Wolf, and Trümpler, "Leuchtende Fenster," 227; Jaritz, "Reiner Rechnungsbücher," 164–65.

24. Caviness, *Stained Glass Windows*, 80.

25. "*E chi volesse fare una bella finestra di vetro, conviene che ci metta tutti i colori.*" Giordano da Pisa, *Prediche*, 1:74.

26. Lagabrielle, "La timide introduction," 134.

27. Wright, *Warm and Snug*, 29.

28. Rauch, "Anmerkungen," 105. See also Helten, *Mittelalterliches Maßwerk*, 144.

29. Rauch, "Anmerkungen," 106. For figures from fourteenth-century France indicating that colored glass was one-third more expensive than blank glass, see Verdon, *Night*, 72.

30. Crowley, *Invention of Comfort*, 40, 63.

31. "*Verreres de la chapelle, des sales et chambres.*" Quoted in Barrelet, *La verrerie*, 48.

32. Lagabrielle, "La timide introduction," 136.

33. Lee, Seddon, and Stephens, *Stained Glass*, 104.

34. *Le ménagier de Paris*, 1:173n4.

35. McGrath and Frost, *Glass in Architecture*, 311; Lagabrielle, "La timide introduction," 134, 138.

36. Lee, Seddon, and Stephens, *Stained Glass*, 20–21.

37. Campbell, *Transoms*; Helten, *Mittelalterliches Maßwerk*, esp. 158; Wigginton, *Glass in Architecture*, 16.

38. Philippe, *Naissance*, 334; Lagabrielle, "La timide introduction," 138.

39. Barz, "Fenster-, Tür-und Toröffnungen," 29; Kirchberger, "Beiträge," 80; Heyne, *Wohnungswesen*, 236.

40. Lagabrielle, "La timide introduction," 133.

41. Barnwell, "Low Side Windows," 64; Turner, *Some Account*, xxix, 75–77; Crowley, *Invention of Comfort*, 41, 63; Godfrey, *Development*, 13; Harden, "Medieval Glass in the West," 99.

42. Quoted in Turner, *Some Account*, 258. See also McGrath and Frost, *Glass in Architecture*, 105; Harden, "Domestic Window Glass," 56.

43. Kühnel, "Alltagsleben," 51.

44. Völckers, *Glas und Fenster*, 31.

45. For France, see Philippe, *Naissance*, 335; Lagabrielle, "La timide introduction," passim; Neveux, "Recherches," 250. For German lands, see Kühnel, "Sachkultur," 17. For Bohemia, see Hlaváček, "Alltag," 314. For England, see Godfrey, *Development*, 13. In Tuscany even later, see Quast, "Fensterverschlüsse," 144–45.

46. Lagabrielle, "Fenêtres des rois," 118; Schürmann and Uekermann, *Das verkleidete Fenster*, 10; Gerner and Gärtner, *Historische Fenster*, 66. Specifically for England, see Barnwell, "Low Side Windows," 64–65.

5
"GLASS WINDOWS MADE OF FABRIC"

1. Friedrichs, *Early Modern City*, 35; Lagabrielle, "La timide introduction," 132; Turner, *Some Account*, xxix, 80–82; Quast, "Fensterverschlüsse," 142, 145.

2. Frugoni, *Day in a Medieval City*, 3; Macfarlane and Martin, *Glass*, 43.

3. Chrétien de Troyes, *Complete Romances*, 432.

4. Schock-Werner, "Bedeutung und Form," 129. On unsealed windows, see also Ostendorf, "Ueber den Verschluss," 178.

5. Thietmar of Merseburg, *Chronicon*, V.6.

6. Kühnel, "Alltagsleben," 38–39; Lagabrielle, "Fenêtres des rois," 99; Schwarz, *Sachgüter*, 38; Schedensack, *Nachbarn*, 31; Thornton, *Renaissance Interior*, 28; Crowley, *Invention of Comfort*, 41.

7. Ladurie, *Montaillou*, 39.

8. Kluge-Pinsker, "Wohnen," 213.

9. Quast, "Fensterverschlüsse," 146; Thornton, *Renaissance Interior*, 29.

10. Quast, "Fensterverschlüsse," 144; Thornton, *Renaissance Interior*, 28. On the variety of medieval shutters, see also Wacker, *Fenster*, esp. 10–11.

11. Farr, *Hands of Honor*, 14. Such regulations were also in effect elsewhere in Europe—for instance, in England: see Palliser, *Tudor York*, 179–80. My thanks to Christopher Friedrichs for these references.

12. Palliser, *Tudor York*, 179–80.

13. Harrison, *Description*, 197.

14. Chambers, *Treatise*, 2:353–54.

15. Thornton, *Renaissance Interior*, 28; Quast, "Fensterverschlüsse," 145.

16. Montaigne, *Travel Journal*, 1133, 1206.

17. Montaigne, *Travel Journal*, 127, 1133, 1206; see also 1114.

18. Anon., *Non-Military Journal*, 13–14. On the Orientalist fascination with the *mashrabiya*, especially in the nineteenth century, see Thürlemann, *Haremsfenster*.

19. Krünitz, *Encyklopädie*, s.v. "Fenster," 588.

20. On the importance of security issues to premodern residents, see Jütte, *Strait Gate*, chap. 2.

21. Antoine, "Maisons rurales," 237; Lagabrielle, "Fenêtres des rois," 101; Turner, *Some Account*, xxix; Thornton, *Renaissance Interior*, 29; Mutz, "Römische Fenstergitter."

22. Kühnel, "Alltagsleben," 49; Heyne, *Wohnungswesen*, 234; Barnwell, "Low Side Windows," 66; Quast, "Fensterverschlüsse," passim.

23. Flood, "Palaces of Crystal," 5.

24. Yamaguchi, "Architecture of the Spanish Philippines," 134. Shells were also commonly used in Mughal architecture: see Dikshit, *History of Indian Glass*, esp. 124.

25. Quast, "Fensterverschlüsse," 142.

26. Erffa, "Verwendung des Glasfensters," 26.

27. Gerlach, "Anfänge," 98.

28. For example, Völckers, *Glas und Fenster*, 15.

29. Lagabrielle, "Fenêtres des rois," 110. According to Mach's estimates, textile fabrics cost two-thirds of the price of glass: Mach, "De verre," 167. See also Woronoff, "Quand l'exception," 135.

30. For lack of transparency, see Garzoni, *Piazza universale*, 1:659.

31. *Dictionary of Architecture*, s.v. "window glazing"; *Encyclopédie méthodique*, s.v. "vitrier," 698–700.

32. Lagabrielle, "Fenêtres des rois," 104; Lardin, "Verre," 90 (Rouen and Normandy).

33. Lagabrielle, "Fenêtres des rois," esp. 102.

34. *Le ménagier de Paris*, 1:173.

35. Plat, *Jewell House*, 77.

36. Schürmann and Uekermann. *Das verkleidete Fenster*, 9; Völckers, *Glas und Fenster*, 15; Meyer, *Schweizerische Sitte*, 24.

37. Völckers, *Glas und Fenster*, 15.

38. *Le ménagier de Paris*; 1:173; Frugoni, *A Day*, 123.

39. Erffa, "Verwendung des Glasfensters," 15, 27; Rauch, "Anmerkungen," 104; Vose, "Dark Ages," 45.

40. Grodecki, *Glasmalerei*, 21; McGrath and Frost, *Glass in Architecture*, 104; Brisac, *Thousand Years*, 185; Frodl-Kraft, *Glasmalerei*, 46.

41. Lagabrielle, "Fenêtres des rois," 97; Quast, "Fensterverschlüsse," 145.

42. Quoted in Demos, *Little Commonwealth*, 29.

43. Mack, "Pastorius," 140.

44. Oliver, *Dwellings*, 79, 130.

45. Lardin, "Verre," 90; Völckers, *Glas und Fenster*, 14.

46. Mach, "De verre," 167.

47. This also posed problems with respect to cleaning the panes: see Montaigne, *Travel Journal*, 898. See also Schock-Werner, "Bedeutung und Form" 124; Lagabrielle, "La timide introduction," 134; Godfrey, *Development*, 205.

48. Thornton, *Renaissance Interior*, 29, 31; Quast, "Fensterverschlüsse," 145. See also the illustration in Gerlach, "Anfänge," 96.

49. Lagabrielle, "La timide introduction," 135; Jütte, "Window Gazes."

50. Krafft, *Reisen*, 230.

51. Lagabrielle, "Fenêtres des rois," 104.

52. Lagabrielle, "Fenêtres des rois," 104; Lagabrielle, "La timide introduction," 139–40; Thornton, *Renaissance Interior*, 28–29; Quast, "Fensterverschlüsse," 145; Bol, "Emerald and the Eye," 90.

53. Quoted in Quast, "Fensterverschlüsse," 151n41.

54. Thornton, *Renaissance Interior*, 29, 370.

55. Inventory of Juan Sánchez Cotán, quoted in Scheffler, *Das spanische Stilleben*, 260 (quote); see also 291. Scheffler goes so far as to claim that the painter's "equation of window and canvas suggests that he subscribed to Alberti's idea of the painting as a window onto nature" (260). As I discuss in Chapter 8, this very assumption is based on a de-historicized interpretation of Alberti's window metaphor.

56. Plat, *Jewell House*, 77.

57. Lardin, "Verre," 90; Quast, "Fensterverschlüsse," 147.

58. Lagabrielle, "Fenêtres des rois," 102.

59. Bol, "Emerald and the Eye," 90.

60. *Oxford English Dictionary* online, s.v. "pane."

61. Lardin, "Verre," 93.

62. Mach, "De verre," 166.

63. Mach, "De verre," esp. 164; Lagabrielle, "La timide introduction," 140–41; Schürmann and Uekermann, *Das verkleidete Fenster*, 10; Kühnel, "Alltagsleben," 50.

64. The best discussions of this subject are Schiaparelli, *Casa fiorentina*, 119–24, and Quast, "Fensterverschlüsse."

65. *Oxford English Dictionary*, s.v. "fenestral."

66. See, for instance, the anonymous, contemporary painting showing the execution of Savonarola in Florence in 1498 (today in the Museo Nazionale di San Marco). See also Schiaparelli, *Casa fiorentina*, 121; Thornton, *Renaissance Interior*, 29.

6

FROM THE HOUSE OF GOD TO
THE HOUSES OF BURGHERS

1. This chapter is derived in part from an article published in *Cultural and Social History* 15, no. 5 (2018), © Social History Society, https://doi.org/10.1080/14780038.2019.1568031.

2. Ueda, *Inner Harmony*; Nishi and Hozumi, *What Is Japanese Architecture?*; Screech, "Glass," esp. 28.

3. See, for instance, Herbig, *Das Fenster in der Architektur*, 7.

4. Oliver, *Dwellings*, 134.

5. Shammas, "Built Environment," 9 (quote); Heyne, *Wohnungswesen*, 236; Steppuhn, "Der (un-)getrübte Blick," 377.

6. Loibl, "Zur Terminologie," 104; Steppuhn, "Der (un-)getrübte Blick," 374. Some scholars disagree, arguing that the reintroduction of crown glass resulted from the Greek campaigns of King Roger II of Sicily in the twelfth century: Strobl, *Glastechnik*, 61; Harden, "Domestic Window Glass," 40–41.

7. Steppuhn, "Der (un-)getrübte Blick," 374; Barrelet, *Verrerie*, 66–67, 85.

8. Harden, "Domestic Window Glass," 41; Steppuhn, "Der (un-)getrübte Blick," 374; Louw, "Window-Glass Making," 52.

9. Louw, "Window-Glass Making," 48. For a critical take on this attribution, see Harden, "Domestic Window Glass," 62.

10. McGrath and Frost, *Glass in Architecture*, 42.

11. Gerlach, "Anfänge," 96; Strobl, *Glastechnik*, 27; Schöne, *Über das Licht*, 36. According to a late medieval account book from Nuremberg, in 1494 one small bullion cost 2 Pfennig, whereas a brand new roof tile cost 0.72 Pfennig. As the modern editor of this source notes, this means that the bullions "were not an extraordinary luxury, but still quite expensive." Dirlmeier, "Alltag," 164.

12. They were melted down with other waste that inevitably resulted from cutting large disks in rectangular panes. This waste amounted to at least 10 percent of the disk: Steppuhn, "Der (un-)getrübte Blick," 375; McGrath and Frost, *Glass in Architecture*, 34; Wigginton, *Glass in Architecture*, 26.

13. Caen et al., "Technical Prescriptions," 167. See also Ng, "Cultural Ecology," 500.

14. Schedensack, *Nachbarn*, 187; Jütte, "Window Gazes."

15. Jütte, "Window Gazes."

16. Shaw, "Construction," 455.

17. Roche, *History*, 115. See also Thornton, *Renaissance Interior*, 275; Shaw, "Construction," 455.

18. *Oxford English Dictionary*, s.v. "light."

19. Schedensack, *Nachbarn*, 187; Shaw, "Construction," esp. 455.

20. Scoville, *Capitalism*, 108.

21. The need of light for medical operations is vividly described in Boccaccio's *Decamerone*, VII.9. On the importance of daylight in anatomical theaters, see Jütte, "Entdeckung," 248.

22. Roth, "Sepher hilchot," 48–50. Such policies were also in place among Christians. In certain parts of Switzerland, for example, it was legally prohibited to assess the value of pawns after sunset: Ekirch, *At Day's Close*, 84.

23. See, for example, Palliser, *Tudor York*, 180.

24. Brant, *Ship of Fools*, 328.

25. "*Also auch wüllen gewand, seyden, marder, zobbeln ynn finstern gewelben odder kreme feyl zu haben und die lufft verstopfen.*" Luther, *Von Kaufshandlung und Wucher* (1524), in *Werke*

15:311–12 (American ed., 45:269). Such arguments and warnings were also common in broadsheets from this period: Goer, "'Gelt ist also,'" 138, 320.

26. *Das Lalebuch*, 47–71.

27. "*Ain staine hause ufmauren ohne fenster und thüren*." Zimmern, *Die Chronik der Grafen von Zimmern*, 2:117–18.

28. "*Dann do konte er am bästen sehen, wo die fenster am notturftigisten*." Zimmern, *Die Chronik der Grafen von Zimmern*, 2:117–18.

29. Alberti, *Art of Building*, 28.

30. Alberti, *Art of Building*, 30. Such prescriptions were later taken up and elaborated by Palladio, who stated that the width of a window should not exceed one-quarter of the breadth of the room, with the height being limited to twice and one-sixth of their breadth. Palladio, *Four Books of Architecture*, 1:25. See also Wigginton, *Glass in Architecture*, 29.

31. Bedal, "Zeitmarken," 146–47. Badstübner, *Funktion des Fensters*, xi; Ng, "Cultural Ecology," 499.

32. Macfarlane and Martin, *Glass*, 43.

33. Le Vieil, *L'art de la peinture*, 235; *Encyclopédie méthodique*, s.v., "vitrier," 698; Belhoste and Leproux, "La fenêtre parisienne," 43. For scholars and their demand for translucent windows, see Bol, "Emerald and the Eye," 93.

34. Da Vinci, *Treatise*, 1:212–13.

35. My thanks to Morgan Ng for this observation.

36. Alberti, *Art of Building*, 28.

37. Apperson and Manser, *Dictionary of Proverbs*, 534.

38. Cavallo and Storey, *Healthy Living*, 71.

39. Biow, *Culture of Cleanliness*, esp. 183; Esch, *Lebenswelt*, 60; Wheeler, "Stench," esp. 25–26.

40. Shaw, "Construction," 452–53.

41. Dumas, "La fenêtre," 159–61; Sturm, *Leben mit dem Tod*, 354; Jütte, *Strait Gate*, 169–70.

42. Vasari, *Technique*, 267.

43. Henderson, *Renaissance Hospital*, 159.

44. Henderson, *Renaissance Hospital*, 159; Mathieu, "Das offene Fenster," 292. In ancient medicine, see Horn, "Respiciens per fenestras," 34.

45. Pepys, *Diary*, February 12, 1666.

46. Guarinonius, *Grewel der Verwüstung*, 1286.

47. Quoted in Corbin, *Foul and the Fragrant*, 216.

48. Corbin, *Foul and the Fragrant*, 216.

49. Quoted in Mathieu, "Das offene Fenster," 295; see also 298.

50. Schiaparelli, *Casa fiorentina*, 120; La Roncière, "Tuscan Notables," 190. On a French hospital that received glass windows as early as the first half of the fourteenth century, see Lagabrielle, "Fenêtres des rois," 113.

51. Henderson, *Renaissance Hospital*, 160.

52. Henderson, *Renaissance Hospital*, 160.

53. Orlin, *Locating Privacy*, 180.

54. Çelebi, *Ottoman Traveller*, 242.

55. Leung, "Evolution," esp. 41, 45; Lei, *Neither Donkey nor Horse*, esp. 37–38.

56. Jannetta, *Epidemics and Mortality*, xix, 5.

57. Jannetta, *Epidemics and Mortality*, 15.

58. Interestingly, even European visitors to Japan, committed as they were to the miasma theory, perceived the realities in Japan to be entirely different from Europe: "The air is extremely wholesome and temperate and thus there are no prevailing maladies, such as the plague, in the kingdom," wrote the Jesuit missionary João Rodrigues around 1600. Quoted in Jannetta, *Epidemics and Mortality*, 31.

59. Cavallo and Storey, *Healthy Living*, 134.

60. Rangone, *Come il Serenissimo*, B3. My thanks to Sabine Herrmann for sharing a digital copy of the treatise with me.

61. Roth, "Sepher hilchot," 49.

62. Kühnel, "Alltagsleben," 50; Thornton, *Renaissance Interior*, 120–21; Cavallo and Storey, *Healthy Living*, 133–34. For complaints about cold air in fifteenth-century letters to the pope, see Esch, *Lebenswelt*, 60.

63. Montaigne, *Travel Journal*, 1078. Wearing warm clothes in the interior was a strategy known throughout the premodern world—and not just in Europe—for coping with cold. For the example of China, see, for example, Knapp, "In Search," 69.

64. McGrath and Frost, *Glass in Architecture*, 105; Harden, "Domestic Window Glass," 56.

65. Kühnel, "Alltagsleben," 50; Wolf et al., "Protective Glazing," 105.

66. Aretino, *Dialogues*, 232: "She who gives herself for less than twenty ducats is like a cloth-covered window [*finestra impannata*], which can be ripped open by the slightest breeze."

67. Plat, *Jewell House*, 77.

68. "*Rompues par des vents impétueux*." Quoted in Philippe, *Naissance*, 59.

69. Schiaparelli, *Casa fiorentina*, 116–17; Kühnel, "Alltagsleben," 49–50.

70. "*Deffendre l'eaue et le vent d'aval contre lequel les dictes fenestres sont*." Quoted in Lardin, "Verre," 90.

71. Thornton, *Renaissance Interior*, 26. On regional differences in France regarding the use and number of fireplaces, see Contamine, "Peasant Hearth," 499–501.

72. Contamine, "Peasant Hearth," 500; Thornton, *Renaissance Interior*, 26.

73. Lagabrielle, "Fênetres des rois," 105–6; Lagabrielle, "La timide introduction," 140.

74. Such an episode from 1498 Florence is described in Landucci, *Diario*, 166.

75. Guidini-Raybaud, *Pictor et veyrerius*, 255; Scoville, *Capitalism*, 108, 162.

76. "*Die fenster, so allein ledlin sindt und der mertheil anstatt der glaß papyrin*." Platter, *Tagebuch*, 151.

77. Montaigne, *Travel Journal*, 1078.

78. Figeac, *L'ancienne France*, 429.

79. Cottin, "La fenêtre," 119, 130; Le Vieil, *L'art de la peinture*, 235.

80. Scoville, *Capitalism*, 108.

81. Borromeo, *Instructiones*, bk. 1, 25.

82. Camille, *Gothic Art*, 48; Lee, Seddon, and Stephens, *Stained Glass*. For the general reluctance of Italian householders to install glass, see Quast, "Fensterverschlüsse," 145. On small windows and the rarity of glass in early modern Spain, see D'Aulnoy, *Relation*, 3:5.

83. Schiaparelli, *Casa fiorentina*, 123; La Roncière, "Tuscan Notables," 190; Quast, "Fensterverschlüsse," 147; Thornton, *Renaissance Interior*, 29.

84. Quoted in Harden, "Domestic Window Glass," 58. See also similar references in Sarti, "Ländliche Hauslandschaften," 186.

85. Goethe, *Italienische Reise*, in *Werke*, 15:29.

86. Quoted in Scoville, *Capitalism*, 108.

87. Schürmann and Uekermann, *Das verkleidete Fenster*, 10; Barrelet, *Verrerie*, 127; Scoville, *Capitalism*, 108–9.

88. Scoville, *Capitalism*, 108–9.

89. Young, *Travels in France*, 16. For another account in the same vein, see Guerrand, "Private Spaces," 389.

90. Young, *Travels in France*, 16.

91. Cavallo and Storey, *Healthy Living*, 134.

92. Schöne and Henkel, *Emblemata*, 1238.

93. Horman, *Vulgaria*, 242.

94. Reichert, *Erfahrung der Welt*, 46.

95. Guarinonius, *Grewel der Verwüstung*, 484. See also his general (polemic) discussion of this subject (482–94).

96. Scamozzi, *Architettura universale*, 321.

97. Alberti, *Art of Building*, 27–29, 146.

98. Oliver, *Dwellings*, 130.

99. Erasmus of Rotterdam, *Opus epistolarum*, 5:613–614 (English edition, 10:471). I have slightly revised the translation. Montaigne, too, mentions that French contemporaries often complained about the "stifling heat" in German stove-heated rooms which "give most of those who are not used to them a headache." (Montaigne, *Essays*, in *Complete Works*, 1008). Montaigne, for his part, admitted that he found more comfort than disadvantage in the German custom (Montaigne, *Essays*, in *Complete Works*, 1008; see also 1078).

100. Shammas, "Domestic Environment," 7.

101. Godfrey, *Development*, 13.

102. Horman, *Vulgaria*, 242.

103. More, *Utopia*, 47 (emphasis mine).

104. See the related orders and expenses recorded in Kempe, *Loseley Manuscripts*, esp. 102–3.

105. Crowley, *Invention of Comfort*, 65; Smith, *Houses*, 266–67; Shammas, "Domestic Environment," 7.

106. Crowley, *Invention of Comfort*, 64.

107. Shammas, "Domestic Environment," 7.

108. For a summary of the "Great Rebuilding" theory, see Shammas, "Early Modern Built Environment," 8–9.

109. Eriksdotter, "Little Ice Age," esp. 24; Fagan, *Little Ice Age*, esp. 90. How to define and date the Little Ice Age remains a complex question, as demonstrated by a recent topic issue on this subject in the *Journal of Interdisciplinary History* 44, no. 3 (2014). But, as Sam White notes in his contribution, "The overall strength of the long-term cooling trend is why climatologists now confidently speak of a 'Little Ice Age' despite its spatial and temporal complexities" (White, "Real Little Ice Age," 347).

110. Eriksdotter, "Little Ice Age," 25; Behringer, *Cultural History of Climate*, 136.

111. Hawkes, *Architecture and Climate*, 4 (quote); Crowley, *Invention of Comfort*, 36.

112. Eriksdotter, "Little Ice Age," 36. See also Meiners's observations regarding the rapid rise of stove-based heating in the sixteenth-century German lands (Meiners, "Stufen des Wandels," 277–79).

113. Meiners, "Stufen des Wandels," 306.

114. Cavallo and Storey, *Healthy Living*, 70–72, 78.

115. Crowley, *Invention of Comfort*, 62; Louw, "'Advantage of a Clearer Light,'" 302.

116. Pepys, *Diary*, 2:197. See also the entry of September 16, 1664, in which Pepys derides the reported inferiority of windows at the Czar's court in Russia.

117. Chamberlayne, *Angliae notitia*, 27.

118. Quoted in Louw, "'Advantage of a Clearer Light,'" 302.

119. Smith, *Wealth of Nations*, 168.

120. Quoted in Midgley, *University Life*, 10.

121. Mączak, *Travel*, 47.

122. Krünitz, *Encyklopädie*, s.v. "Fenster," 596.

123. Reid, "Seventeenth-Century Crisis," esp. 654.

124. Reid, "Seventeenth-Century Crisis"; Richards, "Seventeenth-Century Crisis"; Atwell, "Seventeenth-Century 'General Crisis,'" esp. 673–74.

125. Girouard, *Smythson*, 32, 72 (quote), 290.

126. Girouard, *Smythson*, chap. 3.

127. Girouard, *Smythson*, chap. 2.

128. Girouard, *Smythson*, 101.

129. Girouard, *Hardwick Hall*, 18.

130. Lovell, *Bess of Hardwick*, 410; Girouard, *Smythson*, 153; Crowley, *Invention of Comfort*, 66.

131. Godfrey, *Development*, 205; Girouard, *Hardwick Hall*, 18. On the desire to imitate the "breezy, light-suffused structures associated with Renaissance Italy," see Ng, "Cultural Ecology," 507.

132. Crowley, *Invention of Comfort*, 66.

133. Quoted in Girouard, *Smythson*, 19.

134. Girouard, *Smythson*, 72.

135. Smith, *Houses*, 266.

136. Crowley, *Invention of Comfort*, 37.

137. Wolf et al., "Protective Glazing," 105.

138. North, *On Building*, 62.

139. Alberti, *Art of Building*, 355.

140. Hawkes, *Architecture and Climate*, 47–48.

141. McGrath and Frost, *Glass in Architecture*, 180; Guénoun and Kalmanovich, *Glashäuser*, 19–21.

142. See, for instance, Alberti, *Art of Building*, 145. Of course, this was also known to the Romans: Martial, *Epigrams*, 8.14.

143. McGrath and Frost, *Glass in Architecture*, 460.

144. Vasari, *Technique*, 272.

145. Horman, *Vulgaria*, 242. On such shutters, see also Gerner and Gärtner, *Historische Fenster*, 67.

146. Quoted in Hérold, "Verre des vitraux," 76.

147. Caen et al., "Technical Prescriptions," 169; Lours, "L'éclaircissement," 149; Godfrey, *Development*, 207.

148. Abraham a Sancta Clara, *Etwas für alle*, 517.

149. Letter from Madame de Maintenon to the Duc de Noailles, April 1705, printed in Bowles, *Madame de Maintenon*, 205.

150. Lardin, "Verre," 90.

151. Quoted in Godfrey, *Development*, 207.

152. Löwenstein, *Quellen*, doc. 2454.

153. Crowley, *Invention*, 37. See also Godfrey, *Development*, 207; Orlin, *Locating Privacy*, 179–80.

154. Luther, *Werke* [section *Briefwechsel*], 10:19 (Nr. 3727). For Luther as a home-owner, see also Neser, *Luthers Wohnhaus*, esp. 42.

155. Lagabrielle, "La timide introduction," 135; Lours, "L'éclaircissement."

156. North, *On Building*, 94–95.

157. Tucher, *Baumeisterbuch*, 106 (quote), 246.

158. Tucher, *Baumeisterbuch*, 105.

159. "*Die glesser in den stuben und kamern auf dem sloß pesseren und etlich waschen und fursetzten lossen, wo sein nott was.*" Tucher, *Baumeisterbuch*, 296 (quote), 299–301.

160. Wallace-Dunlop, *Glass*, 174.

161. Dowell, *History of Taxation*, 3:201; Godfrey, *Development*, 207–8; Friedrichs, *Early Modern City*, 39; Schiaperelli, *Casa fiorentina*, 125.

162. Barrelet, *Verrerie*, 67. See also a case of a theft in Bologna in 1498: Nadi, *Diario bolognese*, 235.

163. Crowley, *Invention of Comfort*, 63.

164. *Dictionary of Architecture*, s.v. "window glazing."

165. Godfrey, *Development*, 207–8.

166. For Italy, see Dorigato, *Murano*, 20 (a case from Venice in 1369). For southern Germany, see Montaigne, *Travel Journal*, 1094. For Cologne, see Schmid, *Kölner Renaissance-kultur*, 117.

167. Brown, *Private Lives*, 204–5. For similar cases from sixteenth-century England, see Orlin, *Locating Privacy*, 170.

168. Lardin, "Verre," 91.

169. Coke, *Reports* (pertaining to Herlakenden's Case), pt. 4, 63b (2:448). See also Godfrey, *Development*, 207–8.

170. Crowley, *Invention of Comfort*, 67.

7
GLASS AND CLASS

1. A short section of this chapter is adapted from my article "Smashed Panes and 'Terrible Showers': Windows, Violence, and Honor in the Early Modern City," *West 86th* 22, no. 2 (2015): 131–56. © Copyright 2016 by The Bard Graduate Center: Decorative Arts, Design History, and Material Culture.

2. Scoville, *Capitalism*, 108; Ramsey, "Literary History," 177; Crowley, *Invention of Comfort*, 103.

3. As recorded by a French traveler: "*Lorsque l'on veut parler d'une maison où il ne manque rien, l'on dit en un mot, elle est vîtrée.*" D'Aulnoy, *Relation*, 3:5.

4. Lardin, "Verre," 92; Kühnel, "Sachkultur," 17; Godfrey, *Development*, 13.

5. Montaigne, *Travel Journal*, 1071.

6. Montaigne, *Travel Journal*, 1075, 1111.

7. Quoted in Woronoff, "Quand l'exception," 133; Neveux, "Recherches," 250.

8. Montaigne, *Travel Journal*, 1094.

9. Giesicke and Ruoss, "In Honour of Friendship," 43.

10. Philippe, *Naissance*, 335.

11. Gerber, "Production de cives," 187. For further evidence, see Hirsch, *Der Hof des Basler Bischofs*, 256.

12. Serlio, *On Architecture*, 1:391.

13. Thornton, *Renaissance Interior*, 28.

14. Heberer, *Aegyptiaca Servitus*, 434–35.

15. Scheibelreiter, *Heraldik*, 33–40, 122–24.

16. Hildebrandt and Biewer, *Handbuch*, 20; Scheibelreiter, *Heraldik*, 33–35, 122.

17. Caviness, *Stained Glass Windows*, 70–71; Scheibelreiter, *Heraldik*, 33. On the phenomenon of heraldic windowpanes and the depiction of donors, see also Becksmann and Waetzold, *Vitrea dedicata*; Brisac, *Thousand Years*, 33–34.

18. Frodl-Kraft, *Glasmalerei*, 52.

19. Brisac, *Thousand Years*, 37, 84, 182–83; Rauch, "Anmerkungen," 104; *Grove Encyclopedia of Medieval Art and Architecture*, s.v. "stained glass," 647–48.

20. Garzoni, *Allgemeiner Schawplatz*, 620 (this addition is found in the German edition only).

21. Whitehouse, *Short History*, 39; McGrath and Frost, *Glass in Architecture*, 312; Adam-Veleni and Ignatiadou, *Glass Cosmos*, 33; Dell'Acqua, "*Illuminando colorat*," 147; Frodl-Kraft, *Glasmalerei*, 13.

22. Barovier Mentasti, "Enameled Glass," 253–55, 261; Barovier Mentasti, "Sacro e profane nel Medioevo," 34; McCray, *Glassmaking*, 58, 101; Baumgartner and Krueger, *Phönix aus Asche*, 126–28; Dorigato, *Murano*, 21–22. On the special case of enameled ceramics, see Frodl-Kraft, *Glasmalerei*, 13.

23. Caviness, *Stained Glass Windows*, 39–40, 54; Becksmann and Waetzold, *Vitrea dedicata*, 23; Brisac, "Thousand Years," 131; Lee, Seddon, and Stephens, *Stained Glass*, 100; *Grove Encyclopedia of Medieval Art and Architecture*, s.v. "stained glass," 646.

24. Brisac, *Thousand Years*, 180.

25. Lee, Seddon, and Stephens, *Stained Glass*, 48; Steppuhn, "Der (un-)getrübte Blick," 376; Van Treeck, "On the Artistic Technique," 57.

26. Brisac, *Thousand Years*, 131.

27. Vasari, *Technique*, 308 (editor's note).

28. Vasari, *Technique*, 267.

29. Van Treeck, "On the Artistic Technique," 57.

30. Lee, Seddon, and Stephens, *Stained Glass*, 56; *Grove Encyclopedia of Medieval Art and Architecture*, s.v. "stained glass," 646.

31. Vasari, *Technique*, 266.

32. Vasari, *On Technique*, 268. Seddon has argued, somewhat polemically, that enamel

painting led to the "decline of traditional stained glass" and thus "eventually destroyed the essential quality of coloured glass—its translucency." Lee, Seddon, and Stephens, *Stained Glass*, 100; see also 124.

33. Lagabrielle, "Fenêtres des rois," 114–15.

34. This figure is from the late fifteenth-century Low Countries: Caen and Berserik, "Silver-Stained Roundels," 121.

35. Frodl-Kraft, *Glasmalerei*, 58; Williamson, *Medieval and Renaissance Stained Glass*, 9–10; Witzleben, *Bemalte Glasscheiben*, 9, 12.

36. Vanden Bemden, "Les rondels," 22. For an overview with fine illustrations, see also Witzleben, *Bemalte Glasscheiben*.

37. Raguin, *Stained Glass*, 80; McGrath and Frost, *Glass in Architecture*, 101; Vanden Bemden, "Les rondels," 23.

38. Caen and Berserik, "Silver-Stained Roundels," 122.

39. "*Pincta de gente illustre che ucellano con dame a falconi, aghironi, a quaglioni.*" Thus said a contemporary chronicler, quoted in Thornton, *Renaissance Interior*, 28, 370.

40. Thornton, *Renaissance Interior*, 28.

41. Witzleben, *Bemalte Glasscheiben*, esp. 7, 55; Hess, "Auf der Suche," esp. 206; Kleinmanns, "Fensterglas," 168–69; Schürmann and Uekermann, *Das verkleidete Fenster*, 11.

42. Kemp, *Sermo Corporeus*, chap. 3; Meyer, *Schweizerische Sitte*, 23; Dell'Acqua, "*Illuminando colorat*," 133. A detailed case study is Schleif and Schier, *Katerina's Windows*.

43. Quoted in McGrath and Frost, *Glass in Architecture*, 38. See also Lee, Seddon, and Stephens, *Stained Glass*, 113.

44. Becksmann and Waetzold, *Vitrea dedicata*, 65.

45. Caviness, *Stained Glass Windows*, 59. Kemp does not rule it out that in the end an agreement was reached: Kemp, *Sermo Corporeus*, 221–27.

46. Lee, Seddon, and Stephens, *Stained Glass*, 91.

47. Caviness, *Stained Glass Windows*, 74. This was in line with the Church's vision. The Church rejected the idea that a donation implied ownership of the space or its windows: Becksmann and Waetzold, *Vitrea dedicata*, 84.

48. Becksmann and Waetzold, *Vitrea dedicata*, 65; Caviness, "Biblical Stories in Windows," 126.

49. Becksmann and Waetzold, *Vitrea dedicata*, 69.

50. Kemp, *Sermo Corporeus*, 210, 216.

51. Lardin, "Verre," 92; Becksmann and Waetzold, *Vitrea dedicata*, 84.

52. Donne, *Elegies*, 64–66.

53. Fleming, *Graffiti*, 10, 55. Such windowpanes are rarely on display in museums these days, but one of high quality, inscribed with the names of two young Nuremberg patricians, can be seen in the Germanisches Nationalmuseum in Nuremberg, Inv. Nr. MM259. (It was painted by Dürer's student Hans Süß von Kulmbach.)

54. Erasmus of Rotterdam, *On the Method of Study*, 671.

55. *Richard II*, 3.1.

56. Mohrmann, *Volksleben*, 215–16.

57. Klapisch-Zuber, *La maison*; Jütte, "Living Stones."

58. See, for instance, Carpzov, *Practica nova*, III.109 (99).

59. Schmid, *Kölner Renaissancekultur*, 36–39.

60. A partial German edition is available in Weinsberg, *Das Buch Weinsberg*. On Weinsberg and his family, see esp. Lundin, *Paper Memory*.

61. Weinsberg, *Buch Weinsberg*, 2:283–84.

62. Schmid, *Kölner Renaissancekultur*, 36–39, 113–15.

63. Giesicke and Ruoss, "In Honour of Friendship," 43.

64. In what follows I draw largely on the extraordinarily thorough (if unmistakably patriotic) study by Hermann Meyer, *Schweizerische Sitte*. I have also used Witzleben, *Bemalte Glasscheiben*, esp. 26–40; Rold and Bergmann, "Schaffhausen und Zug"; Giesicke and Ruoss, "In Honour of Friendship"; Hess, "Auf der Suche"; Würgler, *Tagsatzung*, 433–41; Groebner, *Gefährliche Geschenke*, 81–82.

65. Anshelm, *Berner-Chronik*, 2:340–41.

66. "*Gemalt Fenster und Glaßmaler im Schweitzerland.*" Fischart, *Aller Practick Groß-mutter*, n.p.

67. Lee, Seddon, and Stephens, *Stained Glass*, 48.

68. Groebner, *Gefährliche Geschenke*, 81. On the social prestige and political role of heraldic panes, see also Raguin, *Stained Glass*, 53.

69. For northern Germany, see Witzleben, *Bemalte Glasscheiben*, 55; Schürmann and Uekermann, *Das verkleidete Fenster*, 11.

70. "*Schönen eigentlich gemahlten Scheiben.*" Goethe, *Reise in die Schweiz* [1797], entry of October 7, 1797, *Werke* 4/2:739.

71. Garzoni, *Allgemeiner Schawplatz*, 621 (this addition is found in the German edition only).

72. Unless otherwise noted, the following paragraphs draw on Meyer, *Schweizerische Sitte*.

73. Quoted in Meyer, *Schweizerische Sitte*, 11.

74. Segesser, *Amtliche Abschiede*, 1064.

8
FROM SACRED MATERIAL TO SECULAR COMMODITY

1. Macfarlane and Martin go so as far as to claim that "windows with glass and the Renaissance seem deeply linked" (Macfarlane and Martin, *Glass*, 67); see also Friedberg, *Virtual Window*, 12; Wajcman, *Fenêtre*, esp. 95.

2. Dürer, *Schriftlicher Nachlass*, 319. On Dürer's familiarity with the Italian literature, see also the editor's foreword to *Painter's Manual*, 25–28.

3. Alberti, *On Painting*, 39.

4. On the history of this misprision, see Masheck, "Alberti's 'Window.'"

5. Wajcman, *Fenêtre*, 53.

6. Wajcman, *Fenêtre*, 24.

7. Koepnick, "Aesthetics," 18.

8. Elkins, *Poetics of Perspective*, esp. 46–52; Michalsky, "Raum visualisieren," 292.

9. Alberti, *Art of Building*, 146, where he recommends glass windows for the vestibule area of a private villa.

10. Alberti, *On Painting*, 34.

11. Masheck, "Alberti's 'Window,'" 36. See also Alberti, *On Painting*, I.12 (esp. 34).

12. Alberti, *On Painting*, 51.

13. Edgerton, *Mirror*, 127.

14. Da Vinci, *Treatise on Painting*, 1:34.

15. Dürer, *Painter's Manual*, 387. Translation slightly modified. See also Masheck, "Alberti's 'Window,'" 37.

16. Dürer, *Painter's Manual*, 389. Translation slightly modified.

17. Dürer, *Painter's Manual*, 435.

18. Elkins, *Poetics of Perspective*, 51–52.

19. Dürer, *Painter's Manual*, 389.

20. Da Vinci, *Treatise on Painting*, 1:34–35; see also 47, 65, 93–94.

21. Friedberg, *Virtual Window*, 12, 35.

22. Friedberg, *Virtual Window*, 12. See also Elkins, *Poetics of Perspective*, 51–52.

23. Jütte, "Window Gazes."

24. Alberti, *Art of Building*, 119–20. Translation slightly modified.

25. Alberti, *On Painting*, esp. bk. 2.

26. Whitehouse, *Short History*, 44; Whitehouse, "Glass in Medieval Europe," 33.

27. Quoted in Meyer, *Schweizerische Sitte*, 58.

28. Meyer, *Schweizerische Sitte*; Butts and Hendrix, *Painting on Light*; Maissen, "La persistance."

29. Quoted in Litz, *Reformatorische Bilderfrage*, 173.

30. Koerner, *Reformation of the Image*, 91; Caviness, *Stained Glass Windows*, 62. This also happened in Huguenot bastions in France: Davis, "Sacred," 58.

31. Quoted in Raguin, *Stained Glass*, 88.

32. Riviale, *Vitrail en Normandie*, 48.

33. Montaigne, *Travel Journal*, 1090–91.

34. Fuller, *Anglorum speculum*, 420. See also Dörk, "Der verwilderte Raum," 145; Caviness, *Stained Glass Windows*, 63.

35. Quoted in Breeze, "Blessed Virgin," 21.

36. Rosewell, *Stained Glass*, 55; Riviale, *Vitrail en Normandie*, 53, 55. For an instructive example of such a limited replacement, see Phillips, *Reformation of Images*, fig. 16. In Switzerland in the 1580s, Montaigne saw Reformed churches that still had stained-glass windows intact (Montaigne, *Travel Journal*, 1070). Depictions of city saints form a particularly interesting case: while the government of Zurich did not tolerate such images in churches, it allowed them on heraldic panes presented to foreign powers. Maissen, "La persistance," 63–66.

37. Quoted in Phillips, *Reformation of Images*, 95.

38. Caviness, *Stained Glass Windows*, 62.

39. Quoted in Lee, Seddon, and Stephens, *Stained Glass*, 142.

40. Dowsing, *Journal of William Dowsing*, 213.

41. Quoted in Lee, Seddon, and Stephens, *Stained Glass*, 142.

42. Schöne, *Über das Licht*, 39, 48. On blank glass in the Renaissance, see also Gage, "Gothic Glass," 37.

43. Pius II, *Commentaries*, 4:602.

44. Luchs, "Stained Glass"; Blum, *Fenestra prospectiva*, 94.

45. McGrath and Frost, *Glass in Architecture*, 103.

46. Quoted in Dendy, *Use of Lights*, 151.

47. Dendy, *Use of Lights*, 62, 152–53.

48. Quoted in Dendy, *Use of Lights*, 153.

49. Quoted in Dendy, *Use of Lights*, 153.

50. Dendy, *Use of Lights*, chap. 10.

51. Duffy, *Stripping of the Altars*, 451.

52. As Barnwell points out, the decrease of candle smoke and the abolition of incense might also explain why unglazed window slits, which originally served the purpose of ventilation, often were bricked up after the Reformation. Barnwell, "Low Side Windows," 68.

53. Lee, Seddon, and Stephens, *Stained Glass*, 142.

54. Lee, Seddon, and Stephens, *Stained Glass*, 135; Crowley, *Invention of Comfort*, 63.

55. Lee, Seddon, and Stephens, *Stained Glass*, 48; Caen and Berserik, "Silver-Stained Roundels," 122. Where Dutch churches commissioned stained glass in the seventeenth century, they sought historical—not theological—scenes. See van Ruyven-Zeman, "Seventeenth-Century Window Donations."

9
THE RISE OF CRISTALLO

1. Evangelische Kirche in Deutschland, "EKD bedauert 'Bildersturm' der Reformation," press release, July 13, 2015, https://www.ekd.de/pm124_2015_ekd_bedauert _bildersturm_der_reformation.htm.

2. Verità, "Venetian Innovations," 61–62; Trivellato, "Murano Glass," 150–51; McCray, *Glassmaking*, 36, 56, 101–2.

3. Ashtor and Cevidalli, "Levantine Alkali Ashes," esp. 479, 483.

4. A small number of glassmakers in medieval northern Europe did have access to Levantine alkali ashes: see Ashtor and Cevidalli, "Levantine Alkali Ashes," 483; Baumgartner and Krueger, *Phönix aus Sand*, 19, 59. Natron was easier to obtain in the Byzantine Empire and Islamic Levant: McCray, *Glassmaking*, 36. On the history of fluxing agents in the Middle Ages, see also Verità, "Influence," 277; Harden, "Medieval Glass in the West," 98; Dell'Acqua, "Nature and Artifice," 94.

5. Mathesius, *Sarepta*, 273.

6. Agricola, *Ausgewählte Werke*, 8:713.

7. Verità, "Venetian Innovations," 62; Henderson, *Ancient Glass*, 66; Rauch, "Anmerkungen" 105.

8. Ashtor and Cevidalli, "Levantine Alkali Ashes" esp. 482.

9. Ashtor and Cevidalli, "Levantine Alkalli Ashes"; Dungworth, "Innovations," 121; Brondi, *Storia del vetro*, 31; McCray, *Glassmaking*, 40–41, 54, 102. On the mutual influences between the Islamic world and Venice in the field of glassmaking, see also Barovier Mentasti, "Enameled Glass."

10. Verità, "Venetian Innovations," 63; Henderson, *Ancient Glass*, 101; Trivellato, "Murano Glass," 150–51; McCray, *Glassmaking*, esp. 101, 149.

11. Biringuccio, *Pirotechnia*, 131.

12. Corti, "L'industria del vetro"; McGrath and Frost, *Glass in Architecture*, 33; Godfrey, *Development*, 8.

13. The estimates given by Loibl are too high ("Zur Terminologie," 105). The cases

mentioned by Völckers (*Glas und Fenster*, 28–29) refer to the installation of Venetian panes (for instance, in Frankfurt's Weißfrauenkirche and Aschaffenburg Cathedral), but it is not clear whether this implied cristallo glass. It could also have been Venetian *vitrum blanchum*.

14. Pius II, *Commentaries*, 4:602. For Belfiore, see Thornton, *Renaissance Interior*, 28, 370.

15. Keil, *Augustanus Opticus*, 230–31.

16. Filarete, *Treatise on Architecture*, 1:116.

17. Thornton, *Renaissance Interior*, 28.

18. Biringuccio, *Pirotechnia*, 131.

19. Vasari, *Technique*, 267–68.

20. Verità, "Venetian Innovations," 63; Trivellato, "Murano Glass," 165; McCray, *Glassmaking*, 106.

21. "*Ne sono infinite case con . . . finestre tutte de veri. Et sono tanti li veri, che li maistri continuamente conza et mette in opera (i quali si fanno a Muran, come dirò di sotto), che per ogni contra' vi è una bottega de verieri.*" Sanuto, *Cronachetta*, 31. See also Barovier Mentasti, "Sacro e profane nel Medioevo," 31.

22. Quoted in Dorigato, *Murano*, 20. Translation modified after consultation of the original source text.

23. McGrath and Frost, *Glass in Architecture*, 33; Ng, "Cultural Ecology," 501.

24. Vasari, *Technique*, 268. The particular know-how of northern European glassmakers with regard to the production of ordinary glass panes might also explain why, in 1493, the Venetian government authorized a certain glassmaker by the name of "Master Robert of Lorraine" to spend six months on Murano, where he helped to produce window panes (*plastras vitreas pro finestris*). See Hills, *Venetian Colour*, 130.

25. Harrison, *Description*, 199.

26. McGrath and Frost, *Glass in Architecture*, 33.

27. For a nuanced discussion of glassmaking as a state secret in Venice, see McCray, *Glassmaking*, 48.

28. Mathesius, *Sarepta*, 273. See also Agricola, *Ausgewählte Werke*, 8:713.

29. Whitehouse, *Short History*, 71; Veeckman, *Majolica and Glass*.

30. Veeckman and Dumortier, "La production de verres," esp. 73; Dupré, "Value of Glass."

31. Scoville, *Capitalism*, esp. 22.

32. McGrath and Frost, *Glass in Architecture*, 39; Völckers, *Glas und Fenster*, 32–33.

33. For a systematic study of the English transition from wood to coal, see Godfrey, *Development*, chap. 3 and 6, esp. 149. See also Crowley, *Invention of Comfort*, 65; Whitehouse, *Short History*, 47, 78; Crossley, "Outline," 194; Dungworth, "Innovations," 119.

34. Carson, "Eighteenth Century," 117.

35. *Oxford English Dictionary*, s.v. "transparency."

36. Verità, "Venetian Innovations," 65–66; Trivellato, "Murano Glass," 15253; Loibl, "Zur Terminologie," 105; Barrelet, *La verrerie*, 56; McCray, *Glassmaking*, 149; Schwarzenberg, "Color," 30.

37. Dorigato, *Murano*, 138.

38. McGrath and Frost, *Glass in Architecture*, 312.

1. McGrath and Frost, *Glass in Architecture*, 104.

2. Crowley, *Invention of Comfort*, 63; Godfrey, *Development*, 205.

3. McGrath and Frost, *Glass in Architecture*, 105. See also Wigginton, *Glass in Architecture*, 15.

4. McGrath and Frost, *Glass in Architecture*, 105.

5. Grabes, *Mutable Glass*, 4; McGrath and Frost, *Glass in Architecture*, 313.

6. The new translation is from the Global English Study Bible; the older rendering is from the King James Version. On Paul's verse in its historical and linguistic context, see Lindemann, *Der Erste Korintherbrief*, 291–92. See also Crowley, *Invention of Comfort*, 122–24. I am indebted to the late Professor Otto Kaiser for sharing his expertise on this biblical passage.

7. Barovier Mentasti, "Il riflesso della vanità," 82–84; Godfrey, *Development*, 235; McGrath and Frost, *Glass in Architecture*, 313; Grabes, *Mutable Glass*, 4, 72–73; Dorigato, *Murano*, 124, 168–69.

8. Scoville, *Capitalism*, 114; Godfrey, *Development*, 236; Thornton, *Renaissance Interior*, 234–39.

9. Grabes, *Mutable Glass*, 4.

10. Godfrey, *Development*, 236.

11. Barovier Mentasti, "La façon de Venise," 176; Currie, *Inside the Renaissance House*, 76.

12. North, *Of Building*, 53.

13. Crowley, *Invention of Comfort*, 65; McGrath and Frost, *Glass in Architecture*, 35.

14. Pris, *Une grande entreprise*, esp. 1:4–7, 228; Scoville, *Capitalism*, 27, 144; Shovlin, *Political Economy of Virtue*, 34–35.

15. Pris, *Une grande entreprise*, 1:288, 311; McGrath and Frost, *Glass in Architecture*, 35; Dorigato, *Murano*, 124.

16. Pris, *Une grande entreprise*, 2:385; Barovier Mentasti, "La façon de Venise," 176.

17. Feuerstein, *Open Space*, 69; Scoville, *Capitalism*, esp. chap. 4.

18. Dillon, *Artificial Sunshine*, 64.

19. *"Est-ce que j'ai pas fait merveilles? du blé ou ce beau miroir!"* Saint-Simon, *Mémoires*, 2:37.

20. Kohlmaier and Sartory, *Houses of Glass*, 14. On the popularity of mirrors in seventeenth- and eighteenth-century upper-class architecture, see also Feuerstein, *Open Space*, 68–69; Crowley, *Invention of Comfort*, 120–21; 125; Shovlin, *Political Economy of Virtue*, 34–35.

21. See esp. Kantorowicz, "Oriens Augusti," 175.

22. Sedlmayr, *Das Licht*, 30. See also Kantorowicz, "Oriens Augusti," 171–74; Lietz, *Fenster des Barock*, 22.

23. Roche, *History*, 122.

24. Pris, *Une grande entreprise*, 1:311.

25. Scoville, *Capitalism*, 40; McGrath and Frost, *Glass in Architecture*, 36.

26. Völckers, *Glas und Fenster*, 8. See also Scoville, *Capitalism*, 40; Rice and Dutton, *Structural Glass*, 11.

27. Barrelet, *Verrerie*, 81; Pris, *Une grande entreprise*, 1:278.

28. Scoville, *Capitalism*, 40–41; Geotti, "From the Magic," 247–48; Harden, "Domestic Window Glass," 43; Rice and Dutton, *Structural Glass*, 11.

29. Quoted in Barrelet, *Verrerie*, 82.

30. Barrelet, *Verrerie*, 82; Pris, *Une grande entreprise*, 1:14; Scoville, *Capitalism*, 40–41, 47; McGrath and Frost, *Glass in Architecture*, 36.

31. Scoville, *Capitalism*, 109; Falke, *Kunst im Hause*, 276; Schürmann and Uekermann, *Das verkleidete Fenster*, 14; Lietz, *Fenster des Barock*, 50; Gerlach, "Anfänge," 98–99.

32. Völckers, *Glas und Fenster*, 34; Kohlmaier and Sartory, *Houses of Glass*, 46; Pris, *Une grande entreprise* 1:278, 312.

33. Völckers, *Glas und Fenster*, 34. See also Schnapp, "Fragments," 176.

34. Pris, *Une grande entreprise*, 1:294–95; Scoville cites even higher figures (Scoville, *Capitalism*, 40–41).

35. Scoville, *Capitalism*, 40–41, 115, 121.

36. Scoville, *Capitalism*, 95.

37. McGrath and Frost, *Glass in Architecture*, 43; Louw, "Window-Glass Making," 53.

38. Gilboy, *Wages*, 220; see also 116.

39. Louw, "Window-Glass Making," 52–55; Ely, *Crystal Palaces*, 124; Carson, "Eighteenth Century," 131; Dodsworth, "Nineteenth Century," 191.

40. McGrath and Frost, *Glass in Architecture*, 36, 42–43; Louw, "Window-Glass Making," 50; Pris, *Une grande entreprise*, 2:448–49.

41. Scoville, *Capitalism*, 114, 120, 127.

42. Scoville, *Capitalism*, 114; McGrath and Frost, *Glass in Architecture*, 35.

43. Roche, *History*, 122; Lietz, *Fenster des Barock*, esp. 8; Pris, *Une grande entreprise*, 1:312, 2:438. On the prestige associated with oversized mirrors, see Shovlin, *Political Economy of Virtue*, 34–35.

44. McGrath and Frost, *Glass in Architecture*, 311; Lagabrielle, "Avant-propos," v; Muthesius, *Poetic Home*, 185; Morley-Fletcher, "Seventeenth-Century Glass," 115; Lee, Seddon, and Stephens, *Stained Glass*, 142; Witzleben, *Bemalte Glasscheiben*, 39.

45. Quoted in Becksmann, "Die verschollene Denkschrift," 206.

46. Quoted in Becksmann, "Die verschollene Denkschrift," 206. On the declining demand for colored window glass in England, see Godfrey, *Development*, 209.

47. Scoville, *Capitalism*, 109.

48. Lim et. al., *Environmental Factors*, 14; McGrath and Frost, *Glass in Architecture*, 314.

49. Kantorowicz, "Oriens Augusti," 174. See also Jay, *Downcast Eyes*, 87–89.

50. Pris, *Une grande entreprise*, 1:6.

51. Saint-Simon, *Mémoires*, 4:302–4.

52. Scoville, *Capitalism*, 101, 116. On workers' wages, see Roche, *People of Paris*, 87.

53. Louw, "Window-Glass Making," 47. Elsewhere Louw has described the transition to timber as a "revolution in window design" (Louw, "Window on the Past," 46).

54. Badstübner, *Funktion des Fensters*, xiii; Feuerstein, *Open Space*, 75.

55. Quoted in Louw, "'Advantage of a Clearer Light,'" 300.

56. Wigginton, *Glass in Architecture*, 28.

57. Since this passage is not included in the English edition (Çelebi, *Ottoman Traveller*), I am quoting from the German edition: Çelebi, *Im Reiche des Goldenen Apfels*, 210. See also his

description of the same building: "The entire palace receives light from thousands of window which have been adorned, through artful work, with a myriad of beautiful small panes that shine brightly and scintillate" (188).

58. Duller, *Donauländer*, 87. See also Feldern Rolf, *Vaterländisches Lesebuch*, 60.

59. Lietz, *Fenster des Barock*.

60. *Oxford English Dictionary*, s.v. "transparency." According to Schwarzenberg, the salutation *"Ihre Durchlaucht"* implies that "true nobility . . . has nothing to conceal"—a belief that might originate in early Christian ideas about true believers as being "illuminated" (*erleuchtet*, hence also the German *"erlaucht"*). Schwarzenberg, "Color," 29. See also the amusing episode recounted by Gurlitt about a German duke and his penchant for large glass windows: Gurlitt, *Im Bürgerhause*, 165.

61. Goethe, *Poetry and Truth*, 18.

62. Wolff, *Anfangs-Gründe der Baukunst*, 436.

63. Alberti, *Art of Building*, 28.

64. Blumenberg, "Licht als Metaper," 446.

65. Blumenberg, "Licht als Metaper," 446.

66. Louw "'Advantage of a Clearer Light,'" 301. On changing notions of light in the seventeenth century, see also the studies in Bohlmann, Fink, and Weiss, *Lichtgefüge*; on experiments with light as an indicator for timekeeping, Heilbron, *Sun in the Church*.

67. Foucault, "Eye of Power," 153.

68. Blumenberg, "Licht als Metaper," 445. See also Flanders, *Making of Home*, 87; Louw, "'Advantage of a Clearer Light,'" 301; Jay, *Downcast Eyes*, chap. 2.

69. Roche, *History*, 119. See also McMahon, "Illuminating the Enlightenment."

70. Roche, *History*, 121.

71. Schivelbusch, *Disenchanted Night*, 3; Rosseaux, "Sicherheit durch Licht," esp. 810–11; Sarti, *Europe at Home*, 117–18; Kenny, "City Glow."

72. Rosseaux, "Sicherheit durch Licht," 811; Kenny, "City Glow."

73. Schivelbusch, *Disenchanted Night*, 3.

74. Barovier Mentasti, "La tavola di Veronese"; Virdis Limentani, "La fragile apparenza."

75. Worlidge, *Systema horti-culturae*, 35.

76. Sennett, *Conscience of the Eye*, 77–78.

77. Starobinski, *Rousseau*, 13, 254. See also more generally, Sennett, *Conscience of the Eye*, esp. 77; Hood, "Transparency," 5–8; Jay, *Downcast Eyes*, 90–94.

78. Rousseau, *Confessions*, in *Collected Writings*, 5:372.

79. Rousseau, *Confessions*, in *Collected Writings*, 5:375. The trope of the "heart of crystal" also exists in Italian Renaissance literature, but there is no indication that Rousseau was familiar with this tradition. On the Renaissance trope, see Bolzoni, *Il cuore di cristallo*, 120–26.

80. Rousseau, *Institutions chimiques*, 340–46. See also Starobinski, *Rousseau*, 255–56. Rzepka, *Ordnung der Transparenz*, chap. 2, de-emphasizes Starobinski's political reading of Rousseau's discussion of transparency.

81. Rousseau, *Institutions chimiques*, 341.

82. *"Presque tous les usages du verre en général dans la pratique chimique, dans la société et dans le arts, sont fondés sur sa transparence."* Rousseau, *Institutions chimiques*, 346.

83. Rousseau, *Julie, or the New Heloise*, in *Collected Writings*, 6:349. As the editors

point out (6:693), the reference is to Plutarch's *Praecepta gerendae reipublicae*, chap. 4. It should be noted that Plutarch refers to the virtues a public leader should have; Rousseau goes a step further by making openness and transparency a generally desirably virtue for everyone. Interestingly, Rousseau considered windows important enough to elaborate on the need for protecting them. In his pedagogical treatise *Emile, or On Education*, Rousseau advised parents and educators that a window-smashing child should be "[closed] up in darkness in a place without windows." Rousseau, *Emile, or On Education*, in *Collected Writings*, 13:234.

84. Kant, "What is Enlightenment?," in *Basic Writings*, 136–37.

85. Rzepka, *Ordnung der Transparenz*, 47–62, 126.

86. Hood, "Transparency," 6.

87. Hunt, *Politics, Culture, and Class*, 44.

88. Mavidal and Laurent, eds., *Archives parlementaires*, 8:55. My thanks to Katlyn Carter for this reference.

89. Fierro, *Glass State*, 38.

90. Quoted in Etlin, *Symbolic Space*, 28; Etlin, *Architecture of Death*, 255.

91. Etlin, *Architecture of Death*, 255.

92. Etlin, *Symbolic Space*, 28 (first quotation, by Giraud); Etlin, *Architecture of Death*, 255 (second quotation, by a certain contemporary chemist named Dufourni).

93. Etlin, *Symbolic Space*, 28.

94. Bletter, "Interpretation," 312–13.

95. Ginzberg, *Legends*, 1:19.

96. Quoted in Bletter, "Interpretation," 313.

97. Flood, "Palaces of Crystal," 205. On the association of Paradise with crystal and glass in Islam, see Flood, "Palaces of Crystal," section 2, esp. 196, 199.

98. Schwarzenberg, "Cristallo," 68–69.

99. See also Rev. 15:2; Ezek. 1:22.

100. Milton, *Paradise Lost*, VII, 263–65.

101. The term was first used in the 1740s to refer to "an optical instrument or device," specifically "a mechanical peep-show offering views of European capitals, etc., for public entertainment." *Oxford English Dictionary*, s.v. "panopticon."

102. Bentham, *Works*, 4:40.

103. Bentham, *Works*, 4:39.

104. Bentham, *Works*, 4:79–80, 83; 11:96.

105. Foucault, *Discipline and Punish*, 200. On the use of the transparency metaphor in Bentham, see also Rzepka, *Ordnung der Transparenz*, chap. 3, esp. 74–75; Hood, "Transparency," 8–10.

106. Foucault, *Discipline and Punish*, 200.

107. Bentham, *Works*, 4:43.

108. Bentham, *Works*, 4:95.

109. Bentham, *Works*, 10:402.

110. Bentham, *Works*, 11:100.

111. Bentham, *Works*, 11:99.

112. Harou-Romain, *Projet de pénitencier*, 7 (emphasis in the original).

113. Harou-Romain, *Projet de pénitencier*, 8.

114. Foucault, *Discipline and Punish*, esp. chap. 3; Markus, *Buildings and Power*, esp. 123.

115. Foucault, *Discipline and Punish*, 172, 209 ("disciplinary society").

116. Barnstone, *Transparent State*, 33–34; Rzepka, *Ordnung der Transparenz*, 75–76.

117. Foucault, "Eye of Power," 147.

118. Quoted in Foucault, *Discipline and Punish*, 173.

119. Bentham, *Works*, 4:62–63.

120. Gaonkar and McCarthy, "Panopticism," 557; Foucault, *Discipline and Punish*, 249.

121. Bentham, *Works*, 9:203 (emphasis in the original). See also Rzepka, *Ordnung der Transparenz*, 101, 107.

122. Lefebvre, *Production of Space*, 28.

123. Lefebvre, *Production of Space*, 30.

124. Foucault, "Eye of Power," 154. Vidler has argued that Enlightenment thought was not simply about the eradication of darkness and that historians must also explore the "extent to which the pairing of transparency and obscurity is essential for power to operate" (Vidler, *Architectural Uncanny*, 172).

125. Quoted in Collomp, "Families," 502. The quote is by a French Catholic clergyman.

126. Willem Goeree, 1681, quoted in Louw, "'Advantage of a Clearer Light,'" 301.

127. Miège, *New State of England*, 31. The passage is quoted approvingly (and almost verbatim) in Neve's *Dictionary*, s.v. "building" (n.p.).

128. North, *Of Building*, 25.

129. Quoted in Woronoff, "Quand l'exception," 135.

130. Vidler, *Architectural Uncanny*, 169.

131. Sewall, *Diary*, 2:714.

132. Quoted in Vidler, *Architectural Uncanny*, 169.

133. A detailed study of this process is Lours, "L'éclaircissement." See also Roche, *History*, 117–18; Schwarz, *Sachgüter*, 76; Schöne, *Über das Licht*, 36, 39.

134. Krünitz, *Encyklopädie*, s.v. "Fenster," 561.

135. Unger, "Glasmalerei," 67; Lours, "L'éclaircissement," 144, 176, 181; Scoville, *Capitalism*, 108.

136. Schöne, *Über das Licht*, 39.

137. Caviness, *Stained Glass Windows*, 63; Brisac, *Thousand Years*, 131.

138. Quoted in Lours, "L'éclaircissement," 145.

139. Quoted in Lours, "L'éclaircissement," 142.

140. Quoted in Lours, "L'éclaircissement," 142.

141. Borromeo, *Instructiones*, bk. 1, 25.

142. Quoted in Mayer-Himmelheber, "Kunstpolitik," 106–7.

143. Mayer-Himmelheber, "Kunstpolitik," 174–75.

144. Le Vieil, *L'art de la peinture*, 135.

145. Le Vieil, *L'art de la peinture*, 81; Lours, "L'éclaircissement," 93, 149, 167; Schreiber, *Geschichte*, 180.

146. Ordinance reprinted in Richardson and James, *Urban Experience*, 176–77.

147. Suger, *Ausgewählte Schriften*, 362.

148. Lardin, "Verre," 93.

149. Garzoni, *Allgemeiner Schawplatz*, 621 (addition by the German editor).

150. Quoted in Scoville, *Capitalism*, 108. On the decline, see also Le Vieil, *L'art de la peinture*, esp. 62–64; Lours, "L'éclaircissement," 146; Bezut, "Workshop at Sèvres," 97; Witzleben, *Bemalte Glasscheiben*, 39.

151. Le Vieil, *L'art de la peinture*, 81.

152. Lours, "L'éclaircissement," 143–44, 176, 181; Brisac, *Thousand Years*, 142; Morley-Fletcher, "Seventeenth-Century Glass," 115. The same tendency can be observed in Germany: see Unger, "Glasmalerei," 68.

153. Lours, "L'éclaircissement," 147; Brisac, *Thousand Years*, 142; Bezut, "Workshop at Sèvres," 97.

154. Lours, "L'éclaircissement."

155. Quoted in Lours, "L'éclaircissement," 177.

156. Lours, "L'éclaircissement," 169. For similar cases from Reims und Saint-Remi, see Caviness, *Stained Glass Windows*, 64.

157. Eimer, "Einführung," 12. See also Jantzen, *Kunst der Gotik*, 68.

158. Schöne, *Über das Licht*, 36.

159. Lours, "L'éclaircissement," 173, 179.

160. Quoted in Louw, "'Advantage of a Clearer Light,'" 301.

161. Caviness, *Stained Glass Windows*, 64.

162. Quoted in Schreiber, *Geschichte*, 180. Unfortunately, Schneider does not reveal the source of this quotation.

163. Büsching, *Reise*, 70–71. See also Wochnik, "Zur Wechselwirkung," 305; Unger, "Glasmalerei," 68.

164. Lours, "L'éclaircissement," 189; Bezut, "Workshop at Sèvres," 97–98.

165. Caviness, *Stained Glass Windows*, 64.

166. Brisac, *Thousand Years*, 133.

167. Bacher, "Mittelalterliche Glasmalerei," 107.

168. Lours, "L'éclaircissement," 139; Roche, *History*, 117; Caviness, *Stained Glass Windows*, 65; Brisac, *Thousand Years*, chap. 7 and esp. 142. On the nationalist claims regarding medieval stained glass, see also Schumacher, "Zur Rezeption."

11
TOO MUCH GLASS

1. Smith, *Houses of the Welsh Countryside*, 266.

2. Wigginton, *Glass in Architecture*, 6.

3. Herbig, *Das Fenster in der Architektur*, 7.

4. Lagabrielle, "Fenêtres des rois," 113 (emphasis mine).

5. Mandrou, *Introduction*, 55. In a similar (essentialist) vein, Macfarlane and Martin have argued that "windows, mirrors and optical glass" changed "the knowledge base of Europe" (Macfarlane and Martin, *Glass*, 20).

6. Scoville, *Capitalism*, 108.

7. Friedberg, *Virtual Window*, chap. 3 and esp. 103.

8. Armstrong, *Victorian Glassworks*, 133.

9. Lours, "L'éclaircissement," 145.

10. Le Vieil, *L'art de la peinture*. See also *Grove Encyclopedia of Medieval Art and Architecture*, s.v. "stained glass," 655; Bezut, "Workshop at Sèvres," 97.

11. Le Vieil, *L'art de la peinture*, iv.

12. Le Vieil, *L'art de la peinture*, 202.

13. Le Vieil, *L'art de la peinture*, 36.

14. Mercier, *Tableau de Paris*, 149–50.

15. Anon., *Untersuchungen*, 81.

16. Anon., *Untersuchungen*, 18; see also 40.

17. Anon., *Untersuchungen*, 84.

18. Burke, *Philosophical Enquiry*, 122.

19. Burke, *Philosophical Enquiry*, 173–74.

20. Burke, *Philosophical Enquiry*, 102–3.

21. Burke, *Philosophical Enquiry*, 121.

22. Burke, *Philosophical Enquiry*, 122.

23. Heil, *Fenster*, esp. 482; Jütte, "Living Stones," esp. 662–65; Lietz, *Fenster des Barock*, 14–15.

24. North, *Of Building*, 57.

25. North, *Of Building*, 53.

26. North, *Of Building*, 54.

27. North, *Of Building*, 54.

28. Godfrey, *Development*, 206.

29. Bacon, *Essays*, 484.

30. Wotton, *Elements of Architecture*, 56.

31. Ng, "Cultural Ecology," 518–21.

32. "A Proclamation Touching Glasses," royal proclamation of May 23, 1615. Printed in Hartshorne, *Old English Glasses*, 413–14 (quotes at 413).

33. Glantz, "Tax on Light and Air," 19; Ward, "Administration," esp. 524.

34. Dodsworth, "Nineteenth Century," 191; McGrath and Frost, *Glass in Architecture*, 44.

35. Ward, "Administration"; Ely, *Crystal Palaces*, 124; Glantz, "Tax on Light and Air," 19.

36. In Sweden, a window tax was in effect for a few decades (1744–1810). The French tax on windows (and doors) lasted longer, but it was introduced much later (1798–1926). Under Napoleon, the French window tax also applied for a few years to German and Dutch territories under French rule. Schürmann and Uekermann, *Das verkleidete Fenster*, 11; Cieraad, "Dutch Windows," 36. Like its counterpart in England, the French window and door tax met with strong criticism among the population: see, for example, Corrard's sarcastic treatise on this subject: *L'impôt des portes et fenêtres*.

37. Fielding, *Tom Jones*, 260.

38. On the window tax in general, see Ward, "Administration"; Dowell, *History of Taxation*, 3:193–203. For living conditions, see esp. Glantz, "Tax on Light and Air," 14. According to modern economists, "The window tax is a textbook example of how a tax can have serious adverse side effects on social welfare" (Oates and Schwab, "Window Tax," 164).

39. Jean-Marc Daniel, "Quand l'Etat taxait le soleil." *Le Monde*, March 14, 2014. My thanks to Thomas Maissen for bringing this article to my attention.

40. Wotton, *Elements of Architecture*, 55.

41. McClung, *Country House*, 83–84.

42. O'Connor, *Art of Dying Well*, 118.

43. Biringuccio, *Pirotechnia*, 132. For the widespread critique of glass mirrors as vain, brittle, and transient, see Grabes, *Mutable Glass*, 105–6.

44. Gryphius, *Auserlesene Gedichte*, 33.

45. Meisner and Kieser, *Thesaurus philopoliticus*, s.v. "Erfurt"; "Berncastel." For the Latin original, see Publilius Syrus's *Sententiae*, 43 (English translation from the Loeb edition).

46. Farny et al., *Handwörterbuch*, 233; Borscheid and Drees, *Versicherungsstatistik Deutschlands*, 28–29.

47. Scoville, *Capitalism*, 40. On the effects of industrialization, see also Louw, "Window-Glass Making," 53–57.

48. Scoville, *Capitalism*, 97–98, 115, 161. On transportation-related problems and the importance of rivers for the preindustrial transportation of glass in England, see Godfrey, *Development*, 51, 182–83. On similarly high breakage rates in England, see Berg, *Luxury and Pleasure*, 123.

49. McGrath and Frost, *Glass in Architecture*, 44; Louw, "Window-Glass Making," 64; Dodsworth, "Nineteenth Century," 191; Armstrong, *Victorian Glassworks*, 43.

50. Quoted in Louw, "Window-Glass Making," 47.

51. Beckmann, *History of Inventions*, 2:82 (addition to the English edition). See also Louw, "Window-Glass Making," 64; Glantz, "Tax on Light and Air," 18.

52. Quoted in Louw, "Development of the Window," 19.

53. Louw, "Window-Glass Making," 64.

54. Orrinsmith, *Drawing-Room*, 64–65.

55. Orrinsmith, *Drawing-Room*, 64.

56. Wilde, "House Beautiful," 918.

57. Muthesius, *Poetic Home*, 193.

58. Gurlitt, *Im Bürgerhause*, 164.

59. On Britain, see Armstrong, *Victorian Glassworks*, 369. In the French case, this was explicitly decreed in an amendment of March 25, 1803: "*Les propriétaires des manufactures ne seront taxés que pour les fenêtres de leurs habitations personelles.*" Kuhlmann, *De l'impôt des portes et fenêtres*, esp. 4.

60. Chambers, *Treatise*, 2:354.

61. Anon., *Untersuchungen*, 78.

62. Anon., *Untersuchungen*, 78.

63. Krünitz, s.v. "Fenster," 563–64.

64. Muthesius, *Poetic Home*, 184; Friedberg, *Virtual Window*, 111–12; Feuerstein, *Open Space*, 188; Kohlmaier and Sartory, *Houses of Glass*, 21.

65. North, *Of Building*, 53.

66. *Supplément à l'Encyclopédie*, s.v. "fenêtre." (The author's initials—V.A.L.—likely refer to Paul-Joseph Vallet, a police officer and author of several technology-related works.)

67. *Supplément à l'Encyclopédie*, s.v. "fenêtre": "*Les Chinois aiment le grand jour: peut-être que l'usage des grandes fenêtres & le papier blanc, dont on décore les appartements, ont contribué à procurer à ces peuples des yeux à demi-fermés.*" This claim was particularly absurd given

that contemporary European travelers to China often complained that the windows admitted too little light: see, for example, Osbeck, *Reise*, 175.

68. Malter, *Kant in Rede und Gespräch*, esp. 478, 499; Völckers, *Glas und Fenster*, 68.

69. Falke, *Kunst im Hause*, 277; see also 281.

70. Quoted in Isenstadt, "Four Views," 219.

71. Danforth, "Window Glass," 541–42.

72. As reported by Scheerbart, "Die Glasarchitektur," 143.

73. Le Vieil, *L'art de la peinture*, 235; Belhoste and Leproux, "La fenêtre parisienne," 43; Woronoff, "Quand l'exception," 135. See also Orrinsmith, *Drawing-Room*, chap. 5.

74. Lucae, "Macht des Raumes," 296.

75. Lucae, "Macht des Raumes," 296.

76. Falke, *Kunst im Hause*, 281.

77. Scott, *Houses and Gardens*, 66.

78. Jütte, "Window Gazes," 621–22; Shaw, "Construction," 454–55.

79. Gurlitt, *Im Bürgerhause*, 166.

80. Scott, *Houses and Gardens*, 66.

81. Orrinsmith, *Drawing-Room*, 65.

82. Muthesius, *Poetic Home*, esp. 184; Dodsworth, "Nineteenth-Century," 189–90; Giesiecke and Ruoss, "In Honour of Friendship," 44.

83. Falke, *Kunst im Hause*, 283–84. See also Muthesius, *Poetic Home*, 184.

84. Falke, *Kunst im Hause*, vi.

85. Falke, *Kunst im Hause*, 283. See also McGrath and Frost, *Glass in Architecture*, 158. On further nineteenth-century glass techniques meant to prevent intrusive gazes, see Völckers, *Glas und Fenster*, 36.

86. Gurlitt, *Im Bürgerhause*, 167–68.

87. Jean Paul, *Dr. Katzenbergers Badereise*, 171.

88. Baudelaire, *Paris Spleen*, 77.

89. Gerner and Gärtner, *Historische Fenster*, 69.

90. Orrinsmith, *Drawing-Room*, 66.

91. Girouard, *Hardwick Hall*, 36. On the rarity of curtains in Renaissance Italy, see Thornton, *Renaissance Interior*, 29.

92. Thornton, *Renaissance Interior*, 29.

93. See the decrees reprinted in Bistort, *Magistrato alle pompe*, 396, 400 (quote). On Italy, see also Thornton, *Renaissance Interior*, 29. On curtains as objects of conspicuous consumption in France, see Flanders, *Making of Home*, 129.

94. Schürmann and Uekermann, *Das verkleidete Fenster*, esp. 24, 35; Friedberg, *Virtual Window*, 111–12; Ekirch, *At Day's Close*, 150; Schwarz, *Sachgüter*, 38; Flanders, *Making of Home*, 86–87; Muthesius, *Poetic Home*, 194–99.

95. Flanders, *Making of Home*, 86.

96. Gurlitt, *Im Bürgerhause*, 162.

97. Markus, "Function of Windows," 115.

98. Orrensmith, *Drawing-Room*, 67.

99. Falke, *Kunst im Hause*, 292.

100. Schürmann and Uekermann, *Das verkleidete Fenster*, 27; Kohlmaier and Sartory, *Houses of Glass*, 22; Flanders, *Making of Home*, 87, 129–30.

101. Gurlitt, *Im Bürgerhause*, 167.

102. Most recently, see Flanders, *Making of Home*, esp. 85. See also (with some qualifications) Kiem, "Fenster," 92–93. For popular conceptions of this "tradition," see the responses collected in the survey by Vera, "On Dutch Windows," esp. 220.

103. Schürmann and Uekermann, *Das verkleidete Fenster*, 26–27. On the popularity of curtains in the eighteenth-century Netherlands, see also Wijsenbeek-Olthuis, "Social History of the Curtain."

104. Armstrong, *Victorian Glassworks*, 133.

105. Sternberger, *Panorama*, 144.

106. Thus the heading of Sternberger's discussion in *Panorama*, 144–46. See also Isenstadt, "Four Views," 220.

107. Schürmann and Uekermann, *Das verkleidete Fenster*, 59.

1 2
PALACES OF GLASS

1. Armstrong, *Victorian Glass Worlds*, 1. See also Kohlmaier and Sartory, *Houses of Glass*, 22; Hix, *Glasshouse*, 175, 192.

2. Kohlmaier and Sartory, *Houses of Glass*, 1, 18.

3. Kohlmaier and Sartory, *Houses of Glass*, 1.

4. Columella, *On Agriculture*, 161.

5. Martial, *Epigrams*, 8.14.

6. Martial *Epigrams*, 8.68. The translation has "enclosed in transparent glass" (*perspicua . . . gemma*), which I have slightly modified. "Gemma" means "precious stone," so it is debatable whether the reference is to glass (but cf. Whitehouse, *Glass in the Epigrams of Martial*, 80).

7. Martial, *Epigrams*, 8.14.

8. Sperl, "Glas und Licht," 69–70; McGrath and Frost, *Glass in Architecture*, 114.

9. Seneca, *Epistles*, 3:417 (letter 122).

10. McGrath and Frost, *Glass in Architecture*, 114; Hix, *Glasshouse*, esp. 14–17; Kohlmaier and Sartory, *Houses of Glass*, esp. 43.

11. Hix, *Glasshouse*, 16–17.

12. Kohlmaier and Sartory, *Houses of Glass*, esp. 52; McGrath and Frost, *Glass in Architecture*, 115, 124–25; Hix, *Glasshouse*, 16–20.

13. Kohlmaier and Sartory, *Houses of Glass*, 43–44; Feuerstein, *Open Space*, 77.

14. Feuerstein, *Open Space*, 75; Kohlmaier and Sartory, *Houses of Glass*, 4; Hix, *Glasshouse*, 16.

15. Kohlmaier and Sartory, *Houses of Glass*, 52; Hix, *Glasshouse*, 48–56.

16. Hix, *Glasshouse*, 28.

17. Kohlmaier and Sartory, *Houses of Glass*, 44; Hix, *Glasshouse*, 203.

18. Kohlmaier and Sartory, *Houses of Glass*, 45; Feuerstein, *Open Space*, 75.

19. Lim et al., *Environmental Factors*, 16; Kohlmaier and Sartory, *Houses of Glass*, 4.

20. Feuerstein, *Open Space*, 77; Kohlmaier and Sartory, *Houses of Glass*, 59.

21. *Revue générale d'architecture*, quoted in Benjamin, *Arcades Project*, 564.

22. Kohlmaier and Sartory, *Houses of Glass*, 16. On the link between horticultural buildings and nineteenth-century glass architecture, see also Feuerstein, *Open Space*, 74.

23. Ely, *Crystal Palaces*, ii, 2–3; Feuerstein, *Open Space*, 76.

24. Hix, *Glasshouse*, 129.

25. Figures from Beaver, *Crystal Palace*, appendix "Dimensions."

26. Thus the German writer August Reichensberger, quoted in Feuerstein, *Open Space*, 79.

27. Quoted in Benjamin, *Arcades Project*, 184.

28. Quoted in Ely, *Crystal Palaces*, 43.

29. Hix, *Glasshouse*, 175.

30. Kohlmaier and Sartory, *Houses of Glass*, 46; Giedion, *Space, Time, and Architecture*, 251.

31. Wigginton, *Glass in Architecture*, 41.

32. Hix, *Glasshouse*, 184. On Paxton's use of timber in other projects, see Hix, *Glasshouse*, 138.

33. McGrath and Frost, *Glass in Architecture*, 131.

34. Hix, *Glasshouse*, 163.

35. Quoted in Feuerstein, *Open Space*, 79.

36. Armstrong, *Victorian Glass Worlds*, chap. 7; Friedberg, *Virtual Window*, 111–12; Kohlmaier and Sartory, *Houses of Glass*, 4, 22; Hix, *Glasshouse*, 198.

37. Lim et. al., *Environmental Factors*, 18; Wigginton, *Glass in Architecture*, 41.

38. Quoted in McGrath and Frost, *Glass in Architecture*, 139.

39. Hix, *Glasshouse*, 192–93; McGrath and Frost, *Glass in Architecture*, 139.

40. Kohlmaier and Sartory, *Houses of Glass*, 18; McGrath and Frost, *Glass in Architecture*, 138–39.

41. Quoted in McGrath and Frost, *Glass in Architecture*, 134; Ely, *Crystal Palaces*, 123; Hix, *Glasshouse*, 194.

42. The best-known study of nineteenth-century arcades is, of course, Benjamin's *Passagen-Werk*. On Benjamin and his "Arcades Project," see, for example, Hanssen, "Benjamin and the Arcades Project." On the history of the arcade as a building type, see also Feuerstein, *Open Space*, 85–87; McGrath and Frost, *Glass in Architecture*, 145, 244; Giedion, *Space, Time, and Architecture*, 238–40; Hix, *Glasshouse*, 192–93.

43. McGrath and Frost, *Glass in Architecture*, 141.

44. Kluge, *Etymologisches Wörterbuch*, s.v. "Laden."

45. Schivelbusch, *Disenchanted Night*, 146; McGrath and Frost, *Glass in Architecture*, 141. On the history of the shop window, see also Osterwold, *Schaufenster*; Breuss, *Window Shopping*.

46. Lichtenberg, *Briefwechsel*, 1:488.

47. Quoted in Schivelbusch, *Disenchanted Night*, 144.

48. La Roche, *Tagebuch*, 204. Brought to my attention by Schivelbusch, *Disenchanted Night*, 148.

49. Quoted in Schivelbusch, *Disenchanted Night*, 146. See also Louw, "Window-Glass Making," 64.

50. Baudelaire, *Complete Poems*, 262.

51. Schindler, *Rundschau*, 167 (emphasis in the original).

52. Quoted in Ward, *Weimar Surfaces*, 200.

53. Ward, *Weimar Surfaces*, 200.

54. Ward, *Weimar Surfaces*, 227.

55. Quoted in Barnaby, *Light Touches*, 91.

56. Feuerstein, *Open Space*, 102; Ward, *Weimar Surfaces*, 200; Breuss, *Window Shopping*, 20.

57. Benjamin, *Arcades Project*, 150.

58. Giedion, *Space, Time, and Architecture*, 195. A similar perspective is in Schulze, *Glas in der Architektur*, 69; McGrath and Frost, *Glass in Architecture*, 160.

59. Wright, "Meaning of Materials," 197.

60. Louw, "Window-Glass Making," 64; Isenstadt, "Four Views," esp. 220–21.

61. Ward, *Weimar Surfaces*, 200.

62. Sitte, *Art of Building Cities*, 9.

63. Marx and Engels, "Revue: Mai bis Oktober 1850," in Marx and Engels, *Gesamtausgabe*, I/10:458.

64. Quoted in Beaver, *Crystal Palace*, 28.

65. Quoted in Beaver, *Crystal Palace*, 35.

66. Semper, *Style*, 47.

67. Quoted in Feuerstein, *Open Space*, 79.

68. Hix, *Glasshouse*, 198.

69. Lucae, "Macht des Raumes," 303.

70. Lucae, "Macht des Raumes," 296.

I 3
MODERNITY AND THE STRUGGLE
FOR GLASS ARCHITECTURE

1. "*Was kommt, steht im Zeichen der Transparenz.*" Benjamin, "Wiederkehr des Flaneurs," *Gesammelte Schriften*, 8:196–97; Le Corbusier, *City of To-morrow*, 178.

2. Völckers, *Glas und Fenster*, 31.

3. Rice and Dutton, *Structural Glass*, 12; Völckers, *Glas und Fenster*, 39–41; Wigginton, *Glass in Architecture*, 55, 271.

4. Rice and Dutton, *Structural Glass*, 12; Wigginton, *Glass in Architecture*, 55, 271.

5. McGrath and Frost, *Glass in Architecture*, 55; Lim et al., *Environmental Factors*, 27–33; Wigginton, *Glass in Architecture*, 55, 272.

6. Louw, "Window-Glass Making," 55, 57. Panes cut from the disks were also inevitably limited in size: Wigginton, *Glass in Architecture*, 41.

7. McGrath and Frost, *Glass in Architecture*, 49, 78; Völckers, *Glas und Fenster*, 39; Wigginton, *Glass in Architecture*, 55.

8. Wright, "Meaning of Materials," 197.

9. Wright, "Meaning of Materials," 197.

10. Arthur Korn, *Glass in Modern Architecture*, n.p. (introduction).

11. Lim et al., *Environmental Factors*, 36–37; Feuerstein, *Open Space*, 67; Kohlmaier

and Sartory, *Houses of Glass*, 2; McGrath and Frost, *Glass in Architecture*, 167; Wagner, *Marmor und Asphalt*, esp. 40–45.

12. Quoted in Curtis, *Modern Architecture*, 260.

13. Völckers, *Glas und Fenster*, 92; Isenstadt, "Four Views," 221.

14. Hix, *Glasshouse*, 198.

15. Scott, *Houses and Gardens*, 66. Certain other proponents of the Arts and Crafts movement were more open-minded; see Davey, "Window in Arts and Crafts."

16. Benjamin, "Erfahrung und Armut," in *Gesammelte Schriften*, 2:217 (English translation from *Selected Writings*, 2:734).

17. Kohlmaier and Sartory, *Houses of Glass*, 21.

18. Muthesius, *Poetic Home*, esp. chap. 4.

19. Baumhoff, "Das Bauhaus," 587; Eckstein, "Inszenierung einer Utopie," esp. 18. The literature on the Bauhaus is vast. For a good overview, see Fiedler and Feierabend, *Bauhaus*. A fine introduction to the personal politics of the institution is Weber, *Bauhaus Group*.

20. Schulze, *Glas in der Architektur*, 12 ("influences"); Giedion, *Space, Time, and Architecture*, 483 ("hint").

21. Giedion, *Space, Time, and Architecture*, 482; Ward, *Weimar Surfaces*, 65–66. On the Steiff factory in Giengen an der Brenz, designed in 1903 by an anonymous architect, as the first successful realization of curtain-walling and as a possible source of inspiration for Gropius, see Fischer, *Licht und Transparenz*, esp. 178–79.

22. Ward, *Weimar Surfaces*, 66.

23. Rehm, *Bauhausgebäude*, esp. 33–34; Giedion, *Space, Time, and Architecture*, 484–98, 515; Ward, *Weimar Surfaces*, 66; Whiteley, "Intensity of Scrutiny," 8; Thies, "Glasecken," esp. 113.

24. Feuerstein, *Open Space*, 112, 115; Haag, "Mies," 350.

25. Scheerbart, *Glass Architecture*, 41.

26. Scheerbart, *Glass Architecture*, 46.

27. Scheerbart, *Glass Architecture*, 14.

28. See above, Chapter 11.

29. Scheerbart, *Glass Architecture*, 14.

30. Bletter, "Interpretation," esp. 312; Nielsen, *Taut's Design Inspiration*, esp. 4–6.

31. To some extent this was Taut's response to critics who had argued that glass architecture paid too little attention to practical issues. Scheerbart, "Glashäuser," 697.

32. Scheerbart, *Glass Architecture*, 14. Scheerbart also provided support through publications: Scheerbart, "Glashäuser." On the history of Taut's Glashaus, see also Schnapp, "Fragments," 181; Kohlmaier and Sartory, *Houses of Glass*, esp. 20–21; Barnstone, *Transparent State*, 36–37; Bletter, "Interpretation," 324–25; Nielsen, *Taut's Design Inspiration*.

33. For a compilation of the key documents, see *Die gläserne Kette*.

34. Quoted in Bletter, "Interpretation," 328. On the entanglement of expressionist and sachlich visions, see also Bletter, "Mies," esp. 350; Curtis, *Modern Architecture*, 184.

35. Schulze, *Glas in der Architektur*, 20 (quote). See also Giedion, *Time, Space, and Architecture*, 480; Ward, *Weimar Surfaces*, 74–75; Lane, *Architektur und Politik*, 53.

36. Nielsen, *Taut's Design Inspiration*, chap. 2.

37. Schulze's 1929 book *Glas in der Architektur* is a case in point: the illustrations were

provided by the association, and the book's back matter featured advertisements paid for by German glass manufacturers. On industry support for Mies's architecture, see Zimmerman, *Mies van der Rohe*, 15.

38. Rehm, *Bauhausgebäude*, 34; Curtis, *Modern Architecture*, 196.

39. Quoted in Taylor and Bauchet, "Maison de Verre," 173.

40. Frampton, "Maison de Verre," 270; Frampton, "Pierre Chareau"; Taylor and Bauchet, "Maison de Verre"; Le Corbusier, "Glass," 284 (editor's introduction). Nevada glass blocks came on the market in 1928.

41. Rehm, *Bauhausgebäude*, 108–9; Cohen, *Le Corbusier*, 13, 24.

42. Le Corbusier, *Toward an Architecture*, 152.

43. On the struggle for larger windows, see Le Corbusier, *Oeuvre complète*, 5:77. See also his *Precisions*, 51–52. The quote is from *Toward an Architecture*, 172.

44. Cohen, *Le Corbusier*, 24.

45. Hornbein, "Humane and Environmental Architecture," 26–27.

46. Curtis, *Modern Architecture*, 39.

47. Eskilson, *Age of Glass*, 66–72, 77 (with reference to the figure); Giedion, *Space, Time, and Architecture*, esp. 381, 387–88; Wigginton, *Glass in Architecture*, 50; Curtis, *Modern Architecture*, 46–47.

48. On the importance of windows in Wright's architecture, see esp. Pfeiffer, "Frank Lloyd Wright."

49. Giedion, *Space, Time, and Architecture*, 392.

50. Curtis, *Modern Architecture*, 176.

51. Reichlin, "Pros and Cons"; Cohen, *Le Corbusier*, 26.

52. Uhlig and Wolff, "Vier Spots," 31; Colomina, *Privacy and Publicity*, 6–7.

53. Quoted in Reichlin, "Stories of Windows," 105.

54. Cohen, *Le Corbusier*, 26: Colomina, *Privacy and Publicity*, 128–39, 311 (quote at 311); Reichlin, "Pros and Cons"; Reichlin, "Stories of Windows."

55. Quoted in Reichlin, "Stories of Windows," 108.

56. Quoted in Davey, "Window in Arts and Crafts," 53.

57. Schultze-Naumburg, *Gesicht des deutschen Hauses*, 144.

58. Le Corbusier, "Glass," 284, 294 (quote).

59. McGrath and Frost, *Glass in Architecture*, 159.

60. Le Corbusier, "Glass," 297.

61. Riley and Bergdoll, *Mies in Berlin* (catalogue section, 180, 186); Bletter, "Mies," 353; Tegethoff, *Mies van der Rohe*, 66.

62. Korn, *Glass in Modern Architecture*, n.p. (introduction).

63. Quoted in Schulze and Windhorst, *Mies van der Rohe*, 117.

64. Quoted in Schulze and Windhorst, *Mies van der Rohe*, 117.

65. Zimmerman, *Mies van der Rohe*, 39–51; Riley, "Light Construction," 28; Riley and Bergdoll, *Mies in Berlin* (catalogue section, 242); Schulze and Windhorst, *Mies van der Rohe*, 130; Tegethoff, *Mies van der Rohe*, 95.

66. Colomina, *Privacy and Publicity*, 6–9; Uhlig and Wolff, "Vier Spots," 29; Badstübner, *Funktion des Fensters*, xii.

67. Korn, *Glass in Modern Architecture*, n.p. (introduction).

68. McGrath and Frost, *Glass in Architecture* (introduction to first edition [1937]), 21.

69. Benjamin, *Arcades Project*, 4 (translation slightly modified).

70. Benjamin, "Erfahrung und Armut," in *Gesammelte Schriften*, 2:217. See also Mertins, "Enticing and the Threatening," esp. 232; and in more detail, Mertins, "Transparencies Yet to Come."

71. Hilberseimer, "Glasarchitektur," 521.

72. Benjamin, *Selected Writings*, 2:734.

73. Benjamin, *Selected Writings*, 2:734.

74. Benjamin, *Selected Writings*, 2:734.

75. Benjamin, *Selected Writings*, 2:734.

76. Mertins, "Enticing and the Threatening," 232. See also Ascher-Barnstone, "Transparency," esp. 3; Whitelely, "Intensity of Scrutiny," 9.

77. Scheerbart, *Glass Architecture*, 55.

78. Quoted in Schulze, *Glas in der Architektur*, 29.

79. Feininger and Kandinsky quoted in Whiteley, "Intensity of Scrutiny," 10.

80. From a prospectus of the Verein Deutscher Spiegelglas-Fabriken, quoted in Tegethoff, *Mies van der Rohe*, 66.

81. Schulze and Windhorst, *Mies van der Rohe*, 109; Tegethoff, *Mies van der Rohe*, 62.

82. McGrath and Frost, *Glass in Architecture*, 160; Fischer, *Licht und Transparenz*, esp. chaps. 4 and 6.

83. Giedion, *Space, Time, and Architecture*, 497.

84. Kohlmaier and Sartory, *Houses of Glass*, 21.

85. Edel, *Das Glashaus*, passim; see also Kreimeier, *Die Ufa-Story*, 52–54.

86. Quoted in Ward, *Weimar Surfaces*, 146. Interestingly, some of these ideas were received—and explored—as far away as China, at the initiative of Chinese students trained in interwar Germany. On the "large application of glass in a new generation of movie theaters of modernist design" in China, see Bao, *Fiery Cinema*, chap. 4 (quote at 218).

87. Grisko, "Kapitalisierte Phantasie," 286–87; Bock, "Die Glashäuser"; Kreimeier, *Die Ufa-Story*, 214; Ward, *Weimar Surfaces*, 144.

88. Quoted in Grisko, "Kapitalisierte Phantasie," 287.

89. Quotation from the edition of his draft notes in Albera, *S. M. Eisenstein*, 24.

90. Ward, *Weimar Surfaces*, 74.

91. Giedion, *Space, Time, and Architecture*, 480; Barnstone, *Transparent State*, 52; Ulmer and Kurz, *Die Weißenhofsiedlung*, 14; Pommer and Otto, *Weissenhof 1927*, 1; Ward, *Weimar Surfaces*, 74–75; Lane, *Architektur und Politik*, 53.

92. The most comprehensive account is Pommer and Otto, *Weissenhof 1927*.

93. Pommer and Otto, *Weissenhof 1927*, 77–78, 110.

94. Tegethoff, *Mies van der Rohe*, 68 (quote); Schulze and Windhorst, *Mies van der Rohe*, 106–7; Zimmerman, *Mies van der Rohe*, 12, 29.

95. Ulmer and Kurz, *Die Weißenhofsiedlung*, 205. And in more detail, see Pommer and Otto, *Weissenhof 1927*, chaps. 14–15.

96. Pommer and Otto, *Weissenhof 1927*, 28. On the many conflicts preceding construction, see also chap. 4.

97. Anonymous, quoted in Ulmer and Kurz, *Die Weißenhofsiedlung*, 226. On the windows as a subject of public debate, see also Pommer and Otto, *Weissenhof 1927*, 78.

98. Quoted in Schulze, *Glas in der Architektur*, 98.

99. Völckers, *Fenster und Glas*, 118–20.

100. Baumhoff, "Das Bauhaus," 587. See also Rehm, *Bauhausgebäude*, 33; Lane, *Architektur und Politik*, 36.

101. Ward, *Weimar Surfaces*, 66.

102. Karol Teige (1932) quoted in Zimmerman, *Mies van der Rohe*, 51. For further contemporary criticism, see also Sedlák, *Tugendhat House*, 20–21.

14
TRANSPARENCY BETWEEN
TOTALITARIANISM AND DEMOCRACY

1. Quoted in Blau, "Transparency," 58. Moholy-Nagy played a crucial role in establishing the term "transparency" in the lexicon of modern architecture: Forty, *Words and Buildings*, 286.

2. Quoted in Barnstein, *Transparent State*, 37.

3. Gino, "Changing Room," 33.

4. Barnstone, *Transparent State*, 34.

5. Quoted in Knoch, "Schwellenräume," 281.

6. Kafka, *Man Who Disappeared*, 11.

7. Gorky, *In America*, 26.

8. Quoted in Albera, *S. M. Eisenstein*, 26.

9. Albera, *S. M. Eisenstein*, 11.

10. Quoted in Ward, *Weimar Surfaces*, 72–73. See also Barnstone, *Transparent State*, 37–38.

11. Quoted in Alloa, *Architectures of Transparency*, 327. Translation quoted with permission of the University of Chicago Press.

12. Kohlmaier and Sartory, *Houses of Glass*, 24.

13. Kohlmaier and Sartory, *Houses of Glass*, 24.

14. Colomina, *Privacy and Publicity*, 8.

15. Le Corbusier, "Twentieth-Century Building," 146.

16. Quoted in Bletter, "Mies," 354. See also Etlin, *Symbolic Space*, 44; Vidler, "Transparency," 6.

17. Trélat, "La fenêtre"; Schulze, *Glas*, 22; Hilberseimer, "Glasarchitektur," 522; Landsberg, "Die Kulturmission."

18. Scheerbart, *Glass Architecture*, 63.

19. Quoted in Schnapp, "People's Glass House," 46.

20. Schnapp, "Fragments," 181; Schnapp, "People's Glass House," 53.

21. Schnapp, "People's Glass House," 45.

22. Terragni, *Terragni Atlas*, 213.

23. Schnapp, "Fragments," 181. See also Etlin, *Symbolic Space*, 44.

24. *"Ecco il concetto mussoliniano che il fascismo è una casa di vetro in cui tutti possono guardare."* Quoted in Poretti, *La Casa del Fascio*, 52.

25. Terragni, Libeskind, and Rosselli, *Terragni Atlas*, 147.

26. Koepnick, *Framing Attention*, esp. 162; Gerner and Gärtner, *Historische Fenster*, 47.

27. Quoted in Stratigakos, *Hitler at Home*, 25; see also Fest, "Führerbunker," 127.

28. Quoted in Koepnick, *Framing Attention*, 163.

29. Koepnick, *Framing Attention*, 165; Fest, "Führerbunker," 127.

30. Kirkpatrick, *Inner Circle*, 127.

31. Stratigakos, *Hitler at Home*, 2.

32. Stratigakos, *Hitler at Home*, 79.

33. Speer, *Inside the Third Reich*, 86. See also Stratigakos, *Hitler at Home*, 81; Koepnick, *Framing Attention*, 184.

34. Quoted in Stratigakos, *Hitler at Home*, 81 (emphasis in the original).

35. Quoted in Stratigakos, *Hitler at Home*, 81.

36. Kirkpatrick, *Inner Circle*, 97.

37. Kirkpatrick, *Inner Circle*, 96.

38. Charlie Chaplin (dir.), *The Great Dictator* (1940), Warner Home Video Germany, DVD 2007 (my transcription).

39. Stratigakos, *Hitler at Home*, 80, 239.

40. Quoted in Livings, "Ephemere Kulträume," 291.

41. For a rare illustration, see Taylor, *Hitler's Headquarters*, 58.

42. Stratigakos, *Hitler at Home*, 182.

43. Filler, "Hanging Out with Hitler," 38.

44. *"De ces bureaux de travail nous viendrait donc le sentiment de vigies dominant un monde en ordre."* Le Corbusier, *Urbanisme*, 177 (my translation).

45. Quoted in Lane, *Architektur*, 163. For "cathedral of Marxism," see Gilbert Herbert, "Gropius, Walter," in *Grove Art Online*, 2003, https://doi.org/10.1093/gao/9781884446054.article.T035050.

46. Lane, *Architektur*, esp. 163, 204; Curtis, *Modern Architecture*, 354.

47. Hitler, *Deutsche Kunst*, 10.

48. Hitler, *Deutsche Kunst*, 10.

49. Hitler, *Deutsche Kunst*, 13.

50. Baumhoff, "Bauhaus," 593; Eisele, "Adolf H.," esp. 31; Betts, "Bauhaus," 34.

51. Eisele, "Adolf H.," 31. See also Schulze and Windhorst, *Mies van der Rohe*, 157.

52. Lane, *Architektur*, 182.

53. Curtis, *Modern Architecture*, 327.

54. Nerdinger, "Versuchung," 78; Baumhoff, 592; Eisele, "Adolf H.," 37; Cohen, *Mies van der Rohe*, 72–73.

55. Baumhoff, "Bauhaus," 592.

56. Nerdinger, "Versuchung," 84.

57. Völckers, *Glas und Fenster*, 3.

58. Völckers, *Glas und Fenster*, 57.

59. Völckers, *Glas und Fenster*, 50.

60. Völckers, *Glas und Fenster*, 125.

61. Völckers, *Glas und Fenster*, 123, 62.

62. Völckers, *Glas und Fenster*, 90.

63. On the history of this misattribution, see Erich Trunz, "Das Geschlecht, das vom Dunkeln in Helle strebt: Über Goethe-Zitate im Goethe-Jahr," *Die Zeit*, August 4, 1949.

64. Schulze, *Glas*, 22, 100; Trélat, "La fenêtre." See also Colomina, *X-Ray Architecture*; Sadar, *Through the Healing Glass*; Ward, *Weimar Surfaces*, 62–63, 80–81; Holm, "Bürgerliche Wohnkultur," esp. 243–44; Wagner, *Marmor und Asphalt*, esp. 44–45.

65. Völckers, *Glas und Fenster*, 74.

66. Völckers, *Glas und Fenster*, 74.

67. Völckers, *Glas und Fenster*, 74.

68. Völckers, *Glas und Fenster*, 72.

69. Völckers, *Glas und Fenster*, 76.

70. See, for instance, Eddy, "Use of Ultra-Violet Light Transmitting Windows." These studies were known in the German medical literature of the 1930s.

71. Quoted in Eisele, "Adolf H.," 38.

72. Speer, *Inside the Third Reich*, 142.

73. Völckers, *Glas und Fenster*, 80.

74. Fischer, *Licht und Transparenz*, 201.

75. Curtis, *Modern Architecture*, 354; Fischer, *Licht und Transparenz*, esp. 280.

76. Betts, "Bauhaus," 36.

77. Letter from Thomas Mann to Felix Braun, July 31, 1943, in Mann, *Die Briefe*, vol. 2, no. 43/180. See also Valentin, *Steine*, 7.

78. Huber, "JoKarl Huber," 172. I would like to thank Dr. Ursula Huber, the artist's daughter, for sharing her recollections in personal conversations.

79. Huber, "Zum Glasfenster," 3.

80. Beck, "Jokarl Huber," 144; Schmitt, "Moderne Sakralkunst," 61–63; Siedentopf, "Adolf Hitler," esp. 22.

81. Schmitt, "Moderne Sakralkunst," 60.

82. See the biographical entry in the International Architecture Database: "Otto Völckers," Internationale Architektur-Datenbank, https://deu.archinform.net/arch/67409.htm.

83. Barnstone, *Transparent State*, esp. 17.

84. Arndt, *Demokratie als Bauherr*, 19–20.

85. Barnstein, *Transparent State*, xi (quote); Whiteley, *Intensity of Scrutiny*, 13.

86. Barnstone, *Transparent State*, xi.

87. "Building: Prinz Max Palais," Bundesverfassungsgericht, http://www.bundesverfassungsgericht.de/EN/Gebaeude/gebaeude_node.html. On the ideal of transparency in postwar German courthouse architecture, see also Mulcahy, *Legal Architecture*, 152. On Baumgarten's project and the importance of transparency in his oeuvre, see Volkmann, *Paul Baumgarten*, 55–58, 225–29; Menting, *Paul Baumgarten*, 240–41.

88. Koepnick, *Framing Attention*, 248.

89. Quoted in Barnstone, *Transparent State*, 201.

90. Jane Kramer, "Living with Berlin," 54.

91. Badstübner, *Funktion des Fensters*, xv.

92. Nolan, *Transatlantic Century*, 255. On GDR efforts to create a distinctively German and socialist architecture, see, for example, Karrasch, "*Nationale Bautradition.*"

93. On the "showcase of socialism," see Flamm, "Palast der Republik," 668; Wörner, Mollenschott, and Hüter, *Architekturführer Berlin*, 308.

94. Wörner, Mollenschott, and Hüter, *Architekturführer Berlin*, 308.

95. Flamm, "Palast der Republik," 668, 677.

96. Material relics of the Stasi cult around Dzerzhinsky are on display in the Stasi museum in Berlin-Lichtenberg.

97. Fedor, *Russia*, 21, 192.

15
POSTWAR ENTHUSIASM, POSTMODERNIST REJECTION—AND THE PRESENT

1. *BILD*, November 29, 2004.

2. Wigginton, *Glass in Architecture*, 272.

3. Rice and Dutton, *Structural Glass*, 12.

4. Quoted in Wigginton, *Glass in Architecture*, 64.

5. Lim et al., *Environmental Factors*, 30; Rice and Dutton, *Structural Glass*, 12; Wigginton, *Glass in Architecture*, 64, 284; Achilles and Navratil, *Glass Architecture*, 10–11.

6. Whiteley, "Intensity of Scrutiny," esp. 10. On England (and the particular case of public libraries), see Black, *Libraries of Light*. On France, see below, as well as Vidler, *Architectural Uncanny*, 219–25; Forty, *Words and Buildings*, 288. But see also Geroulanous, *Transparency*, 115, which has unearthed a critique of transparency in 1950s and 1960s French intellectual circles and argues that, in this period, "French thinkers tended to equate a 'transparent society' with a totalitarian one."

7. Schudson, *Right of the Rise to Know*, 5.

8. Schudson, *Right of the Rise to Know*, 16; see also Fenster, "Transparency in Search of a Theory"; Ananny and Crawford, "Seeing without Knowing," esp. 3–4.

9. Quoted in Rosen, *Brandeis*, 42.

10. Brandeis, *Other People's Money*, 92. Brandeis first used the line in an article published in 1913.

11. Quoted in Hood, "Transparency," 11.

12. Whiteley, "Intensity of Scrutiny," esp. 11–12.

13. Garner, "Glass between the Wars," 241.

14. Wright, "The Meaning of Materials," 201–2.

15. Wright, *Natural House*, 51.

16. Wright, *Natural House* 40.

17. Wright, *Natural House*, 53.

18. Wright, *Natural House*, 53.

19. Wigginton, *Glass in Architecture*, 89.

20. "Plans for U.N. Home Call for City of Glass," *Chicago Tribune*, September 17, 1947.

21. Sennett, *Conscience of the Eye*, 111; in the same vein, see Whiteley, "Intensity of Scrutiny," 10.

22. Schulze and Windhorst, *Mies van der Rohe*, 286; Zimmerman, *Mies van der Rohe*, 67–69, 73–78; Lim et al., *Environmental Factors*, 41–42; Curtis, *Modern Architecture*, 407.

23. Curtis, *Modern Architecture*, 405.

24. Brand, *How Buildings Learn*, 170.

25. Isenstadt, "Four Views"; Isenstadt, "Rise and Fall."

26. Lane, *Houses for a New World*, 24.

27. Quoted from the poster reproduced in Petty, "Scopophobia/Scopophilia," 48.

28. Quoted in Petty, "Scopophobia/Scopophilia," esp. 52.

29. The 1953 article by Edwin Bateman Morris is quoted in Isenstadt, "Rise and Fall," 302–3.

30. Isenstadt, "Four Views," 214, 226; Petty, "Scopophobia/Scopophilia," esp. 46, 52.

31. Zimmerman, *Mies van der Rohe*, 63–65 (quote at 63).

32. Vandenberg, *Farnsworth House*, 16.

33. Quoted in Vandenberg, *Farnsworth House*, 19–21.

34. Hornbein, "Humane and Environmental Architecture," 27; Brüning, "Glossary," 619.

35. Le Corbusier, "Glass," 307 (quote).

36. Le Corbusier, "Glass," 287–88 (editor's introduction).

37. Schulze and Windhorst, *Mies van der Rohe*, 260.

38. Vandenberg, *Farnsworth House*, 23.

39. Vandenberg, *Farnsworth House*, 23. See also Schulze and Windhorst, *Mies van der Rohe*, 260.

40. Zimmerman, *Mies van der Rohe*, 76; Schulze and Windhorst, *Mies van der Rohe*, 334.

41. McGrath and Frost, *Glass in Architecture*, 686; Wigginton, *Glass in Architecture*, 72; Eskilson, *Age of Glass*, 173–74.

42. Leong and Jovanovich Weiss, "Air Conditioning," esp. 121.

43. Markus, "Function of Windows," 97.

44. Leong and Jovanovich Weiss, "Air Conditioning," 121; Hornbein, "Humane and Environmental Architecture," 27.

45. Quoted in Schulze and Windhorst, *Mies van der Rohe*, 357.

46. Schulze and Windhorst, *Mies van der Rohe*, 357.

47. Zimmerman, *Mies van der Rohe*, 85.

48. Lane, *Houses for a New World*, 25.

49. Spigel, "Suburban Home Companion," 202.

50. Rudofsky, *Behind the Picture Window*, 195.

51. The 1953 article in the *Journal of the American Institute of Architects* is quoted in Isenstadt, "Rise and Fall," 303.

52. Quoted in Feuerstein, *Open Space*, 157.

53. Quoted in Vandenberg, *Farnsworth House*, 15. See also Colomina, *Domesticity at War*, 164.

54. Vandenberg, *Farnsworth House*, 25.

55. Sennett, *Conscience of the Eye*, 113. Similarly, Quetglas, *Der gläserne Schrecken*, 78. On privacy concerns in late twentieth-century domestic architecture, see also Whiteley, "Intensity of Scrutiny," 15.

56. Schulze and Windhorst, *Mies van der Rohe*, 292.

57. Schulze and Windhorst, *Mies van der Rohe*, 293.

58. Quoted in Schulze and Windhorst, *Mies van der Rohe*, 293.

59. Schulze and Windhorst, *Mies van der Rohe*, 293.

60. Giedion, *Space, Time, and Architecture*, 614.

61. McGrath and Frost, *Glass in Architecture*, 479.

62. Quoted in Cartwright, *Screening the Body*, 155. See also Colomina, *Domesticity at War*, 146.

63. Colomina, *X-Ray Architecture*.

64. Colomina, *Domesticity at War*, 153.

65. McGrath and Frost, *Glass in Architecture*, 113.

66. Feuerstein, *Open Space*, 189.

67. "Walking Tour with Philip Johnson, 1991," The Glass House, http://theglasshouse .org/explore/brick-house/. See also Colomina, *Domesticity at War*, esp. 177–88.

68. Auer, "Begehrlicher Blick," 39.

69. Rudofsky, *Behind the Picture Window*, 194; see also 159.

70. Mumford, *City in History*, 310.

71. Quoted in Petty, "Scopophobia/Scopophilia," esp. 54. On the "backlash against the picture window," see also Koolhaas, *Elements of Architecture*, 6:58; Banham, "Modern Monuments," 371.

72. Stamp, "Anti-Ugly Action," 81. My thanks to Professor Stamp for sharing this article. On bold and idealistic experiments with glass in 1960s Britain, see Black, *Libraries of Light*, esp. 96.

73. Rowe and Slutzky, *Transparency*.

74. Rowe quoted in Anthony Vidler, "Robert Slutzky: An Appreciation," The Cooper Union, http://archweb.cooper.edu/exhibitions/spectral/appreciation.html.

75. Kepes, *Language of Vision*, 77.

76. Forty, *Words and Buildings*, 287.

77. Quoted in Vidler, "Robert Slutzky."

78. Vidler, "Transparency: Literal and Phenomenal." For a critique of Rowe and Slutzky's approach, see Mertins, "Transparencies Yet to Come"; see also Blau, "Transparency," esp. 51.

79. Hornbein, "Humane and Environmental Architecture," 27. For a wide-ranging critique of architectural transparency, see also the contributions in the topic issue of *Daidalos* 33 (1989).

80. Auer, "Begehrlicher Blick," 43.

81. Whiteley, "Intensity of Scrutiny," 12; Achilles and Navratil, *Glass Construction*, 75; Brand, *How Buildings Learn*, 170.

82. Vidler, *Architectural Uncanny*, 291; Whiteley, "Intensity of Scrutiny," 12. Forty has argued that "postmodernism rejected transparency (in all senses)" (Forty, *Words and Buildings*, 288).

83. Jameson, *Postmodernism*, 42.

84. Forty, *Words and Buildings*, 288.

85. Vidler, *Architectural Uncanny*, 219.

86. Fierro, *Glass State*, 166.

87. Fierro, *Glass State*, esp. 7, 235.

88. Ayers, *Architecture of Paris*, 206.

89. The boom of glass architecture in recent French architecture is discussed in great detail in Fierro, *Glass State*. On the Fondation Cartier, see Fierro, *Glass State*, 123. On skirts, see Gerhard Matzig, "Der Stein der Weisen: Architektur mit Beton," *Süddeutsche Zeitung*, May 14, 2009.

90. Teresa Roelcke, Volkmar Kabisch, and Sebastian Pittelkow, "Alles im Eimer," Tagesschau, October 29, 2021, https://www.tagesschau.de/inland/wasserschaden-bundestag-101.html.

91. For surveys (and illustrations) of this phenomenon, see Kristal, *Immaterial World*; Feuerstein, *Open Space*.

92. Harry Bartnick, "Give Boston's City Hall a Much-Needed Makeover," *Boston Globe*, July 26, 2015. My thanks to Daniel Merzel for pointing this out and sharing the reference.

93. Martin Gropp, "Apples Raumschiff," *Frankfurter Allgemeine Zeitung*, February 22, 2016.

94. Gropp, "Apples Raumschiff," 18. My thanks to Martin Gropp for providing me with the English transcript of his interview.

95. Lucy Kellaway, "Apple Has Built an Office for Grown-Ups," *Financial Times*, July 3, 2017, 14.

96. John Tenanes, "Expanding Our Home in Menlo Park," Facebook press release, September 4, 2018, https://newsroom.fb.com/news/2018/09/expanding-our-home-in-menlo-park/.

97. Sarah Pines, "Unsere Zukunft hat die Farbe von veganem Apfeleis," *Frankfurter Allgemeine Zeitung*, January 7, 2019, 11.

98. Tenanes, "Expanding Our Home."

99. Pines, "Unsere Zukunft," 11.

EPILOGUE

1. William Gibson, "The Future of Secrecy," *New York Times*, December 6, 2016, international edition, S3.

2. Kantorowicz, "Oriens Augusti," 175.

3. Foucault, "Eye of Power," 152.

4. Ascher-Barnstone, "Transparency," 3. See also Gino, "Changing Rooms," 33. In Forty's dictionary of key terms of modern architecture, one entry is dedicated to "transparency": Forty, *Words and Buildings*, 286–88. See also Blau, "Transparency," 50, which argues that "transparency has been a constant trope of the architectural discourses of modernity."

5. Wigginton, *Glass in Architecture*, 24.

6. Terragni, *Terragni Atlas*, 39.

7. On toughened glass, see Wigginton, *Glass in Architecture*, 77.

8. Riley, "Light Construction," 33.

9. Achilles and Navratil, *Glass Construction*, 17–19; Riley, "Light Construction," 33–34; "Problemlöser für ein gutes Lebensgefühl: Interview with Bernhard Helbling," *Frankfurter Allgemeine Zeitung*, March 20, 2012, suppl. *Faszination Fenster*, n.p.; Lukas Weber, "Klarer Blick," *Frankfurter Allgemeine Zeitung*, March 22, 2016, T1.

10. Clara Schick, "Manche Fenster führen ein Schattendasein," *Frankfurter Allgemeine Zeitung*, March 3, 2016. On "smart windows," see also Wigginton, *Glass in Architecture*, 75.

11. Achilles and Navratil, *Glass Construction*, 75.

12. Mays, "De Blasio's 'Ban' on Glass."

13. Mark Chambers, director of the Mayor's Office of Sustainability, New York, quoted in Mays, "De Blasio's 'Ban' on Glass."

14. Fierro, *Glass State*, x.

15. Whiteley, "Intensity of Scrutiny," 14.

16. Koolhaas, "Junkspace," 410.

17. Mulcahy, *Legal Architecture*, 96. See also Whiteley, "Intensity of Scrutiny," 14; Le Dantec, "La transparence," 99.

18. Ananny and Crawford, "Seeing without Knowing," 3.

19. Farrell, *One Nation under Goods*, 24.

20. Benjamin, *Arcades Project*, 532. See also Fuller, "Welcome to Windows 2.1," 164.

21. Barr and Broudy, *Designing to Sell*, 44.

22. Farrell, *One Nation under Goods*, 9.

23. Quoted in Leong and Jovanovic Weiss, "Air Conditioning," 112.

24. Horst W. Opaschowski, *Pädagogik der freien Lebenszeit* (Opladen: Leske und Budrich, 1996), 22; Jütte, "Window Gazes," esp. 612–13.

25. Friedberg, *Virtual Window*; Koepnick, *Framing Attention*, esp. 6; Koolhaas, "Junkspace," 421.

26. "Wohnwelten der Zukunft," *Frankfurter Allgemeine Zeitung*, March 9, 2016, suppl. *Faszination Fenster*, V1.

27. Jacobs, *Death and Life*, 54.

28. Quoted in Colomina, *Domesticity at War*, 183.

29. De Certeau, *Practice*, 92. See also Pile, *Body and the City*, 223, which argues that such panorama windows "construct the city as a framed view."

30. Sennett, *Conscience of the Eye*, xii; 108. See also Quetglas, *Der gläserne Schrecken*, 78.

31. Sennett, *Conscience of the Eye*, 108. See also Fuller, who speaks of modern windows as "vision machines" (Fuller, "Welcome to Windows 2.1," 163).

32. Urry, "City Life and the Senses," 392; Achilles and Navratil, *Glass Construction*, 27–28.

33. "Zürcher Gespräche (III): Interview mit Santiago Calatrava," *Neue Zürcher Zeitung*, November 16, 2015, international edition.

34. Heil, *Fenster als Gestaltungsmittel*, 492; Gottlieb, *Window in Art*, 383–85; Hans Kollhoff, "Wer wollte nicht das Fenster öffnen?" *Frankfurter Allgemeine Zeitung*, July 26, 2017.

35. Friedensreich Hundertwasser, "Window Dictatorship and Window Rights," Hundertwasser Archive, http://www.hundertwasser.at/pdf/fensterrecht_eng.pdf.

36. To be sure, restoring the importance of the nonvisual senses in our approach to the natural world is not an end in itself and certainly is not a solely aesthetic task. As Soper has pointed out, we still need to ask ourselves how different regimes of sensory perception contribute to the appropriation and cultural construction of the natural world. In other words, the history of sensory perception is always also a history of human attempts to subject nature to human will and to impress a sense of order on the world that surrounds us; see Soper, "Privileged Gazes."

37. See esp. Shelton, *Learning from the Japanese City*.

38. Nishi and Hozumi, *What Is Japanese Architecture?*, 67, 75; Shelton, *Learning from the Japanese City*, esp. 28–31; Screech, "Glass," esp. 28–29.

39. Macfarlane and Martin, *Glass*, 188.

40. Sand, "Property in Two Fire Regimes," 47.

41. Screech, "Glass," 29.

42. Sand, *House and Home in Modern Japan*, 249. See also Herold, "Eigenheiten," 88.

43. Nishi and Hozumi, *What Is Japanese Architecture?*, 74.

44. In general, there is no such thing as "right" lighting levels; the perception of what constitutes sufficient light is culturally determined and varies greatly among different societies: see Rapoport, *House Form and Culture*, 62; Oliver, *Dwellings*, esp. 137–38.

45. Nishi and Hozumi, *What Is Japanese Architecture?*, 131.

46. Tanizaki, *In Praise of Shadows*, 29.

47. Ando, [Untitled], 256. On ways to reconcile the Japanese tradition of "soft lighting" with modern Western architecture, see Yagi, *Japanese Touch*, 70–71. See also, more generally, Shelton, *Learning from the Japanese City*.

48. Brin, *Transparent Society*, 26.

49. Bachelard, *Poetics of Space*, xxxvii.

50. On the long and powerful afterlife of Plato's allegory, see esp. Blumenberg, *Höhlenausgänge*.

51. Joyce, *Ulysses*, 66.

BIBLIOGRAPHY

Abdel Gelil, Nermine. "A New Mashrabiyya for Contemporary Cairo: Integrating Traditional Latticework from Islamic and Japanese Culture." In *Journal of Asian Architecture and Building Engineering* 5 (2006): 37–44.

Abraham a Sancta Clara. *Etwas für alle: Das ist: Eine kurtze Beschreibung allerley Stands-Ambts-und Gewerbs-Persohnen*. Nuremberg: Weigel, 1699.

Achilles, Andreas, and Diana Navratil. *Glass Construction*. Basel: Birkhäuser, 2009.

Adam, Jean-Pierre. *Roman Building: Materials and Techniques*. Translated by Anthony Mathews. New York: Routledge, 2005.

Adam-Veleni, Polyxeni, and Despina Ignatiadou, eds. *Glass Cosmos*. Thessaloniki: Archaeological Museum of Thessaloniki, 2010.

Agricola, Georgius. *Ausgewählte Werke*. Edited by Hans Prescher. 11 vols. Berlin: Deutscher Verlag der Wissenschaften, 1955–99.

Albera, François. *S. M. Eisenstein, Glass House: Du projet de film au film comme projet*. Dijon: Les presses du réel.

Alberti, Leon Battista. *On the Art of Building in Ten Books*. Translated by Joseph Rykwert, Neil Leach, and Robert Tavernor. Cambridge, MA: MIT Press, 1988.

—. *On Painting*. Edited and translated by Rocco Sinisgalli. Cambridge: Cambridge University Press, 2011.

Aldrete, Gregory S. *Daily Life in the Roman City: Rome, Pompeii and Ostia*. Westport, CT: Greenwood Press, 2004.

Alloa, Emanuel. "Architectures of Transparency." *Res* 53/54 (2008): 321–30.

Ananny, Mike, and Kate Crawford. "Seeing without Knowing: Limitations of the Transparency Ideal and Its Application to Algorithmic Accountability." *New Media and Society*. December 13, 2016. DOI: 10.1177/1461444816676645.

Ando, Tadao. [Untitled]. In Lampugnani, *Architecture of the Window*, 254–61.

Anon. *A Non-Military Journal, or Observations Made in Egypt by an Officer upon the Staff of the British Army*. London: Wilson, 1803.

—. *Untersuchungen über den Charakter der Gebäude: Über die Verbindung der Baukunst mit den schönen Künsten und über die Wirkungen, welche durch dieselbe hervorgebracht werden sollen*. Lepizig: Haug, 1788. Reprint, Nördlingen: Uhl, 1986.

Anshelm, Valerius. *Die Berner-Chronik*. 6 vols. Bern: Wyss, 1884–1901.

Antoine, Annie. "Maisons rurales de Haute-Bretagne au XVIIIe siècle: Les débuts d'une enquête." In *La maison rurale en pays d'habitat dispersé de l'Antiquité au XXe siècle*, edited by Annie Antoine, Martine Cocaud and Daniel Pichot, 227–40. Rennes: Presses universitaires de Rennes, 2005.

Apperson, George Latimer, and Martin H. Manser, eds. *Dictionary of Proverbs*. Ware: Wordsworth Editions, 2006.

Aretino, Pietro. *Dialogues*. Translated by Raymond Rosenthal. London: Allen, 1972.

Ariès, Philippe, and Georges Duby, eds. *A History of Private Life*. Cambridge, MA: Harvard University Press, 1987–91.

Armstrong, Isobel. *Victorian Glass Worlds: Glass Culture and the Imagination, 1830–1880*. Oxford: Oxford University Press, 2008.

Arndt, Adolf. *Demokratie als Bauherr*. Berlin: Archibook-Verlag, 1984.

Arnulf, Arwed. *Architektur-und Kunstbeschreibungen von der Antike bis zum 16. Jahrhundert*. Munich: Deutscher Kunstverlag, 2004.

Ascher-Barnstone, Deborah. "Transparency: A Brief Introduction." *Journal of Architectural Education* 56 (2003): 2–5.

Ashtor, Eliyahu, and Guidobaldo Cevidalli. "Levantine Alkali Ashes and European Industries." *Journal of European Economic History* 12 (1983): 475–522.

Atwell, William S. "A Seventeenth-Century 'General Crisis' in East Asia?" *Modern Asian Studies* 24 (1990): 661–82.

Auer, Gerhard. "Begehrlicher Blick und die List des Schleiers." *Daidalos* 33 (1989): 36–53.

Ayers, Andrew. *The Architecture of Paris: An Architectural Guide*. Stuttgart: Menges, 2004.

Baatz, Dietwulf. "Fensterglastypen, Glasfenster und Architektur." In *Bautechnik der Antike: Internationales Kollquium in Berlin vom 15. bis 17. Februar 1990*, edited by Adolf Hoffmann et al., 4–13. Mainz: Zabern, 1991.

Bachelard, Gaston. *The Poetics of Space*. Translated by Maria Jolas. Boston: Beacon Press, 1994.

Bacher, Ernst. "Mittelalterliche Glasmalerei im Rückblick." In Westermann-Angerhausen, *Himmelslicht*, 107–10.

Bacon, Francis. *Essays or Counsels Civil and Moral*. In *Works*, edited by James Spedding, Robert Leslie Ellis, and Douglas Denon Heath, 6:377–517. London: Longmans, 1861–79.

Baddeley, St. Clair. "Window Glass." *Notes and Queries* 9 (1902): 271–72.

Badstübner, Ernst. *Die Funktion des Fensters von der Romantik bis zur Gegenwart*. Leipzig: Prisma-Verlag, 1970.

Badstübner, Ernst, et al., eds. *Licht und Farbe in der mittelalterlichen Backsteinarchitektur des südlichen Ostseeraums*. Berlin: Lukas, 2005.

Banham, Reyner. "Modern Monuments." In Gannon, *Light Construction Reader*, 371–73.

Bao, Weihong. *Fiery Cinema: The Emergence of an Affective Medium in China, 1915–1945*. Minneapolis: University of Minnesota Press, 2015.

Bargebuhr, Frederick P. *The Paintings of the "New" Catacomb of the Via Latina and the Struggle of Christianity against Paganism*. Heidelberg: Winter, 1991.

Barnaby, Alice. *Light Touches: Cultural Practices of Illumination, 1800–1900*. London: Routledge, 2017.

Barnstone, Deborah Ascher. *The Transparent State: Architecture and Politics in Postwar Germany*. London: Routledge, 2005.

Barnwell, P. S. "Low Side Windows: Ventilating a 170-Year Old Controversy." *Ecclesiology Today* 36 (2006): 49–76.

Barovier Mentasti, Rosa. "Enameled Glass between the Eastern Mediterranean and Venice." In *Venice and the Islamic World, 828–1797*, edited by Stefano Carboni, 253–75. New Haven: Yale University Press, 2007.

———. "Il riflesso della vanità." In *Trasparenze e riflessi*, 77–84.

———. "La façon de Venise." In *Trasparenze e riflessi*, 171–80.

———. "La tavola di Veronese." In *Trasparenze e riflessi*, 85–134.

———. "Sacro e profane nel Medioevo." In *Trasparenze e riflessi*, 11–34.

———, ed. *Trasparenze e riflessi: Il vetro italiano nella pittura*. Verona: Banco popolare di Verona e Novara, 2006.

Barr, Vilma, and Charles E. Broudy. *Designing to Sell: A Complete Guide to Retail Store Planning and Design*. New York: McGraw-Hill, 1990.

Barrelet, James. *La verrerie en France de l'époque gallo-romaine à nos jours*. Paris: Larousse, 1954.

Barry, Fabio. "The House of the Rising Sun: Luminosity and Sacrality from the Domus to Ecclesia." In *Hiertopy of Light and Fire in the Culture of the Byzantine World*, edited by Alexei Lidov, 82–104. Moscow: Theoria, 2013.

Barz, Dieter. "Fenster-, Tür-und Toröffnungen an den Burgen des 11. bis 13. Jahrhunderts in der Pfalz und im Elsaß." In *Fenster und Türen in historischen Wohn-und Wehrbauten*, edited by Barbara Schock-Werner and Klaus Bingenheimer, 26–31. Stuttgart: Theiss, 1995.

Battaglia, Roberto. *La cattedra berniniana di San Pietro*. Rome: Reale Istituto di Studi Romani, 1943.

Baudelaire, Charles. *Complete Poems*. Edited by Walter Martin. New York: Routledge, 2002.

———. *Paris Spleen, 1869*. Translated by Louise Varèse. New York: New Directions, 1970.

Baumgartner, Erwin, and Ingeborg Krueger, eds. *Phönix aus Sand und Asche: Glas des Mittelalters*. Munich: Klinkhardt und Biermann, 1988.

Baumhoff, Anja. "Das Bauhaus." In *Deutsche Erinnerungsorte*, edited by Hagen Schulze and Etienne François, 2:584–600. Munich: C. H. Beck, 2009.

Beaver, Patrick. *The Crystal Palace: A Portrait of Victorian Enterprise*. Chichester: Phillimore, 1986.

Beck, Otto. "Jokarl Huber (1902–1996)." *Heilige Kunst* 28 (1996): 143–46.

Beckmann, John. *A History of Inventions, Discoveries, and Origins*. Translated by William Johnston. 2 vols. London: Bohn, 1846.

Becksmann, Rüdiger. "Die verschollene Denkschrift des Jean-Adolphe Dannegger oder die verpaßte Chance einer Wiedergeburt der monumentalen Glasmalerei in Straßburg um 1750." In *Le vitrail et les traités du Moyen Âge à nos jours*, edited by Karine Boulanger and Michel Hérold, 205–24. Bern: Peter Lang, 2008.

Becksmann, Rüdiger, and Stephan Waetzold. *Vitrea dedicata: Das Stifterbild in der deutschen Glasmalerei des Mittelalters*. Berlin: Deutscher Kunstverlag, 1975.

Bedal, Konrad. "Zeitmarken in den traditionellen Baukultur: Ein gewagter Versuch an Hand nord-und süddeutscher Beispiele." In *Wandel der Alltagskultur seit dem Mittelalter*, edited by Günter Wiegelmann, 139–59. Münster: Coppenrath, 1987.

Behringer, Wolfgang. *A Cultural History of Climate*. Translated by Patrick Camiller. Cambridge: Polity, 2010.

Belhoste, Jean-François, and Guy-Michel Leproux. "La fenêtre parisienne aux XVIIe et XVIIIe siècles: Menuiserie, ferrure et vitrage." In *Fenêtres de Paris: XVIIe et XVIIIe siècles*, edited by Guy-Michel Leproux, 15–43. Paris: Commission du vieux Paris, 1997.

Benjamin, Walter. *Das Passagen-Werk*. Edited by Rolf Tiedemann. 2 vols. Frankfurt am Main: Suhrkamp, 1983. Translated by Howard Eiland and Kevin McLaughlin as *The Arcades Project* (Cambridge, MA: Harvard University Press, 1999).

———. *Gesammelte Schriften*. Edited by Rolf Tiedemann and Hermann Schweppenhäuser. 14 vols. Frankfurt am Main: Suhrkamp, 1972–89.

———. *Selected Writings*. Edited by Marcus Bullock and Michael W. Jennings. 4 vols. Cambridge, MA: Belknap Press, 1996–.

———. "Theses on the Philosophy of History." In *Illuminations*, 245–55. London: Random House, 1999.

Bentham, Jeremy. *The Works of Jeremy Bentham*. Edited by John Bowring. 11 vols. Edinburgh: Tait, 1838–43.

Beretta, Marco. "Between Nature and Technology: Glass in Ancient Chemical Philosophy." In *When Glass Matters: Studies in the History of Science and Art from Graeco-Roman Antiquity to Early Modern Era*, edited by Marco Beretta, 1–30. Florence: Olschki, 2004.

Beretta, Marco, and Giovanni Di Pasquale. "Introduzione." In Beretta and Di Pasquale, *Vitrum*, 19–36.

———, eds. *Vitrum: Il vetro fra arte e scienza nel mondo romano*. Florence: Giunti, 2004.

Berg, Maxine. *Luxury and Pleasure in Eighteenth-Century Britain*. Oxford: Oxford University Press, 2005.

Betts, Paul. "The Bauhaus and National Socialism—a Dark Chapter of Modernism." In Fiedler and Feierabend, *Bauhaus*, 34–41.

Beyer, Annette. "Die Orientierung griechischer Tempel: Zur Beziehung von Kultbild und Tür." In Heilmeyer and Hoepfner, *Licht und Architektur*, 1–9.

Bezut, Karole. "The Stained-Glass and Painting-on-Glass Workshop at Sèvres, 1827–1854." In *The Sèvres Porcelain Manufactory: Alexandre Brongniart and the Triumph of Art and Industry, 1800–1847*, edited by Derek E. Ostergard, 97–111. New Haven: Yale University Press, 1997.

Biernoff, Suzannah. *Sight and Embodiment in the Middle Ages*. New York: Palgrave Macmillan, 2002.

Binding, Günther. *Die Bedeutung von Licht und Farbe für den mittelalterlichen Kirchenbau*. Stuttgart: Steiner, 2003.

Biow, Douglas. *The Culture of Cleanliness in Renaissance Italy*. Ithaca, NY: Cornell University Press, 2006.

Biringuccio, Vannoccio. *Pirotechnia*. Edited and translated by Cyril Stanley Smith and Martha Teach Gnudi. New York: Basic Books, 1959.

Bistort, Giulio. *Il magistrato alle pompe nella republica di Venezia: Studio storico*. Venice: Deputazione Veneta di Storia Patria, 1912. Reprint, Bologna: Forni, 1969.

Black, Alistair. *Libraries of Light: British Public Library Design in the Long 1960s*. New York: Routledge, 2017.

Blau, Eve. "Transparency and the Irreconcilable Contradictions of Modernity." *Praxis* 9 (2007): 50–59.

Bletter, Rosemarie Haag. "The Interpretation of the Glass Dream: Expressionist Architecture and the History of the Crystal Metaphor." In Gannon, *Light Construction Reader*, 311–35.

———. "Mies und die dunkle Transparenz." In Riley and Bergdoll, *Mies in Berlin*, 350–57.

Blum, Gerd. *Fenestra prospectiva: Architektonisch inszenierte Ausblicke: Alberti, Palladio, Aguc-chi*. Berlin: De Gruyter, 2015.

Blumenberg, Hans. *Höhlenausgänge*. Frankfurt am Main: Suhrkamp, 1989.

———. "Licht als Metapher der Wahrheit: Im Vorfeld der philosophischen Begriffsbildung." *Studium Generale* 10 (1957): 432–47.

Boccaccio, Giovanni. *Decameron*. Translated by J. G. Nichols. New York: Knopf, 2009.

Bock, Hans-Michael. "Die Glashäuser." In *Das Ufa-Buch: Kunst und Krisen, Stars und Regisseure, Wirtschaft und Politik*, edited by Hans-Michael Bock and Michael Töteberg, 22–23. Frankfurt am Main: Zweitausendeins, 1992.

Bohlmann, Carolin, Thomas Fink, and Philipp Weiss, eds. *Lichtgefüge des 17. Jahrhunderts: Rembrandt und Vermeer, Leibniz und Spinoza*. Munich: Fink, 2008.

Bol, Marjolijn. "The Emerald and the Eye: On Sight and Light in the Artisan's Workshop and the Scholar's Study." In *Perspective as Practice: Renaissance Cultures of Optics*, edited by Sven Dupré, 71–101. Turnhout: Brepols, 2019.

Bolzoni, Lina. *Il cuore di cristallo: Ragionamenti d'amore, poesia e ritratto nel Rinascimento*. Turin: Einaudi, 2010.

Borromeo, Carlo. *Charles Borromeo's Instructiones fabricae et supellectilis ecclesiasticae, 1577*. Translated by Evelyn Carol Voelker. Published (posthumously) at http://evelynvoelker .com/.

Borscheid, Peter, and Anette Drees. *Versicherungsstatistik Deutschlands, 1750–1985*. St. Katharinen: Scripta Mercaturae Verlag, 1988.

Bowles, Emily. *Madame de Maintenon*. London: Kegan, Paul, and Trench, 1888.

Brand, Steward. *How Buildings Learn: What Happens after They're Built*. London: Phoenix Illustrated, 1997.

Brandeis, Louis D. *Other People's Money: And How the Bankers Use It*. Mansfield Center, CT: Martino Publishing, 2009.

Brant, Sebastian. *The Ship of Fools*. Translated by Edwin H. Zeydel. New York: Dover Publications, 1962.

Breeze, Andrew. "The Blessed Virgin and the Sunbeam through Glass." *Celtica* 23 (1999): 20–29.

Breuss, Susanne. *Window Shopping: Eine Fotogeschichte des Schaufensters*. Vienna: Metroverlag, 2010.

Brin, David. *The Transparent Society: Will Technology Force Us to Choose between Privacy and Freedom?* New York: Perseus, 2008.

Brisac, Catherine. *A Thousand Years of Stained Glass*. Translated by Geoffrey Culverwell. New York: Doubleday, 1986.

Brödner, Erika. *Wohnen in der Antike*. Darmstadt: Wissenschaftliche Buchgesellschaft, 1989.

Broise, Henri. "Vitrages et volets des fenêtres thermales à l'époque impériale." In *Les thermes romains: Actes de la table ronde organisée par l'École française de Rome*, 61–78. Rome: École française de Rome, 1991.

Brondi, Maria Badano. *Storia del vetro: Il vetro preindustriale dalla Liguria a Newcastle*. Genoa: De Ferrari, 1999.

Brown, Patricia Fortini. *Private Lives in Renaissance Venice: Art, Architecture, and the Family*. New Haven: Yale University Press, 2004.

Brüning, Ute. "Glossary." In Fiedler and Feierabend, *Bauhaus*, 616–22.

Büchsel, Martin. "Ecclesiae symbolorum cursus completus." *Städel-Jahrbuch* 9 (1983): 69–88.

———. "Licht und Metaphysik in der Gotik: Noch einmal zu Suger von Saint-Denis." In Badstübner et al., *Licht und Farbe*, 24–37.

Buck-Morss, Susan. *The Dialectics of Seeing: Walter Benjamin and the Arcades Project*. Cambridge, MA: MIT Press, 1989.

Burke, Edmund. *A Philosophical Enquiry into the Sublime and Beautiful*. Edited by David Womersley. London: Penguin, 1998.

Büsching, Johann Gustav. *Reise durch einige Münster und Kirchen des nördlichen Deutschlands im Spätjahr 1817*. Leipzig: Hartknoch, 1819.

Butts, Barbara, and Lee Hendrix. "Drawn on Paper, Painted on Glass." In Butts and Hendrix, *Painting on Light*, 1–16.

———, eds. *Painting on Light: Drawings and Stained Glass in the Age of Dürer and Holbein*. Los Angeles: J. Paul Getty Trust, 2000.

Caen, Joost, and Cornelis J. Berserik. "Silver-Stained Roundels and Unipartite Panels in the Low Countries: Donations and Designs." In *Les panneaux de vitrail isolés*, edited by Valérie Sauterel and Stefan Trümpler, 121–32. Bern: Peter Lang, 2010.

Caen, Joost, et al. "Technical Prescriptions and Regulations for Craftsmen in the Southern Netherlands during the Sixteenth, Seventeenth and Eighteenth Centuries: A Confrontation of Archival and Material-Technical Information Regarding Glazing and Stained-Glass Windows." In Lagabrielle and Philippe, *Verre et fenêtre*, 159–70.

Camille, Michael. *Gothic Art: Glorious Visions*. New York: Abrams, 1996.

Campbell, Anthony. *Transoms in the Windows of Gothic Churches on the European Mainland*. Cologne: Kölner Architekturstudien, 2004.

Campbell, James. *Brick: A World History*. London: Thames and Hudson, 2016.

Careri, Giovanni Francesco Gemelli. *Giro del mondo del dottor D. Gio. Francesco Gemelli Careri: Parte terza contente le cose più ragguardevoli vedute nell'Indostan*. Naples: Roselli, 1708.

Carpzov, Benedikt. *Practica nova Saxonica rerum criminalium*. Wittenberg: Heirs of Schurer, 1635.

Carson, John. "The Eighteenth Century, 1770–75." In Klein and Lloyd, *History of Glass*, 117–44.

Cartwright, Lisa. *Screening the Body: Tracing Medicine's Visual Culture*. Minneapolis: University of Minnesota Press, 1995.

Cavallo, Sandra, and Tessa Storey. *Healthy Living in Renaissance Italy*. Oxford: Oxford University Press, 2013.

Caviness, Madeline H. "Biblical Stories in Windows: Were They Bibles for the Poor?" In *The Bible in the Middle Ages: Its Influence on Literature and Art*, edited by Bernard S. Levy, 102–47. Binghamton, NY: Medieval and Renaissance Texts and Studies, 1992.

————. *Stained Glass Windows*. Turnhout: Brepols, 1996.

Çelebi, Evlyiâ. *Im Reiche des Goldenen Apfels: Des türkischen Weltenbummlers Evlyiâ Çelebi denkwürdige Reise in das Giaurenland und in die Stadt und Festung Wien anno 1665*. Edited and translated by Richard F. Kreutel, Erich Prokosch, and Karl Teply. Graz: Styria, 1987.

————. *An Ottoman Traveller: Selections from the Book of Travels of Evliya Çelebi*. Edited and translated by Robert Dankoff and Sooyong Kim. London: Eland, 2010.

Chamberlayne, Edward. *Angliae notitia; or, the Present State of England*. London: T. N., 1669.

Chambers, William. *A Treatise on the Decorative Part of Civil Architecture*. 2 vols. London: Priestley and Weale, 1825.

Chambon, Raymond. "The Evolution of the Processes Used for the Hand-Fashioning of Window Glass from the Tenth Century to the Present." In *Advances in Glass Technology: History Papers and Discussions of the Technical Papers of the VI International Congress on Glass*, edited by Frederick R. Matson and Guy E. Rindone, 2:165–78. New York: Plenum Press, 1963.

Chaucer, Geoffrey. *The Riverside Chaucer*. Edited by Larry Dean Benson. 3rd ed. Oxford: Oxford University Press, 1987.

Chrétien de Troyes. *The Complete Romances*. Translated by David Staines. Bloomington: Indiana University Press, 1990.

Christensen, Lars Thøger, and Joep Cornelissen. "Organizational Transparency as Myth and Metaphor." *European Journal of Social Theory* 18 (2015): 132–49.

Cieraad, Irene. "Dutch Windows: Female Virtue and Female Vice." In *At Home: An Anthropology of Domestic Space*, edited by Irene Cieraad, 31–52. Syracuse: Syracuse University Press, 1999.

Codex epistolarum Tegernseensium. Edited by Karl Strecker. Vol. 3 of *Monumenta Germaniae Historica: Epistolae Selectae*. Berlin: Weidmannsche Buchhandlung, 1925.

Cohen, Jean-Louis. *Le Corbusier, 1887–1965: The Lyricism of Architecture in the Machine Age*. Taschen: Cologne, 2006.

————. *Mies van der Rohe*. London: Spon, 1996.

Coke, Edward. *Reports of Sir Edward Coke*. Edited by John H. Thomas and John F. Fraser. 6 vols. London: Butterworth, 1826.

Collomp, Alain. "Families: Habitations and Cohabitations." In Ariès and Duby, *History of Private Life*, 3:493–29.

Colomina, Beatriz. *Domesticity at War*. Cambridge, MA: MIT Press, 2007.

————. *Privacy and Publicity: Modern Architecture as Mass Media*. Cambridge, MA: MIT Press, 1996.

————. *X-Ray Architecture*. Zurich: Müller, 2019.

Columella. *On Agriculture*. Vol. 3, books 10–12. Translated by E. S. Forster and Edward H. Heffner. Cambridge, MA: Harvard University Press, 1955.

Contamine, Philippe. "Peasant Hearth to Papal Palace: The Fourteenth and Fifteenth Centuries." In Ariès and Duby, *History of Private Life*, 2:425–506.

Coolman, Boyd Taylor, and Dale M. Coulter, eds. *Trinity and Creation: A Selection of Works of Hugh, Richard and Adam of St Victor*. Turnhout: Brepols, 2010.

Corbin, Alain. *The Foul and the Fragrant: Odor and the French Social Imagination*. Translated by Aubier Montaigne. New York: Berg, 1986.

Corrard, Joseph. *Le célibat et l'impôt sur les célibataires: L'impôt des portes et fenêtres, critique humoristique*. Le Mans: Imprimerie de Monnoyer, 1907.

Corti, Gino. "L'industria del vetro di Murano alla fine del secolo XVI in una relazione al Granduca di Toscana." *Studi veneziani* 13 (1971): 649–54.

Cottin, François. "La fenêtre et le verre à Lyon aux XVIIe et XVIIIe siècles." In *Mélanges de travaux offerts à maître Jean Tricou*, 111–37. Lyon: Audin, 1972.

Cramp, Rosemary. "Window Glass from the British Isles, 7th to 10th Century." In Dell'Acqua and Silva, *Il colore nel medioevo*, 67–85.

Crossley, David. "An Outline of the Manufacture of Broad Glass in England, c. 1300–1900." In Lagabrielle and Philippe, *Verre et fenêtre*, 193–97.

Crowley, John E. *The Invention of Comfort: Sensibilities and Design in Early Modern Britain and Early America*. Baltimore: Johns Hopkins University Press, 2001.

Crowley, Patrick R. "Crystalline Aesthetics and the Classical Concept of the Medium." *West 86th* 23 (2016): 220–51.

Currie, Elizabeth. *Inside the Renaissance House*. London: Victoria and Albert Museum, 2006.

Curtis, Emily Byrne. *Glass Exchange between Europe and China, 1550–1800: Diplomatic, Mercantile and Technological Interaction*. Ashgate: Farnham, 2009.

Curtis, William J. R. *Modern Architecture since 1900*. 3rd rev. ed. London: Phaidon, 1996.

D'Aulnoy, Marie-Catherine. *Relation du voyage d'Espagne*. 3 vols. Paris: Barbin, 1691.

da Vinci, Leonardo. *Treatise on Painting: Codex Urbinas Latinus 1270*. Edited and translated by A. Philip McMahon. 2 vols. Princeton, NJ: Princeton University Press, 1956.

Danby, Miles. "Privacy as a Culturally Related Factor in Built Form." In *Companion to Contemporary Architectural Thought*, edited by Ben Farmer and Hentie Louw, 137–42. London: Routledge, 1993.

Danforth, R. E. "Window Glass as a Factor in Human Evolution" *Scientific Monthly* 8 (1919): 537–41.

Das Lalebuch: Wunderseltszame/abentheuerliche/unerhörte /und bisher unbeschriebene Geschichten und Thaten der Lalen zu Lalenburg. [Strasbourg], 1597. Reprint, Göppingen: Kümmerle, 1982.

Davey, Peter. "The Window in Arts and Crafts and Art Nouveau." In Lampugnani, *Architecture of the Window*, 44–57.

Davis, Natalie Zemon. "The Sacred and the Body Social in Sixteenth-Century Lyon." *Past and Present* 90 (1981): 40–70.

De Certeau, Michel. *The Practice of Everyday Life*. Translated by Steven Rendall. Berkeley: University of California Press, 1984.

Deichmann, Friedrich Wilhelm. "Entstehung der christlichen Basilika und Entstehung des Kirchengebäudes: Zum Verhältnis von Zweck und Form in der frühchristlichen Architektur." In *Rom, Ravenna, Konstantinopel, Naher Osten: Gesammelte Studien zur spätantiken Kunst und Geschichte*, 35–46. Wiesbaden: Steiner, 1982.

Dell'Acqua, Francesca. "The Christ from San Vincenzo al Volturno: Another Instance of 'Christ's Dazzling Face.'" In *Les panneaux de vitrail isolés*, edited by Valérie Sauterel and Stefan Trümpler, 11–22. Bern: Peter Lang, 2010.

———. "Enhancing Luxury through Stained Glass, from Asia Minor to Italy." *Dumbarton Oaks Papers* 59 (2005): 193–211.

———. "Glass and Natural Light in the Shaping of Sacred Space in the Latin West and in the

Byzantine East." In *Hierotopy: Creation of Sacred Spaces in Byzantium and Medieval Russia*, edited by Alexei Lidov, 299–324. Moscow: Progress-Tradition, 2006.

———. *"Illuminando colorat": La vetrata tra l'età tardo imperiale e l'alto medioevo: Le fonti, l'archeologia*. Spoleto: Centro italiano di studi sull'alto medioevo, 2003.

———. "Le finestre invetriate nell'antichità romana." In Beretta and Di Pasquale, *Vitrum*, 109–20.

———. "Nature and Artifice: Transparent Streams of New Liquid." *Res* 53/54 (2008): 93–103.

———. "Plaster Transennae and the Shaping of Light in Byzantium." In *La mémoire des pierres: Mélanges d'archéologie, d'art et d'histoire en l'honneur de Christian Sapin*, edited by Sylvie Balcon-Berry, Brigitte Boissavit-Camus, and Pascale Chevalier, 337–47. Turnhout: Brepols, 2016.

Dell'Acqua, Francesca, and Romano Silva, eds. *Il colore nel medioevo: Arte, simbolo, tecnica*. Lucca: Istituto storico lucchese, 2001.

Delmedigo, Joseph Solomon. *Sepher mazref la-chochma*. Jerusalem, 1980.

Demangel, Robert. "Fenestrarum Imagines." *Bulletin de Correspondance Héllenique* 55 (1931): 117–63.

Demos, John. *A Little Commonwealth: Family Life in Plymouth Colony*. Oxford: Oxford University Press, 2000.

Dendy, D. R. *The Use of Lights in Christian Worship*. London: S. P. C. K, 1959.

Depaule, Jean-Charles. *A travers le mur*. Paris: Centre de Création Industrielle, 1985.

Deschamps, Paul, and Victor Mortet, eds. *Recueil de textes relatifs à l'histoire de l'architecture et à la condition des architectes en France au moyen âge*. 2 vols. Paris: Picard, 1911–29.

Dialogus inter Cluniacensem monachum et Cisterciensem. In *Thesaurus novus anecdotorum*, edited by Edmond Martène. 5:1569–1654. Paris: Delaulne, 1717.

The Dictionary of Architecture. Issued by the Architectural Publication Society. 8 vols. London: Richards, 1853–92.

Die gläserne Kette: Visionäre Architekturen aus dem Kreis um Bruno Taut, 1919–1920. Leverkusen: Museum Leverkusen, 1963.

Dikshit, Moreshwar G. *History of Indian Glass*. Bombay: University of Bombay Press, 1969.

Dillon, Maureen. *Artificial Sunshine: A Social History of Domestic Lighting*. London: National Trust, 2002.

Dirlmeier, Ulf. "Alltag, materielle Kultur, Lebensgewohnheiten im Spiegel spätmittelalterlicher und frühneuzeitlicher Abrechnungen." In *Mensch und Objekt im Mittelalter und in der Frühen Neuzeit: Leben, Alltag, Kultur*, edited by Gerhard Jaritz, 157–80. Vienna: Österreiche Akademie der Wissenschaften, 1990.

Dodsworth, Roger. "The Nineteenth Century." In Klein and Lloyd, *History of Glass*, 169–98.

Donne, John. *The Elegies, and the Songs and Sonnets*. Edited by Helen Gardner. Oxford: Clarendon Press, 1965.

———. *The Major Works*. Edited by John Carey. Oxford: Oxford University Press, 1990.

Dorigato, Attilia. *Murano: Island of Glass*. Translated by Jeremy Scott. San Giovanni Lupatoto: Arsenale, 2003.

Dörk, Uwe. "Der verwilderte Raum: Zum Strukturwandel von Öffentlichkeit in der frühneuzeitlichen Stadt am Beispiel Berns." In *Zwischen Gotteshaus und Taverne: Öffentliche*

Räume in Spätmittelalter und Früher Neuzeit, edited by Susanne Rau and Gerd Schwerhoff, 119–54. Cologne: Böhlau, 2004.

Dowell, Stephen. *A History of Taxation and Taxes in England: From the Earliest Times to the Present Day*. 4 vols. London: Longmans and Green, 1884.

Dowsing, William. *The Journal of William Dowsing: Iconoclasm in East Anglia during the English Civil War*. Edited by Trevor Cooper. Woodbridge: Boydell Press, 2001.

Drerup, Heinrich. "Bildraum und Realraum in der römischen Architektur." *Mitteilungen des Deutschen Archäologischen Instituts: Römische Abteilung* 66 (1959): 147–74.

Duffy, Eamon. *The Stripping of the Altars: Traditional Religion in England, 1400–1580*. New Haven: Yale University Press, 2005.

Duller, Eduard. *Die malerischen und romantischen Donauländer*. Leipzig: Wigand, 1847.

Dumas, Geneviève. "La fenêtre dans les traités de peste de la région de Montpellier aux XIVe et XVe siècles." In *Par la fenestre: Études de littérature et de civilisation médiévales*, edited by Chantal Connochie-Bourgne, 157–65. Aix-en-Provence: Publications de l'université de Provence, 2003.

Dungworth, David. "Innovations in the 17th-Century Glass Industry: The Introduction of Kelp (Seaweed) Ash in Britain." In *Les innovations verrières et leur devenir*, edited by Sophie Labgabrielle and Corine Maitte, 119–23. Paris: Verre et histoire, 2013.

Dupré, Sven. "The Value of Glass and the Translation of Artisanal Knowledge in Early Modern Antwerp." In *Nederlands Kunsthistorisch Jaarboek* 64 (2014): 139–61.

Durand de Mende. *The Rationale Divinorum Officiorum of William Durand of Mende*. Edited and translated by Timothy M. Thibodeau. New York: Columbia University Press, 2007.

Dürer, Albrecht. *Dürers schriftlicher Nachlass*. Edited by Konrad von Lange and Franz Louis Fuhse. Halle: Niemeyer, 1893.

———. *The Painter's Manual: A Manual of Measurement of Lines, Areas, and Solids by Means of Compass and Ruler*. Translated by Walter L. Strauss. New York: Abaris, 1977.

Eckstein, Kerstin. "Inszenierung einer Utopie: Zur Selbstdarstellung des Bauhauses in den zwanziger Jahren." In *Bauhaus-Ideen, 1919–1994: Bibliografie und Beiträge zur Rezeption des Bauhausgedankens*, edited by Christina Biundo et al., 15–29. Berlin: Reimer, 1994.

Eddy, Walter H. "The Use of Ultra-Violet Light Transmitting Windows." *American Journal of Public Health and the Nation's Health* 18 (1928): 1470–79.

Edel, Edmund. *Das Glashaus: Ein Roman aus der Filmwelt*. Siegen: Böschen, 2013.

Eder, Gabriele. "Licht und Raumform in der spätantiken Hallenarchitektur." In Heilmeyer and Hoepfner, *Licht und Architektur*, 131–39.

Edgerton, Samuel Y. *The Mirror, the Window, and the Telescope: How Renaissance Linear Perspective Changed Our Vision of the Universe*. Ithaca, NY: Cornell University Press, 2009.

Eimer, Gerhard. "Einführung in die Thematik." In Badstübner et al., *Licht und Farbe*, 11–21.

Eisele, Petra. "Adolf H. beim Zeitungslesen unter dem Adventsbaum: Zur Rezeption der Gestaltungsprinzipien des Bauhauses im Nationalsozialismus." In *Bauhaus-Ideen, 1919–1994: Bibliografie und Beiträge zur Rezeption des Bauhausgedankens*, edited by Christina Biundo et al., 30–41. Berlin: Reimer, 1994.

Ekirch, Roger A. *At Day's Close: Night in Times Past*. New York: Norton, 2006.

Elkins, James. *The Poetics of Perspective*. Ithaca, NY: Cornell University Press, 1994.

Ely, Ronald S. *Crystal Palaces—Visions of Splendor: An Anthology*. Leicester: Sceptre Print, 2004.

Encyclopédie méthodique par ordre des matières. Paris: Panckoucke, 1782–1832.

Enders, Siegfried. "Zur historischen Bauweise." In *Wohnen in Japan: Ästhetisches Vorbild oder soziales Dilemma?*, edited by Renate Herold, 31–58. Berlin: Erich Schmidt, 1987.

Engels, Friedrich. *The Condition of the Working Class in England in 1844*. Translated by Florence Kelley Wischnewetzky. In *Karl Marx/Friedrich Engels Gesamtausgabe* (MEGA), 30:369–555. Berlin: Akademie Verlag, 2011.

Engle, Anita. *Light, Lamps and Windows in Antiquity*. Jerusalem: Phoenix, 1987.

Erasmus of Rotterdam. *On the Method of Study*. Translated by Brian McGregor. In *Collected Works of Erasmus*, 24:661–691. Toronto: University of Toronto Press, 1978.

———. *Opus epistolarum*. Edited by P. S. Allen. 12 vols. Oxford: Clarendon Press, 1906–58. Translated by R. A. B. Mynors and D. F. S. Thomson as *The Correspondence of Erasmus* (Toronto: University of Toronto Press, 1974–).

Erffa, Hans Martin von. "Die Verwendung des Glasfensters im frühen deutschen Kirchenbau." PhD diss., Ludwig Maximilians University Munich, 1951.

Eriksdotter, Gunhild. "Did the Little Ice Age Affect Indoor Climate and Comfort? Re-Theorizing Climate History and Architecture from the Early Modern Period." *Journal for Early Modern Cultural Studies* 13 (2013): 24–42.

Esch, Arnold. *Die Lebenswelt des europäischen Mittelalters: Kleine Schicksale selbst erzählt in Schreiben an den Papst*. Munich: C. H. Beck, 2014.

Eskilson, Stephen. *The Age of Glass: A Cultural History in Modern and Contemporary Architecture*. London: Bloomsbury, 2018.

Etlin, Richard. *The Architecture of Death: The Transformation of the Cemetery in Eighteenth-Century Paris*. Cambridge, MA: MIT Press, 1984.

———. *Symbolic Space: French Enlightenment Architecture and Its Legacy*. Chicago: University of Chicago Press, 1994.

Fabri, Felix. *The Wanderings of Felix Fabri*. Translated by Aubrey Stewart. 2 vols. New York: AMS Press, 1971.

Fagan, Brian. *The Little Ice Age: How Climate Made History, 1300–1850*. New York: Basic Books, 2002.

Fajt, Jiří, Jan Royt Jan, and Gottfried Libor. *The Sacred Halls of Karlštejn Castle*. Prague: Central Bohemia Cultural Heritage Institute, 1998.

Falke, Jacob von. *Die Kunst im Hause: Geschichtliche und kritisch-ästhetische Studien über die Decoration und Ausstattung der Wohnung*. 5th rev. ed. Vienna: Gerold, 1883.

Farny, Dieter et al., eds. *Handwörterbuch der Versicherung*. Karlsruhe: VVW, 1988.

Farr, James R. *Hands of Honor: Artisans and Their World in Dijon, 1550–1650*. Ithaca, NY: Cornell University Press, 1988.

Farrell, James J. *One Nation under Goods: Malls and the Seduction of American Shopping*. Washington, DC: Smithsonian Books, 2003.

Fedor, Julie. *Russia and the Cult of State Security: The Chekist Tradition, from Lenin to Putin*. Routledge: New York, 2011.

Feldern Rolf, Mathilde. *Vaterländisches Lesebuch für Kinder des österreichischen Kaiserstaates*. Vienna: Mechitaristen Congregations-Buchhandlung, 1841.

Fenster, Mark. "Transparency in Search of a Theory." *European Journal of Social Theory* 18 (2015): 150–67.

Fest, Joachim. "Der Führerbunker." In *Deutsche Erinnerungsorte*, edited by Hagen Schulze and Etienne François, 1:122–37. Munich: C. H. Beck, 2009.

Feuerstein, Günther. *Open Space: Transparency, Freedom, Dematerialisation*. Stuttgart: Menges, 2013.

Fichtenau, Heinrich. *Living in the Tenth Century: Mentalities and Social Orders*. Translated by Patrick J. Geary. Chicago: University of Chicago Press, 1991.

Fiedler, Jeannine, and Peter Feierabend. *Bauhaus*. Cologne. Könemann, 1999.

Fielding, Henry. *The History of Tom Jones, a Foundling*. Ware: Wordsworth Editions, 1999.

Fierro, Annette. *The Glass State: The Technology of the Spectacle: Paris, 1981–1998*. Cambridge, MA: MIT Press, 2003.

Figeac, Michel, ed. *L'ancienne France au quotidien: La vie et les choses de la vie sous l'Ancien Régime*. Paris: Armand Colin, 2007.

Filarete. *Treatise on Architecture*. Edited and translated by John R. Spencer. 2 vols. New Haven: Yale University Press, 1965.

Filler, Martin. "Hanging Out with Hitler." *New York Review of Books* 62, no. 20 (2016): 36–40.

Fischart, Johann. *Aller Practick Großmutter*. [Strasbourg], 1593.

Fischer, Rudolf. *Licht und Transparenz: Der Fabrikbau und das Neue Bauen in den Architekturzeitschriften der Moderne*. Berlin: Mann, 2012.

Flamm, Stefanie. "Der Palast der Republik." In *Deutsche Erinnerungsorte*, edited by Hagen Schulze and Etienne François, 2:667–82. Munich: C. H. Beck, 2009.

Flanders, Judith. *The Making of Home: The 500-Year Story of How Our Houses Became Homes*. London: Atlantic Books, 2014.

Fleming, Juliet. *Graffiti and the Writing Arts of Early Modern England*. London: Reaktion Books, 2001.

Fleming, Stuart J. *Roman Glass: Reflections of Everyday Life*. Philadelphia: University of Pennsylvania Museum of Archaeology and Anthropology, 1997.

Flood, Finbarr Barry. "The Ottoman Windows in the Dome of the Rock and the Aqsa Mosque." In *Ottoman Jerusalem, the Living City, 1517–1917*, edited by Sylvia Auld and Robert Hillenbrand, 431–63. London: Altajir World of Islam Trust, 2000.

———. "Palaces of Crystal, Sanctuaries of Light: Windows, Jewels, and Glass in Medieval Islamic Architecture." PhD diss., University of Edinburgh, 1993.

———. "Stucco and Glass Window-Grilles from the East and West Palaces." In *Raqqa IV: Excavations of the Deutsches Archäologisches Institut at Raqqa, Syrian Arab Republic*. Forthcoming.

Flusser, Vilém. "Häuser bauen." In *Architekturwissen: Grundlagentexte aus den Kulturwissenschaften*, edited by Susannae Hauser, Christa Kamleithner, and Roland Meyer, 2:283–85. Bielefeld: Transcript, 2013.

Fontaine, Souen Deva, and Danièle Foy. "De pierre et de lumière: Le lapis specularis." In Foy, *De transparentes spéculations*, 159–63.

———. "Des fermetures de verre pour les oculi." In Foy, *De transparentes spéculations*, 33–36.

———. "La modernité, le confort et les procédés de fabrication des vitrages antiques." In Foy, *De transparentes spéculations*, 15–24.

Forssbæck, Jens, and Lars Oxelheim. "The Multifaceted Concept of Transparency." In Forssbæck and Oxelheim, *The Oxford Handbook of Economic and Institutional Transparency*, 3–30.

———, eds. *The Oxford Handbook of Economic and Institutional Transparency*. Oxford: Oxford University Press, 2015.

Forty, Adrian. *Concrete and Culture: A Material History*. London: Reaktion, 2016.

———. *Words and Buildings: A Vocabulary of Modern Architecture*. London: Thames and Hudson, 2004.

Foucault, Michel. *Discipline and Punish: The Birth of the Prison*. Translated by Alan Sheridan. New York: Pantheon, 1977.

———. "The Eye of Power." In *Power/Knowledge: Selected Interviews and Other Writings, 1972–1977*, edited by Colin Gordon, 146–65. Brighton: Harvest Press, 1980.

Foy, Danièle. "La suprématie du verre soufflé en cylindre: Panneaux et vitraux du Vᵉ au IXᵉ siècle." In Foy, *De transparentes spéculations*, 59–64.

———, ed. *De transparentes spéculations: Vitres de l'Antiquité et du Haut Moyen Âge (Occident-Orient)*. Bavay: Musée/site d'archéologie Bavay-Bagacum, 2005.

Foy, Danièle, and Souen Deva Fontaine. "Diversité et évolution du vitrage de l'antiquité et du haut moyen âge: Un état de la question." *Gallia* 65 (2008): 405–59.

Frampton, Kenneth. "Maison de Verre." In *Rereading Perspecta: The First Fifty Years of the Yale Architectural Journal*, edited by Robert A. M. Stern et al., 268–75. Cambridge, MA: MIT University Press, 2004.

———. "Pierre Chareau: An Eclectic Architect." In Gannon, *Light Construction Reader*, 375–86.

Franz, Heinrich Gerhard. "Neue Funde zur Geschichte des Glasfensters." *Forschungen und Fortschritte* 29 (1955): 306–12.

———. "Transennae als Fensterverschluß: Ihre Entwicklung von der frühchristlichen bis zur islamischen Zeit." *Istanbuler Mitteilungen* 8 (1958): 65–81.

Friedberg, Anne. *The Virtual Window: From Alberti to Microsoft*. Cambridge, MA: MIT Press, 2006.

Friedrichs, Christopher R. *The Early Modern City, 1450–1750*. London: Longman, 1995.

Frodl-Kraft, Eva. *Die Glasmalerei: Entwicklung, Technik, Eigenart*. Vienna: Schroll, 1970.

Frugoni, Chiara. *A Day in a Medieval City*. Translated by William McCuaig. Chicago: University of Chicago Press, 2005.

Fryer, John. *A New Account of East-India and Persia in Eight Letters*. London, 1698.

Fuchs, Aharon Ron, and Michael Meyer-Brodnitz. "The Emergence of the Central Hall House-Type in the Context of Nineteenth Century Palestine." In *Dwellings, Settlements, and Tradition: Cross-Cultural Perspectives*, edited by Jean-Paul Bourdier and Nezar Al-Sayyad, 403–24. Lanham, MD: University Press of America, 1989.

Fuchs, Günter. "Die Funktion der frühen römischen Marktbasilika." *Bonner Jahrbücher* 161 (1961): 38–46.

Fukuyama, Francis. "Why Transparency Can Be a Dirty Word." *Financial Times*, International Edition, August 9, 2015.

Fuller, Gillian. "Welcome to Windows 2.1: Motion Aesthetics at the Airport." In *Politics at the Airport*, edited by Mark B. Salter, 161–73. Minneapolis: University of Minnesota Press, 2008.

Fuller, Thomas. *Anglorum speculum: or The Worthies of England, in Church and State*. London, 1684.

Gage, John. "Gothic Glass: Two Aspects of a Dionysian Aesthetic." *Art History* 5 (1982): 36–58.

Gai, Sveva. "Vitres et vitraux du palais impérial de Charlemagne à Paderborn." In Foy, *De transparentes spéculations*, 83–85.

Gannon, Todd. "Introduction." In Gannon, *Light Construction Reader*, 17–21.

———, ed. *The Light Construction Reader*. New York: Monacelli Press, 2002.

Gaonkar, Dilip Parameshwar, and Robert J. McCarthy Jr., "Panopticism and Publicity: Bentham's Quest for Transparency." *Public Culture* 6 (1994): 547–75.

Garner, Philippe. "Glass between the Wars." In Klein and Lloyd, *History of Glass*, 221–42.

Garzoni, Tomaso. *La piazza universale di tutte le professioni del mondo*. Edited by Giovanni Battista Bronzini. Florence: Olschki, 1996.

———. *Piazza Universale: Das ist: Allgemeiner Schawplatz/Marckt und Zusammenkunfft aller Professionen/Künsten/Geschäfften/Händeln und Handtwercken*. Frankfurt am Main: Merians Erben, 1659.

Geotti, Anna. "From the Magic of Fused Glass to Intelligent Glass." In *Glass throughout Time: History and Technique of Glassmaking from the Ancient World to the Present*, edited by Rosa Barovier Mentasti et al., 245–64. Milan: Skira, 2003.

Gerber, Christoph. "Production de cives et de manchons dans le Jura central suisse au début du XVIIIe siècle: L'exemple de la verrerie de Court-Chaluet." In Lagabrielle and Philippe, *Verre et fenêtre*, 187–92.

Gerevini, Stefania. "*Christus crystallus*: Rock Crystal, Theology and Materiality in the Medieval West." In *Matter of Faith: An Interdisciplinary Study of Relics and Relic Veneration in the Medieval Period*, edited by James Robinson and Lloyd De Beer, 92–99. London: British Museum Press, 2014.

———. "'Sicut crystallus quando est obiecta soli': Rock Crystal, Transparency, and the Franciscan Order." *Mitteilungen des Kunsthistorischen Instituts in Florenz* 56 (2014): 255–83.

Gerlach, Christoph. "Die Anfänge von Glasverschlüssen." In *Fenster und Türen in historischen Wohn-und Wehrbauten*, edited by Barbara Schock-Werner and Klaus Bingenheimer, 94–103. Stuttgart: Theiss, 1995.

Gerner, Manfred, and Dieter Gärtner. *Historische Fenster: Entwicklung, Technik, Denkmalpflege*. Stuttgart: Deutsche Verlags-Anstalt, 1996.

Geroulanos, Stefanos. *Transparency in Postwar France: A Critical History of the Present*. Stanford: Stanford University Press, 2017.

Giedion, Sigfried. *Space, Time, and Architecture: The Growth of a New Tradition*. 5th rev. and enlarged ed. Cambridge, MA: Harvard University Press, 2008.

Giesicke, Barbara, and Mylène Ruoss. "In Honour of Friendship: Function, Meaning, and Iconography in Civic Stained-Glass Donations in Switzerland and Southern Germany." In Butts and Hendrix, *Painting on Light*, 43–55.

Gilboy, Elizabeth W. *Wages in Eighteenth-Century England*. Cambridge, MA: Harvard University Press, 1934.

Gilson, Etienne. *La philosophie de Saint Bonaventure*. Paris: Vrin, 1924.

Gino, Alex. "Changing Rooms." *Journal of Architectural Education* 56 (2003): 32–36.

Ginzberg, Louis. *Legends of the Jews*. 2 vols. Philadelphia: JPS, 2003.

Giordano da Pisa. *Prediche*. Edited by Domenico Moreni. 2 vols. Florence: Magheri, 1831.

Girouard, Mark. *Hardwick Hall*. London: National Trust, 1989.

———. *Robert Smythson and the Elizabethan Country House*. New Haven: Yale University Press, 1983.

Glantz, Andrew E. "A Tax on Light and Air: Impact of the Window Duty on Tax Administration and Architecture, 1696–1851." *Penn History Review* 15 (2008): 1–23.

Godfrey, Eleanor S. *The Development of English Glassmaking, 1560–1640*. Oxford: Clarendon Press, 1975.

Goer, Michael. "'Gelt ist also ein kostlich Werth': Monetäre Thematik, kommunikative Funktion und Gestaltungsmittel illustrierter Flugblätter im 30jährigen Krieg." PhD diss., University of Tübingen, 1981.

Goethe, Johann Wolfgang von. *The Auto-Biography of Goethe: Truth and Poetry: From My Own Life*. Translated by John Oxenford. Cambridge: Cambridge University Press, 2013.

———. *The Poems of Goethe*. Translated by William Gibson. London: Simpkin Marshall, 1883.

———. *Sämtliche Werke: Münchner Ausgabe*. 33 vols. Munich: Hanser, 1985–98.

Gorky, Maxim. *In America*. Honolulu: University of the Pacific Press, 2011.

Gottlieb, Carla. *The Window in Art: From the Window of God to the Vanity of Man: A Survey of Window Symbolism in Western Painting*. New York: Abaris, 1981.

Grabes, Herbert. *The Mutable Glass: Mirror-Imagery in Titles and Texts of the Middle Ages and the English Renaissance*. Translated by Gordon Collier. Cambridge: Cambridge University Press, 1982.

Gregory of Tours. *Glory of the Martyrs*. Translated by Raymond van Dam. Liverpool: Liverpool University Press, 1988.

Grisko, Michael. "Kapitalisierte Phantasie." In Edel, *Das Glashaus*, 273–307.

Grodecki, Louis. *Romanische Glasmalerei*. Translated by Liliane Châtelet-Lange. Fribourg: Office du Livre, 1977.

Groebner, Valentin. *Gefährliche Geschenke: Ritual, Politik und die Sprache der Korruption in der Eidgenossenschaft im späten Mittelalter und am Beginn der Neuzeit*. Constance: UVK, 2000.

Grose, David F. "Early Imperial Roman Cast Glass: The Translucent and Colourless Fine Wares." In *Roman Glass: Two Centuries of Art and Invention*, edited by Martine Newby and Kenneth Painter, 1–18. London: Society of Antiquaries of London, 1991.

———. "The Origins and Early History of Glass." In Klein and Lloyd, *History of Glass*, 9–38.

The Grove Encyclopedia of Medieval Art and Architecture. Edited by Colum P. Hourihane. 6 vols. Oxford: Oxford University Press, 2012.

Gryphius, Andreas. *Auserlesene Gedichte*. Edited by Wilhelm Müller. Leipzig: Brockhaus, 1822.

Guarinonius, Hippolytus. *Die Grewel der Verwüstung Menschlichen Geschlechts*. Ingolstadt: Angermayr, 1610.

Guarnieri, Chiara. "Il lapis specularis nel mondo romano: Lo stato dell'arte e prime linee di ricerca." In *Il vetro di pietra*, 233–39.

————, ed. *Il vetro di pietra: Il lapis specularis nel mondo romano dall'estrazione all'use*. Faenza: Carta Bianca, 2015.

Guénoun, Gabriel, and Jean-Claude Kalmanovich. *Glashäuser zum Wohnen: Anbauten, Veranden, Wintergärten, Gewächshäuser: Konstruktion, Sonnenenergienutzung, Bauausführung*. 2nd rev. ed. Wiesbaden: Bauverlag, 1985.

Guerrand, Roger-Henri. "Private Spaces." In Ariès and Duby, *History of Private Life*, 4: 359–449.

Guidini-Raybaud, Joëlle. *Pictor et veyrerius: Le vitrail en Provence occidentale, XIIe–XVIIe siècles*. Paris: Presses de l'université de Paris-Sorbonne, 2003.

Günter, Roland. *Wand, Fenster und Licht in der Trierer Palastaula und in spätantiken Bauten*. Herford: Beyer, 1968.

Gurlitt, Cornelius. *Im Bürgerhause: Plaudereien über Kunst, Kunstgewerbe und Wohnungs-Ausstattung*. Dresden: Gilbers'sche Königliche Hof-Verlagsbuchhandlung, 1886.

Haller, Annette, ed. *Das Protokollbuch der jüdischen Gemeinde Trier, 1784–1836*. Frankfurt am Main: Peter Lang, 1992.

Han, Byung-Chul. *Transparenzgesellschaft*. Berlin: Matthes und Seitz, 2013.

Hanssen, Beatrice, ed. *Walter Benjamin and The Arcades Project*. London: Continuum, 2006.

Harden, Donald B. "Domestic Window Glass: Roman, Saxon, and Medieval." In *Studies in Building History: Essays in Recognition of the Work of B. H. St. J. O'Neil*, edited by Edward M. Jope, 39–63. London: Odhams Press, 1961.

————. "Medieval Glass in the West." In *Eight International Congress on Glass, 1968*, 97–111. Sheffield: Society of Glass Technology, 1969.

Harou-Romain, Nicolas-Philippe. *Projet de pénitencier*. Caen: Lesaulnier, 1840.

Harris, Dianne, and D. Fairchild Ruggles, eds. "Landscape and Vision." In Harris and Ruggles, *Sites Unseen: Landscape and Vision*, 5–29. Pittsburgh: University of Pittsburgh Press, 2007.

————. *Sites Unseen: Landscape and Vision*. Pittsburgh: University of Pittsburgh Press, 2007.

Harrison, William. *The Description of England: The Classic Contemporary Account of Tudor Social Life*. Edited by Georges Edelen. Mineola: Dover Publications, 1994.

Hartshorne, Albert. *Old English Glasses: An Account of Glass Drinking Vessels in England, from Early Times to the End of the Eighteenth Century*. London: Arnold, 1897.

Hasler, Rold, and Uta Bergmann. "Schaffhausen und Zug: Zeitdokumente zur Entstehung von Einzelscheiben in Schaffhauser und Zuger Werkstätten." In *Les panneaux de vitrail isolés*, edited by Valérie Sauterel and Stefan Trümpler, 133–46. Bern: Peter Lang, 2010.

Hawkes, Dean. *Architecture and Climate: An Environmental History of British Architecture, 1600–2000*. New York: Routledge, 2012.

————. *The Environmental Tradition: Studies in the Architecture of Environment*. London: Spon, 1996.

Heberer, Michael. *Aegyptiaca Servitus: Das ist/Warhafte Beschreibung einer Dreyjährigen Dienstbarkeit/So zu Alexandrien in Egypten jhren Anfang und zu Constantinopel jhr Endschafft genommen*. Heidelberg: Gotthard Vögelin, 1610. Reprint, Graz: Akademische Druck-und Verlagsanstalt, 1967.

Heil, Elisabeth. *Fenster als Gestaltungsmittel an Palastfassaden der italienischen Früh-und Hochrenaissance*. Hildesheim: Olms, 1995.

Heilbron, John L. *The Sun in the Church: Cathedrals as Solar Observatories.* Cambridge, MA: Harvard University Press, 1999.

Heile, Irmgard. "Licht und Dach beim griechischen Tempel." In Heilmeyer and Hoepfner, *Licht und Architektur*, 27–34.

Heilmeyer, Wolf-Dieter. "Über das Licht im Pantheon." In Heilmeyer and Hoepfner, *Licht und Architektur*, 107–10.

Heilmeyer, Wolf-Dieter, and Wolfram Hoepfner. *Licht und Architektur.* Tübingen: Wasmuth, 1990.

Helbling, Bernhard. "Problemlöser für ein gutes Lebensgefühl: Interview with Bernhard Helbling." *Frankfurter Allgemeine Zeitung*, March 20, 2012, suppl. "Faszination Fenster."

Helten, Leonhard. *Mittelalterliches Maßwerk: Entstehung, Syntax, Topologie.* Berlin: Reimer, 2006.

Henderson, John. *The Renaissance Hospital: Healing the Body and Healing the Soul.* New Haven: Yale University Press, 2006.

Henderson, Julian. *Ancient Glass: An Interdisciplinary Exploration.* Cambridge: Cambridge University Press, 2013.

Henke-Bockschatz, Gerhard. *Glashüttenarbeiter in der Zeit der Frühindustrialisierung.* Hanover: Hahnsche Buchhandlung, 1993.

Herbig, Reinhard. *Das Fenster in der Architektur des Altertums: Baugeschichtliche Studien.* Athens: Hestia, 1929.

———. "Fenster an Tempeln und monumentalen Profanbauten." *Jahrbuch des Deutschen Archäologischen Instituts* 44 (1929): 224–62.

———. "Fensterstudien an antiken Wohnbauten in Italien." *Mitteilungen des deutschen archäologischen Instituts: Römische Abteilung* 44 (1929): 260–321.

Hermansen, Gustav. *Ostia: Aspects of Roman City Life.* Edmonton: University of Alberta Press, 1982.

Hérold, Michel. "Le verre des vitraux (XVe–XVIe siècles): Approche méthodologique." In Lagabrielle and Philippe, *Verre et fenêtre*, 69–79.

Herold, Renate. "Eigenheiten des Bauens und Wohnens—naturbedingt?" In *Wohnen in Japan: Ästhetisches Vorbild oder soziales Dilemma?*, edited by Renate Herold, 81–95. Berlin: Erich Schmidt, 1987.

Hess, Daniel. "Auf der Suche nach einer helvetischen Identität: Die Erfindung der 'Schweizerscheibe.'" In *Les panneaux de vitrail isolés*, edited by Valérie Sauterel and Stefan Trümpler, 205–20. Bern: Peter Lang, 2010.

Heyne, Moriz [sic]. *Das deutsche Wohnungswesen von ältesten geschichtlichen Zeiten bis zum 16. Jahrhundert.* Leipzig: Hirzel, 1899. Reprint, Meerbusch: Erb, 1985.

Hilberseimer, Ludwig. "Glasarchitektur." *Die Form* 4 (1929): 521–22.

Hildebrandt, Adolf Matthias, and Ludwig Biewer. *Handbuch der Heraldik.* 19th ed. Hamburg: Nikol Verlag, 2007.

Hills, Paul. *Venetian Colour: Marble, Mosaic, and Glass, 1250–1550.* New Haven: Yale University Press, 1999.

Hirsch, Volker. *Der Hof des Basler Bischofs Johannes von Venningen (1458–1478): Verwaltung und Kommunikation, Wirtschaftsführung und Konsum.* Ostfildern: Thorbecke, 2004.

Hitler, Adolf. *Die deutsche Kunst als stolzeste Verteidigung des deutschen Volkes.* Munich: Zentralverlag der NSDAP, 1934.

Hix, John. *The Glasshouse*. London: Phaidon, 1996.

Hlaváček, Ivan. "Zum Alltag des Rates der Prage Neustadt im Spiegel der Rechnungen vom Anfang des 15. Jahrhunderts." In *Symbole des Alltags, Alltag der Symbole*, edited by Gertrud Blaschitz et al., 309–22. Graz: Akademische Druck-und Verlagsanstalt, 1992.

Höcker, Christoph. *Metzler Lexikon antiker Architektur*. Stuttgart: Metzler, 2004.

Hodges, Richard. "A Fetishism for Commodities: Ninth-Century Glass-Making at San Vincenzo al Volturno." In *Archeologia e storia della produzione del vetro preindustriale*, edited by Marja Mendera, 67–90. Florence: Giglio, 1991.

Holm, Christiane. "Bürgerliche Wohnkultur im 19. Jahrhundert." In *Das Haus in der Geschichte Europas: Ein Handbuch*, edited by Joachim Eibach and Inken Schmidt-Voges, 233–53. Berlin: De Gruyter, 2015.

Holtsmark, Erling B. "The Bath of Claudius Etruscus." *Classical Journal* 68 (1973): 216–20.

Honroth, Margret. *Vom Luxusobjekt zum Gebrauchsgefäß: Vorrömische und römische Gläser*. Stuttgart: Landesmuseum Württemberg, 2007.

Hood, Christopher, and David Heald. *Transparency: The Key to Better Governance*. Oxford: Oxford University Press, 2006.

———. "Transparency in Historical Perspective." In Hood and Heald, *Transparency*, 3–23.

Horman, William. *Vulgaria*. London: Pynson, 1519.

Horn, Hans-Jürgen. "Respiciens per fenestras, prospiciens per cancellos: Zur Typologie des Fensters in der Antike." *Jahrbuch für Antike und Christentum* 10 (1967): 30–60.

Hornbein, Victor. "A Humane and Environmental Architecture." In *In the Cause of Architecture*, edited by Frederick Gutheim, 24–29. New York: Architectural Record, 1975.

Huber, Ursula. "JoKarl Huber and Hildegard Huber-Sasse: Leben für das Malen von innen." In *Das Künstlerdorf: Von Spitzweg bis Campendonk*, edited by Renata von Fraunberg, 166–83. Munich: Apex, 2013.

———. "Zum Glasfenster von JoKarl Huber 'Leben Jesu' in der Taufkapelle der Stadtpfarrkirche St. Peter und Paul in Weil der Stadt." Unpublished manuscript, 2007.

Hunt, Lynn. *Politics, Culture, and Class in the French Revolution*. Berkeley: University of Berkeley Press, 1984.

Hutter, Heribert. *Glasmalerei im Mittelalter*. Vienna: Rosenbaum, 1963.

Ingravallo, Vega, and Maria Stella Pisapia. "Trasparenze antiche dalle città Vesuviane: Frammenti di lapis specularis da Pompei e da Ercolano." In Guarnieri, *Il vetro di pietra*, 161–68.

Isenstadt, Sandy. "Four Views, Three of Them through Glass." In Harris and Ruggles, *Sites Unseen*, 213–40. Pittsburgh: University of Pittsburgh Press, 2007.

———. "The Rise and Fall of the Picture Window." In *Housing and Dwelling: Perspectives on Modern Domestic Architecture*, edited by Barbara Miller Lane, 298–306. New York: Routledge, 2007.

Isidore of Seville. *The Etymologies of Isidore of Seville*. Translated by Stephen A. Barney et al. Cambridge: Cambridge University Press, 2006.

Jacobs, Jane. *The Death and Life of Great American Cities*. New York: Vintage Books, 1961.

Jameson, Fredric. *Postmodernism, or, The Cultural Logic of Late Capitalism*. Durham, NC: Duke University Press, 1991.

Jannetta, Ann Bowman. *Epidemics and Mortality in Early Modern Japan*. Princeton, NJ: Princeton University Press, 1987.

Jansen, Stephan A., Eckhard Schröter, and Nico Stehr, eds. *Transparenz: Multidisziplinäre Durchsichten durch Phänomene und Theorien des Undurchsichtigen*. Wiesbaden: VS Verlag, 2010.

Jantzen, Hans. *Kunst der Gotik: Klassische Kathedralen Frankreichs: Chartres, Reims, Amiens*. Berlin: Reimer, 1987.

Jaritz, Gerhard. "Die Reiner Rechnungsbücher (1399–1477) als Quelle zur klösterlichen Sachkultur des Spätmittelalters." In *Die Funktion der schriftlichen Quelle in der Sachkulturforschung*, edited by Heinrich Appelt, 145–249. Vienna: Österreichische Akademie der Wissenschaften, 1976.

Jay, Martin. *Downcast Eyes: The Denigration of Vision in Twentieth-Century French Thought*. Berkeley: University of California Press, 1993.

Jean Paul. *Dr. Katzenbergers Badereise*. Stuttgart: Reclam, 1986.

Jordan, Borimir, and John Perlin. "Solar Energy Use and Litigation in Ancient Times." *Solar Law Reporter* 1 (1979): 583–94.

Joyce, James. *Ulysses*. Dublin: O'Brien Press, 2013.

Jütte, Daniel. *The Age of Secrecy: Jews, Christians, and the Economy of Secrets, 1400–1800*. Translated by Jeremiah Riemer. New Haven: Yale University Press, 2015.

———. "Living Stones: The House as Actor in Early Modern Europe." *Journal of Urban History* 42 (2016): 659–87.

———. *The Strait Gate: Thresholds and Power in Western History*. New Haven: Yale University Press, 2015.

———. "'They shall not keep their doors or windows open': Urban Space and the Dynamics of Conflict and Contact in Premodern Jewish-Christian Relations." *European History Quarterly* 46 (2016): 209–37.

———. "Window Gazes and World Views: A Chapter in the Cultural History of Vision." *Critical Inquiry* 42 (2016): 611–46.

Jütte, Robert. "Die Entdeckung des inneren Menschen, 1500–1800." In *Erfindung des Menschen: Schöpfungsträume und Körperbilder, 1500–2000*, edited by Richard van Dülmen, 240–58. Vienna: Böhlau, 1998.

Kafka, Franz. *The Man Who Disappeared (America)*. Translated by Ritchie Robertson. Oxford: Oxford University Press, 2012.

Kalas, Rayna. *Frame, Glass, Verse: The Technology of Poetic Invention in the English Renaissance*. Ithaca, NY: Cornell University Press, 2007.

Kant, Immanuel. *Basic Writings of Immanuel Kant*. Edited by Allan W. Wood. New York: Random House, 2001.

Kantorowicz, Ernst H. "Oriens Augusti. Lever du Roi." *Dumbarton Oaks Papers* 17 (1963): 117–77.

Karrasch, Alexander. *Die "Nationale Bautradition" denken: Architekturideologie und Sozialistischer Realismus in der DDR der Fünfziger Jahre*. Berlin: Mann, 2015.

Keil, Inge. *Augustanus Opticus: Johann Wiesel (1583–1662) und 200 Jahre optisches Handwerk in Augsburg*. Berlin: Akademie Verlag, 2000.

Kemp, Wolfgang. *Sermo Corporeus: Die Erzählung der mittelalterlichen Glasfenster*. Munich: Schirmer-Mosel, 1987.

Kempe, Alfred John, ed. *The Loseley Manuscripts*. London: Murray, 1836.

Kenny, Nicolas. "City Glow: Streetlights, Emotions, and Nocturnal Life, 1880s–1910s." *Journal of Urban History* 43 (2017): 91–114.

Kenzari, Bechir, and Yasser Elsheshtawy. "The Ambiguous Veil: On Transparency, the Mashrabiy'ya, and Architecture." *Journal of Architectural Education* 56 (2003): 17–25.

Kepes, Gyorgy. *Language of Vision*. Mineola, NY: Dover, 1995.

Kessler, Cordula M., Sophie Wolf, and Stefan Trümpler. "Leuchtende Fenster: Glas als Werkstoff und seine Herstellung." In *Die Zeit Karls des Grossen in der Schweiz*, edited by Markus Riek, Jürg Goll, and Georges Descoeudres, 224–27. Sulgen: Benteli Verlag, 2013.

Kessler, Herbert L. "'They preach not by speaking out loud but by signifying': Vitreous Arts as Typology." *Gesta* 51 (2012): 55–70.

Kiel, Yishai. "Gazing through Transparent Objects in Pahlavi and Rabbinic Literature: A Comparative Analysis." *Bulletin of the Asia Institute* 24 (2014): 25–36.

Kiem, Karl. "Fenster weit und breit." *Daidalos* 33 (1989): 88–93.

Kirchberger, Stefan. "Beiträge der Archäologie Süd-und Südwestdeutschlands zu Tür- und Fensterverschlüssen." In *Fenster und Türen in historischen Wohn- und Wehrbauten*, edited by Barbara Schock-Werner and Klaus Bingenheimer, 79–87. Stuttgart: Theiss, 1995.

Kirkpatrick, Ivone. *The Inner Circle*. London: Macmillan, 1959.

Kitschelt, Lothar. *Die frühchristliche Basilika als Darstellung des himmlischen Jerusalem*. Munich: Neuer Filser-Verlag, 1938.

Klapisch-Zuber, Christiane. *La maison et le nom: Stratégies et rituels dans l'Italie de la Renaissance*. Paris: Éditions de l'École des hautes études en sciences sociales, 1990.

Klein, Dan, and Ward Lloyd, eds. *The History of Glass*. London: Orbis, 1984.

Kleinmanns, Joachim. "Fensterglas—Glasfenster: Die Entwicklung im norddeutschen Profanbau bis 1800." *Jahrbuch für Hausforschung* 50 (2004): 161–71.

Klinkott, Manfred. "Fenstergeschichte im Hausbau." In Uhlig, Kohler, and Schneider, *Fenster* 34–47.

Kluge, Friedrich. *Etymologisches Wörterbuch der deutschen Sprache*. Berlin: De Gruyter, 1967.

Kluge-Pinsker, Antje. "Wohnen im hohen Mittelalter (10.–12. Jahrhundert, mit Ausblicken in das 13. Jahrhundert)." In *Hausen, Wohnen, Residieren (500–1800)*, vol. 2 of *Geschichte des Wohnens*, edited by Ulf Dirlmeier, 85–228. Stuttgart: Deutsche Verlags-Anstalt, 1998.

Knapp, Ronald G. "China's Houses, Homes, and Families." In *House, Home, Family: Living and Being Chinese*, edited by Ronald G. Knapp and Kai-Yin Lo, 1–9. Honolulu: University of Hawaii Press, 2005.

———. "In Search of the Elusive Chinese House." In *House, Home, Family: Living and Being Chinese*, edited by Ronald G. Knapp and Kai-Yin Lo, 37–71. Honolulu: University of Hawaii Press, 2005.

Knoch, Habbo. "Schwellenräume und Übergangsmenschen: Öffentliche Kommunikation in der modernen Großstadt, 1880–1930." In *Ortsgespräche: Raum und Kommunikation im 19. und 20. Jahrhundert*, edited by Alexander Geppert, Uffa Jensen, and Jörn Weinhold, 257–84. Bielefeld: Transcript, 2005.

Koepnick, Lutz. "The Aesthetics of the Interface." In *Window/Interface*, edited by Sabine Eckmann and Lutz Koepnick, 15–49. St. Louis: Mildred Lane/Kemper Art Museum, 2007.

—————. *Framing Attention: Windows on Modern German Culture.* Baltimore: Johns Hopkins University Press 2007.

Koerner, Joseph Leo. *The Reformation of the Image.* London: Reaktion Books, 2004.

Köhbach, Markus. "Die Beschreibung der Kathedralen von Iasi, Kaschau und Wien bei Evliyà Çelebi: Klischee und Wirklichkeit." *Südost-Forschungen* 38 (1979): 213–22.

Köhler, Jan Thomas. "Basilika und Thermenfenster: Die Verwendung des Lichts in der Architektur der Spätantike." In Heilmeyer and Hoepfner, *Licht und Architektur,* 123–30.

Kohlmaier, Georg, and Barna von Sartory. *Houses of Glass: A Nineteenth-Century Building Type.* Translated by John C. Harvey. Cambridge, MA: MIT Press, 1986.

Koolhaas, Rem. "Junkspace." In *Harvard Design School Guide to Shopping,* edited by Chuihua Judy Chung, Jeffrey Inaba, Rem Koolhaas, and Sze Tsung Leong, 408–21. Cologne: Taschen, 2001.

—————, ed. *Elements of Architecture.* 15 vols. Milan: Marsilio, 2014.

Korn, Arthur. *Glass in Modern Architecture.* Translated by N. N. London: Barrie and Rockliff, 1967.

Krafft, Hans Ulrich. *Reisen und Gefangenschaft Hans Ulrich Kraffts.* Edited by K. D. Hassler. Stuttgart: Litterarischer Verein, 1861.

Kramer, Jane. "Living with Berlin." *New Yorker,* July 5, 1999, 50–62.

Kreimeier, Klaus. *Die Ufa-Story: Geschichte eines Filmkonzern.* Munich: Hanser, 1992.

Kreusch, Felix. "Beobachtungen zu Gipsfenstern." *Architectura* 8 (1978): 39–48.

Krinsky, Carol Herselle. *Synagogues of Europe: Architecture, History, Meaning.* New York: Dover Publications, 1996.

Kristal, Marc. *Immaterial World: Transparency in Architecture.* New York: Monacelli Press, 2011.

Krünitz, Johann Georg, ed. *Oekonomische Encyklopädie.* 242 vols. Berlin: Pauli, 1773–1858.

Kuhlmann, Frédéric. *De l'impôt des portes et fenêtres: En ce qui concerne les établissements industriels.* Lille: Danel, 1843.

Kühnel, Harry. "Das Alltagsleben im Hause der spätmittelalterlichen Stadt." In *Haus und Familie in der spätmittelalterlichen Stadt,* edited by Alfred Haverkamp, 34–65. Cologne: Böhlau, 1984.

—————. "Die Sachkultur bürgerlicher und patrizischer Nürnberger Haushalte des Spätmittelalters und der frühen Neuzeit." In *Haushalt und Familie in Mittelalter und früher Neuzeit,* edited by Trude Ehlert, 15–31. Sigmaringen: Thorbecke, 1991.

Kurmann, Peter, "'Architektur in Architektur': Der gläserne Bauriß der Gotik." In Westermann-Angerhausen, *Himmelslicht,* 35–43.

Kurmann-Schwarz, Brigitte. "'Fenestre vitree [. . .] significant Sacram Scripturam.' Zur Medialität mittelalterlicher Glasmalerei des 12. und 13. Jahrhunderts." In *Glasmalerei im Kontext: Bildprogramme und Raumfunktionen,* edited by Rüdiger Becksmann, 61–73. Nuremberg: Germanisches Nationalmuseum, 2005.

La Roche, Sophie von. *Tagebuch einer Reise durch Holland und England.* Offenbach: Weiß und Brede, 1786.

La Roncière, Charles de. "Tuscan Notables on the Eve of the Renaissance." In Ariès and Duby, *History of Private Life,* 2:157–309.

Lacerenza, Giancarlo. "Simboli del mistero: Vetri e finestre nel giudaismo fra età romana e medioevo." In Dell'Acqua and Silva, *Il colore nel medioevo,* 183–94.

Lagabrielle, Sophie. "Avant-propos." In Lagabrielle and Philippe, *Verre et fenêtre*, v–vii.

———. "La timide introduction du vitrage dans les demeures médiévales: L'exemple du Midi de la France." In "La maison au Moyen Âge dans le Midi de la France." Special issue, *Bulletin de la Société Archéologique du Midi de la France* (2002): 129–44.

———. "Les fenêtres des rois et des princes, XIVe–XIVe siècles." In Lagabrielle and Philippe, *Verre et fenêtre*, 97–118.

———, ed. *Le verre: Un Moyen Âge inventif*. Paris: Éditions de la Réunion des musées nationaux, 2017.

Lagabrielle, Sophie, and Michel Philippe, eds. *Verre et fenêtre de'l Antiquité au XVIIIe siècle: Actes du premier colloque international de l'association Verre et Histoire*. Paris: Verre et histoire, 2009.

Lampugnani, Vittorio Magnago, ed. *The Architecture of the Window*. Tokio: YKK Architectural Products, 1995.

Landsberg, Max. "Die Kulturmission des Glases: Ein vergessenes Stück Geschichte." *Deutsche Bauzeitung* 8 (1929): 89–94.

Landucci, Luca. *Diario fiorentino dal 1450 al 1516*. Florence: Sansoni, 1883. Reprint, Florence: Studio Biblos, 1969.

Lane, Barbara Miller. *Architektur und Politik in Deutschland, 1918–1945*. Translated by Monika and Klaus-Dieter Weiß. Braunschweig: Vieweg, 1986.

———. *Houses for a New World: Builders and Buyers in American Suburbs, 1945–1965*. Princeton, NJ: Princeton University Press, 2015.

Lane, Frederic C. *Venice: A Maritime Republic*. Baltimore: Johns Hopkins University Press, 1973.

Langlois, Jean-Yves, and Jacques Le Maho, "Les origines du vitrail (Ve–XIIe siècle)." In Lagabrielle, *Le verre*, 32–37.

Lardin, Philippe. "Verre et verriers dans la construction normande à la fin du Moyen Âge." In Lagabrielle and Philippe, *Verre et fenêtre*, 87–96.

Latour, Bruno. "The Moral Dilemmas of a Seat Belt." Translated by Lydia Davis. Available at https://courses.ischool.berkeley.edu/i290-tpl/s11/w/images/6/69/The_Moral_Dilemmas_of_a_Safety-belt.pdf. Accessed November 9, 2016.

Le Corbusier, *The City of To-morrow and Its Planning*. Translated by Frederick Etchells. New York: Dover, 1987.

———. "Glass, the Fundamental Material of Modern Architecture" (1935). Edited by Tim Benton and translated by Paul Stirton. *86th West* 19 (2002): 282–308.

———. *Oeuvre complète*. Edited by Willy Boesiger and Oscar Stonorov. 8 vols. Zurich: Les Éditions d'architecture, 1991.

———. *Precisions on the Present State of Architecture and City Planning*. Translated by Edith Schreiber Aujame. Cambridge, MA: MIT Press, 1991.

———. *Toward an Architecture*. Translated by John Goodman. London: Lincoln, 2008.

———. "Twentieth-Century Building and Twentieth-Century Living." In *Raumplan versus Plan Libre: Adolf Loos and Le Corbusier, 1919–1930*, edited by Max Risselada, 145–49. New York: Rizzoli, 1988.

———. *Urbanisme*. Paris: Crès, 1925. Reprint, Paris: Éditions Vincent, Fréal, 1966.

Le Dantec, Jean-Pierre. "La transparence et le secret: Questions d'architecture." *Traverses* 3 (1992): 92–99.

Le ménagier de Paris: Traité de morale et d'économie domestique composé vers 1393. Edited by Jérôme Pichon. 2 vols. Paris: Crapelet, 1846.

Le Roy Ladurie, Emmanuel. *Montaillou: The Promised Land of Error.* Translated by Barbara Bray. New York: Braziller, 1978.

Le Vieil, Pierre. *L'art de la peinture sur verre et de la vitrerie.* Paris: Delatour, 1774.

Lee, Lawrence, George Seddon, and Francis Stephens. *Stained Glass.* London: Mitchell Beazley Publishers, 1976.

Lefebvre, Henri. *The Production of Space.* Translated by Donald Nicholson-Smith. Oxford: Blackwell, 1991.

Legner, Anton. "Karolinische Edelsteinwände." In *Kaiser Karl IV.: Staatsmann und Mäzen,* edited by Ferdinand Seibt, 356–62. Munich: Prestel, 1978.

———. "Wände aus Edelstein und Gefäße aus Kristall." In *Die Parler und der Schöne Stil, 1350–1400,* edited by Anton Legner, 5:173–82. Cologne: Museen der Stadt Köln, 1978–80.

Lei, Sean Hsiang-lin. *Neither Donkey nor Horse: Medicine in the Struggle over China's Modernity.* Chicago: University of Chicago Press, 2014.

Leong, Sze Tsung, and Srdjan Jovanovich Weiss. "Air Conditioning." In *Harvard Design School Guide to Shopping,* edited by Chuihua Judy Chung, Jeffrey Inaba, Rem Koolhaas, and Sze Tsung Leong, 93–127. Cologne: Taschen, 2001.

Leung, Angela Ki Che. "The Evolution of the Idea of Chuanran Contagion in Imperial China." In *Health and Hygiene in Chinese East Asia: Policies and Publics in the Long Twentieth Century,* edited by Qizi Liang and Charlotte Furth, 25–50. Durham, NC: Duke University Press, 2010.

Lewis, Gertrud Jaron. *By Women, for Women, about Women: The Sister-Books of Fourteenth-Century Germany.* Toronto: Pontifical Institute of Mediaeval Studies, 1996.

Lichtenberg, Georg Christoph. *Briefwechsel.* Edited by Ulrich Joost and Albrecht Schöne. Munich: C. H. Beck, 1983–2004.

Lichtenberg, Heinrich. *Die Architekturdarstellungen in der mittelhochdeutschen Dichtung.* Soest: Jahn, 1931.

Liefkes, Reino, ed. *Glass.* London: V&A Publications, 1997.

Lietz, Sabine. *Das Fenster des Barock: Fenster und Fensterzubehör in der fürstlichen Profanarchitektur zwischen 1680 und 1780.* Munich: Deutscher Kunstverlag, 1982.

Lim, B. P., et al. *Environmental Factors in the Design of Building Fenestration.* London: Applied Science Publishers, 1979.

Lindemann, Andreas. *Der Erste Korintherbrief.* Tübingen: Mohr Siebeck, 2000.

Litz, Gudrun. *Die reformatorische Bilderfrage in den schwäbischen Reichsstädten.* Tübingen: Mohr Siebeck, 2007.

Liu, Lihong. "Vitreous Views: Materiality and Mediality of Glass in Qing China through a Transcultural Prism." *Getty Research Journal* 8 (2016): 17–38.

Livings, Frances. "Ephemere Kulträume: Raum und Material nationalsozialistischer Masseninszenierungen, 1933–1939." PhD diss., University of Hamburg, 2003.

Löhr, Christoph. "Griechische Häuser nach 348 v. Chr.: Hof, Fenster, Türen." In Heilmeyer and Hoepfner, *Licht und Architektur,* 10–19.

Loibl, Werner. "Zur Terminologie des historischen Flachglases." In *Glashütten im Gespräch: Berichte und Materialien vom 2. Internationalen Symposium zur archäologischen Erfor-*

schung mittelalterlicher und frühneuzeitlicher Glashütten Europas, ed. Peter Steppuhn, 103–7. Lübeck: Schmidt-Römhild, 2003.

Lours, Mathieu. "L'éclaircissement des églises parisiennes au XVIIIè siècle: Gestion et spiritualité." *Paris et Ile-de-France* 52 (2001): 139–98.

Louw, Hentie. "'The Advantage of a Clearer Light': The Sash-Window as a Harbinger of an Age of Progress and Enlightenment." In *Companion to Contemporary Architectural Thought*, edited by Ben Farmer and Hentie Louw, 300–308. London: Routledge, 1993.

———. "The Development of the Window." In *Windows: History, Repair, and Conservation*, edited by Michael Tutton, Elizabeth Hirst, and Jill Pearce, 7–96. Shaftesbury: Donhead, 2007.

———. "A Window on the Past: What the Study of Historic Fenestration Practices Can Tell Us about the Nature of Architecture." In *Practice and Science in Early Modern Italian Building: Towards an Epistemic History of Architecture*, edited by Hermann Schlimme, 43–50. Milan: Electa, 2006.

———. "Window-Glass Making in Britain c. 1660–c. 1860 and Its Architectural Impact." *Construction History* 7 (1991): 47–68.

Lovell, Mary S. *Bess of Hardwick: Empire Builder.* New York: Norton, 2006.

Löwenstein, Uta, ed. *Quellen zur Geschichte der Juden im Hessischen Staatsarchiv Marburg, 1267–1600.* 3 vols. Wiesbaden: Kommission für die Geschichte der Juden in Hessen, 1989.

Lucae, Richard. "Über die Macht des Raumes in der Baukunst." *Zeitschrift für Bauwesen* 19 (1869): 293–306.

Luchs, Alison. "Stained Glass above Renaissance Altars: Figural Windows in Italian Church Architecture from Brunelleschi to Bramante." *Zeitschrift für Kunstgeschichte* 48 (1985): 177–224.

Lundin, Matthew. *Paper Memory: A Sixteenth-Century Townsman Writes His World.* Cambridge, MA: Harvard University Press, 2012.

Luther, Martin. *Werke. Kritische Gesamtausgabe* [Weimar ed.]. Weimar: Böhlau, 1883–. Where applicable, English translations are taken from Jaroslav Pelikan and Helmut T. Lehmann, eds., *Luther's Works* (St. Louis: Concordia, 1955–86).

Macfarlane, Alan, and Gerry Martin. *Glass: A World History.* Chicago: University of Chicago Press, 2002.

Mach, Jordi. "De verre et de toiles: Les cloisons de fenêtres au château royal de Perpignan, XIVᵉ–XVᵉ siècles." In Foy, *De transparentes spéculations*, 164–68.

Mack, Rüdiger. "Franz Daniel Pastorius: Sein Einsatz für die Quäker." *Pietismus und Neuzeit* 15 (1989): 132–71.

Mączak, Antoni. *Travel in Early Modern Europe.* Cambridge: Polity, 1995.

Mavidal, J., and E. Laurent, eds. *Archives parlementaires de 1787 à 1860: Recueil complet des débats législatifs et politiques des chambres françaises.* 96 vols. Paris, 1867–1990.

Maissen, Thomas. "La persistance des patrons: La représentation de Zurich avant et après la Réforme." In *La ville à la Renaissance: Espaces—représentations—pouvoirs*, edited by Marie-Luce Demonet and Robert Sauzet, 59–80. Paris: Honoré Champion, 2008.

Malte-Brun, Conrad. *Précis de la géographie universelle ou Description de toutes les parties du monde sur un plan nouveau d'après les grandes divisions naturelles du globe.* 5th ed. Paris: Claye et Taillefer, 1845–47.

Malter, Rudolf, ed. *Immanuel Kant in Rede und Gespräch*. Hamburg: Meiner, 1990.

Mandrou, Robert. *Introduction to Modern France, 1500–1640: An Essay in Historical Psychology*. Translated by R. E. Hallmark. London: Arnold, 1975.

Mann, Thomas. *Die Briefe Thomas Manns: Regesten und Register*. Edited by Hans Bürgin and Hans-Otto Mayer. 5 vols. Frankfurt am Main: Fischer, 1976–87.

Marinelli, Sergio. "Trasparenze e riflessi di un dio minore." In Barovier Mentasti, *Trasparenze e riflessi*, 3–9.

Markus, Thomas A. *Buildings and Power: Freedom and Control in the Origin of Modern Building Types*. London: Routledge, 1993.

———. "The Function of Windows: A Reappraisal." *Building Science* 2 (1967): 97–121.

Martial. *Epigrams*. Edited and translated by D. R. Shackleton Bailey. 3 vols. Cambridge, MA: Harvard University Press, 1993.

Marx, Karl, and Friedrich Engels. *Gesamtausgabe* [MEGA]. Berlin: Dietz, 1972–.

Masheck, Joseph. "Alberti's 'Window': Art-Historiographic Notes on an Antimodernist Misprision." *Art Journal* 50 (1991): 34–41.

Mathesius, Johann. *Sarepta: Oder Bergpostill: Sampt der Jochimßthalischen kurtzen Chronicken*. Nuremberg: Newber, 1564. Reprint, Prague: Národní technické muzeum, 1975.

Mathieu, Jon. "Das offene Fenster: Überlegungen zu Gesundheit und Gesellschaft im 19. Jahrhundert." *Annalas da la Societad Retorumantscha* 106 (1993): 291–306.

Mayer-Himmelheber, Susanne. *Bischöfliche Kunstpolitik nach dem Tridentinum: Der Secunda-Roma-Anspruch Carlo Borromeos und die mailändischen Verordnungen zu Bau und Ausstattung von Kirchen*. Munich: Tuduv-Verlagsgesellschaft, 1984.

Mays, Jeffery C. "De Blasio's 'Ban' on Glass and Steel Skyscrapers Isn't a Ban at All." *New York Times*, April 25, 2019, https://www.nytimes.com/2019/04/25/nyregion/glass-skyscraper-ban-nyc.html.

McClung, William A. *The Country House in English Renaissance Poetry*. Berkeley: University of California Press, 1977.

McCray, W. Patrick. *Glassmaking in Renaissance Venice: The Fragile Craft*. Aldershot: Ashgate, 1999.

McGrath, Raymond, and A. C. Frost. *Glass in Architecture and Decoration*. London: Architectural Press, 1961.

McMahon, Darrin. "Illuminating the Enlightenment: Public Lighting Practices in the Siècle des Lumières." *Past and Present* 240 (2018): 119–59.

Meid, Michiko. "Einfluß westlicher Architektur und Ausstattung in Japan." In *Wohnen in Japan: Ästhetisches Vorbild oder soziales Dilemma?*, edited by Renate Herold, 59–79. Berlin: Erich Schmidt, 1987.

Meiners, Uwe. "Stufen des Wandels: Aspekte der Periodisierug der bürgerlichen und bäuerlichen Kultur im Münsterland, 1550–1800." In *Wandel der Alltagskultur seit dem Mittelalter*, edited by Günter Wiegelmann, 275–308. Münster: Coppenrath, 1987.

Meisner, Daniel, and Eberhard Kieser. *Thesaurus philopoliticus oder Politisches Schatzkästlein*. Frankfurt am Main, 1625–31. Reprint, Unterschneidheim: Uhl, 1992.

Menting, Annette. *Paul Baumgarten: Schaffen aus dem Charakter der Zeit*. Berlin: Mann, 1998.

Mercier, Louis-Sébastien. *Tableau de Paris*. Vol. 12. Amsterdam, 1788.

Mertins, Detlef. "The Enticing and the Threatening Face of Prehistory: Walter Benjamin and the Utopia of Glass." In Hanssen, *Walter Benjamin*, 225–39.

————. "Transparencies Yet to Come: Sigfried Giedion and the Prehistory of Architectural Modernity." PhD diss., Princeton University, 1996.

Meyer, Carol. "Crown Window Panes: Constantine or Justinian?" In *Essays in Ancient Civilization Presented to Helene J. Kantor*, edited by Albert Leonard, Jr., and Bruce Beyer Williams, 213–19. Chicago: Oriental Institute of the University of Chicago, 1989.

Meyer, Hermann. *Die schweizerische Sitte der Fenster- und Wappenschenkung vom XV. bis XVII. Jahrhundert*. Frauenfeld: J. Huber, 1884.

Michalsky, Tanja. "Raum visualisieren: Zur Genese des modernen Raumverständnisses in Medien der Frühen Neuzeit." In *Ortsgespräche: Raum und Kommunikation im 19. und 20. Jahrhundert*, edited by Alexander Geppert, Uffa Jensen, and Jörn Weinhold, 287–310. Bielefeld: Transcript, 2005.

Midgley, Graham. *University Life in Eighteenth-Century Oxford*. New Haven: Yale University Press, 1996.

Miège, Guy. *The New State of England under Their Majesties K. William and Q. Mary*. London: H. C., 1691.

Milner, Matthew. *The Senses and the English Reformation*. Farnham: Ashgate, 2011.

Milton, John. *Paradise Lost*. Edited by Alastair Fowler. New York: Routledge, 2013.

Mohamed, Jehan. "The Traditional Arts and Crafts of Turnery or Mashrabiya." Capstone for master's thesis, Rutgers University–Camden, 2015.

Moholy-Nagy, László. *Von Material zu Architektur*. Munich: Langen, 1929. Reprint, Mainz: Kupferberg, 1968.

Mohrmann, Ruth-Elisabeth. *Volksleben in Wilster im 16. und 17. Jahrhundert*. Neumünster: Wachholtz, 1977.

Montaigne, Michel de. *Travel Journal*. In *The Complete Works*, translated by Donald M. Frame, 1049–1270. New York: Knopf, 2003.

More, Thomas. *Utopia*. Edited by George M. Logan and Robert M. Adams. Cambridge: Cambridge University Press, 2003.

Morley-Fletcher, Hugo. "Seventeenth-Century Glass." In Klein and Lloyd, *History of Glass*, 93–116.

Möseneder, Karl. "Lapides vivi: Über die Kreuzkapelle der Burg Karlstein." *Wiener Jahrbuch für Kunstgeschichte* 34 (1981): 39–69.

Mulcahy, Linda. *Legal Architecture: Justice, Due Process, and the Place of Law*. Abingdon: Routledge, 2011.

Mumford, Lewis. *The City in History: Its Origins, Its Transformations, and Its Prospects*. Harmondsworth: Penguin, 1961.

Muthesius, Stefan. *The Poetic Home: Designing the Nineteenth-Century Domestic Interior*. London: Thames and Hudson, 2009.

Mutz, Alfred. "Römische Fenstergitter." *Jahrbuch der Schweizerischen Gesellschaft für Urgeschichte* 48 (1960–61): 107–12.

Nadi, Gaspare. *Diario bolognese*. Edited by Corrado Ricci and Bacchi della Lega. Bologna: Romagnoli dall'Aqua, 1886.

Naumann-Steckner. "Depictions of Glass in Roman Wall Paintings." In *Roman Glass: Two Centuries of Art and Invention*, edited by Martine Newby and Kenneth Painter, 86–98. London: Society of Antiquaries of London, 1991.

Nerdinger, Winfried. "Versuchung und Dilemma der Avantgarde im Spiegel der Architekturwettbewerbe, 1933–1935." In *Faschistische Architekturen: Planen und Bauen in Europa, 1930 bis 1945*, edited by Hartmut Frank, 65–87. Hamburg: Christians, 1985.

Neser, Anne-Marie. *Luthers Wohnhaus in Wittenberg: Denkmalpolitik im Spiegel der Quellen*. Leipzig: Europäische Verlagsanstalt, 2005.

Neuheuser, Hanns Peter. "Mundum consecrare: Die Kirchweihliturgie als Spiegel der mittelalterlichen Raumwahrnehmung und Weltaneignung." In *Virtuelle Räume: Raumwahrnehmung und Raumvorstellung im Mittelalter*, edited by Elisabeth Vavra, 259–79. Berlin: Akademie Verlag, 2005.

Neve, Richard. *The City and Country Purchaser's and Builder's Dictionary: Or, the Complete Builder's Guide*. 3rd ed. London, 1736.

Neveux, Hugues. "Recherches sur la construction et l'entretien des maisons à Cambrai de la fin du XIVe siècle au début du XVIIIe." In *Le bâtiment: Enquête d'histoire économique XIVe–XIXe siècles*, edited by Pierre Chaunu, 189–283. Paris: Mouton, 1971.

Ng, Morgan. "Toward a Cultural Ecology of Architectural Glass in Early Modern Northern Europe." *Art History* 40 (2017): 496–525.

Nielsen, David. *Bruno Taut's Design Inspiration for the Glashaus*. New York: Routledge, 2016.

Nightingale, Georg. "Glass and the Mycenean Palaces of the Aegean." In *The Prehistory and History of Glassmaking Technology*, edited by Patrick McCray, 205–26. Westerville, Ohio: American Ceramic Society, 1998.

Nishi, Kazuo, and Kazuo Hozumi. *What Is Japanese Architecture? A Survey of Traditional Japanese Architecture*. Translated by H. Mack Horton. Tokyo: Kodansha, 1996.

Nixon, John. "A Dissertation on the Antiquity of Glass in Windows. In a Letter to the Rev. Tho. Birch, D. D. Secret. R. S." *Philosophical Transactions* 50 (1758): 601–9.

Nolan, Mary. *The Transatlantic Century: Europe and America, 1890–2010*. Cambridge: Cambridge University Press, 2012.

Norberg-Schulz, Christian. *Meaning in Western Architecture*. London: Studio Vista, 1975.

North, Roger. *Of Building: Roger North's Writings on Architecture*. Edited by Howard Colvin and John Newman. Oxford: Clarendon Press, 1981.

Oates, Wallace E., and Robert M. Schwab. "The Window Tax: A Case Study in Excess Burden." *Journal of Economic Perspectives* 29 (2015): 163–80.

O'Connor, Mary Catharine. *The Art of Dying Well: The Development of the Ars moriendi*. New York: Columbia University Press, 1942.

Oliver, Paul. *Dwellings: The Vernacular House World Wide*. London: Phaidon, 2003.

Onasch, Konrad. *Lichthöhle und Sternenhaus: Licht und Materie im spätantik-christlichen und frühbyzantinischen Sakralbau*. Dresden: Verlag der Kunst, 1993.

Onians, John. "Sign and Symbol." In *Companion to Contemporary Architectural Thought*, edited by Ben Farmer and Hentie Louw, 510–17. London: Routledge, 1993.

Opaschowski, Horst W. *Pädagogik der freien Lebenszeit*. Opladen: Leske und Budrich, 1996.

Orlin, Lena Cowen. *Locating Privacy in Tudor London*. Oxford: Oxford University Press, 2007.

Orrinsmith, Lucy. *The Drawing-Room: Its Decoration and Furniture*. London: Macmillan, 1878.

Osbeck, Peter. *Reise nach Ostindien und China*. Rostock: Koppe, 1765.

Ostendorf, Friedrich. "Ueber den Verschluss des Profanfensters im Mittelalter." *Centralblatt der Bauverwaltung* 21, no. 29 (1901): 177–80.

Osterwold, Tilman. *Schaufenster: Die Kulturgeschichte eines Massenmediums*. Stuttgart: Württembergischer Kunstverein, 1974.

Ovid. *Amores*. Edited by Walter Marg and Richard Harder. Munich: Heimeran, 1968. Translated by Tom Bishop as *Amores* (New York: Routledge, 2003).

Palladio, Andrea. *The Four Books of Architecture*. Translated by Isaac Ware. London: Isaac Ware, 1738. Reprint, New York: Dover Publications, 1965.

Palliser, David M. *Tudor York*. Oxford: Oxford University Press, 1979.

Pavlovskis, Zoja. *Man in an Artificial Landscape: The Marvels of Civilization in Imperial Roman Literature*. Leiden: Brill, 1973.

Pepys, Samuel. *The Diary of Samuel Pepys*. Edited by Robert Latham and William Matthews. 11 vols. London: Bell, 1970–83.

Petronius. *Satyricon*. Translated by Sarah Ruden. Indianapolis: Hackett, 2000.

Petty, Margaret Maile. "Scopophobia/Scopophilia: Electric Light and the Anxiety of the Gaze in American Postwar Domestic Architecture." In *Atomic Dwelling: Anxiety, Domesticity, and Postwar Architecture*, edited by Robin Schuldenfrei, 45–63. New York: Routledge, 2012.

Pfeiffer, Bruce Brooks. "Frank Lloyd Wright: A Quest for Light and Space." In Lampugnani, *Architecture of the Window*, 78–87.

Philippe, Michel. *Naissance de la verrerie moderne, XIIe–XVIe siècles: Aspects économiques, techniques et humains*. Turnhout: Brepols, 1998.

Phillips, John. *The Reformation of Images: Destruction of Art in England, 1535–1660*. Berkeley: University of California Press, 1973.

Philo of Alexandria. *The Embassy to Gaius*. Edited and translated by F. H. Colson. Cambridge, MA: Harvard University, 1962.

Pile, Steve. *The Body and the City: Psychoanalysis, Space and Subjectivity*. London: Routledge, 1996.

Pius II. *The Commentaries of Pius II*. Translated by Florence Alden Gragg. 5 vols. Northampton, MA: Smith College, 1937–57.

Plat, Hugh. *The Jewell House of Art and Nature. Conteining divers rare and profitable inventions, together with sundry new experimentes in the Art of Husbandry, Distillation, and Moulding*. London: Short, 1594.

Platter, Felix. *Tagebuch (Lebensbeschreibung), 1536–1567*. Edited by Valentin Lötscher. Basel: Schwabe, 1976.

Pliny the Elder. *Natural History*. Edited and translated by H. Rackham et al. 10 vols. Cambridge, MA: Harvard University Press, 1938–63.

Pliny the Younger. *Letters and Panegyricus*. Translated by Betty Radice. 2 vols. Cambridge, MA: Harvard University Press, 1969.

Pöhlmann, Robert. *Die Übervölkerung der antiken Großstädte im Zusammenhange mit der Gesammtentwicklung städtischer Civilisation*. Leipzig: Hirzel, 1884.

Pommer, Richard, and Christian F. Otto. *Weissenhof 1927 and the Modern Movement in Architecture*. Chicago: University of Chicago Press, 1991.

Poretti, Sergio. *La Casa del Fascio di Como*. Rome: Carocci, 1998.

Pris, Claude. *Une grande entreprise française sous l'Ancien-Régime: La manufacture royale des glaces des Saint-Gobain, 1665–1830*. 2 vols. New York: Arno Press, 1981.

Publilius Syrus. "Sententiae." In *Minor Latin Poets (I)*, translated by J. Wight Duff and Arnold M. Duff, 14–111. Cambridge, MA: Harvard University Press, 1934.

Quast, Matthias. "Fensterverschlüsse im Sieneser Profanbau zwischen dem 14. und dem 16. Jahrhundert und ihre Rolle bei der Entwicklung der Fassadenarchitektur." *Burgen und Schlösser* 43 (2002): 141–51.

Quetglas, Josep. *Der gläserne Schrecken: Mies van der Rohes Pavillon in Barcelona.* Translated by Kirsten Brandt. Basel: Birkhäuser, 2001.

Raguin, Virginia Chieffo. *Stained Glass: Radiant Art.* Los Angeles: J. Paul Getty Museum, 2013.

Ramazzini, Bernardino. *Diseases of Workers: De morbis artificum.* Translated and edited by Wilmer Cave Wright. New York: Hafner, 1964.

Ramsey, Rachel. "The Literary History of the Sash Window." *Eighteenth Century Fiction* 22 (2009): 171–94.

Rangone, Tommaso. *Come il Serenissimo Doge di Vinegia . . . e li Venetiani possano viver sempre sani.* Venice: Bindoni, 1577.

Rapoport, Amos. *House Form and Culture.* Englewood Cliffs, NJ: Prentice-Hall, 1969.

Ratzka, Thomas. "Atrium und Licht." In Heilmeyer and Hoepfner, *Licht und Architektur,* 95–106.

Rauch, Ivo. "Anmerkungen zur Werkstattpraxis in der Glasmalerei der Hochgotik." In Westermann-Angerhausen, *Himmelslicht,* 103–6.

Rehm, Robin. *Das Bauhausgebäude in Dessau: Die ästhetischen Kategorien Zweck, Form, Inhalt.* Berlin: Mann, 2005.

Reichert, Folker. *Erfahrung der Welt: Reisen und Kulturbegegnung im späten Mittelalter.* Stuttgart: Kohlhammer, 2001.

Reichlin, Bruno. "The Pros and Cons of the Horizontal Window: The Perret-Le Corbusier Controversy." *Daidalos* 13 (1984): 65–78.

———. "Stories of Windows." In Lampugnani, *Architecture of the Window,* 104–19.

Reid, Anthony. "The Seventeenth-Century Crisis in Southeast Asia." *Modern Asian Studies* 24 (1990): 639–59.

Rice, Peter, and Hugh Dutton. *Structural Glass.* London: Spon, 1995.

Richards, John F. "The Seventeenth-Century Crisis in Southeast Asia." *Modern Asian Studies* 24 (1990): 625–38.

Richardson, R. C., and T. B. James, eds. *The Urban Experience: English, Scottish and Welsh Towns, 1450–1700.* Manchester: Manchester University Press, 1983.

Richer of Saint-Rémy. *Histories.* Edited and translated by Justin Lake. 2 vols. Cambridge, MA: Harvard University Press, 2011.

Riegl, Alois. *Spätrömische Kunstindustrie.* Vienna: Österreichische Staatsdruckerei, 1927. Reprint, Berlin: Mann, 2000.

Riley, Terence. "Light Construction." In Gannon, *Light Construction Reader,* 23–41.

Riley, Terence, and Barry Bergdoll, eds. *Mies in Berlin: Ludwig Mies van der Rohe: Die Berliner Jahre 1907–1938.* Munich: Prestel, 2001.

Riviale, Laurence. *Le vitrail en Normandie entre renaissance et réforme, 1517–1596.* Rennes: Presses universitaires de Rennes, 2007.

Roche, Daniel. *A History of Everyday Things: The Birth of Consumption in France, 1600–1800.* Translated by Brian Pearce. Cambridge: Cambridge University Press, 2000.

———. *The People of Paris: An Essay in Popular Culture in the 18th Century.* Translated by Marie Evans. Berkeley: University of California Press, 1987.

Rosen, Jeffrey. *Louis D. Brandeis: American Prophet*. New Haven: Yale University Press, 2016.

Rosewell, Roger. *Stained Glass*. Oxford: Shire Publications, 2012.

Rosseaux, Ulrich. "Sicherheit durch Licht? Zur Entwicklung von öffentlichen Straßenbeleuchtungen in frühneuzeitlichen Städten." In *Sicherheit in der Frühen Neuzeit: Norm, Praxis, Repräsentation*, edited by Christoph Kampmann and Ulrich Niggemann, 806–12. Cologne: Böhlau, 2013.

Roth, Avraham Naftali Zvi. "Sepher hilchot malveh ve-loveh." *Hebrew Union College Annual* 26 (1955): 39–74 [Hebrew section].

Roth, Joseph. "Das Schaufenster." In *Der Neue Tag: Unbekannte politische Arbeiten 1919 bis 1927: Wien, Berlin, Moskau*, 127–28. Cologne: Kiepenheuer und Witsch, 1970.

Rousseau, Jean-Jacques. *The Collected Writings of Rousseau*. Edited by Roger D. Masters and Christopher Kelly. 13 vols. Hanover, NH: University Press of New England, 1990–2010.

———. *Institutions chimiques*. Edited by Christophe van Staen. Paris: Champion, 2010.

Röver, Elgin. "Einleitung." In Heilmeyer and Hoepfner, *Licht und Architektur*, xi–xiv.

Rowe, Colin, and Robert Slutzky, *Transparency*. With a commentary by Bernhard Hoesli and an introduction by Werner Oechslin. Basel: Birkhäuser, 1997.

Rudofsky, Bernard. *Behind the Picture Window*. New York: Oxford University Press, 1955.

Ruggles, D. Fairchild. "Making Vision Manifest: Frame, Screen, and View in Islamic Culture." In Harris and Ruggles, *Sites Unseen: Landscape and Vision*, 131–56.

Rykwert, Joseph. "Windows and Architects." In Lampugnani, *Architecture of the Window*, 12–23.

Rzepka, Vincent. *Die Ordnung der Transparenz: Jeremy Bentham und die Genealogie einer demokratischen Norm*. Münster: Lit, 2013.

Sadar, John Stanislav. *Through the Healing Glass: Shaping the Modern Body through Glass Architecture, 1925–35*. New York: Routledge, 2016.

Saint-Simon, Louis de Rouvroy. *Mémoires complets et authentiques du Duc de Saint-Simon*. Edited by Adolphe Chéruel. 20 vols. Paris: Hachette, 1856–58.

Sand, Jordan. *House and Home in Modern Japan: Architecture, Domestic Space, and Bourgeois Culture, 1880–1930*. Cambridge, MA: Harvard University Press, 2003.

———. "Property in Two Fire Regimes: From Edo to Tokyo." In *Investing in the Early Modern Built Environment: Europeans, Asians, Settlers, and Indigenous Societies*, edited by Carole Shammas, 35–66. Leiden: Brill, 2012.

Sanuto, Marino. *Cronachetta*. Venice: Visentini, 1880.

Sarti, Raffaela. *Europe at Home: Family and Material Culture, 1500–1800*. Translated by Allan Cameron. New Haven: Yale University Press, 2002.

———. "Ländliche Hauslandschaften in Europa in einer Langzeitperspektive." In *Das Haus in der Geschichte Europas: Ein Handbuch*, edited by Joachim Eibach and Inken Schmidt-Voges, 175–94. Berlin: De Gruyter, 2015.

Sauer, Joseph. *Symbolik des Kirchengebäudes und seiner Ausstattung in der Auffassung des Mittelalters, mit Berücksichtigung von Honorius Augustodunensis, Sicardus und Durandus*. 2nd ed. Freiburg im Breisgau: Herder, 1924.

Scamozzi, Vincenzo. *L'idea della architettura universale*. Venice, 1615. Reprint, Ridgewood, NJ: Gregg Press, 1964.

Schedensack, Christine. *Nachbarn im Konflikt: Zur Entstehung und Beilegung von Rechtsstreitigkeiten um Haus und Hof im frühneuzeitlichen Münster*. Münster: Aschendorff, 2007.

Scheerbart, Paul. "Die Glasarchitektur." In *Gesammelte Werke*, 10:141–46.

———. *Gesammelte Werke*. Edited by Uli Kohnle. 10 vols. Bellheim: Phantasia, 1986–95.

———. "Glashäuser: Bruno Tauts Glaspalast auf der Werkbund-Ausstellung in Cöln." In *Gesammelte Werke*, 10:693–700.

———. *Glass Architecture*. Edited by Dennis Sharp and translated by James Palmes. New York: Praeger, 1972.

Scheffler, Felix. *Das spanische Stilleben des 17. Jahrhunderts: Theorie, Genese und Entfaltung einer neuen Bildgattung*. Frankfurt: Vervuert, 2000.

Scheibelreiter, Georg. *Heraldik*. Vienna: Oldenbourg, 2006.

Schiaparelli, Attilio. *La casa fiorentina e i suoi arredi nei secoli XIV e XV*. Florence: Sansoni, 1908.

Schindler, Friedrich. "Rundschau von Wien's Neubauten und Spaziergang durch dessen neue Straßen (kein Fantasiebild)" (1866). In *Wien wird Weltstadt: Die Ringstraße und ihre Zeit*, edited by Michaela Pfundner, 122–203. Vienna: Metroverlag, 2015.

Schivelbusch, Wolfgang. *Disenchanted Night: The Industrialisation of Light in the Nineteenth Century*. Translated by Angela Davis. Oxford: Berg, 1988.

Schleif, Corine, and Volker Schier. *Katerina's Windows: Donation and Devotion, Art and Music, as Heard and Seen through the Writings of a Birgittine Nun*. University Park: Pennsylvania University Press, 2009.

Schlink, Wilhelm. "The Gothic Cathedral as Heavenly Jerusalem: A Fiction in German Art History." In *The Real and Ideal Jerusalem in Jewish, Christian and Islamic Art: Studies in Honor of Bezalel Narkiss*, edited by Bianca Kühnel, 275–85. Jerusalem: Hebrew University, 1998.

Schmaltz, Karl. *Mater Ecclesiarum: Die Grabeskirche in Jerusalem: Studien zur Geschichte der kirchlichen Baukunst und Ikonographie in Antike und Mittelalter*. Strasbourg: Heitz, 1918.

Schmandt, Matthias. *Judei, cives et incole: Studien zur jüdischen Geschichte Kölns im Mittelalter*. Hanover: Hahn, 2002.

Schmid, Wolfgang. *Kölner Renaissancekultur im Spiegel der Aufzeichnungen des Hermann Weinsberg, 1518–1597*. Cologne: Kölnisches Stadtmuseum, 1991.

Schmidt, Fritz, and Ulf Dirlmeier. "Geschichte des Wohnens im Spätmittelalter." In *Hausen, Wohnen, Residieren (500–1800)*, vol. 2 of *Geschichte des Wohnens*, edited by Ulf Dirlmeier, 229–346. Stuttgart: Deutsche Verlags-Anstalt, 1998.

Schmitt, Elmar. "Moderne Sakralkunst in Weil der Stadt: Das Schaffen des Künstlerehepaars Prof. Jokarl Huber und Hildegard Huber-Sasse." In *St. Peter und Paul, Weil der Stadt: Geschichten und Bilder*, edited by Wolfgang Schütz, 60–70. Weil der Stadt: Katholische Kirchengemeinde, 1989.

Schmoll gen. Eisenwerth, J. A. "Fensterbilder: Motivketten in der europäischen Malerei." In *Beiträge zur Motivkunde des 19. Jahrhunderts*, edited by Ludwig Grote, 13–165. Munich: Prestel, 1970.

Schnapp, Jeffrey T. "Fragments of a Cultural History of Glass." *West 86th* 20 (2013): 173–94.

Schock-Werner, Barbara. "Bedeutung und Form mittelalterlicher Raumverschlüsse nach den Bildquellen." In *Fenster und Türen in historischen Wohn-und Wehrbauten*, edited by Barbara Schock-Werner and Klaus Bingenheimer, 122–30. Stuttgart: Theiss, 1995.

Scholz, Harmut. "Ornamentverglasungen der Hochgotik." In Westermann-Angerhausen, *Himmelslicht*, 51–62.

Schöne, Albrecht, and Arthur Henkel. *Emblemata: Handbuch zur Sinnbildkunst des XVI. und XVII. Jahrhunderts.* Stuttgart: Metzler, 1996.

Schöne, Wolfgang. *Über das Licht in der Malerei.* Berlin: Mann, 1994.

Schreiber, Heinrich. *Geschichte und Beschreibung des Münsters zu Freiburg im Breisgau.* Freiburg im Breisgau: Wagner, 1820.

Schudson, Michael. *The Rise of the Right to Know: Politics and the Culture of Transparency, 1945–1975.* Cambridge, MA: Harvard University Press, 2015.

Schuller, Manfred. "5000 Jahre Bauen mit Licht." In *Dom im Licht, Licht im Dom: Vom Umgang mit Licht in Sakralbauten in Geschichte und Gegenwart,* edited by Regensburger Domstiftung, 21–58. Regensburg: Schnell und Steiner, 2004.

Schultze-Naumburg, Paul. *Das Gesicht des deutschen Hauses.* Munich: Callwey, 1929.

Schulze, Franz, and Edward Windhorst. *Mies van der Rohe: A Critical Biography.* Chicago: University of Chicago Press, 2012.

Schulze, Konrad Werner. *Glas in der Architektur der Gegenwart.* Stuttgart: Zaugg, 1929.

Schumacher, Claudia. "Zur Rezeption der Glasmalerei im 19. Jahrhundert." In Westermann-Angerhausen, *Himmelslicht,* 111–16.

Schürmann, Thomas, and Egbert Uekermann. *Das verkleidete Fenster: Die Kulturgeschichte der Gardine 1800 bis 2000.* Cloppenburg: Niedersächsisches Freilichtmuseum, 1994.

Schwarz, Dietrich W. H. *Sachgüter und Lebensformen. Einführung in die materielle Kulturgeschichte des Mittelalters und der Neuzeit.* Berlin: Erich Schmidt Verlag, 1970.

Schwarz, Michael Viktor. "Kathedralen verstehen (St. Veit in Prag als räumlich organisiertes Medienensemble)." In *Virtuelle Räume: Raumwahrnehmung und Raumvorstellung im Mittelalter,* edited by Elisabeth Vavra, 47–68. Berlin: Akademie Verlag, 2005.

Schwarzenberg, Erkinger. "Color, Light and Transparency in the Greek World." In *Medieval Mosaics: Light, Color, Materials,* edited by Eve Borsook, Fiorella Gioffredi Superbi, and Giovanni Pagliarulo, 15–34. Milan: Silvana, 2000.

———. "Cristallo." In Beretta and Di Pasquale, *Vitrum,* 61–70.

Scott, M. H. Baillie. *Houses and Gardens.* London: Newnes, 1906.

Scoville, Warren. *Capitalism and French Glassmaking, 1640–1789.* Berkeley: University of California Press, 1950.

Screech, Timon. "Glass, Paintings on Glass, and Vision in Eighteenth-Century Japan." *Apollo* 147, no. 433 (March 1998): 28–32.

Scriptores historiae augustae. Translated by David Magie. 3 vols. London: Heinemann, 1921–32.

Sedlák, Jan. *The Tugendhat House.* Brno: Fotep, 2012.

Sedlmayer, Hans. *Das Licht in seinen künstlerischen Manifestationen.* Mittenwald: Mäander Kunstverlag, 1978.

Segesser, Anton Philipp, ed. *Amtliche Sammlung der ältern eidgenössischen Abschiede: Die eidgenössischen Abschiede aus dem Zeitraume von 1500 bis 1520.* Lucerne: Meyer, 1869.

Selbmann, Rolf. *Eine Kulturgeschichte des Fensters von der Antike bis zur Moderne.* Berlin: Reimer, 2010.

Selle, Gert. *Die eigenen vier Wände: Zur verborgenen Geschichte des Wohnens.* Frankfurt am Main: Campus, 1993.

Semper, Gottfried. *Style in the Technical and Tectonic Arts; Or, Practical Aesthetics.* Translated by Harry Francis Mallgrave and Michael Robinson. Los Angeles: Getty Publications, 2004.

Seneca. *Epistles*. Translated by Richard M. Gummere. 3 vols. Cambridge, MA: Harvard University Press, 1917–25.

Sennett, Richard. *The Conscience of the Eye: The Design and Social Life of Cities*. New York: Norton, 1990.

———. "Plate Glass." *The Raritan* 6 (1987): 1–15.

Serlio, Sebastiano. *On Architecture*. Translated and edited by Vaughan Hart and Peter Hicks. 2 vols. New Haven: Yale University Press, 1996–2001.

Sewall, Samuel. *The Diary of Samuel Sewall, 1674–1729*. Edited by M. Halsey Thomas. 2 vols. New York: Farrar, Straus and Giroux, 1973.

Shammas, Carole. "The Domestic Environment in Early Modern England and America." *Journal of Social History* 14 (1980): 3–24.

———. "The Early Modern Built Environment Globally: The State of the Field." In *Investing in the Early Modern Built Environment: Europeans, Asians, Settlers, and Indigenous Societies*, edited by Carole Shammas, 1–31. Leiden: Brill, 2012.

Shaw, Diane. "The Construction of the Private in Medieval London." *Journal of Medieval and Early Modern Studies* 26 (1996): 447–66.

Shelton, Barrie. *Learning from the Japanese City: West Meets East in Urban Design*. London: Spon, 1999.

Shovlin, John. *The Political Economy of Virtue: Luxury, Patriotism, and the Origins of the French Revolution*. Ithaca, NY: Cornell University Press, 2006.

Sidonius. *Poems and Letters*. Edited and translated by W. B. Anderson. 2 vols. Cambridge, MA: Harvard University Press, 1936–65.

Siedentopf, Adrian. "Adolf Hitler versucht den Menschensohn: Ein Beispiel des Widerstands in der Kunst: Das Glasfenster von JoKarl Huber in der Stadtpfarrkirche St. Peter und Paul in Weil der Stadt." Bachelor's thesis, Ludwig Maximilians University Munich, 2013.

Simson, Otto von. *The Gothic Cathedral: Origins of Gothic Architecture and the Medieval Concept of Order*. New York: Harper and Row, 1962.

Sitte, Camillo, *The Art of Building Cities: City Building According to Its Artistic Fundamentals*. Translated by Charles T. Stewart. New York: Reinhold, 1945.

Skrabei, Christine. "Fenster in griechischen Tempeln." In Heilmeyer and Hoepfner, *Licht und Architektur*, 35–42.

Smith, Adam. "The Wealth of Nations." In *The Essential Adam Smith*, edited by Robert L. Heilbroner and Laurence J. Malone, 149–320. New York: Norton, 1987.

Smith, Peter. *Houses of the Welsh Countryside: A Study in Historical Geography*. 2nd enlarged ed. London: Her Majesty's Stationery Office, 1988.

Soper, Kate. "Privileged Gazes and Ordinary Affections: Reflections on the Politics of Landscape and the Scope of the Nature Aesthetic." In *Deterritorialisation: Revisioning Landscape and Politics*, edited by Mark Dorrian and Gillian Rose, 338–48. London: Black Dog, 2003.

Speer, Albert. *Inside the Third Reich: Memoirs*. New York: Simon and Schuster, 1970.

Speer, Andreas. "Lux mirabilis et continua: Anmerkungen zum Verhältnis von mittelalterlicher Lichtspekulation und gotischer Glaskunst." In Westermann-Angerhausen, *Himmelslicht*, 89–94.

Sperl, Dina. "Glas und Licht in Architektur und Kunst." In Heilmeyer and Hoepfner, *Licht und Architektur*, 61–71.

Spigel, Lynn. "The Suburban Home Companion: Television and the Neighborhood Ideal in Postwar America." In *Sexuality and Space*, edited by Beatriz Colomina, 185–217. Princeton, NJ: Princeton Architectural Press, 1992.

Spinazzola, Vittorio. *Pompei alla luce degli scavi nuovi di Via dell'Abbondanza (anni 1910–1923)*. Rome: Libreria dello Stato, 1953.

Stambaugh, John E. *The Ancient Roman City*. Baltimore: Johns Hopkins University Press, 1988.

Stamp, Gavin. "Anti-Ugly Action: An Episode in the History of British Modernism." *AA Files* 70 (2015): 76–88.

Starobinski, Jean. *Jean-Jacques Rousseau: Transparency and Obstruction*. Translated by Arthur Goldhammer. Chicago: University of Chicago Press, 1988.

Statius. *Silvae*. Edited and translated by D. R. Shackleton Bailey. Cambridge, MA: Harvard University Press, 2003.

Stehr, Nico, and Cornelia Wallner. "Transparenz: Einleitung." In Jansen, Schröter, and Stehr, *Transparenz*, 9–19.

Steppuhn, Peter. "Der (un-)getrübte Blick nach draußen: Zur Entwicklungsgeschichte des Glasfensters, in Europa." In *Centre, Region, Periphery: Medieval Europe*, edited by Guido Helmig et al., 1:371–78. Hertingen: Wesselkamp, 2002.

Stern, E. Marianne. "Ancient Glass in a Philological Context." *Mnemosyne* 60 (2007): 341–406.

———. "Glass and Rock Crystal: A Multifaceted Relationship." *Journal of Roman Archaeology* 10 (1997): 192–206.

———. "I vetrai dell'antica Roma." In Beretta and Di Pasquale, *Vitrum*, 37–60.

———. *Roman, Byzantine, and Early Medieval Glass, 10 BCE–700 CE: Ernesto Wolf Collection*. Ostfildern-Ruit: Hatje Cantz, 2001.

———. "Roman Glassblowing in a Cultural Context." *American Journal of Archaeology* 103 (1999): 441–84.

Sternberger, Dolf. *Panorama of the Nineteenth Century*. Translated by Joachim Neugroschel. New York: Urizen Books, 1977.

Stratigakos, Despina. *Hitler at Home*. New Haven: Yale University Press, 2015.

Strobl, Sebastian. *Glastechnik des Mittelalters*. Stuttgart: Gentner, 1990.

Sturm, Patrick. *Leben mit dem Tod in den Reichsstädten Esslingen, Nördlingen und Schwäbisch Hall: Epidemien und deren Auswirkungen vom frühen 15. bis zum frühen 17. Jahrhundert*. Ostfildern: Thorbecke, 2014.

Suger of Saint-Denis. *Abt Suger von Saint-Denis: Ausgewählte Schriften: Ordinatio, De consecratione, De administratione*. Edited by Andreas Speer and Günther Binding. Darmstadt: Wissenschaftliche Buchgesellschaft, 2000.

Supplément à l'Encyclopédie ou Dictionnaire raisonné des sciences, des arts et des métiers. 4 vols. Amsterdam: Rey, 1776–77.

Symphosius. *The Aenigmata*. Edited by T. J. Leary. London: Bloomsbury, 2014.

Tanizaki, Jun'ichirō. *In Praise of Shadows*. Translated by Thomas J. Harper and Edward G. Seidensticker. London: Vintage, 1991.

Taylor, Brian Brace, and Bernard Bauchet. "The Maison de Verre." In *Pierre Chareau: Mod-*

ern Architecture and Design, edited by Esther da Costa Meyer, 173–89. New Haven: Yale University Press, 2016.

Taylor, Michael D. "The Iconography of the Façade Decoration of the Cathedral of Orvieto." PhD diss., Princeton University, 1969.

Tegethoff, Wolf. *Mies van der Rohe: The Villas and Country Houses*. Cambridge, MA: MIT Press, 1985.

Terragni, Attilio, Daniel Libeskind, and Paolo Rosselli, eds. *The Terragni Atlas: Built Architecture*. Milan: Skira, 2004.

Thébert, Yvon. "Private Life and Domestic Architecture in Roman Africa." In Ariès and Duby, *History of Private Life* 1:319–405.

Theis, Lioba. "Architektur und liturgische Ausstattung byzantinischer Kirchen." In *Byzanz, das Licht aus dem Osten: Kult und Alltag im Byzantinischen Reich vom 4. bis 15. Jahrhundert*, edited by Christoph Stiegemann, 19–28. Mainz: Zabern, 2001.

———. "Lampen, Leuchten, Licht." In *Byzanz, das Licht aus dem Osten: Kult und Alltag im Byzantinischen Reich vom 4. bis 15. Jahrhundert*, edited by Christoph Stiegemann, 53–64. Mainz: Zabern, 2001.

Theophilus. *The Various Arts: De diversis artibus*. Edited and translated by C. R. Dowell. Oxford: Clarendon Press, 1986.

Thesaurus proverbiorum medii aevi. 13 vols. Berlin: De Gruyter, 1995–2002.

Thies, Harmen. "Glasecken." *Daidalos* 33 (1989): 110–19.

Thietmar of Merseburg. *Thietmari Merseburgensis episcopi chronicon*. Edited by Robert Holtzmann. Berlin: Weidmann, 1935.

Thornton, Peter. *The Italian Renaissance Interior, 1400–1600*. London: Weidenfeld and Nicolson, 1991.

Thürlemann, Felix. *Das Haremsfenster: Zur fotografischen Eroberung Ägyptens im 19. Jahrhundert*. Munich: Fink, 2016.

Torriti, Piero. *The Cathedral of Orvieto: A Gem of Italian Gothic Architecture*. Florence: Bonechi, 2006.

Treeck, Peter van. "On the Artistic Technique of Glass Painting in the Age of Dürer and Holbein and Its Conservation Problems." In Butts and Hendrix, *Painting on Light*, 57–65.

Trélat, Emile. "La fenêtre étudiée comme source de lumière dans la maison." *Revue d'hygiène et de police sanitaire* 8 (1886): 647–56.

Trivellato, Francesca. "Murano Glass: Continuity and Transformation, 1400–1800." In *At the Centre of the Old World: Trade and Manufacturing in Venice and the Venetian Mainland, 1400–1800*, edited by Paola Lanaro, 143–84. Toronto: CRRS, 2006.

Tucher, Endres. *Baumeisterbuch der Stadt Nürnberg, 1464–1475*. Edited by Matthias Lexer. Stuttgart: Litterarischer Verein, 1862.

Turner, Thomas Hudson. *Some Account of Domestic Architecture in England*. Oxford: Parker, 1877.

Ueda, Atsushi. *The Inner Harmony of the Japanese House*. Tokyo: Kodansha, 1990.

Uhlig, Günther, Niklaus Kohler, and Lothar Schneider, eds. *Fenster: Architektur und Technologie im Dialog*. Braunschweig: Vieweg, 1994.

Uhlig, Günther, and Jan A. Wolff. "Vier Spots aus der Kulturgeschichte von Fenster und Tür." In Uhlig, Kohler, and Schneider, *Fenster*, 20–33.

Ulmer, Manfred, and Jörg Kurz. *Die Weißenhofsiedlung: Geschichte und Gegenwart*. Stuttgart: Hampp, 2009.

Unger, F. W. "Glasmalerei (historisch)." In *Allgemeine Encyclopädie der Wissenschaften und Künste*, edited by J. G. Ersch and J. G. Gruber, 69:39–72. Leipzig: Brockhaus, 1859.

Urry, John. "City Life and the Senses." In *A Companion to the City*, edited by Gary Bridge and Sophie Watson, 388–97. Oxford: Blackwell, 2000.

Valentin, Sonja. *Steine in Hitlers Fenster: Thomas Manns Radiosendungen "Deutsche Hörer!," 1940–1945*. Göttingen: Wallstein, 2015.

Van Ruyven-Zeman, Zsusanna. "Seventeenth-Century Window Donations by the City of Amsterdam for Parish Churches in Amsterdam." In *Glasmalerei im Kontext: Bildprogramme und Raumfunktionen*, edited by Rüdiger Becksmann, 257–71. Nuremberg: Germanisches Nationalmuseum, 2005.

Vanden Bemden, Yvette. "Les rondels, cousins mal aimés des vitraux?" *Vitrea: Revue du centre international du vitrail* 1 (1988): 22–23.

Vandenberg, Maritz. *Farnsworth House: Ludwig Mies van der Rohe*. London: Phaidon, 2003.

Vasari, Giorgio. *Vasari on Technique*. Edited by G. Baldwin Brown and translated by Louisa S. Maclehose. New York: Dover Publications, 1960.

Vattimo, Gianni. *The Transparent Society*. Translated by David Webb. Cambridge: Polity Press, 1992.

Veeckman, Johan, ed. *Majolica and Glass from Italy to Antwerp and Beyond: The Transfer of Technology in the 16th–Early 17th Century*. Antwerp: City of Antwerp, 2002.

Veeckman, Johan, and Claire Dumortier. "La production de verres à Anvers: Les données historiques." In Veeckman, *Majolica and Glass*, 69–78.

Vera, Hernan. "On Dutch Windows." *Qualitative Sociology* 12 (1989): 215–34.

Verdon, Jean. *Night in the Middle Ages*. Translated by George Holoch. Notre Dame, IN: University of Notre Dame Press, 2002.

Verità, Marco. "Influence of the Islamic Tradition on the Chemistry and Technology of Venetian Glass." In *Venice and the Islamic World, 828–1797*, ed. Stefano Carboni, 276–79. New Haven: Yale University Press, 2007.

———. "Venetian Innovations in Glassmaking and Their Influence on the European Glass History." In *Les innovations verrières et leur devenir*, edited by Sophie Lagabrielle and Corine Maitte, 61–67. Paris: Verre et histoire, 2013.

Veyne, Paul. "The Roman Home: Foreword." In Ariès and Duby, *History of Private Life*, 1:315–17.

Vickers, Michael. "Antiquity and Utopia: The Paradox in Glass Studies." In *The Prehistory and History of Glassmaking Technology*, edited by Patrick McCray, 17–31. Westerville, Ohio: American Ceramic Society, 1998.

Vidler, Anthony. *The Architectural Uncanny: Essays in the Modern Unhomely*. Cambridge, MA: MIT Press, 1992.

———. "Transparency: Literal and Phenomenal." *Journal of Architectural Education* 56 (2003): 6–7.

Vipard, Pascal. "L'usage du verre à vitre dans l'architecture romaine du Haut Empire." In Lagabrielle and Philippe, *Verre et fenêtre*, 3–10.

Virdis Limentani, Caterina. "La fragile apparenza dell'armonia: I vetri nelle nature morte olandesi del Seicento." In Barovier Mentasti, *Trasparenze e riflessi*, 181–86.

Vitruvius. *De architectura libri decem*. Edited by Curt Fensterbusch. Darmstadt: Wissenschaftliche Buchgesellschaft, 1976.

Völckers, Otto. *Glas und Fenster: Ihr Wesen, ihre Geschichte und ihre Bedeutung in der Gegenwart*. Berlin: Bauwelt Verlag, 1939.

Volkmann, Barbara. *Paul Baumgarten: Bauten und Projekte, 1924–1981*. Berlin: Akademie der Künste, 1988.

Vose, Ruth Hurst. "From the Dark Ages to the Fall of Constantinople." In Klein and Lloyd, *History of Glass*, 39–65.

Wacker, Alfons Johann. *Das Fenster im deutschen Wohnhaus: Entwicklung des Steinstützen-, Blendrahmen-, Zargen-, und im besondern des altbayerischen Stockfensters*. Danzig: Kasemann, 1938.

Wagner, Monika. *Marmor und Asphalt: Soziale Oberflächen im Berlin des 20. Jahrhunderts*. Berlin: Wagenbach, 2018.

Wajcman, Gérard. *Fenêtre: Chroniques du regard et de l'intime*. Lagrasse: Verdier, 2004.

Wallace-Dunlop, M. A. *Glass in the Old World*. London: Field and Tuer, [1882].

Wallraff, Martin. *Christus verus sol: Sonnenverehrung und Christentum in der Spätantike*. Münster: Aschendorff, 2001.

Ward, Janet. *Weimar Surfaces: Urban Visual Culture in 1920s Germany*. Berkeley: University of California Press, 2001.

Ward, W. R. "The Administration of the Window and Assessed Taxes, 1696–1798." *English Historical Review* 67 (1952): 522–42.

Warton, Thomas. *The History of English Poetry: From the Close of the Eleventh to the Commencement of the Eighteenth Century*. 3 vols. London: Taylor, 1840.

Weber, Nicholas Fox. *The Bauhaus Group: Six Masters of Modernism*. New Haven: Yale University Press, 2011.

Weinsberg, Hermann. *Das Buch Weinsberg: Kölner Denkwürdigkeiten aus dem 16. Jahrhundert*. Edited by Konstantin Höhlbaum et al. 5 vols. Leipzig: Dürr, 1886–1926. Reprint, Düsseldorf: Droste, 2000.

Wenzel, Siegfried, ed. and trans. *Fasciculus morum: A Fourteenth-Century Preacher's Handbook*. University Park: Pennsylvania State University Press, 1989.

Westermann-Angerhausen, Hiltrud. "Glasmalerei und Himmelslicht: Metapher, Farbe, Stoff." In Westermann-Angerhausen, *Himmelslicht*, 95–102.

————, ed. *Himmelslicht: Europäische Glasmalerei im Jahrhundert des Kölner Dombaus, 1248–1349*. Cologne: Schnütgen-Museum, 1998.

Westermann-Angerhausen, Hiltrud, and Dagmar Täube, eds. *Das Mittelalter in 111 Meisterwerken aus dem Museum Schnütgen Köln*. Cologne: Greven, 2003.

Wheeler, Jo. "Stench in Sixteenth-Century Venice." In *The City and the Senses: Urban Culture Since 1500*, edited by Alexander Cowan and Jill Steward, 25–38. Ashgate: Aldershot, 2007.

White, Sam. "The Real Little Ice Age." *Journal of Interdisciplinary History* 44 (2014): 327–52.

Whitehouse, David. *Glass: A Short History*. Washington, DC: Smithsonian Books, 2012.

————. "Glass in the Epigrams of Martial." *Journal of Glass Studies* 41 (1999): 73–81.

————. "Glass in Medieval Europe." In Whitehouse, *Medieval Glass*, 24–61.

————. *Medieval Glass for Popes, Princes, and Peasants*. Corning, NY: Corning Museum of Glass, 2010.

————. "Window Glass between the First and the Eighth Centuries." In Dell'Acqua and Silva, *Il colore nel medioevo*, 31–43.

Whiteley, Nigel. "Intensity of Scrutiny and a Good Eyeful: Architecture and Transparency." *Journal of Architectural Education* 56 (2003): 8–16.

Wigginton, Michael. *Glass in Architecture*. London: Phaidon, 1996.

Wijsenbeek-Olthuis, Thera. "The Social History of the Curtain." In *Inventaires après-décès et ventes de meubles: Apports à une histoire de la vie économique et quotidienne (XIVe–XIXe siècle)*, edited by Micheline Baulant et al., 381–87. Louvain-la-Neuve: Academia, 1987.

Wilde, Oscar. "The House Beautiful." In *Collins Complete Works of Oscar Wilde: Centenary Edition*, 913–25. Glasgow: HarperCollins, 1999.

Williamson, Paul. *Medieval and Renaissance Stained Glass in the Victoria and Albert Museum*. London: V&A Publications, 2003.

Wimmel, Walter. "Luna moraturis sedula luminibus: Zu Properz I, 3, 31/32." *Rheinisches Museum für Philologie* 110 (1967): 70–75.

Witzleben, Elisabeth von. *Bemalte Glasscheiben: Volkstümliches Leben auf Kabinett-und Bierscheiben*. Munich: Callwey, 1977.

Wochnik, Fritz. "Zur Wechselwirkung von Glasmalerei und äußerer und innerer Farbfassung von Sakralbauten in der Mark Brandenburg und in den angrenzenden Territorien." In Badstübner et al., *Licht und Farbe*, 281–325.

Wolf, Sophie, et al. "Protective Glazing: The Conflict between Energy-Saving and Conservation Requirements." In *Recent Advances in Glass, Stained-Glass, and Ceramics Conservation*, edited by Hannelore Roemich and Kate van Lookeren Campagne, 99–107. Zwolle: Spa, 2013.

Wolff, Arnold. "Die Kathedrale." In Westermann-Angerhausen, *Himmelslicht*, 17–21.

Wolff, Christian. "Anfangs-Gründe der Bau-Kunst." In *Anfangs-Gründe aller mathematischen Wissenschaften, erster Theil*. Frankfurt am Main, 1750. Reprint, Hildesheim: Olms, 1973.

Worlidge, John. *Systema horti-culturae: Or, the Art of Gardening*. London, 1700.

Wörner, Martin, Doris Mollenschott, and Karl-Heinz Hüter. *Architekturführer Berlin*. Berlin: Reimer, 1991.

Woronoff, Denis. "Quand l'exception devient (presque) la règle: Remarques sur le vitrage en France, XVIe–XVIIIe siècles." In Lagabrielle and Philippe, *Verre et fenêtre*, 133–36.

Wotton, Henry. *The Elements of Architecture*. London: Bill, 1624.

Wright, Frank Lloyd. "The Meaning of Materials: Glass." In *In the Cause of Architecture*, edited by Frederick Gutheim, 197–202. New York: Architectural Record, 1975.

————. *The Natural House*. New York: Horizon Press, 1954.

Wright, Lawrence. *Warm and Snug: The History of the Bed*. Stroud: Sutton, 2004.

Würgler, Andreas. *Die Tagsatzung der Eidgenossen: Politik, Kommunikation und Symbolik einer repräsentativen Institution im europäischen Kontext, 1470–1798*. Epfendorf: Bibliotheca Academica Verlag, 2013.

Yagi, Koji. *A Japanese Touch for Your Home*. Tokyo: Kodansha International, 1982.

Yamaguchi, Kiyoko. "The Architecture of the Spanish Philippines and the Limits of Empire." In *Investing in the Early Modern Built Environment: Europeans, Asians, Settlers, and Indigenous Societies*, edited by Carole Shammas, 119–38. Leiden: Brill, 2012.

Yamasaki, Kazuo. "A Brief History of Glassmaking in Japan." In *Glass and Religious Man*, edited by Anita Engle, 95–108. Jerusalem: Phoenix, 1982.

Young, Arthur. *Travels in France during the years 1787, 1788, and 1789: Undertaken more particularly with a View of ascertaining the cultivation, wealth, resources, and national prosperity, of the Kingdom of France.* London: Rackham, 1792.

Zedler, Johann Heinrich, ed. *Grosses vollständiges Universal-Lexicon aller Wissenschafften und Künste, welche bißhero durch menschlichen Verstand und Witz erfunden und verbessert worden.* 68 vols. Halle: Zedler, 1731–54.

Zimmerman, Claire. *Mies van der Rohe, 1886–1969: The Structure of Space.* Cologne: Taschen, 2004.

Zimmern, Froben Christoph von. *Die Chronik der Grafen von Zimmern.* Edited by Hansmartin Decker-Hauff and Rudolf Seigel. 3 vols. Darmstadt: Wissenschaftliche Buchgesellschaft, 1964–72.

ACKNOWLEDGMENTS

THIS BOOK TOOK SHAPE after I joined New York University. I would like to thank my department colleagues for welcoming me to their community and for many stimulating conversations. I am particularly grateful to the Andrew W. Mellon Foundation and the Dean of Humanities for their generous support of my work through the NYU Urban Humanities Initiative.

I would also like to thank David Armitage, Thomas V. Cohen, Finbarr Barry Flood, Christopher R. Friedrichs, Stefanos Geroulanos, Sophie Lagabrielle, Thomas Maissen, Morgan Ng, Jennifer Rampling, Kerry Wallach, Christian Wildberg, and Winnie Wong. I am particularly grateful to Daniel Merzel for his eagle-eyed reading of the entire manuscript as well as for incisive comments at every stage.

It has been a pleasure to continue the collaboration with Yale University Press. I would like to thank my editor, Jennifer Banks, for her all-around support. Heather Gold, Jeffrey Schier, and Abigail Storch expertly steered the manuscript through the publication process. Laura Hensley meticulously copy edited the final version. Many thanks also to the two anonymous readers of the manuscript.

I am, as ever, deeply grateful to my parents for their encouragement and support.

INDEX

Page numbers in *italics* refer to illustrations.

CREDITS

The photographers and the sources of visual material are as follows. Every effort has been made to supply complete and correct credits; if there are errors or omissions, please contact Yale University Press so that corrections can be made in any subsequent edition.

Fig. I.1: Andreas Praefcke, Wikimedia Commons

Fig. I.2: Berthold Werner, Wikimedia Commons

Fig. I.3: © Finbarr Barry Flood

Fig. I.4: Vrajesh jani, Wikimedia Commons

Fig. I.5: Emzett85, Wikimedia Commons

Fig. I.6: © Finbarr Barry Flood

Fig. I.7: © Finbarr Barry Flood

Fig. I.8: The Metropolitan Museum of Art, New York, Gift of Estate of Samuel Isham, 1914

Fig. I.9: Image courtesy of The American Jewish Historical Society

Fig. 1.1: Library of Congress, LOT 13550, no. 147

Fig. 1.2: The Swedish Pompeii Project. Photo: Thomas Staub

Fig. 1.3: Photo P. Lucci. Soprintendenza ABAP Ravenna, Italy

Fig. 1.4: Spinazzola, *Pompei*, 70

Fig. 1.5: D. Foy, Aix-Marseille Université, CNRS Centre Camille Jullian

Fig. 1.6: The Metropolitan Museum of Art, New York, Gift of Henry G. Marquand, 1881

Fig. 1.7: D. Foy, Aix-Marseille Université, CNRS Centre Camille Jullian

Fig. 1.8: Souen Fontaine

Fig. 1.9: Wolfgang Nutsch (partly after Brisac, *Thousand Years*, 180–81)

Fig. 1.10: Baatz, "Fensterglastypen," 9

Fig. 1.11: Greg Willis, Wikimedia Commons

Fig. 1.12: Fczarnowski, Wikimedia Commons

Fig. 1.13: Fabrizio Bisconti, ed., *Temi di iconografia paleocristiana* (Vatican City: Pontificio Istituto di Archeologia Cristiana, 2000), pl. 57

Fig. 1.14: Berthold Werner, Wikimedia Commons

Fig. 2.1: Jürg Goll, Müstair

Fig. 2.2: Hans Bernhard, Wikimedia Commons

Fig. 2.3: gnosne, Wikimedia Commons

Fig. 2.4: Georges Jansoone, Wikimedia Commons

Fig. 2.5: Carlo Pelagalli, Wikimedia Commons

Fig. 2.6: The Metropolitan Museum of Art, New York, Gift of J. Pierpont Morgan, 1917

Fig. 2.7: © Finbarr Barry Flood

Fig. 3.1: Uoaei1, Wikimedia Commons

Fig. 3.2: Shadowgate, Wikimedia Commons

Fig. 3.3: The Metropolitan Museum of Art, New York, The Cloisters Collection, 1956

Fig. 3.4: The Metropolitan Museum of Art, New York, The Cloisters Collection, 1956

Fig. 3.5: Jacques76250, Wikimedia Commons

Fig. 3.6: Vassil, Wikimedia Commons

Fig. 3.7: © Finbarr Barry Flood

Fig. 3.8: Reinhardhauke, Wikimedia Commons

Fig. 4.1: British Library, Add. Mss. 24189, fol. 16; author's reproduction of public domain image

Fig. 4.2: Remi Mathis, Wikimedia Commons

Fig. 4.3: © Guillaume Piolle/CC BY 3.0, Wikimedia Commons

Fig. 4.4: Magnus Manske, Wikimedia Commons

Fig. 4.5: The Metropolitan Museum of Art, New York, The Cloisters Collection, 1956

Fig. 5.1: Yale University Art Gallery. Lent by Dr. and Mrs. Herbert Schaefer

Fig. 5.2: Yale University Art Gallery. Lent by Dr. and Mrs. Herbert Schaefer

Fig. 5.3: Jennifer Rampling

Fig. 5.4: The Walters Art Museum, Baltimore

Fig. 5.5: The Walters Art Museum, Baltimore

Fig. 5.6: © Galleria Nazionale dell'Umbria

Fig. 5.7: © Galleria Nazionale dell'Umbria

Fig. 5.8: Galleria Palatina, Palazzo Pitti, Florence; author's reproduction of public domain image

Fig. 6.1: Jane023, Wikimedia Commons

Fig. 6.2: Author's collection

Fig. 6.3: Javier Kohen, Wikimedia Commons

Fig. 6.4: Manfreeed, Wikimedia Commons

Fig. 6.5: Roemer Visscher, *Sinnepoppen* (Amsterdam: Blaeu, 1614). Rijksmuseum, Amsterdam

Fig. 6.6: Stefan W, Wikimedia Commons

Fig. 6.7: Barry Skeates from Newbury, UK, Wikimedia Commons

Fig. 7.1: The J. Paul Getty Museum, Los Angeles. Digital image courtesy of the Getty's Open Content Program

Fig. 7.2: The Metropolitan Museum of Art, New York, Purchase, Bequest of Kate Read Blacque, in memory of her husband, Valentine Alexander Blacque; Bequest of Thomas W. Lamont and Gift of J. Pierpont Morgan, by exchange; and Rogers Fund, 1982

Fig. 7.3: © Victoria and Albert Museum, London, no. 465-1905

Fig. 7.4: Gemäldegalerie der Staatlichen Museen zu Berlin—Preußischer Kulturbesitz; author's reproduction of public domain image

Fig. 7.5: Schürmann and Uekermann, *Das verkleidete Fenster*, 13

Fig. 7.6: Giogo, Wikimedia Commons

Fig. 7.7: © Victoria and Albert Museum, London, no. C.430–1919

Fig. 7.8: Sidonius, Wikimedia Commons

Fig. 8.1: The Metropolitan Museum of Art, New York, Gift of Henry Walters, 1917

Fig. 8.2: © Museum of London

Fig. 8.3: © Victoria and Albert Museum, London, no. C.62–1927

Fig. 8.4: Courtesy of Michael J. Dixon

Fig. 8.5: Photo by David Iliff; License: CC BY-SA 3.0, Wikimedia Commons

Fig. 9.1: Wellcome Collection, London

Fig. 9.2: The Metropolitan Museum of Art, New York, Edward C. Moore Collection, Bequest of Edward C. Moore, 1891

Fig. 9.3: Hans Sachs and Jost Amann, *Das Ständebuch* (Frankfurt am Main, 1568; reprint, Aarhus: Aarhus University Press, 2009), 1:113

Fig. 9.4: The Metropolitan Museum of Art, New York, Gift of J. Pierpont Morgan, 1917

Fig. 9.5: The J. Paul Getty Museum, Los Angeles. Digital image courtesy of the Getty's Open Content Program

Fig. 10.1: Photo: Myrabella/Wikimedia Commons/CC BY-SA 3.0

Fig. 10.2: Arnaud 25, Wikimedia Commons

Fig. 10.3: Charles Coulston Gillispie, ed., *A Diderot Pictorial Encyclopedia of Trades and Industry* (New York: Dover, 1959), pl. 273

Fig. 10.4: The J. Paul Getty Museum, Los Angeles. Digital image courtesy of the Getty's Open Content Program

Fig. 10.5: Dennis Jarvis, Wikimedia Commons

Fig. 10.6: Norbert Schnitzler, Wikimedia Commons

Fig. 10.7: Wikimedia Commons

Fig. 10.8: Miguel Hermoso Cuesta, Wikimedia Commons

Fig. 11.1: Wikimedia Commons

Fig. 11.2: 2 Cod Ms Uffenbach 40c, Niedersächsische Staats- und Universitätsbibliothek Göttingen

Fig. 11.3: Meisner and Kieser, *Thesaurus philopoliticus*, 1:14

Fig. 11.4: *Punch, or, the London Charivari*. Wellcome Collection, London

Fig. 11.5: The Metropolitan Museum of Art, New York, Purchase, Fletcher Fund, Joyce F. Menschel Gift, Louis V. Bell Fund, Alfred Stieglitz Society and W. Bruce and Delaney H. Lundberg Gifts, 2010

Fig. 12.1: Roger Ward (Flickr), https://flic.kr/p/dktkir, CC BY 2.0

Fig. 12.2: The J. Paul Getty Museum, Los Angeles. Digital image courtesy of the Getty's Open Content Program

Fig. 12.3: The Metropolitan Museum of Art, New York, David Hunter McAlpin Fund, 1952

Fig. 12.4: KoS, Wikimedia Commons

Fig. 12.5: chensiyuan, Wikimedia Commons

Fig. 12.6: Wikimedia Commons

Fig. 13.1: Oana Popa, Wikimedia Commons

Fig. 13.2: Clemensfranz, Wikimedia Commons

Fig. 13.3: Spyrosdrakopoulos, Wikimedia Commons

Fig. 13.4: *Jahrbuch des Deutschen Werkbundes 1915* (Munich: Bruckmann, 1915), 77

Fig. 13.5: © Finbarr Barry Flood

Fig. 13.6: J. Crocker, Wikimedia Commons

Fig. 13.7: Andreas Praefcke, Wikimedia Commons

Fig. 13.8: vicens, Wikimedia Commons

Fig. 13.9: © Finbarr Barry Flood

Fig. 13.10: Ward, *Weimar Surfaces*, 46

Fig. 13.11: harald909, Wikimedia Commons

Fig. 13.12: *Das Buch für Alle: Illustrierte Familienzeitung*, no. 5 (1918): n.p.

Fig. 13.13: Oskar Kalbus, *Vom Werden deutscher Filmkunst*, vol. 1, *Der stumme Film* (Altona-Bahrenfeld: Cigaretten-Bilderdienst, 1935), 99

Fig. 13.14: Fred Romero, Wikimedia Commons

Fig. 14.1: Giuseppe Albano, Wikimedia Commons

Fig. 14.2: Bavarian State Library Munich/Image Archive

Fig. 14.3: Courtesy National Archives, photo no. 242-EB-3–41D

Fig. 14.4: Völckers, *Glas und Fenster*, 81

Fig. 14.5: *Das Taschenbuch Schönheit der Arbeit* (Berlin: Verlag der Deutschen Arbeitsfront, 1938), 67

Fig. 14.6: Adrix3000, Wikimedia Commons, with permission of Dr. Ursula Huber

Fig. 14.7: Author's collection

Fig. 14.8: BlazeMKD86, Wikimedia Commons

Fig. 14.9: Jean-Pierre Dalbéra, Wikimedia Commons

Fig. 14.10: BEBUG/Bild und Heimat, Berlin; author's collection

Fig. 15.1: Billie Grace Ward, Wikimedia Commons

Fig. 15.2: AlasdairW, Wikimedia Commons

Fig. 15.3: Photo: Chris Schroeer-Heiermann

Fig. 15.4: Author's collection

Fig. 15.5: Author's collection

Fig. 15.6: Victor Grigas, Wikimedia Commons

Fig. 15.7: Library of Congress, Prints & Photographs Division, photograph by Carol M. Highsmith, LC-DIG-highsm-04817

Fig. 15.8: Geographer at English Wikipedia, Wikimedia Commons

Fig. 15.9: Fletcher6, Wikimedia Commons

Fig. 15.10: Gregory Varnum, Wikimedia Commons